# Gideon Welles

Gideon Welles, Secretary of the Navy, 1861–1869. Library of Congress.

# Gideon Welles

## Lincoln's Secretary of the Navy

JOHN NIVEN

New York   Oxford University Press   1973

For Drake, Kathy,
and especially for Peter

# PREFACE

DESPITE THE IMMENSE BODY of diaries and papers Gideon Welles left to posterity, his life poses a difficult problem to the biographer. Clearly, Welles was a highly sensitive individual, a reticent man, who preferred the background to the limelight. Yet at the same time he was fiercely ambitious. That he should have devoted his career to politics, which is among the more public of vocations, seems somewhat paradoxical until one begins to understand the limited number of options open to a young man of Welles' temperament in the 1820's.

In no sense was Welles the voluble egotist or the courthouse lawyer, with an eye on the main chance, which then and now make up the professional politician. From the beginning he was an oddity in his chosen role. What made this shy moralist so successful in a profession conspicuous for its easy virtue? What made this essentially introverted individual mark out for himself a career where the prize more often than not went to the brash, the self-confident, the compulsively gregarious, those very qualities he lacked to a marked degree?

To be sure, Welles had a talent for organization and an extraordinary capacity for work. But so did many other public men of his generation. He was also a compulsive writer who depended upon the art of written persuasion for partisan advantage with which he easily identified his own personal advancement. But any number of his political contemporaries began their careers as journalists and for reasons similar to Welles'.

Perhaps the answers lie in Welles' inherent moralism, in his dogmatic sense of his own mission, which seems to have raised his political and editorial efforts above those of his associates. For he was no mere place-hunter, no political hack. He believed almost as an article of faith that certain underlying principles should govern American life. Welles was a complex individual who, amidst the clutter, the constant change, the frenetic movement of the antebellum United States, still managed to adapt lofty Jeffersonian credos to the earthiness of practical politics without losing his principles or his sense of perspective. He never deviated from his vision of the Union as a limited government, where the rights of states were the surest protection for the rights of man. And if the means he used did not always square with his high-minded rhetoric on the subject, the ends he sought were unwaveringly idealistic until the cataclysm of the Civil War and Reconstruction.

Welles was a wire-puller for thirty-five years, a politician's politician, who worked in the relative obscurity of the local and regional party organization. He did not become a national figure until his fifty-ninth year, when Lincoln appointed him Secretary of the Navy. From then until his retirement in March 1869, he played an important role as an administrator and as a counselor for Presidents Lincoln and Johnson.

During most of this turbulent period, he kept a diary of the historic events he was privileged to observe at first hand. Welles' Civil War and Reconstruction diaries, thousands of pages of manuscript, make up the most vivid and certainly the fullest inside account we have of those trying times. As such they have misled generations of historians who blindly exploited them, while failing to distinguish Welles' personal reflections from the many objective statements, analyses and descriptions he also made. Welles meant his diaries to be historical sources, but he also used them as a mode of release from the constant tensions he labored under. And it is just this quality of highly personal judgment which can be as fatally misleading to the careless historian as it is fruitful to the biographer.

This then is the biography of an eminent journalist, politician, statesman, and administrator. But it is preeminently the story of a reflective nineteenth-century man who observed his contemporaries with a keen eye, critical, shrewd, pungent and concise, and always vivid and realistic.

I am deeply grateful to many individuals and institutions who have helped me in various ways. Summer grants-in-aid from the American Philosophical Society and the American Council of Learned Societies made it possible for me to complete necessary research in New York and New England. A Senior Research Grant from the Smithsonian Institution in 1966 enabled me to work at the Library of Congress and the National Archives during a year's leave of absence. The Claremont Graduate School, over a period of time, purchased a microfilm copy of the major Welles collection in the Library of Congress. It also provided funds for typing, for the acquisition of pictures, and for additional microfilm and for xerox materials.

Personal obligations are legion. The support and encouragement of

Allan Nevins, my teacher and dear friend, helped me over many moments of flagging spirit. Professor Bennett Wall of Tulane University read early drafts of the manuscript, and he, too, bolstered my confidence when the going seemed rough.

Friends and colleagues have given generously of their talents, time, and interest. At Claremont, my colleagues Leland Carlson, Barnaby Keeney, Harry Jaffa, John H. Kemble, Alfred R. Louch, Leonard W. Levy, and Charles Lofgren read all or parts of the manuscript. Dr. Alan Brownsword of the Department of Health, Education and Welfare made available to me the results of several years of research in Connecticut politics during the early nineteenth century. His assistance in helping me unearth primary source materials, his enthusiasm for the project, and his wise counsel were invaluable. In moving among the treacherous rocks and shoals of Welles' career during the Civil War and Reconstruction, Professors Ari Hoogenboom and Hans Trefousse of the City University of New York, E. B. Long of the University of Wyoming, and Hal Bridges of the University of California, Riverside, rescued me time and again from errors of fact and judgment.

For their unfailing assistance, I wish to thank the staffs of the manuscript departments of the Library of Congress; the Huntington Library; the New York Public Library, the New-York Historical Society; the Connecticut Historical Society; the New Hampshire Historical Society; the Eleutherian Mills Historical Library; the Illinois Historical Society; the Chicago Historical Society; the New York State Library at Albany; Honnold Library at Claremont, California; the Sterling Library, Yale University; the Houghton Library, Harvard University; the John Hay Library, Brown University; the University of Rochester Library; the Library of the University of California at Los Angeles; the Firestone Library, Princeton University; the Pierpont Morgan Library; and the Butler Library, Columbia University. The staff of the National Archives were invariably helpful.

Larry Burgess of the Lincoln Shine, Redlands, California, supplied me with copies of important manuscripts, as did Thomas Welles Brainard of Melody Farms, South Coventry, Connecticut, who is a descendant of Gideon Welles. Professor David Williams, of California State University at Long Beach, microfilmed for me the Welles correspondence in the Stephen A. Douglas papers at the University of Chicago.

For all the Welles family pictures, I am indebted to Thomas Welles Brainard and Suzanne Welles Brainard and they are reproduced with their permission. Thomas G. Welles, of Coventry, Connecticut, gave me access to valuable family letters in his possession.

Milton Kaplan, Director of the Library of Congress' picture division personally helped me select and provided prints of all the Library of Congress photos that appear as illustrations. Charles Haberlein of the Naval Photo Center at the Washington Navy Yard and Robert Carlisle of the Navy Department's Information Office supplied the photograph of the original *Monitor* and crew. Pictures of Welles are reproduced with the permission of the National Archives. Philip K. Lundeberg of the Naval History Division, Smithsonian Institution, has helped me in many ways and I wish here to acknowledge his assistance. I wish also to thank Sheldon Meyer and Caroline Taylor of the Oxford University Press for their interest, understanding, and passion for clarity and accuracy. I am grateful to Mrs. Orin Tramz, who typed the manuscript and who helped me with the notes.

J.N.

*Claremont, California*
*May 1973*

# CONTENTS

# Gideon Welles

# CHAPTER 1

# A Roving Disposition

It was a fine morning in late April of 1846. For two weeks mild winds from the southwest had coaxed out what was left of winter in Hartford.[1] Blooming cherry trees and damson plums and yellow splashes of forsythia brightened dreary dooryards. New leaves on the elms and lindens along Main and State streets cast a fretwork of light and shadow on the uneven brick walkways.

Gideon Welles, politician and sometime journalist, should have been in good spirits when he boarded the "English style" coach of the New Haven train on the first leg of a journey to Washington, for he was sensitive to the beauties of nature and enjoyed travel. But on this rare April day he seemed preoccupied, indifferent to his fellow passengers, blind to the sparkling panorama of the Connecticut River valley, whose rounded hills, pale green with new growth, sloped down to the water's edge. A week earlier he had accepted an appointment as Chief of the Bureau of Provisions and Clothing in the Navy Department. The decision had not been an easy one. A man of independent means, he was reluctant to leave the security of his comfortable home, his family and friends, for the uncertainties and the rough bachelor life of Washington. He did not know what would be expected of him, what duties the office entailed, whether the tenure was sound.

One can imagine that he did not bandy words with the New Haven's garrulous conductor, who had amused Charles Dickens three years before. Even in the best of moods, Welles was rarely expansive in public. He preferred to listen to and observe strangers, to record their interests and their foibles, rather than engage in casual conversation. Balding, with an oversized head for his slender build, long clean-shaven face, heavy, cleft, receding chin, he looked older than his forty-three years. Steel spectacles completed the image—an inconspicuous middle-aged person of sedentary habits.

Welles may have looked inconspicuous, but he was known at least by reputation to every important public man in the nation. Many he numbered as close personal friends. For more than twenty years he had been a political figure in New England, an influential editor, a maker of governors and congressmen, a dispenser of patronage. It was true that he was a bookish man; and it was equally true that he had injured his eyesight composing editorials, proofreading, and writing letters under poor light in the cramped, cluttered office of the *Hartford Times*. Physically, however, Welles did not lead a sedentary life. He had walked or ridden hundreds of miles in all kinds of weather, attending political meetings, visiting with local party bosses. He had traveled over much of the Northeast and the Middle Atlantic states. He had been as far west as Milwaukee, as far south as Washington. In fact, he had visited the capital at least once a year since 1829, customarily in January, after the new session of Congress convened. As familiar with primitive frontier conditions as with Washington soirées, on his many journeys he had braved the elements in drafty stage coaches and on horseback, dared the disease and borne the discomfort of squalid, ill-kept taverns and overcrowded drawing rooms.

An intensely ambitious man who craved the prestige and visible recognition of a distinguished public office, he had planned and plotted and worked—yet to what avail? To become a bureau chief in the Navy Department? This was scarcely Welles' notion of a prestigious office or even one that engaged his interest, much less his competence. He was painfully aware that he was taking a calculated risk—that his faction of the party was not on the best of terms with the Administration. When he had accepted, he had acted impulsively, and he knew it. What he did not know was that, without planning, plotting, or going through agonizing reflection, he had made the wisest decision of his life. New issues and new political alignments arising from the Mexican War would give broad scope to his talents. The political connections he would establish in Washington would prove invaluable. He was moving from journeyman to craftsman in his chosen trade. His credentials were not as tangible as he had hoped; they were credentials, nonetheless. He could practice his art where it counted, at the center of national affairs. Recalling the doubts and fears of that day some months later in his Washington boardinghouse, he jotted a revealing phrase in his diary:

"It is the duty of man to acquiesce in his destiny and submit to circumstances he can not control."

Welles believed himself a nonconformist in religious matters, a free thinker, who reserved his sharpest editorial barbs for the rigidities and intolerance of orthodox Calvinism. Yet this calm rationalist, this enlightened Jeffersonian, had never quite escaped from the dogmatic convictions of his Puritan forebears. Implanted deep within his character was the lurking sense that God moved in mysterious ways. That belief was at once a refuge during times of stress and a goad to his ambition.

Welles had absorbed these precepts intuitively from his total environment, not from specific parental guidelines. His easy-going, indulgent father, Samuel Welles, thought all Congregationalists were meddlesome prigs—their dogma pure cant masking selfish purposes. In formal religious matters he leaned toward the Episcopalian Church, more as gesture of defiance than from any settled conviction. To his skeptical mind, life was a lottery with many more blanks than prizes. Young Gideon accepted these notions as a matter of course, and he believed that he too was free of Calvinist bigotry. But he was less secure, less casual, than his father, infinitely more sensitive to community opinion. While he absorbed the forms and would practice the style of a freethinker, the ordered, moralistic universe of Jonathan Edwards had found a lodgment in the deepest recesses of his mind. He would emulate his father's strict business habits, his fierce family loyalty, his politics. He could not accept his essential pragmatism. The father took men as they were, neither saints nor devils; the son strove for perfection, even though he knew it was unattainable here below.

Samuel Welles was a stocky, bald-headed, nearsighted man of marked independence. Moderately prosperous, always busy with various enterprises, he enjoyed shocking his family and the community in his home town of Glastonbury, Connecticut with his radical opinions. An ex-captain of the militia, farmer, and owner of a small store in 1784 he married Anne Hale, slight, dark-haired daughter of a neighbor, Gideon Hale. Townsfolk whispered that Samuel had made a good match. Gideon Hale was well off by Glastonbury standards—a justice of the peace, a member of the General Assembly and like his new son-in-law a farmer, but a far more successful one. Hale had earned solid gold louis supplying Rochambeau's army while Samuel had been away from home serving in the militia, which had been called out in 1781 to defend the state against Benedict Arnold's invasion. Hale owned the only "carriage" in Glastonbury, which he put at the disposal of the bridal pair.[2] He also presented his son-in-law with a house, and from time to time would lend him money to enlarge his business—debts Samuel Welles would repay many times over.

A year after their marriage, Anne Welles gave birth to a son, Oliver, who was followed by another son, Chauncey, in 1786. The second birth was difficult and in some way injured the mother. She remained more or less an invalid until she died. Though frail and weak, spending most of her time indoors, and frequently not leaving her bedroom for days on end, she was determined to have more children even if it cost her her life. Eleven years after Chauncey's birth, Samuel, Jr., was born. She almost died then and she never walked another step. Yet five years later this frail woman, then thirty-eight, became pregnant again. On July 1, 1802, she was safely delivered of a fourth son. He was named Gideon after her aged father, who, with her mother and her spinster sister, Hannah Hale, had been members of the Welles household for some years. The indomitable Anne Welles bore a fifth child, Thaddeus, in 1806. This final effort cost whatever small reserves of strength and energy remained. She lingered on for ten years, withdrawn into a world of her own. "Poor afflicted woman," her son described her years later, ". . . I remember her pale, emaciated, helpless. Her large dark eyes that were beautiful were interesting to the last."[3]

When Gideon was born Samuel Welles was forty-eight years old, and he was about to enter the most prosperous and active period of his busy life. His fellow townsmen had already honored his success by electing him First Selectman, and then a member of the General Assembly. By 1802 he had made Glastonbury one of the few Jeffersonian enclaves in Federalist Connecticut.[4] Samuel's political principles were a mixture of opportunism and conviction. He never forgot the day when his own father had come home to die, a physical wreck after surviving almost three years as a British prisoner of war in a rotting hulk moored on the Hudson River. Eighteen months later Samuel himself had marched off with his militia company to defend Connecticut from Tryon's invasion, and again to combat Arnold's foray. These experiences made him a confirmed nationalist and an even more confirmed Anglophobe. Samuel's hatred of the British and of all Tories led him to accept without question the radical ideology of the Revolution. Jefferson and Tom Paine were his political mentors, France the great benefactor of American independence. His trips into the countryside to purchase the cheese, the gin, the onions, and the horses he would ship to the West Indies brought him close to the local farm community. Blunt and direct, Samuel found a receptive audience for his ideas.

As he became more affluent in the 1790's, his prestige increased among the poorer folk with whom he dealt. To them he seemed the very embodiment of what two contemporary observers called "that spirit of trade which attaches an undeserved importance to property."[5] His business success may have impressed those who occupied the free benches and the gallery in Glastonbury's First Church, but it did not endear him to the better folk who rented their pews in front of the pulpit. His nonconformity in religious matters was another sore point, for at that time the Congregational church and its secular arm, the Federalist party, were the ruling powers of the state.

Members of the oligarchy were not adverse to profiting from Welles' shrewd commercial ventures, however. Many of them, including the pastor of the First Church in Hartford, Nathan Strong, that monument of orthodoxy, were partners in his profitable voyages to the West Indies. But socially there was no room for a man so brash in his manner, so independent and self-assured in his politics and religion.

In many respects a clear-headed, enlightened individual, Samuel Welles was curiously sensitive to these petty distinctions—the lilliputian grandeur of Connecticut's ruling class in the late eighteenth century. Excessively proud of his forebears, he put great stock in the fact that he was a direct descendant of Thomas Welles, third Governor of the colony, and that his ancestors were among the original proprietors of the town. When partisan lines were drawn more tightly after Jefferson's election, he and his family were not counted among the "better" people of Glastonbury. Years later, his son recalled, bitterly, that the Jeffersonians in Connecticut "were proscribed and regarded as an inferior caste, a degraded race, like the Soodras in India, the Israelites in Egypt or the Jews in Europe . . . aliens and strangers in their native land."[6] To a convivial man like Samuel Welles, the slurs and snubs were humiliating experiences, but he refused to be intimidated. His political principles hardened into a dogmatism as inflexible as that of the most uncompromising Federalists. He pitted his pride against the community prejudice, his driving ambitions against the Trumbulls, the Walcotts, the Ellsworths, the Goodriches—too long had they reigned. He won political control of Glastonbury, which for more than forty years would be a political fief of his own family. In the larger sphere of state affairs, he contributed substantially to the downfall of Church-State rule.

Genial, rough in manners, a thoroughgoing paternalist, Samuel Welles made his home and his other properties havens of refuge for veterans of the French and Indian Wars and the Revolution, many of whom were "men of broken fortunes and impoverished habits."[7] It was an exciting household for an impressionable boy. The anecdotes of the old French war and the Revolution were as thick and heady as the hard cider and the flip Samuel Welles dispensed of an evening to loosen the tongues of the old warriors. Young Gideon's active mind was saturated with stories of adventure interlaced with the nationalism and the idealism of the Revolution. Inevitably, these tall tales were couched in Jeffersonian terms, if not by the spouting veterans around the hearth in the kitchen; then by Samuel Welles himself.

There was less of this hospitality after 1807, when the Jeffersonian Embargo completed a series of British and French restrictions that crippled the re-export trade of maritime New England. After managing to get off a last cargo to the West Indies before the law went into effect, Samuel Welles decided that his political principles meshed with his prudence. In supporting his party's policy, he was being a loyal Jeffersonian who had weighed the future of the West Indies trade in the balance and found it wanting. Welles sold his ships, closed his store, and, at the age of fifty-eight, invested much of his capital in loans on good security and became a partner in a local wollen mill. Though his style of living had to undergo some retrenchment, he could now spend more time at home with his family.

Samuel Welles was concerned about his sons, who were not measuring up to his standards of accomplishment. As if to make up for the years he had neglected the parental role, he began a strict regimen of work and character-building on the accepted Puritan model. Yet he was neither a martinet nor a Calvinist patriarch. And even if he had possessed the implacable determination of a Cotton Mather, he could not have coped with his firstborn—the twenty-seven-year-old Oliver. This unstable young man, whom Samuel sought to involve in his various enterprises, found relief from all too frequent clashes with parental authority at cousin Jonathan Welles' tavern. Samuel, Jr., too, though much younger and more responsive, seems to have resisted his father whenever possible by indulging in forbidden pastimes. Only Gideon and little Thaddeus tried to conform, either because of their tender years or because their personalities were more malleable. They worshipped their father and sought to obey his mandates, but they too soon learned that sudden tears and stammered apologies would turn away paternal wrath.

Both Gideon and Thaddeus attended the local district school, but its meager educational fare was not stimulating enough, at least not for

Gideon, who had an active mind and scholarly tastes. He soon became bored with recitations of Jedediah Morse's *Geography*, and he quickly learned all there was to learn from Nathan Daboll's *Arithmetic* and Noah Webster's *American Spelling Book*. When he discovered that his knowledge of the rudimentary curriculum was as accurate and extensive as the schoolmaster's, he lost all interest in study. "The result was," he explained, "my mind was getting visionary and unsettled and though I had not become vicious like others in similar situations, I was beginning to indulge in mischievous pranks."[8]

During this stage of adolescent drift and listlessness Gideon had his first experience with death in his immediate family. He was deeply affected at first, so deeply that his father worried about his sanity. In the fall of 1815, Gideon's aged and much-loved grandparents died within two weeks of each other. Then, on January 11, 1816, Anne Welles died suddenly of pneumonia. Though his mother had been a remote figure for as long as he could remember, Gideon felt the loss of her gentle presence keenly. His father's marriage a few months later to Anne Welles' spinster sister, Hannah, probably was another disturbing factor. But the accidental drowning of his gay, impulsive, older brother, Samuel Jr., in the spring of 1818, plunged him into acute melancholia. He spent hours brooding over family gravestones, or taking long, solitary walks.[9]

Samuel Welles was now sixty-four years old—his eldest son an alcoholic, his second son and namesake dead, his third son, Gideon an enigma. His business affairs were in a perilous state as the gathering depression threatened his mill interests and other investments. If the old man was in a despairing mood, he gave no sign of it. That summer and fall he worked hard as one of the leading delegates to the constitutional convention which finally disposed of Connecticut's colonial charter and decreed religious toleration in the state. But he was worried about Gideon, about his mental health, his lack of ambition, his moody silences. He believed the boy to have ability; he knew him to be obedient and industrious. Perhaps further education away from home would help.

A nominal Episcopalian, Welles had learned of the church's academy at Cheshire. Its struggles against the Congregational church and Yale College appealed to his independent spirit. While in Hartford at the convention, he talked with Samuel Foot, a fellow delegate and an Episcopalian. Foot explained that his two sons were attending the academy and that it was flourishing under the guidance of the Reverend Tillotson Bronson.[10]

Samuel Welles wanted Gideon to have some say in such an important matter as his future education. He counted, however, on his ability to persuade his son that the Cheshire move would be a wise one. Indeed, anticipating a favorable decision, he had already written Bronson, who had accepted the youth in the collegiate program and arranged to have him board with his assistant, Asa Cornwall.[11] When Samuel Welles returned home from the May session of the 1819 legislature, he broached the subject, stressing "in kindly terms" that Gideon ought to begin preparing himself "for the duties of life." He noted that his son had "a natural diffidence" that made him awkward among strangers. New surroundings would instill confidence and self-reliance—the educational program at Cheshire would prepare him for a professional career. "I assented to what I could not contradict," said Gideon, ". . . and it was settled that evening that in three weeks' time I should leave."[12]

Early Tuesday morning, September 21, 1819, Gideon, with young Thaddeus for company, left Glastonbury on horseback for their one-day ride to Cheshire.[13] They reached the town at seven-thirty that evening and walked their horses down the broad Main Street to Bronson's house, passing groups of students on the way. "Many of them eyed me . . . some with rudeness," the self-conscious young man noted, "and all appeared acquainted with each other." He was a stranger, an outsider; would he ever be anything else? "Who and what were these lads and which of them were to be my associates?" he asked himself. "Which were the mischievous and vicious boys that were to annoy me?" Mercifully for Gideon, the Bronson home ("one of the best in appearance in the village") was only a few minutes' walk from the tavern. He was relieved when Mrs. Bronson ushered them in, though he was awed by her "majestic and lady-like appearance."[14] Nor was he reassured when Bronson strode awkwardly into the parlor to greet them.

Tillotson Bronson was fifty-seven years old.[15] Of medium height, he looked "spare and sickly" to Gideon, who noticed that his face was deeply pitted from smallpox scars. Despite the principal's unprepossessing appearance, his precise, yet hesitant enunciation, the monotonous timbre of his voice, he was a scholar of some distinction in mathematics and natural philosophy. Considered an "excellent teacher," it was admitted that he was a poor speaker who relied upon argument rather than eloquence in the classroom or at divine services. His administration of the academy had been one of unremitting labor with few tangible results. He had rescued the infant institution from certain collapse in 1806, and slowly, through the years, with the help of one assistant, he had built up its reputation. The Episcopal diocese contributed much advice and no funds, yet Bronson had managed.

Gideon, of course, had no knowledge of the principal's "heroic" qualities, nor would he have been impressed if he had. Rather, he was critical of Bowden Hall, a small two-story brick building which was the school's only facility, and the academy's nondescript library—177 volumes.[16] When Thaddeus left that night, Gideon was so badly shaken that many years later he would say, "it was to me one of the most painful moments of a varied and chequered life. . . ."[17] Fortunately, his father's friend, newly elected Congressman Samuel A. Foot, looked after him, and Foot's two sons, Andrew and John, both of whom had attended the academy for some years, were friendly and helpful.[18] But Gideon never really took to life at Cheshire. He would not look back on the two years he spent there with any sense of fondness or feeling of accomplishment. That he worked hard is evident from his copy books, and he did make some firm friends. Otherwise the experience was not particularly satisfying, either to him or to his father. He was now more at ease with strangers, less awkward in social situations. He had learned some Latin and less Greek—which he would promptly forget—and had been impressed by Bronson's lectures on "the rise and progress of the mechanical arts." But as far as Samuel Welles could judge, Cheshire seemed merely to have increased his son's penchant for idle scribbling and vague hopes of an impossible literary career. He reminded Gideon that the family assets were dwindling and that he had to support Oliver. There was young Thaddeus also.

During the summer of 1820, father and son had several conversations about the future. Samuel Welles stressed either the law or business as worthy careers for a young man. When Gideon expressed the hope of a college education, his father replied, rather sharply, that college would be expensive and that the costs would have to be deducted from Gideon's portion of his estate. This comment rankled. When Gideon returned to Cheshire for his last term, he wrote a long and serious letter to his father, reviewing their talks. He recalled Samuel Welles telling him that a college education had been offered to Oliver. "I presumed," said Gideon rather archly, "no such thing would ever [have] been thought of him. And if Thad has a mind now to get an education, I dare say nothing will ever be said on the subject." "Why then," he asked in an aggrieved tone, "is it [said] to me."

Gideon was dubious about the law as a career. The preceding summer, at his father's suggestion, he had borrowed from a neighbor Blackstone's commentaries on the common law. He had found the work

tedious, the measured style heavy and distasteful. He also took stock of
the legal profession in the state and decided it was so overcrowded that
struggling lawyers were tempted to adopt unethical practices. "Many,"
he moralized, "will follow a profession to advantage, but more will de-
grade themselves by it." Gideon had a higher regard for a career in
manufacturing or commerce; but what he really wanted was to continue his schooling at Yale, Harvard, or Brown—colleges most of his
classmates were planning to attend. As he told his father, a liberal
education would never be lost; "in the wreck of fortune and the loss of
property, he has that which the hungry creditor cannot deprive him."[19]
Neither his arguments nor his rhetoric convinced Samuel Welles.
When he returned to Glastonbury in the summer of 1821, his future
was still unresolved. Sometime during that winter he agreed to try his
hand at business. He concluded a partnership with Ransome Tomlinson, a local surveyor, and, with a loan from his father, tried the whole-
saling of merchandise. Whatever the reasons—lack of experience,
competition, hard times, insufficient capital, or a combination of these
factors—the venture failed within six months. Gideon resumed his
former occupation of helping to manage his father's affairs. For a time
he served as tax collector for the town.[20]

These routine tasks were boring, and continued dependence on his
father was humiliating. He decided he had no talent for business enterprise. The law seemed equally discouraging. He was again reading
Blackstone and other ponderous volumes prescribed for the student of
law, but the language seemed just as sterile and incomprehensible as
ever. And he had come to the tentative conclusion that he would never
be able to speak well in public. How could he ever be a successful
lawyer with such a handicap? "My life," he wrote a Cheshire schoolmate, "has been nothing but [a] scene of inconsistencies, no form and
permanent resolution, with a roving disposition which my pecuniary
resources will not support."[21] In October of 1822, Samuel Welles gave
his son an opportunity to gratify his "roving disposition" by sending
him to Pennsylvania. It was to be a business trip, but the elder Welles
hoped his relatives and in-laws in Pennsylvania—several of whom were
lawyers—would persuade the reluctant Gideon to follow the legal
profession.

Samuel Welles had just learned that an interest he held in Pennsylvania lands which he had thought worthless might have some value.
Some thirty years earlier, he, Joel Barlow, and Oliver Walcott, Jr., had
acquired on a speculation the title to 20,000 acres of land in the Wyoming Valley of northeastern Pennsylvania, near the great bend of the

Susquehanna River.[22] They had bought the parcel very cheaply from the Connecticut-chartered Susquehanna Company, with the knowledge that they might not have a clear title. Both Connecticut and Pennsylvania claimed the land under colonial charter grants.[23] New surveys were being conducted in Bradford County during 1822, and they inspired rumors that clear titles might be issued to the Connecticut claimants. The information Samuel Welles received was convincing enough for him to decide upon a prompt investigation. He asked Gideon to leave immediately for Towanda, Pennsylvania, a frontier village near his land claims and the home of his brother-in-law, Reuben Hale. This meant that young Welles would be exposed to the hardships of travel in wilderness regions during winter months. Towanda was over 300 miles distant, and it would be December at the earliest before he could begin his return trip. Yet he did not trouble himself with any doubts about the hazards of a long journey in unseasonable weather. Gone were the painful soul-searchings that had characterized his first separation from the family. He was clearly thrilled at the prospect. He had never met his Pennsylvania relatives, though he had corresponded with them. He was curious about the frontier, where so many former Connecticut residents now lived. His romantic notions were fired at the thought of adventure in the new West. More important, perhaps, the trip would defer (or might even solve) the troublesome problem of a career.

A carefree Welles left Glastonbury in mid-October. By the twenty-second he was at Palmer's Hotel in Albany, New York, waiting for the stage to Utica and points west. Thus far he enjoyed the journey. Albany seemed a foreign city, with "quaint Dutch houses and sharp gables unlike anything I had ever seen." The Capitol he thought "magnificent"—far superior to that wonder of New England, the Boston State House. But his evening ride to Schenectady, with nine other passengers through "sterile and uninteresting country," over a wretched road, dampened his high spirits.[24] They did not improve until he reached Little Falls on the Mohawk and was able to observe the work going forward on the Erie Canal. From there until he reached the canal village of Montezuma, where he turned south toward the Pennsylvania line, the "great work" was constantly in view. For the trip from Utica to Montezuma— a distance of about 80 miles—Welles decided to try the novelty of a canal boat.

After a sleepless night in the overcrowded cabin, he was more than happy to exchange the mephitic interior of the boat for the drafty discomfort of the stage. He also counted himself lucky to have an interesting coach companion, Judge Joshua Forman, who traveled with him as far as Ithaca. Forman could have been modeled directly on Fenimore Cooper's Judge Marmaduke Temple. Forty-six years old when Welles met him, he was one of the leading promoters of western New York. Expansive, affable, and shrewd, he discoursed endlessly on a variety of topics—the glittering future of the canal, the coming importance of Syracuse, the state of politics in New York. Forman was close to Governor DeWitt Clinton, and he expected to reap immense profits on his Syracuse land holdings when the canal was completed. To the impressionable young man, this middle-aged speculator embodied all those dynamic qualities he was beginning to associate with the Empire State—qualities he felt were lacking in New England. He warmed instinctively to Forman's easy, intimate manner. For the first time in his life he was being treated as an equal by a successful older man. There was none of that condescension which passed for friendliness at home, that labored cordiality of the seniors who chose to include the young folk in the conversation. The few days in Forman's company did much for Gideon's self-esteem.

A month after leaving Albany he reached his Uncle Reuben's house in Towanda, where he was warmly received by his relatives—and by the entire community. Towanda was still an isolated frontier village. The arrival of a visitor from distant Connecticut at this time of year was an event. After the hardships of the journey, Welles was pleased by the spacious comfort of Uncle Reuben's big white house, perched on a bluff overlooking the confluence of Towanda Creek and the Susquehanna.

Reuben Hale had prospered since he purchased his first tract of land along the creek in 1799. A typical Yankee settler, he combined farming with a saw mill, a distillery, and a variety of local offices, including that of justice of the peace—a distinction his brother-in-law, Samuel Welles, was never to attain. Gideon enjoyed his stay with the Hales. Uncle Reuben's wife, the former Wealthy Tracey, also of Connecticut stock, was a well-educated woman who had been the first schoolteacher at Towanda. Mentally and physically vigorous, she ran an orderly household where the traditional New England respect for learning and religion had not been weakened by frontier life. Welles, though he was satisfied with, even impressed by, the standards of the Hale household, was still highly critical of Towanda. He had assumed that a county seat, even in the wilds of Pennsylvania, would have some distinction. What he found was a hamlet, its one main street clinging precariously to the steep bluffs above the Susquehanna.

A country man, Welles approved of the rich soil around the town. Good crops of wheat, he was told, were raised even on the hilltops. But he was appalled at the backward farming methods, the primitive tools and household utensils in common use. Livestock were few in number, thin, and rangy. Grazing land was being developed, but as yet it consisted largely of hundreds of acres of girdled trees, whose dead trunks and peeling bark cast a gloom over the rugged countryside. The only goods that brough money into the area were animal pelts, whiskey, lumber, and shingles.[25] Towanda's major problem, as Welles soon learned from Uncle Reuben and from George Scott—the prothonotary, and the editor of the four-page weekly paper, the *Settler*—was the almost total lack of transportation. The Susquehanna was navigable for a few summer months, but it was always treacherous. The area needed roads, bridges, and canals—a system of internal improvements that presidential candidate Henry Clay was then urging upon the federal government.

George Scott's tiny office at the Court House doubled as a meeting place for the local politicians, and Welles spent a good deal of time there. He had first visited Scott to inquire about his father's land claims, which he soon learned were valueless. His business accomplished, Welles could have returned home, but it was now December and there were other relatives in Mifflin County whom he wanted to visit. He also enjoyed talking with Scott and with other Bradford county notables (including his cousin, Charles F. Welles) who came to discuss politics. Like Judge Forman, the local politicians at George Scott's treated Welles as an equal, even to the extent of asking his advice regarding the imminent presidential canvass. Quite probably Welles helped Scott with his editorial labors. These new and exhilarating interests no doubt acclimated him to the crude environment of a Pennsylvania frontier village. He needed little urging from his relatives to postpone his return home until spring.

Welles wrote his father that his claim was worthless, that only original Pennsylvania titles would be recorded. He also proposed that he wait until spring before journeying home. Worried about the perils of winter travel, Samuel Welles approved his son's delay in returning. Yet these "perils" did not interfere with Gideon's traveling in central Pennsylvania. He spent some time with his Uncle Elias Hale, Reuben's younger brother, who lived in Lewiston (later, Lewistown), 150 miles southwest of Towanda. Elias Hale, a graduate of Yale and one of the leading lawyers in Mifflin County, had also prospered on the Pennsylvania frontier.[26] As at Towanda, Welles was warmly received, though

Elias' wife, Aunt Jane, seems not to have been attracted to the shy, homely young man. This may have been prompted by Welles' resistance to Uncle Elias' arguments in favor of law as a career; or, perhaps Samuel Welles had written his Lewiston in-laws about his difficulties with his impractical, imaginative son.

In the late spring of 1823, Welles left for Connecticut, traveling overland from Lewiston to Philadelphia, on to New York, then by steamboat to New Haven and turnpike to Glastonbury. It was good to be home among the placid meadows and the flowering orchards, the fields freshly turned to await the sowing of crops. How different it was from the romantic grandeur of the wild Susquehanna Valley or the stump-littered hillsides of Towanda! Welles had gained a new appreciation for his native heath—its tidy aspect, its ancient trees and compact villages. Still, he missed the freedom and the casualness of the boisterous frontier settlements, the variety and interest of travel.

The long journey had failed to recoup the family fortunes in Pennsylvania lands, but it had been an unforgettable experience for Gideon Welles. He had seen something of the world outside of the ordered confines of southern New England. He had been jostled in crowded stages, shared rough and frequently dirty beds with strangers in illkept taverns, met and conversed with frontier politicians, lawyers, and land speculators. He had noted different traditions and cultures and the clashes of ethnic groups among the heterogeneous populations of New York and Pennsylvania. His observation of the conflicting forces, restlessness, and boundless individual optimism of the frontier confirmed for him that Jefferson's political ideas were right. At every hand he found evidence of communities working out their own problems in their own way without those artificial constraints his father said served merely the special interests of remote operators in Boston, New York, and Philadelphia. He was beginning to convince himself that the only way to avoid tyranny, yet maintain national unity and progress, was through states' rights.[27]

However beneficial the trip was to Welles personally, it had only postponed the immediate problem of his career. He had now passed his twenty-first birthday, yet he was as unsettled as ever in grappling with the problems of a man's estate. During the summer of 1823, he sought escape from his fears and worries in the writing of fictional sketches that dealt with ruined maidens, vile seducers, heroic Indians, mistaken identities, shipwrecks, and the like. Oddly enough, they found favor with Samuel Woodworth, author of "The Bucket," and editor of the *New York Mirror*, a ladies weekly magazine that had just begun publication in New York City.

Under the pen name "Morton," Welles sent the *Mirror* his first production—"The Deserted Orphan." In the September 13 issue he read what he scarcely dared hope—that "the beautiful little story of the deserted orphan by Morton will appear next week."[28] Thus encouraged, Welles published four more stories in the *Mirror*. One, "Edward and Isabella" a lachrymose romance, filled two full pages in the eight-page magazine.[29] A proven author, Welles' reputation soared among the Glastonbury literati, but it failed to make any impression on his father. Old Samuel, practical and direct, could see no future in unpaid sketches for literary weeklies. There was no telling where this might have led had not the *Mirror* providentially changed editors in the summer of 1824. Its new editor, George Pope Morris, rejected several of Morton's manuscripts.[30] Other editors to whom they were submitted did likewise. Reluctantly, Gideon again started casting about for a suitable career.

For several years, during times of personal anxiety, Welles had solicited advice from Cheshire classmates. Most of his intimate friends were established in worthwhile occupations or were studying for collegiate degrees. Only Welles, older than all of them, was still at home, still dependent upon his father for support. Before he left on his Pennsylvania trip, one of his friends had recommended the new American Literary, Scientific, and Military Academy, which Captain Alden Partridge had founded three years before at Norwich, Vermont.[31] Welles had not forgotten the suggestion.

During the winter of 1823-24 he secured a copy of the academy's bulletin. That exuberant prospectus seemed most impressive. More importantly, Samuel Welles was impressed too. He approved of the emphasis on practical subjects such as bookkeeping, modern languages, mathematics, and surveying. His financial situation had improved since he had, in effect, rejected Gideon's request for a college education in 1821. He was now willing to pay the $250.00 it would cost for Gideon to spend a year at Norwich.[32] The blasting of his brief literary career prompted Gideon to accept his father's offer. He enrolled as a cadet in early August 1824.[33]

The first impression Welles had of the academy could not have been favorable. He saw a plain, four-story brick building with a peak roof, standing starkly on a treeless enclosure, without even an ornamental cupola to break the harsh lines of its hundred-foot front. Welles had

seen mills in Connecticut that were more attractive. The academy's
five-acre campus had been tramped into bare earth by the marching
cadets. There were brick sentry boxes on either side of the main gate,
but no paved walkway from the gate to the building itself. Like all
entering students, Welles was escorted by one of the cadet sentries to
the superintendent's office on the second floor. Here he met the redoubtable Partridge, who entered him on the rolls; personally collected the fees for uniforms, tuition, and board; and assigned his
quarters.[34]

Partridge was then forty years old, a gaunt, sharp-featured man of
average height and austere demeanor.[35] The interview was short, as the
superintendent cultivated a brusque manner when dealing with cadets.
Given one day off to settle himself, Welles was dismissed without being told where to report or whom to consult about classes and the
academy routine.[36] This was his first brush with Partridge's casual
administrative procedures, which had already caused severe disciplinary
problems at Norwich.

Old "Pewt," as Partridge was know to both West Point and Norwich cadets, was a man of undoubted talent, but he was completely
miscast in the role of a school administrator. He was an admirable
drillmaster, a competent, practical mathematician, and a gifted promoter. But he was too domineering, and too suspicious of his subordinates, to be an effective manager of an educational institution. Nor
had he been able to rise above the sly, grasping ways of the proverbial
Yankee. When superintendent of West Point, he had directed that
public institution as a private affair—a sort of aid society for hungry
Partridges and impecunious friends. These and other irregularities
resulted in his removal from the superintendancy of West Point, and,
ultimately, in his court-martial for insubordination. For the remainder
of his life (he died in 1853), the embittered Partridge attacked West
Point with an acrid hostility—in pamphlets, in lectures, in casual conversation.[37] Unquestionably, Welles' later antipathy toward the cli-
quism of West Point and what he regarded as the aristocratic pretensions of its graduates can be traced to Partridge's monomania on the
subject. The administrative laxity of which Partridge had been accused
by his colleagues at West Point was also evident in his management
of the academy at Norwich. Welles soon discovered that the institution
was run for the exclusive profit of Partridge and his family.

The cadets all lived in identical rooms, eighteen by twenty-four feet,
each of which had a fireplace, chairs, wooden bunks with straw mat-
tresses, a closet, a pair of andirons, and a fireplace shovel. They them-

selves supplied all other furniture and bedding. Rooms were adequate for two cadets,[38] but during Welles' year at Norwich, Partridge increased enrollment dramatically, from 162 to 400 students.[39] This put an unbearable strain on facilities and faculty. As many as six cadets were now housed in a single room. Since Partridge seemed interested only in the fees and kept his own counsel, anyone was admitted if he had a letter from a parent, the necessary cash, and was at least nine years old. A harried faculty of twelve was able to preserve the semblance of education only by recruiting about ten of the recent graduates or senior cadets as instructors. Even with these hastily extemporized measures, it was impossible to cope with the horde of adolescent boys and unruly young men.[40]

To a man of Welles' temperament and orderly habits, life in the barracks was a rude shock. The atmosphere was more like that of a frontier tavern than a dormitory in a military academy. He was also dismayed when he learned that most of Captain Partridge's elaborate catalogue of courses simply did not exist. He had come to Norwich for what he supposed would be a solid, practical education. He soon discovered that in most instances the educational level there was about the same as that of Cheshire. The library had been described as holding a respectable 1000 volumes (200 more than the University of Vermont had); but that proved to be a gross exaggeration.[41] It did, however, contain a good collection of newspapers, most of which were received in exchange for the paid advertising of the Academy. Here, at least, Welles could escape the noise of the barracks while, at the same time, gratifying his taste for political news and other editorial matter. By the end of the academic year, he had given up completely his hopes for a college education. Pride would keep him from telling his father or any member of his family about the time wasted at the academy. For want of anything better, he decided that he would resume his study of law. When he returned to Glastonbury in August 1825, he discussed the matter with his father.

Samuel Welles needed Gideon to help him with the management of his loan and mortgage business. Oliver, who had married, was more of a burden on his resources than ever. Thaddeus, nineteen years old, was operating the family farm and would maintain the home in Glastonbury. If Gideon was serious about the law, his father thought it best for him to study in Hartford. There the opportunities for instruction and practice were much more promising than in Glastonbury. He would also be near enough to assist in his father's business affairs.

As he had so many times before, Samuel Welles came forward to help his son. He approached William W. Ellsworth, the most prestigious lawyer in Hartford County, who agreed to accept the younger Welles as a law student. In the fall of 1825, Gideon Welles was boarding at the Franklin House in Hartford, grappling again with Hale and Blackstone, and conning, without much interest, Zephaniah Swift's discursive work on Connecticut law.

# CHAPTER 2

# Gentleman-Editor
# (1825-1828)

G<small>IDEON</small> W<small>ELLES</small> <small>HAD FALLEN</small> into the habit of conducting his personal correspondence during the evening hours after ten o'clock, when the quiet of the city was broken only by the church bells tolling the hour and the periodic tramping of the watch. Curfew rang at nine, with one hour's grace given for the streets to be cleared. Rarely would a tippler or roisterer dare break the rest of Hartford citizens by challenging the burly watchmen who prowled the dark, deserted streets with club, lantern, and dog.[1]

On an August night in 1826, Welles was answering a letter of inquiry from Samuel Southworth of Providence, Rhode Island. Southworth, the editor of the *Literary Cadet,* a weekly journal devoted to the presidential ambitions of Henry Clay, had learned that Welles was writing editorials for the *Hartford Times and Weekly Advertiser.* He was hopeful that the Hartford paper might be converted to the Clay cause, and he was curious about Welles, about his background, his attitudes on public questions, his political influence. Prudently, Welles refused to be drawn out on presidential candidates or on current issues; but he was less reserved when it came to describing himself. Referring, rather expansively, to his father as a Revolutionary veteran and a "successful merchant," Welles wrote, "his affection and indulgence has [sic] permitted me against my own best interests to grow up careless and indifferent of the future."[2]

Almost a year had slipped by since he had begun the study of law with Ellsworth. Yet he had been unable to resist the easy camaraderie of the *Times* office, the intrigues at the State House, the pleasures of writing romantic sketches and political editorials and seeing them published. He had also, he knew, stolen time from his law books to talk politics with fellow boarders in the club-like atmosphere of the Franklin House. During his first six months in Hartford, Welles tried earnestly to steep himself in the law, but he was unable to maintain the level of interest and attention that Ellsworth demanded of his clerks.

Quite probably the frosty Ellsworth repelled the insecure young man. That distinguished lawyer was the scion of a great Federalist family, self-assured, dignified, cold, and formal in bearing. Thomas S. Williams, his partner and brother-in-law, was a warmer person, and what law Welles did learn came from Williams' instruction. To the relief, no doubt, of both Ellsworth and Williams, Welles soon decided that he would never master the legal profession. They offered no obstacle to his withdrawal and dissolved the arrangement on amicable terms.[3] Being a student of Ellsworth had had its compensations, however, if not in a professional, at least in a social sense—*entrée* into the tight little social circles of Hartford, teas at the Ellsworth's, literary afternoons at the Sigourney's, solemn assemblies at the City Hall.

Hartford had always seemed a pleasant and interesting place to Welles. Scarcely eight miles distant from Glastonbury, it was the local metropolis—the market center, the state capital on alternate years, the social and cultural arbiter of the region. Though it was little more than a large town—it had a population of about 6000—Welles considered Hartford a city of style, culture, and opportunity. In reality, it was a dull, commercial place, "plodding, mercantile and mechanical in character," a contemporary of some taste decided, adding that "the leading men were thrifty mechanics, with a few merchants and many shopkeepers."[4]

In 1825 the city meandered for about a mile along the west bank of the Connecticut River. Some thirty streets, unpaved and undrained, either terminated at the river or dwindled off into the countryside. Inland and coastal shipping, together with their attendant service industries—retail and wholesale merchandising, insurance, and banking—were the economic mainstays.[5] When winter ice did not block river traffic, the wharfs along Front Street, on the river's edge, were crowded four deep with a motley of small boats, sloops, brigs, and barges. Imports of sugar, molasses, and coffee transshipped from Baltimore, New York, and Boston were either sold locally or processed, packaged, and conveyed to towns and villages along the Connecticut River valley. Much of the merchandise borne by flatboat up the river was exchanged for return cargoes of salt beef, salt pork, and lumber from as far north as Littleton, New Hampshire. Locally owned coasters then transported the bulk of the produce direct to Southern ports for the plantation trade.[6]

As befitted a capital of "the land of steady habits," Hartford had changed little in outward appearance since Revolutionary days. The State House, which dominated the central square, had been erected in 1796. Just south of it, Henry L. Ellsworth, twin brother of Welles' law teacher, recently had built Central Row on speculation. The State House, designed by Bullfinch, was traditional in style, as was Central Row, a gambrel-roofed brick building. On Main Street, a Wadsworth still occupied the family mansion where Washington and Rochambeau had planned the seige of Yorktown. Lafayette, who was feted in a downpour when he visited Hartford in 1824, found the same solid brick buildings, the same wide, muddy Main Street he remembered from 1781.[7]

Yet in many subtle ways the city had changed. Bewigged and powdered gentlemen no longer dominated its economic or its social life. John Morgan and John Caldwell, former nabobs of the West Indies trade, still walked the streets in knee breeches and white top boots. Once considered the richest men in Hartford, they were now almost destitute, victims of the commercial decline that had followed the Napoleonic Wars. Morgan, tall and spare, eked out a living as the city's measurer of firewood, his goldheaded cane, Welles remarked, "almost the only relic of better days." His friend and former business associate, Captain Caldwell, a huge man "who made a fine appearance," existed on a small claim he had received under the provisions of "the Florida treaty with Spain."[8] John Trumbull, the last of the Hartford wits, was finishing out his days as a Supreme Court Judge. Forty years had passed since he and his fellow bards had evoked the muse with their rustic ironies and their patriotic narratives. In taste as in trade, the expansive rum-flavored humor of the Revolutionary generation was no longer the mode in Hartford.

Leading citizens dealt in such prosaic items as provisions, hardware, iron, paint, dyestuffs, and dry goods, and engaged in banking or insurance on the side. These busy, earnest individuals, and their equally busy but fanciful wives, no longer fought the Revolution with John Trumbull's *McFingal*, or thrilled at Joel Barlow's *Vision of Columbus*. They read Irving and Scott avidly and whispered about Byron's immorality (exposed in pirated editions of his poetry) at afternoon teas. Lydia Huntley Sigourney reigned as poet-laureate of Hartford, commemorating local and national events and providing a stream of occasional pieces for the newspapers and the annuals.

Mrs. Sigourney was unusually gifted in imitating poetic styles and equally talented in judging the latest sentimental tastes of her various publics. Soon to be styled the "American Hemans," she dealt profitably with death and morality—the noble passing of prominent people, infants, consumptives, and missionaries, "the loving Christian family." Trumbull's *McFingal* went through thirty editions during his lifetime, earning him fame without fortune. Mrs. Sigourney, of a more practical generation, knew the merits of discreet advertising; she made a comfortable living from her literary productions.[9]

Welles was an occasional visitor to the white-pillared Sigourney mansion just beyond the Hartford city line. He, too, remembering poignantly his invalid mother and others of the family dead—his brother Samuel and his grandparents—responded to her personality, her plaintive, wistful verse. Sharp-featured, pedantic Charles Sigourney, the poet's consort, a hardware merchant and a bank president, dispensed pompous hospitality. He had not as yet suffered the financial reverses which would embitter his later days, nor had he come to resent the business-like determination that the "American Hemans" kept concealed behind her demure charm. "Muse's time at Sigourney's and he gives us a treat tomorrow," wrote Welles to his friend and Norwich classmate, Henry Mitchell, "I wish you were here to participate in the cup of friendship."[10]

Welles had broadened his circle of acquaintances. At the Sigourney's he met Isaac Toucey, the solemn, aspiring lawyer, and high-spirited Samuel Goodrich—at that time a publisher and bookseller, but already on the road to riches as "Peter Parley," author of textbooks for children. He was also introduced to John G. Brainard, a consumptive poet of local consequence who was the editor of the *Connecticut Mirror*. Despite the elegance (in Hartford terms) of the Sigourney "afternoons," the atmosphere was too conventional and stiff for Welles' tastes. He found the less genteel, Jeffersonian surroundings of the *Times* office more congenial, if less elegiac, than the Parnassus on the wooded hill.

The *Hartford Times and Weekly Advertiser* had the smallest subscription list and the least patronage of the four newspapers then being published in Hartford. Just reorganized for the third time in less than a year, its new publishers, John Russell and Benjamin Norton, were trying to settle unpaid bills while dunning delinquent subscribers and advertisers.[11] They must have been glad to see Welles with his sheaf of sketches and fictional pieces. Russell, a printer by trade, was wholly occupied in getting out the paper and doing the job work. Norton, a capable journalist, lacked creative ability. John Milton Niles, who had the editorial direction of the paper, was equally inept at providing the romantic sketches, poems, and feature material that the public demanded of its newspapers. In September 1825, the *Times* began printing Welles' literary sketches—historical vignettes, romantic stories of local flavor, even an occasional poem. Soon he would be writing editorials too.

The young law student was attracted to the *Times* through its editor, whom his father had known and respected for a number of years. Since 1817, when Niles founded the *Times* as the only paper of strict Jeffersonian sentiments in the state, the Welles family had been faithful subscribers. Niles was a self-taught country lawyer from Windsor, an uncompromising Jeffersonian in politics, a forceful writer of vigorous editorials. In appearance, he was a slovenly little man with flaming red hair worn long and parted on the side. Small, penetrating eyes and a deep frown, almost a scowl, gave him a rather fierce expression that was belied by his calmness of temper. He was, in the words of an observer, "plain, undemonstrative, awkward, without the polish which comes from intercourse with what is called 'good society,' possibly with some of the bitterness which comes from continual opposition."[12] When Welles first met him he was thirty-eight years old, Judge of the Hartford County Court, and author of several books, the most notable of which was a pedestrian *Life of Oliver Hazard Perry*. Intense and highly ambitious, he had raised himself to an influential position in Hartford County by constant application. The second son of a poor, self-educated farmer, he had helped support a large family when both his parents died during an epidemic. While laboring with his older brother on the farm, he managed to read enough law to be admitted to the bar. He was a compulsive worker, and he accepted any law work he could find, however trivial and toilsome, did his share of heavy farm labor, wrote for pleasure and profit, always sought to improve his knowledge by wide, if unsystematic, reading, and plunged ardently into local politics.

For a young man of Niles' background and limited formal education, it was well nigh impossible to penetrate the family-conscious Federalist party. Nor was he by taste or inclination attracted to Federalism. He was, and always would remain, one of those yeomen farmers whom Jefferson thought of as the root and branch of American democracy. Considering his background, one is not surprised that he admired John Trenchard's and Richard Gordon's *Independent Whig*, with its clearly expressed natural rights philosophy, its insistence on religious toleration, its optimistic view of popular government.[13] As William Livingston and his circle had utilized *The Independent Whig* for their attacks on the Anglican oligarchy in New York just before the Revolution, so Niles had reprinted these venerable essays to attack Connecticut's Standing Order and demand Toleration after the War of 1812. The homespun lawyer-editor was also attracted to the skeptic David Hume, whom he thought "the most profound philosopher of modern times." He was untroubled, apparently, by their fundamental differences in approach and outlook. Although Niles rejected Hume's Tory views of English history, he delighted in quoting them out of context to prove the opposite of what Hume intended.

Niles' salty, self-assured arguments against the revered British constitution were vastly appealing to Welles, who also relished his pointed criticism of American preparation for the law. Why is so much time spent, Niles queried, studying the "common law of England, of their statutes and the British Constitution . . . while a few weeks may suffice for learning the constitution and laws of the United States?" He had harsh things to say in the same vein about American schools and colleges. Public opinion, the cornerstone of American democracy, rested on a knowledge of the "true theory and principles of their own system of government." Yet, said he, "this is greatly, almost entirely neglected. The few books on this subject, designed for schools, have been defective and of bad tendency."[14] Niles, like other self-taught men of his generation, was fond of drawing object lessons from history. When he first met Welles he had just finished reading Sismondi's *History of the Italian Republics of the Middle Ages* and was full of fears that the United States would lose its liberties as had Venice and Florence and Genoa.

After seven years of floundering, Welles had hit upon a teacher and a program of education that was far more interesting and enlightening than the humdrum of Cheshire, the chaos of Norwich, or the arid ecstasy of Ellsworth and Williams when they uncovered a tort in an action for lascivious carriage. Through the readings Niles suggested, and their discussions, not only of political theory but of practical politics, an art in which the older man qualified as a master, Welles soon outstripped his teacher. And being of a younger generation, he saw more clearly how political doctrine could have emotional as well as didactic appeal.

Niles had been a close associate of Jefferson's supporters in the state —Abraham Bishop of New Haven and Alexander Wolcott of Middletown. As a journalist and a partisan organizer, he had rendered invaluable service to the minority Jeffersonian party. During years of political proscription and social ostracism, his commitment to its principles never flagged. Jefferson's philosophy and the simple republicanism of John Taylor and Nathaniel Macon seemed to exemplify all the political and social truths he had uncovered in his reading or in his observations of life in Windsor and in Hartford. To Niles, with his countryman's passion for his native ground, states' rights was the best means of protecting individual liberties while preserving local institutions. The visible form of the Federalist-Congregationalist oligarchy may have been altered by Toleration, but its substance and its aims had not changed. If anything, he deemed its influence more pervasive than before; hidden behind the structure of town power, it had implanted itself in the county apparatus of the Republican party. In his opinion, Federalists posed the same threat to the liberty of the individual, and to his material advancement, that the Tories had presented before the American Revolution. Welles agreed substantially with his mentor's reading of the situation and the issues involved.

Under Niles' tutelage, Welles found both theoretical and practical confirmation for his germinal ideas on government. Already a firm believer in the cohesive strength of local pride and tradition, he was able to rationalize that states' rights, not federal power, were the bulwarks of any democratic nation. He agreed with Jefferson: that when the liberty of individuals was securely established within each state, a majority of enlightened citizens would safeguard the proper division of powers. There could be no collision of vital interests. Sectionalism or a combination of states against the nation was treason to Welles, as it was to Niles. The Hartford Convention had been a conspiracy of a Federalist minority to wreck the Union for its own selfish benefit.

Welles' early notion of states' rights and the Union was a naïve, impractical approach to the problems of sovereignty. In his exclusive emphasis on the political adjustment, he ignored economic and social differences among the various states and sections. At the time, however, his viewpoint seemed a viable rationale for Connecticut, with its homogeneous population, culture, and tradition, and its absence of any disruptive frontier influence. States' rights, or more properly, state nationalism, was not then, nor would it ever be, an adequate solution to the functional diversities that cut across political boundary lines. But politicians are not apt to be troubled by future imperatives. Welles and Niles were dealing with the hard realities of the situation as it existed in Connecticut. If the young man were to make any mark in public affairs, if he were to set his sights beyond the green hills of Glastonbury, a formula must be devised to undermine the local power of the old Federalist families. Appeals to state pride were useful. The image of that old devil, Boston—its wealth, its pretensions, its cultural and political influence among the gentry of his own state—might be turned to advantage.

Welles was quite certain that the economic future of Connecticut was bound securely to the increasing prosperity of the great port of New York, not, as formerly, to the special interests of purse-proud Bostonians. His own personal observations of the Erie Canal and of the Long Island Sound traffic had satisfied him of New York's crucial importance. Niles supplied an additional argument when he called attention to the New York market for manufactured products. As he was fond of pointing out, Connecticut was poor in everything but its enterprising population. One of the most densely peopled of all the states, it had an abundance of cheap, skilled labor. Connecticut shipyards could underbid most of their competitors in other states. Fabled "Yankee notions," carried far and wide by peddlers, were the results of hard work and inventive talent, honed on the grinding wheel of harsh necessity. The burgeoning population of New York was both an expanding market for these wares and a logical shipping point for their carriage into the interior or to points south. A glance at the map of Connecticut and Rhode Island that Niles tipped into his *Gazetteer* should have convinced the obstinate farmer or the pompous squire that New York was about 300 miles or three days by sail closer to national markets than Boston was, and from two to four days closer overland. If anyone wanted further proof, he need only scan the shipping lists: they would have disclosed eight steamboat lines running from Connecticut ports directly to New York and more than half of the state's exports being absorbed by the polyglot metropolis.[15]

Yet ties of culture and kinship and tradition are hard to break. Political habits are influenced by emotional attitudes that have nothing to do with economic factors. A Fairfield county farmer may have disposed of his scant surplus in the New York market, but he clung to his sense of New Englandism. The thirty miles that separated Manhattan Island from the Connecticut border might have been 3000 miles in terms of social outlook. Even the prosperous expatriates who lived and labored in the metropolis were self-consciously Yankee, never "Yorker."[16]

Welles himself shared some of these prejudices, but the more he and Niles pondered ways and means of turning New Englandism to their particular advantage, the more obvious it seemed to them that the sense of Yankee identity need not be bound up with Boston. In fact, the traditional allegiance, as they saw it, had worked to the disadvantage of their native state, tarnishing its loyalty to the Union and reducing its impact on national affairs. Welles had vivid memories of the Hartford Convention, that meeting of disgruntled Federalists who opposed "Mr. Madison's war" and threatened the integrity of the Union. Unquestionably, he had heard the oft-repeated comment of the embattled Republicans that the Convention was "hatched in the purlieus of Hell." The "purlieus," it was plain to the Connecticut Jeffersonians, were in or near Boston.[17] Fisher Ames, Timothy Pickering, and others of the Essex Junto were cast as the great devils in the conspiracy; their Connecticut associates, David Daggett, Roger Griswold, and John Cotton Smith, imps of the perverse. Welles needed no prompting from his father or from Niles to see in the Convention a callous betrayal of Connecticut's independence, and one designed by and for the exclusive commercial interests of Boston merchants. The New Englandism of 1814, in his view, cast sinister shadows over the New Englandism of 1826—it was still a scheme to exploit the five other states in the region for the sole benefit of eastern Massachusetts. He maintained that for a quarter of a century Connecticut had been a political (if not an economic) satellite of the Bay State. Since the days of Oliver Ellsworth, Roger Sherman, and Oliver Wolcott, there had been no Connecticut man who could match the eloquence and influence of a Daniel Webster or an Edward Everett, not one who commanded the respect of a Josiah Quincy or a Joseph Story. It was mortifying when Webster loftily remarked on the floor of Congress that he spoke for New England. To a young man of Welles' ardent temperament Webster's utterances were simply recent and galling examples of Connecticut's absolute decline in political influence.

What lay behind the trumpeting nationalism of Boston's eloquent spokesman? What did it portend for New England? Was it the same Webster of 1813 who had so remorselessly attacked President Madison for warmongering, who had sided with Timothy Pickering in almost every measure which that bitter Federalist could devise to badger the Jeffersonians in Congress? After reading Webster's great speech on Clay's "American Policy," Welles was certain he had not changed, that he remained an inveterate enemy of states' rights, and that his nationalism, as before, was but a subterfuge to "Bostonize" the entire region. Eager for issues, restless in their minority position, Welles and Niles were not overscrupulous in imputing selfish, sectional motives to Webster, whether a reasonable doubt existed or not. Nor did they fail to

notice the policies being developed by that other Massachusetts statesman, President John Quincy Adams. Webster may have been an independent in politics, or a crypto-Federalist as Welles suspected. But
there was no denying that Adams the Republican and Webster the ex-
Federalist thought along similar centralist lines. A close student of recent political history, Welles could not have assigned the same invidious role to Adams that he reserved for Webster. He could, and did,
declare that the extension and the consolidation of national power
which both the President and Webster espoused would lead to the
same end—curtailment of states' rights and, ultimately, the rights of individuals. Meanwhile, the old Federalist-merchant ring in Boston
would, as they had in the past, bend Adams' nationalist policies to
its own advantage. Welles' rationale of the state of the nation fit precisely the impressions Niles had been gathering for some time.

In his editorial direction of the *Times*, Niles had one eye on the
situation in Washington and the other on various local issues, such as
one-party rule through legislative caucus, which he had so carefully
kept before the public for seven years. There was an air of expectancy
around the *Times* office during 1825 and 1826, a sense of impending
change, which Gideon Welles found most stimulating.

Niles had at once recognized young Welles' writing skill. He was
also impressed by his knowledge of local and national politics. As his
interest in the law flagged, Welles' visits to the *Times* office became
more frequent. There, over the rhythmic crash of the old flatbed press
in the next room, Welles, Niles, and Norton ranged over the political
topics of the day—the charge of a corrupt bargain between Adams and
Clay, the issue of districting in the state, the latest Federalist intrigue,
the replacement of old Governor Oliver Wolcott.

In political matters it was a congenial group. Welles' inherited
Jeffersonian bias was buttressed by Niles' old Whig views, his close
analysis of John Taylor's tedious but illuminating (to Connecticut
Jeffersonians) *Inquiry into the Principles and Policies of the Government of the United States*. On the presidential question they all
thought Andrew Jackson was the only prominent man who combined
Jeffersonian principles with what they regarded as American—not New
England nor Southern nor Western—interests. Indeed, so harmonious
were their attitudes on public questions that Niles soon asked his new
acquaintance to try his hand at editorial writing. Welles produced a
series of slashing attacks on the Adams administration which delighted
Niles but called forth bitter protests from both Republican and Federalist newspapers in the state. Even one of Welles' closest friends,

Henry Mitchell, who shared his political views, criticized him as being "unjust to Mr. Adams" and thought his editorials were not written with "your accustomed coolness and candor."[18]

Despite the success of his journalistic efforts, Welles was still troubled by his seemingly purposeless existence. He had abandoned all thought of a legal career. The family loan business claimed only a portion of his time. A total commitment to politics and journalism did not seem either socially or economically desirable. During the winter of 1826 he grew increasingly restless and depressed. He felt he needed a change of scene to compose himself and to gain a fresh perspective. The possibility of a foreign mission was appealing. On impulse, he wrote Gideon Tomlinson and Samuel A. Foot, Connecticut Congressmen and friends of his father, asking them to use their influence in obtaining an appointment for him as a Secretary of Legation. Tomlinson's reply was friendly and vague. But the crusty Foot administered a stern and well-deserved lecture on Welles' youth, his inexperience for such a post, his lack of political prestige. The young man was hurt by the rebuke as much from its censorious tone as from the obvious truth it contained.[19] Yet by probing his weaknesses, Foot had done him a service. Now Welles understood clearly what he had suspected but had refused to admit to himself. There was no easy escape from the realities of life—his father's influence and support reached to a certain point, but beyond this he must make his own way. Gideon Welles, at the age of twenty-four, was finally breaking through the protective chrysalis that had encased him since childhood.

Meanwhile, he was being drawn further into journalism and politics. The Jeffersonian faction in the state was showing unmistakable signs of revolt, as the leading spirits saw possibilities for office and patronage if Jackson triumphed in 1828. A majority of the Republicans were solidly behind Adams. Most of the Federalists, too, had reconciled themselves to the President's apostasy of 1809. When they compared the turncoat Adams with the savage, presumably militaristic hero of New Orleans, they may have shuddered, but he was obviously the better of two evils. At least he was a New England man.

Welles' political antennae had grown sensitive since his association with the men of the *Times*. Writing his friend Henry Mitchell early in 1826, he ventured a prediction: "There is . . . a ferment already in the country, a storm gathering and the result will be like the Jeffersonian election of 1800."[20] Welles had made an accurate judgment on the political situation everywhere except in his own region. The ferment was little more than froth on the surface in New England, and barely that in Connecticut. To be sure, signs of public unrest were apparent to the eye of a sensitive observer even in conservative Connecticut. For a generation, itinerant evangelists had been lashing out at orthodoxy—political and religious—and their efforts were beginning to yield results, especially among the younger men and women.

The average citizen was a subsistence farmer, as his father and grandfather had been before him. A brief period of commercial affluence during the early phases of the Napoleonic Wars had made little impression on the stolid countryside. The nascent manufacturing interest had not as yet drawn appreciable numbers of the farm population to the cities and towns. Emigration to the West had tapered off, though there was a steady flow of younger farm families to western New York and the Pennsylvania and Ohio frontiers.

Immersed in his endless struggle with the refractory soil, the Connecticut farmer viewed the outside world with some suspicion. He was literate, but his reading did not extend much beyond the family Bible and perhaps a newspaper that found its way into the countryside. He had little time and few advantages to widen his knowledge. Beyond his daily labor, religion was of prime interest—as it had been since the days of Thomas Hooker. But it was religion of a new style, with a political flavor—more dramatic, more personal, earthier than the Great Awakening of Wesley, Whitefield, and Edwards.

Horace Bushnell, born on a farm in Litchfield County in the same year as Welles (1802), recalled that: "The house was a factory on the farm, a grower and producer for the house. Harnessed all together into the producing process, young and old, male and female, from the boy that rode the plough horse to the grandmother knitting under her spectacles, they had no conception of squandering lightly what they had all been at work, thread by thread, and grain by grain, to produce."[21] Small wonder that the farmer seemed so prudent, that his prejudices and traditions had such deep roots. Yet the very nature of his existence had made him unusually responsive to emotional appeal. And religious revivals, which had started again in 1790, provided him with an outlet for his social wants—a measure of relief from his hardscrabble existence.

The second Great Awakening, unlike its earlier counterpart, had been spearheaded by a host of colorful, itinerant preachers—Lorenzo Dow, John Maffitt, "Doctor" Warren, Jesse Lee, Elder Washburn. Many, like Washburn and Lee, had well-deserved reputations for putting their listeners into hypnotic trances. "This was not a state of distress caused by conviction of sin," wrote Frances Calkins, a local historian who actually observed such Methodist meetings, "but was understood to be a condition of indescribable rapture. . . ." Elder Washburn, who presided at a New London meeting, reported that "twenty persons fell to the floor and lay helpless from one to seven hours."[22] The message these preachers carried was similar to that of Wesley and Whitefield—equalitarian, individualist, essentially nonintellectual. But the style was new—intensely personal, argumentative, brimming over with dry wit and crude anecdotes, bristling with concrete examples drawn from the immediate locale, an evangelism that fused religious zeal with the more secular aspects of mass democracy and partisan politics.[23]

The exhorters were sketching an outline (unwittingly, of course) for future political activity. They were demonstrating how to arouse public opinion in rural, and even in urban, areas, how to exploit the emotions and utilize the prejudices of the masses—the uninformed electorate. Here was Dow, for example, on Connecticut's Sunday blue law. "There are some people," he said, "[who] instead of worshipping and serving the Lord, they only worship *Sunday*! being Sunday Christians and Monday Devils! whose religion is only in the head, not in the heart. Hence, if the head were cut off, soul and body would go to the devil!" Doubtful logic, but simple and effective metaphor! Jacksonian and Whig editors would owe a heavy debt to the style of the "Cosmopolite" when they lashed out at their political opponents.

Dow and his fellow exhorters were innovators in persuasive techniques, not just in Connecticut, but throughout the nation. They were the connection between evangelical religion as politics and evangelical politics as religion. For it was the sectarian movement itself, of which they were but a part, that was providing a model for future party organization. Thomas Jefferson, rationalist and Deist, saw clearly before he died the thrust of sectarian rivalry. "We have most unwisely committed to the hierophants of our particular superstition the direction of public opinion," he wrote in 1820. "The people in mass are . . . as wax in the hollow of their hands."[24]

Had Jefferson been a younger man when he discovered the power of the evangelists, he too might have studied their appeal and bent it to his own ideological ends. For no politician of his generation was more skillful in molding public opinion. But the actual use of the revivalist touchstone in political activity was left to his successors, who were less fastidious than he. While men such as Welles, Niles, Isaac Hill, and Amos Kendall shared Jefferson's distaste for sectarian frenzies, they made no effort to quarantine themselves from the contagion, if indeed that had been possible. Without premeditation, they copied the style of the exhorters in their partisan papers, because they knew it was effective with their audiences.

In time the creeds of the competing denominations, with their emotional attachments, sense of identity, mission and group action, would be translated by the political organizers and wire-pullers into competing party doctrines. The sectarian drive for higher education, "so deliberate, self-conscious and explicit," as Bernard Bailyn has written, was training a new generation of denominational ministers; it was also training a new generation of political men who had been taught to think and act in the equalitarian tradition of the second Great Awakening.[25] William Tudor, that astute compiler of New England quirks and quiddities, described it well: "We have so many professional men," he wrote, "so many sects with their wire-drawn subtleties, so many legislators and the habit in general of taking an interest in one or all of these pursuits that conversation is too often infected with their peculiar pendantry."[26] Writing fifteen years later, when revivalist techniques had been rather completely borrowed and secularized in politics, Michel Chevalier was astonished at the ritualistic tone of party contests. His vivid descriptions of Democratic parades clearly establish their evangelical character. He was struck by their resemblance to religious processions he had seen in Mexico and in Europe—the torches, the mottoes, the transparencies, "the halting places"—all the symbolic trappings and varieties of quasi-mystical experience.[27] Tocqueville, who visited the United States three years earlier, had generalized in a similar vein: "Every religious doctrine," he wrote in one of his pocket notebooks, has a political doctrine which by affinity is attached to it."[28] Gideon Welles would have cheerfully applied such a notion to New England Federalism, while rejecting its application to Jacksonian Democracy. Yet he did not scruple to employ both the form and substance of the second Great Awakening in his political and editorial work. He owed more to the itinerant evangelists than he knew, or would have cared to admit.[29]

# CHAPTER 3

# Apprenticeship
# in Politics

"BIGOTED, HIDEBOUND, ARISTOCRATIC, proud, arrogant and contemptible," said Gideon Welles, describing his political opponents to a friend in February 1828.[1] After two years of discussion and planning, of editorial writing by day and political correspondence at night, of journeying to this town or that in winter cold and summer heat, he was admitting his apparent failure to a Middletown friend. Even his fellow townsmen had rejected him after one term in the legislature. It was most galling to be supplanted by an Adams man in the next session.

Now committed to a career of journalism and politics, Welles was savoring the intimations of power and influence to be gained in politics. He thoroughly enjoyed the manipulative arts, and the fact that public men as far away as Tennessee read his editorials and his letters, not always with approval, but with interest. He corresponded with Congressmen on equal terms, and had a hand in making a governor of his own state. Welles had worked desperately hard for two years with little to show for his efforts. Still, the experience had done much for his self-confidence, had surfaced latent qualities he never thought he possessed. Persuasive editorials flowed as effortlessly from his pen as the sketches and short stories of former days. And they were infinitely better: taut, crisp, well-shaped pieces, full of fact and argument, but rarely missing the opportunity for a well-turned epigram if it would serve a purpose or the ironic phrase if it would sharpen a point. He found to his astonishment that he had an aptitude for political management. In dealing with politicians, most of whom were older than himself, he learned when to be frank and candid, when to be cautious and deceptive, when to be threatening or conciliatory. Tactlessness was a major weakness that he recognized and worked hard to control. It was trying for one who could be so sensitive to accept on an impersonal basis the rough and tumble of the career he marked out for himself. He set high, almost quixotic, standards for his own conduct and was invariably upset when his chosen associates did not conform to what he understood to be the essentials of character and responsibility. In time, and with much effort, he would condition himself to the treachery and ruthlessness of the political world, the graft and the greed, the false witness of erstwhile friend or secret foe. But unlike many of his colleagues, he made a clear distinction between his private convictions and his public posture, between the means he employed and the ends he cherished. Never during his forty-five years of public life did he confuse his politics with his principles. Nor did he accept the easy, arrogant role of the cynical manager who viewed his fellow politicians as a pack of knaves and the public a pack of fools—the one to be trumped, the other led. So he gained a measure of circumspection during these early years in politics, concealing his righteous indignation at questionable practices, venting his sense of outrage in his secret diary or his private correspondence, and always striving to raise the moral tone of political leadership.

Despite the checkrein imposed on his political ambitions in 1828, Welles could take some satisfaction in the progress of the *Times*. Two years before, at Niles' behest, he had assumed editorial direction of the paper. Doing much of the work himself—editorials, political correspondence, sketches, and exchange articles—he added vigor and variety to the four-page journal. Within a few months these improvements were reflected in rising circulation and advertising revenues. By January 1827, Welles felt justified in enlarging the pages of the *Times* and in changing its format. There was no doubt now that the paper was making an impression. It was being quoted favorably by such influential journals as the *Albany Argus, The United States Telegraph,* and M. M. Noah's *New York Enquirer.* Within the state its new influence could be gauged in the mounting tempo of attacks made upon it by the Adams Republican and the Federalist press. In fact just one month before Welles denounced the Adams Republicans as "bigoted" and "aristocratic," they had established a new paper in Hartford—*The New England Review*—to assist the staid *Courant* and the colorless *Mercury* in counteracting the *Times'* popularity. For its editor they chose a young journalist, George D. Prentice, who had made a local reputation for his sardonic wit while editor of the *New London Ga-*

*zette.* He was soon to prove Welles' peer in editorial writing, and his superior in the practice of ridicule and innuendo.[2]

Welles was pleased by his quick success as an editor, but he still regarded journalism as merely an avocation. His prime motivation for accepting an editorial post had been to further the political ambitions of his own Hartford circle. Niles, of course, was the acknowledged leader, though Welles was now on such close political and personal terms with him that, if Niles moved up the political ladder, he himself would move also. As a working team they aimed beyond the restricting confines and petty jealousies of state politics. Both were clever enough to gamble on the probable election of Andrew Jackson to the presidency in 1828 and were relying on it to build up their reputations; yet neither thought of himself as a political opportunist.

Their reading of exchange newspapers from the South and West convinced them that Jackson was the choice of the common man. Distinguished Jeffersonians such as Littleton Tazewell of Virginia, who stood at the head of the Virginia bar, if not the nation's, were openly supporting Jackson.[3] In neighboring New York State, Martin Van Buren had withdrawn his support from the stricken William H. Crawford and was backing Jackson. For some years Van Buren's growing power and prestige had counted heavily with the Connecticut Jeffersonians. His political organization was considered a model of functional efficiency; his close alliance with the Virginia dynasty, proof of his orthodox republicanism; the political stronghold he had built in New York, a massive counterpose to a "Bostonized" New England.

If men of such sterling qualifications could testify that the Old Hero was the legitimate heir of Jefferson, Welles reasoned, then Jackson was neither centralist nor sectionalist. Satisfied on this score, Welles saw no reason why he and Niles should not share in the blessings Jackson would bring when virtue was restored to the land. A first and crucial step in this direction was control of the Republican party in the state. When Welles assumed the editorship of the *Times* in 1826, the political situation seemed as favorable as it would ever be for grasping the reins of power.

The Republican party in Connecticut had never been a viable political entity. Assembled from disparate parts, it achieved its purpose in drawing up the Constitution of 1818 and in breaking down Federalist rule. No single power center existed. Unity had been maintained after a fashion through the shifting alliances of county leaders, who agreed on the slate for the Senate, for state officers, and for Congressmen. Nominations were then ratified by a party legislative caucus and pre-

sented to the people. Since the Federalists after 1820 offered no opposing ticket, annual and biennial elections were mere formalities.
Few issues ruffled a deceptive political calm.[4]

Although for six years the Federalists had not contested the Republican ticket, they did maintain their organization in the towns. A respectable minority of Federalist representatives was elected each year
to the lower house of the legislature. Party policy for them was one of
watchful waiting. When it seemed expedient, they would support
whichever Republican faction seemed most congenial to their views.
A floating minority, the Federalists contributed to the unstable condition of the Republican party, effectively blocking unified action and
weakening any specific sense of party doctrine. Most of the leading Republicans, Niles among them, at one time or another courted them
when it seemed advantageous to strike a bargain.

In 1826 Niles and a former political rival, Noah Phelps, joined
forces to achieve an uneasy control of the Hartford County organization. Phelps, an inveterate officeseeker, was hoping for a congressional
seat; Niles was aiming for control of the state organization so that he
could at an appropriate time, swing it over to Andrew Jackson.[5] Both
men, of course, concealed their real aims in their communication with
other county leaders. Ostensibly, they sought a reshuffling of the state
administration that would force old Governor Wolcott out of office
and ultimately destroy the mischief-making potential of the Federalists. Republican leaders in Litchfield, Tolland, and Middlesex seemed
friendly to the Niles-Phelps overtures. The southern counties, including New Haven—solid Adams territory—actually anticipated Niles and
Phelps by coming forward with a similar proposition,[6] an unexpected
turn of events that should have alerted the Hartford schemers to trouble ahead. Probably it did, because both Niles and Phelps were well
seasoned in the cut and slash of state politics and had no illusions
about the motives of the New Haven group. That former Congressman Samuel Foot and his associate, Congressman Ralph Ingersoll,
should come bearing gifts could have meant nothing more than an expression of their own particular interest in unseating Wolcott. Niles
must have assessed their intentions accurately as they did his, but he
was glad to accept their support.

Foot's sphere of influence was wider and more highly integrated
than that of the Niles-Phelps coalition. Supreme in New Haven, he
and Ingersoll had a good working alliance with party leaders in all of
the southern counties. The trim, self-assured Foot was in the prime of

life, energetic and ambitious, a cunning politician whose immediate goal was a seat in the United States Senate. His lieutenant, Ingersoll, was the abler man, more flexible in his dealings, more tactful than the overbearing Foot.[7] An urbane lawyer and a master of intrigue, Ingersoll enjoyed political combat for its own sake. Power interested him also—not the trappings of high public office, but the sure feel of control in his own hands, the satisfaction of directing a well-constructed machine that would respond precisely to his command. Let Foot have the glory, he would be content with the power, at least for the time being.

For almost ten years Ingersoll's political ambitions had been contained by the placid and, to him, meaningless course of the Republican party. Ingersoll had captained the Tolerationist forces in the legislature during the heated sessions of 1817 and 1818. Only twenty-eight years old at the time, he easily outmaneuvered the Federalists in debate, while behind the scenes he divided their strength and skillfully held their Tolerationist wing to its bargain with the Jeffersonian minority. It was an admirable performance that earned the grudging regard of the defeated old-line Federalists. "Young Hotspur," they had dubbed him after one of his ferocious onslaughts in the General Assembly, a tribute to his fighting qualities that overlooked the careful, calculating side of his personality.[8] Ingersoll was a man of expediency rather than principle—never impetuous without purpose.

It was now expedient to work with any faction that would remove Wolcott from the political scene. The New Haven lawyer saw as clearly as Niles that the Governor was a major obstacle to his personal ambition. Wolcott's following of conservative Republicans and Federalists had to be smashed before he could reorganize the party to his own satisfaction. Though Foot deemed Niles and Phelps upstarts who were beneath contempt, he was persuaded by the arguments of his younger colleague that a temporary alliance would be of immediate advantage.

Niles and Welles considered that Wolcott—a man of great ability and influence—had been gradually "Federalizing" the Republican party since his election in 1818. More significantly, the Governor had exerted his influence to squelch the Crawford candidacy in 1823 and would very likely oppose Jackson in 1828. They, like Ingersoll, had come to the conclusion that no one could assume party leadership while Wolcott remained in office—a potent factor in their accepting assistance from the basically hostile New Haven faction. The choice of the new combination to succeed Wolcott was Gideon Tomlinson, a popular, easygoing Congressman from Fairfield County who was regarded as manageable—"a sleek little governor of whom little was to be expected, but who if elected would do no harm."[9]

To the dismay of the forces arrayed against him, Wolcott, with Federalist support, narrowly defeated Tomlinson in 1826. It was his last victory, however; he made no effort to deal with the party chieftains or again seek Federalist support. He was sixty-six years old and longed for retirement to his farm in Windsor. Only a strong sense of duty had prompted him to seek re-election.

Wolcott was a distinguished man. He had been a devoted friend of Alexander Hamilton, succeeding him as Secretary of the Treasury. Washington had respected his fiscal abilities, and John Adams, no mean judge of talent, had continued Wolcott as Secretary of the Treasury despite his close association with Hamilton. A gifted administrator, he was neither a strong executive nor a successful party leader. In many ways he resembled the Adamses in their talents and their political ineptitude, but he was much warmer in personal relations, less egotistical—a portly, reticent, old-fashioned gentleman.

During the early years of his governorship, he had applied all of his skill and experience toward refashioning his backward little state into a progressive commonwealth on the Hamiltonian model. In message after message, he recommended internal improvements, tax reforms, mechanic lien laws, state aid for agriculture and industry. Gideon Welles, who opposed these "Federalizing" tendencies, still admired him as one of the greatest governors in Connecticut history. "He was a statesman among statesmen," wrote Welles in retrospect. "His messages and state papers have a vigor and power, and display a maturity of thought and scope and grasp of mind, which are seldom surpassed in similar communications."[10]

Wolcott failed in his efforts to ensure the orderly development of his native state. At the end of his long public career he had gained the unenviable distinction of being a prophet without honor in his own land. The last and the best of the Federalist dynasty, he and his kind would be succeeded by a new generation of public men, less talented, more flexible—professionals in the art of the possible. Wolcott could no more have understood the coming style of popular politics than Jonathan Edwards could have comprehended the vulgarisms and rustic wit of Lorenzo Dow or Elder Warren. Essentially an eighteenth-century rationalist, Wolcott was out of touch with the emotional needs and the restless, though undefined, aspirations of the people.

The Governor was shunted aside—or more properly, made no contest—but his removal from the scene did not yield the benefits expected by "the Hartford radicals," as the Niles' group called themselves. Their bid for control of the state organization was a complete fiasco. Ingersoll had seen to that. Acting swiftly yet discreetly, he encouraged a group of restive Republicans in Hartford County to challenge the Niles-Phelps coalition. Far from unifying the party under their control, the radicals found that they had to fight for their political lives in their home territory.

Spurred on by public opinion, most of the newspapers were demanding that the state be divided into election districts and that district conventions take over the nominations. The issue was a hoary one in state politics. Over the years the Jeffersonian minority had constantly urged districting, not only for state senators but for Congressmen and for presidential electors as well. They had assumed, correctly, that districting would assist a minority faction in gaining some representation in the state senate, perhaps even a Congressman. Niles had been a vigorous supporter of the reform, which suited his political principles— mass suffrage and popular participation—and his position within the party. But by 1826 his influence among the Republican leaders had broadened considerably. While opposing caucus nominations, he and Welles were uncertain about which of the many districting proposals they would support. The decision was made for them by a direct challenge to Niles' county leadership from an able, aggressive Wethersfield lawyer, Martin Welles, Ingersoll's chief collaborator in Hartford County.

Martin Welles was a man of heavy build, hard-featured, with pendulous underlip and grim expression sharpened by the small, steelrimmed spectacles he wore. He was also a man of high intelligence, fine diction, and commanding presence. Formerly a Federalist, he was now a Republican and had served two terms in the legislature as a representative from Wethersfield. Almost at once he made an impact on the legislature, which promptly elected him clerk—an influential post—and reelected him in the next session. Briefly he cooperated with the Hartford radicals, but in 1826, with powerful support from New Haven, he began to interfere seriously with their plans.

Capitalizing on a local issue, prison reform, he managed to block Noah Phelps' nomination for Congress in the legislative caucus, and had himself selected for the state senate. If the radicals were to survive within the party, Martin Welles, with his Federalist and New Haven connections, must be beaten down. The way ahead was clear; the Hartford radicals would support county conventions and stigmatize

the regular nominations as examples of caucus dictation. Such actions
were to be regularized in the future by a constitutional amendment
that would provide election districts for the upper house of the legislature. And depending upon the circumstances, they would seek legislation for the districting of congressional seats and presidential electors.

Once their decision was made, Gideon Welles opened a correspondence with friendly state leaders. He had two objectives in mind: to
learn their opinions on districting, so that the political strength of the
movement could be more accurately measured, and to gain their support for a districting plan that was proportional.[11] In principle, the
Welles-Niles districting plan was democratic and Jeffersonian—one citizen, one vote; in practice, it would favor the political aims of the radicals. Hartford County, the most populous in the state, would have
more districts, and hence more weight in the upper house of the legislature, than any other in the state. Should congressional districts be
established, the Hartford area could always count on at least one Congressman, perhaps more. Should presidential electors be apportioned
on the same basis, a minority, if well organized, might well carry some
of the districts and be reflected in the votes cast by the state.[12] It seems
likely that Republican leaders in other counties saw through Welles'
pious arguments that proportional districting was the democratic way.
All of them professed a cautious support for districting, but all were
vague about how it should be implemented. Not one would commit
himself to the proportional idea.[13] Welles' correspondence on the subject had served only to demonstrate that popular agitation against the
caucus system was making an impression on county leaders.

The ambiguous response on the vital issue of proportional as opposed to county representation prompted Welles to move carefully and
deliberately. In November 1826 he sent out a circular letter to political
friends in the towns of his own county, inviting them to a meeting
where caucus nominations and districting would be discussed.[14] The
meeting was held in late December, and, while sternly condemning the
caucus, the delegates took no action on the regular ticket.[15] Welles'
maneuver, much to his surprise, set off a chain reaction of county
meetings which did make changes in the ticket. Emboldened by this
unexpected turn of events, the Hartford radicals saw an opportunity
to consolidate their power in the county. Rashly, they called a second
convention in February and substituted Niles for Martin Welles as a
candidate for the state senate.[16] No other changes were made in the
slate—a fact that cast some doubt on the sincerity of Welles' strictures
against the caucus system in the *Hartford Times*.

Martin Welles was vulnerable on many points—his caucus nomination, his refusal to back districting, his arrogant and open opportunism. Had districting been in force, Niles would have beaten him handily, for Niles carried Hartford, New Haven, and Litchfield counties, the most populous areas in the state. But Welles, bearing the organization label, triumphed over the insurgents, who were badly divided among themselves. Gideon Welles and John M. Niles had poked a nest of wasps when they held the first county convention to discuss caucus nominations. By election time virtually every newspaper in the state had its own list of candidates. In such a confused situation, the regular organization scored an easy victory.[17]

The election did reveal that an overwhelming majority of those who voted were in favor of some districting plan. "King Caucus" was being forced to abdicate. Though the Hartford radicals had lost the election, they might gain their immediate objectives in another way. Gideon Welles was elected to the lower house as a member from Glastonbury. He would act as floor leader for a districting law based on "democratic" principles.[18]

The new member from Glastonbury was familiar with legislative proceedings. He had been a frequent visitor to the State House when his father was a member, and, like most children in those days of limited recreation, he enjoyed the special festivities of "election day" —the militia parades, the annual "election cake," the informal hospitality that custom decreed. Now he was a member himself, as both his father and grandfather had been before him.

Everything seemed fresh and interesting to his uncritical eye. He did not concern himself about the stark discomfort of the representatives' hall on the second floor of the State House. He found no fault with the bare wooden benches on which the representatives sat facing each other across the long central aisle. Even the wretched acoustics of the place, the fact that the speaker presiding on a platform at one end of the hall could scarcely be heard at the other, did not curtail his satisfaction at being an elected representative of the people. If he was dismayed at all during the session, it would have been because of his inability to engage in debate. Painfully self-conscious, he could not match wits with the experienced attorneys who were the leading members of the house. Though a majority of the legislators were farmers, the tone of debate was set by the lawyers. And this usually took the form of special pleading where subtle distinctions were asserted and small points maintained in a typical courtroom manner.[19]

Unwilling to take the floor, Welles worked behind the scenes discussing proposed legislation in the lobby or escorting key members to the *Times* office for a glass of French brandy and some quiet conversation. He was not appointed to the house committee raised to consider districting; nevertheless, working tirelessly in his quiet way, he persuaded the Republican caucus to exclude as "quids" some dubious members, then to vote unanimously for a bill embodying single districts based on population. He and Niles also convinced a majority of the districting committee to report favorably on a proportional bill.

At this point they ran into overwhelming opposition. It was voiced about that proportional legislation, especially for presidential electors, would injure the prospects of John Quincy Adams in the state.[20] From his seat in the state senate, Martin Welles exerted his powerful influence to advance this idea. The result was that sufficient Republicans bolted the caucus and joined with the Federalists to amend the bill by removing its proportional feature.

The term in the legislature provided valuable experience for Welles. He began the process of evaluating the strengths and weaknesses of his new acquaintances—a matter of vital importance to a political tyro. His rebuff in the districting affair impressed upon him the need for tact and patience in dealing with political friends as well as opponents. Martin Welles had proven a formidable antagonist and, if anything, had increased his influence in the state. The member from Glastonbury boasted that "Martin Welles showed his teeth several times but could not bite." The record shows otherwise. Gideon Welles had been outmaneuvered on several important occasions by the masterful Wethersfield lawyer.

The New Haven faction was more to be feared than Martin Welles. Samuel Foot, its titular leader, was now in the United States Senate, where he was gaining a national reputation of sorts. Congressman Ralph Ingersoll and his spokesman Joseph Barber of the *New Haven Register,* though temporarily cooperating on the issue of districting, were openly bidding for the dominant party role in the state, and an immediate problem was their well-known partiality to Adams' reelection. Already definite signs were appearing that the New Haven group would again join with Martin Welles and other Adams Republicans to "proscribe" the Jacksonians.

Near the close of the session, Welles wrote a conciliatory letter to Joseph Barber, explaining his vote on districting and expressing the hope that differences over presidential candidates would "not enter into the great question—the preservation of the party." For now, clearly, Jackson had not the remotest chance of winning the electoral vote of the state. A correspondent from Fairfield County wrote Welles that the only supporters of Jackson in his area were "three Federalists of the old stamp plus two apostate Republicans." Governor Tomlinson, a native of Fairfield, was exerting all the prestige of his office for Adams. The editor of the influential Bridgeport *Farmer* was merely biding his time before attacking the Jackson movement. "I must say," wrote one of Welles' correspondents from that quarter, "of our old school democrats—the weight of talent is against us."[21]

So disquieting was the flow of pessimistic reports that the self-appointed Jacksonian leaders became concerned lest they had misread the Old Hero's popularity in the country. Someone, they felt, ought to visit other states and gain fresh impressions concerning the relative strengths of the two candidates. A group of Pennsylvania wool producers had just issued a call for a national tariff convention to meet in Harrisburg on July 27, 1827, and it was announced that a Connecticut meeting would be held early that month to select delegates. Andrew Judson, one of the defeated Jacksonian candidates for a congressional nomination, had heard that the Harrisburg convention was being planned as an electioneering device for Adams and Clay. Might not the Middletown meeting have similar political motives? He urged that a Jackson man or two attend, a suggestion Welles was quick to accept.[22] Welles and Henry L. Ellsworth, who was then leaning toward the Jacksonians, attended the Middletown meeting, where they were placed on the slate of delegates for the Harrisburg meeting. Contrary to Judson's fears, the state convention had no political overtones, but of the seven Connecticut delegates who did journey to Harrisburg (Ellsworth dropped out), Welles was the only avowed Jacksonian.[23] At 11 a.m. on July 21, Welles boarded the *McDonough* for his steamboat trip to New York. In high spirits, he looked forward to the change, variety, and excitement of travel. He was eager to meet and cultivate politicians outside of his state, to exchange views, and to reinforce, if possible, convictions he had formed but had not tested.

Welles had devoted a good deal of his time the previous summer to "examining the grounds of political division with a somewhat critical eye, from the first rise of parties." In his study of party formation, he decided that a fundamental difference in principle existed between the "centralist" position of Hamilton and the "democratic" doctrine of Jefferson. Conversations with Niles strengthened his belief that there were certain abiding principles in American politics. Jefferson had expounded these to Welles' satisfaction. The Virginian's political philosophy, once accepted, became a fixed ideal—no wavering, no "half-way covenant" for Welles. Issues might change, Welles decided, but democratic principles were eternal. In forming his conclusions he noted what he took to be a Hamiltonian departure from strict Jeffersonian doctrine during the Madison and Monroe administrations. But the only departure he considered serious was national appropriation for internal improvements, a clear and present danger to state, and hence, individual, freedom. He had no position on the Second Bank of the United States. Poorly informed on the tariff question, he was undecided whether higher duties on various key products were compatible with his political philosophy or not.[24]

As the *McDonough* moved downstream, Welles was busy as usual gaining impressions of people, of scenery, of local history to be used later for feature material in the *Hartford Times*. Though these pieces were meant to be descriptive, he always strove for the light touch. "Saybrook (Pittipaug)," he jotted down in his Diary, "renowned for valor, bravery, chivalry in the glorious defense of the place when a monstrous army of one hundred and fifty Englishmen met and gloriously frightened eight hundred militia. . . ." "Many worthy men in Saybrook," he quickly scribbled as an afterthought, "not to be blamed for the conduct of the militia in 1814." Welles enjoyed the comparative comfort of steamboat travel (spiced with some danger from the possibility of boiler explosion), but he was too reserved to strike up acquaintances among so many strangers. In the closer intimacy of the stagecoach in which he traveled from Philadelphia, he was able to cast off his shyness and indulge his curiosity, his essentially gregarious nature. "I like a stage coach," he said. "Friendly feelings are for the moment created and though that feeling may be ephemeral in the bosoms of some, it is not the case for all." When it came to overnight accommodations, he was not so expansive. Hot, dusty, and tired after a long, stifling stage ride "on a sultry day," he reached Harrisburg at seven in the evening of July 29. Some sixty delegates had already arrived, lodgings were scarce and expensive. He finally obtained a bed at Wilson's, "the best house in town," but to his disgust found that "six of us were crowded into a small room."[25]

Welles attended all the sessions but took no active part in the proceedings. He was far more interested in the various personalities present and the possible backstairs politics than he was in the debate over tariff schedules. Disappointed that presidential politics were not evident on the floor, he contented himself with the conjecture that "our opponents have found it policy to keep silent and maneuver in the background." "It cannot be supposed," he wrote one of his new correspondents—James A. Jones, editor of the *Philadelphia Palladium*—"that such men, all supporters of Adams and Clay, as Jonathan Roberts, J. G. Wright, Bell, Bartlett, Sprague, Robbins, Lawrence, and Hall should be long together without concerting some scheme to press the coalition."[26] Welles met and talked with several Jackson men and some who were partial to Jackson but not quite ready to move. He met Simon Cameron at Harrisburg, and he observed (correctly) that the shrewd Pennsylvanian "was not fully prepared to commit himself for Jackson." The young editor was most impressed by old Mathew Carey, the eminent Philadelphia publisher, with whom he would later correspond.[27]

Welles made no contribution to the convention, except to sign, with other Connecticut delegates, the high tariff memorial to Congress authored jointly by Carey and Hezekiah Niles. Then he journeyed westward, stopping for a few days with his Hale cousins in Lewiston before reaching his planned destination, Pittsburgh. By mid-September he was back in Hartford with a notebook of fresh material, a good many political contacts in other states, and information for his father on the investment possibilities of western Pennsylvania.

Much had happened in state politics during his six-week absence. The Adams Republicans, guided deftly by the irrepressible Ingersoll, had composed their factional differences and were moving vigorously to isolate the Jacksonians. All of the Republican and Federalist papers except the *Hartford Times* and the *New Haven Herald* (a High Federalist sheet) were supporting Adams. Their editorial pages were freighted with personal and political attacks on Jackson, who was pictured as an autocrat, a sectionalist, a frontier ruffian, an ignorant, bloody-minded, military tyrant. His supporters in the state, when they were not ridiculed as a corporal's guard of political hacks, were branded as self-seeking adventurers who would ride any demagogue's coattails.

The young editor found himself the spokesman for the Jacksonians in the state, at a time when they were being assailed by most of the other journals in Connecticut. Though he had the added burden of directing the political campaign as well, he gloried in what he chose to regard as the lonely grandeur of his position. But he had to summon all of his physical and mental resources to cope with the heavy demands of publishing a newspaper and launching a new party.

Preliminary measures had been taken during the legislative session in Hartford the previous May to organize the friends of Jackson in the state. They agreed on a Jacksonian electoral ticket even if—as they were certain—the party organization came out for Adams. No move was contemplated until they could assess the outcome of the state elections in the spring of 1828; nor would any independent action be taken to launch a separate state ticket for 1829 until the presidential election was decided in November.

Welles himself had outlined this calculating course—in effect, he had made a realistic appraisal of Jacksonian weakness in the state. He hoped that the state ticket could be kept separate from presidential politics and that he and his associates could remain in good standing within the party yet continue their active support for Jackson. If Jackson lost the election, their already tenuous political position would be dealt a mortal blow. If he won, however, it could be immensely strengthened. Should their opponents make the presidential issue a test of party loyalty, Welles wanted the test deferred until Jackson's strength in the country was more fully developed. Any premature action, he thought, would arouse the opposition and probably reduce the popular vote in the state for the Old Hero. Welles assumed that Adams would carry Connecticut; still, he needed a good showing for Jackson if he and his friends were to make any impression outside of their embattled enclave. Considering the circumstances, it was the best plan possible, but the entire strategy rested on the shaky assumption that the Adams Republicans could be persuaded to divorce the state campaign from the national one for the sake of party unity. Welles had gravely underestimated the political expertise of Ingersoll and Martin Welles. When he returned from Harrisburg, the Adams press was demanding that the Hartford radicals be read out of the party.[28]

Responding in the columns of the *Hartford Times,* Welles declared that presidential politics had not been an issue in the state since 1816, and should not be made one now. Through the fall and winter he continued to press for party harmony in the face of mounting evidence that the Jacksonians were being deliberately and effectively isolated. Welles also sought unsuccessfully to head off a public celebration in Middletown on the anniversary of Jackson's New Orleans victory, lest it widen the breach in the party. But by now his patience was nearing an end. In mid-December he wrote one of his correspondents in Litchfield County that an independent stand might have to be taken. "I do not wish the Republican party dismembered," he said, ". . . but if those who differ from us in opinion attempt to proscribe us, let us not suffer lamely."[29]

As yet the Jacksonians had no formal organization. Welles, a one-man committee of correspondence, kept in touch with alleged supporters in the various towns. They were well organized only in Hartford County, where Noah Phelps had used his position as sheriff to pack the county committee—which then dutifully renominated Niles for state senator on the regular Republican ticket. In presenting the slate the *Hartford Times* warned that only Federalists would profit if the regular ticket was not supported.

The opposition moved rapidly against Niles. Martin Welles had foreseen such a move, and on March 2, 1828 the *American Mercury* published a call for a second nominating convention, to be composed exclusively of Adams men.[30] Gideon Welles was shocked to note that George Merrick, a Glastonbury friend on whom he had counted for support in his own bid for re-election to the legislature, had signed the call, along with Jonathan Welles, a bitter opponent (as only a relative could be) in town politics. The Adams convention that met on March 7 promptly nominated Martin Welles—a signal for the Adams Republicans in other counties to purge any convention candidate suspected of being sympathetic to Jackson. "The administration folks," wrote Andrew Judson from the eastern part of the state, "are doing everything possible to prevent the election of a single Jackson man to either house. I find them extremely bitter towards Judge Niles."[31]

Welles strove with all his might to stem the tide. He filled the columns of the *Hartford Times* with bitter attacks on Adams, he pronounced the coffin handbills charging Jackson with the murder of militia men an insult to common sense, he raised the specter of Federalism, and he even tried convincing Joseph Barber of the *Register* that the presidential test was a plot to disrupt the party—an effort, he must have known, was well nigh hopeless. The Adams press had managed to identify Jackson as a symbol of tyranny in the popular mind. Welles and his group were so closely tied to his candidacy that a vote for any of the Jacksonian candidates was a vote for military despotism.

The regular ticket won in two counties—New Haven and Fairfield—only because all of the candidates were firm Adams men. About twenty would-be Jacksonians were elected to the 1828 legislature, which had 280 members. Small recompense for a campaign so bitter that there seemed little hope of reconciliation between the two factions. As one of the state's Congressmen wrote Welles, "the work is done, the Republican party will harmonize no more."[32]

# CHAPTER 4

# Rewards
# for the Faithful

WELLES HAD BECOME so deeply involved in the campaign and had taken so much abuse that he viewed the Adams triumph in the state as a personal defeat. Close friends, he learned, had defected to the enemy. Political associates he counted on for support had, he felt, bowed to expediency. He could forgive his friend Henry Mitchell, who voted against Niles because he was a fledging lawyer; Welles knew what obligations he had been forced to accept. But when a seasoned politician yielded to the pressure of Adams men, Welles was not so tolerant.

Loyalty to one's political friends and principles, he sternly reminded one erring state senator, must never be compromised.[1] He made his point clear to the small group of Jacksonian leaders. If they were to succeed, they had to trust each other. Once a decision was taken, there was to be no wavering, even if it entailed a personal sacrifice. As Welles saw it, personal ambition—"men not measures," a slogan he was fond of quoting—had perverted the Republican party and sapped its strength. The Jacksonians alone remained faithful to the democratic principles on which the party had been founded. It was their duty to uphold and propagate these principles through an inflexible organization. In maintaining a united front they would capitalize on the inherent divisions of their opponents, yet still act as defenders of the true faith.

The course of action he was demanding closely resembled that of the Albany Regency in New York politics. Welles was not acquainted with Martin Van Buren, nor with any of his henchmen. He was, however, an avid reader of the New York press, and it is likely that he was influenced by the Regency pattern of organization.[2] Whatever the model, Welles and Niles had fashioned an initial organization within four months of their defeat. On May 15, 1828, about thirty "friends of Jackson" from every county in the state met in New Haven. They appointed committees to call county conventions which would nominate Jackson electors whose names would be ratified at a general meeting in August. These groups were also charged with the formal organization of a political party—the appointment of county committees of "vigilance and correspondence." And they were expressly requested to carry the organization right down to the basic units of local government, the towns. Town elections would be held in the fall. It was hoped there would be a Jackson candidate for each one of the more than 800 local offices, an ambitious program for the infant party, which numbered about 1000 firm supporters in the state.

Spurred on by Welles and Niles, the Hartford Jacksonians held their first county convention on June 12, 1828. Well over 100 delegates, from all but "two or three of the most distant and remote towns" attended the meeting. The convention not only nominated presidential electors, but it issued a call for a state convention to be held in Middletown on August 12. It also approved an address to the people of Connecticut to be printed in sufficient quantities to blanket the state.

Niles was the author of this document, though Welles read and criticized the first draft before final copying. It was a cogent, well-reasoned paper, frankly aimed at the intelligent and articulate, rather than the average voter. At least one realistic Jacksonian criticized it for being too candid, "in admitting or seeming to admit the qualifications of Jackson for the presidency to be inferior to those of Adams." He advised that Jackson's heroic qualities be played up, that the people could understand and appreciate the simple themes of patriotism and courage.[3] But Welles and Niles were better informed about the state of the popular mind than he. The campaign to stereotype Jackson as an autocratic despot had done its work too well. As Andrew Judson described it to Welles, "Our people are remarkably obstinate in this business . . . not that they like Adams, but that they fear Jackson." At this initial stage of organization it made far more sense to concentrate efforts on community leaders rather than on the general public. If they could be persuaded, they could then explain the Jackson cause to their friends and neighbors.

In other counties the Jackson men followed Hartford's example, but their meetings were poorly attended. Thus, the state convention at Middletown was scarcely a representative one, nor could its members boast of pure Jeffersonian lineage. Prentice's acrimonous *New England Review* was probably not far off the mark when it described the assembled delegates as "Democrats, Federalists, quids, straddlers, and twaddlers, in fact all sorts of not exactly four-footed beasts, but creeping things in great multitudes. . . ."[4]

Even the Hartford County delegation, a clear majority of the convention, was not entirely free of "eleventh hour" men. Henry L. Ellsworth, Hartford's leading real estate speculator, played a prominent role. Formerly a strict Federalist, he had supported the Hartford Convention, but unlike other members of his prestigious family, Ellsworth had become an apostate and joined the Toleration forces in 1816. For the next ten years he had been a prodigal son—and something of a pariah in the political and social world of Hartford. He was spurned by his former Federalist friends, and his new Tolerationist colleagues had not altogether trusted him. His business affairs suffered; his family relations were affected. "There was a time," he recalled, "when I thought I should be thankful for a shelter anywhere from the religious, political and pecuniary persecutions. . . . I suffered much in feeling and in property." Ellsworth joined the *Times* group for purely opportunist reasons. Welles and Niles were quite aware of this, but their position was such that they welcomed any support, even Ellsworth's. Commenting on the Ellsworth conversion, the caustic Prentice of the *Review* said ". . . he was taken by the hand by Noah A. Phelps, while Niles wiped his face and he became as pure a Republican as the *Times* could wish. . . ."[5]

Since most of the delegates were from Hartford County, the *Times* men easily dominated the proceedings. They saw to it that they controlled a majority of what they euphemistically styled the central committee, which was appointed by the convention. There was some grumbling at the time, and there would be more after the election, but it was apparent that Hartford had the strongest organization and the most alert leadership. Welles and Niles would not tolerate any overt challenge at this formative stage. They brushed aside all criticism of their high-handed tactics as mere quibbles, and, in demanding a concerted effort, they stressed the importance of individual leadership in bringing out the Jackson vote.

The apparent popularity of Old Hickory outside of New England was beginning to influence various key individuals who had remained neutral. A small but steady accretion of federal officeholders (mainly postmasters) gave the new party an appearance of some strength. A few Federalists would support Jackson because they still considered Adams a traitor to the cause. Other citizens would not vote for President Adams because he was a Unitarian—anthema to orthodox Congregationalists and free-swinging Methodists alike.[6]

Niles' address had also made an impression, especially that part which dealt with economic affairs. He argued that Adams was a creature of Massachusetts interests, and then he made the point that Massachusetts was receiving a lion's share of federal money for internal improvements. He opposed such appropriations, but if they had to be made, Connecticut must not be deprived of a just proportion. Describing Massachusetts as a commercial state and Connecticut as a manufacturing state, he pointed out that many Massachusetts Congressmen had voted against the tariffs of 1824 and 1828. Selfishly, they had determined to advance the interests of their own state to the detriment of the rest of New England. Niles' arguments appealed especially to the producers and manufactureres of wool, a small though influential group. But in a general sense his strictures reached a wider audience: all those—and there were many in the state—who resented the pretensions of Boston. New Englandism, in Niles' rhetoric, was the catspaw of overweening, purse-proud Boston merchants.

The Hartford Jacksonians bargained hard with their slender stock of political wares, and they were gratified at evidences of increasing support. None harbored any illusions of carrying the state, however. All they wanted was a respectable showing—a sufficient vote to improve their claim to a share of the federal and state offices on their own terms. Meanwhile, for the long run, they worked to extend their organization outside of Hartford County. Communication links were established with every town and even, it was claimed, every school district where a known Jacksonian lived. Bundles of the *Hartford Times*, packages of Niles' address, handbills, and ballots by the thousands were sent to the towns for distribution in the countryside. No friendly visitor left the *Times* office without a supply of these materials, for the costs of paper and printing had been borne largely by the Hartford group, and not enough money remained to underwrite mailing expenses.[7]

As expected, Adams carried the state in November. But considering that the campaign had been the first effort of a new and still incomplete organization, the Jacksonians made an impressive showing—

4500 votes out of about 18,000 cast. Welles felt they would have done better had not the districting amendment, which was being voted on at the same time, brought out a large number of Federalist-Adams men.[8] He had hoped for a higher vote; still a good beginning had been made.

The Jackson landslide outside of New England vindicated Welles' judgment as a politician and an editor. His paper had been the first in the region to support the Old Hero. His small band of loyal Jacksonians had organized a new party and fought hard. They may have been defeated, but with support from the new administration there was every reason to expect that a Jackson stronghold could be built in Connecticut.

The major question facing the young editor was how to reach the highest levels of influence surrounding the President-elect. More than a year earlier Welles had written Judge John Overton of Nashville, one of Jackson's closet friends in Tennessee, suggesting they correspond and asking for the names of other influential men who might want to exchange information with him. Overton had never replied. At Harrisburg Welles had acquired some correspondents in other states, but none were close to the inner circle. Noah Phelps had established contact with Martin Van Buren a few months earlier, and he brought back encouraging words from Albany—but nothing more.[9]

The Connecticut men had fought their campaign almost entirely on their own. What encouragement they got from the outside came from two Jacksonian editors—the acerbic Isaac Hill of the *New Hampshire Patriot* and Duff Green of Jackson's Washington paper, *The United States Telegraph*. Jovial General Green, a Western promoter and an expansive partisan, was sure to cut a swath in the new administration. He was known to be on intimate terms with Jackson, and had family ties with Vice President-elect John C. Calhoun. More important, Welles could reach Green directly through Benjamin Norton, his friend and former associate on the *Times*.

Some months earlier, Norton had accepted an editorial position on the *Telegraph*. He had originally been sent to Washington by a group of Connecticut paper manufacturers to arrange a contract for newsprint with Duff Green, whom they expected would be awarded the government printing. After Norton made an arrangement with Green for his paper supply, he stayed on as his assistant editor.[10] From Washington he kept his Hartford friends informed of impending developments and boosted their stock with the politically knowledgeable Green. Welles, on his side, had been most hospitable to the *Telegraph* in the columns of the *Times*, so much so that his journalistic rival, George D. Prentice of the *New England Review*, dubbed him "one of Duff Green's two penny trumpets."[11] Isaac Hill could also be counted on for support, though no one in Hartford at the time—least of all Welles—suspected how much Jackson admired him for his devotion to the cause.

Hill was a hard-eyed, thin-lipped Yankee who had hacked his way out of the backwoods of the Massachusetts frontier to a commanding position in New Hampshire politics. Lame, frail, and stooped, he walked with a shuffling gait that made him seem much older than his thirty-nine years. As editor-proprietor of the *New Hampshire Patriot*, one of the leading, and certainly the most controversial, of the Jeffersonian papers in New England, Hill had edged himself into virtual control of his state's legislative caucus. Few Jeffersonian Republicans, if they aspired to any prominence, could afford to neglect either the *Patriot* or the activities of Isaac Hill. By 1828 he had not only consolidated his power at home but had gained a national reputation for his venomous editorials and his uninhibited political style. Ever suspicious and calculating, he was a cool, thoroughly ruthless operator who prowled among the various Republican factions in New Hampshire, leaving a twisted trail of personal feuds and partisan rancor behind him. His closest associates he deemed potential rivals; his most dangerous rivals, potential associates. No one spoke and wrote for the common man in purer democratic accents, but many a New Hampshirt Jeffersonian doubted the sincerity of his words and could point to actions that mocked his democratic principles. Tireless in his quest for wealth and power, Hill struck at anyone in his way, choosing with care the appropriate weapon for the task and timing the execution so that it would achieve maximum impact. Somewhere buried deep in his past, in the miserable poverty of his childhood, perhaps, or the shame of his father's insanity, or the consciousness of his physical handicap, lay the complex elements of a driving ambition that guided his conduct along devious paths. Yet even his enemies—and they were legion—were compelled to respect his journalistic skills, his talent for organization, his swift and accurate appraisal of any political situation.[12]

Niles had known him casually for over a decade, and had exchanged the *Times* for the *Patriot* since he founded his paper in 1817. Far from Hill's stalking ground, Niles and Welles were inclined to discount what they heard or read about his dubious reputation. On occasion the *Patriot* seemed excessively bitter and vindictive to Welles, but he was in complete agreement with its general policies. Hill himself was pleasant and open, and always entertaining when he limped into the *Times* office for a brief stopover on one of his political or business junkets to other states. Niles especially liked to match his own impressive stock of bizarre facts and obscure literary allusions with the garrulous, self-taught New Hampshire editor, whose background so resembled his own. Welles also found Hill interesting, the more so because he was deep in the counsels of Senator Levi Woodbury, latterly New England's most prominent Jacksonian.

Hill, of course, like Duff Green, made no bones about the rewards to be expected by the faithful. Shortly after the Jackson triumph, Welles was gratified when the *New Hampshire Patriot* put these sentiments into print. "A band of New England Democrats," it declared, "have encountered the dominant party at vast odds—they have suffered every species of persecution and contumely. Shall these men not be protected by the Administration of the people under General Jackson?"[13] Unfortunately, in Connecticut the Welles-Niles faction needed support to protect itself from friends, not from enemies.

After the isolation of the Hartford radicals in the spring election, Welles had wanted to exclude from leadership all who were not what he considered original Jacksonians. By this he meant that small group who were known to have supported the General between 1825 and 1827, and who frankly espoused Republican principles. More realistic politicians had overruled him. Just prior to the Middletown convention in August, they had suggested a fusion of anti-Adams Federalists and Jacksonians, if and when a state ticket was nominated. Arguing that this would be their only chance of success, they recalled the Toleration precedent, when Jeffersonians and factional Federalists had combined in 1817 to defeat the Congregational establishment.[14] After Jackson's triumph, Welles, as chief correspondent, was besieged on all sides to ascertain whether a deal might be made with the defeated Adams men. He was willing to accomodate them, provided the fusion was on "fair and honorable" terms. "Our friends who supported Mr. Adams," he wrote the editor of the Bridgeport *Farmer,* "should unite with us and give us a share of the offices. If the Jacksonians are proscribed in the state," he warned the editor, "our opponents must expect from the national government a return in part of this favor. As they mete out to others, so will it be meted out to them."[15]

Welles was clearly demanding major concessions; and he was quite unwilling to dilute party ranks further by admitting large numbers of former opponents. "I want no trimmer—no half way wind-and-water politicians, who are professedly loyal to all, and honest to none," he wrote a party supporter in southeastern Connecticut. His uncompromising attitude, as it had before, alarmed the more realistic managers of the party, several of whom immediately challenged his stand. An influential Jacksonian from Fairfield County urged "that the Federalists who fought with us for Jackson and even those who join us now . . . should be admitted into the ranks of the Jackson-Republican party." Niles, Phelps, and Ellsworth agreed.[16]

Much against his will, Welles modified his harsh line, though he insisted that former Federalists had to meet the test of "genuine Democratic principles." "Nor must they," he said, "expect that they are to be promoted at once to the exclusion of Republicans." He was also willing to accept the nomination for state offices of "some honest Democrats" who had supported Adams. In stipulating state offices, Welles and his Hartford friends made it clear that the Jacksonians must have a major share of the congressional nominations. When their convention met at Middletown on January 8, 1829, it elected a central committee and nominated four "pure Jacksonians" to run for the six congressional seats—Niles and Judson being the most prominent candidates.[17] William H. Ellis, a New Haven meat dealer and party stalwart, summed up the central committee's policy in a toast he proposed at the banquet for the delegates: "The Jacksonians who came in at the eleventh hour, they shall have every man his penny; but let them wait for the change."[18] Ellis's toast was an open avowal that the members of the central committee would divide most of the federal patronage among themselves. Beyond that boastful earnest of their intent, everyone was in the dark, not knowing how much patronage they could expect or what they should do to obtain it. All of the Jacksonian leaders were candidates for some post. Men such as Noah Phelps and Ellis were openly insistent, while Niles, Judson and Crawford, who were candidates for Congress or the state senate, bided their time, awaiting the verdict of the people. Welles was the only one who pressed for a policy on patronage that would strengthen the party, not just reward faithful service.[19] Though not immune to the emoluments of office, he kept his own counsel and was considered objective enough to be charged with representing the committee in Washington. Arrangements were completely informal. No guidelines or instructions were agreed upon, but it was expected that Phelps and Ellis, at least, would be placed. Appointment policy, like party organization, was in a state of flux.

Welles must have wondered whether the party in Connecticut could survive its national success. In the exuberance of Jackson's victory, party leaders acted impulsively when they thought they were acting realistically. Again he counseled prudence, arguing that discipline be maintained until the situation could be properly assessed. He was unable to convince his associates. The Middletown convention, as he had foreseen, proved a chaotic, unmanageable affair. Although party leaders were able to agree upon a slate for congressional and state nominations, even the most optimistic doubted whether it would be supported. The candidates themselves scrambled for personal support, making promises that undermined discipline. As the *Middletown Gazette* observed: "Jackson was the watchword . . . but it would have required more than the presence of the chieftain, commanding as he is, to have calmed the spirits his name had raised."[20]

When Welles boarded the New Haven stage for the first leg of his trip to Washington, he could count on little assistance and less constructive advice from home. He would be on his own in the capital city, a frightening prospect for a young man of twenty-six with less than three years of political experience, and all of that in Connecticut. Accustomed to planning ahead, he knew that his own future and that of his close political friends depended upon such a nebulous thing as influence in Washington. His only currency was the blessing of the Hartford-dominated central committee, rather small change if any outsider probed the actual condition of the state organization. It was common knowledge that several ambitious individuals were ignoring the committee and trying to develop Washington contacts in their own interest or that of others. Welles could expect no help from the congressional delegation, most of whom would be pitted against him. Norton, of course, was on the scene and seemed eager—too eager—to be of service. In his letters home he had dwelt glowingly on his close connections with important figures in Washington whom he declared were in Jackson's confidence. When Niles learned that he was angling for the Hartford post office—the most lucrative federal position in the state—he wrote Norton inquiring about his intentions, only to receive what he deemed an insulting reply. Welles patched up their differences after Norton claimed he had been misrepresented. Despite his denials, the Hartford men remained uneasy about his motives, which seemed to dovetail neatly with those of the Jacksonians who were by-passing the central committee.[21] Forewarned by these developments, Welles steeled himself for what he assumed would be a delicate and difficult task in Washington.

On a cold, blustery day in early February 1829, Welles caught his first glimpse of the Capitol dome—that "inverted wash bowl"—rising out of the distant countryside. It had been a tedious five-day trip, entirely by stage before the final five-hour run from Baltimore to Washington. He would be happy to reach Mrs. Taylor's boardinghouse near the Capitol, where he was fortunate to have accommodations.

Gradually the farmhouses and barns (dilapidated and unkempt to a New Englander's tidy eye) became more numerous, but nothing indicated a city until his stage skirted the Capitol and rolled down Pennslyvania Avenue. From his vantage point Welles could survey the entire unpaved thoroughfare and with a sweep of the eye take in most of Washington. He could not have been impressed. About one mile to the south stood the President's house, majestic and forlorn. The trees President Adams had planted around it would in time soften the stark outline; now they merely emphasized its drab angularity. Grouped around the White House were the executive department buildings— War, Navy, Treasury—unimposing brick structures in the Greek revival mode. Between the Capitol and the White House, along both sides of the avenue, straggled the business and residential section of the city. As at Hartford, many of the narrow two- and three-story residences and boardinghouses had shops on the ground floor.

Washington was twice as large as Hartford, yet to Welles it must have appeared much smaller, scattered as it was helter-skelter over the countryside. There was less purposeful bustle, fewer wagons and drays, more carriages and cabs, more idlers on the sidewalks than at home. This was his first visit to a Southern town, and, like most New Englanders, he probably felt a bit out of place. The large numbers of Negroes (more than he had ever seen before), the casual appearance and more casual conduct of the whites all seemed a trifle strange. It was different yet similar, as if he were looking at a prismatic image of Hartford or Glastonbury through a camera lucida, the image slightly distorted, bright but not clear.[22]

Gatsby's Hotel, where most of the Jacksonian leaders were holding court, was Welles' first stop after he settled himself. To the young Connecticut visitor it was not a particularly reassuring place. The public rooms and cavernous bar of the rambling, barracks-like building were jammed with visitors from all over the Union. Some had come merely for the trip, or to witness the inauguration, but most were there for more practical reasons. As it was known that the President-elect had taken rooms at Gatsby's, hopeful place-seekers were constantly pouring in and out of the public rooms. In all this motley Welles was unable to find a familiar face. "Washington is filled with strangers," he wrote Niles, "almost all of whom have some object in view similar to myself." He had hoped to have Isaac Hill as a traveling companion and was disappointed when the New Hampshire editor altered his plans at the last minute. Welles had come on alone.[23] He would have to depend on Norton for personal introductions, much as he disliked the prospect, until Hill arrived.

Norton was very obliging. He introduced Welles to Duff Green and to Amos Kendall, the Frankfort, Kentucky, editor of the *Argus of Western America*, one of the most influential Jacksonian papers in the west. The tall, spare Green, who knew Welles by reputation, was all easy affability. Amos Kendall, pale and thin, with striking, prematurely white hair, was more reticent. Though he had lived for a number of years in Kentucky, he had been born in Massachusetts and educated in New Hampshire. Welles was drawn to this self-effacing, soft-spoken man, probably because of their similar personalities and backgrounds. He also liked the sociable Green, but he seemed too open, too frank, too engaging. Kendall was more his kind.

Isaac Hill finally arrived on February 8, much to Welles' relief. "He is very friendly," he reported to Niles, "and I have no doubt will be of great use to us." Hill, who immediately closeted himself with Postmaster General McLean, would not be available for a day or so. And Welles, determined to employ his time profitably, sought interviews with Kendall and Green. He found Kendall at his lodgings, in the home of the Reverend Obadiah Brown, on the south side of E. Street between Eighth and Ninth Streets. In the friendly atmosphere of Brown's parlor, the Kentucky editor shed his reserve. Welles was impressed by his learning, his taste for literature, his quiet humor. Brown, who joined in the conversation was unlike any Baptist minister Welles had ever met. No sober cleric he, but a warm-hearted, hospitable man who enjoyed good food, good drink, and the spice of politics. Pastor of the city's First Baptist Church, he led a double life, serving God on Sundays and Caesar on week days as a $1400-a-year clerk in the Post Office Department.[24] Brown's witty caricatures of Washington society soon had Welles and Kendall roaring with laughter. For the first time since he left Hartford, Welles was able to unbend, to cast caution and doubt aside.

Politics, of course, claimed first priority. Welles asked Kendall his opinion on the appointment policy of the new administration. He was reassured to learn that "removals will invariably take place," though Kendall did qualify his reply by adding that only those would be removed who "have been violent in their opposition, or made the best use of their status to injure the cause of Jackson." Pausing for a moment, Kendall looked directly at Welles and said, "this point [must] be distinctly made out and submitted to the President." As he rose to leave for his appointment with Green, both Brown and Kendall urged him to call again, an invitation he was delighted to accept.[25]

Welles had several urgent reasons for having a long talk with Green. Norton had dropped all pretense and was openly pressing for the Hartford post office. He was also, Welles had learned, telling such important men as Postmaster General McLean and Senators Eaton and Ingham that he was the controlling influence among the Connecticut Jacksonians. Welles suspected, correctly that Norton was trying to undercut him at home. "I wish Norton well, but his claims are most presumptuous," he wrote Niles, ". . . to hear his talk, one would suppose that he constituted the very backbone of the party." It was most important to learn just how much influence Norton had with Green. If it should prove necessary, he must convince the powerful journalist that he, not Norton, was the chosen representative of the party in Connecticut.

Another reason for a confidential chat with Green had to do with the political situation in Washington. From what he could sift out of the newspapers, and from what he overheard at Gatsby's, the subject of Jackson's successor was already being discussed privately. Party leaders were busily denying such talk, but Welles was not convinced. "Van Buren," he noted, "has more friends here than either Calhoun or Clay and nearly as many as both." If factions were developing at this early date, he wanted to be sure he chose the right side. All of his inclinations were for Van Buren and New York; but he was realistic enough to tread warily—premature action could be dangerous.

The editorial office of the *Telegraph*, where Green held court, was thronged with visitors, though the hour was late. Welles has some difficulty working his way through the noisy group to a place where he could catch the editor's eye. Green recognized him at once and, beckoning him to follow, stepped into the press room. When they were alone Green astonished his visitor by roundly condemning Norton's political activities. As if he were imparting confidential information, he warned that "there was some log-rolling, or something else unknown to the Jackson party in Connecticut." His candid remarks about his own assistant were reassuring to the worried Welles, who reported home that "Duff Green knows him [Norton] as well as you, or I, or any person."[26]

Had Welles been more experienced in the personal politics of Washington, he would have realized that the veteran editor was merely fencing with him; he had no intention of dropping Norton at this time. Green, who was just beginning his campaign for the Calhoun succession, was intent on mustering all possible support. The editor of the *Times* was certainly important enough to be wooed, and if possible, to be won over to the Calhoun cause. Beyond this immediate objective, Green planned no further action until he gathered some hard facts about the state of the party in Connecticut. He still did not know who represented the Jacksonians, or indeed, whether an effective organization existed. He was open and direct about the succession, however. Welles learned that he would back Calhoun, "but will go with the party if they say differently."[27]

On the following day, Isaac Hill was free for a long talk. He ranged broadly over the Cabinet and appointment situation as he saw it. Welles acted the role of the interested listener, never intrusive, deferring to the older man, following his train of thought carefully, adjusting his questions to Hill's commentary when it seemed appropriate. He did mention his troubles with Norton, his anxieties about major appointments in Connecticut, his meetings with both Kendall and Duff Green. But he did not elaborate; nor did he say anything specific about his information on Calhoun and the succession.

As the New Hampshire editor talked on, Welles realized that he was dealing with an exceptionally keen though curiously unstable mind. Since Hill was volatile and vain, wary yet revealing in his conversation, it seemed best to let him take the lead, to play up to his sense of self-importance. The tactic worked. Hill became expansive before such a willing audience, and gave him a shrewd estimate of the Cabinet situation with special reference to New England. Senator Levi Woodbury, he said, was the region's best candidate but probably would not be selected because New Hampshire, along with all of the New England states, had gone for Adams. Yet Woodbury still had a chance, since he occupied a middle ground between Calhoun and Van Buren. The *Times*, Hill urged, should join the *Patriot* in advancing Woodbury's claims. He added that he and Woodbury would exert all of their influence to assist Welles in gaining his appointments.

That evening Hill took Welles to a reception at Woodbury's lodging. Welles found the Senator to be a tall, balding man, inclined to corpulence, rather formal in manner, with an air of imperturbable dignity. Obviously briefed by Hill, the stately Woodbury unbent sufficiently to receive Welles with marked attention. He guided him through the crowded drawing room to a quiet corner, where he assured him that he would have no problem in obtaining the collectorships at New Haven and Middletown.[28]

Welles was flattered by the attention he was receiving from Green, Hill, Woodbury, and Kendall, yet he was increasingly disturbed by information from home. Norton was encouraging rival candidates for several posts. All were pressing their claims, and without reference to him. He was beginning to worry about his own friends in Hartford, particularly Noah Phelps, whom he knew to be in touch with Norton. Nor did the rumor-ridden, intrigue-laden atmosphere of Washington improve his spirits. The weather was unseasonably bad—cold and wet. His clothes were always damp from walking through the rain across open fields and over muddy lanes as he made his daily calls. When he had to take a hack, which was frequent, he found the fares double what they were in Hartford. It was difficult to get a good night's sleep at Mrs. Taylor's, where he was sharing a small room with several other place-seekers. A constant hum of conversation went on in the corridors, and in adjoining rooms. The sudden uproar of some drunken frolic on the street below would often bring him bolt upright in bed at night.

Welles was not a novice to this kind of existence. On previous trips he had found that the spice of change more than compensated for the discomfort. But what would have been a minor annoyance under other circumstances he found acutely depressing in Washington. He spent hours waiting in crowded lobbies or corridors—then perhaps had a brief interview—and all too frequently was given ambiguous replies to his requests for aid. Frustrated, lonely, his self-confidence shaken badly by his failure to keep all the irons in the fire, he agonized over whether he had been too hasty in his judgments. Perhaps he had been unduly critical of Norton. "If I have made a mistake," he wrote home, "I will bow most cheerfully to your decision." Niles answered reassuringly in a series of letters, but he was also disturbed by the conflicting pressures and claims of would-be officeholders. "I fear that we shall appear like a hungry, if not unprincipled, set of fellows," he exclaimed, "I wish our friends could have some degree of moderation and be governed by a spirit of compromise and forebearance.[29]

By the time Welles received Niles' comforting words his outlook had improved considerably. Jackson had arrived in Washington and settled himself in a suite of rooms at Gatsby's, which was dubbed the "Wigwam" by some waggish place-seeker, a name that promptly caught on.[30] There had been more evening conversations in Parson Brown's hospitable parlor, and Amos Kendall had widened Welles' circle to include a select group of leading Jacksonian journalists. Isaac Hill was a frequent visitor now, along with the suave M. M. Noah of the New York *Courier and Enquirer* and bluff Nathaniel Green of the *Boston*

*Statesman.* Welles' self-esteem began to recover under the warming ministrations of the convivial Brown and the stimulating discussions with his fellow journalists that went on far into the night. Most of them were ready conversationalists—all seemed knowledgeable politicians. Kendall, the only one present who could claim a personal relationship with the President-elect, soon asserted a kind of primacy in his tactful way. It was he who decided that the editors should pay their respects to Jackson in a group—a gesture he felt would appeal to the General's well-known sentimental instincts. Would they not stand before him like so many battle-scarred veterans who had defended his honor and the memory of his revered Rachel? The group, twelve in all, met Jackson on February 11—one day after his arrival in Washington. Their interview was brief because the Old Hero was constantly being interrupted, despite the best efforts of Major Donelson, his nephew and private secretary, to preserve some order in appointments. He had a cordial greeting for each one. Welles was struck by his "penetrating" eye and his conversation, which he noted was "fair easy and affable."[31]

That Kendall's gesture had made an impression on Jackson was soon manifest in the sudden attention paid the editors by the expectant placemen at Gatsby's and by the friendly interest of more exalted personages. Levi Woodbury personally told Welles "that General Jackson will do all in his power to sustain the democracy of New England, that he will appoint his friends to office and turn out his enemies." Jackson spoke so highly of the meeting with his editorial champions that Duff Green lost no time in contacting each one personally for one of his confidential chats. In Welles' case he took the additional precaution of having Norton pledge his complete loyalty. Though much relieved at the rapid improvement in his prospects, Welles was not content to let matters take their own course. While maintaining cordial relations with Duff Green, he was leaning toward the Van Buren men, especially Woodbury and Hill. Woodbury, of course, would be the key figure in steering the Connecticut appointments through the Senate.

Welles had already acted to keep his part of the bargain with Hill. He wrote Niles, who was editing the *Times* in his absence, outlining a series of articles that would boost Senator Woodbury and at the same time stress the importance of federal appointments to the party in Connecticut. "Send a paper containing these articles to each of the Jackson Senators," he wrote. "State also our unfortunate situation, unrepresented as we are in Congress . . . and the need we have of the protecting arm of the general government."[32] Welles was also trying to ingratiate himself with all the Cabinet hopefulls—a particularly frustrating effort, since each day, it seemed, the slate would undergo another change. At one time he heard from an authoritative source that his friend Isaac Hill was in line for Postmaster General, only to have his hopes dashed when he learned John McLean would be continued in that office. Woodbury was spoken of for the Treasury, then Henry Baldwin, a Connecticut man who now lived in Pittsburgh. The appointment finally went to Samuel Ingham, a Pennsylvanian and a supporter of Calhoun. For home consumption, Welles drew the best possible picture of the Cabinet appointments, even though he knew that the exclusion of New England would be politically damaging. "The appointment of Ingham will be extremely fortunate for the collectors," he reported to Hartford, "as he is a thorough party man and fearless." Essentially, he had to agree with Niles, who had written that "the Cabinet will have the appearance of confirming what our opponents have asserted that the influence of New England is annihilated by the late triumph."[33]

After all the nervous strain of the preceding two weeks, Welles was caught up in the hurly-burly of the Jackson inauguration, and he was shocked at what he saw. For once his New England sense of propriety overcame his abstract notions about the sovereignty of the people—overcame even his habit of describing what he must have known was an historic event. "After the fatigues of yesterday," he scribbled in a note to Niles, "I have no disposition to write."[34] He never would record his impressions of the mob scene at the White House when the people claimed their victory. It may have been too vulgar, or too frightening, to recall.

By now he was very tired. He wanted desperately to leave the hectic, confusing, vital, yet somehow anomalous atmosphere of Washington. But he had to get his appointments through, if he and those who were depending on him at home were to have any future in politics. No less important were all the minor essentials of patronage that had to be arranged—government printing for "loyal" newspapers, small town postmasterships, lesser customs officials, and the like. Most of the minor patronage could not be handled until he reached home, where, together with his friends, he could make a systematic appraisal of the party situation on a state-wide basis. Still, recommendations had to be scanned and noted, papers filed in the appropriate departments or withdrawn. Tedious work involving frequent trips to the departments had to be done, and always he had to balance conflicting claims with political pedigrees. Since he could not confer with the congressional delegation, he had to seek advice from home, which meant further delay and more work—heavy writing chores at night after long days at the executive offices.

Major appointments were the most taxing, and Noah Phelps the most insistent on his list of office seekers. "I wish you could dispose of him as soon as possible," wrote Niles, who was vexed at Phelps' constant importunities. Welles managed to have a brief talk with the President on the Connecticut patronage, and Hill and Kendall used their influence at the White House. By the third week in March the Jackson men had overcome the partisan opposition in the senate, which was led by Daniel Webster. Mindful to the end how important it was to strengthen his own influence, Welles asked for and received the signed commissions of appointment. These he would carry in his carpetbag and personally present to the new officers. He had but one regret as he prepared for his trip home; he would miss meeting Martin Van Buren, the new Secretary of State, who was not due in Washington for another week. But all of his requests for printing contracts were filed with the Acting Secretary, James Hamilton. He did not anticipate difficulties, and if any should arise, he felt reasonably sure his interests would be protected. Thanks to his own patient industry and Brown's cheerful fireside, he had made some valuable connections close to the new administration.

The Hartford post office appointment was the only important piece of unfinished business. Welles had asked that any action on this post be deferred until after the state election in April. His friends assured him that no problem would arise, despite the chaos in the Post Office Department. John McLean had resigned as Postmaster General four days after the inauguration. He was replaced by Major William T. Barry of Kentucky, a pleasant, undistinguished man, more a social lion than an administrator. Barry was not known to be in the Van Buren camp, but he was certainly not devoted to Calhoun, as McLean had been. It was expected that he would be generous with the vast patronage at his disposal. Welles had no misgivings about the Hartford post office appointment. Unknown to him, however, Barry was indolent and careless, an amiable, irresponsible, political hack who was soon to be overwhelmed by the responsibilities of his department. The Hartford post office was not as secure as Welles thought. He had done his spade work thoroughly, but he had not reckoned with such a bumbler as the new Postmaster General, or the long-range plans of Duff Green.[35]

When Welles arrived in Hartford, he found his friends in a gloomy state of mind, already conceding defeat in the state election. The appointments he brought with him helped restore flagging spirits and

contributed substantially to the prestige of the Hartford group. Unfortunately, they came too late to have any material effect on the
election. If anything, Welles' success cost the Jacksonians the support
of a good many cooperating Federalists, who saw no future in a party
where government patronage was controlled by such an outspoken
critic of their past policies.

Niles had described the political situation as "disgusting." "If we
were in a reputable minority, but were organized as a party and had
an organized majority against us," he told Welles, "this would be an
agreeable state of parties to what now exists. There is [sic] now but two
parties in the state, the old Federal party and the *Times* party. The
Republican party is completely broken up and the Jackson party is
not organized except those who follow your paper."[36]

The imminent failure of the Jackson ticket was disappointing to
Welles after his success in the struggle over the appointments. Though
he had mentioned it to no one, he wanted the Hartford post office for
himself, yet if Niles lost his election to Congress, Welles was committed
to support him for the office. He was the senior man, the honored
founder of the *Times*, the stalwart fighter for Jeffersonian principles,
and, more than any claims of merit or service to the cause, he was
Welles' closest friend. As much as he might covet the post, Welles
would never jeopardize their relationship.

In Connecticut the Hartford post office was the prime political
plum, worth over $3000 a year in salary and fees, besides valuable
patronage, negotiation of mail contracts, rent for premises, and a half-
dozen clerks. Duties were modest: monthly and annual reports to Washington, collecting and disbursing of funds, general supervision of the
office. It would have meant financial security to Welles, most tempting
to a young man with no independent source of income beyond the small
sums he accepted for his work on the *Times*. The position would have
raised his status in the community, strengthened his prestige in politics,
provided for his immediate future—a wife and family perhaps. And the
post office appointment would relieve him from editorial drudgery so
that he could devote more of his energies to the essential job of
organizing the party.

Welles had already hinted delicately to Niles that the party would
suffer if he, its most active and efficient man, were buried in the post
office. Niles parried this suggestion, declaring that his prestige in the
state, and hence his political effectiveness, depended on a public office.
Should he fail again in his bid for Congress, as seemed likely, he had
to have the post office or retire from politics. The truth of Niles' bitter

comment was soon obvious—the *Times* party against all. Not one of
the Jackson candidates for Congress or for the state senate was elected;
nor did any of them even make a good showing.[37]

Welles had expected defeat, and well before the election he had
immersed himself in his editorial work, in his planning for the May
legislative session, and in next year's political canvass. Federal patronage claimed major attention too. He was busy selecting candidates and
securing recommendations for posts in the various key towns. It would
take at least a month before a suitable list could be prepared for his
return trip to Washington. The Hartford post office appointment
claimed the highest priority and required the most careful handling.
Besides Niles, several men of importance to the Jacksonian movement
coveted the office. Welles had to maneuver carefully so as not to offend,
or arouse jealousy, or risk alienating a segment of the county organization. By the second week in April, he had managed the delicate operation to everyone's satisfaction. He had just completed his final arrangements for a return trip to Washington when news reached Hartford
that Jonathan Law, the incumbent postmaster, had been removed and
Norton appointed in his place.

This turn of events, entirely unexpected, and highly damaging to
Welles personally, was a stunning blow. He had assured all of his
associates that the appointment was secure. They, relying on his previous success, had seen no reason to doubt his word. Now his status in
the movement, his authority as its spokesman and chief organizer, was
being directly challenged. If nothing could be done to reverse the action, if he lost the confidence of his political friends, it would take
years to restore his prestige, years of editorial hackwork, political
drudgery, and little or no recognition. Beyond his acute embarrassment
and the threat to his own political career loomed the impact of such
dramatic failure on the state of the party, its cohesion, its sense of
identity and mission. In his judgment (prejudiced to be sure, but also
the result of careful observation) Norton simply did not have the
imagination, the tact, and the intimate knowledge of state affairs to
use the power of the office effectively. Clearly, he was a creature of Duff
Green, and hence of Calhoun, responsive to them and their ambitions
rather than to the local constituency. The Connecticut Jacksonians
were hard enough pressed without having the patronage of the most
lucrative federal office in the state diverted to other hands. In Hartford
County, where the Jacksonians were strongest, the post office was absolutely crucial. What then should be done?

In the emergency Welles acted coolly and deliberately. He recognized the need for a distinguished name to impress the powers in Washington, and he recalled that Henry Ellsworth was an old acquaintance of Levi Woodbury. As a son of the great jurist Oliver Ellsworth, second Chief Justice of the Supreme Court and author of the great judiciary act which bore his name, Henry Ellsworth would render invaluable service in legitimizing the status and the claims of the Hartford group. Under plea of extreme urgency, he was persuaded to accompany Welles on a quick trip to the capital. Doubtless Ellsworth saw through Welles' motives; doubtless also he weighed the perils to his own political aspirations if they did not succeed, for he was both ambitious and able. But, like Welles and Niles, he had no alternative. He was so closely identified with them now that his career would be in jeopardy if outsiders dictated and controlled the appointment. He had no choice but to accept. Within a few hours he and Welles were bound for Washington, which they reached after a record three days of travel. There followed a strenuous round of talks with Hill, Woodbury, Kendall, and Van Buren, whom Welles met for the first time. The Ellsworth name, as Welles had expected, did carry a good deal of weight, especially with Van Buren and Woodbury. Ellsworth himself proved an earnest and persuasive advocate.

It soon became clear that Postmaster General Barry had acted on a general recommendation for Norton that had been signed by Maine, Massachusetts, and New Hampshire men. The document, addressed to the President, had been routinely forwarded to the Post Office Department. Swamped under a flood of similar testimonials, Major Barry had overlooked the fact that no Connecticut names appeared on the recommendation. The evidence is circumstantial, but Duff Green had probably taken advantage of Barry's inexperience and carelessness to press for Norton's appointment.[38] What must have baffled Welles was that his presumed friends—Hill, Woodbury, and Kendall—all of whom had assured him that the appointment could be safely deferred, had done nothing to forestall action on it. Kendall and Hill, of course, were seeking posts for themselves and for others to whom they owed deeper obligations than to Welles. Yet both men enjoyed Jackson's confidence. And Major Lewis, one of the President's two secretaries, kept them informed of pending appointments in which they had expressed an interest. Woodbury could have delayed Norton's confirmation in the Senate until he heard from Connecticut. Most damning of all in Welles' eyes was that none of these gentlemen had written him at any stage in the proceedings. Norton himself had informed Hartford after he had been confirmed.

The most likely explanation for their conduct is that they assumed Norton was Green's candidate and were unwilling to challenge the redoubtable editor, or his more redoubtable master, John C. Calhoun. None of them could be sure of Welles' and Niles' standing among the Connecticut Jacksonians, nor, in fact, could they rule out the possibility that Green had made an arrangement with Welles on Norton's appointment. So confused were the lines of communication between Washington and the state organizations, so tangled and intrigue-laden was the whole problem of federal appointments, that even such politically astute men as Hill and Kendall were reluctant to interfere before they had solid evidence. There were just too many intangibles.[39]

Welles and Ellsworth were able to clear up all doubts about their own and the party's position in Connecticut. More to the point, they convinced even the cautious Van Buren that a great blunder had been made and that it must be rectified immediately. Major Barry offered no obstacle, readily conceding his mistake and promising to take up the matter personally with the President. The decline in Duff Green's influence and the rise of the Van Buren faction in the Kitchen Cabinet had had some effect on Major Barry's willingness to reverse himself. "The character of the whole farce," said Isaac Hill, "is fully understood both by the President and Major Barry."[40]

On April 20 Ellsworth wrote Niles that "our anxiety is over—Norton is removed—you are appointed—notice of both goes by the mail that carries this."[41] Norton had been postmaster for one day. A brilliant display of political influence, the change of postmasters created a sensation in Hartford. "As old as I am," wrote Hartford Federalist George Goodwin to his friend, David Daggett of New Haven, "I do not remember to have witnessed such excitement as there is at this time in the city on account of the Post Office." Those who had ascribed Welles' previous success to actions of other men or to the merits of the candidates themselves were now convinced that he really was a political power. His lightning coup had widespread effects throughout the state. The *Times* party was almost immediately acknowledged as the controlling influence among Connecticut Jacksonians. Niles might have had the post office, but aspiring politicians and hungry editors looked to Welles for the patronage. He was the wire-puller with the right connections. After three years of labor and many disappointments, he felt that he was now in a position to organize a party. Only three months had elapsed since he had journeyed alone to Washington and had not seen a friendly face in the crowd at Gatsby's.[42]

# CHAPTER 5

# Assignment in
# Washington

THE EDITORIALS IN THE *Hartford Times* during the fall of 1829 bore an unmistakable stamp of optimism. Friends noticed that Welles was in a mellow mood, that he even had kind words for the Adams Republicans. Nor were these changes in his attitude and in the policy of the *Times* an ingenious snare to catch opponents off-guard, as the *New England Review* so captiously described them. Welles and Niles were completely sincere; for they were quite certain they had a winning combination that would ultimately establish their political control. Welles, who was inclined to look on the dark side, to temper Niles' enthusiasm with sober appraisals, for once matched the confidence of his associate.[1]

In the full flush of his victory over Norton he had gone to the state legislature, where most of the influential Republican members had courted him. With only thirty-nine avowed Jacksonians, Welles was able to control an all-faction Republican caucus that chose the delegates for the primary meetings in the new senatorial districts. Men of the "right stamp," he was convinced, would be selected as delegates to both senatorial and state conventions. With federal patronage at his command, how could it be otherwise? As the editor of the Bridgeport *Farmer* wrote of the Republican party, in an enthusiastically mixed metaphor, "this child of ours is to be nursed by yourself, and we are extremely happy to have it in our power to name so good a godfather. . . ."[2] Loyal Jacksonians were nominated in fifteen out of twenty-one senatorial districts, and the state ticket was divided between representatives of the two groups, to the apparent satisfaction of each. There seemed good and sufficient reasons for Welles to congratulate himself. He, after all, was the principal architect of an impending victory which would include a United States Senator—possibly his friend Niles—to replace the hated Foot, whose term would expire in the new year.

In his preoccupation with local arrangements, Welles had over-simplified an unstable political situation. His generation had inherited a host of problems that the Virginia dynasty had first raised, then glossed over. States' rights, Jefferson's policy of local power and locally inspired piecemeal development, was congealing into regional rights, which were far more threatening to the integrity of the Union than the narrow and wavering challenge of the Hartford Convention had been. Conflicting forces were polarizing within an improvised structure of Union. The nation lurched unevenly along uncharted paths of economic change, industrializing in some areas, expanding plantation agriculture in others, opening up vast new farming regions in the West to emigrants from the older states and from abroad. Politics, as practiced in Washington, mirrored the turbulent crosscurrents of this atomistic growth. For the moment, Andrew Jackson, with his immense prestige, his tenacious will, and his political acumen, had them under control. But even he was unable or unwilling to dampen the fierce personal rivalries in Washington, as representatives of emerging regional interests sought to widen their personal influence. Every state was fast becoming a political battlefield where leading contenders maneuvered for the presidential succession. Until this issue was settled, Welles and his associates could not be sure about the federal patronage, so essential to the well-being of their party.

Persuasive rhetoric helped significantly in competing for votes, in overcoming the apathy of the electorate, or, as Welles was fond of putting it, in "concentrating public opinion." But there was no substitute for a government printing contract in converting an important newspaper or in building a corps of loyal party workers. Members of the organization desired tangible proof that their services were appreciated, as well as the financial independence to perform the all-important but tedious and time-consuming party chores. Welles had to deliver that proof along with a reasonable security of tenure, at least while Jackson remained in office. He also had to expand the organization—more jobs, more demonstrations of pulling the right wires in Washington—if his minority faction was ever to become a majority party in the state. Success had to be continuous in this perilous profession, a factor that he now understood.

Others within his group felt as well qualified as he to be the controlling influence. They resented "dictation," complained darkly of the "Hartford junto" or the "*Times* regency," and journeyed to Washington, sometimes clearing their trips with Hartford, more frequently not. William Ellis, who owed his job as customs collector at New Haven to Welles, was in constant touch with such powers as Levi Woodbury, Secretary of the Treasury, Samuel Ingham, Amos Kendall, and Duff Green of the *United States Telegraph*, confidential adviser to Jackson, confidant of Calhoun. Noah Phelps, the collector at Middletown, also under obligation to Welles, was pursuing an independent, undercover course aimed at making himself the master of the party. Within Welles' own Hartford group, a newcomer, Isaac Toucey, an ambitious ex-Federalist lawyer, was intriguing with Phelps. And Henry Ellsworth, who had helped Welles in the Norton affair, was undercutting his political brethren as he desperately sought public office to solve his many financial difficulties.

These competitive, calculating men did not lack an audience in Washington. In fact there were so many conflicting claims and so many individual opinions that department heads must have often been in a quandary. Ellis, as guilty as any in pushing himself forward, complained angrily about the lack of any policy on appointments. "Why, what the devil does all this mean," he wrote Welles from the national capital. "Here are petitions and remonstrances and counter-petitions and counter-remonstrances and everything is so snarled up that the different departments are obliged to apply to Sam Foot. . . . Now, for God's sake won't you begin, and look out that we get better organized . . . and if all goes to pot at home we must sustain ourselves as an Administrative party or our hopes here are all at an end."[3]

By December of 1829 Welles again had to make a show of strength. Ellis was complaining about postmasters in the New Haven vicinity who should be "reformed." His Hartford associates had decided that a government printing contract might purchase the support of the *New Haven Register*. Adams appointees still controlled the customs house and the post office in New London. Niles had tried his hand several weeks earlier and failed to have them removed. He managed to have several long but inconclusive conversations with a wary Van Buren, whom he finally ran to earth in Richmond, Virginia, where a galaxy of politicians had gathered for the state's constitutional convention. Previously, Niles had made a direct approach to Secretary Ingham, who was either too busy or not at home. Ingham, who typed the stocky, little postmaster as a Van Buren man, had other plans for the Treasury patronage in New England.[4]

If Niles had been unaware of Ingham's preferences, his treatment was a sign, however obscure, that Calhoun was still searching for political footholds in the Northeast. His presidential ambitions were confirmed dramatically for Welles when he visited Duff Green shortly after the first session of the twenty-first Congress convened, about mid-December of 1829. The normally suave editor "shocked and disgusted" Welles when he asked him flatly to bring the *Times* out for Calhoun at an early date in the new year. He added that John McLean, formerly Postmaster General and now a Jackson appointee to the Supreme Court, was willing to run with Calhoun for the Vice Presidency. Green explained that Calhoun's "claims could not be postponed another four years." Taken aback, Welles objected to the question of the succession being brought up at such an early date. Jackson had only been in office for six months. Might he not be a candidate for re-election? He also raised the possibility of divisions in the party, alluding to Van Buren and others who might not support Calhoun. The *Telegraph* editor, in his most confidential manner, replied that "these preliminary steps were confined to a few in each state." "It is important," he stressed, "to have the party act in concert, which could be effected in no other way as by having active and influential men in each state early engaged for Mr. Calhoun." Green declared emphatically that "General Jackson was himself opposed to his re-election but Van Buren and Eaton desire it in order to throw Calhoun off the course." If Van Buren "would waive any pretensions he might have to the presidency and consent to be placed on the ticket as vice-president to Mr. Calhoun, harmony would be restored. . . . Mr. C. and his friends would consent to that arrangement, provided Mr. Van Buren would cease pressing General Jackson as a candidate for reelection." Should Jackson make a personal decision to run again, Green thought Calhoun "would not probably" oppose him, "but," he added, "Judge McLean would be a candidate, and would command a heavy support in the west, which with the Federalists in the east, together with the anti-Masons who would unite on him and his Methodist brethren . . . would secure his election."[5]

Welles was deeply disturbed. He respected Green as a knowledgeable politician, editor of the administration's paper, an intimate of the President and of most Cabinet members. How much did Jackson know about Calhoun's plans? What of Van Buren? Was Green's assessment accurate? Would the New Yorker protect his friends? Would he strengthen their position, or would he defer to Calhoun's "prior claims?" John McLean was a new element. That craggy-faced operator, who would be a presidential hopeful for the next thirty years, had just been appointed an Associate Justice of the Supreme Court after turning down three Cabinet posts. It was common knowledge in Washington that he still retained his influence with hundreds of postmasters all over the country. Either allied with Calhoun or as an independent candidate, McLean could be a dangerous opponent of Van Buren.

The tangled web of the succession, Welles decided, was the major reason for the vexing slow-down on appointments and the mysterious delay in the award of printing contracts. Yet he would not commit himself to Duff Green; nor for the moment would he communicate his information to any of Van Buren's friends in Washington. He did not trust Calhoun, whom he had never met but whose speeches over the years he had studied carefully. As he had traced the sinuous course of the great Carolinian, Welles had come to the conclusion that he was not "a democrat from principle but from circumstances." It would not do to act rashly in the matter. He must consult with trusted friends in Hartford before he made any moves in this perilous game.

Welles could spare only a few days in Washington because of an impending state-wide party convention at home. Though he did not see Van Buren, he received assurances from the State Department that the *Hartford Times*, the *Register*, and the *New London Centinel* would all be awarded contracts for printing the laws. With the Post Office and Treasury departments he was no more successful than Niles had been. In the case of the Treasury, the reason seemed obvious—there would be no favors from Ingham unless Welles supported Calhoun. Duff Green had made that clear. The Post Office Department was a different matter. Here Major Barry had frozen all new appointments until the political situation in the various states was clarified. The easygoing Postmaster General had acted precipitously in too many instances, and, as Ellis informed Welles, he wanted no more embarrassing Norton affairs. Nevertheless, the *Times* editor impressed the Connecticut Congressmen (all of whom were his political foes) as a man with the right connections. "Such is the influence that Gideon Welles *et id omne genus*, seemed to have acquired over the functionaries of the government," confessed Congressman William Storrs, that "I . . . anticipate but little success. The delegation of our state have not . . . any reason . . . to suppose their recommendation would have much weight."[6]

Welles returned home. After consulting with Niles on January 6, he wrote a long, carefully phrased letter to Green. His object was to heal what he assumed was an impending break between Calhoun and Van Buren. New England Federalists, he told Green, would not support either man. The "democrats," however, "are friendly to both, and nothing would induce them to do aught prejudicial to either." Welles thought that any association with McLean, a former Federalist and a turncoat Adams Republican, would hurt the party. "There is a deep and strong feeling among the Republicans against Mr. McLean," he warned Green, adding, "I am satisfied that any show of favor or friendship towards a union with that gentleman would have a tendency to alienate the democracy of the north. . . ."[7]

Even as Welles was penning his letter to Green, events were occurring in Washington which would make reconciliation between Calhoun and Van Buren all but impossible. Welles of course was fully aware of the social rift within the Cabinet over Peggy Eaton, wife of the Secretary of War. The wives of Vice President Calhoun, Secretaries Branch and Ingham, and Attorney General Berrien would not receive the comely, vivacious Mrs. Eaton because it had been alleged that she had led an immoral life before she married Eaton. Jackson demanded proof. When none of the charges could be substantiated, he brought pressure on Calhoun and the Cabinet members to have their wives accept Mrs. Eaton socially. Van Buren, a widower, and Major Barry, whose family had remained in Kentucky, were only too happy to oblige. The rest of the Cabinet refused. As Calhoun phrased it delicately in a note to Jackson, "the laws of the ladies are like the laws of the Medes and the Persians and admit neither of argument nor of amendment." Calhoun's rare attempt at humor was missed by the angry President, who was beginning to suspect that the whole affair was a contrivance to embarrass his administration. At the height of the petticoat rebellion, Jackson was confronted with defiance from another quarter—the Senate refused to confirm a batch of appointments (mainly journalists) he had made to important posts. Since most of the rejected men were friendly to Van Buren, the source of the opposition seemed obvious. Calhoun, however, preserved a discreet silence. Only once was he required to show his hand. In this instance he cast the deciding vote to confirm Amos Kendall, a Van Buren partisan, as fourth auditor in the Treasury Department. Such a show of impartiality did not impress the President, who saw in it further evidence of Calhoun's intriguing nature.[8]

Welles watched the events in Washington carefully. When he learned on April 17 that the Senate had rejected Isaac Hill by a large majority for the post of second auditor in the Treasury Department, he wrote the New Hampshire editor, asking for information on how he might condemn the vote in the *Times.* Hill replied in a long, angry letter, hinting broadly that Calhoun had been responsible and vowing revenge. "Had the rejection been only by two or three," he said, "I would have returned to New Hampshire without one pang or regret . . . I return, as it is, wounded to be sure, but I trust not incurably. . . ." Though Hill still professed friendship for Duff Green, he left no doubt that he thought the *Telegraph* editor's "usefulness to the Democratic party is on the wane."

This was the opening Welles had been waiting for. On April 24 he included in his answer to Hill a brief account of his conversation with Green the previous December. "General Green did not know me, or he would not have talked to me in this manner. He has probably not been as free with you, for he knew you better," Welles said. In the May 3 edition of the *Times*, he gave Hill's version of his rejection, implicating Green, though not by name, and alluding only indirectly to Calhoun.[9]

By now Hill felt he was surrounded by enemies in high places. Immediately after his rejection, friends in New Hampshire began soliciting support for his election to the Senate. Woodbury, who Hill thought was still hoping for a Cabinet post, had "repeatedly declared that he would resign his place and decline a re-election." But then the overwrought editor received a request "from Boston to forego the proffer of my friends in New Hampshire and assist in re-electing Woodbury to the Senate." At about the same time he learned that David Henshaw, the new customs collector at Boston, and his close associates were "deep on Gen. G[reen]'s paper, who is said to be involved already more than $60,000." "They must lose thousands," he wrote Welles, "if he falls—as fall he certainly will." Henshaw, a wholesale druggist, owed his post largely to the influence of Green and Calhoun. He had used the rich patronage of the customs house to make himself master of the Jacksonian party in Massachusetts.[10]

Distrusting the ambitious, grasping Henshaw, Hill saw the outlines of a conspiracy directed at himself and at Van Buren, whom he was supporting against Calhoun. As Hill pieced the intrigue together, Henshaw would help Woodbury to secure another term in the Senate in return for his tacit espousal of Calhoun and his support of Green's application for the government printing. Woodbury, backed up by the Henshaw machine in Boston and by Calhoun and Green in Washington, would pose a serious, if not fatal, threat to Hill's political future. No doubt the worried editor was engaging in some rather fanciful speculations as he gave vent to his fears in his letters to Welles, but he was too sagacious a politician, the veteran of too many party skirmishes, to see phantoms where none existed. Where he probably erred was in his estimate of Woodbury's position. It seems most likely that Henshaw and Green were building support for Calhoun in New England and that they regarded Woodbury as a key figure in their planning. By the same token, Hill was considered a prime obstacle, since he was one of Van Buren's most active and influential lieutenants in the region. If Woodbury could isolate Hill in New Hampshire without dividing the party, a heavy blow would be struck against a dangerous adversary.

In many ways Woodbury would have been receptive to overtures from Green and Henshaw. He had some old scores to settle with Hill, and for personal as well as political reasons he was most eager to retain his Senate seat. During early May of 1829, Henshaw visited Washington, where he spent a good deal of time with Woodbury and Calhoun, both of whom, Hill acidly observed, were "unwearied in their civilities and attentions." "Woodbury," he remarked to Welles, "if saved at all, calculates to be saved through them."[11] The crafty New Hampshire Senator, however, had been conducting his own surveys of the power struggle in Washington. Although he must have been tempted by Henshaw's offer of assistance, he was, after all, a seasoned politician who would never take unnecessary chances. At the moment, Calhoun was out of favor with the President and Van Buren's star was rising. It would not do to make any frontal assault on Isaac Hill, who stood high in the Jackson camp, had friends in Boston too, and was as popular in New Hampshire as he. The evidence points to an arrangement, possibly engineered by Hill and Kendall, in which the President let it be known that he would shortly reorganize his Cabinet and that Woodbury would be offered a post provided he did not stand for a second term in the Senate and would support Hill.

Welles knew comparatively little of these intricate maneuvers save what he heard from Hill and what he read in the *Telegraph* and the *Intelligencer*. The net result of all the reports and rumors emanating from the capital was that Welles marked down Woodbury and Henshaw as doubtful quantities. He continued to trust Hill implicitly, accepting without question his assertion that Calhoun was plotting to take over the party in New England.

During his dialogue with Hill, Niles heard from Duff Green, complaining that Welles' article in the *Times* on Hill's rejection had been "unjust . . . and doubly so towards the V.P." He wanted Welles to write another editorial—as Niles explained it, "to set the matter right and remove the erroneous impressions your article was calculated to produce." Ever wary of the shifting center of power, Welles complied. In a most adroit article that appeared on June 1, he managed to defend Hill yet, at the same time, deny that he had meant to implicate either Calhoun or Green in his rejection.[12]

There matters rested for the next six months, and during that time Calhoun's standing with the President continued to decline. Jackson learned that the Vice President, when he was Monroe's Secretary of War, had wanted him court-martialed for his unauthorized foray into West Florida. Nullification was still being threatened by the South Carolina delegation in Congress. But a more serious blow to Calhoun's immediate prospects was the collapse of his plans to defeat Van Buren in New England. Hill returned to Washington in triumph as Woodbury's successor in the Senate. Yet the Vice President had not given up his ambition for the presidency, nor had Jackson committed himself to a second term. Even the Kitchen Cabinet, now entirely composed of Van Buren partisans, had to tread carefully.

Amos Kendall was anxious to combat the *Telegraph*'s influence by establishing a new administration paper in Washington, but he was very circumspect when it came to planting the idea in Jackson's mind. The President retained his fondness for Green, despite that editor's well-known partiality for Calhoun. Others close to Jackson admired Green's editorial abilities, his early and valuable services to the Jackson cause, and his undoubted prestige among politicians and journalists in the various states. It was hoped that he might be persuaded to abandon Calhoun and, if not actually support Van Buren, at least remain neutral in the impending contest. Jackson finally accepted the argument that Green needed help, but only after Kendall assured him that the new press would assist, not compete with, the *Telegraph*. On these rather tentative terms, Francis Preston Blair, Kendall's successor as editor of the *Argus of Western America*, reluctantly agreed to accept editorial responsibility for a new administration organ.[13]

The first issue of the *Globe*, as Blair named his new paper, announced, disingenuously, that its sole mission was to defend Republican principles and the Jackson administration. But most seasoned observers, not the least Duff Green, were skeptical about Blair's professions of high-minded principle, and Welles and Niles, original subscribers as well as experienced editors, had not read many issues before they detected its latent bias for Van Buren. Letters from Washington confirmed their judgment. Though both men favored Van Buren, they had maintained cordial relations with Duff Green. Only in his confidential correspondence with Hill had Welles indicated his preferences, which were always couched in terms of complete loyalty to the President. While communications with Washington had been uncertain and information conflicting, he maintained a prudent stance. The establishment of the *Globe* had cleared up much of the political static, and to Welles the signal seemed clear—it was time to take a stand. Perhaps he could break through the jamming that had blocked new appointments in Connecticut for more than a year—but he knew better than to approach the subtle Van Buren directly.

Months earlier, Welles had written Ellis, who was then in Washington, to ask if Secretary Van Buren would care to have some confidential information on political matters. Van Buren would be more than happy to receive correspondence, Ellis reported back, saying "that you may write him fully and freely and communicate to him any information you think proper either as relates to him or yourself and that the strictest confidence will be observed." Ever discreet, Van Buren cautioned that he would "not answer any enquiries respecting future operations."[14] On December 27, 1830, Welles wrote the Secretary, giving him the substance of Green's conversation on the Calhoun candidacy. He did not mention that he had previously acquainted Isaac Hill with the facts; and he disclaimed any ulterior motive in disclosing the information. He was prompted to write, he explained, for "the good of the democratic party, and your own welfare in which I have long taken a deep interest." It was just such a letter that a sincere and modest young man would write to a statesman he admired. Van Buren read it with interest, not only for the facts it contained, but for the warm expression of support from a New England editor. He knew that Green had been trying to build up support for Calhoun well before Jackson's inauguration. And what really caught his eye was Welles' precise account of his opponent's planning at an early stage. Here was a man who obviously kept memoranda of important discussions, a valuable witness, if one were needed.[15]

Welles had been in Washington for two weeks when he made his disclosures to Van Buren. His primary mission was to have the collector at New London (formerly an Adams Republican, now in the Calhoun camp) removed and Thomas Mussey, a man loyal to Hartford, appointed in his place. He had not been at the capital long when Duff Green sent a message asking for a private talk in the *Telegraph* office.

Welles had expected that the *Telegraph* editor would seek him out, but he had not expected Green would be so candid in denouncing Van Buren. Green opened the conversation by alluding to the "sorrows of Calhoun," whom he called "the pillar of strength to the democratic party." He charged Van Buren with direct responsibility for stirring up the West Florida incident which had hurt Calhoun with the President. Stating that "the whole matter would be laid before the people," he assumed Welles would publish in the *Times* "any communications . . . Mr. Calhoun and his friends . . . may wish to make . . . at the proper time." Then Green attacked the *Globe*, declaring angrily that it was "wrong in Mr. Van Buren, Major Barry and the President to encourage the establishment of a rival newspaper in Washington." "The *Globe* is not only to interfere with me," he remarked heatedly, "it is to affect seriously our eastern friends, particularly our Boston friends. Van Buren and Barry . . . intended to withdraw their printing from all other quarters and give it to Blair to support his press, and himself." In a remarkable display of self-interest, Green said he would "probably have to expose . . . this whole system, and it remained to be seen whether a paper which was uncalled for by the people, which they refused to support, was to be sustained by the people's money in order to please Van Buren."

On the following day Welles visited Green again, this time in an effort to enlist his aid in the matter of the New London collectorship. Accompanied by several Connecticut associates, he found Green with Andrew Dunlap, the Attorney General of Massachusetts, who was a prominent member of David Henshaw's "customs house clique." Though Welles was unable to get any promise of support from Green, he and his friends were treated to another diatribe against Van Buren and the Kitchen Cabinet. "Gentlemen," Green said as they were leaving, "you will take notice I am no longer a supporter of this Administration." Welles had done more listening than talking. As soon as he returned to Gatsby's he made a full memorandum of both conversations. Probably sensing it might be misconstrued if it were known that he had seen Van Buren, he did not request an interview. He did, however, visit Amos Kendall and gave him a detailed verbal account of what had happened.

When he arrived back in Hartford, there was a letter awaiting him from Kendall. "I am told . . . ," he read, "that the *Telegraph* will assume a hostile tone as soon as the election for printer is over. . . . If he should take a stand against the President, it may be important to show what his private speculations were in December, 1829." Kendall wanted the details in writing. Would Welles supply them, "to be used only in the event of his desertion?" Welles replied in early February of 1831, giving the statement and also referring Kendall to his correspondence with Isaac Hill during the past year. "Should it be necessary," he wrote, "I would not withhold the statement I have made verbally to you . . . but unless it be of great importance, I should prefer that my name should not appear."[16]

During the third week of February 1831, Calhoun began an elaborate defense of his position on the West Florida affair in the *Telegraph*. Kendall, who now had Welles' statement and extracts from his letter to Hill, was eager to publish them in the *Globe*. Their appearance before the public, he thought, would cast further doubt on Calhoun's credibility. A more compelling reason, perhaps, was the opportunity the correspondence afforded to destroy Green's influence with the President—and if possible, with those party leaders who were still loyal to the *Telegraph*. Rumors of Green's disloyalty had been floating around Washington for more than a year, but Welles apparently was the only one who could or would furnish hard facts. As Kendall remarked to Welles, "the next *Globe* will assert without any reference to you, the fact of Green's intriguing to bring out Calhoun in 1829. He will deny it, of course. The proof must then be had."[17]

Green did deny the *Globe* assertion, and Welles was reluctant at this stage to be drawn openly into the controversy. Well aware of Green's capacity for innuendo, for quoting out of context, for slashing, damaging personal attacks, he was concerned also about the confidential nature of his conversations and his letters on the subject. He was reasonably certain that he had not committed any major indiscretion, but, since he did not have copies of all his letters, he could not be sure. After much soul-searching, he agreed to be named the source for the *Globe* statement, an acknowledgment that was immediately taken up by the opposition press in Connecticut. Woodward's *Connecticut Herald* used it for a savage indictment of Welles which must have scored deeply. He was accused of being "destitute of *principle* or of *honor*," not "the fit companion of gentlemen. With the daring of the highwayman, the impudence of a mendicant, he worms himself into the society and confidence of honorable men, only to stab when he is detected or to betray when disappointed."[18]

Fortunately for Welles' peace of mind, Calhoun's version of the West Florida affair did not have the impact on the public that Duff Green had thought it would. Jonathan Harvey, a New Hampshire Congressman, wrote Welles that, instead of forcing the Van Buren group to come to terms, it had brought Calhoun out in the open as "an enemy to the President and the Democratic party." Kendall substantiated Harvey's comment when he noted "there is every indication that Calhoun's friends begin to think his publication a bad business and wish for peace." It was clear, however, that Kendall, having gained the initiative, would accept nothing less than an unconditional surrender. "Peace may be granted them," he wrote, "but they must lay down their arms." Welles could expect only a brief respite, for, with Calhoun now largely discredited in the President's eyes, Kendall and Blair were determined to smash Green, their competitor, once and for all. The *Times* editor was slated to be one of the major weapons in the onslaught.[19]

On March 10 Kendall again urged Welles to permit publication in full of his conversations with Green, insisting that it would do him no injury. He offered a plan which he thought would spare Welles from any public vendetta with the redoubtable Green. "We can push him to call on you, if you prefer it," he suggested, "or we can give one or both of these extracts without stating that you consented to the publication which you can negative if he shall apply to you but affirm that they contain the truth." While Welles agonized over his dilemma, the *Globe* opened a drum-fire attack on the *Telegraph*; and finally, on March 18, Green erupted with a furious rebuttal. "War, open war is now the cry," exulted Amos Kendall. "In this day's paper, Green releases everybody from confidence in relation both to his conversations and correspondence and challenges the whole out! What a fool! Well, I think he should have it all. It is time to put him down." Kendall wanted Welles to prepare a complete statement of his conversations with Green.

Earlier, Welles had relayed to Kendall the details of his second interview with Green in January, at which several Connecticut friends and Andrew Dunlap had been present. Now Kendall wanted their corroborating statements. "It is desirable," he said, "to get so much proof that there can be no gain-saying." Step by step, the soft-voiced, self-effacing Kendall was managing the affair with masterful aplomb. He knew how to arouse Green's splenetic nature, and he also knew that an angry man was a man who made mistakes. "Blair is not expected back for a week," he advised Welles. "Nothing will be done here but to provoke Green by a few short hits, until B's return. It is probable he will then be taken in hand."[20]

As March wore on the *Globe* continued to insist it had irrefutable evidence of Green's disloyalty to the administration. The embattled editor of the *Telegraph* repeatedly denied the assertion. On April 6 the *Globe* for the first time printed a substantial part of Welles' letter to Isaac Hill in a two-column attack on Green. Blair had deleted Green's comment, as reported by Welles, that if Jackson were a candidate in

1832, Calhoun "would not probably" oppose him. Instead, he emphasized that part of the letter which quoted Green as stating that Calhoun's "claims could not be postponed another four years." Green immediately demanded of Welles copies of all correspondence that had
passed between them. Assuming that "their confidential conversations
had been either misunderstood or misrepresented," he requested that
the letters be made public. The *Telegraph* of April 6 carried Green's
letter together with his editorial comment, declaring he had a letter of
Welles' dated March 31, 1830, "that controverted the *Globe*'s positive
proof."[21] The allusion to Welles in the counterattack of the *Telegraph*
was a matter of serious concern to Amos Kendall, who had never
doubted Welles' loyalty or the truth of his assertions. Could Welles
have been playing both sides, or had he been indiscreet, or was it
merely another example of Green's blustering? If Green did have some
incriminating correspondence, their own reputations and the future of
the *Globe* could be in serious jeopardy. Hitherto Jackson had accepted
Kendall's criticism of the *Telegraph* and had rather grudgingly agreed
to the establishment of the *Globe*. Should Green prove that Blair and
Kendall had misrepresented the case, had in fact made a most serious
charge on contradictory evidence, it would be most embarrassing.

The President had decided that the Cabinet must be reorganized so
that Calhoun's influence in it would be terminated, but he was quite
capable even at this late date of changing his mind.[22] Rumblings of
concern came from the White House through Major Lewis, the President's closest friend and a Van Buren partisan. Jackson had been following the controversy with keen interest. He was disturbed by Green's
confident statement that he had ample evidence to disprove the charges
in the *Globe*. At Van Buren's request, Major Lewis wrote Welles on
April 7, 1831, seeking to clarify the situation. "Green," he said, "seems
to think or rather affects to believe that the letter is not genuine; but if
it be, he says he has ample means of vindication which he will lay before the public. What can he mean? What are his means of vindication
of which he speaks? Has he any letters of yours which may, by possibility, conflict with the extract published in the *Globe*?" Van Buren was
concerned because his letter from Welles contained the phrase deleted
from the Hill extract published in the *Globe* that Calhoun probably
would not oppose Jackson's re-election. Careful as always, he warned
Welles, through Lewis, to keep him clear of the imbroglio, "not to refer to any letter you may have written to this place, during the year
1830, unless you have a copy of it. There is one gentleman here," continued Lewis, "to whom you have written, I would particularly cau-

tion you not to refer should you deem it necessary to say anything in your paper in relation to this matter." Kendall, writing the next day, also warned Welles, "not to answer Green hastily."[23]

Schooled in the rough-and-tumble journalism of frontier Kentucky, Kendall was more confident than Lewis that Welles could handle any apparent discrepancy, provided there was no major contradiction; yet he was concerned. Should Welles prove loyal but indiscreet, as Kendall suspected was the case, could he maintain himself against such a veteran journalist as Green? The *Times* editor was young, comparatively inexperienced, little known outside of his native state. "It is an important moment for Welles," Kendall wrote Niles, "if he can sustain himself nobly against Green, he will rise in the party. I beg you, therefore, to counsel with him freely. . . . I will aid Welles with all my might. He must not be injured by such a knave and hypocrite as Green. But W[elles] must not use my name. I will correspond hereafter through you."[24]

Kendall was correct in assuming Welles to be loyal, but he had erred in judging him to be either indiscreet or rash; and he had underestimated his journalistic capacity, which was clearly superior to Green's. Welles did not reply to Green's request for copies of their correspondence until April 14, 1831, when he asked that a copy of his letter of March 31, 1830 (the one Green wanted to publish), be sent to Hartford for his examination. Regarding Green's letters to him, Welles wrote that they were deposited at his home in Glastonbury. It would take at least two weeks before he could transmit copies.

The *Telegraph* editor would not wait. He denied, truthfully enough, that he had said Calhoun would oppose Jackson if he ran for a second term, but, rather than confine himself to this, his strongest point, he launched a general attack on Van Buren, Eaton, and Lewis. They were, he asserted, a band of conspirators, hiding behind Jackson's popularity, influencing the President, against his better judgment, to stand for re-election, so that Van Buren could have the nomination in 1836. Green admitted that he told Welles either Calhoun or McLean would be a stronger candidate than Van Buren even in his own state of New York. "It may be," he said, "that I expressed an opinion that in case General Jackson was not a candidate, Mr. Calhoun's friends would not consent to his postponement." Referring to Welles as a man to whom he had given his confidence, and with whom he had conversed as a gentleman of honor, Green said scornfully, "it now appears that he was a mere jobber for office hunters, and that he sought my confidence to betray it." He then offered Welles' letter of March 31, to show, as he put it, "how far I was deceived." Welles had written that he thought it was impolitic to mention whether Jackson would be a candidate in 1832. He also expressed himself as favoring one term for the presidential office, "but if the party say otherwise, I feel it my duty to submit." And recognizing Jackson's popularity with the voters, he did not think it would be wise "to counteract the tide that is slowly setting in our favor, by denying that which is doing most for our benefit."[25]

Apparently Green thought Welles' neutral stance on a second term marked him as a Calhoun supporter; for the enraged editor now considered that anyone who wanted the President re-elected was in league with Van Buren. He was mistaken. Had he read the letter carefully, he would have noted Welles' belief that there were impressive political advantages in a second term for Jackson. At least this was Amos Kendall's verdict. Relieved of his anxiety, the able manipulator congratulated Welles "that the *Telegraph* magazine has exploded without doing you any injury . . . your letter . . . is such a one as every true Republican might be proud of having written." More gratifying was Van Buren's, and indirectly, the President's, approval, conveyed again through Major Lewis. Jackson had been completely satisfied with Welles' conduct. "The secret working of Duff Green, Calhoun and Co.," wrote the President to his old friend General John Coffee, "is clearly developed . . . the plot unmasked . . . and Duff and Calhoun have politically destroyed themselves, never to rise again."[26]

What might have developed into a journalistic duel between the *Hartford Times* and the *U. S. Telegraph* was overshadowed by the resignation of every member of the Cabinet except Major Barry, a maneuver made by the President to rid himself of Calhoun's supporters, yet maintain a semblence of party unity. For the next several months the Welles-Green affair would bob about in the wake of the Cabinet upheaval. Welles was cited in the public controversy between Ingham and Eaton; and, at the suggestion of Kendall, the *Hartford Times* used the reference to belabor Calhoun and the *Telegraph* during the summer of 1831.[27] The opposition press in Connecticut, taking its cue from the *Telegraph*, abused Welles unmercifully. John Greenleaf Whittier, who had replaced Prentice on *The New England Weekly Review*, outdid them all in his vicious personal attacks, which stigmatized Welles as this "jobber for office hunters—the fool and pimp of Amos Kendall," guilty of "ineffable, inimitable meanness . . . contamination in his very shadow."[28] Overly sensitive to such personal imputations, Welles must have writhed under Whittier's merciless lashing; yet he knew that anyone who became identified in a well-publicized quarrel must expect to be a target for open attack. However galling these partisan thrusts, Welles enjoyed the satisfaction of having acquitted himself admirably in a contest with one of the most powerful editors in the Union. He was well aware that his stock had risen among Jackson's confidential advisers. To many he may have seemed a controversial figure, but he was the only Jacksonian politician in the state who could claim a measure of national prominence.[29]

# CHAPTER 6

# Conflict and
# Compromise

WELLES HAD SEEN the party grow from a handful of dedicated men in Hartford—a mere faction of a faction—to a state-wide organization. The Jacksonians were still in a minority, but each year they were gaining, and triumph at the polls seemed not far off. Welles thought 1833 would be the year. Although he was planning for it, he was far too experienced in politics to assume that he could win a prized nomination without a struggle. Within his own county organization, he was secretly opposed by two clever men—Henry L. Ellsworth and Isaac Toucey. In other counties restive party leaders regarded with suspicion any move of Welles or Niles, who were discovering that even patronage could not buy steady loyalty.

Everyone, it seemed, was experimenting with political techniques—combining and separating, advancing toward one goal, retreating from another. Local interests were fragmented and fiercely competitive. In Litchfield the farmers continued their age-old feud with the lawyers; in New Haven, Yale College interfered in local and state politics to pursue its own ends, while the counties east of the Connecticut River distrusted the counties west of it. Each little "village-city" had its own pretensions, its own aspirations, its own special champions. And the industrial revolution just beginning in the state was heightening local attachments, as competitive (and always marginal) enterpreneurs fiercely defended their market territory against all rivals. Connecticut was entering its long travail that would eventually, and with much anguish, produce a new social order. Important changes had occurred, even in the five years of Welles' active participation in politics. Small factories were cropping up everywhere; banks and insurance companies were being formed and seeking charters from a suspicious, farmer-dominated legislature; canals were being built and railroads projected.

A more important sign of the times, at least for an aspiring politician, was the significant change that was occurring in education and in the public attitude toward learning. In the preceding thirty years some 200 denominational academies and a dozen colleges had been founded in New England. By 1830 Connecticut alone had about thirty new academies and two new colleges, a private school, and a college population near 5000. And many of those who were not fortunate enough to gain a higher level of formal education threw themselves into ambitious programs of self-improvement through reading and study.[1] What Samuel Goodrich described so aptly as the age of talk was the age of study as well. Young men such as Elihu Burritt of New Britain, who outdid even Isaac Hill or Bronson Alcott in his passion for self-improvement, were ransacking the pitiful, hoary stocks of local libraries or neighborhood collections. Working at hard labor from ten to twelve hours a day, they managed somehow to master stupendous quantities of miscellaneous information—about the resources of Vermont, for example, or the Roman consuls from the beginning of the Republic to the reign of Augustus—some 650 of them.

Most young people addicted to the vogue of study were seeking knowledge they felt might prove useful in advancing themselves. Niles taught himself Latin with the help of a neighbor because he had been told a mastery of at least one classical language was absolutely essential for a "poor farm boy to get ahead." A bemused Hawthorne observed the youthful keeper of a "temperance hotel" in Hartford "reading a Hebrew Bible in the bar, by means of a Lexicon and an English version."[2]

The books they read were rarely of modern vintage; rather, they were ancient or outdated works—the collection of a long-dead minister or squire that happened to be available in a country village. Whatever may have been the strange and wonderful results of their untutored labors, some wheat was gleaned out of all the chaff. Far more important than the quality of their reading was the fact that it made little difference to the ambitious farm boy, clerk, or apprentice whether he met the test of an educated man. With no basis for comparison, he thought he did. So did his family and neighbors. His numbers helped swell the ranks of graduates from the new academies and colleges. By the mid-1830's there was scarcely a hamlet in Connecticut that did not boast of one or two young folk who felt they had prepared themselves for an improvement in their prospects.

Much of the impetus for identifying education with social mobility (in effect, secularizing the old Puritan ethic) seems to have been provided by the activities of the competitive Protestant sects, reinforced by the ideas of Thomas Jefferson. Samuel Goodrich, who considered Jefferson a demagogue, remarked sourly that his philosophy had "percolated through the blood and bones of society . . . not only the politicians, but the preacher, the lawyer, the editor, the author, all took to talking, speechmaking, lecturing in a new sense—that is, to seduce the multitude."[3] Goodrich, a good Federalist son of a Federalist father, could not resist the partisan fling; and, accurate observer that he was, for once he failed to realize he was witnessing a significant change in the American character. His age of talk reflected a dawning belief that education in an open society was the American equivalent of good birth in a closed society.

In due course this popular notion would cause the social unrest that welled up in the politics of the Jackson administration. Connecticut, along with other Northern states, was beginning to experience one of the classic problems of an emerging industrial society. There were too many educated, semi-educated, and self-educated individuals for the non-agricultural economy to absorb. Aspirations were high, opportunities in other than farm employment few. Education had broadened the horizons of a growing middle class; yet it had also sharpened their prejudices against manual labor as ill-rewarded, confining to the body and the spirit, harsh, degrading. Even in Connecticut, one of the most traditional of all states, a land of self-sufficient farmers, there was an increasing surplus of lawyers, ministers, schoolteachers, small manufacturers—individuals whom the *Hartford Times* was fond of calling "distressed young men."

Politics and its concurrent activity, journalism, seemed likely to develop a possible outlet for many of these restless spirits who preferred gardening to farming. Public office traditionally conferred status. Why should it not provide a livelihood, too? Welles thought it should—an attitude he shared with most working politicians of his generation. If the Jacksonian spirit was entrepreneurial in its economic thrust, it was even more so in its political behavior. William L. Marcy's aphorism— "to the victor belongs the spoils"—would have been more accurately phrased as "to the victor belongs the career." Though Welles and Ellsworth were notable exceptions, the new politics was practiced by new men, men who had hauled themselves out of the farm or the forge. The pungent humor of the barnyard or the country workshop lingered in their rustic wit and rural ways. Calloused hands still gripped the new steel pens as if they were scythe handles; grammar was frequently more direct than proper.

"Let me get a clip at him," Gurdon Russell, a farmer's son, remembered General Nathaniel Terry saying, after Niles spoke at a town meeting in Hartford. "No bloodhound," said Russell, "could have been more fierce or confident. . . . But Mr. Niles would not stay fixed." The self-taught lawyer-politician was more impressive, Russell thought, than "the elegant, autocratic" General Terry, representative of Federalism which was nearly dead. Niles had convinced Russell because of his "great knowledge of facts and the power of logical reasoning, and practical acquaintance with the affairs of life." Direct and matter-of-fact when dealing with a local audience, Niles let his country twang speak for itself when he told an anecdote or indulged in a witticism. He pronounced "point" "pint," and "party" "porty," but he knew also how and when to impress with his erudition, a technique of persuasion that General Terry never could master. Niles always reminded his audience that he was not born to his learning, that he had acquired it himself, "by hard study and under unfavorable circumstances." He was respected the more for it. Russell, a young man at the time, admired him as "a sturdy defender of the democracy now beginning to be felt in the state." His father thought more of Niles' style and the content of his remarks. Said the elder Russell: "He has got a head."[4]

Niles was an ambitious man, as self-seeking as any of the new political breed; but he was also a man of principle, loyal to his friends and to his party. In contrast, most of Connecticut's new politicians, whether Jacksonian or Whig, let their interests rule their actions. Once an office—any office—had been achieved, return to a hardscrabble farm or a country law practice was unthinkable. Most would compete savagely to gain a position, and would utilize any means—ethical or not—to hold it or to advance their income and their prestige.[5]

National and local positions available were increasing as new states came into the Union and new territories were organized. Social and economic reform measures in the older states—at first pushed by the Jacksonians, soon championed by their opponents—also provided new jobs. The over-all increase of the population and of economic activity required more public services, hence more government positions in the post offices, in the customs houses, even in the Army and Navy.[6] Public service was not exactly a new frontier, but there were sufficient new possibilities to excite strenuous rivalry. The Jacksonians, despite their full-blown rhetoric on the subject, were careful to confine themselves to general principles, and they were never known to be laggards in the pursuit of office—local, state, or federal. As Samuel Kellogg, a close friend of Welles, exclaimed: "God knows that if the Jackson party lacks talents there is no lack of applicants for office amongst them. . . . I sometimes think that the Whigs have good reason to bestow upon us the epithet of hungry cormorants or a set of jackals following the camp merely for the sake of the garbage."[7]

The difficulty, of course, was that, like the economy, the government could not be made to grow fast enough to accommodate even a fraction of the ambitious claimants. The struggle for office, elective or appointive, became a frenzied affair of unrestrained competition, marked by secret intrigues, sudden betrayals, jealousies, mutual recriminations. Under the circumstances it was difficult for such able organizers as Welles or Niles to maintain any sense of party regularity. Complaining about the selfish course of a would-be candidate for the United States Senate, Niles lamented, "It is thus the personal objects of individuals that embarrass all general objects."[8]

Gideon Welles and his fellow Jacksonians had not envisaged such a free-for-all competition. Effective persuaders, they had an implicit faith in their program, certain that their opponents who occupied state and federal offices had become the masters rather than the servants of the people. The opposition, of course, had similar views. John J. Crittenden, the eminent Kentucky Whig, sounded much like Welles when he wrote to David Daggett that "our politics partake too much of the *personal*, and too little of *principle*. . . . For my own part, tho' not insensible to personal distinctions and preferences, I care but little comparatively about the individual that is advanced. I wish to see the Dynasty of the *Masters*, exchanged for one of Public *Servants*."[9]

Believing that their principles were the only correct principles, the Jacksonians saw their task as that of convincing the people of the truth and making it stick through political organization and political advertising in the editorial columns of their partisan sheets. They soon discovered that inventing and merchandizing a political program was not quite the same as selling Yankee notions. Within their own ranks the distribution of offices was a constant problem. Where one "common man" was as good as another, who was to decide on the candidate? Honesty, loyalty, devotion to the cause became the tests; but the party had too many honest men and loyal workers, too few rewards for the faithful. What of the opposition they meant to overthrow? Proscription, or "rotation in office," as it was more euphemistically termed, could be tried only once. Influenced by Jefferson's and Madison's teachings, Welles and his group had thought, naïvely, that when they gained control, their "correct principles" would prevail and factional strife would disappear. They soon discovered that the opposition had its own interpretation of correct principles, that that this commanded its own share of public opinion. The Jacksonians had brought about free competition in the political marketplace; they now had to abide by the results. Tenure became uncertain, not only for the officeholder, but for the party leaders themselves. Welles commented on the personal character of Jacksonian politics in one of his fragmentary jottings written years later. "I looked upon the contest," he wrote, "as one of personal rivalry among aspiring men. Such I am inclined to think was and is with many, perhaps a majority of every party, the impelling motive. . . ."[10]

When the Jacksonians recognized (as they soon did) that the old Jeffersonian party system was gone forever, they accepted the realities of political life. In doing so, they adopted many of the promotional techniques the revivalists had been using with such success. The printed word bore testimony to the feverish style of the itinerant preacher. Jacksonian newspapers teemed with vivid words and pejorative phrases: "whiffling weathercocks," "trimmers," "twaddlers," "dodgers," "butter milks," "wigs," "vigs," "nigs" were but a few of the epithets Welles used to describe his political opponents. When a defense of their position seemed indicated, the Jacksonians fell back on glowing rhetoric. They would restore the good old days of the simple, rural Republic—the civic virtues, the American Arcady. Should the occasion demand it, they would illustrate their precepts with tangible examples. In 1834, for instance, when Congress changed the monetary ratio to favor the minting of gold, Jacksonian leaders in Connecticut purchased several thousand dollars' worth of the new eagles. These were shown around for the credulous to admire, the skeptical to bite, and the opposition to scorn. American gold pieces had not been in general circulation since the War of 1812, and there had been precious few of them even then. The opposition was quick to imitate these promotional devices, especially the parades, the slogans, and the harangues. When Michel Chevalier was visiting the United States in 1835, he said, with conviction: "It is the democratic party that gets up the most brilliant and animated."[11]

Important changes in political behavior were becoming so obvious that even the most stolid of party leaders could not fail to observe them. Public interest was quickening in political affairs. Active participation in party work was no longer being considered the exclusive province of a small elite group. Welles himself was in touch with a score of ardent party workers all over the state—men who had rarely concerned themselves with politics before. He and his associates had done much to stir up public interest in political issues, real or imaginary. This was a practical necessity in their struggle to establish position and identity in the political marketplace. Their opponents, too, had been actively cultivating public opinion and strengthening their organization with new blood. But neither party had apparently foreseen the possibility that competition might arise from another quarter, that a third party movement might develop with its own appeal to the electorate, its own set of ambitious managers.

It came as a shock to Welles when he learned that the New York Anti-Masonic movement had leaped over the state boundary and was being organized into a distinct political entity. A Mason himself, he was aware of the excitement in New York over the alleged kidnapping and murder of William Morgan for planning to reveal the secrets of the order. He also knew something of the activities of Thurlow Weed and William H. Seward, who had formed a vigorous political movement on the Anti-Masonic issue. Deeply involved at the time with his own party work, Welles paid little attention to what he dismissed as purely a New York affair. Nor had there been any need for politicians in Connecticut to concern themselves. The "Land of Steady Habits" seemed impervious to all the activity that was going on just west of its borders. As late as February 1828, Jeremy Cross, a New Haven exporter of Masonic regalia, wrote a friend who was organizing new lodges in South America that nothing was "stirring" in the state.[12]

The excitement of the Jackson-Adams contest brought much of the latent Anti-Masonic feeling into the open, especially in the rural eastern counties, where almost immediately it assumed a political complexion. Wherever Baptists and Methodists were numerous, Anti-Masonry attracted converts. At first this posed a more serious problem for the Jacksonians than for their opponents. William Ellis complained from New Haven that "unfortunately the greater part of those who formerly went with me as democratic Jacksonians have gone over stock and flute to the Anti-Masonic party. Some three or four are Methodists who lead them on." But Congregationalists, too, were impressed by the Anti-Masonic rhetoric. Old John Cotton Smith, the state's last Federalist governor, an educated man who should have known better, fell an easy victim to the campaign. He decided that Masonry was "radically unsound, and that in its operation, whatever may have been the original intention, it is essentially anti-Christian."[13]

Welles' initial reaction to the new organization was one of alarm. He feared a coalition between the Anti-Masons and the Federalists that would dominate local elections was in the making. When a fusion did not materialize, he began to wonder whether the movement might not be turned to Jacksonian advantage. There was no doubt in his mind that Anti-Masonry had popular appeal, but it seemed unable to develop an effective leadership. No Thurlow Weed appeared to convert the party into a strong political force. That it had no aims beyond the uprooting of Masonry was evident in the behavior of its members in the legislature. The *Hartford Times* remarked that "on no question has a third party appeared. There has been a fraternal embrace, or rather, an 'Indian hug' between the Nationals and the Anties." By 1831, however, the new party was hurting the Republicans more than the Jacksonians in the elections, though it was cooperating with them in the legislature. Welles was particularly impressed by its success in kindling political interest where none had existed before. "The public mind in our country," he wrote Phelps, "must have something to feed upon, if wholesome fare is not to be obtained they will take what is pernicious and harmful." Why not, he suggested, remove the cause by having the various lodges give up their charters and voluntarily dissolve Masonry in the State? "It would unquestionably lead to harmony in society . . . something in a country like ours is due to public opinion."

The suggestion that the society disband met with little favor from the Masons he approached. Most of them were determined to resist what they regarded as persecution by unprincipled demagogues seeking political advantage at their expense. "Do you suppose," asked Phelps in reply, "that if the charters were surrendered and the Lodges broken up the Anti-Masons would be satisfied? Nothing will satisfy them but renouncing the order and joining their party."[14]

Phelps was being realistic, but he had not understood the real tenor of Welles' remarks. A veteran politician of the old style, he thought of the public as so many cyphers, so many vacuous entities that were incapable of making independent judgments and were to be manipulated by leaders such as himself. He made no effort to understand public opinion in any meaningful sense. Phelps's political world was one of deals and alliances with fellow bosses. Why should anyone bother with the sentiments of the average citizen, when his vote (if he were persuaded to exercise it) could be bought for a glass or two of rum? The Anti-Masonic movement was simply an expression of an out-group which represented a vague threat to the leadership of the two parties. He might be prepared at some time in the future to counsel a deal with Anti-Masonic leaders if this seemed expedient, but he could not imagine ever trying to compete with them for voters.

Welles thought differently. The Anti-Masonic movement had answered a question that had been troubling him for some time—what should be done to overcome voter apathy? Since he had first engaged in political work, he had been trying without much success to increase the rural vote and the Jacksonian share of it. Now, suddenly, hundreds of new voters were supporting Anti-Masonic candidates in local elections. He considered the movement to be a specious one, but, unlike many of his colleagues, he insisted on taking it seriously. His first reaction to its success at the polls—that the lodges bow to public opinion and dissolve themselves—had been hasty and wrong. He deserved the rebuke he received from his fellow Masons. His conclusion, however, had been right. The average citizen needed issues "to feed upon," issues he could understand, presented in terms that would engage his interest.[15]

As Welles read the columns of Hartford's *Anti-Masonic Intelligencer*, he began to understand more fully the importance of style in bidding for broad support. Though he had always been aware of this, he had more often than not fallen into the habit of countering the opinions of opposing editors rather than in taking his case directly to the public. The Anti-Masonic argument had a familiar ring. Basically, it rehearsed the old sectarian arguments, but with an important difference. The Anti-Masons claimed to have uncovered a *real* plot—a conspiracy in high places that was determined to subvert individual liberties in the interest of a tyranical secret order. They supplied facts, dates, gory details. They emphasized mysterious, evil forces which they likened to popery. It was not an appeal for the exercise of freedom of conscience, but a clarion call to save the Republic and the Christian religion from imminent destruction.[16]

Welles realized that there was little truth in the Anti-Masonic position, that it was aimed frankly at ignorance, prejudice, and suspicion. He agreed with the Bridgeport *Republican Farmer*, "that we cannot as honest men look on and see the lawless and causeless enthusiasm now attempted . . . without entering our solemn protest." But he was impressed and not a little disturbed at how the free citizenry could be so easily persuaded to whore after a false god. If this kind of direct approach was necessary to generate political enthusiasm, then responsible men should utilize it for the public good. And by responsible men Welles meant the Jacksonians. While he would never, as editor of the

*Times* or as a writer on political affairs, indulge in the wild accusations and the fictitious claims of the Anti-Masons, he would change his approach and his appeal. As Phelps and other associates had predicted, the Anti-Masonic movement did die out in Connecticut; but it was the first organized political expression of an essentially religious impulse —evangelical, fundamentalist, crusading. And as such, it would have a mighty influence on the ritual, and the style, of American political institutions.[17]

In a more immediate and practical context, the Anti-Masonic excitement had almost no impact on the presidential contest in Connecticut. It was apparent as the election approached that a majority of the Anti-Masons would support Clay against Jackson. The new National Republican party was trying the same fusion tactics that the Jacksonians had used and found wanting. Ellsworth, who knew more of their difficulties than any other Jacksonian (his brother was a leading National Republican), described their condition to Van Buren: "Federalists, Clayites and Anti's have united as National Republicans, but their party is already filled with jealousy."[18]

Welles and his associates had not the slightest doubt that Jackson would be re-elected and that his popularity would carry over to his running mate, Martin Van Buren. They were concerned, as they had been in 1828, about the showing they themselves would make in the state. By May it was distressingly clear that many of their supporters would vote for Clay. "When political honesty becomes better policy and a surer prospect to office, than trimming and political knavery," exclaimed an angry Niles, "we may reasonably expect a change in our politics." Of course it was not entirely "trimming and political knavery" that benefited Clay. Jackson's Indian removal policy and his stands on the tariff and on the Bank were not popular among the more conservative voters. The National Republicans had also borrowed many of their opponent's organization techniques and had made some improvements of their own.[19]

Clay carried the state by over 6000 votes, but the Jacksonians had tripled their vote over 1828. If Wirt's vote were added to Clay's, the relative position of the two parties remained unchanged, as the *Middletown Gazette* pointed out. Despite the truth of this assertion, the Jacksonians took comfort in the fact that they had polled almost as many votes as their friends in Massachusetts had.[20]

Most perplexing to Welles was what to do about these Clay Democrats. One of his correspondents in Litchfield wrote that "the twaddlers of this county are coming out for the Administration like sheep over a wall." He would spurn them, and he urged the same policy on Welles. "Much depends on you sir," he said, "if you hold on for the next six months, as you have for a year past, I cannot doubt that we shall have the soundest party that we have ever had in this state. . . ."

Phelps urged a different course: "We have no terms to make with the Clay Democrats. Let us adhere to principles—nominate for offices none but good and true men and others will come in and support us." Welles took Phelps and other party leaders at their word, and on December 31, 1832, he laid down the policy for the spring campaign in the *Hartford Times*. The nominees must be "unflinching democrats" whose pedigrees went back to 1828 or earlier. With an obvious reference to himself, he stipulated some further qualifications: "It is too common for weak politicians to advocate a surrender of the best and firmest friends of democracy, merely because from their fidelity and integrity they have rendered themselves obnoxious to the federalists." Jacksonians, then, would not proscribe Clay Democrats if they gave assurances of their loyalty and agreed that they did not have first claim to office.

Most experienced politicians thought that the Democrats would win handily in 1833. The National Republicans, after Clay's defeat, were warring among themselves. Clay Democrats had no option but to support the regular Democratic ticket. Jackson's firm handling of the Nullification controversy had met with strong approval, especially from the old-line Federalists in both major parties. Since the presidential election the Democrats had acquired significant newspaper support, including that of the *Register* and the Bridgeport *Republican Farmer*. In Hartford, Phelps, Niles, Toucey, and others had established a new paper, the *Jeffersonian*, to assist the *Times*.[21] Phineas T. Barnum, the future showman, surveyed the political scene in Fairfield County, found it to his liking, and decided to try his hand at being a Democratic editor. Hungry for office, he opened such a scurrilous attack on his political opponents that he found himself in jail for libel instead of in the post office at Bethel. After his release from jail, Barnum learned that it was "an unvariable rule" in the Post Office Department not to bestow an office upon a practicing editor. Unperturbed by this administration ruling, Barnum nominated his father, Philo, in his place. For the first time since their establishment as a party, the Democrats, as the Jacksonians now called themselves, had at least one newspaper in every county and important town.[22]

Confident of party success in the spring campaign, Welles was determined to run for Congress. He had certainly earned the nomination, and he was by all odds the best qualified man the Democrats could put up in Hartford. But having the best qualifications did not mean that he was the best candidate. His most serious handicap was his position as editor of the *Times* and as chief party organizer. In both areas of responsibility he had compiled a distinguished, if not brilliant, record. Yet paradoxically, his success had made him a highly controversial candidate, and hence a weak one; for the nominee had to have the united support of his own party and substantial help from outside. Welles could not count on either. Over the preceding five years he had built up a reputation as the most dedicated and the most inflexible party man in the state. Outspoken, inventive, thorough in preparation, he was a hard fighter for any cause he believed in. This combative spirit, so effective on the editorial page, carried over into the council chamber, where diplomacy, not polemics, was the important thing. Observing so clearly himself what ought to be done, he was impatient and apt to be overly critical of associates less gifted than he. His constant insistence upon principles was irritating to many, even to close friends such as Niles, who found him annoyingly sensitive and stubborn when they proposed any move that smacked of expediency. Welles, of course, recognized that converts had to be made if the party was ever to build up its organization. Yet he found it difficult to accept these individuals, much less work with them. He distrusted their motives, not without reason, and he was quick to challenge their loyalty in party councils.

On their side, many resented Welles. Few had been spared his vitriolic pen in the past, when they were in the opposition. The more conservative converts did not approve of his conduct of the *Times*—his contempt for sectarian religion, his criticism of banks, lotteries, and all special charters. As a partisan editor, Welles was also open to the charge that he was using the editorial chair to advance his own interests rather than the party's.

In the past Niles had encouraged Welles' ambition but, aware of his weaknesses, strove to temper it with caution. He wanted to spare his friend a mortifying defeat which he felt would be inevitable. Concerned about the fragile condition of party unity, he wanted no disruption during the early stages of its development. There was also an element of self-interest in Niles' attitude of restraint. Welles could not be spared. He was the one indispensable man. When he left Hartford for brief trips to Washington or vacations in Pennsylvania he could always expect letters from home decrying his absence. Nothing, it seemed, ever went right in the *Times* office when he was away. "Are you sensible how much you are wanted at home?" asked Niles in January 1832. "Never was there a time when you was [*sic*] more wanted," he continued, his irritation evident in his grammatical slip. "Now is a crisis in our affairs, and there is a diversity of opinion among our friends. . . ."[23]

Welles' awareness of his value to the party spurred his ambition. Merit and faithful service, he reasoned, ought to be recognized. He had wanted to run for Congress in 1831, when it was thought the fusion arrangement with the Adams Republicans would assure victory for the regular candidates. At that time Niles had advised him to go slow. "If you keep back," he said, "your course is more certain, you are daily strengthening your hold on the confidence of the party and a few years will place you in the very front rank in this county, if not in the state." Fortunately, Welles heeded this sound advice. The coalition did not hold together in the congressional race, and had he been nominated he would have been defeated.

When he told Niles that he wanted to run in 1833, the older man offered no objection, and by early December of 1832 they had worked out a slate. Since congressmen were elected at large, they started the slow process of sounding out party leaders. Opposition developed at once, though no important figure chose to make an open issue of it at that stage. Most of the criticism was directed at Welles and at Dr. Samuel Simons, his hand-picked candidate for Congress from Fairfield County. Henry W. Edwards, the choice of the *Times* office for the governorship, seemed to meet with general approval. A long-time foe of the Ingersolls, he had been selected at Welles' suggestion to counter their influence in New Haven. Edwards was willing to run, but he felt that the party would not win unless certain Clay Democrats received congressional nominations.

Welles brushed aside all objections as merely the grumbling of a few disappointed office-seekers; but behind the scenes opposition was crystallizing fast. Noah Phelps viewed Welles' nomination as a serious challenge to his own party influence. For three years, step by step, Phelps had been constructing a personal following in Middletown. Now, despite his assertions to the contrary, he was deep in negotiations with the Clay Democrats and certain disappointed National Republicans. He was also in touch with his chief, Secretary of the Treasury Louis McLane, who was trying to undermine Van Buren's support in the North. Welles' policy of disciplining all former opponents of the administration threatened to wreck Phelps' plans. A congressional delegation of staunch Van Buren supporters headed by Welles would be a distinct setback to McLane, and for Phelps it could mean a subordinate role in the party, an end to his ambitions, perhaps even his office as collector at Middletown.

The alarmed Phelps made secret overtures to two men within the Hartford County organization whom he knew resented the power of the *Times* office—Henry Ellsworth and Isaac Toucey. Ellsworth, who had lost a small fortune in a carpet-mill speculation, was desperate for any office which might help him recoup. Toucey, a handsome, successful lawyer who had married into a wealthy Hartford family, was eager for the honor and distinction of public office. Originally a Federalist (when it was profitable to be one), he was an Adams Republican for a brief period but quickly accepted a Jacksonian nomination for Congress in 1831 when it was thought he might split the opposition. Cold, calculating, subtle, Toucey considered Welles an ineffectual dilettante and Niles a crude and dangerous visionary. He was most receptive when Phelps outlined a working alliance if the *Times* group succeeded in controlling the congressional nominations. An essential first step, they agreed, would be to establish a new Democratic paper in Hartford, ostensibly to assist the *Times*, but, if a fight developed, to represent their own interests exclusively. At Toucey's suggestion, Thomas Hart Seymour, a young, attractive member of one of Hartford's leading families and a Norwich classmate of Welles, was selected as the editor of the paper. All went according to plan. Toucey and Ellsworth had no difficulty in persuading the *Times* men that a new paper (which they proposed to call the *Jeffersonian*) would help the cause. Niles even agreed to purchase stock in the enterprise.[24]

Meanwhile, on the surface at least, the Welles-Niles ticket seemed to be moving ahead smoothly. The Democratic convention, meeting in Hartford on January 30, 1833, sanctioned their plan that the congressional nominations be made by the county delegations, which in turn obediently approved their slate. The state ticket encountered no difficulty. Phelps had learned the day before the convention that Welles would not withdraw his candidacy. Though he attended the afternoon session, he left before the congressional nominations were announced. A long and bitter attack on Welles and on the "management" of the *Times* office had already been set in type at the office of the Middletown *Witness*, Phelps' paper, before the collector reached home. The indictment appeared on February 3, and it was followed on the sixth by an equally scathing attack from Seymour's *Jeffersonian*.

Welles was shocked. Toucey and Ellsworth disclaimed any responsibility for Seymour's tirade but raised the question of party unity and delicately suggested that Welles withdraw. Niles, who was skeptical about the extent of the opposition, counseled an open letter to the county delegates which would test the political climate before any decision was made. Accordingly, Welles drafted a circular requesting that the county delegates reconsider their previous action, without, however, removing himself as a candidate. The county delegates, as Niles had expected, took no further action in the matter. Opposition in Hartford, he thought, must be limited to a few envious individuals who had managed to impress the inexperienced Seymour. He and Welles may have had some inkling that Toucey and Ellsworth were implicated, but they let the matter rest.

The *Witness*, however, seemed so obviously linked to Phelps that Welles decided upon a resolute course of action. He wrote a stern letter to the collector, reminding him of their long association and of his political obligations. Phelps replied immediately, denying that he had any connection with the *Witness* or that he was in any way responsible for its editorial policy. Bitterly critical of the convention proceedings, he lashed back at Welles. "I went to Hartford," he complained, "under high expectation of success and that all there would be right. I returned politically sick. I do not complain that my advice was not taken, for it was not asked by the prevailing party . . . there was too much management there. . . ." Further angry correspondence passed between the two men—Welles charging "ingratitude," the collector insisting he had acted in good faith. The exchange served no purpose except to make reconciliation all but impossible. Welles decided he had only two options: either to have the collector summarily removed or to withdraw from the race himself. For as Phelps had surmised, the Clay Democrats would take advantage of the split and refuse to support the regular ticket.[25]

On February 15, 1833, Welles left for Washington as he had planned, so that there would be no conflict of interest between the *Time*'s position and his own candidacy. Grimly determined to discipline Phelps, he went straight to Isaac Hill, who was sympathetic but doubted whether Secretary McLane's approval could be obtained, and certainly not in time to affect the election in Connecticut. His judgment with respect to McLane proved accurate.

Welles knew that he was beaten. His only chance to hold the dissidents in line—a prompt display of his influence in Washington—had come to naught. He had already learned from William Holland, a professor at Hartford's Washington College, that the Clay Democrats would not support him in Hartford County. Holland explained that "they dare not rebel, *en masse*; but they can not, on the other hand cordially cooperate. There is no man they have so much feared, in the state, as yourself. They can not now zealously electioneer for your success."[26]

As Welles saw it, a little group of conspirators had ruined the best chance, perhaps the only chance, the party would ever have of winning an election honestly and on its own terms. Disappointed and discouraged, he was mortified that the Washington influence he had counted on as a last resort had failed him. He was ready to give up— to give up his candidacy, his connection with the *Times*, his interest in politics. Had it not been for Niles he might well have done so. The doughty little postmaster, who recognized the symptoms of despair in his sensitive friend, managed to bolster him up. "Let not your heart be troubled," he wrote, ". . . those who are assailing you, under a pretense of regard for the general good, will in the end suffer much more than you." At the same time he took steps to silence the attacks of the *Jeffersonian* and to force the Hartford County organization into line.[27]

When Welles returned from Washington in mid-March, he had recovered his poise and was able to view the situation more realistically. Neither he nor the party had anything to gain by his withdrawal from the race. The congressional ticket (much altered from its original form by withdrawals and last-minute substitutions) was doomed anyway. Better to go down in defeat and retain the moral advantage than to retire in the face of the enemy. The Jacksonians lost all of the congressional districts but carried the state. Clearly, the personal vendetta against Welles had robbed the party of a complete triumph. His rivals had not weakened Van Buren as they had planned, nor were they able to alter the policy of the *Hartford Times*. They had been motivated by fear, by jealousy, and by notions of temporary expediency. For Welles, the experience, though painful and humiliating, was not without value. He realized in retrospect that he had been as guilty as any in his desire for public office.

In the future he would continue his insistence on binding principles in politics, but he would be more circumspect regarding his own political career, more realistic in his judgments of what could be accomplished through influence in Washington. His friends there on whom he had counted for support—Kendall, Hill, Van Buren—had entrenched themselves in the administration. Feeling themselves reasonably secure, they were not as responsive to party quarrels in the various states as they had been when Calhoun was a dangerous rival. Welles would never again take anything for granted in politics.

# CHAPTER 7

# Struggle for Ascendancy

GIDEON WELLES HAD BECOME cynical about many things, but not about the capacity of the people to support honest, democratic government. Though impatient with the slow processes of indoctrinating the popular mind, he never doubted that in the end the community would right itself and come round to "the old tried and true principles of individual liberty and equality of opportunity." The chief obstacles were the men of expediency—those political freebooters who sought personal gain exclusively, who advanced their own private interests over the public good. Welles found no fault with personal ambition—indeed, he had more of that character trait than most—but personal ambition for its own sake, without any sense of public purpose, he loathed with all the intensity of a practicing moralist. He would certainly have agreed with Nathaniel Hawthorne's ironic estimate of Democratic politicians as men whose "consciences are turned to India rubber, or to some substance as black as that, and which will stretch as much."[1]

Where Hawthorne despaired of any change for the better, Welles believed there was a practical solution for the problem. If all special privilege laws were rooted out and general legislation substituted in their place, he theorized, then self-interest would force the amoral politician to identify his own welfare with the public good. For some time Welles, and Niles too, had been reading William Leggett's political articles in the New York *Evening Post*. Leggett's reduction of all social and economic issues to the principle of general legislation that would favor no special group or interest appealed to Welles' fundamentalist political beliefs. More significantly, it offered a practical method that could translate Jeffersonian ideals into a program of social reform, compelling the most unregenerate politician to work for the common welfare.[2]

Several years before Leggett had formulated his political theories, Welles had been attracted to the equalitarian program of the Workingmen's party. Connecticut, like other industrializing states, had suffered from the downward price spiral of manufactured goods that set in after 1828. The situation was less serious than it was in the New York City or in the Boston area, though it bore heavily enough on the textile manufacturing counties of New London and Windham, which employed two-thirds of the state's 10,000 factory workers. Even during prosperous times, working conditions in the struggling textile factories were bad—long hours, twelve on the average, and low wages, one dollar a day for men, less than half that for women.

Henry Ellsworth, who made a survey of Connecticut industry in 1832, declared that the manufacture of woolen cloth "has very generally been disastrous," and that there was not one woolen factory in the state whose stock was near par. The largest mill in Connecticut could be purchased in the spring of 1832 at a 50 per cent loss on capital investment to its owners.[3]

Under the circumstances, mills curtailed operations, cut wages, and in some cases lengthened hours in order to remain solvent. Whenever possible, they discharged men and replaced them with women and children, in an effort to reduce overhead. It had been this particular aspect of hard times that aroused the wrath of an intense New London physician, Dr. Charles Douglas, whose practice brought him into the homes of the textile workers. An idealist, a romantic, a man of conviction, Douglas took his political guidelines directly from his highly selective readings of Paine, Jefferson, Adam Smith, Jeremy Bentham, and Robert Owen, the English industrialist and social reformer.

This crusading doctor had been an interested observer of the ten-hour agitation in New York City, where he was attracted to the theories of young Robert Dale Owen and Frances Wright, both of whom were clamoring publicly for the rights of the working man. In early December of 1829, Douglas organized the Mechanics and Laboring Men's Association in New London—a workingmen's group devoted to political action along the lines of the Wright-Owen program. Douglas was a doctrinaire reformer who much preferred public life to the practice of medicine. Politics bored him, though he was a gifted organizer; journalism he found tedious, though he was an excellent writer, with a clear, vigorous style.[4]

In many respects Douglas and Welles were complete opposites, and, as a result, each supplied something the other lacked. Bitterly hostile to the new factory system, Douglas was a monomaniac on the subject of the exploited, underprivileged workers and their families. While not indifferent to the plight of the worker in a depression economy, Welles viewed their distress as one of the lesser social evils that could be cured by the abolition of special privilege. Industry, he felt, was a constructive force that would strengthen the economy of the state and eventually raise living conditions.

Douglas's reformist zeal made an impression on Welles, who began to recognize that mills, like banks and all other economic institutions, owed certain obligations to the public. He was sensitive to the complaint that factory children, as well as farm children, were being deprived of an education. The health and welfare of factory women touched a responsive chord. He shared also the New London reformer's antipathy toward banks, subscribing cautiously to the productionist theory of the workingmen. "We come, then," he wrote in one of his editorials for the *Hartford Times*, "to the abstract proposition, that labor is the only source of wealth . . . the idea is a startling one—but reflection will show that it legitimately arises from the facts of the case."

Welles first met Douglas through Thomas Mussey, who had been elected to the 1830 legislature as a Workingmen's candidate. He was attracted to Douglas, who spoke so convincingly about human rights and was teeming with facts and figures about the state of farmers and workers in New England. The skill with which Douglas and Mussey had organized their movement in New London had also made an impression, and so had the undeniable popularity of the Workingmen's party in certain areas of southeastern Connecticut. The Hartford faction needed to expand its influence in New London and Windham counties, long a bastion of the Adams Republicans and now being infected with Anti-Masonic fever. Further, Douglas and Mussey gave assurances that they would support Van Buren over all potential rivals. Welles was ready to help them as much as he could.

Original Adams appointees who had switched their loyalty to Calhoun still controlled the New London customs house. Shielded by Secretary of the Treasury Ingham, they had managed to resist all efforts to have them removed. Now that their terms of office were about to expire, it seemed appropriate to make another push. Mussey was designated for the collectorship. New Haven collector William Ellis, who knew about the plan and was trying to steer a course between Calhoun and Van Buren, warned Welles that such an appointment would have

dire consequences. The Workingmen, he said, "oppose regular nominations and in my opinion are decidedly opposed to Gen. Jackson. If
Van Buren fails in his own state it will be entirely owing to this viler
than the vilest of parties, the Fanny Wright workerism." Suspecting
that Ingham had told Ellis to oppose any change in the New London
customs house, Welles reacted sharply to his allegations. Ellis backed
down. "I feared that he was so prominent and well known to our
friends at Tammany . . . ," he wrote Welles, "that his appointment
might injure us with them. . . ." By this time the efforts of the Hartford group to have Mussey appointed collector were public knowledge,
so its political prestige was again at stake. Niles thought that the appointment was crucial, that if they failed it would be "entirely fatal to
all our hopes and all our prospects in this state."[5]

Welles hurried off to Washington (a portion of his expenses paid by
Mussey) determined to pull every possible wire. He found Ingham as
obdurate as ever, and he was not surprised at the coolness of Woodbury, now a lame-duck Senator. Jackson, well aware of Calhoun's intrigues, listened to Hill's account of New London appointments with
interest. He promised favorable action. True to his word, the President
submitted Mussey's name to the Senate, which promptly rejected him.
Nevertheless, the Hartford men were relieved, and no one more so
than Niles, who felt that if they had failed to have Mussey nominated
"there would have been no course for us, but to remain a small minority . . . a mere state party without any reference to national politics."[6]

What underlay Niles' comment was the unstable relationship that
existed between local and national politics. It was not only that lines
of communication were vague and wavering; the ambitions of the powerful and the aspiring in Washington also projected themselves on a
smaller scale in the states. Federal patronage, an obvious link, did not
as yet conform to any policy on distribution. Each removal and each
new appointment was battled through as an individual case. Welles
continued to act independently and to compete with other would-be
wire-pullers in his own party. The Hartford men had early cast in their
lot with Van Buren. But the Secretary of State, who played his own
game in Washington, either was not sure they were the proper people
to support or was unwilling to risk a direct confrontation with his
powerful rivals until it became absolutely necessary.

Louis McLane, Van Buren's choice to replace Ingham after the Cabinet upheaval, soon began a series of complex intrigues to make himself
heir-apparent, and, for the brief period that he held the Treasury portfolio, he used the power of his office against the Welles-Niles faction in

the state. The customs collectors, whose affairs fell within the Treasury Department, had to be in close official contact with the Secretary. In the natural order of things they were responsive to suggestions, hints, or other subtle pressures from Washington. Conversely, officeholders solicited their chiefs' aid to improve their own political position at home.

Behind all of the personal politics, the jungle warfare, that raged in the Democratic party, loomed the controversy over banking, highlighted by the struggle over the Bank of the United States. The Bank, which was central to the reform program that the Hartford men finally embraced, was one of the major reasons for the fierce struggle that threatened to splinter party organization during the first ten years of its existence. Welles' attitude toward banking, like his political philosophy, had been influenced by his father's views. Old Samuel Welles had an abiding distrust of the money men. In his opinion, banking was another aspect of Federalism, an outgrowth of Hamilton's funding plan (which he had bitterly opposed as organized thievery), an oppressive system of class and privilege. A year after Samuel's death in 1834, Gideon was still attacking Hamilton's financial policy. "The funding act," wrote the younger Welles, "was the most audacious of legalized speculations and fraud which history affords an example." To this corrupt scheme, he added, "most of the early fortunes of the illustrious families in the union owed their origin." The Bank of the United States, according to Welles, was "designed to concentrate and perpetuate the wealth created by the funding act."[7]

Connecticut had no banks until 1792, when two were organized on the pattern of Hamilton's Bank of New York. One was in Hartford and the other in New London. By 1796 five banks were doing business in the state. As the new banks soaked up the available funds, profit sharing—Samuel Welles' customary method of financing his operations —became more difficult, and finally it became impossible. Before that time Samuel Welles had raised capital at little or no interest, with the lender sharing the risk on the expectation of profit from the ventures. Now, all too frequently, he had to pay interest on his debt and carry the entire risk himself. His temper, one may surmise, was not improved by the fact that he was personally contributing to the affluence of the Federalist-Congregational oligarchy, which controlled the banks. Later, after he abandoned his trading ventures, he invested much of his funds in personal loans and mortgages. Thus he entered into direct competition with the banks, a situation which he found invariably irksome and at times unprofitable.

Aside from these special reasons, Samuel Welles could have had no quarrel with the management of Connecticut's banks during the first quarter-century of their existence. The state did not experience its first banking failures until 1825, when New Haven's Eagle Bank and the neighboring Derby Bank closed their doors. An account of gross mismanagement in their affairs soon became public knowledge, generating a wave of anti-bank sentiment. Alert for popular issues, Gideon Welles sensed a latent hostility toward banking among the country members of the legislature during his first term as a representative; but it was not until the 1829 session that he began to think seriously of banking in a political context.

As one of the leading operators behind the scenes in the house, Welles was aware of the pressures being exerted by numerous groups for bank charters. Agreeably surprised by the negative reaction of his fellow legislators, most of whom were not Jacksonians, he moved rapidly to mobilize them against all new banking incorporations. Following his lead, a majority in the legislature blocked every application. Experience had shown him that the granting of bank charters could be made decidedly unpopular with the public. If and when renewed efforts were made to introduce new bank bills in the legislature (and Welles had no doubt that they would come), he was prepared to capitalize on them as a prime political issue. What he did not foresee was that the issue would be bound up in national politics, and that a majority of his own party would go against him.

Organized banking in Connecticut was a relatively novel method of supplying credit. Since the average citizen did not understand its workings, banks became a prime subject for misrepresentation. In some mysterious process, banks manufactured money which varied in worth—and which might suddenly prove valueless. Many a trusting farmer had been bilked of reward for his hard-earned labor when he accepted at par value out-of-state notes for his produce. Memories of worthless Revolutionary War paper was still fresh in the minds of the older generation. The argument that the chartering of more banks would flood the state with unredeemable paper money and make a few insiders rich at the expense of the many, Welles was convinced, could not fail to impress even the most ignorant farmer.

Yet, after all the editorials he had penned against special legislation, after all the time he had spent fighting the money men, Welles was astonished by the unseemly scramble of his own party to charter new banks in the legislative session of 1833. When the Democrats finally gained a majority, they acted, Welles thought, in a wholly irresponsi-

ble manner, permitting more banks to be chartered than in any previous session. Dr. Douglas, who was now editing the *New England Ar-
tizan*, a Workingmen's paper in Boston, was sharply critical of the
Connecticut Democrats. Welles, who had not been a member of that
legislature, agreed with him completely, and took pains to disassociate
himself from his political friends in that body. "The policy of incorpo-
rating institutions for banking purposes, and thus concentrating wealth
we have always doubted . . . ," he wrote in the *Times*. "Had these
men who were for increasing these privileges voted a repeal of the re-
strictive laws on banking—and left this business like that of merchandizing open to all . . . they would have carried out their doctrines and
wishes of abolishing monopolies."[8]

Meanwhile, he kept himself posted on the opposition that was
gathering in Washington to the Bank of the United States. Kendall
and others at the capital supplied him regularly with information so
that the *Hartford Times* could keep abreast of the administration line
in the struggle between Jackson and Nicholas Biddle, the imperious
president of the Bank of the United States. Henry Ellsworth, a director
of the Hartford branch of the Bank, turned over to Welles whatever he
learned about policy (which was not much) at board meetings. All factions of the Democratic party in the state greeted with unfeigned enthusiasm Jackson's ringing veto of the Bank recharter bill and then his
removal of the government deposits.[9]

The legislature might not have chosen to take his advice and pass a
free banking law, but Welles saw nothing wrong in supporting the incorporation of a Democratic bank. Good politics and better business
would be served by a friendly bank in Hartford that might receive on
deposit a share of the federal funds being removed from the Bank of
the United States. After all, the funds had to be placed somewhere. It
was unthinkable to Welles that a Democratic administration should
place a part of the people's money in the hands of bitter political opponents who were managing the established banks in the city. He had
rationalized his position neatly in terms of political necessity and civic
virtue. His name and Niles' appeared with those of a score of other local Democrats on the memorial praying for the incorporation of the
Farmers and Mechanics Bank of Hartford.

The new bank lost no time in applying for government funds. On
September 24, 1833, while the deposit question was still being debated
in the Cabinet, Niles himself drafted a formal request to William
Duane, Ingham's replacement in the Treasury. He prepared also a
brief prospectus of the new bank, which Welles endorsed. By early No-

vember word was received from Washington that the bank had been selected as a depository.[10]

The Farmers and Mechanics Bank had already gotten off to a prosperous start. It began doing business with a capital of $500,000, which within a few months was increased to $1 million. So popular was the institution that the "poor farmers and mechanics" of the neighborhood oversubscribed by $600,000 when the new stock issue was thrown on the market. The directors approved the doubling of capital on purely business grounds, but, as Welles and Niles were to discover, this policy was the prelude to a reconstruction of the board.[11] The original membership of the board of directors reflected a rough balance between those loyal to the *Times* office and those who followed an independent course in party politics. When the capital was doubled, the balance of power tipped toward the monied elements in the community—businessmen and lawyers for the most part, who were eager to join with the Clay Democrats and beat down what they regarded as the radical influence of the *Times* faction. The ultimate clash between the two groups, however, was postponed by Nicholas Biddle's rash counterattack against the administration during the winter and spring of 1834.

In an effort to force a reversal of Jackson's policy on deposits, Biddle deliberately created a money panic. Desperate businessmen in New Haven and Hartford responded with mass meetings demanding the return of all government deposits to the Bank of the United States. James Brewster, manufacturer of carriages and at that time the largest employer in New Haven, stated explicitly to a public meeting that, if the existing pressure continued much longer, he would be forced to discharge his workmen and discontinue his business. Welles himself confirmed that the panic was most severe among merchants and manufacturers in New England. "The Bank," he wrote in March 1834, "is making shipwrecks of thousands, involving many enterprises and meritorious individuals. . . . It [the Bank] serves to admonish the people and especially those entrusted with political power to beware how they commit the prosperity and welfare of their citizens into irresponsible hands."[12] Sound Democratic doctrine this, yet he had failed to apply it at home when he helped raise up the Farmers and Mechanics Bank, a power he would not be able to control.

Biddle's money panic shook the confidence of many who had supported the Democrats the previous year, and since the Connecticut election was the first political test of the removal policy, the opposition was eager to make it a popular referendum against the President. Senator Nathan Smith, a warm supporter of the Bank, wrote David Daggett, "if the nomination made by the Jackson convention shall prevail, it will be regarded as unequivocal evidence that the state is Jackson and that all the high-handed measures of the government are sanctioned through the ballot box." William W. Ellsworth was more emphatic. He urged his fellow National Republicans to support Anti-Masonic candidates, if necessary, and not risk a third party division. "We had better yield anything and everything to rescue such an important election," he said.

The National Republicans were unable to keep the Anti-Masons from running a separate ticket, but they were able to attract enough Clay Democrats and frightened Jacksonians to gain a plurality in the state. Though the election was scarcely a decisive referendum on Jackson's bank policy, it was sufficient to elect ex-Senator Samuel Foot to the governor's chair and reduce the Democrats to a helpless minority in the new legislature.[13]

Welles had borne the brunt of the coalition's vigorous campaign. Largely through his efforts, the Jacksonians had not only held together but had increased their vote by almost 3000 in the state. Nor did his labors cease on election day. As one of the eighty-five Democratic members elected to the assembly, he was relied upon to lead his minority in the well-nigh impossible job of resisting the vindictive National Republicans.

Well before the organization of the legislature, the National Republicans had concluded an effective working arrangement with the newly elected Anti-Masonic members. Their objective was a clean sweep of every local officeholder who was a Jacksonian Democrat or who had on any occasion supported that ticket. They were, it was true, following the example set by the Jacksonians in 1829 and 1833. But in both of those years the removal policy had been selective and relatively moderate. Now the coalition seemed determined to show the Democrats just how far their "rotation in office" policy would be carried. Welles fought the majority with a variety of tactics—parliamentary delays, publicity in the *Times* and other Democratic papers, private interviews with opposition members, debate on the floor. All to no avail. The "Panic Session" mentality, as he called it in the *Times*, made his efforts an exercise in Sisyphean futility. Badgered as he was, he still indulged in some wry humor at the majority's expense:

> The Legislature of this state adjourned on Friday morning after a session of thirty days, which was principally spent in legislating Democrats out of office and legislating Federalists into their places. We shall give a list of the killed, wounded and missing as soon as a report can be made out.[14]

With the fatigue and frustration of the "Panic Session" behind him, Welles looked forward to at least five months of routine political correspondence and editorial work. He would not, he thought, have to begin planning for the spring campaign until December. Then two events occurred almost simultaneously which, though unrelated, thwarted his hopes for a quiet summer.

In early July, Levi Woodbury was appointed Secretary of the Treasury to replace Roger B. Taney, whom the Senate had refused to confirm. A few weeks later three of Connecticut's Congressmen (all pro-Bank partisans) resigned, forcing a special election and another test of the deposit policy. It is quite likely that the National Republicans—then in the process of coalescing all anti-Jackson elements into the new Whig party—had decided on the special election as a device for launching their new organization. Whatever the motivation, the special election was a challenge that forced Welles into another round of strenuous political activity. The Woodbury appointment was quite another matter, more disturbing than the prospect of a fall campaign.

His relations with the new Secretary had cooled perceptibly over the years. He recalled all too well the winter of 1830, when the delphic New Hampshire politician seemed on the verge of joining the Calhoun faction in a bid for control of the party in New England. Woodbury, he knew, was still close to David Henshaw, whose Boston Customs House clique had earned an unsavory reputation in regional politics.

Welles had other reasons, too, for being concerned. He had met with a virtual snub from the Secretary on the Mussey appointment. Later Woodbury had been unwilling to exert any of his formidable influence when Welles, in his hour of desperate need, appealed to him for aid in disciplining Noah Phelps. Indeed, there was some reason to believe that Phelps would enjoy as much protection under Woodbury as he had previously enjoyed under Ingham and McLane.[15]

For some time it had been apparent that Henry Ellsworth aspired to party leadership. In his constant search for public office, he had ranged himself in direct, though covert, opposition to the *Times* office. Welles had no positive proof of his singular conduct, but there were rumors enough to excite apprehension. These were soon confirmed when Ellsworth joined the conservative faction of the party to block Welles' nomination for Congress in the special election. The primary meeting had been a stormy affair, during which the president of the Farmers and Mechanics Bank, with Ellsworth's help, had succeeded in pushing through the nomination of a fellow bank director, Luther Loomis, for Congress. Both Welles and Niles had been startled at this sudden and unexpected display of what they chose to regard as the interference of a corporate enterprise (and a bank at that) in party politics.[16] They were not surprised that Ellsworth had finally shown his hand but decided to take no action for the time being. Woodbury might be in the background—it seemed the better part of prudence to wait and see. Welles supported the Loomis nomination in the *Times*, yet published a series of attacks on the candidate from anonymous correspondents. These articles and letters alluded to his former support of the Bank of the United States. They hinted broadly that Nicholas Biddle was infiltrating the Democratic party through men like Loomis.

In the special election the Whigs eked out marginal victories. If they had been hoping for a decisive referendum against Jackson's bank policies, they were again disappointed. "I fear after all," wrote that whimsical old Federalist Calvin Goddard to Daggett, "that Jacksonism may endure longer than your Eagle pen."[17]

If the Democrats would compose their differences they seemed certain to win the spring election. Welles, who had been watching Ellsworth and the bank men, was not so sure. Signs were multiplying that they aimed to capture the county organization as a prelude to making themselves masters of the party in the state. Whether Levi Woodbury was behind it or not, the *Times* group would fight for its position and what it regarded as uncompromising principles. For the bank faction had made it plain that one of the major reasons in opposing Welles and Niles was the radical course of the *Times*—its affinity for the Workingmen's movements, its espousal of general incorporation laws, its opposition to bloc or factional alliances.

In early October 1834 Welles learned that a small group of local capitalists was about to establish another Democratic paper in Hartford. The paper was to be named the *Patriot and Democrat*, and John B. Eldridge, a journalist who fitted perfectly Welles' definition of a "whiffling weathercock," was retained as its editor. Formerly the editor of the *New London Centinel*, an Adams Republican paper, Eldridge had been a delegate to the Boston Workingmen's Convention of 1832. Just before accepting the editorial direction of the *Patriot and Democrat*, he had been the proprietor of the Springfield, Massachusetts, *Whig*, a pro-Henshaw organ.

Welles acted vigorously to meet the threat. On October 27 he published a long editorial in the *Times* in which he referred to the bank men as a cabal, "destitute of any principles, and fluctuating in their opinions and actions." The Democratic party had nothing to fear from open enemies, "only from factions and secret foes," he said. Alluding to the new paper about to be published, he declared flatly that the *Times* would oppose it. How, he asked, could such a partisan conservative like Eldridge be so suddenly converted into an honest Democrat and a supporter of Van Buren?[18]

Brave words, these. They merely concealed the fact that Welles and Niles were thoroughly alarmed. Was it possible, they wondered, that Van Buren might disavow his friends who had come out boldly for reform legislation in the various states? Welles remembered the warnings of Ellis some years before, that Tammany Hall, Van Buren's New York City machine, was opposed to the Workingmen. Since then he had been working closely with Workingmen radicals such as Dr. Douglas, Mussey, and Theophilus Fisk, the New Haven anti-clerical propagandist and reformer. Woodbury was conservative by the standards of the *Hartford Times.* Presumably, he enjoyed the Vice President's confidence—he was certainly supporting his candidacy. Could it be that he was acting through Ellsworth and the bank men in accordance with Van Buren's wishes?[19]

Welles had met and was on terms of political intimacy with Silas Wright, William L. Marcy, and others of the Albany Regency. He admired them all, especially Preston King, a junior member of the Regency—corpulent, genial, and wise in the ways of politicians.[20] No criticism of Welles' editorial or political conduct had appeared in the Regency press or in the all-powerful *Washington Globe,* no hints of political deviation in his correspondence with Democratic friends in New York. Yet, as he and Niles knew, Van Buren rarely entrusted his personal views even to his closest friends. They could not be sure about two crucial things—whether Woodbury was behind the bank faction, and, if he was, whether he had Van Buren's sanction and active support. It was a trying situation.

Both men had been loyal to Van Buren since 1829; both had staked their political fortunes on his election in 1836. Since then they had worked out a reform program which they believed in time would command broad popular support. They believed in their program and had testified to that belief repeatedly in public print and private correspondence. It was inconceivable to them that any party could exist— much less flourish—merely on loyalty to one man or on tenure of office. Andrew Jackson, with all his charismatic qualities, had stood for something, and his policies had not disappointed such democratic idealists in the Northern states as Welles, Niles, and Douglas.

What the Hartford radicals had not fully evaluated at this point was that there were basic and necessary differences between presidential politics as practiced in Washington and local politics as practiced in Hartford or New Haven. Van Buren did not possess the heroic qualities of a Jackson. He could not afford to be so independent of the great sectional chiefs within the party, nor could he profess openly his personal views on great public issues without risking a breach that might defeat him. Where Jackson could and did follow an undeviating course, Van Buren fashioned a careful, politically discreet, balancing act. If one considers his public image, his was a realistic assessment of the political situation as it existed during the year 1834-35. Levi Woodbury, an habitual temporizer, a careful calculator of interests scarcely less able than Van Buren himself, was shaping his course accordingly. That he was an ambitious man is not to be denied; that he could be implacably ruthless in dealing with rivals is well-documented in his New Hampshire career. What seems most likely is that, after some initial resentment, he had accepted the inevitable and was supporting Van Buren as the Democrat who had the best prospects of winning the nomination in 1836.[21]

Meanwhile, he was planning ahead for his own nomination in 1840 or 1844, when he assumed New England's chances for the nomination would come round again. The early differences that once existed between Woodbury and Isaac Hill had long since been smoothed over. That brazen, irrepressible editor of former days was now the courted Senator Hill, a powerful figure in Washington. And with his obvious success and prestige he had shed most of his strident radicalism. He too, for personal and political reasons, saw much to be gained from curbing the presumed "excesses" of the New England radicals. Still sharing the confidence of men like Welles, Niles, Douglas, and Fisk, Isaac Hill was the ideal link between the Girondists in Washington and the Jacobins in Boston and Hartford.

Woodbury saw clearly, as did Van Buren, that the party in New England and elsewhere must have a broader base of support than its noisy radical-Workingmen element. Even Welles was aware of this fact. As Reynolds Webb, an old crony who lived in New Haven, wrote him in January 1835: "In our part of the state we have many Democrats, who still regard the bank as a useful and safe institution—and consider the removal of the deposits as unjust."[22] The Bank issue, widely popular as it was, had already alarmed conservatives in the Northeast and in the Middle Atlantic states. The theme of "equal rights" which Welles was advocating in the *Times* bid fair to alienate many influential Democrats who were either enjoying or lusting after the exclusive benefits of special charters—banks, turnpikes, canal companies, railroads, and commercial ventures. Might not the politically astute Secretary of the Treasury have feared that similar agitation would be directed against the great land speculators, his friend Ellsworth among them? Might not "equal rights" for the East come to mean homestead laws for the West?

Woodbury's objective, it seems, was to devise a party formula that would hold the radicals yet at the same time would prove palatable to the special interest groups. After six years of rule, the Democratic leadership in Washington had outgrown its primitive blindman's buff gropings for power sources in the states, its rankling feuds and personal rivalries. Jacksonian principles were still being trumpeted, and men like Welles and Niles continued to cherish them. But behind the generalities with their special meaning to the believers the sources of party power in the Northeast were moving beyond state lines. Within the state organizations, vertical cleavages were developing manifest differences of opinion on economic and social matters, though nothing as yet was clear-cut.

In this fluid situation the men in Washington were trying to identify the adhesive agents—those functional similarities that made for a relatively stable party on a national scale. Increasingly, they sought to intervene in—to manipulate, if you will—the state machines. Accommodation, after all, was the only course; for they dealt with contesting factions, with competing political alignments on regional levels, and with three distinct cultures in the making—Western, Southern, and Northern. The questions of the black man and of slavery, then but small clouds on the political horizon, were also troublesome factors.

To cope with these complex problems, Hill, Woodbury, and others of their Washington circle were evolving a flexible policy which varied with their understanding of party composition in state and region. But they continued their search for a common denominator, some mutuality of interest in class, in motive, in section on which all could rally. Conciliation, compromise, and adjustment seemed in order if any harmony was ever to be imposed on the Democratic party. This would necessarily interfere with the accustomed independence of state leaders. In the interest of adjustment, the Washington managers were building countervailing powers within state organizations. The Connecticut radicals already had some inkling of this interference in their own party affairs. Unsure of themselves, of their power at home, and of their prestige in Washington, they feared a concerted effort was underway to deprive them of their influence and their standing in the party. Their information from Washington was usually more inaccurate than not, and even if their communication had been less distorted, they would have misinterpreted the attitudes and many of the moves of the high command. The local politicians were seeing only one small segment of the party spectrum. Absorbed in the affairs of their own state, they could not evaluate in any meaningful terms the condition of the party as a whole.

The careful balancing of men and measures now being attempted by the national leaders of their party had been tried before in Connecticut, and always, as far as Welles could see, with disastrous results. He was never more decided that a man's political principles must be inflexible—almost articles of faith—than he was during the winter of 1834-35. Yet it was just at this time that Levi Woodbury, through Henry Ellsworth, began a major effort to wrest party leadership from the radical faction in the interest of consolidating the party, not just in Connecticut, but throughout New England.

# CHAPTER 8

## Loco-Foco

To Welles the bank men were more than just party rivals; they were a set of unprincipled rascals bent on seizing power to enrich themselves at the expense of the people. Levi Woodbury, on the other hand, thought of the bank group in Hartford and the later ones established in New London (the Whaling Bank circle) and New Haven (around the Mechanics Bank) as political nuclei for attracting businessmen and the more conservative elements of society everywhere to the Democratic party. William Ellis, the New Haven collector, was already "wholly involved" in the affairs of the New Haven Merchants and Mechanics Bank.[1] The Secretary was not disposed to proscribe the radicals; he seems to have been fully aware of their energy, their talents, and their loyalty to Van Buren. But on most questions involving factionalism within the party, Woodbury consistently lent his influence as a makeweight against them.

Niles had sized him up years before when he was a house guest of Henry Ellsworth: "There was something in his countenance which I did not like—which indicated reserve, selfishness, faithlessness, a disagreeable squinting towards obliquity and knavery." Later Woodbury himself let slip his connection with the Henshaw machine in a roundup of political news he sent to Hartford. Welles could have known nothing of the Secretary's grand design, but he would have been less the politician he was if he had not noted a certain feeling of being "out of favor at court."[2]

After the Democratic defeat in the special election, the radicals again decided to run Welles as a candidate for Congress. This time they were more interested in plumbing the strength of the bank faction and drawing out its Washington connections than in securing his nomination. An early and rather surprising manifestation of Washington's intent came from Isaac Hill, who had heard that Welles would be a candidate and urged him to withdraw. Certain key phrases in Hill's letter alerted Welles and Niles to possible difficulties ahead. They considered the New Hampshire Senator a sincere friend, a close political ally, perhaps the only man of influence at the capital on whom they could rely. Yet here he was asking that Welles move aside "so the party will unite in supporting any uniform Democrat." The words "unite" and "uniform" had a menacing cast. To a perceptive man like Welles, they could only mean that he was considered unreliable by his closest friends in Washington.[3]

If Welles was shaken by this intelligence, he gave no sign of trimming his sails to the variable winds from the south. In an editorial he wrote on December 20, 1834, he warned that "the rush of twaddlers into our ranks will increase our numbers, but will not add to the strength of the party." Resorting to a favorite theme, he declared emphatically that "a check is to be put to the rage for incorporations, and the Bank mania . . . special legislating and special privileges will meet no countenance." When the state convention met in Middletown on January 28, 1835, he and his radical supporters, or Loco-Focos, as the opposition called them, committed the party to a forthright declaration of support for "equal rights."[4]

The document itself bore all the marks of Welles' Anglophobia, his partisan interpretation of history (the Whigs were the legitimate successors of the Federalists, and the Federalists of the Tories), his anticlericalism. He went to great lengths in denouncing the evil genius of Alexander Hamilton, whom he implied was disloyal to democratic principles—at heart an Englishman and a royalist. "It is openly and boldly avowed," charged Welles, "that there were two principles of government—*force* and *fraud*—and as our system did not admit of the first, we must rely on the last, and be content with liberty in the English sense." With all of his insinuations, all of his voter-appealing bombast, Welles was clear and explicit when he discussed his theory of "equal rights" and tried to explain why it was essential in a democratic state:

> In free communities, like the states of this union, there is a reciprocal action and reaction between public sentiment and legislation. Whilst the laws are in some measure influenced and controlled by popular opinion, on the other hand legislation reacts upon and often controls public sentiment. . . . It is vain to expect a well-balanced government without a well-balanced society.[5]

The "Panic Session" of the legislature had repealed the districting law for the election of Congressmen; therefore the state convention referred all such nominations to "popular conventions" in the former districts. The Loco-Focos spared no effort to recruit as much support for Welles as possible, and before the district convention assembled in late February it was clear they had the upper hand. It was also clear that if Welles were nominated, the party would split, certainly in Hartford County, probably in other counties as well.[6]

Levi Woodbury was not the only powerful New Englander in Washington who thought Welles a positive threat to the Van Buren candidacy in Connecticut. Isaac Hill, who had written Welles earlier suggesting he withdraw, had not received any assurances that he would. From what he read in the *Hartford Times,* in the new *Patriot and Democrat,* and in his correspondence with various Connecticut politicians, he judged that the radicals would force the issue. There were more than the usual comings and goings between Woodbury's handsome residence on Lafayette Square and Hill's boardinghouse on Pennsylvania Avenue near Sixth Street. During January, when the weather permitted, the little New Hampshire Senator, too frugal to pay the hack fare, could be seen limping along the avenue on his way to Woodbury's house. The almost daily visits between the two bespoke something important in New England politics. Unquestionably, the Connecticut situation claimed precedence in their conversations, because sometime in mid-January Hill wrote a rather peremptory letter to Niles. Welles must withdraw; Niles must see that he did![7]

The Hartford postmaster was as responsive to Washington influence as any working politician, but in this instance he was outraged at the commanding tone of Hill's letter. His suspicions—mere niggling doubts before—were fully aroused. He showed the letter to Welles, and after a brief discussion in the *Times* office they decided to have it out with the New Hampshire Senator once and for all. If he and Woodbury and Ellsworth were associated with the bank faction, if they were determined (as Welles believed) to make the party in Connecticut an appendage of the Henshaw machine in Massachusetts, then it would be better to make a stand now rather than be maneuvered out of their position in the party and have their program of reform go by default. Welles was not deterred by the fact that Isaac Hill was one of the most influential men in Washington, a leading member of the Kitchen Cabinet. He minced no words when he replied for Niles. The tone of Hill's letter, he said, was scarcely that of a man who had professed warm friendship for many years, nor was it the language which gentlemen used in communicating with each other. Welles said nothing about his own candidacy except to imply that Hill was being unduly influenced by others who *did* have a direct interest in it.

Hill did not respond directly to Welles, but he did write Niles on February 21 complaining "that the *Times,* and particularly our friend Welles, take ground too exclusive." He branded the position of the Loco-Focos "as a personal dispute." If it continued, he predicted, there would be a schism and the state would be lost by the party. "The men whom he [Welles] now opposes," said a petulant Hill, "Phelps, Ellis, Dodd, Loomis, and others were first introduced to me by Welles himself as Democrats worthy of confidence. It will be impossible that all Mr. Welles' friends on his mere move believe that all these men are without the pale of the democratic party."

Finally, in early March, a full week after Welles had stepped aside in favor of Isaac Toucey as a compromise candidate, and more than a month after he had received Welles' letter of rebuke, Hill replied in tones of a well-meaning friend, wrongfully accused. He denied that he had been influenced by anyone in Washington or Connecticut, but said he had gleaned his information solely from the *Hartford Times.* The reason he had written as he had was that he feared a division of the party if Welles ran, "and that this would paralyze the Democrats in Connecticut." They resumed their former relationship, but Welles never again completely trusted the New Hampshire Senator.[8] Indeed, on the same day he received Hill's grudging explanation, Welles decided to take his troubles directly to the top. He wrote Vice President Van Buren, saying that "our domestic troubles have been misconstrued or misunderstood by our friends." He had had enough, he said; he had worked for the party, hard and loyally, without pay and in fact at "some pecuniary sacrifice" for ten years. His reward for all these services was abuse from a professed Democratic paper and underhanded attacks from members of his own party in Connecticut and in Washington—a group he stigmatized as men "who act without sincerity, and who want office without commanding confidence." The only leading politician in the state still "retaining power and influence whom you can trust," he said, was Niles. In him, "you will always find an honest and sincere friend."[9]

Welles' avowal to Van Buren that he was about to resign his editorship of the *Times* was no idle threat. Again a candidate for the legislature, and certain of re-election, he intended to serve for the session, then terminate his editorial duties. He would write occasional pieces on political topics (for such writing had become more than a habit—it was now one of his chief recreations) and would devote full time to politics. Welles' father had died the previous year, leaving him enough money so that by judicious management he could afford a certain independence. Though he denied to Van Buren that he had any interest in a government office, he was not averse to accepting a post if one came his way. Connecticut had not received any position of consequence from the Jackson administration. All party leaders—radical and conservative alike—felt that the claims of the state had been studiously ignored.

With the strong prospect of victory at the polls in the spring election, the justice of Welles' complaints and the pleas of other Democrats finally made an impression in Washington. Word came through that a Connecticut man was in line for the next vacancy in one of the departments, and that almost certainly Ellsworth would get the post. Quite obviously, Welles and Niles would not support him. On January 7 Welles wrote Woodbury that Ellsworth did not enjoy the confidence of the party in the state. As they expected, the Secretary replied in a curt note defending his friend and chiding Welles for not being more specific in his allegations.[10]

Some time during the next fortnight, Woodbury had second thoughts on the subject. On January 30 he assured Welles that no appointment would be made without the unanimous approval of the party leadership in the state, a promise he would not keep. Silas Wright may have been responsible for Woodbury's apparent change of mind. Welles had written the New York Senator, one of Van Buren's closest associates, asking him to block an Ellsworth appointment. Wright had thought Ellsworth "a very useful man with you, one whom you wanted to keep in office." He had been about to join with his colleague Senator Tallmadge in recommending the Hartford conservative when Welles' letter arrived. In his usual candid manner, Wright admitted to the communication problem that was confusing party policy. "I thank you sincerely for it [the letter]," he wrote, "as we are apt to do mischief unnecessarily here, when we suppose we are doing our friends [a] service." But he pointed out that he thought Ellsworth stood "very high in the confidence of the President, and if so may get a place, for as you know, no man was ever more devoted to his friends or those he considers such, than he is." Wright's letter was friendly and gracious. He must have known of Welles' radical leanings, but, though he was scarcely a reformer himself, there was not the slightest hint of disapproval.[11]

With Welles out of the running, the Democratic state and congressional ticket swept the state. Conservatism may have dominated the ticket, but it did not control the platform, which Welles had written. Nor had the *Times* wavered in its support of a reform program. Even the *New Haven Palladium,* an opposition paper, paid it the compliment of being "consistent and straight ahead . . . much as we detest the political character and principles of the *Times*."[12]

Whatever his difficulties within the party at home and in Washington, everyone assumed Welles would play the leading role in the next legislature. Radicals were quick to send in their advice or recommendations. Dr. Douglas wanted abolition of imprisonment for debt, a drastic curtailment of new bank charters, and heavier taxes on existing banks—or, as he explained it, "they should be compelled to deposit an additional portion of ill-gotten gains in the public chest." Douglas wrote in his customary, acid style—bitingly critical of employers, and highly skeptical of lawyer-legislators, many of whom he felt had adopted the reform mantle for their own selfish purposes. On abolition of imprisonment for debt, he urged the Massachusetts law—in his eyes, a model of brevity, clarity, and honest intent. "Do not be influenced by the New York law," with its vague provisions, its extreme length and complexity, the work of a "cunning lawyer, who while he labored to quiet the people," warned Douglas, ". . . took good care to shape that law as to make it as profitable to the members of his profession as possible." Closer to Welles' heart was Douglas's deep concern for effective legislation that would ensure working children "such an education as a self-governing people, of a right ought to have." "As things now are," he wrote with burning conviction, "their minds, their morals and their bodily energies, are all left a prey to the avaricious employers who care for nothing else but to force as much labor out of them as possible."[13]

Much as he sympathized with Douglas' righteous indignation, Welles would not proceed until he had an expression of opinion from the Van Buren forces in New York. Whom should he consult? Who best reflected the ideas of the Vice President—Senator Wright or the state officers, Governor William L. Marcy, Azariah Flagg, John A. Dix, Benjamin Butler? All were political associates of Van Buren; all were experienced, sagacious men, masters not just of the art of the possible, but of the practical as well. Despite an embarrassment of talents, Welles went outside of the old Regency organization; he asked Churchill C. Cambreleng for advice. A long-time friend of Van Buren, Cambreleng was accounted one of the nation's leading experts on commercial and fiscal affairs. Welles could not have found a better person for a discreet sounding of opinion in the highest party circles, and, with the possible exception of Wright, he could not have tapped a better mind.

Cambreleng, now in his fiftieth year, was a round, little man of ripe wisdom and rare wit. Southern by birth but not by inclination, he had spent most of his adult years in the North or abroad. Only a slight trace of the North Carolina tidewater lingered in his soft, rolling speech and his courtly address. He was then serving his seventh term in Congress, where he was one of its most popular members, noted for his kindliness and unfailing good humor. Cambreleng chaired three powerful House committees—Commerce, Foreign Affairs, and Ways and Means—and was chief Jacksonian whip. More important than his ability, his prestige, and his friendship with both Jackson and Van Buren was that he alone of the regular New York Democrats had been partial to the Workingmen's movement since its inception.[14] Welles had met Cambreleng many times on his visits to Washington. The introspective New Englander fell an easy prey to the expatriate Southerner's charm, his good sense, and, of course, his powerful connections. He had not corresponded with Cambreleng before, nor had any of his political associates, as far as he knew, an important consideration.

On April 6, 1835, before the official canvass had been completed in the state, Welles wrote a long, candid letter to Cambreleng, who was then in New York, asking for his advice on the legislative session ahead. So anxious was he for a reply that he wrote again on the thirteenth, and finally, on the fifteenth, he received the long-anticipated answer. When he read the letter he instantly understood the reason for delay. Cambreleng had not written merely a summary of his views, nor a polite expression of generalities, as Welles had feared he might. Rather, he had supplied a treatise on government and politics, a blueprint for legislation and reform, an affirmation and a demonstration that political and economic freedoms were not mutually exclusive. It was an impresive effort. If, as Welles hoped, it represented Van Buren's thinking, all would be well.

Clearly, Cambreleng had been influenced by Leggett's and Theodore Sedgewick's articles in the *Evening Post* on the virtues of general legislation. The burden of his work was on this subject, but his discourse was more pointed, less rhetorical, than the essays of his journalistic friends. Although he was indebted for many of his ideas to Adam Smith and Jeremy Bentham and even, paradoxically, to Alexander Hamilton, he had constructed a frame of reference that was uniquely American, practical and impractical by turns, opportunistic, yet intensely Jeffersonian in spirit. In its insistence on the benefits, and the importance, of manufacturing, it was mercantilistic, but on its rejection of planning, of state control, and of exclusive privileges such as perpetual charters or tariffs, Cambreleng followed current Jefferson-Jackson opinion. Competition was essential, but it must not be impeded by either state intervention or state enterprise.

When the New York Congressman began to discuss specifics, however, he became more Hamiltonian in his outlook. While still holding out an option for cooperative undertakings by interested communities, he advanced a plan whereby individuals could launch public works for profit and be granted limited monopolies for their risk. "If the work is not made by the county for free use," he said, "then by subscription the profits of the improvement [are] to be wholly divided among the proprietors, for the first ten years, as a premium to undertake the enterprise." After that he proposed an annual reduction of rates and tolls, "so as to yield an annual interest not exceeding, say 1 or 2 percent, beyond the lawful rate (6% in most states)." Mergers, consolidations, and franchises would be permitted with "other associations or counties" so as to provide "a continuous line of improvement." All could be accomplished, Welles was glad to see, under a general law of incorporation which would ensure economic and political democracy, purify politics, and encourage enterprise "in seeking out new avenues of commerce."

Utopian in his ideas about general laws of incorporation, Cambreleng was realistic enough to recognize that, the wider the distribution of ownership and management in a given enterprise, the less the chance that unrestrained competition among communities would fragment the economy. He was for "healthy rivalry," not guerilla warfare.[15]

Cambreleng's letter was most helpful to Welles. In the main, he dealt with subjects which the *Times* office men had been considering for some time, and, in general, they agreed with what he had to say. Though Cambreleng, Welles, Niles, even Dr. Douglas at this time were basically agrarian in outlook, they, unlike their revered mentors, Jefferson, John Taylor of Caroline, and Nathaniel Macon, were prepared to make an accommodation with the new technology and its concomitants—canals, railroads, steamboats, factories, banks. But their insistence on "equal rights" indicated that the future they imagined was to be both progressive and dynamic—entrepreneurial, classless, equalitarian—where if the state acted at all, it acted in the Jeffersonian sense, not to regulate, but to restrain.

Of the group, Niles, more than Welles or Cambreleng, or even Douglas, feared the economic encroachments of emergent capitalism upon individual liberty. "The vital principles of our system," he told a Boston audience in 1839, "are popular power and equal rights," which included "just representation . . . without reference to property; and secondly, universal and equal suffrage." The strength of American democracy lay in its moral power. "As popular sovereignty is the foundation of our political system," he said, "equal rights are the basis of our social system."[16] Civil liberty could never be maintained "where there is great inequality in the social condition of the people."

Niles' concerns about the future were proper concerns, but he was unable to gauge the depth or the sweep of the industrial revolution then just beginning. He and Welles were both caught in the web that had entrapped Montesquieu and Delolme; they were confusing the forms of the political process with the substance of economic growth. Thus, Welles and his colleagues set out to chart the future, not from an economic or even a rational base, but from a political one that placed the burden and the promise on the individual. Like the Progressives sixty years later, the Jacksonians invented their legislative devices and their political slogans to support them. Woodrow Wilson's demand that democracy be given back to the people would have rung as true to Gideon Welles as it did to Ray Stannard Baker. And the Jacksonians, like their lineal descendants, had great faith that their legislative nostrums—general laws of incorporation, free banking, general bankruptcy acts—would create a proper social order that would not anticipate but would apparently keep up with the *manifest* needs of the people. They would live long enough to realize the inadequacy of their much-touted reforms, their misplaced faith in a maxim—the sovereignty of the people in the states—rather than in constructive, accumulative plans of development with adequate agents for design and control.

Though Connecticut was in no way comparable to New York, which was a veritable North in microcosm, Welles set out to incorporate many of the ideas of Cambreleng, Douglas, and Niles in his contemplated reform program. The Democrats had large majorities in the General Assembly and an able leader on the floor of the House in Perry Smith, a swarthy, deep-browed lawyer who closely resembled Daniel Webster.[17] Niles was ready with his shrewd advice, his persuasiveness in caucus, and his purse, if necessary. From Windham County came the portly, expansive Chauncey F. Cleveland, who represented the Loco-Focos in eastern Connecticut. Sly and unpredictable he certainly was, but he was also one of those horse-trading Yankees who made a clear distinction between life's practical aspects and its moral duties. He could be counted among the reliables. In Hartford and New Haven counties, the key areas, a dozen Loco-Focos—in and out of the legislature would be on hand to keep the conservative Democrats in check. Governor-elect Edwards was cooperative and agreed to recommend a reform program that might have been written in the *Times* office.[18]

From Washington—so long the source of criticism and restraint, the apparent citadel of chilly conservatism—came words of encouragement. Amos Kendall, who had not written his friends in Hartford for some time, penned a letter to Niles praising Welles and offering advice. All constructive Democrats in Washington, he said, were hoping that the Connecticut legislative session would be a model for reform programs in other states. Jackson had gone as far as he could to carry out reform in the federal government; the rest had to be done in the states, where special interests had been entrenched since Federalist days and were beyond the reach of Washington. In Kendall's words, "the whole of our *Nobility system* embracing in the long list of Corporations of every name and character . . . by them [the states] . . . must be overthrown. General Jackson has crippled the *monarchs,* but the lords of this system yet domineer over our people." Welles enjoyed an enviable position. "If he acts wisely and perseveres in executing a program featuring equal rights, he may," said Kendall, "cause himself to be marked among the first reformers of the age."[19]

Isaac Hill was even more effusive than Kendall in his praise of Welles, and equally positive that if Welles remained at home in command of the new reform program, a great future awaited him. "Your field," he advised, "is your own native state. I would not in your circumstances, leave it for any position at Washington. You are yet comparatively young, and office more acceptable than any abroad will come to you in due time." Welles must have been amused when Hill apologized for his intervention the previous year. "I know," he continued, "that a number of your politicians one year ago were extremely timid. I felt the effects of that timidity at Washington and it cut me to the quick. But I have great charity for the timidity of such men as Ellis, who has always been *ready* to do much for the cause." Had he searched his memory he would have recalled that Welles' rebuke for his accepting the advice of the conservatives had caused him "deep and agonizing pain." And surely Hill did not improve his standing or the sincerity of his apology when he boosted the *Patriot and Democrat* by saying in the same letter that "an additional democratic paper might be of advantage to you at Hartford."[20]

Welles knew, and Hill knew also, that Ellsworth was still the favored candidate for the next job vacancy in Washington. Where did this leave him and his friend Niles, the architects of the Democratic triumph in Connecticut? Both were determined to push their program through the legislature, but both also expected, in accordance with party practice, that they and their faction as the victors deserved some material consideration. Yet there would be no reward for the present. Hill had promised that he would press an appointment for Niles directly with the President, but nothing ever came of this. Welles applied to Kendall, who answered that he had thought of the patent office, until he learned it would be offered to Ellsworth. Welles wrote also to Martin Van Buren, suggesting "a good office for Niles." He had heard that Kendall might be promoted to Postmaster General. Might not his former position as fourth auditor be offered to Niles? Blair replied for the Vice President, acknowledging the justice of Niles' claims: "but alas," said he, "the 4th auditorship had already been offered some one else." Blair excused himself lamely: "If it had been known in time, I believe Niles would have gotten it."

On May 11, Kendall informed Niles that Ellsworth had been appointed Commissioner of the Patent Office through Woodbury's influence. He had not been consulted about the appointment, but implied that if he had been, he would have been guided by their wishes. "I consider you and Mr. Welles pre-eminent in your state." Flattery, however sincere and well-meant, was no palliative for the hard and cold facts. If there was one major fault in the Jackson administration, Welles concluded, that fault must lie in its appointment policy.[21]

With nothing immediately available for Niles in Washington, he would, of course, retain his postmastership. Thus, Welles had to fall back on a state appointment. Two positions of importance were at his disposal. One, the house speakership, carried local prestige and much party importance, but a trivial remuneration. The other, though less influential, was one of the most lucrative offices in the state—the comptrollership. Welles chose the income rather than the prestige. The speakership went to Chauncey Cleveland.

In accepting the position of comptroller, Welles made a wrong decision regarding his political future. He was probably motivated by family responsibilities—he had recently married. Though he did not discourage the persistent rumors that he was a man of means, he must have thought he needed the extra income. He also shrank from the oratorical and forensic efforts expected of the speaker and the fact that he would have been on constant public display during the session. Had he taken the trouble to examine the political careers of the various speakers, he would have noted that thirteen of the fifteen who had held that office since 1817 had gone on to higher positions. All but two had served in Congress, most more than one term. Three—Gideon Tomlinson, Samuel Foot, and Henry W. Edwards—had been at one time or another elected to the governorship, to the House of Representatives, and to the United States Senate. His associate, Cleveland, whose post as speaker he could have had, would be elected governor twice and would serve two terms in Congress.[22]

Welles had not heeded Kendall's sound advice—that he personally and publicly steer the reform program through the legislature. While he was a decisive influence in framing and pushing through the program, an effort that would not be completed until 1837, he operated from his secluded, private office on the first floor of the State House, not from the noisy and public representative's hall upstairs. Welles did most of the work, but Cleveland got most of the public acclaim and, except among the knowledgeable, most of the credit from the party sachems in Washington.

The 1835 session, despite all the Jacksonian rhetoric expended, all of the advice received, all of the work—the arguments in caucus, the debates on the floor, the committee reports, the glasses of ardent spirits in the *Times* office—did not set the model of reform which Amos Kendall had hoped it would. Nor did the session realize all of Welles' expectations. Yet, as the *Times* stated, "the last Legislature is deserving of great credit for commencing a new era and laying the foundation for future improvement." Its achievements, however, were in the main negative ones. No new bank charters were granted. Small bank notes —those under three dollars—were prohibited; Welles had wanted five-dollar notes also banned. The legislature expressly forbade the incorporation of monopolies, in accordance with Cambreleng's suggestion. Welles, when chairman of the committee on corporations, had been directly responsible for this law. He had also written the majority report, which condemned special charters, and presented a carefully wrought bill for a general incorporation law. After he resigned his seat to assume the comptrollership, Perry Smith took over as floor leader. Assisted by Speaker Cleveland, the Loco-Focos managed to ram the general incorporation bill through the house, but, because of conflicting railroad interests, it took them so long that there was not enough time to secure the concurrence of the Senate.

In fact, railroad promoters had been a troublesome source of log-rolling to the Loco-Focos from the outset. Neither Smith nor Speaker Cleveland, with Welles and Niles in the background, could defeat the three private railroad charters before the legislature. Nor could they even bring the promoters to accept Cambreleng's limited-monopoly idea as a compromise solution. The legislature granted them all special privileges, such as route monopolies (with no specified dates of termination), tax-free bond issues, and other exclusive features common to the turnpike-canal charters of an earlier age. On the governmental and judicial side, the legislature restored the congressional districting law and set in motion a constitutional amendment restricting superior and supreme court terms to five years instead of life tenure.

Not altogether dissatisfied with the results of the session, the Loco-Focos learned that party organization as it functioned in the legislature was still far from complete. The *Times* explained that the party not only had its open enemies—the Whigs—to contend with, "but the prejudices and fears of timid and erring friends." There were also "*corporation democrats,* and the latter had it in their power to, and frequently did, defeat the democrats."[23]

The Loco-Focos were undeterred. They had gained valuable experience—it was one thing to win an election, it was quite another to carry a program through a legislative body. Fortunately, they would be given the opportunity of completing their legislative reforms. For the Democrats under the leadership of the Loco-Focos would win in 1836 and in 1837. When the Whigs took over in 1838, Connecticut *did* enjoy the brief distinction of being one of the few states in the Union with a nearly complete set of Jacksonian measures.

The assessment and taxing of corporate property had been increased in 1836 and equalized in 1837. A mechanics lien law was passed; imprisonment for debt was abolished. By giving or withholding benefits, mainly through the taxing power, the old perpetual charters were put on the road to extinction. And crowning their achievement was the first general incorporation law in the land, authored by Welles and passed by the 1837 legislature. Even the Whig majority of 1838, while it suspended the small-note prohibition, approved legislation requiring Connecticut banks to redeem these notes ($3.00 or less) on demand in specie or lose their charters.[24] In only one major respect were the years of radical Democratic rule disappointing to reformers such as

Charles Douglas and Thomas Mussey. No acts were passed, no bills even reported, to protect the health and morals or ensure the education of factory children. Possibly, the farmers in the legislature saw in such humanitarian legislation an opening wedge to restrain them from exploiting their own children. But it is more likely that the small number of children—less than 1000—working in all Connecticut mills had not seemed to pose a problem that required legislative action. Their health may well have been impaired, but their education, such as it was, did not differ in quality from that being received by farm boys and girls. Mill owners at this time customarily slowed down or even terminated operations during the fall months, when the district schools were in session. There was nothing philanthropic about this; it was simply a matter of economics and markets.[25]

The three-year rule of the Loco-Focos was maintained, but not without the party schism that Isaac Hill had feared in 1834. And the scars left by this internal struggle were not to be completely healed until the 1870's, near the end of Welles' life. During 1835 the bank faction and its press, the *Patriot and Democrat,* seemingly bowed to the Loco-Focos. Eldridge wrote several editorials in the *Patriot and Democrat* which were not far from Welles' views on incorporations. But there is no doubt that the "timid and erring friends" and the "corporation democrats" of whom the *Times* complained darkly were associated with a conservative bloc. Besides, the Loco-Foco program, modest as it was, seems to have promoted further distrust among the influential, propertied men as to the ultimate intentions of the Welles-Niles group.[26] Presumably, others were chagrined that few if any exclusive privileges could be secured in the future. But, more than anything else, the rhetoric of the Loco-Foco press incited imaginary fears from the conservatives and overly extravagant expectations from the reformers.

The Loco-Foco program of general legislation made scarcely a ripple in the relations between the people and their government. Since its general direction was declaratory, not regulatory, and since there were no provisions for investigative or supervisory commissions, compliance with Loco-Foco legislation rested on community sentiment. Surprisingly, the radical Jacksonians had done their work well in the important area of public acceptance. No one challenged the general incorporation law in the courts or in the political sphere; banks, by and large, complied with the small-note restrictions; and tax assessment and equalization met with no determined resistance.

After the panic and depression of 1837, many in their economic distress would look back on the period of the Bank war and Loco-Foco ascendancy as a time of radical legislation undertaken by profligate demagogues in the interest of promoting class warfare. Nothing could have been further from the truth. Welles, in one of his more eloquent statements of their position, declared that he and his associates simply wanted justice: "the rich desire to be, and must be, protected in their property, and I would contend for this right for them with the same zeal that I do for the right of the poor man to that freedom which he inherited from his God, and of which no human law should deprive him . . . it is a misfortune to be poor, but not a crime. . . ."[27] The charge that the radical Democrats were led by poor men bent on plundering the rich was equally without foundation. Even Whig newspapers at the time had harped on the fact that Welles and Niles were men of means and that Ralph Ingersoll of New Haven was a "rank aristocrat."[28]

Significantly, the Whig party, which won in 1838 by picturing their opponents as reckless extremists, did little or nothing to alter the private enterprise ethos that Welles and his party associates in New York and Massachusetts had instilled. For it was difficult, if not impossible, to quarrel with a program which merely asserted in legislative form that economic activity, like political activity, was a privilege of the freeborn citizen.

Loco-Foco rhetoric was another matter. The violent tone of the *Times* and of other radical newspapers, especially their apparent hostility to banking, was in part responsible for a rift in the party. Those managers in Washington, men of the Woodbury-Hill stamp who were trying to build a national organization along moderate, if not conservative, lines, who sought the allegiance of commercial soft-money men imagined the Welles circle to be far more radical than it was. They seemed to fear that the Loco-Focos, if unchecked, would produce a basic, ideological conflict within the Northern Democracy. This impression might well have been fostered by the newer brand of Southern politicians, who were even then demanding special privileges for plantation agriculture, and who read with dismay of the "equal rights" agitation in Northern papers such as the *Hartford Times*. The conservatives at home and in Washington should have rested easily. Connecticut radical Democrats were merely expressing the political democracy of Jefferson, John Taylor, and Nathaniel Macon in economic terms. To have seen any sinister assaults on property in their program would have been a tortuous construction even for the most sectional of Southern spokesmen.

# CHAPTER 9

# Niles, Welles and Co.

A WINTER JOURNEY from New England to Washington during the 1830's was apt to be a rigorous, even a perilous, undertaking. Connecticut Senator Nathan Smith was a heavy man of sedentary habits, just short of his sixty-sixth year and the hardships he encountered on his way to the capital for the first session of the twenty-fourth Congress were too much for a man of his age and physical condition. He survived the ordeal—a northeaster followed by a vicious cold snap—only to collapse and die, apparently of a stroke, on December 5, two days after reaching Washington. The news of Smith's death reached New Haven on December 8, 1835, and Hartford the next day—a brief time lag that was to have important political consequences.[1]

Welles immediately got a letter off to the Governor urging Niles' appointment to the Senate. But Governor Edwards, with unseemly haste, had already called together a small group of New Haven politicians, and after discussing the situation, had offered the seat to Ralph Ingersoll. Not all of the Governor's advisers agreed with his decision. Some, like Ellis, said frankly that it was both discourteous and indiscreet not to have consulted with Hartford on such an important matter. The Governor's motives, they held, would surely be questioned. Even Ingersoll's brother, Charles, thought it highly improper to bestow such a distinguished post upon one who had only recently become a Democrat. Ingersoll himself was "half inclined to accept," but his usual good political sense asserted itself, and he declined. After receiving Welles' letter, the Governor lost no time appointing Niles to the vacant seat in Washington.[2]

Unquestionably, Niles would be taking a calculated risk in accepting the senatorial appointment. The Democrats would have to win in the spring election, because the legislature then elected would in turn elect a Senator to serve out the remainder of Smith's term, three years in this instance. If they won, the Loco-Focos would still have to control the majority in the legislature, no easy task in the light of their experience with the last one. If the Democrats lost, his term would end after the short session of Congress. He was willing to take the gamble, but he made one stipulation: Welles and only Welles should succeed him as Hartford postmaster. At all costs the Hartford post office must be kept in reliable hands. Evidently, the New Haven men had come to the same conclusion and were willing to support such an arrangement, "though no concern of ours," as Ellis hastily added.[3] After having his suspicions aroused by the Governor's less than open course on Niles' appointment, Welles was gratified that the Edwards-Ellis-Ingersoll faction seemed friendly and would not interfere, for the bank Democrats in Hartford had already announced their opposition to him in the *Patriot and Democrat*.

With such a valuable position as the postmastership at stake, several of the bank Democrats were candidates, but the choice soon narrowed down to James Dodd, president of the Farmers and Mechanics Bank. Dodd himself approached the Connecticut congressional delegation through Isaac Toucey, while his agents sought out Amos Kendall, the new Postmaster General. If Welles were made postmaster, they said, they and their friends would oppose Niles' election to the Senate the following spring. Kendall asked about Welles' qualifications for the office. Was he honest? Did he have business experience? Had he served the party? None of his visitors denied Welles' qualifications or claims; they simply repeated that his appointment would disrupt the party. With more feeling and spirit than he usually permitted himself in public, Kendall interjected, "if there was any such association or organization in Hartford, the quicker it was broken up the better."[4] Dodd's representatives got a much more cordial reception from Congressman Toucey, who had his own reasons for acting against Welles. He "was no doubt disposed," said Niles after the fact, "to strengthen the [bank] faction feeling . . . he had more of a hold on them than on the other division of our party, which he knew had not very strong confidence in him." The dignified Congressman, with his elegant dress and his carefully cultivated manner, had little difficulty in persuading his rustic colleagues that they should all support Dodd. In his deliberate manner, Toucey pointed out they had not heard from Welles and that he already was occupying "an honorable appointment as any state can give

him, which he had held less than one year. . . ." Having drafted
Dodd's testimonial, which was then signed by all of the delegation and
by Henry Ellsworth, he arranged an interview with President Jackson.
In handing the testimonial to the President, Toucey said that it represented not only the unanimous opinion of Connecticut's Democratic
congressional delegation but of the party as well. He took care not to
mention Niles, whom he knew would be arriving shortly—and would
press for Welles' appointment.

Forewarned by Amos Kendall, President Jackson was ready with
some sharp questioning when the Connecticut delegation appeared.
Addressing himself only to Toucey, who had spoken for his colleagues,
Jackson asked: "On what grounds do you object to Mr. Welles? Is he
not an honest man?"

"Unquestionably, we mean no imputation on his integrity," replied
Toucey.

"Is he capable?"

"Most certainly."

"Is he faithful and true to the Constitution?" asked the President.
Has his conduct been "at all questionable?"

Under the barrage of presidential questions, Toucey was unable
to make a clear case against Welles. Nor was he able to convince Jackson that Welles would not be acceptable to the Hartford Democracy.
"Personally I am better acquainted with Mr. Welles than with you
all," said the President as he concluded the interview, "I have considered him one of the most reliable friends I have in the state, and confess I am amazed at this movement."[5]

When Niles arrived in Washington on December 21 to take his seat
in the Senate, both Kendall and Silas Wright told him about Toucey's interview with Jackson. One week later, Niles received a long
letter from Albert Day, who had been a director of the Farmers and
Mechanics Bank and was fast becoming one of the richest wholesale
merchants in Hartford. He too was irritated at the "unpolitic" course
of the congressional delegation. "No doubt can be entertained," wrote
Day, "that Mr. Welles would be the choice of seven eighths of the
friends of the Administration, besides, his fitness for the office has not
[been] and can not be questioned." With this testimonial, among others, and with the support of Kendall and Wright, Niles wrote Welles
that he had nothing to fear. "Had old Jo. [Joseph Pratt, one of Dodd's
emissaries] brought home Dodd's commission," commented one of
Niles' trusted friends, "adieu to all your hopes of greatness. Your Bank
Democratic friends have no love for you and had your influence 'at

court' been on the wane, they would soon have put you in Coventry."
The new Senator's influence at court was higher perhaps than even
he realized at the time. When Amos Kendall reminded the President
on January 7 that the Hartford post office appointment ought to be
made, Jackson scrawled on the note: "Let the individual recommended by Mr. Niles be appointed. . . ."⁶

The bank faction may have been defeated in Washington, but it was
still determined to wrest the leadership of the county machine from
Welles, then deal with Niles at the next legislative session. The *New
Haven Palladium,* a Whig paper, which could afford to be objective
when it was not being mischievous for partisan purposes, described
the situation as a struggle between radicalism and conservatism. Welles,
Niles, and the *Hartford Times* made up the "radical faction," said the
*Palladium,* "the projectors of the boldest measures, on the issue of
which they will hazard 'neck or nothing.'" James Dodd, Luther
Loomis, William Holland, and the *Patriot and Democrat* led the other
group, which the *Palladium* stigmatized as "a cautious, cringing, ser-
vile faction, that ground their claims for patronage upon the popularity
of a party that had existed some twenty years ago."

New Haven Democrats had originally thought of the contest as purely
a Hartford affair, but they began to have some doubts when they learned
that the entire congressional delegation had backed Dodd. "Has it
come to this," asked the normally timid Ellis, "that we have put down
the U. S. Bank for interfering in our elections and appointments; and
are we to have the little fingers of our state deposit banks, stronger
than the loins of the U. S. Bank?" Ellis sounded a note of caution,
though; he advised Welles to wait until the bank faction opened the
attack and then defend himself. Governor Edwards had no love for
Hartford or its boisterous Loco-Focos, yet he told Ellis that "the interference of any corporation by its President and directors in the appointments to office is not to be tolerated." There was a touch of Jonathan Edwards' zeal in his mild-mannered, middle-aged grandson's
exclamation: "If this is what we gain, dictation in appointments from
democratic banks, God save us from such democratic institutions."
Ralph Ingersoll was equally vehement. Writing what Niles described
as "a very sensible and very friendly" letter, he vigorously supported
Welles' appointment and suggested that the motives of "the bankites"
be explored by the *Times.* Though Ingersoll assumed there would be
more agitation in Hartford, he did not think it would spread to other
counties. "We shall do everything in our power this way to calm the
troubled waters."⁷

Ingersoll was mistaken on this score. The quarrel between pro- and anti-bank forces had already spread to other areas. Thomas Mussey and Ingoldsby Crawford, leaders of the Loco-Focos in New London, were engaged in a similar contest with the local deposit bank for political control of the county. "In fact," said Mussey, "since his satanic majesty old Nick has lost his empire over the Union, the petty imps are determined if possible to establish regencies in the *several states.*" Ingersoll also misjudged the temper of party leaders in Washington when he advised an exposé in the *Times* of the bankites. Welles had written both Silas Wright and Isaac Hill early in January, explaining that he thought the bank faction was jeopardizing his and Niles' position in the party. Welles wanted to launch a full-scale attack against them in the *Times.* What would they advise? Wright thought that "an attack upon the bank . . . at this time, and under present circumstances would be unadvisable and unfortunate." "Besides," he said, "the bank is a deposit Bank, and an attack upon it as a political machine would confirm the slanders of the opposition as to the banks generally which hold government deposits, would annoy the President and Secretary of the Treasury." In an obvious reference to the Van Buren candidacy, Wright said it would "do great harm here." Hill echoed these sentiments, remarking that Thomas Hart Benton had told him "the Bank of the Metropolis [Washington, D.C.] was at this moment in the hands of the opposition."[8]

Welles heeded the advice, despite extreme provocation from the *Patriot and Democrat,* until January 21, 1836, when a public collision between the two factions in Hartford ruled out any truce. The occasion was the primary meeting of the local party organization; at stake was control of the Hartford Democracy. Joseph Pratt (one of Dodd's unsuccessful envoys to Washington) as chairman of the Hartford committee, had called a special meeting in a surprise move and packed the Hall with bank partisans. His object was to strip the new postmaster of his power by excluding all of his friends from the town committee. With the city of Hartford as a base, the conservatives would then go after the county organization. Pratt's plan almost succeeded, for the bank men maintained careful security. Welles knew nothing about the meeting (it had not been announced in any paper) until a few hours before it was to convene in Belden's Hall. By moving quickly, he got enough supporters there to raise emotions, though not enough to break up the meeting. So heated were the exchanges that, after the radicals stalked out, the furious bank men passed a series of extremely rash resolutions dealing with the recent appointments.

Niles' nomination to the Senate was "disapproved by the Democracy of Hartford" and was held to be "unacceptable to the Democracy of the State." As for Welles, his appointment was "the evident result of intrigue and misapprehension at Washington, as contrary to the voice of the Democratic party in this city, and dangerous to its harmony and welfare, and disrespectful to the Democracy of the state of Connecticut through their Representatives in Congress." After reading out of the party its new United States Senator and its most prominent officeholder, the reckless "bankites" went on to accuse Democratic Governor Edwards of being a political renegade. For good measure, by implication they condemned the Postmaster General as being either a fool or an intriguer. Kendall may have been an intriguer, but he was no fool. It was dangerous business to make public statements that reflected upon the political character of this powerful man. In the expert hands of Welles and his friends of the *Times* office, the resolutions were used with telling effect. He and his little group of skillful men had shown conclusively that the bank men were complete innocents when it came to cut-and-slash politics. The Loco-Focos may have been less than competent in business affairs, but they were experts in their own sphere—the manipulation of opinion, whether in the small confines of a town meeting or in the larger context of a partisan campaign.

Eldridge and Holland of the *Patriot and Democrat*—more at home in the world of politics and journalism than their banker friends—recognized the mistake at once, and they did all they could to rectify it in the columns of their paper. They denied that anyone had meant to impugn the character and judgment of Governor Edwards or of Postmaster General Kendall. In six columns of close type they gave their history of the appointments and their version of the town meeting. Much thought and care went into their indictment of Welles and Niles. As many facts as they could gather were marshalled, in and out of context, to create the impression that the two men had been engaged in a conspiracy of long standing. Information gaps were bridged by clever deductions or rhetorical questions. They explored the profit motive. Niles had received "not less than $17,500" of the public money during his tenure of office, excluding other fees and perquisites that did not show up in his official salary. He and Welles together were now enjoying an official income which they estimated to be in excess of $6000 a year. This sum included Welles' compensation as comptroller of the state—a position he was about to resign.[9]

Before Welles received word from Washington he had answered the

*Patriot and Democrat* in a slashing attack that filled three columns of the *Times*. He avoided the mistake of Holland and Eldridge, however, by refusing to deal with personalities in abusive or scurrilous terms. He handled them sharply enough, but he kept his language within the bounds of decorum. He also made it plain that the *Times* had been silent under extreme provocation and was now only defending itself—that the responsibility for a rupture, if it came, must lie with the other side. Niles was delighted with Welles' response, adding only the injunction: "Be decided and firm, but not violent, speak the truth boldly and fearlessly." "After all," he concluded, "the whole state and the party leaders in Washington are your audience—it is up to our friends outside of Hartford to determine which is the party and which a faction."

On January 30 the *Patriot and Democrat* replied to Welles' article of the twenty-fourth in another abusive piece, this one concentrating its fire upon Niles. Continuing in his former style, Welles answered. He reviewed Niles' long services to the party and the state. When he could find specific allegations among the innuendoes, the hearsay and the rumors, he countered them with facts, giving names, dates, and sources. Welles was less tolerant, however, when he dealt with Holland's and Eldridge's careers.

Both had been involved in the Workingmen's movement. Eldridge had been a delegate to the 1832 convention of the "New England Association of Farmers, Mechanics and Other Workingmen." For a time he had been active among "the workies" in Springfield, Massachusetts. Then, mysteriously, he had become the proprietor of the *Springfield Whig*, where he had taken a violent anti-Workingman position. Now he was, presumably, a Democrat. Welles concluded that Eldridge was simply a pen for hire, devoid of principles, political or otherwise. The political career of William Holland was similarly checkered. At one time an admirer of Frances Wright ("the red harlot of infidelity") and Robert Dale Owen, Holland had been a frequent contributor to Owen's radical sheet, *The Free Enquirer*. Furthermore, he had once been an Adams Republican, had switched to Clay in 1832, and had then joined the Democracy, but only after Jackson's re-election. Both Eldridge and Holland had been disloyal to their Workingmen friends, their National Republican friends, their Whig friends. Was there any reason to believe they were or could be loyal to the Vice President?

Considering the brief history of political parties since Jackson's first election, Welles was not being scrupulously fair. The Workingmen had never been able to build a distinct organization. It must be admitted, however, that most of their former leaders were now counted among the Loco-Foco branch of the Northern Democracy. Charles Douglas and Thomas Mussey, the most prominent of the Connecticut "workies," were loyal supporters of the Hartford radicals. Welles himself was not unfriendly to the reforms proposed by Owen and Wright and others, but he knew his reading public well and he knew their memories were short. A detailed account of political inconsistency carried much more force in 1836, after the two parties were firmly established, than would have been the case in 1829, when all was in a state of flux. When Welles' narrative was combined with the facts of a radical past, of hints that infidelity and atheism once learned were never forgotten, he had the better of the argument. The Anti-Masonic-revivalist style Welles was using, perhaps unconsciously, had again proven its worth, at least in the opinion of the leaders in Washington. Isaac Hill told Niles that he thought Welles had used "the Professor of Languages pretty much up and that you ought to call a halt." Van Buren also advised Welles through Niles to break off. The prevailing sentiment was that the *Times* had scored a complete victory in the editorial duel, and that its continuance "will write these men into consequence." Much now depended upon Niles. He must quash the Hartford bank faction and stamp out all the other insurgencies or threatened insurgencies that were cropping up throughout the state.[10]

To a very considerable extent Niles was on trial himself in Washington, on trial before the most critical audience in the nation—the United States Senate. Here he was, a "short thick-set man" of fifty who had visited the capital only once before in his life, moving as a peer among such national monuments as Webster, Calhoun, Clay, Benton. From his dingy room at the post office in Hartford, Niles had, in the space of a week, been transported to the awesome dignity of the United States Senate. He walked over thick Brussels carpeting to his mahogany desk, where he sat in a well-upholstered mahogany chair. Glancing nervously about him, as he must have done, he saw the slender, fluted pillars that supported the semicircular gallery, the crimson drapes, the eagle-embellished rostrum of the Vice President. That lofty personage himself was as arresting as a stout, little man could be, always affecting some vivid combination of sartorial splendor that set him apart from the somber dress of his senatorial colleagues. To Niles' undiscerning eye, the chamber and its occupants must have seemed the epitome of elegance, grandeur, and power. No wonder the little, self-taught law-

yer, with his rustic airs and country twang, had "a super-abundance
of stiffness in all his movements," or that "he was brushed up and
looked better" than he ever did in Hartford.[11]

At first he acted with the care and reticence which he had been advised was the traditional posture of a new Senator. When approached
by Senator William C. Rives, who was just observing the amenities,
Niles decided that the Virginian was trying "to form a personal party."
Benton's initial cordiality met with the same cautious response. Niles
had been told that the Vice President was excessively concerned with
senatorial cliques. "The mere appearance of something of this kind,
I am satisfied," he wrote Welles, "gives Mr. Van Buren some uneasiness."

Diffidence may have been customary for new Senators, but Welles
felt that neither Niles nor the party could afford it. He was concerned
about the incipient revolt that seemed to be gaining momentum each
day. Niles had only a few months to establish himself with the managers in Washington, and, more particularly, with the people of his
own state. This meant speeches in the Senate—not just brief remarks
on trivial matters, but significant, well-turned-out displays of eloquence
on subjects of importance to the Connecticut voters and to party leaders. These Welles would have published in the *Times,* and the *Register*
if it could be persuaded, then published as pamphlets and distributed
where they would do the most good. A debate or two with a Webster
or a Calhoun would furnish excellent editorial copy for the New
England press, be it Whig or Democratic.

Niles had not been in his seat more than a week when Welles and
other friends in Hartford began demanding action. The new Senator,
overawed as he was by his surroundings, quailed at the thought of addressing the august body, much less engaging Calhoun or some other
public grandee in debate. The United States Senate was not the Hartford State House, and these people were not simple farmers or country lawyers. "I must act with judgment and caution," he wrote Welles,
masking his lack of confidence, but he added, truthfully enough, that
new members were not expected to speak, merely to vote.[12] Yet the
new Senator heeded the urgency in the pleas of his friends and, courageous as always, resolved on the plunge. His first effort was a purely
extemporaneous comment on a resolution proposed by Thomas Hart
Benton to which Clay had objected. The junior Senator from Connecticut caught the eye of the Vice President and was recognized. Everyone turned toward the compact figure as he rose awkwardly from
his desk, some with curiosity, some with barely concealed amusement.

Clay, who had just finished speaking, stretched out his long frame at his desk, took a pinch of snuff, and appeared to be completely indifferent.

"I spoke for from twenty to twenty-five minutes," said Niles, "with as much coolness as ever I did in my life." His subject was what he called "partial legislation"—a topic, he remarked, "which has not often been heard in the Senate, where three-fourths of the whole Legislature is in violation of the great principles of general sound rules of action and equal rights." Those who had been prepared for a stuttering, shambling display of ill-digested notions, or, even more hopefully, for one of those embarrassing lapses in speech that betrayed the impetuous novice, were disappointed. He had been nervous enough, but by a great effort of will he spoke as well as any senatorial veteran, his rhetoric at times approaching eloquence. Even Clay turned to listen, and, on the conclusion of Niles' remarks, tall, handsome Whig Senator John M. Clayton of Delaware, no mean orator himself, crossed over to Niles' desk in full view of the galleries to extend his personal congratulations. Other Senators crowded around him to give theirs.[13]

On adjournment, Vice President Van Buren, who had listened carefully to Niles, offered him a ride to his lodgings, an invitation he was flattered to accept. As they rode together down Pennsylvania Avenue, Van Buren asked, "Where, Mr. Niles, have you acquired the habit of public speaking?" "Have you been much in the Legislature, sir?" "I told him," said Niles, "I had been a member one session of four weeks . . . the whole of my experience." Van Buren replied that he had "seldom heard anyone speak with more coolness or in such a manner, so that every word seemed to be precisely as it should be, and where it should be."

The Vice President was well known for his flattery, but the sincerity of his comments on this occasion and the marked display of attention he had immediately shown Niles meant much. Van Buren measured out carefully his personal relations with the Senators at this crucial point of his career. It would appear that he was genuinely impressed, that if the Loco-Foco faction in Connecticut had such men in its ranks, perhaps he had been misinformed. "After the first plunge [that] is always the most dreaded," as Ralph Ingersoll had written, complimenting Niles on his maiden effort, the junior Senator joined frequently in the verbal skirmishes of the Senate session.

Genuine recognition of his merit came when his party colleagues selected him as the final speaker in a debate they anticipated with John C. Calhoun. Calhoun had given notice that he intended to an-

swer Silas Wright, who was making a major address on national defense. Garrett Wall, a New Jersey Senator of some skill in debate, was
to lead off in countering the expected attacks on administration policy.
Niles would follow. Word that Calhoun would probably speak on the
intriguing topic soon became public knowledge in the boardinghouses,
hotel lobbies, and oyster bars. Thus, on February 18 the Senate gallery was crowded with spectators. Many members of the diplomatic
corps, also attracted by the importance of the subject, were present in
their reserved seats near the rostrum.

Wright concluded his carefully documented address during the early
afternoon of February 15. Calhoun rose to reply. As usual, he was
dressed in black broadcloth, swallowtail coat, and high, white, standing collar, a costume which always added a dimension of power and
dignity to his tall, lean figure, his ruff of stiff, greying, black hair, his
deep-set, dark eyes. He spoke softly, but the chamber was so quiet that
every word could be heard distinctly in the galleries. In his initial remarks he criticized the state of national defense; then, to the delight of
the galleries and the Whig Senators, he shifted, launching a personal
attack on Jackson and on the "spoils system" as practiced by the New
York Democracy. Wall answered in what was not one of his better
efforts, accusing Calhoun of a "breach of decorum." Calhoun's South
Carolina colleague, William B. Preston, serving his first term in the
Senate, replied to Wall in a manner so scathing, yet so well phrased,
that the New Jersey Senator, after a concluding remark or two, sat
down abruptly.[14]

At this point Niles rose and was recognized. During the entire debate, he had kept his eyes on the desk in front of him, not daring to
survey the gallery or the diplomats in their dress uniforms, heavy with
gold lace. A ripple of unconcealed laughter greeted Niles when he
began to speak—his rural twang, his stiff gestures, were a droll comparison to the polished address of the preceding speakers. What he had
to say, however, was not the homespun, ungrammatical discourse his
audience had expected. He concentrated on Calhoun's charge that the
Democratic party was ruled by spoilsmen. In doing so, he reviewed
some unsavory actions on the part of Calhoun's partisans, and then
began with rising eloquence to describe the Carolinian's political
course since 1816. He had scarcely commenced speaking when Daniel
Webster and several of his fellow Whigs left the Chamber. Calhoun,
the subject of Niles' discourse, did not join them. Though he and
Preston left their desks, they took up a position out of sight behind the
Vice President's rostrum, where they could listen, yet remain unob-

served.[15] "The gallery," said Isaac Hill, "true to the wishes of the malignants, attempted to do their part towards drowning his [Niles'] voice." Undaunted by any of this commotion, Niles "warmed with his subject . . . forced the attention of those who would have shut the ears of the whole world to what he said . . . he drew such a picture of Calhoun and of the other leaders of the disjointed party acting in opposition as made them writhe." When the little Senator sat down mopping his scarlet face with a huge, red handkerchief, an incident that should have convulsed any audience, there was no laughter in the Chamber. Instead, there was a brief silence, then spontaneous applause when Silas Wright and Wall led a group of Democratic Senators to congratulate him. "On the whole," wrote the happy but weary Niles, "it was a great triumph; it was a proud day to me, more so than I ever expect [to] see again if I was to be here many years." He had made his mark at what cost of human effort and mental agony only Welles and the beloved Sarah Niles perhaps could imagine. "My character here is now established," he said after the debate, "for good or for evil with friends and enemies, not only on the floor of the Senate but in the galleries with the letter writers and the retainers of Clay, Calhoun and Co."[16] The *Hartford Times* could now boast that finally, after thirty years, the state had a man in the Senate worthy of an Oliver Ellsworth—a voice which would speak out for Connecticut and make its influence felt in national affairs.

This was all to the good; still, of overriding importance was the publicity—the news features, the editorial matter, the pamphlet material. Both Welles and Niles wanted favorable comment, of course, but, like their fellow Democrat P. T. Barnum, they recognized the value of any publicity, even adverse. Niles exulted in the violent criticism of his remarks by the *Baltimore Patriot* and other Whig papers. "You will see," he wrote Welles, "that I have become of consequence enough to be attacked here as well as at home." An immediate dividend was that the *Globe* would publish his entire speech. Blair had also offered to combine it with other remarks he had made in pamphlet form for distribution in the various states. Some Democratic Senators were already clamoring for copies.[17]

Niles' triumph came none too soon. In early March he heard that Henry W. Edwards was a candidate for the Senate. Ralph Ingersoll, it was said, would replace him as Governor if Edwards were elected by the legislature. When the Democrats won again—this time by a landslide—in the spring election, competition became more intense. Niles' speeches and his well-conducted publicity campaign made him the leading contender. Even so, he took no chances, and during the month of March he was active in the more important Senate debates. In addition he made formal speeches on such popular subjects as the expunging resolution (erasing the Senate censure of Jackson for removal of the deposits), the tariff, and the currency question. These displays imposed a great strain on his physical and mental resources. In a letter to Welles he remarked that each fresh triumph built up further expectations from his colleagues and from his friends at home. "I seem like the idle boy," he said, "who ventured into deep water borne up by bladders and wholly unconscious of the dangers." As Niles implied, he had to depend upon himself when it came to engaging the oratorical giants of the day. The printed word was a different matter, but, alas, here he had to rely exclusively on Welles and the *Times*. After his initial gesture of support, Blair, from whom he had expected much, proved disappointing. The *Globe* had little to say about the Senator's remarks, and that little was indifferently reported.

Though new to his duties in the post office, which he had assumed in late December 1836, Welles shouldered a major burden of managing Niles' campaign. With the Connecticut audience in mind, he edited all material carefully before he would permit it to be published in the *Times*. On more than one occasion, he added or deleted entire sections. Welles was also the final authority on all pamphlet production and distribution outside of the Hartford area.[18]

With the May session of the legislature approaching, the bank faction made another desperate effort to defeat Niles—this by an arrangement with the Whigs. The move miscarried because Toucey, Ellsworth, and Noah Phelps refused to be a party to it. Much as they desired Niles' repudiation, they had long since agreed that discretion was the only safe course. Hill, and presumably Woodbury, had caught Van Buren's hint that the Connecticut election was "the most important in the Union." The New Hampshire Senator had observed Niles in action and was impressed. He and Woodbury had likewise noticed Van Buren's marked partiality. Welles' appointment as postmaster, the publishing of Niles' speech in the *Globe,* Kendall's defense of Niles and Welles in a public letter to the *Times,* were all portents of White House approval too. Hill and Woodbury had not interfered when Niles brought the New London Loco-Focos and the bank faction there into an armed truce. Whatever pressure had been applied by the deposit bank in New Haven seems to have been relaxed. These limited moves were the extent of their support—if support it could be called.[19]

The *Patriot and Democrat* still carried on its campaign against Niles

—with somewhat less confidence than before, but with as much acrimony. As late as April 25, two weeks before the election in the legislature, the *New Haven Register* was still abusing Niles, Welles, and the "Hartford regency." Democratic papers in other states generally ignored the Connecticut campaign. Niles was particularly incensed at "the criminal neglect of the *Globe* and some other papers abroad." In Connecticut, the *Times* was his only steadfast advocate. One or two other Democratic papers gave him fitful support, while the rest stood clear of the contest. The anxious Senator was irritated too at "the cold indifference [with] which a considerable portion of the office holders and office seekers, looked on, and carefully abstained from taking any part. . . ." Despite his fears and frustrations, Niles easily won re-election to the Senate for the three years of Smith's unexpired term. And the legislature was more responsive to the Loco-Focos than it had been during the previous sessions.[20]

Another Senator was to be chosen to replace Gideon Tomlinson for the full six-year term. Welles' man was Perry Smith, who had taken over as party floor leader in the 1835 legislative session after Welles had been elected comptroller. Originally from Litchfield, but now practicing law in Fairfield County, Smith had a convincing geographic argument. The western counties deserved consideration too. Perry Smith was elected handily—a telling demonstration of Loco-Foco power. Tartly appraising the legislature's performance in this and in its other work, the *New Haven Palladium* declared that it had been controlled by the "decided radicals . . . completely governed by Niles, Welles and Co."[21]

The two men—Niles in the Senate, and Welles in Hartford—had almost alone achieved a striking victory. "It has vindicated my conduct and yours in regard to state matters and generally," wrote Niles. Yet complete as their triumph was, they had neither vanquished the bank faction at home nor improved their position in Washington significantly. The aged and enfeebled Jackson, looking forward to retirement, had come more and more to rely on his own Cabinet advisers in party affairs. Blair, who idolized Jackson, followed the Executive line. As a result, the *Globe* was neglecting its party constituents in Congress and was paying almost no attention to the party in the states. It had given no aid or comfort to Niles during the height of his senatorial campaign. The Connecticut Senator was not alone in his complaints. "In one mess," he observed, "all complain of it, indeed it can be considered only as a mere executive organ and not the organ of the party, or even of Congress." In justice to Blair, it would have been impossible to satisfy all of the claims put upon him and the *Globe*. Party representatives in Congress were an unmanageable lot, each member placing his own interests first. Niles himself testified to this. Speaking of the party's senatorial caucus, he said that members met every Saturday evening to discuss policy for the next week: "We have the most disorderly meetings I ever attended, where the numbers were so small. All seemed disposed to talk and none to listen. It is found difficult to decide anything and when we have come to our decision, it has yet amounted to little or nothing as questions have usually taken a different course in the Senate."[22]

The organization men—those chiefly grouped around the President, with Blair as their spokesman—were trying to impose some pattern of national organization, some adjustment that would override the feuds and the factions in the various states, some policy that would harmonize the various sections, which were rapidly becoming more and more independent of each other. On New England matters, Jackson looked more to Woodbury and his ally in the Senate, Isaac Hill, than he did to any of the congressional delegations, which were usually badly divided among themselves. Blair echoed what he deemed to be Jackson's sentiments. One of Welles' early complaints about the conduct of the *Globe* was its neglect of state campaigns. While Jackson was President and Henry Clay his chief political opponent, Blair *did* over-emphasize Tennessee and Kentucky politics. When Van Buren succeeded to the Presidency, Blair, to Welles' disgust and probable alarm, dropped his interest in Tennessee and shifted it to New Hampshire. He continued, of course, to devote major attention to Kentucky politics. Woodbury, it would seem, was being groomed for the presidency, or at least it appeared so to many New Englanders.

These two gentlemen, Woodbury and Hill, had by no means given up their notions of balancing conservative and radical influence in the northeast. Amos Kendall, who leaned toward the Loco-Focos, had been the chief radical influence "at court," but he was now the most overworked man in Washington. As the new Postmaster General, he was cleansing the Augean stables which his careless predecessor, Major Barry, had made of the Department. He simply had neither the time nor the interest to quarrel with Woodbury and Hill over New England problems. Van Buren preferred to remain above it all. Cautious, discreet, wholly dependent on Jackson's popularity, he would not risk alienating the powerful Secretary of the Treasury, whom he knew the Old Hero admired. And at this stage of his career Van Buren was as interested in building a national party as Woodbury was. Preeminently the organization man—the team player—he too was seeking the party formula that would reconcile Lofo-Foco and bankite, Northerner and Westerner and Southerner. While Woodbury remained in power and influence, the radical Democrats in Connecticut were deprived of complete party control, and the conservative wing gradually increased its strength. Welles and Niles had been wary of the Secretary almost from the beginning of the Jacksonian Presidency. By 1837 Welles had no doubt about his interference in Connecticut party matters. "Mr. Woodbury," he wrote Van Buren, "believes he is using Ellsworth and thinks he can use Holland, while these gentlemen are using and will use him."[23]

During the years ahead Welles would come to understand the moves and the motivations of the master-players, the delicate equipoise they sought through party management. He would not, however, wholly accept their ironclad definition of organization, which he felt led directly to the "tyranny of party" and the eventual destruction of democratic ideals. Once the party became an end in itself, rather than an instrument for the public good, it became an alien thing. "The disciplining and training of the different organizations," he wrote, "becomes in time effective, controlling . . . the timid, and cowing even the resolute, so that in our elections the exercise of private judgment is often sacrificed to the tyranny of party." Welles wanted both organization and the right of the "resolute" individual to be heard in the organization. To the end of his days he prized his right of dissent, yet after a lifetime of stubborn fighting for his views, he would have to confess that the realists, not the idealists, always prevailed.[24]

# CHAPTER 10

# A Persistent Suitor

VAN BUREN WAS PRESIDENT-ELECT; Niles was in the Senate. Welles was now postmaster of Hartford, his faction in the ascendency, his political prestige in the state at a high point. He had never been so content and happy as he was during the winter of 1836-37. But it had been a long and lonely pull, ten years of hard labor since he first walked into the *Times* office with his sheaf of sketches, ten years of boardinghouses and hotels, an angular, homely bachelor, the butt of opposition editors when they caught him off guard. Once he was seen trudging to Glastonbury pushing his week's laundry ahead of him in a wheelbarrow. On another occasion, he was observed crossing the Connecticut River Bridge with a load of sweet potatoes sent him by a Washington friend. The appearance of the earnest editor bent over his barrow of sweet potatoes had been too droll to escape the pen of George Prentice of the *New England Review*. One of his little pun-studded sketches on Gideon and his "sweet" was relished by Welles' opponents and even brought a chuckle in the *Times* office.

Those first ten years in Hartford had been busy, productive, but somehow empty for Welles. Marriage and a family seemed increasingly remote. He was envious as, one after another, of his friends and acquaintances left the convivial bachelor circle at the Franklin House and set up their own households. His brother Oliver, living in East Hartford and still partially dependent on his father, had long since acquired a family, which Welles visited from time to time. Even his younger brother, Thaddeus, was engaged.

Welles surveyed the eligible young women of Hartford and Glastonbury with a critical eye, perhaps too critical, for his flirtations were never more than that. And he congratulated himself that he had avoided the allurements of the once charming Lucy Hollister. She had first spurned his attentions when he was a student at Cheshire, then indicated her availability when Welles achieved a brief literary fame among the Glastonbury literati. Their paths had not crossed for years until, one day in October 1833, Welles met her on Main Street in Glastonbury. He barely recognized Lucy in the matronly figure who greeted him. She is "really and truly massive," wrote Welles to his cousin Reuben Hale, shocked at the ravages of time, saddened by the memories of the past they evoked, "she is gone and with her the gay vision of childhood and early youth. . . ."[1]

Since 1826 Welles had lived in a man's world, a world in which he sublimated his emotions in work and travel. He continued to improve and enlarge the *Times*, which by the mid-1830's was being published twice a week. In 1834 he started a country edition also. As he had done since his first connection with the paper, he wrote most of the editorials himself—and this included proof reading, a tedious task that could not be entrusted to the careless Russell.

Chief organizer for the Democratic party, Welles diligently expanded his political correspondence in and out of the state. The occasional passerby who happened along deserted Main Street at midnight, if he glanced up at the fourth floor of Jabez Ripley's United States Hotel, would have seen the fitful light of a whale oil lamp glimmering from Welles' window. There he did most of his political writing at night in his own room, conscientiously copying the more important letters for his own file. In October 1828, he had moved from the Franklin House to more comfortable and convenient quarters at the United States Hotel. Room and board were cheap enough—less than $5.00 a week. Ripley's hostelry was new, his table reputed to be the best in Hartford. The only disagreeable factor in the change of residence was that Welles had to endure the company of George D. Prentice, who also lived and boarded there. The two men were barely on speaking terms. Otherwise, the hotel was admirably suited to Welles' comfort, his needs, and his interests. It was the common meeting place for local politicians and, during the Hartford session of the General Assembly, state officers, editors, and lawyers.

Customarily, Welles spent an hour or two before his nightly chores lounging in Jabez Ripley's barroom with friends over a glass of wine or a drop of brandy. He still found time to write fictional and historical sketches, many of which he used for filler in the *Times*. But apart from their practical application he also found in this kind of writing a release from his constant involvement with political subjects. Probably because of his father's Episcopalian connections, and certainly because of his innate aversion to Yale, he was attracted to the newly established Washington (later Trinity) College in Hartford. There he met William M. Holland, whom he found interesting and congenial until their falling out over politics. Holland introduced him to Park Benjamin, then an undergraduate, a young man with massive chest and powerful arms who was completely paralyzed below the hips. In 1827 Benjamin had led a group of undergraduates away from Trinity's only literary club, the Atheneum, and set up a new association, the Parthenon. Welles was elected an honorary member, a tribute to his literary tastes and his conversational abilities.[2]

In July 1830, much to Welles' relief, Prentice of the *Review* announced he was leaving for Kentucky, where he planned to write a biography of Henry Clay. It was announced that John Greenleaf Whittier would replace him. Whittier was almost unknown at the time, save to a few minor litterateurs and journalists in the Boston area. Welles knew more about him than most Hartford people did because of his poetic contributions to the *Review* and the praise bestowed upon him by Prentice. The *Times* editor had little personal respect for Prentice, but he rated his literary judgment as high as he did his editorial ability.

Welles expected that the editorial style of the shy young Quaker from Haverhill, Massachusetts, who had written such touching pieces for the *Review*, would be a welcome release from the cudgeling he had taken from Prentice. He assumed that the *Review* would present the same arguments for the American system and the same bias for Henry Clay, but without the fire or the exuberant invective of its former editor. In this hope he was quite mistaken. Whittier's concept of brotherly love obviously did not include political journalism. Whittier's wit, when he chose to employ it, was sharp as a needle point, and Welles was soon being neatly punctured by the modest Quaker poet. He must have writhed inwardly when Whittier ridiculed a bit of careless doggerel that Russell had found on his table and thoughtlessly inserted as filler in the *Times*. "And here is something of a tender nature," wrote Whittier in the *Review*—"Shades of Moore and Anacreon, let Gideon be heard."

> Yet fearless and careless
> I freely will declare,
> That it teazes yet half pleases
> Me, to see a pretty fair.

"There," concluded Whittier, "I have done with the poetry of my brother editor. As a poet, an orator, and a politician, he is like 'a city on a hill.'³" Prentice at his keenest had never used quite so sharp an instrument. Yet curiously enough, Welles seems to have passed off Whittier's personal sallies without taking deep offense. He even made a tentative overture to the poet-editor that they become better friends, outside of the newspaper office, of course. "I wish you well," Welles wrote, "and should be pleased to be more intimately acquainted than I would permit myself to be with your predecessor." Whittier spurned Welles' proffer of friendship because at the time he believed he had been libeled by the *Hartford Times*. "Sir," he had written Welles, so angry that he did not employ the customary Quaker style of discourse, "if you know of anything against my character—a character dearer to me than life itself—then in God's name publish it to the world as becomes a man, but deal no longer in dark insinuations." The article that had incensed Whittier was a hard-hitting, personal attack that had been penned by Welles, but it did not refer to the new editor, nor even, except by implication, to the *Review*. It was directed against Prentice, who, Welles maintained, had left a series of unpaid bills in Hartford and, though not a member of the bar, was passing himself off as a lawyer in Kentucky.

Welles was frankly puzzled by the young Quaker's heated allegation. He replied that he was not conscious of any slur on Whittier's character in the article referred to, either direct or implied. Apparently either Whittier, in the turmoil of the newspaper office, had confused the *Times* with the *Columbian Register*, which *had* made an insidious attack on his character, or he had been told that Welles had inspired, perhaps had even secretly written, this vicious, piece. On July 23 the *Register* had cast doubt on the poet-editor's masculinity, describing him as the "pretty maiden Whittier." Welles offered to print a retraction of any libelous *Times* story, along with any letter Whittier wished to write under his own name that specified where he had been libeled. Since neither letter nor retraction appeared in subsequent issues of the *Times*, we must conclude that Whittier realized his mistake.⁴

Though Welles would have welcomed a friendship with Whittier, the young man preferred to move in more select circles. He was clasped to the bosom of Mrs. Sigourney, accepting tea in the white-pillared mansion, yet certainly declining her husband's more stimulating "cup of friendship," which Welles had enjoyed some years before. Others of Whittier's Hartford friends belonged to the old conservative aristocracy of the city—Jonathan Law, whom Niles had replaced as postmaster (and with whom Whittier boarded), Joseph Trumbull, and Judge John Russ, ex-Federalists all. Martin Welles, bitter political and personal enemy of the *Times* men, was also friendly with Whittier, a relationship that was prompted by their mutual interest in prison reform, for the imperious, argumentative Martin Welles was neither a genial nor an easy man to know on any terms of intimacy. Other Whittier friends, such as Dr. Eli Todd, Frederick A. P. Barnard (whom Welles also knew as a friend of Park Benjamin), and Isaac Toucey were asssociated with Dr. Gallaudet's school for the deaf and dumb or the new mental institution—the Hartford Retreat—which was already gaining for itself a more than local reputation for treatment of the mentally ill.

In later years Welles would take a lively interest in these humanitarian projects, but now, despite his solemn cast of mind, he was ready for nothing more than a casual interest in philanthropy. Whittier, the younger man, was deadly serious about social reform. Priggish, dedicated, abstemious, he would have found Welles' friends too frivolous and convivial for his elevated tastes. A confirmed abolitionist, Whittier preferred not to associate with those who did not share his extreme views on the slavery question. Welles, like other leading Democrats, saw the abolitionists as a dangerous, irresponsible lot. He detested slavery as much as Whittier, but he would not jeopardize the Constitution and the Union to stamp it out where it lawfully existed. Abolition was unlawful, potentially subversive, a threat to the nation; slavery was a local institution, a matter for the states to decide.

Beyond their differences over abolition, their opposing convictions ruled out anything but the most formal civilities. A nonconformist who attended Episcopal services, Welles was a member of St. John's Lodge No. 4—Hartford's oldest Masonic organization. He had a fancy too for military organizations and served a number of years as an officer in the Connecticut militia.[5] Whittier, a devout Quaker and a confirmed pacifist who hated all things military, held Welles in the same contempt he reserved for that epitome of militarism, Andrew Jackson. He believed the *Times* editor was a militarist at heart, his profession of faith in the common man a cloak for autocratic tendencies.

After the *Patriot and Democrat* was established and Holland became connected with it, Welles' interest in the Parthenon came to an abrupt end. In this case politics had been responsible for terminating a brief but enjoyable friendship. Rarely did he allow political views to interfere with his personal affairs, but William M. Holland and, later, Thurlow Weed and U. S. Grant were notable exceptions to this sensible rule. Increasing factionalism among the Democrats in Hartford

County did, however, restrict Welles' meager socializing to old and trusted friends—Niles; Loraine T. Pease and his son Elisha, of neighboring Enfield; Dr. Allan, a commercial druggist; Albert and Calvin Day, prosperous dry goods merchants; Samuel Kellogg, a Micawberish character with a ready wit, a dozen children, and a nagging wife. Whenever he could, Welles went off to Glastonbury, where he visited his aged father and his younger brother, Thaddeus, to whom he was very close.

Of all his friends and associates, Niles claimed first preference. Their taste for government and politics was similar. Both enjoyed gardening, and Welles spent many a happy hour puttering around Niles' orchards and grape arbors. As he helped the older man with planting and pruning, they discussed the characteristics of newly introduced French pears or whether such European grapes as muscats or oportos would graft well on familiar American stock. The red-haired, red-faced, unkempt Niles, who had no children of his own, took a fatherly interest in his young friend, and Welles reciprocated. He shared many of his confidences with the older man and always respected his opinion, even when he disagreed with it. What their friendship meant to Welles is best described in a letter he wrote suggesting a pattern of life for a young relative: "He should live with a friend whose opinion he regarded, whom he believes a friend and whom he would respect, whose advice he would listen to, and in short, one by whom, when there was occasion, he would permit himself to be governed."[6] His relationship with Niles went deeper than any other friendship he would form in later years. He was, however, becoming attached to his mother's Pennsylvania relatives, particularly the Lewiston branch. He persuaded his Uncle Elias to send his two oldest boys, Reuben and George, to Captain Partridge's Academy, now located in Middletown. George Hale remained only a year, returning to Lewiston when Partridge moved the Academy back to its original site in Norwich, Vermont. Reuben completed his course. In 1832 he accompanied his cousin Gideon to Washington, where they stayed at Gatsby's for a week or two before they continued on to Lewiston.

In Lewiston, Reuben paraded a bevy of local girls before Welles' appraising eye. Two young ladies caught his fancy. Lucy Alexander "is the main star," he confided to his cousin, "but Jane Houston is not without interest." Neither of the Pennsylvania girls responded to his tentative advances. Perhaps they found him too stiff and shy—he was certainly far from handsome; even then he was beginning to lose his thin, sandy hair. Reticent, easily embarrassed in the presence of the opposite sex, Welles could not have seemed much of a catch for the gay Lewiston and Bellefonte girls or their ambitious mothers. By now this area of Pennsylvania had cast off its frontier appearance—the crude primitivism that had so dismayed Welles on his first visit ten years earlier. But it still retained one characteristic of its recent past, a shortage of eligible and attractive young women. Lewiston, Bellefonte, and Towanda were not particularly good hunting grounds for a balding, nearsighted bachelor with marriage in mind.

Not long after Welles returned to Hartford from Lewiston early in 1833, Elias Hale died. His widow, Jane, was left relatively prosperous, but there were six children, four of whom were minors, and a complicated estate to be settled. Reuben, the eldest, who was clerking for an established lawyer in nearby Bellefonte, acted as executor. He leaned on Welles for advice and for the collection of certain debts owed the estate by Glastonbury relatives. Welles did what he could. He refused, however, to utilize against impecunious relatives the debt imprisonment law still on the Connecticut statute books. Apparently, Reuben and Aunt Jane Hale agreed with him, for they did not prosecute Elias Hale's penniless brother, Hezekiah, who was indebted to the estate for a large sum.

In his letters to Pennsylvania, Welles constantly urged Aunt Jane Hale to permit the younger children to visit their Connecticut relatives. Perplexed by the sudden responsibilities of widowhood, especially the future of her younger sons, John and James, and the education of her daughters, Mary Jane and Caroline, she was cautiously receptive to a family visit. Reuben and George thought that the girls should have the cultural polish of an Eastern school. They also agreed with Welles that there were more and better job opportunities for the younger brothers in Connecticut. The income from Elias Hale's estate would not stretch sufficiently to provide further education for all the minor children. Thus, James and John preferred to try their hands at the business prospects in Hartford so glowingly described by Welles. All were eager for the trip, and when old Samuel Welles added his invitation to that of his son, Jane Hale capitulated. Her youngest child, Caroline, would remain with her at home. Reuben would also stay for the summer to complete his law studies and wind up the estate. Dr. Curtin, a Lewiston physician, and his wife, a Glastonbury girl (one of Welles' childhood friends), agreed to chaperone the group. In early June, five Pennsylvania Hales converged on Hartford, to be distributed among various relatives in Glastonbury. Welles had made all the arrangements. He met them with four hacks at the steamboat landing near the foot of

Front Street. A wagon was in readiness for their luggage, which he himself accompanied on horseback to see that none of it became dislodged. But after performing these chores, he could not spare any time for the various reunions in Glastonbury because of urgent political commitments.[7]

President Jackson had already started the triumphal procession which would take him as far north as Concord, New Hampshire. Welles had been appointed one of Governor Edwards' special aides for the gala event. Both he and Niles were also members of Hartford's reception committee and would join the presidential party in New York City, for after the celebration they were to act as escorts through Connecticut. It is quite probable that Welles had the President's visit in mind as a special attraction for his Pennsylvania relatives. No doubt the part he expected to play in this national event was also calculated to impress them.

If this had been one of his motives, he succeeded admirably.[8] No member of the family was present at the ludicrous scene in New York when the wooden bridge between Castle Garden and the mainland gave way, dumping most of the presidential party into the shallow water and mud below. The President, who led the party on horseback, his tall beaver hat draped with a weeper (a badge of mourning he still wore in memory of his beloved Rachel), reached dry land safely. Most of those behind him, on horseback or in carriages, went down with the bridge, Welles and Niles among them. Fortunately, no one was hurt, but dignities were certainly ruffled from the drenching. Governors, Congressmen, Cabinet members, mayors, and magnates struggled ashore, some wigless, some horseless, all soaked to the skin. It took several hours before the horses and carriages could be disentangled and the illustrious ones made presentable enough to begin the parade. The President retired to a near-by hotel until all was in readiness for the march up Broadway.

Happily for Welles, the tour through Connecticut was free of such incidents, which were already being humorously caricatured by "Major Jack Downing" in the opposition press. Welles, crowded in with the dignitaries on the steamboat *Splendid*, felt for the first time in his life a vicarious sense of personal importance, sharing as he did in the public and official displays of honor for the President and his party. The buildings and warehouses surrounding the *Splendid*'s berth at the battery were crowded with New Yorkers who cheered long and loud as the little steamboat cast off. Then came the measured rumble of "a twenty-four gun salute as she passed the sloop of war *Vincennes*, moored near the Narrows—"her yards manned with sailors, the officers in full dress, all flags and pennants flying."

At six the next morning the presidential party left New Haven for Hartford. The procession moved north at a leisurely pace along the turnpike, which was lined with thousands of country folk who had come with their families from miles around to see the President. At Berlin, near the southern boundary of Hartford County, Mayor Williams and other city officials stood ready to escort the presidential party. The visiting Pennsylvania Hales were on hand to watch the grand parade through the city of Hartford. None had ever seen such a colorful display. And there, riding in the first carriage behind the President—who was on horseback, as usual—was cousin Gideon with Vice President Van Buren and Governor Edwards. How important he seemed as he whispered a word to the Vice President or the Governor or searched the crowd for his friends and relatives.[9]

The procession passed by the *Times* office, which stood on State House Square, and Welles looked up to wave a greeting, catching the eye of Mary Jane as she stood with her brothers at one of the windows. To an impressionable sixteen-year-old girl, cousin Gideon must have seemed scarcely less notable than Vice President Van Buren himself. Later in the day, when Jackson received at the State House, there was a personal compliment for Mary Jane from the Old Hero and from each member of the Cabinet in turn. All the other relatives, too, Welles introduced personally. It was a pleasurable and exhilarating day for the careworn editor, who had shown his relatives, his friends, and his political opponents that he was not only known to the greats of the nation, but enjoyed their confidence as well. Secretary Woodbury and Vice President Van Buren were especially cordial. Welles had some cause for complaint about Woodbury's previous treatment of him, yet the Secretary could not have been more complimentary.

Welles accompanied the presidential party when it boarded the steamboat *Water Witch*, which the ladies of Hartford had decorated with evergreens for the trip down-river. He was enjoying himself thoroughly, and he was reaping much political advantage from the tour. He had had a conversation or two with Van Buren and with Major Donelson, the President's nephew and one of his private secretaries. Jackson, who was beginning to feel the strain of the trip, always had a kind word when they met. Secretary of War Lewis Cass was jovial and companionable; Woodbury showed him "marked attention." Welles made himself useful in a variety of ways, yet he took care never to be obtrusive, and he was rewarded by being made a permanent member of the party for the remainder of the trip, a mark of high respect indeed.[10]

In his semi-official capacity, he attended all of the social functions where most of the feminine wealth and beauty of New England were on display. At Boston, as befit its pretensions, "we saw," said Welles, "the largest number . . . some were as handsome as I ever beheld . . . as wealthy as in the Union." Though he found the vivacious belles attractive, he wrote humorously to Reuben Hale, "I passed the ordeal as cold as an icicle, and as firm as a stoic." Feigned indifference merely concealed the fact that Welles, whatever his official connection might be, was an awkward, far from handsome, nobody from Connecticut. Among the sophisticated, inbred society of Boston, where family and money counted, who among the young and beautiful had ever heard of him? And he was certainly not the man to make up for these differences with any elegance of wit or manner. He had to confess to his cousin Reuben, who was far more gifted in the social graces: "I wish you could have had my place, for I believe you would have enjoyed it more and improved it better."[11]

Though Welles was unable to scale the lofty citadel of Boston fashion and society, he made a conquest in Hartford. Young Mary Jane Hale, naïve and gay, had been dazzled by her cousin's importance. To her youthful, uncritical eye, he was a man of affairs who seemed to know everybody from President Jackson to Bishop Brownell, who, in full canonicals, was almost as impressive as the President. Yet this busy cousin of hers was thoughtfulness itself. Courteous and attentive to his aged father, affectionate toward his younger brother Thaddeus, he treated Mary Jane and her brothers as equals and companions, suggested tours to Talcott Mountain, and arranged picnics in Glastonbury and rambles that included points of interest or culture in Hartford. Between times he was in the city, writing those endless columns whose finer points he was ever ready to discuss with his visiting relatives. Mary Jane learned he was a poet and a writer of stories as well as a politician and an editor—what surer way to the heart of a young Pennsylvanian girl, brought up strictly in remote and provincial Lewiston?

In Boston, the President suddenly became ill, and the cavalcade was abruptly halted. Welles immediately rushed home to make good his promise to Aunt Jane. He enrolled Mary Jane in the city's finest private school for girls—the Hartford Female Seminary. He did not do this until he had been assured by Niles, Professor Holland, and "several others on whose judgement I most rely" that the Seminary "has the highest reputation and is considered the best school" in town.[12]

Welles made an excellent choice. The Hartford Seminary had been founded ten years earlier by Catherine Beecher, eldest of the Beecher brood and a gifted educator. Ill health finally forced her to resign in 1832, but her position had just been assumed by John P. Brace, who carried on the enlightened tradition she pioneered. Mary Jane found herself among the young female elite, not only from the Hartford area, but from other sections of the state and from other states as well. The course of study was elaborate—music, drawing, geometry, geography, *belles lettres*—and it must have proved a challenge to a girl of Mary Jane's youth and background. Welles, concerned about her morals as much as he was about her education, put aside his anti-sectarian bias and arranged for her to board with Dr. North, whose house was conveniently close to the *Times* office—"only about fifteen rods west," he explained to Reuben. As for Dr. North, Welles would have preferred someone less religiously oriented. "A clever fellow," he wrote, "an ultra Calvinist, and the worst that I know of him is [that] he has at some former period been touched with fanaticism." "He will not, I think," continued Welles, "molest Jane with his notions, and has, I imagine, got pretty much over them himself." The important thing of course was that Mary Jane's social life during out-of-school hours would be strictly supervised, and she would be living almost next door to Welles' office. Tea in the afternoon with Dr. North and his family, not to mention the brown-eyed Mary Jane, would be an event after the daily stint on the second floor corner of Central Row.[13]

During the remainder of the summer of 1833 Welles saw much of Mary Jane, either at Dr. North's or on weekend trips to Glastonbury. The more she was in his company, the more he began "to question whether my feelings towards Mary were not nearer and dearer than those of friendship." Behind her demure yet sparkling pose, Mary Jane Hale was uncommonly perceptive for a girl who had just passed her sixteenth birthday. Under her gentle persuasion, Welles spoke of his ambitions, his frustrations, his work, and his friends. He talked of Washington, describing vividly for her the great personalities, those demi-gods of the Republic, who had been myths rather than men to her. Mary Jane soon came to appreciate that there were rare, if not great, qualities in this far from handsome man, twice her age, so shy and self-effacing at large social gatherings, yet so warm and stimulating, even forceful, among small groups—and always, it seemed, so kindly and considerate. She, too, began to think in terms "dearer than those of friendship," though neither communicated their feelings to the other.

They were so much together that sharper eyes than theirs took note of the occasional glances timidly exchanged at the various social affairs in Glastonbury. By fall, when Reuben Hale finally arrived from Pennsylvania, rumors concerning their relationship were all over town. They had even reached the ears of old Samuel Welles, to whom discretion (except in business affairs) had never been a virtue. One morning, while having breakfast with his two sons and Reuben Hale, the elder Welles, "in his blunt manner," alluded to the possible engagement of Gideon and Mary Jane. The old man favored such an alliance. Though the two were first cousins, he was not disturbed. He had grown up in a society where marriages of close relatives were a common occurrence. Gideon Welles was both startled and embarrassed by his father's forthright utterances. "It was the first allusion," he would explain later in an apologetic tone, "that had ever been made in my presence to a topic that so nearly concerns me."[14] Reuben Hale made no response. Nor did he encourage further conversation on the subject either then or at any time during his visit. After the incident at his father's table, Welles soon discovered from other sources the extent of the rumors. He concluded, and rightly so, that Reuben was aware of them, yet Reuben's reticence on the subject he found most disconcerting. Had not he and Reuben the year before agreed to exchange confidences? Still, Reuben kept his own counsel, and Welles was too shy to approach him directly on a matter of such delicacy. The month Reuben remained in Glastonbury was a time of trial and anxiety. Welles did take some solace from Reuben's silence: "knowing as I did the talk abroad, I gathered hope from the reserve, and permitted myself to indulge a belief that . . . you would not disapprove of my attachment." But he was troubled because he had fallen deeply in love with Mary Jane.[15]

On the day of Reuben Hale's departure, while Welles and Mary Jane were riding to Hartford together, he steeled himself to profess his love for her. Once he had stammered out his declaration, he gathered courage and "offered her all." He explained his financial affairs (not altogether promising at that time), his habits, his likes and dislikes— "everything has been communicated to her," he wrote, "and my temporal welfare is in her hands." Mary Jane sat composed during this outpouring, neither encouraging nor discouraging his suit. Welles took comfort from this and thought she was "not indifferent to my happiness and trust we may share the world . . . together."[16] She refused, however, to make any avowal of affection for him. Welles, who had business in Washington, accompanied Reuben as far as Amboy, New Jersey. Several times during the trip he had been on the point of confiding in his cousin, but was not able to summon up the courage. On his return, while riding with Mary Jane to Glastonbury, "we talked over the subject, but so reserved was Mary, and such the objections she raised that I almost despaired of success." Eventually Mary Jane's heart prevailed over her hesitation. Secretly, they pledged themselves to each other.[17]

It would have been unthinkable for Welles to communicate directly with Aunt Jane. Reuben was the male head of the family, at least in name (Jane Hale was a strong-minded woman), and propriety dictated that Welles write him first. He had other reasons, too, for taking Reuben into his confidence. A close friend as well as a cousin, Reuben, he assumed, would be on his side should there be any objections. Mary Jane not only agreed; she insisted that her brother be consulted. On November 6 Welles wrote Reuben Hale, declaring his love for Mary. He asked him to use his "good offices with other relatives . . . should you approve my sentiments and actions."[18]

There, he had done it. Now came the anxious period waiting for a reply. If the mails went through without delay or mishap, and if Reuben answered promptly, Welles could expect a letter in a week to ten days. By November 15 Postmaster Niles had noticed Welles' mounting interest in the Pennsylvania mail. Young John Hale, who was boarding in Hartford and attending Trinity College, relieved Welles' fears a trifle by explaining that Reuben was probably not at Lewiston but attending court in Huntingdon. Yet the impatient lover was in an agony of suspense, turning over and over in his mind what Reuben might say. "There are moments," he said, "when I cannot control my mind sufficiently to ward off doubts or to suppress hope." Mary Jane did not help matters by exercising that ancient feminine perogative of acting the coquette. Though Welles pleaded to have her miniature taken for him, she would not consent, nor was she willing to encourage him further until Reuben, "her favorite brother," was heard from. She even expressed some doubt that he would approve. This remark cast Welles into the depths of despair, or as he put it, brought "my mind into a state of almost nervous excitement."[19]

Finally, on November 23, the long-expected letter arrived. He dared not open it in the post office or at the *Times*, fearing that if it contained bad news he could not control himself in a public place. He waited until he could be alone in his room at the United States Hotel before he broke the seal, "and then it was done I confess with apprehension." When he read the opening lines in which Rueben approved of the match, he put down the letter. "Conjecture my feelings, I cannot describe them. It was one of those moments of unalloyed happiness, that we seldom experience in this world, but which once experienced can never be forgotten." Welles, in all his happiness, was much too practical a man to assume that Reuben's consent was all that was necessary. A most formidable problem yet remained—the consent of Aunt Jane, without which Mary Jane had said she could not marry him. He was wary about Jane Hale, in whom he had detected a certain, indefinable coolness toward him beneath her cordiality. He had to have Reuben's advice on how she should be approached. Whatever course he suggested, Welles would follow to the letter.[20]

Meanwhile, John Hale had grown restive under the strict tutelage of Professor Beardsley at Trinity. Welles had painted in bright terms the business opportunities of Hartford, but the young man had been unable to find a situation that appealed to him. He spoke of going to New York or Philadelphia in search of a position, a possibility that alarmed Welles. More a man of the world than he would admit, he feared the temptations that the big city would hold out to such a restless, naïve, young person as John Hale. These fears he had communicated to Reuben, who passed them on to Aunt Jane. That matriarchal figure peremptorily ordered her young son to return home. There would not be, if she could help it, any exposure to the oyster houses, the dramshops, or to the painted ladies of the sinful metropolis for any of her male offspring. John obeyed, much to his disgust, leaving for Lewiston in mid-November, before Welles had heard from Reuben.[21]

John Hale was aware of the rumors that existed of an engagement between his sister and Welles. Both Mary Jane and her ardent suitor now worried that he would inform his mother and put such a construction on the news that he would prejudice her against their romance. When Aunt Jane wrote her daughter in early December, absolutely forbidding any match and urging her to return to Lewiston at once, the lovers were certain that John Hale had been responsible. They were mistaken; Reuben had explained the situation before his brother's arrival.[22]

Welles was disconsolate when he learned of Jane Hale's decision, but he would not give up. Speaking through Reuben, he pleaded with his formidable aunt that Mary Jane be at least permitted to remain for the winter and complete her school term. "Aunt will," he hoped, "on further reflection, think that this is best for Mary. She will part with her at some day, and perhaps for some more distant and less hospitable region." Welles, trying to anticipate Jane Hale's objections, wrote that he would make any sacrifices and would "accede to any terms that Aunt may please to require." Two days later, he wrote directly to Jane Hale for the first time, repeating in substance what he had already written to Reuben.[23]

She did not reply to Welles; instead, she wrote her daughter, demanding that she return home at once. As Mary prepared to obey her mother's summons, Reuben advised Welles that "nothing can prevail on [Mother] to let her remain in Connecticut." He had ridden in a heavy snowstorm from Bellefonte to Lewiston, hoping that he might persuade his mother to change her mind. She had made her decision, however, and Reuben could not move her. All he could recommend to the now-distraught Welles was that he accompany Mary Jane as far as Philadelphia, and then, if he had business in Washington, to remain there for a possible trip to Lewiston. Welles agreed: "as to going to Washington, I can make *business* there at any time, *especially* if I may take *Lewiston in my route.*"[24]

Welles and Mary Jane left Hartford on December 26, reaching Philadelphia two days later. He lingered there with her, visiting friends until January 2, and then left sadly for Washington. The capital, which he had come to enjoy, seemed a prison to him; even politics had lost its savor. He amused himself as well he could by roaming about the city, attending presidential levees, reading and writing in the Library of Congress.[25] By January 14 he was becoming restless and extremely depressed. In addition, he was worried about Mary Jane, who as far as he knew had not as yet reached Lewiston. He was much relieved when he heard from Reuben that she had arrived safely on January 20, 1834. In the next mail his hopes for a visit to Lewiston were dashed. Neither Reuben nor Mary Jane could make any impression on their mother, who said she would prefer that Welles not visit Lewiston on his return to Hartford. He had no alternative but to return home. The spring campaign was already beginning, Biddle's money panic was at its height, and the Democrats were under heavy attack. Welles' presence was demanded.[26]

He returned to Hartford in mid-January, depressed beyond measure, only to receive another crushing blow to his all but shattered romance. Aunt Jane wrote him a stern letter forbidding any further correspondence between him and her daughter. At this point most men in his position would have given up. Welles would not. He wrote letters to Reuben which were meant for Mary Jane, and he buried his disappointment and his heartbreak in fighting as he had never fought before to hold the party together in the face of wholesale desertions. In the midst of the campaign, Russell, the publisher of the *Times*, became ill. Welles had to take over all his responsibilities—overseeing the compositors, handling the business details, making up the paper, besides attending to his own heavy editorial and political duties.[27]

In early May, Mary Jane defied her mother and wrote directly to Welles. When she told her mother about it, Jane Hale decided on direct action—a lecture to Welles on his conduct and a demand that he stop bothering her daughter. She was still adamantly opposed to the marriage. "I will never change my opinion," she wrote Welles in late June, ". . . drop all correspondence—if there are any more letters . . . they will be sent back. Just let my child alone." Again, Reuben Hale interceded with his angry parent. Mary Jane, too, became more critical. At least Welles ought to be permitted a visit as a relative, if not as a suitor.[28]

Finally, in August, Jane Hale capitulated to the extent of not opposing a visit. She must have realized by now that her continued opposition was alienating both Reuben and Mary Jane. When Welles learned of this auspicious change he dropped everything—his newspaper duties (Russell was still sick, but Niles agreed to carry on temporarily), the special congressional election campaign just beginning, the grave illness of his father—for a lightning trip to Lewiston. He and Mary Jane had several lengthy discussions with her mother. They must have been convincing, because on the day he left Welles said, "Aunt treated me with the utmost kindness and affection and was all that I could wish and feel."[29]

The happy man hurried home and buried himself in his newspaper and political chores, while maintaining a stream of letters to Pennsylvania. There was still nothing definite from Lewiston. By November it was clear that the eighty-year-old Samuel Welles was dying. Welles and his brother, Thaddeus, took turns at his bedside. Oliver had broken with his father. Neither he nor his son Joseph "called to see him or inquired concerning him." On November 13, 1834 at eleven in the morning, the old man died, thus breaking Welles' final, personal link with the past—with the Revolutionary generation. He was able to view the event with a calmness and resignation that was unusual in such a sentimental man. He had worshipped his father, perhaps more as a symbolic figure than a real person. Though he would cherish his memory, he had finally, at the age of thirty-two, gained his personal independence.[30]

On the practical side, Samuel Welles had divided his estate of about $25,000 (the probate figure, it was probably closer to $50,000) equally between Gideon and Thaddeus. Oliver, it would appear, had been given his legacy earlier. He was not mentioned in the will, but Samuel Welles' notions of fairness to his family would indicate that provision must have been made for his unfortunate eldest son. Samuel Welles' death removed Jane Hale's most important objection to her daughter's marriage. Welles now had sufficient means to support a family. In view of his penchant for exaggerating his financial affairs, he probably led his Aunt to believe that his father's estate was much larger than it actually was. The wedding date was set in accordance with Welles' wishes. They were married on July 16, 1835, just after Mary Jane's eighteenth birthday.[31]

# CHAPTER 11

# Hard Times

STATE COMPTROLLER WELLES brought his bride to Hartford during the late summer of 1835. As was traditional with young couples of their social class, they boarded in a suite of rooms at the United States Hotel. Devoted to his gay young wife, Welles gave as much time as he could borrow from his many tasks to provide her with whatever simple diversions the little city offered. They visited Sinclair's "peristrephic panorama," which depicted the life of Napoleon, marveling at the realism of Waterloo, saddened by the simple burial at St. Helena.[1] There were lectures at the college, and variety shows and concerts, but no plays (they were forbidden by municipal ordinance) at the city's three private and two public halls.

Though Welles clung to his nonconformist beliefs, he attended Christ Church with Mary Jane. During the many weekends they spent in Glastonbury, where he maintained his legal residence, the couple attended St. Luke's, the only Episcopal church in town. Their social life was centered in Hartford—teas and suppers with the Calvin Days, the Major Allens, the Nileses. Welles purchased a pianoforte for Mary (he had dropped the "Jane"), and enjoyed listening to her sing and play the sentimental ballads of the day. He indulged her one extravagance, a stylish wardrobe, considering her most glamorous in black silk.

When he became postmaster of Hartford, in January 1836, Mary was pregnant. Her health and his new public responsibilities made it necessary for them to find a permanent home in the city. The fact that both of them enjoyed gardening was further incentive for the move. They would rent a house at first, while they looked for a suitable purchase, preferably near the Nileses on Main Street, within walking distance of the post office and the *Times*.

Welles' happiness was complete—he had a charming young wife, the prospect of a family, a home of his own, a position of social, economic, and political importance. His financial circumstances were excellent— he had in excess of $5000 a year, an income that placed him in the top stratum of Hartford society. Most of his friends supported their families comfortably on a fifth of that amount. Yet the Welleses did not live ostentatiously. Mary was a frugal housekeeper, and the rental of their comfortable but by no means elaborate house was relatively modest. Welles was able to save perhaps three-fourths of his annual income, which he invested prudently—some in Western lands through Henry Ellsworth, the remainder in personal loans, mortgages, and stock in local enterprises. He looked ahead to a period of domestic tranquillity for at least the next six years, during which he would manage the post office, conduct his own business affairs, and pursue his hobby of writing political articles on topics of current interest. He would continue his work as chief correspondent and party organizer, but he wanted to free himself from the daily drudgery of the editorial chair. His plans were realized in part when he turned over the editorial direction of the *Times* to Alfred E. Burr, an able young printer and writer who had attracted his attention, but he still averaged a nine-hour day. What many would consider a normal work load seemed light to Welles, who reveled in his new-found freedom from the discipline of the daily deadline.[2]

The respite, if one may call it that, lasted barely a year. Had it not been for his Federal salary, his visions of financial independence would have vanished. The great panic of 1837 and the long depression that followed was about to break. His investments in Western real estate for a time would yield a fraction of their former income. Finally, the economic collapse would initiate a period of intense political activity that would far surpass any of his former labors.

Welles had foreseen possible disaster in the multiplication of state banks, railroad projects, and other internal improvements. He and his friend Niles had been worried also about the distribution of the Treasury surplus, which would add some $20 million of specie to the overheated economy. Niles had voted for it in the Senate, but reluctantly, explaining that, at the time, distribution seemed the only way for the Treasury to dispose of "the huge and embarrassing surplus."[3] The deposit banks, Welles feared, would be the major beneficiaries of distribution. This heavy infusion of federal funds would strengthen the resources of existing banks while encouraging the incorporation of new banks. Too many bank notes were circulating now, and at substantial discounts. Distribution would simply increase the issues. He also worried about the political implications of Connecticut's share—upwards of $750,000—on the party organization. Then there was the most vexing question of all: how would the first installment be distributed, on what basis, and for what ends? The only practical way, he thought, was payment to the towns on a proportional basis. But this meant that the more urban towns such as Hartford and New Haven would receive much larger shares than the rural townships. The old cry of dictation would be raised, the city-country conflict aggravated.

Governor Edwards called a special session of the legislature in December 1836, to devise a means for the use of the money. Surprisingly, the legislators drew up a compromise plan that was acceptable to most of the towns. The funds would be turned over to them on a proportional basis to be managed as the towns saw fit, the proceeds to endow local schools. Thus, the measure would provide some abatement in property taxes, and that found favor with farmers and urban householders alike. Town fathers saw an opportunity for more low-interest personal loans, while local politicians grasped at the patronage potential in administering the funds.

Welles himself had offered the most radical plan. In the *Hartford Times*, under the pseudonym "Hampden," he suggested that this allotment and all subsequent sums be used as the capital for a state bank, wholly controlled by state authorities with appropriate safeguards for their good conduct. Such a bank, he argued, would force the private banks to mend their ways on note credit and on political activity or force them out of existence.[4] Of all the ideas advanced, that of Dr. Douglas was the most farsighted and probably would have been the most beneficial. Arguing from the Benthamite slogan—the greatest good for the greatest number—Douglas proposed that the capital be lent to citizens at 6 per cent, the income to be used for the founding of what he called "manual labor schools." These institutions would educate teachers "of common schools," who would then teach mechanical skills and generally improve the wretched state of primary education throughout Connecticut. Students would be drawn, in accordance with Douglas' humanitarian instincts, from among the poorest families, and orphans would "be preferred in the selection." Though poor, they also had to have demonstrable skills; their selection was to be made on a merit basis. Neither Welles' plan, nor Douglas', nor a host of others favoring special interests—the colleges, private academies, railroads, turnpikes, and the like—aroused any marked interest among the legislators. Under the circumstances, the unimaginative plan they adopted was sensible; above all, it avoided any serious political divisions.[5]

Preoccupied with the political implications of distribution, Welles did not at first connect it with the financial collapse, which began in May 1837. The speculative instincts of the state banks and their "rag" currency, he thought, were primarily responsible. Well before the panic, two Connecticut banks, the Stamford Bank and the old City Bank in New Haven, were under a cloud, their officers suspected of gross mismanagement. In early 1836, more than a year before the panic, the "young Democrats" of New Haven were circulating a petition that the financial affairs of both banks be investigated by a committee to be raised at the special session of the legislature. Welles saw to it that the Democratic majority in the legislature did not become so wholly involved in the distribution issue that it overlooked the petition of the "Young Democrats." Despite the delaying tactics of bank partisans, the legislature did appoint a special investigating committee and gave it powers to examine all books and records. The City Bank was of particular interest to Welles, because Governor Edwards and William Ellis had for sometime been closely associated with its officers and directors. Ellis used it for the deposit of his customs collections and Edwards was a large stockholder in his own right and as the executor voted the stock of the Eli Whitney estate.[6]

When the special committee finally made its report, which demonstrated mismanagement in both institutions, all Connecticut banks, in concert with those of New York and Boston, had suspended specie payment. The coincidence raised up the specter of the Eagle and Derby Bank failures—seeming to prove the validity of the anti-bank editorial policy Welles had been pursuing in the *Times* for seven years. Suspension had influenced the committee report too. A majority recommended that the charter of both banks be rescinded. The legislature promptly repealed the Stamford bank charter, but bank Democrats and Whigs in New Haven and Fairfield counties were strong enough to save the City Bank in the house, only to have the vote reversed in the senate. Welles had a hand in that. Then he and his loyal band of Loco-Focos in the house managed to stir up enough country members so that a majority concurred with the senate action.

Foolishly, Governor Edwards vetoed the act repealing the City Bank charter. Though the Governor had the constitutional right to veto a legislative act, in practice he had violated the long-standing precedent of legislative supremacy.[7] A more flagrant abuse of his power was his intimate association with the bank in question. The conflict of interest was so open and brazen that Welles seized upon it to purge Edwards, whom he had suspected of disloyalty ever since his strange behavior in the appointment of Niles to the United States Senate. How could a party whose official slogan was "equal rights" retain as its titular leader a man who did not apply "equal rights" to his own official conduct? Welles and his associates would not tolerate what they regarded as treason to party principles. A measure of the disaster Edwards had brought upon himself can be seen in the attitude of the party leadership in New Haven, the Governor's home territory. In response to a sharp summons from Hartford, Ellis, who had favored the bank, quickly withdrew the customs funds. The Ingersolls, who were certainly not unfriendly to the City Bank, fell quickly into the ranks behind Welles and the Loco-Focos. Levi Woodbury, who had been nurturing the City Bank and its political influence, had drawn back as soon as he detected a probable insolvency.[8]

As panic deepened into depression, Welles' political burdens grew heavier. The *Patriot and Democrat* group opened a skirmishing action on "the Hartford regency"—part of a national conspiracy, thundered Eldridge, that was destroying the people's confidence in banks and perpetuating the depression. Truman Smith, another member of that ubiquitous Connecticut clan, was stirring up the Whigs to what he sensed would be winning issues in the campaign of 1838: the reckless financial measures of the Jackson administration and hard times. Smith, a giant of a man (he stood six feet seven inches and weighed 300 pounds), was an adroit propagandist, an energetic and capable organizer. Having finally found a strong leader and a plausible issue, the Whig party was developing a hard, lean muscular look that boded ill for the Democrats, who were still unable either to drive off or to contain their troublesome conservative faction. Welles anticipated a difficult contest.[9]

Much would depend, he thought, on the new administration's patronage policy. Long overdue was a thorough overhaul of federal appointments in the state, the removal of weak men like Ellis and obvious enemies like Phelps ("pseudo Democrats," as Dr. Charles Douglas called them), and their replacement with energetic, loyal organizers who would invigorate the entire party apparatus.[10] Increased federal subsidies for loyal newspapers (more extensive printing of official news and announcements) would make them less dependent on local advertising revenue, especially from Whig sources. There were still areas of the state where no Democratic paper existed. Money must be raised to establish them, and Welles counted on some assistance for this purpose from the federal government through official advertising. An avowed object was to have Ellsworth removed, not only because of the hostile influence he represented in Washington, but because his place, the Patent Office, was a valuable asset in bartering for the loyalty, the influence, and especially the organization work that Welles deemed necessary to win the state election. A final and urgent requirement was, as Welles put it, a reform in the Executive appointment policies. In plain words, he was asking that more federal jobs be awarded Connecticut.

No Connecticut man had held a Cabinet post since the administration of John Adams, when Oliver Walcott was Secretary of the Treasury. Henry Ellsworth, the Commissioner of Patents, was the only federal officeholder representing Connecticut. Even Rhode Island, Niles said in disgust, had two *chargés d'affaires*. "For more than a quarter of a century," he complained indignantly, "Massachusetts was New England as to federal appointments and for some years New Hampshire has been New England." Connecticut Democrats recognized that their state, one of the last Federalist bastions in the Union, could scarcely have expected recognition from the Republican dynasty that had held the presidential office since 1801. Nor did they have just cause for complaint during the Jackson administration, when their state twice cast its electoral vote for his opponents. Since 1835, however, the Democrats had been in complete control. Connecticut had cast its vote for Van Buren, and Niles had done his best to defend the administration on the Senate floor.

Of course the opposition, whether the conservatives in the Democratic party or the Whigs, had made political capital out of Welles' failure to do more for the state. These negative pinpricks served only to amplify the need for more federal patronage of any class, including fifth-rate $500-a-year clerkships. Niles was more concerned than Welles about this particular situation. Highly critical of the monopoly held by local Washingtonians on the minor offices, he castigated "the miserable lopers in the District . . . who seize the spoils while the hardworking Democrats in the states get nothing."[11]

From Connecticut it seemed that everything was working at cross purposes in Washington. The *Globe* was praising the deposit banks as democratic institutions, an editorial policy that Welles thought politically unwise and morally unjustifiable. He decided that the paper lacked spirit and interest, its columns jammed with editorial matter that bore little relevance to the important issues of the day. "I frankly say," he wrote Silas Wright, "that I think there is a want of tact, of energy, of industry and of skill on the part of the *Globe*." Welles had sensed in the vigor of the Whigs a "determination to oppose the next administration violently and implacably, whatever may be its acts. . . ." All the more reason, he felt, that the administration paper in Washington should set forth clearly the challenges to be faced and provide some outline of how they might be met. He was anxious about the state of public opinion, both national and local. The *Globe* had been expressly established to set the guidelines for the Democratic press. From where Welles stood, it was failing in this vital function. Blair was living in the past, editing the paper to suit Jackson, when he should be looking ahead to anticipate the policies of the new administration.[12]

Some of Welles' criticisms were apt. Blair was still relying on his old editorial formulas, still tilting for the Old Hero whose villains should have been largely imaginary ones by now. Yet the fault was Jackson's, not Blair's. He had dictated his successor with the understanding that his policies would be continued. The Jackson mystique continued to pervade Washington during the early months of 1837 and would continue to do so well after March 4. If the President-elect himself seemed as entranced as ever by the dominating personality of the imperious old man in the White House, it would seem a trifle unjust to criticize the editor of the *Globe*, who owed everything to Jackson.

Niles and his party associates in the Senate were unable to penetrate the cloak of secrecy which Van Buren cast over his moves and his purposes. "No one unless it be Mr. Wright," said Niles, "appears to have been consulted. . . ." Senator James Buchanan of Pennsylvania had buttonholed him on the subject. A shrewd operator with a disconcerting habit of peering obliquely at one, Buchanan was well known among the Democratic Senators for trading confidences. "Of course I told him nothing," Niles wrote Welles. As Niles remembered the conversation, "Buchanan thought all the secretaries would be retained & that the change of Administration would only be a succession not a new administration." If this were true, and Niles was inclined to think so, then it would confirm what had been charged by the Whigs and "is precisely what Mr. VB ought to have avoided." He predicted gloomily that the new administration "will commence so radically wrong, that it will be found difficult, if not impossible, to get right." He doubted whether the party could be held together for the next four years, "by a timid, cautious, temporizing course of policy. . . ." "VB wants to do justice to his Eastern friends & particularly Connecticut," Niles observed perceptively, "but the problem is his stock in trade is small as it has all been disposed of by his predecessor."[13]

By the summer of 1837 Welles' faith in the President as a politician's politician had been considerably shaken. He wondered how Van Buren would act to meet the financial crisis. Would he propose novel and dramatic measures that would capture the imagination of the people—would he dismantle the deposit banking system, for example, and take the federal government out of the banking business? (Welles favored that possibility.) Or would he let the economic distress run its course? These were tormenting questions to state leaders who were already under heavy attack from their own constituents, not to mention the partisan opposition. That the Whigs were clamoring for the recharter of a National Bank was to be expected, but it was startling and not a little shocking that many good Jacksonian Democrats were joining in the demand. "This is real pressure," warned John Cotton Smith, a Litchfield associate who was nephew of the last Federalist Governor, "different from the fictitious pressure of '34."[14] The Whigs had an issue. After his disappointment on patronage, Welles was doubtful that the administration would devise and push the kind of bold measures he believed necessary to cope with the challenge. The original Jacksonians whom he had praised eight years before and among whose members he counted himself seemed prematurely aged in their political life. Were Blair, Kendall, Hill, the President, so bereft of ideas, so politically inert, that they were unaware of the dangers creeping up around them? In response to Welles' Macedonian cries came a kind of bland resonance that all would be well if he relied on the old Jacksonian maxims and the time-tested tactics of '28.

What he could not accomplish by letter, perhaps he might by personal interview. At least he could brief the important personages in Washington on the campaign he had just waged against the Whigs in Connecticut. Some plain talk might help dissipate the political haze that had settled over the White House. In mid-May of 1837, Welles, his young wife, and their infant daughter, Anna Jane, left Hartford for a long-delayed visit to Lewiston. They spent some time in New York, then went on to Philadelphia, where they separated, Mary and Anna Jane traveling to Lewiston, Welles going on to Washington. He paid his formal visit to the President, then hurried to the Post Office Department for a talk with Kendall about political and patronage problems, returning soon after midday to his room at Gatsby's. There, to his surprise and delight, he was greeted by a presidential messenger, who handed him an invitation to dine informally at the White House that evening. The time set for dinner was 4 p.m., giving Welles ample time to eat a light lunch, organize his thoughts, and change into more formal attire. When he arrived at the White House he found that the President's son and private secretary, Martin, Jr., and Levi Woodbury were the only other guests.

Van Buren may have had his faults as a public man, but these were not for lack of social grace. One of the most accomplished hosts in the nation, he entertained with a flair whether his guests numbered thirty or three, although his dinners were apt to be elaborate—a soup, a fish, then six or seven meat and game courses, as many different wines, followed by at least four different desserts. After he had put his Connecticut guest at ease, they went in to dinner.

In marked contrast to the rather splendid and formal cuisine, Van Buren was relaxed, affable, and entertaining, "very easy in his manners, plain, direct, straightforward in all his remarks, and very social." For three hours, during the innumerable courses, the wines, the liquors, he led the discussion on political and economic topics. When the opportunity afforded itself, Welles complained about the conduct of the *Globe*. Neither Woodbury nor the President responded directly to his criticism of Blair's editorial conduct, but the President did ask if William Holland, Welles' editorial and political gadfly, had the ability to conduct a new administration paper in Washington. Van Buren knew of the feud between the two men; and one can only suppose that his question was posed more to test the political atmosphere in New England than to elicit an opinion which he knew would be biased. It was an awkward moment for Welles, what with Levi Woodbury, massive and taciturn, sitting opposite him across the presidential table. Welles managed to divert the conversation to New England matters after a word or two about Holland's undoubted ability as a writer.

Talk passed to other topics. Van Buren queried his Connecticut guest on the financial crisis. He had already called a special session of Congress to convene on the first Monday in September for the express purpose of devising measures to meet it. How severe was financial distress in the Northeast? What were the political implications? What measures ought to be taken by the administration to relieve distress? And how should the party react to Whig charges that the Democrats had deliberately led the nation into financial ruin for political advantage?

Welles replied that economic distress in New England was general, that the Whigs were capitalizing on it and would, he predicted, make the rechartering of the Bank of the United States a major issue in the 1838 campaign. He acknowledged that the Democrats in Connecticut would have a hard fight on their hands. Defeat was likely unless the administration came out with a vigorous new program—divorcing the government from the state banks, for example. New England, he mentioned, was being flooded with worthless paper currency from Western banks, and the people had lost confidence in the deposit bank system.

During the long trip to Lewiston, Welles pondered the implications of his conversation with Van Buren and Woodbury. On June 9, 1837, shortly after his arrival in Pennsylvania, he wrote a long letter to the President, reiterating what he had said about the *Globe* and stating again that Holland had "ability, acquirements, and, I think, industry, but I have very little confidence in his honesty and sincerity." Welles was unusually candid in suggesting that Henry Ellsworth, through Woodbury, was responsible for recommending Holland to the President. "Perhaps, Mr. Ellsworth had not said much to you on the subject, but I presume he has to Mr. Woodbury. . . ."[15]

Welles' choice for editor of the new paper was William Leggett, then editing his own journal, the *Plain Dealer*, in New York City. Welles thought Leggett was not only a brilliant journalist, but one of the finest exponents of "pure democracy" in the land. Admitting that Leggett had recently been at odds with the administration on its anti-abolition policy, Welles was quite certain that he could be brought around easily to the President's views on this controversial subject. In fact, he went further, suggesting that Leggett was "not such an abolitionist, as the interested would represent him to be." Unknown to Welles, the President admired Leggett, but he must have recoiled in horror at the thought of such a radical editing the administration's official paper in Washington. Welles, so practical in most things, seems to have been governed more by his heart than his head in recommending the erratic Leggett for the most sensitive editorial post in the nation. Yet his grasp of the problems besetting the administration and of Van Buren's public image was insightful. The party, in the Northern states, at least, had to shake off the Jackson aura. It had to evolve some imaginative program, like "divorcement," that he and his associates could use to stimulate public opinion. Van Buren desperately needed a man of Leggett's creative qualities, but of sounder health and more stable behavior. Bryant could have done the job, or Welles himself, or perhaps even James Gordon Bennett, but the President approached none of these editors. Blair remained the spokesman.[16]

During the summer of 1837—a month after Welles dined at the

White House—Van Buren queried a small group of congressional leaders for suggestions on how to deal with the financial crisis. Niles, who had impressed the President by his sound grasp of political and economic affairs, was included among the select list. On June 10, 1837, Van Buren wrote him for advice. Highly flattered that the President should think him worthy of the task, he began a comprehensive analysis which took him three weeks to prepare. Welles had just returned from Pennsylvania, and when he learned of the President's urgent request, he showed Niles a letter on the subject he had prepared but never mailed.

Welles thought that a majority of the people would oppose any attempt by the federal government to bail out or bolster up the deposit banks, but he conceded that in any discussion of possible alternatives "there is general diversity and doubt." Banking had been so long established "and is so interwoven with all business transactions—the present generation has been so accustomed to paper money and incorporated banks—men know so little and have thought so little of society without them," it would be difficult to arrive at any consensus worthy of the name. He cited as examples of the prevailing confusion the chaotic actions of the various state legislatures after suspensions. Welles saw two completely opposite alternatives—paper money to be abolished as a currency, or banking "be left like all other business to free competitors, subject to general laws but open to private enterprise." On federal policy he wanted "the government divorced from banks of every description." He had no more faith, he said, "in a cordon of state banks than in one United States bank."

With Welles' document as a beginning, he and Niles hammered out a seventeen-page letter to the President that supported the sub-treasury plan and tried to anticipate objections to it. Gradually they came to the conclusion that no distinction existed between money as a public medium of exchange and credit as a private medium of exchange. Niles summed up the interests involved: currency, the banking system—both state and national—commerce to some extent, politics and political principles, division of power between state and federal governments and even the distribution of power within the federal government between the Executive and the Legislative branches.

With a problem involving so many diverse factors, the two men could find no easy or simple solution. The state banking system, they thought, might be resumed, but only after "a restriction upon the issue of bills of a high denomination" and the establishment of a sound and uniform ratio of specie to note issue for all banks. By divorcing itself from the banks, the federal government could provide the standard. Then, said they, "the specie rises to its proper level, and the paper remaining where it was, the difference between the two becomes apparent." Remove this "factitious connection between credit & currency whereby they act and react upon each other, to the great derangement of each," and let the state banking system "stand upon its own strength or fall by its weakness." They admitted that there was not enough specie in the country for the government to hoard through its revenue powers, that this would have a depressing effect on the normal operations of the business world. But spartan measures had to be adopted—the nation's credit was involved, and if that fell, everything would go. Eventually, state bank and credit policy would be forced to adopt the metallic standard, bank notes rising and falling in value according to the specie in their vaults.[17]

It was a thoughtful paper, whose principal weaknesses were a heavy emphasis on constitutional limitations of federal power and a rigid adherence to bullionist theory on money and credit. Admirable for an emergency situation, the Niles-Welles laissez-faire approach would restore the public credit, so essential for foreign exchange, but would let private credit shift for itself. Meanwhile, public debate in the various party presses had reached a high pitch on what course the administration should take. The hard-money line of Benton and of the more radical Democrats in the North and West was coming under heavy attack. Thomas Ritchie's *Richmond Enquirer* joined with the conservative Democratic papers in New York City in ridiculing any exclusively metallic currency. The deposit bank system was defended as the only practical and constitutional method to save the economy without resorting to another national bank. What was needed, they declared, was a more complete involvement of federal resources with the state banks. And Senator Nathaniel Tallmadge of New York echoed their sentiments in a public letter. At home, the *Patriot and Democrat* joined the hue and cry, belaboring the *Times* and Bryant's *Evening Post* for their stands on hard money and the separation of the banks from the state. When the *Globe*, on July 22, complimented Tallmadge's letter, ridiculing "the chimerical scheme of an exclusive metallic currency," Welles was outraged.[18]

He wrote Van Buren a vigorous letter protesting the *Globe*'s policy and advising the President that it was lacking "in firmness and consistency at this crisis." The most efficient party workers, he maintained, "are totally and absolutely opposed to the incorporative banking system. I earnestly, sincerely beg that the administration may not be in any way connected with these pernicious institutions." Welles' letter reflected his own personal concerns that the conservatives had captured the President. In common with other radical Democrats, he had been uneasy about the administration's attitude toward reform since Van Buren's lackluster inaugural. All of his doubts, however, were dispelled when he read the President's message to the special session of Congress. Van Buren came out strongly for the sub-treasury system along lines suggested in the Welles-Niles memorandum. "The great issues are now found for discussion and guidance of public opinion for years to come," wrote the relieved Senator Niles, with pardonable expansiveness, to his co-worker in Connecticut.[19]

Debate in the Senate began at once. Senator William C. Rives of Virginia led off with a defense of the deposit banks, as expected, but the unpredictable Calhoun supported the administration plan. There would be no solid South against the administration's new policy, as some Northerners had feared. Niles dominated the second day of debate. After he had spoken for ten minutes, everyone realized that his was going to be one of the most comprehensive explanations of the proposed financial measures. For three hours he ranged over the entire field of banking, currency, and credit as he understood it. Step by step, he analyzed and dismissed each of Rives' contentions, declaring that, in sum, they would merely encourage speculation and inflation and would result in the total destruction of the nation's credit. He admitted, as he had earlier advised Van Buren, that the independent treasury system would work temporary hardship on the already hard-pressed business community. To ease the transition, he recommended an emergency issue of treasury notes. The *Globe*, which had previously been temporizing on the independent treasury question, was impressed. For the first time in eighteen months his speech was given full coverage and was well reported. The old man at the Hermitage read Niles' remarks and praised them warmly.[20]

As the debate over the independent treasury continued through the fall of 1837, Niles added to his stock of arguments, always seeming to anticipate Rives' various points and making effective rebuttals. His comments followed the orthodox hard-money theme with one notable exception—a speech he made on September 23, 1837, in which he sought to explain a paradox that troubled many close students of the problem. Since 1831 American imports had exceeded exports, and for the preceding three years the exchange had totaled almost $120 million against the United States. Yet during this same period there had accumulated a surplus of specie from foreign exchange in excess of

$32 million. "This," said Niles, "is in direct violation to the ordinary laws of trade," unprecedented in this country and perhaps in any other. He attributed the apparent contradiction to "the agency of credit in our foreign trade, and by loans and the sale of stocks in England not connected with trade." Bankers in Europe who dealt in American securities and "who loaned credit to our importing merchants as long as American merchants could import goods on credit obtained abroad," created a favorable exchange. Niles had cast new light on a complex problem, and made an original contribution to the debate. Martin Van Buren would draw heavily on these ideas for his third annual message, in which he traced the panic and depression through the banking system of the United States to its ultimate source—as he put it, "the money power in Great Britain."[21]

The radical Jacksonians were educating themselves in the intricacies of international finance. At the same time they were broadening their argument against "the money power" to include a popular whipping boy—Great Britain. It was a canny political stroke, yet it was also essentially a valid assessment of one aspect of the depression of 1837. Senator Niles and his collaborator Gideon Welles had set a train of thought in motion that would be a recurring theme in the entire Progressive tradition—the conspiracy of international bankers who stood ready at any opportune time to rob American prosperity for their own corporate gain.

The phalanx of speakers for the administration made a much better showing than the opposition did, but the issue was doubtful even after Calhoun confided to Niles "that the whole state rights party of the South was coming into support of the bill." On October 3 Niles jubilantly reported to Welles that "the great reform bill" had passed in the Senate. His optimism was premature. The House defeated the measure by thirteen votes. There were enough conservative Democrats from Virginia and New York, inflationists and deposit-bank men, to give the Whigs a majority. Niles stated flatly that "all the gambling land speculators E & W voted against the bill." He had known the vote would be close but had hoped to the last that the administration forces would eke out a victory. When John J. Crittenden, the Whig Senator from Kentucky, brought the news to the Senate chamber from the House, Henry Clay sprang up, grinning broadly, and led his party colleagues in three "Hurrahs." "Our friends," said Niles, "meet the reverse firmly & do not appear to be at all discouraged."[22]

But one powerful figure in the Democratic party was discouraged. William L. Marcy, Governor of New York, had been aghast at the

President's course. His own administration was inextricably involved with the New York state banks. He feared dire political consequences, a conservative-radical split over the independent treasury system. Sorely beset by illness and other personal difficulties, the overworked Governor had stolen a few weeks from the cares of his office to visit his mother in Southbridge, Massachusetts. On his return, he stopped over in Hartford and made directly for the post office.

Postmaster Welles was surprised and flattered when a clerk announced the burly, dark-visaged Governor. Still far from well, Marcy was troubled that his friends and political associates seemed not to understand his dilemma. The two men talked for the better part of the day—Marcy half-apologizing for his early and intemperate opposition to the Van Buren administration, Welles explaining his reasons for supporting the President's financial measures. The discussion in some measure quieted Marcy's fears of a "political tempest." As he was leaving in the late afternoon, he said that his administration would not be "antagonistic to . . . Van Buren and in due time he trusted all would come right."

In view of Marcy's splenetic references some months before about a "Jacobinical spirit abroad," about "the hideous monster of locofocoism," his sudden descent upon Welles, whom he knew to be as radical on banks as any in the party, is somewhat mysterious. He may have wanted to understand more perfectly the radical position, its rationale for the independent treasury system. More probably, he wanted political information about the state of affairs in New England. His apologetic attitude suggests that he was mending fences and meant to have Welles convey this to Washington. Yet Welles made no reference to the visit in his daily correspondence with Niles nor in his frequent letters to Van Buren and Wright.[23] A sixth sense must have warned him to keep clear from New York politics, where the opposing factions were beginning to line up and where intervention on his part would be misconstrued. He had enough on his hands trying to carry his own state for the party without meddling in New York affairs. Though Niles had acted the disinterested statesman during the great debate, he was also running for re-election to the Senate. His great independent treasury speech, which made up seven columns in the *Globe*, was edited, reprinted in the *Times*, bound in pamphlet form, and broadcast throughout Connecticut. The state's delegation in the House had voted solidly for the administration bill, but Niles was critical of their behavior— "entirely indifferent & inactive as to any influence at home."[24]

Well before the election, the congressional delegation was so frightened of arousing further hostility from the state banks they stayed away from the party caucuses that were trying to revive the independent treasury bill. "If we escape a defeat," Niles wrote Welles in early 1838, "it will astonish all here, friends and foes." Until the very end, however, he hoped that the Democrats would retain control of the state senate. When he learned of the Whig sweep—they had taken control of both houses of the legislature and had won by a majority of about 4000 votes—he had grave doubts whether the party would recover. By his analysis there were some 16,000 "sound and firm" Democrats and about the same number of orthodox-Whigs. "All the rest," he said, "are mere floating votes upon which there can be no dependence. Of this number from 2-3,000 are twaddlers or mercenaries who fight for *pay*; the others are in a dependent condition hanging onto the bank factions and wealthy individuals in business . . . exposed to intimidation, caution & bribers."[25]

Niles' own personal disappointment was acute, though he tried to make light of it. He had come to enjoy Washington. He was working hard, driving himself beyond his physical resources, but he had made many close friends and he felt he had "acquired a reputation here and in the country." Even Henry Clay admired the pluck and the analytical ability of the plainspoken Connecticut Senator—"a man of high and honorable feelings . . . of superior order of talents."[26]

As soon as it was learned in Washington that Niles would not be reelected, many came forward to assist in securing him a Cabinet appointment. Rumor had it that there would be several resignations in the near future, and Niles certainly deserved consideration. He did nothing to discourage these moves on his behalf, but privately he was not optimistic that they would lead anywhere. Well acquainted with the President's political style, he judged that when and if Van Buren made any changes personal qualities would have little to do with his decision. "He wants to reinforce his Administration & it certainly wants it enough & he thinks Connecticut is of but little consequence. . . ."[27] Undeterred, Welles cautiously approached Silas Wright about a Cabinet post for Niles.

Wright answered in his usual candid manner. The Attorney General, Benjamin Butler, had tendered his resignation, and he was reasonably certain that Mahlon Dickerson would soon leave the Navy Department. Lest Welles misinterpret him, however, he said, "I have had but one rule for my own conduct upon these points . . . and that is never to speak to the President in relation to the selection of a member of his cabinet, but upon his own solicitation." He confirmed Niles'

earlier judgment that neither post would go to Connecticut despite the
President's high regard for its Senator. While Levi Woodbury remained in the Cabinet, Van Buren simply could not name another
New Englander. And he could not spare Woodbury for reasons of state
as well as politics. The heavy-featured, heavy-bodied, slow-moving
Woodbury was anything but slow-thinking. A superb administrator
and a tireless worker, he was managing with distinction the complicated affairs of the Treasury Department and the deposit banks, seeking to rescue as much of the government's funds as possible without
further depressing the economy. Politically, Woodbury's friendship
with Jackson, his strong ties with the conservative but loyal wing of
the party, made him invaluable to a man of Van Buren's temperament.
For the President was still trying desperately to balance sectional and
factional interests and still deemed himself under heavy obligation to
the Hermitage. The popular mind of the South and the West viewed
New England with distrust—a land of fanatical abolitionists, cranky
Congregationalists, Websterian bankers, and fraudulent peddlers. In
Van Buren's judgment, one member of the Cabinet from New England
was all the party would tolerate.

Woodbury had been a strong advocate of the deposit bank system.
He had also sought to strengthen the conservative elements in the various states by his policies and his patronage. This Van Buren knew and
probably sanctioned, yet when the deposit system proved inadequate to
the crisis of 1837, Woodbury rallied behind the sub-treasury plan. The
powerful Secretary had by no means given up his long-range plans of
blending conservative and radical Democrats in the North; but, after
Tallmadge and Rives openly opposed the administration on the sub-
treasury issue, he ceased to encourage the conservative bank factions in
Connecticut and elsewhere. When the *Patriot and Democrat,* which
was openly espousing the recusant Democrats, charged that the federal
government had offered bribes to secure its support, Woodbury acted
promptly to disassociate himself from the Hartford bank faction. Henry
Ellsworth wrote Welles directly, denying that any bribe was offered
and in effect reading the *Patriot and Democrat* out of the party.[28] Although this was welcome news, Welles continued to distrust Woodbury, whom he knew was friendly with conservative Democrats—men
such as Toucey, Judson, and Phelps—in his own state. They had all at
one time or another supported the bank faction, but now found it expedient to disavow their former connections. At the earliest opportunity, Welles thought, Woodbury and his "twaddlers" would again
oppose him. For five years, it seemed, whichever direction he took, he

was sure to find the burly figure of the Secretary and his ubiquitous associate, Henry Ellsworth, squarely in his path. Right now Woodbury's presence in the Cabinet was blocking the advancement of his friend Niles, and with it his own political future.

Though he had given up all hope of a Cabinet appointment, Niles resolved to continue building his reputation as a spokesman for the administration on the Senate floor until the end of his term. His course was not entirely disinterested. He might, in the time remaining, enlarge Van Buren's obligation to him. Niles spoke repeatedly on topics of national interest and made a specialty of attacking Tallmadge and Rives whenever they sniped at the administration. On many occasions he drew praise from the Hermitage. "I have read Mr. Niles' reply with great pleasure," wrote Jackson to Blair, "it is just such a reply as Rives merited & has prostrated this apostate in the minds of all honest and impartial men, forever." Much of Niles' material and most of his ideas were supplied by Welles in his personal correspondence and in the editorials he wrote for the *Times*.[29]

While the industrious Niles was defending administration policies with wit and vigor, the President had another opportunity to gratify his ambition, by appointing him Attorney General. Felix Grundy, an old Jacksonian from Tennessee who had replaced Benjamin Butler, resigned from the Cabinet when he was elected to the Senate. But Van Buren appointed Niles' friend—the rich and talented bibliophile Henry D. Gilpin—instead. It was still the safer course, apparently, to have Pennsylvania and New York (James K. Paulding had received the Navy Department) represented in the Cabinet than to have two men from the six New England states. Niles was better qualified than either man for either post. Paulding, a popular author, had served as naval agent in New York, a sinecure post; Gilpin was more of a raconteur and literary dilettante than a lawyer.

Just before the end of Niles' term, Levi Woodbury was appointed Chief Justice of the New Hampshire Supreme Court. For a few days there was speculation that he might retire from the Cabinet, and Niles' hopes for his place rose accordingly. He took the unusual step of asking Welles to plead his suit personally with Van Buren. "I know," he wrote, "that the President has great confidence in you, not only in your democracy & attachment to him but also in your talents, judgment & discretion."[30] But Woodbury decided to stay on, and nothing came of it. Niles' term expired. He journeyed home in mid-June, his personal and political future at a low ebb. A year earlier his paper mill in

Windsor had burned down, involving him and his brother, Richard, in heavy losses. He still had enough income for his modest wants, but he was comparatively poor, which meant that he would have to devote a good deal of time to his private affairs. His years in Washington, while they had been rewarding, had been frustrating too. He returned to Hartford in an embittered mood, angry at what he chose to regard as shabby treatment accorded him by the leader of his party. Disillusioned with politics, worried about his investments, he seemed tired and strangely withdrawn for such an outgoing man.[31]

After a few months of rest, he regained his composure, improved his business affairs, and renewed his interest in politics. He accepted his party's nomination for the governorship in 1839, when he knew defeat was certain, and again in 1840, when no one else was willing to risk his political reputation against the Whig juggernaut.

Welles took personal charge of both campaigns, as he had done for several years past. Refusing to admit, even to himself, that the Democratic cause in 1840 was hopeless, he mobilized all of the federal officeholders. Believing that men will listen to a speaker when they cannot be persuaded to read a paper of any kind, he put together a list of the party's best orators. The speakers, including candidate Niles, were sent on what Welles called "missionary tours" throughout the state. "We want missionary efforts—preaching—stirring up at this time of all others," he wrote Chauncey Cleveland in March 1840. Of course he did not neglect the power of written persuasion. In fact, he converted the *Times* into a propaganda sheet, printing extra editions of the paper for the political guidance of party workers and the political education of the average readers. Bundles of Niles' and Toucey's speeches on the independent treasury were franked out to loyal postmasters in the state. Where any were deemed doubtful—and some were—these materials were sent to a more trustworthy man.

Welles did concede privately that "the Whigs are desperate as devils." For two years they had controlled a majority of the towns, and now they were barring Democratic leaders from examining the voter registry lists. Truman Smith, under the expert tutelage of Thurlow Weed, was exerting constant pressure. Like the Democrats, Whigs all over the nation looked to the Connecticut election as the first test of the Harrison-Tyler ticket, and like the Democrats before them, they leaned heavily on promotional techniques—more heavily than their opponents ever had—to influence the vulgar or the ignorant. "The Federal electioneers," said a Litchfield Democrat, "acted up strictly according to the instructions of their circular." Those who were in debt were offered "loans and accommodations . . . bank and factory screws were applied with all their prodigious force."[32]

The continuing depression was a major theme of the campaign. Democrats insisted it was being perpetuated by the banks—that the independent treasury system was the all-purpose remedy. Whig speakers and pamphleteers ridiculed these arrangements and advanced two novel ideas of their own which made direct appeals to workingmen and debtor elements everywhere. Both were simplicity themselves. One dealt with the currency, the other with the tariff. On currency, the Whigs preached quantity—the more bank bills in circulation, the easier for them to find their way into a laborer's pocket. Hard-pressed Democrats found that the money approach to the working man "has been one of the hardest things we have had to encounter. . . ." The tariff issue in the hands of the Whigs became an equally clever and equally spurious device to catch votes. First suggested by "Honest John" Davis of Massachusetts, in a speech on the Senate floor, the party line on the tariff contrasted the pauper condition of labor in Europe with what was described as the free condition of labor in the United States. Low wages and unemployment were specifically a result of the steady reduction of the tariff on key industries under the Compromise Act of 1833.

Besides such planned publicity and specific instances of intimidation, the Whig leadership purchased votes with a prodigality hitherto unmatched, offering free newspapers, pamphlets, refreshments, colorful parades. Niles estimated that from $40,000 to $50,000 was being spent in the state for campaign purposes, $14,000 in Hartford County alone. The Democrats were also carrying the burden of the depression, which was now more than three years old, and they faced the opposition of abolitionists and temperance men. Neither of these pressure groups had a distinct organization as yet, but each would vote the Whig ticket rather than deliver the state to what they regarded as the party of slavocracy and drink. Their ranks would be swelled by over 1000 bank Democrats who were expected to be in the Whig ranks for the first time. That the Niles ticket in defeat was able to poll 26,000 votes, almost 3000 more than the previous year, was a political miracle, considering the odds against it.[33]

In May of 1840, Welles attended the Democratic convention in Baltimore that renominated Van Buren for the presidency. After the proceedings he went on to Washington with a pocketful of grievances against the national management of the party and the conduct of the

*Globe.* He had experienced at first hand the power and the tactics of the new Whig organization. The party chieftains must be made to recognize the dangers which lay ahead. Silas Wright was the only person of consequence who took Welles seriously. "Even he was not fully aware of the storm that was raging, though he was the only member of Congress whom I saw that took any rational view of the subject . . . a strange and fatal security was prevailing at Washington." Ordinarily he would have followed Wright's policy and not presumed to advise the President unless called upon to do so. That he took the unusual course of appealing to Van Buren shows how gravely he viewed the situation.

The President received him graciously, as usual. After the amenities, his visitor came directly to the point. Drawing on his own observations of the Whig campaign in Connecticut, he proposed that the party be completely reorganized and that "two or three efficient editors [should be] appointed to assist Blair in conducting the *Globe.*" The President listened intently to Welles' soft-spoken but earnest indictment of party management. If he felt that the Hartford postmaster had broken the rules of decorum or had seemed presumptuous, he gave no sign of irritability. Leaning back on a richly brocaded sofa, Van Buren heard him out. As he had done before, he asked Welles for suggestions of editors who might help with the *Globe.* Without hesitation, Welles named Isaac Hill. He told Van Buren that Hill was "always irritable and often perverse in conversation," but, as an editor, "he possesse[s] great tact and unwearied industry."

Welles knew that Van Buren disliked Hill, but the times demanded that all personal considerations be put aside. The President mulled over what he said for a moment, then rose indicating the interview was over. He walked to the door with Welles, and apparently in an effort to cheer him up, said a few kind words about the *Times* and the good fight the Democrats had waged in Connecticut. If he had meant to be thoughtful (which he probably had), the overly sensitive, deadly serious Welles took Van Buren's soothing remarks as mistaking "my convictions for despondency."[34]

The editor's frank comments did make more of an impression on the President than Welles had thought at the time. A regular reader of the *Hartford Times,* Van Buren had told Niles before Welles' visit that he considered it and *The Patriot* of New Hampshire (Hill's paper) "two of the ablest Democratic journals in the country." One of the nation's shrewdest politicians, the President would never dismiss lightly the views of an editor whose ability he admired and whose loyalty he knew to be beyond suspicion. "I was not as insensible to the dangers which surrounded me in 1840," he wrote Welles at a later date, "as I appeared to be, but for the best reasons abstained from emphasizing my apprehension."[35]

Only a day or so after that conversation (or, possibly, the same day), Amos Kendall, pleading ill-health, resigned as Postmaster General. The President immediately came to a decision which, considering the close timing and the unwonted speed of his action, must have been influenced by Welles' remarks. He tendered the office of Postmaster General to Niles. There is no doubt that Van Buren's conscience had been troubled for some time about his failure to reward in any significant fashion the loyal Democracy of Connecticut, the ability and industry of its ex-Senator. Yet the appointment must be viewed also from its practical aspects.

The Welles' interview had alerted Van Buren to the fact that the administration needed a man like Niles, whose ready pen and quick, logical mind would be of invaluable assistance during the hard campaign ahead. If anyone could invigorate the *Globe*, it would be Niles, with Welles behind him. For once the immediacy of the campaign problem had overcome Van Buren's fears of having two men in the Cabinet from New England. Niles gratefully accepted the post on May 12. As he had been the most vigorous and certainly the most eloquent Senator from Connecticut since the days of Oliver Ellsworth, so now he had become the first Cabinet member from the state in over forty years.[36]

The new Postmaster General was delighted to be back in Washington, delighted at his reception from old friends. Vice President Richard Mentor Johnson greeted him with a great hug, Secretaries Forsyth and Poinsett, though less demonstrative, beamed. At first he was overwhelmed by his new and unfamiliar duties, but he soon grew accustomed to the routine of the department, "the herculean labors of the service" he had been led to expect. Indeed, he became so immersed in his administrative work that he neglected his political chores—a bureaucratic vice that he had frequently attacked in the past. When Welles wrote him in early August, calling attention to the inadequacies of the *Globe*, he defended Blair, refusing to admit the truth of his friend's charges.[37]

Welles' remarks had been very much to the point. The editorial force of the *Globe* had been declining steadily since 1837. Niles claimed that Blair had insufficient help, but he soon learned that the slight, peppery editor would not delegate any of his authority to an assistant.

Nor would he accept any material for publication unless it filled at least one column with a minimum of editing. Blair much preferred an article or a speech that would fill from five to six columns. Imperceptibly, the dynamic editor of the Jackson administration had fallen into slothful ways, and by now quantity and ease of page makeup, rather than quality, marked his conduct of the *Globe.* Welles was correct when he said the average reader simply would not wade through six or seven columns of fine type when it was obvious the editor had not bothered to remove the turgidities and the digressions.

Apart from his unflattering remarks about makeup, Welles was specifically critical of the *Globe*'s abandonment of "equal rights" and its refusal to consider corporations and special privileges as issues in the campaign. He remembered all too clearly when Blair had seemed about to espouse the cause of the deposit banks three years before. To Welles, fundamental Democratic principles were being disregarded on this, the eve of what he knew was going to be a desperate contest. He wanted the *Globe* to launch a slashing attack on political interference by corporations. He wanted it to expose what he considered the cant of "Honest John" Davis and the paper-money slogans. Above all, he and other radical Democratic editors wanted fresh ideas from Washington which they could exploit as the Whigs were doing. How, Welles asked, could he carry the battle into the enemy territory by attacking the abolitionists as the *Globe* was doing, with five- and six-column rebuttals to their arguments? That issue had best be buried for the time being, he thought. Nor did he think it wise to impugn with such vehemence Harrison's patriotism, his character, or his mental abilities. True, the Whig candidate refused to be drawn out on any of the leading issues of the day. His ambivalence should be hit hard, but not by libeling the old Indian fighter and war veteran, who, in the popular mind, retained much of Jackson's folk-hero characteristics. He had beaten the British at the Battle of Thames, an engagement that ranked with New Orleans as a great military victory in the War of 1812. He had proven himself an able commander of troops, a good administrator, and his senatorial career had been unexceptionable. Leave Harrison alone, Welles counseled; attack the Whig politicians who were using him (and, in Welles' mind, most shamelessly) for their own special ends.

His criticism of the *Globe* and his analysis of the weaknesses in the Democratic campaign strategy were in the main correct. But it would take some time before reports from other field workers and editors would be able to penetrate the protective screen around Van Buren.

Niles, though he excused Blair, was still fresh enough from active campaigning to recognize the truth of Welles' over-all comments. He relayed them to Amos Kendall, whose health had improved and who was now assisting Blair in the conduct of the *Globe*. That veteran journalist and keen politician was highly indignant. In his reply to Niles, he justified the Democratic line, defending the *Globe* vehemently. Though he was one of the cleverest editors and manipulators of the hero symbol, he was falling into the same trap he himself had helped design for John Quincy Adams in 1828. The sacred vestments of American nationalism, the heroic mantle of Andrew Jackson, was now on the other side. How it got there, by what cynical operators was it being used, and for what selfish ends? This was the crux of Welles' position. It was a good position, probably the only kind of campaign strategy that had any chance of success, but it took smashing Whig victories in Kentucky and Indiana to shake Kendall out of his complacency. On August 13, after hearing the discouraging news, he virtually admitted to Welles that he had been wrong. "The Democratic party," he said, "have contented themselves with talking and working themselves into a self-deceiving confidence which deceives also their friends abroad."[38]

Niles, emerging from the new and unfamiliar administrative problems of the Post Office Department, was able to pay more attention to the campaign. His reaction was more immediate and explosive than Kendall's. "There is a strange confidence bordering on infatuation in certain high functionaries here that bodes us no good," he wrote Welles. It had dawned on Niles, as it had on Kendall, that the rules of the political game were undergoing a sudden and rapid change. "This is a new era in political warfare," he mused, "and the old modes of conducting campaigns being abandoned on one side & new weapons & modes of fighting adopted, we are compelled to meet them in this with the same weapons or such others as these new tactics may require." As for the *Globe,* he retracted his defense of a week before. "Blair," he said, "has done nothing and is doing nothing. He has not a single copy of any speech or document on hand." The criticism may have been just, but the fault was not Blair's alone.[39]

The adroit fiscal hand of Blair's partner, John C. Rives, must be held responsible for many of the *Globe*'s editorial weaknesses. By 1835 he had made himself and Blair rich men. Though the editor of the *Globe* still possessed a lean and hungry look, he was more interested in his country house at Silver Spring, his growing family, and his increasing wealth than in giving his paper the close attention it demanded. One may forgive Blair for eschewing the labor of the editorial office, but not for his obstinacy in holding onto the reins when his major interests lay elsewhere. Evidences of Rives' business-management policies—profit over party success—had been accumulating for some years. Niles and other Senators had listed this error among the bill of complaints they filed against the *Globe* as early as 1836. Yet not only had these same sharp practices continued, they had increased.

Welles must have viewed the singular and rapid change of opinion in Washington with some grim satisfaction. Unfortunately, it had come too late. And Kendall, whom Welles regarded as "an admirable essayist," had become too much of a mandarin in thought and style to do the kind of job he judged essential. The President refrained from using the prestige and power of his office to assist his immensely capable, and by now thoroughly alarmed, political managers. Besides Kendall, Welles and Niles were supplying Blair with material; so also were Silas Wright and James Buchanan. As late as September 1840, after half a dozen important states had gone Whig by large majorities, Niles reported "the President still stands firm & thinks he will be elected."[40] Niles had been deceived by Van Buren's outward demeanor. Actually, as the President would explain to Welles in 1843, "I gave up in fact all hopes of the election the moment I saw the Whigs were determined to carry it at all costs & by any means and were plentifully supplied with the sinews of war."[41]

For months the streets of Hartford—normally dark, quiet, and very nearly deserted after sunset—were alive with Whig torchlight parades. Small contingents from neighboring towns would make their noisy way past the *Times* office, groaning, cat-calling, and firing blank charges at the upper windows of Central Row. They were on their way to the Whig log cabin that had been knocked together on the corner of Trumbull and Asylum Streets. The anticipated uproar on their return caused Welles to abandon his customary evening talks at the *Times* office, for it could be expected that the cider, whiskey, and rum dispensed by the Whig workers in wooden dippers and gourds would have done their work well. Late in the campaign Alfred Burr, who was now editing the *Times,* found it expedient to darken the windows of the office when the Whigs held mass rallies in the city. Whig managers converted the state into one huge Methodist camp meeting, where the rhetoric and the parades were heightened by campaign songs (gospel style) and catchy slogans, liquor (where appropriate—Whig managers did not want to lose the temperance vote), broadsides, badges, pamphlets, and speeches.

It must have seemed like a Mad Hatter's Tea Party when starchy old Federalists such as General Nathaniel Terry and Timothy Pitkin donned coonskin caps at great Whig rallies. The more cynical Democratic leaders charged demogoguery and resolved to out-Herod Herod in the next campaign. Others, of a more idealistic bent, were sorely troubled at the ease with which their revered common man deserted the party of the common man for the Whig show in the big tent. After witnessing this spectacle, Welles would never again be able to recapture the verve he once possessed, the optimism, the sheer wonder of unleashing for the general good the promethean forces of democracy. Unwilling to admit that he and others of his kind bore a large share of the responsibility for the Whig-showmanship of 1840, he began to search for a new moral cause that would purify a debased electorate. He would not be quite the Democrat he was before, but he loved his party and its Jeffersonian principles as Bunyan's Christian loved Zion. Ahead lay the narrow road, straight as a rule, and bordered on both sides by political, social, and economic perplexities. Would they and their party survive the perilous journey? This was the question Welles asked himself after the Whig triumph of 1840.[42]

# CHAPTER 12

# Low Ebb

THE YEARS BETWEEN 1840 and 1845 were a time of personal distress and of mounting frustration for Welles. The visible recognition he craved, the ironclad control of the party he desired, had not been realized. Twice he was elected comptroller of the state, an honorable though scarcely prestigious office. His desire for a federal post of appropriate status and dignity had become almost an obsession. He was no longer able to tolerate the inconstancy of men on whom he had relied and to whom he had given his friendship and support. If for no other reason than his accumulated grievances, he needed the satisfaction of showing his enemies and rivals that he was an influential man among the great of the Democratic party.

Welles' personal life in Hartford—so pleasant during the early years of his marriage—had been marred by sickness and sorrow. He had recently lost his second son, Edward, a winsome lad of four, and was grieving deeply. Mary was unwell. Anna Jane, his eight-year-old daughter, on whom he doted, had never really recovered from a near-fatal attack of typhoid fever. She and his first-born son, Samuel, an eight-months-old baby, had been stricken at the same time. Little Samuel suffered great pain before he died, and the daughter hovered between life and death for weeks until her fever finally subsided. Welles was beginning to despair whether she would ever enjoy a normal, happy life, or would even reach maturity. While he watched his daughter—the victim of some mysterious, chronic complaint, unable to play with other children—memories of his own fragile, bed-ridden mother crowded his mind, contributing to his sorrow, his sense of helplessness.[1] Long-thwarted ambition, personal tragedy, and some economic distress (for two years now he had received no outside income) undermined the control he usually imposed on his emotions. All of his pent-up anguish, his feelings of hostility, came to a head in early December 1844, and, unfortunately, they were discharged upon his only real friend, Niles, who had been re-elected to the Senate two years before.

Shortly after Niles reached Washington for the short term of the twenty-eighth Congress, he was approached by an old associate and fellow mess-mate, John Fairfield of Maine. The slight, swart Senator wanted to be New England's representative in the new Polk administration. Witty and popular, Fairfield had served in Congress, had been twice elected Governor of Maine, had been a leading candidate for the vice presidential nomination, and had certainly been a major factor in swinging his state behind Polk. Fairfield did not aspire to a major position in the Cabinet. He had his sights set on the Navy Department, a post of material interest to his own state and to all of maritime New England.[2] Niles had scarcely settled himself in Washington when the Maine Senator, handing him a sheaf of recommendations, asked if he would deliver them and a recommendation of his own to the President-elect. Without pausing to reflect on its possible consequences, the Connecticut Senator was happy to comply with a legitimate request from a long-time friend and political associate.

Unaware of any injudicious action, Niles detailed the entire transaction to Welles. The letter, with its praise of Fairfield's qualities, put Welles into a cold fury. Such ingratitude! was his immediate response, such a callous indifference to the welfare of a friend who had been so loyal and self-sacrificing for almost twenty years! Niles' letter contained not even a hint that Welles had any claims, no inquiry as to whether the Senator should make any effort in his behalf. In his reply Welles could not suppress his disappointment.[3]

Niles now realized that he had unwittingly offended his closest friend. He regretted his action and was willing to try for a recommendation from the Connecticut delegation, or if Welles preferred, from himself alone, though he was not optimistic about either course. "If it fails in its immediate object," he wrote, "it may lead to the offer of some other place which you may be disposed to accept," but his gesture of good faith came too late. Welles had already mailed a stinging indictment which charged Niles with "a coolness and want of zeal" in advancing his interests. The Senator was shocked at this intemperate outburst. Angry, repentant, and defensive by turns, how was he to know that Welles desired any service from him, when the subject had never been mentioned? "I had thought of you for the post office department," said Niles, "but," and here he made a practical assessment of the situation, ". . . I had so little confidence in the success of the attempt that I doubted whether it would be worth the while to make the attempt."[4]

Niles was being brutally candid. If party considerations were to determine the makeup of Polk's Cabinet, Fairfield stood first in New England. If personal obligations were to be the criteria, then George Bancroft had the better claim, for he had been instrumental in effecting Polk's nomination at Baltimore, and his ties with Van Buren and Wright were as close as Welles'—though somewhat tarnished by his actions at the convention. Both men enjoyed national reputations— Bancroft as the nation's foremost historian, Fairfield as a distinguished public man for the previous decade. "They have held high stations," Niles reminded Welles, "and although distinguished official stations do not afford any conclusive evidence of a man's talents, qualifications or merits, yet there is more importance attached to them than they deserve. . . ."[5]

Meanwhile, Welles had recovered his poise. On December 14, he explained the personal and political tensions he had been under and begged the Senator's forgiveness. Niles accepted the apology gratefully. A rupture in their relations, which would have wounded both, was narrowly averted. Never again during Niles' lifetime would Welles permit himself to doubt his friend's honesty and sincerity. That he had done so in that near-fatal letter of December 8 shows the toll that the past four years had taken on his normally controlled temperament. To his friends in Hartford, he seemed the same thoughtful husband and loving parent, the good neighbor, freely giving of himself to the cultural and material improvement of his city. But inwardly, his self-control had been eroding for some time, a process that had started when the new Whig administration had summarily dismissed him from the Hartford post office in late March 1841, even though his term of office as specified in his commission had not yet expired.[6]

After the debacle of 1840, the Connecticut Democrats wandered in the political wilderness for two years. By 1842, however, the fortunes of the political wheel finally came round to their advantage. President Tyler had been read out of the Whig party, which was now floundering without strong Executive support. The easing, to some extent, of the depression offered Democratic editors and orators an opportunity to reassert their economic and social doctrines, and they quickly grasped it.

Welles had not changed his mind about the evils of corporations.

"We must shake them off," he wrote Franklin Pierce, whose recent resignation from the Senate he lamented, "and preserve individuality, which always carries with it a responsibility that corporations do not and can not [have], or surrender our liberties."[7] But, much to his regret, he was forced to make some compromises with his political conscience. Noah Phelps, whom he detested, went on the ticket. His personal choice for the governorship, Chauncey Cleveland, proved to be not as reliably radical as Welles had assumed; nor was he pleased with the new congressional delegation. He had unsuccessfully opposed the nomination of Thomas H. Seymour for Congress from the Hartford district; he liked Seymour personally, but distrusted his judgment.[8]

None of his colleagues, except Niles, could be considered sources of strength for what Welles thought was the only important political question: Van Buren's renomination for the 1844 election. He had, as he would say later, "identified any political aspirations I may have entertained" with the ex-President's candidacy.[9]

Niles was crucial to his planning. Welles expected him to push Democratic–Van Buren principles on the Senate floor with the same vigor and ability that he had shown during his earlier term. As in 1836, Welles was ready to supply him with ideas, arguments, and telling phrases which would be used in speeches or in debate on the Senate floor, reprinted in the party press, or, if especially pertinent and effective, published in pamphlet form.

Everything was knocked askew during the winter of 1842-43 when Senator-elect Niles became seriously ill. He had not seemed able to cope with day-to-day problems since the death of his devoted wife, Sarah, after a short illness on November 23, 1842. In the early spring of 1843 he suffered a complete nervous breakdown, becoming more irrational as the weeks went by. "It is melancholy, most melancholy to see him," Welles wrote to Van Buren on June 13. "His physicians think he may travel in two or three weeks—I shall be satisfied if he can be got abroad in double that period." By mid-July neither Welles nor Niles' brother, Richard, felt they could cope any longer with his deteriorating condition. The afflicted man would be rational at times, then he would sink into a fantasy world of vivid hallucination.[10] During one of his infrequent periods of normal behavior, Welles prevailed upon him to visit a mutual friend, Dr. Amariah Brigham, who had left Hartford to superintend the New York State Asylum in Utica.

At the peak of his all-too-brief career (he died at fifty), Brigham was one of the best known, most controversial figures in American medicine. A pioneer specialist in mental disorders, and a fine surgeon in the tradition of Philip Syng Physick and Benjamin Rush, he, like them, had spent years in medical apprenticeship, including study abroad. He moved to Hartford during the early 1830's, just when the city was experiencing the height of the second Great Awakening. Alarmed at the sudden rise in the incidence of hysteria, he linked such mental disorders directly to emotions stirred up by the revivals in progress. A man of action as well as a scientist, Brigham published two books in quick succession on abnormal behavior, stressing the connection between religious excesses and mental diseases. In fact, he made bold to charge revivalism with major responsibility for an admitted increase of insanity. These polemical works brought down on his head every evangelist of note and many distinguished members of the orthodox ministry as well. Criticism, if anything, sharpened his interest in mental disorders. He broadened his novel psychological studies, and he fearlessly lectured on such sensitive topics as the mental aspects of sex to medical and lay audiences. Yet his interests were not confined exclusively to the professional sphere. Well-versed in subjects other than medicine, he was soon drawn into the Welles-Niles circle. Through their efforts, and over sectarian and political opposition, Brigham was appointed superintendent of the Hartford Retreat, a position he left in 1842 to manage the larger New York State Asylum. It was quite in keeping for Welles to suggest a visit to the congenial Brigham, and for Niles to be receptive. After all, Brigham was an old friend and a true Democrat.[11]

In late July 1843, the dutiful Welles accompanied his emotionally disturbed friend to Utica. Shocked at the sick man's appearance, Dr. Brigham persuaded Niles to remain with him at the asylum. Despite the careful attention he received, his physical and mental condition grew worse during the remainder of the summer and fall. He refused to eat, lost weight, and had fewer rational moments. "His whole thoughts are absorbed & his mind overwhelmed, with the idea that he is condemned of God—cast off—to be eternally damned, that he can not die—though he wishes to—that he is to be buried alive . . . that he had not been baptized properly by the right name. I have great anxiety about him and regard his recovery as doubtful," said the experienced physician, who had rarely seen a case of this kind that did not terminate fatally.[12]

Yet Brigham persisted, with gentle but firm efforts, in directing his patient's interests away from himself to other topics. Even during Niles' worst periods of depression, Brigham commented, ·"occasionally I can interest him a little in other subjects and he will read the newspapers, etc., but this lasts only for a short time." His mode of treatment, more intuitive than scientific, eventually began to achieve some results. By January of 1844, Niles had, in Brigham's words, "regained his flesh & began writing friends, taking an interest in his business & giving directions how it should be managed." Welles and Richard Niles took turns making the tedious trips to Utica, so that every two weeks the convalescing Senator could count on a visit from his best friend or his brother. Both men were concerned about the political situation, and after consulting with Brigham, Welles broached the idea of an early return to Washington. The Doctor approved for therapeutic reasons—warmer weather, the diversion of renewing old acquaintances. But the patient flatly refused to go south. The mere thought of the Senate raised feelings of complete inadequacy. It had taken all the energy and strength he could muster to make a mark in that chamber five years earlier, when his mental and physical resources were unimpaired. All he wanted was repose, his home, and his garden. He wrote a letter of resignation to Governor Cleveland, which he asked Welles to deliver personally.[13]

A month later Niles was so much better that his correspondence was almost entirely devoted to politics—both state and national. He was under the impression that he had resigned, yet there was no query nor any mention of the fact that his letter had not been acknowledged. He finally learned the truth when he read an extract from one of his political letters in the *Hartford Times*. Welles had written a preface in which he pointed out that Niles was almost entirely recovered, and would probably take his seat in the near future. Though he regretted that his letters of resignation had not been forwarded, he said nothing more on the subject. Dr. Brigham added an encouraging postscript. He thought Niles well enough to make the Washington trip, "immediately, I hope after your election." Toward the end of March, the patient physician persuaded Niles that the warmer weather of the capital would be beneficial. Brigham arranged for one of his staff to accompany Niles as far as Albany, where they would put up at the Eagle Tavern. Niles' personal attendant, Mr. Lillybridge, would be a member of the party and would be prepared "to go farther if you think best." He was emphatic on the point that Welles, and Welles alone, should accompany Niles to Washington. "I fear," he said, "that with his brother, he would worry about business." The date appointed for the Albany meeting was Wednesday, April 10.[14]

All went off as Brigham had planned. The weather in Washington was unseasonably warm, which, as Dr. Brigham predicted, did seem to improve Niles' mental outlook. He visited old friends, and even went with Welles and most of official Washington to the Navy Yard, where they watched their fellow townsman, Samuel Colt, blow up "a ship under full sail" with a submarine explosive.[15]

Niles' arrival in Washington immediately put Welles under strong pressure from the Democratic Senators, who needed his vote. Sympathetic friends—Silas Wright, Thomas Hart Benton, Governor Fairfield of Maine—had to be cautioned by Welles lest in their eagerness for Niles' presence in the Senate they put undue strain on his morbidly sensitive state of mind. It was all so frustrating. "He is at times evidently strongly disposed to take his place, and yet always has a dread and reluctance . . . I am absolutely at a loss what to think or do concerning my poor friend," the impatient Welles complained to his wife.[16] Besides shielding Niles from his party colleagues, he had to fend off inquisitive Whigs, who were hoping to disqualify him on the grounds of insanity or inability to perform the duties of his office. The Democrats had been beaten in the Connecticut state election. Whig Governor-elect Baldwin and party boss Truman Smith were calling for an official inquiry into Niles' condition as soon as the new legislature was organized in May. The Whig press claimed that he had been a raving lunatic, that he had been chained in a cell at Utica, that his presence in Washington was merely a shabby political trick to have Connecticut represented by an incompetent.[17] Colonel Niles arrived on April 15 to take over, and the very weary Welles hastened back to Hartford.

A week after Welles' departure, Niles was persuaded to visit the Senate with his brother and Fairfield. His appearance on the floor provoked a fury of partisan attack that could not be concealed from him. He was distressed, yet to the great relief of all concerned did not relapse into his former condition. Indeed, he seemed to improve and began attending the sessions daily. Still, he refused to take what was to him the mighty step of submitting his credentials. "I can induce him to do anything, to ride, walk or go into the Senator's rooms & talk & everything but to take his seat in the Senate, a thing," wrote Colonel Niles, "that can not be forced upon him & must be done from the impulse of his own feelings."[18] The very next day he impulsively blurted out to his brother that the legislature "would probably declare his place vacant when it meets next Wednesday week." Colonel

Niles had not planned it that way, but his brother needed just this kind of shock to nerve him into action. On his own volition Niles inquired of Ohio's Senator Allen whether objections would be made if he took his seat. The raffish, hard-drinking Allen thought not, nor did Wright and other Democratic Senators Niles consulted. Only Fairfield believed they should be prepared for any eventuality. He asked Niles frankly what he would do if objections were raised. "Will you stand your ground or will you say nothing & shrink under it?"

Niles thought he would say nothing.

"But of that," thought his brother, "I am not certain."[19]

Welles had already anticipated an *ad hoc* Senate committee of inquiry, and one of his first actions on reaching home was to contact Dr. Brigham. He had two requests: Would Brigham write Niles a letter that would strengthen his confidence in himself? Would he write another letter, for publication in the *Times,* rebutting the Whig image of the Senator as a mental incompetent? Well-informed of Niles' situation in Washington, Brigham was alarmed at the erroneous accounts he read of the Senator's condition in the Whig press and was most happy to comply. He wrote Niles uring him to take his seat in the Senate: "*you must act . . .* you must engage in some active duties as a resource against disease." To Welles Dr. Brigham gave a full account of Niles' original condition and his recovery, omitting any clinical details, but describing fully Niles' accommodations—no chains, no padded cell, no restrictions of any kind.[20]

By then, Fairfield had presented Niles' credentials to the Senate. Brigham's letter had been the deciding factor. On April 30 Colonel Niles wrote Welles jubilantly, "the die is cast, the great agony is over." Several Whig Senators raised objections. Foremost among them was the bibulous Edward Hannegan of Indiana, who proposed a special committee of investigation. The Democrats had anticipated just such a maneuver and were prepared. They made no objections to the raising of a committee, for they had arranged its composition beforehand: two Whigs, Hannegan and John M. Berrian of Georgia, two Van Buren Democrats, Wright and Benton, and one Calhoun Democrat, George McDuffie of South Carolina. Colonel Niles had "no apprehension of the result." Nor, in fact, did that old Federalist Elizur Goodrich of New Haven, who tartly remarked to Simeon Baldwin "perhaps they cannot reject him merely for imbecility of intellect—as there is no precise state whereby to measure a Senator's understanding."[21]

The next two weeks were painful ones for Niles. Whenever Wright, who acted as chairman, tried to assemble the committee, either Berrian or Hannegan would absent himself. Wright, Fairfield, and Richard Niles eased him over his bad moments while bringing pressure to bear on the Whigs for their discourteous treatment of a fellow Senator. Wright wanted a unanimous report, and he finally got one. On May 16 the Senate, without a word of protest, accepted the recommendation of the committee that Niles be seated. He was immediately sworn in.[22]

This was a great relief to Welles. Niles, to whom he had assigned a major role in sustaining the Van Buren candidacy throughout New England had been of no assistance at all during the critical period of early 1843. Quite the contrary, his protracted illness had put such a strain on Welles that he had been unable to function at peak efficiency. Those semi-monthly trips to Utica wore him down physically and always left him emotionally upset. With Niles absent from Washington, he had lost his best correspondent. All the intricate maneuvers, the rumors, the gossip, the evaluations which he expected the Senator would report in his valuable letters were not available to him. He heard now and then from Silas Wright, but the New York Senator was much too busy for the volume of correspondence Welles needed. Seymour wrote him frequently—brief, offhand letters, containing less hard information than Welles could read in the *Globe,* the *Intelligencer,* or the *Evening Post.*

At home, party affairs were developing a menacing cast. Governor Cleveland, who owed his post more to Welles than to anyone else in the party, was ambiguous on Van Buren. Though hardened by years of political combat, Welles had been shocked when Isaac Hill turned renegade and supported John Tyler. There were rumors that David Henshaw was reassembling his old conservative clique under presidential auspices in Massachusetts. Senator Woodbury of New Hampshire, still presumably a Van Buren man, did not condemn Hill, as party leaders in his own state were doing. Others, too, among them Andrew Judson, Henry Ellsworth, and Noah Phelps, were delicately testing the political crosscurrents. The *Patriot and Democrat* faction, which had supported the Harrison-Tyler ticket in 1840, was ready to back any conservative move against the Welles-Niles leadership and the Van Buren candidacy. In April 1843, Tyler dropped all pretense of remaining neutral in the impending presidential contest and conducted a purge of Whig officeholders throughout New England. On the national scene he introduced the Texas question, which immediately became an explosive political issue. Distracted by Niles' illness, his communications with Washington sporadic, his relations with Governor Cleveland uncertain, Welles was decidedly skeptical of his personal control over Connecticut's congressional delegation.[23]

From the beginning Welles had believed that Calhoun was behind all of Tyler's moves, that he was the real candidate and Tyler the stalking horse. Events during the spring of 1843 seemed to confirm his judgment. A new Democratic paper, the *Spectator,* was established in Washington to promote Calhoun, the *Globe* having come out squarely for Van Buren. Robert Barnwell Rhett, Calhoun's sagacious manager, was in close touch with Northern conservatives. He recognized that Van Buren was by all odds the popular choice of the party in New England, but with the active assistance of the Tyler patronage he saw a reasonable chance of securing a number of Calhoun delegates from Van Buren's home territory if nominations were made by district rather than by general convention. Rhett had the audacity to approach Blair and ask him to print in the *Globe* an article presenting this position as the democratic way of selecting delegates. Blair promptly refused because, as he later explained to Andrew Jackson, it would defeat the organization of the party and set "the presidency up at auction in the House of Representatives." The *Spectator,* the *Charleston Mercury,* the Hartford *Patriot and Democrat* and other Southern or conservative Democratic papers did carry the Rhett proposal. Welles saw through the scheme as quickly as Blair had. He was relieved when he learned that New York would nominate delegates by general convention. And he assured Van Buren that he would do everything in his power to prevent district nominations in Connecticut. Yet he was worried.

In the short space of two weeks, while he was absent from Hartford trying to help Niles adjust to the Washington scene, party sentiment at home had changed dramatically. There was a widespread impression that Van Buren could not be elected. "It pervaded our ranks," Welles said, "to an extent that I could not have believed." A sense of discretion kept him from communicating his fears openly to Van Buren or to any of his lieutenants at this early date. But a careful reader, and Van Buren was certainly that, could not have missed the implied warnings he inserted in his frequent letters to Kinderhook.[24]

Welles wanted a national convention as soon as possible. "The movement has been too long delayed. It should have been held next month, so that we might have presented a united front." The longer the convention was postponed, he argued, "the greater will be bickering and heart-burnings among ourselves, and enmities created against our own friends instead of the Whigs." As the situation stood, he predicted with accuracy, "the convention can not take place sooner than next fall—it will most likely go over to next spring."[25] Had Van Buren acted on this advice, he might well have gained the nomination. He did not, however, and in the end he allowed Wright to agree on further postponement of a tentative fall date that permitted a final merger between the Calhoun and Tyler factions. A party split was now a distinct possibility unless a new candidate were nominated who could satisfy the South and beat Henry Clay.

In Connecticut, as in other New England states, Whig forces were organizing rapidly around Clay, while the Democrats, abetted by Tyler officeholders, were still striving to contain a vigorous Calhoun movement. The President may not have been aware of this, for he had ambitions of his own, or he may have been deliberately encouraging his minions to kill off Van Buren first, Calhoun being marked out as the next victim. Whatever the motives, his appointees in Connecticut were all on the Calhoun bandwagon during the spring and summer of 1843. Word was broadcast that Levi Woodbury would be Calhoun's running mate, a move that did not surprise Welles.[26]

Of graver concern was the popularity of Calhoun in New England. "Many of our sterling Democrats," wrote a valued political friend to Welles "are partial to the 'Southern' but . . . seem willing to go with the majority whether it be for VB or Calhoun." While Judson was working feverishly to reinvigorate the conservatives in Hartford County, the Calhoun forces were developing their major strength in New Haven, where the Carolinian had many social and political ties. It was to New Haven that Levi Woodbury repaired for a lecture on free trade after his appearance in New York City. "Mr. Woodbury," observed Welles acidly, "without intending to leave his foot on the sand, lingered on the road from Washington to Portsmouth while an important election was pending in New Hampshire." Welles was "surprised and mortified to find all of the Ingersolls except Ralph . . . active supporters of Calhoun." They remained closeted with Woodbury before and after his talk. A few days later the chief "Tyler" Democrat of Massachusetts, David Henshaw, conferred with the same group, moving freely among the members of the legislature, which was then in session. He "was particularly active for Calhoun."[27]

Welles remained hopeful about Governor Cleveland, but as he explained to Van Buren, he "is too much of a schemer and too much the creature of expedients and policy to be a safe man." Stalwart old Perry Smith was much more emphatic. He could never understand why Welles had placed so much confidence in Cleveland. "I consider him a mere bag of chaff," wrote Smith, ". . . the nucleus of all the dodging part of our party." For the others, the New Haven Calhounites, Smith reserved his choicest epithet—"political pustules." Welles was probably right when he estimated that four-fifths of the party were for Van Buren. But the Calhoun-Tyler men were a close-knit, well-financed, articulate group, deeply rooted in the county organizations. Texas was proving to be a popular issue with the rank and file. From their limited view of national events and politics, Calhoun seemed just as true a Democrat as Van Buren and, unlike the cautious New Yorker, had taken a decided stand in favor of the admission of Texas as a state. Tyler's assault on Whig officeholders convinced many that he would be "welcomed" into the party.[28]

As much as he raged privately, Welles had to pick his way with care. He even felt it necessary to tell his radical friend, Dr. Douglas, that he "was not so prejudiced for or against anyone that I can not listen to argument and yield to reason." To Ralph Ingersoll he was especially deferential. The elderly New Haven lawyer was the only member—though the senior and most important—of that influential family still supporting Van Buren. But by August of 1943, at the peak of the Calhoun boom, Welles could contain himself no longer. A letter went forward to Silas Wright outlining the situation and spelling out the facts in detail. Three of the four Connecticut Congressmen were Calhoun men, he told Wright, information that astounded the overworked Senator. After alerting Wright to the problems Van Buren faced in Connecticut, and, by implication, throughout New England, Welles learned from Ingersoll that all the New Haven city delegates to the state convention were for Calhoun and Rhett's district system. Bad news, though not unexpected. He redoubled his efforts to infuse Van Buren sentiment through the state organization, in which, as corresponding secretary, he held a commanding position. A majority of the Democratic press took its cue from the *Hartford Times,* but the *New Haven Register* was a major exception.[29] At Welles' suggestion, the *Times* calmly and logically discussed the merits of all the candidates, including Calhoun, which did much to undercut the opposition.

Over the short term, Welles reaped a maximum of dividends from the state convention for the Van Buren cause. He saw to it that the delegates were elected by a general vote; and although at least three of the six were considered unreliable, he maneuvered the doubtful ones into a position where they had to declare themselves openly for Van Buren on the convention floor. He also had the meeting endorse the New Yorker by a substantial majority (162 to 69). In a final stroke before adjournment, he persuaded the convention to adopt a resolution declaring that each state should determine for itself how its delegates were selected. "I congratulate you on this result, which I knew we should have," Welles wrote Van Buren on October 26, "but I can assure you we have had infinite trouble to obtain it."

The management of the convention was a fine exercise in political tactics, nothing more. Welles knew, and his opponents knew, that he needed a Democratic victory in the spring campaign to stiffen the back-bones of the alleged Van Buren delegates. The odds were against him because the Whigs were thoroughly organized, abundantly supplied with campaign funds, less beset by factionalism. Even so, Welles almost made it. The Whig state ticket won by an average of only 1200 votes, with about 6000 more votes cast than in 1842.[30]

After the election—which Reverdy Johnson of Maryland considered proof-positive of Whig victory in November—other state and local elections showed unusual strength for Clay. With the evidence before him, Welles reluctantly came round to the opinion that Van Buren could not beat "Harry of the West." Calhoun, now Tyler's Secretary of State, had by no means given up. David Henshaw, the new Secretary of the Navy, was still working hard with Woodbury and Isaac Hill to strengthen the anti-Van Buren forces. Welles thought it most unlikely that the party would accept either Tyler or Calhoun as a candidate, but he was quite sure that both would combine to eliminate Van Buren.

The ex-President had a majority of the delegates from the Northern and Western states, more than enough to defeat the combination. Yet most of these delegates outside of his own state could not be counted on after the first ballot. Rhett's *Spectator* had already served notice that a two-thirds rule for nomination would be insisted upon. "I am satisfied," wrote Welles to Silas Wright, "that if the sentiment of our state is any indicator, that some new and extraordinary man is necessary." Calhoun would be a fatal candidate: "The Grecian horse came in with armed men against us when he united with us." Van Buren's letter against immediate annexation of Texas in the *Globe* merely confirmed his doubts. A more emphatic expansionist than his Albany Regency friends, Welles had hoped Van Buren would accept Texas, even though the issue "has been brought forward in the most odious and disgraceful form that it could be presented."

Meanwhile, the man he had most counted on to keep the Connecticut delegates in line, Ralph Ingersoll, their unofficial chairman, was openly expressing himself against Van Buren in Washington. Silas

Wright learned that President Tyler spoke "very strongly of nominating Ingersoll" for the vacancy that existed in the Supreme Court. "I have many reasons," Wright wrote Benjamin Butler on May 10, 1844, "to suspect that Ingersoll has been tampered with lately. . . ."[31]

Ingersoll's posture at the convention—whether dictated by self-interest or not—disappointed Welles. He voted with two other Connecticut delegates for the two-thirds rule, and he was only willing to support Van Buren on the first ballot. When the Connecticut delegates learned that Bancroft would swing Massachusetts to former Representative James K. Polk of Tennessee, they voted for him on the ninth and final ballot.

The campaign was hotly contested. Polk, who had served seven terms in Congress and had been an effective Speaker of the House and a Governor of Tennessee, was scarcely the dark horse the Whigs branded him. But his reputation was a pale shadow of that enjoyed by Henry Clay, or even by Van Buren, for that matter. Nor could this rather prim, plain figure with his cold grey eyes bear any favorable comparison with the warm scintillating "Harry of the West," whose public career almost spanned the history of the young nation. Yet Clay went down to defeat, in part because Van Buren and his followers fell into line behind Polk. Silas Wright resigned from the Senate and ran for Governor of New York, lending his wide popularity to the Democratic presidential candidate. Clay lost New York by the narrowest of margins, and with it he lost the election.

After Polk's victory, Welles saw grave problems ahead unless the President-elect recognized that the Baltimore delegates did not represent the majority of the party in the state. "Anti-Van Buren men in Connecticut," he said, "expect to be first rewarded by the new Administration, but if Polk does this he will commit an error. Niles must point him in the right direction."[32]

Welles was concerned about the organization they had labored so long to build in Connecticut. The fate of their controlling faction, he saw clearly enough, depended upon their influence with the new administration. "You have seen the movement of Van Ness & his associates in New York where Wright was insulted and Tyler applauded," he reminded the Senator. "Many here believe that the Polk administration is to be a continuance of Tyler's and that Mr. Calhoun is to be the master spirit." Niles needed no prompting to see that without the strong support of the administration his friends at home would be in serious trouble. But he needed time during which he could strengthen his ties with the new administration, for he had little or no influence with the President-elect. Three letters had gone to Polk "proferring my suggestions & advice & rec'd no reply to any of them . . . your idea that it depends more on myself than any other man to set Mr. Polk in the right path as regards New England is probably very wide of the truth."[33]

Polk's Cabinet appointments—conservatives and Southerners in the main—were as disconcerting to Niles and Welles as they were to most radical Democrats. This unpleasant fact was made especially evident to Niles when he found that he could make no headway with Cave Johnson, the new Postmaster General, nor obtain any satisfaction from Robert J. Walker at the Treasury or Buchanan at State. He saw the President only twice by appointment. On both occasions, Polk was polite, cool, noncommittal.

Weary and morose, his self-confidence not fully restored, when Congress adjourned Niles' only thought was to return home as quickly as possible for much needed rest and recuperation. Welles would have to take over what looked like a losing proposition. Every conservative leader in the state was flocking to the capital. Welles knew he had to go (the radicals must press their claims or lose by default), but he dreaded the trip. He arrived in Washington on April 18, 1845, to find the anti-Van Buren Democrats were operating at forced draft the most heated patronage engine he had ever seen.[34] Yet he could not have asked for a more friendly reception, and at first he thought all would be well. Marcy was cordial, even solicitous. Buchanan invited him to dinner. Secretary of the Navy George Bancroft greeted him effusively whenever they met. He "has bowed lowest, talked loudest, shook my hand the hardest," said Welles, who probably from personal pique considered Bancroft the "coldest and as it appears to me, the most insincere" in the Cabinet. Welles may have been put off by Bancroft's nervous manner and his shrill voice, once described as "an unearthly yell," more penetrating than any "among the entire tribes of the Sauks and the Foxes . . . when [he] was a little excited."[35]

At an evening reception in the White House, the President recognized Welles and introduced him personally to the first lady, the accomplished Sarah Childress Polk, whose jet black hair and dark brown eyes reminded him of Mary. A few moments later, while Welles was talking with Amos Kendall, Polk made his way through the throng and drew him aside for "a fifteen minute chat." The reserved President proved to be direct and voluble, at least on this occasion. He spoke of the Connecticut appointments, alluding to those at New London and New Haven. Norris Wilcox, a Niles-Welles man, had been

appointed collector at New Haven, but Charles Lester, a Tyler appointee and a thorn in their side, was being retained in the New London customs house. Polk was perfectly willing to remove him if that
was the wish of the party in Connecticut. That "plain little six pence,"
James K. Polk, "is very well and very kindly disposed," Welles thought,
"he aims to do right and has very honest intentions." He would soon
change his mind.[36]

A day or so later Welles was shocked to read in the *Washington
Union* that Stephen Lounsbury had been named collector at Bridgeport. He had not been consulted, nor had his friend Dr. Simons, ex-
Congressman from the district. Lounsbury, once a Federalist and an
Adams Republican, a Calhoun-Tyler stalwart, was a bitter political
enemy of Simons and a carping critic of *Times* "dictation." What
could this mean? Welles had taken the President's remarks literally.
He had prepared from memory a list of "reliable" men whom he
thought would be appointed on his advice to replace Tyler postmasters, collectors, and their deputies. He already had made an appointment to see Robert J. Walker to discuss Treasury patronage. Before
he visited the Secretary, he managed to examine the papers in the
Lounsbury case and found, as he expected, that the selection had been
made exclusively on the ground that Lounsbury had opposed Van
Buren. Welles decided that he must force the issue with the Secretary.

Walker, short, bald, energetic, seemed buried in papers when Welles
was ushered into his room. He greeted his visitor brusquely, showing
a want of civility that provoked Welles into an immediate and pointed
criticism of the Bridgeport appointment. "The intent of the administration and the democratic party in Connecticut," snapped Welles,
"ought to be identical." The Secretary replied: "the complaints [are]
that a few men control things with [you]." "The same charge," said
Welles, with a rasp to his voice, "is more legitimately applied to Washington than Connecticut." Walker gave him the impression that all
the incumbents—Tyler men without exception, barring Wilcox in New
Haven—would retain their offices. It had not been a friendly interview.
After a perfunctory handshake, Walker turned back to his papers.
Welles was not successful with post office appointments either. He
could not even arrange an interview with Cave Johnson, the Postmaster General. After these rebuffs he concluded that the Polk administration would follow a policy of balancing factions rather than relying
upon merit and proven political principle to strengthen the organization. As he expressed it first to Niles, then to Van Buren, "the policy

of the administration, as avowed by themselves, is to conciliate all who belong to the democratic party. . . ."[37] Welles could not remember when he had worked so hard and so long for such trifling results.

As soon as the twenty-ninth Congress convened in December 1845, a host of angry and powerful Democrats stood ready to do battle with the administration over patronage. Senator Niles, recently remarried, completely rested, and quite fit, was one of the leading spirits among them. On the evening of December 14 he called by appointment on the President, determined to demand what he considered his and Connecticut's rights. His temper was not improved by a downpour which soaked him through as he waited for a hack. Aware that Niles' rather abrupt demeanor was not caused solely by his sodden condition, and deducing the reasons for it, Polk led him over to the blazing fire. "I had no opportunity to scold," said Niles, "as he at once agreed to all I said." In the matter of local appointments, Polk said that he was "willing to correct them at New London & Bridgeport." As to federal appointments, a sore point with Niles, the President remarked that he had "for some time intended to do something for Welles and Douglas." "Douglas," said Niles, "is a zealous & good man in his way, but he is not to be compared with Welles, either as to his qualifications for office, or standing with the party." Polk agreed, praising Welles in "the highest terms." The office he had in mind, however, seemed hardly to square with his extravagant remarks. And the manner in which it was presented was, to say the least, unfortunate. "He intended," said Niles, "to give you the place of 3d ass't PMG unless Mr. [Cave] Johnson should conclude to discontinue that office as he had expressed the opinion that it was unnecessary." One can imagine the rather tense situation in the Welles' household at Hartford after he received that letter.[38]

However tactless his suggestion, Polk was resolved to gratify Niles, if only because he needed the Senator's vote in what he knew would be a stormy session. He would not give all that was asked, for he too was following the same policy of balance that Van Buren and Woodbury had blocked out earlier. He did not remove any Tyler appointees until a full year after his inauguration, though he did accept Niles' recommendations for their replacement. He would appoint Welles to a position in the Navy Department, which was by no means equivalent in prestige to heading the Patent Office or the Pension Bureau, or even to the posts of the chief clerks and the assistant secretaries of the major departments. A few months later he would balance Welles' junior appointment by awarding Ralph Ingersoll (no radical) with a more senior one, in fact, the fourth highest rank of the foreign posts—Minister to Russia.

When the President made up his mind on an appointment, he moved cautiously but inexorably toward his goal. For some time he had been concerned about the efficiency of the military departments in purchasing and shipping supplies. Though he had no reason to doubt the honesty of the senior Army and Navy officers who staffed the bureaus in Washington, it was their competence in dealing with shrewd, hard-bargaining suppliers that bothered him. Of more immediate moment, he was moving toward a probable war with Mexico and needed his best senior officers at sea or in the field. William B. Shubrick was then heading the Naval Bureau of Provisions and Clothing. A minor hero of the War of 1812, Shubrick, now fifty-five years old, stood eleventh on the list of captains. He was in the prime of life with a distinguished naval career behind him. A fine deepwater sailor, he had served as a squadron commander, enjoyed the reputation of being a good fighter, and, if Fenimore Cooper was any judge, was the best ship handler in the Navy. Polk wanted such men at sea, not bound to a desk in Washington.

Orders placing Shubrick in command of American naval forces in the Pacific were already being drawn when Polk mentioned casually to Niles at a meeting on New Year's Eve that he expected a vacancy in the Bureau of Provisions and Clothing. The President said he had suggested Welles' name to Bancroft, "& that he (Mr. B.) replied that he knew you well and that there could be no better man for the place in the country." It was still uncertain, but if it did materialize, "he hoped you would accept it for a time until there should be something you might like better," Niles wrote.[39]

If there had not been one of those recurring crises in his personal and political affairs, Welles would not have accepted the position. He was worried about his family. His only son, Edgar, had reached the precarious age of two years and was susceptible to colds, Anna Jane's health was extremely delicate, and his wife was far from well. Mary Welles, who had been painfully afflicted with rheumatism the previous winter, was pregnant again. Doctor Taft, the family physician, had just given the usual medical prescription for Welles' wife's condition and the welfare of the children—a warmer climate. State politics, always turbulent and troublesome, had taken another difficult turn. Welles was in the thick of the patronage battle that Niles was fighting on a higher level in Washington. It was another one of those savage affairs where old friends and associates were quarreling, and where Welles, trying to mediate, was being assailed by all. As Niles put it, the job in Washington would be "a good retreat on your part from the Post Office squabble." With many lingering doubts about Bancroft, the prestige of the position, the policy of the administration, and the condition of his wife, Welles finally decided to chance the uncertainties of Washington.[40]

# CHAPTER 13

# Mutual Fears

WELLES ARRIVED IN Washington on April 25, 1846. He heeded Niles' suggestion that officeholders, even senior ones, should keep clear of the messes that catered to Congressmen. While he roomed at Mrs. Scott's, where Senators Niles and Fairfield and Congressman Preston King of New York lived and dined, he took his meals at Mrs. Daniels' on Fourth Street. His mess-mates there were all civil servants like himself—some senior, some junior. Though this involved an inconvenience, Welles was able to maintain his political and personal ties yet not break the unwritten code of official Washington.

For the first time in many years he was able to explore the community apart from the federal establishment. Thinking back to the city as it was in 1829, he found it much improved in physical appearance. Most of the major streets now had "finely paved brick walks." The tacky, temporary structures that once lined both sides of Pennsylvania Avenue had been replaced by "very creditable buildings." The city's moral tone, he thought, had improved too. "There is less drinking—less gambling—less lewdness," he observed. On a house-hunting ramble with the affable Preston King, Welles was delighted with Georgetown—"some pleasant residences . . . places that please my fancy and where with pleasant neighbors, I should think one might have a cheerful home. . . ."[1] He missed his family and, though uncertain about the immediate future, decided to set up a household.

As the only civilian among the bureau chiefs, and a political appointee at that, Welles found himself in a peculiar situation. His associates were polite, but beyond the formal amenities he was excluded by a wall of indifference that forbade any social exchange.[2]

Although the position of a bureau chief was no sinecure, it was much sought after by senior professional officers. What would soon be referred to nostalgically as the old Navy was a close-knit group, almost a club, of senior and junior officers with family and social ties that transcended the purely professional aspects of a naval career. It was quite natural that they would resent the intrusion of Welles, a civilian, and worse yet, a politician. Senior naval officers had to work with politicians—the Secretary, for instance, and members of Congress, but never had they been required to accept a politician as a professional associate. Welles' appointment, moreover, meant one less senior berth. In a navy where there never were enough senior positions, where gifted naval officers such as John A. Dahlgren and David Dixon Porter remained lieutenants for twenty years, the loss of a bureau to a civilian had repercussions all down the line.

While Welles' nomination was pending before the Senate, Joseph Smith, Chief of the Bureau of Yards and Docks, organized the Navy officer corps to oppose confirmation of the appointment. On February 20, 1846, Smith complimented Lieutenant Andrew H. Foote on using his political influence to oppose Welles. "You have done a good thing for the service by 'putting in your oar' to keep all the bureaus in the Navy," he said. "It is strange," he continued, "that the Navy can not furnish a head of a bureau capable of knowing what seamen want and how to furnish stores."[3] Foote and Welles had been schoolboys together. They had drifted apart but were still friends. In later years when Welles became Secretary, Smith would be one of his closest advisers, and Foote would renew their old intimacy on the warmest terms. But in 1846, the perogatives of the service and its limited scope for promotion dictated their narrow view of the very real needs of a wartime navy. For there was not an officer in the fleet who had a modicum of Welles' experience in business, politics, and general administration. Few could match his industry or ability in areas other than strictly naval affairs.

A good appointment or not, Welles' presence in the department was bitterly resented. Of all the bureau chiefs, only Commodore Morris, their titular head, showed any semblance of friendliness. Morris bore the reputation of being the strictest disciplinarian in the fleet, but he was shrewd enough to unbend and be accommodating when ashore. He was also a Connecticut man, sharing with Welles an abiding pride in his native state. Lewis Warrington, Chief of the Bureau of Ordnance and Hydrography, a heavy, taciturn Virginian, cold and reserved even among his naval colleagues, treated Welles with studied indifference,[4] as an interloper and a Yankee to boot. Warrington, as Welles observed, "never had the politeness to call on me and I have never had an opportunity to return his call." He concluded that the old Commodore had "a muddy mind," a personal rather than a rational judgment. Warrington seems to have been the only senior officer who recognized the importance of Dahlgren's novel ideas about heavy ordnance, and somehow he found the necessary funds to begin the work.

Joseph Smith was more hostile to Welles than Warrington was. At a reception given by Secretary Bancroft, he was actually rude to his new associate. Oddly enough, Welles was inclined to excuse his behavior as unintentional. "Smith is not a considerate man," he confided to his diary, "though I think well disposed. He has not much presence and no manners. . . ."[5] The frosty attitude of the service chiefs was difficult for someone as acutely sensitive as Welles, but far more trying was his relationship with the Secretary of the Navy, George Bancroft. He was irritated at Bancroft's ceremonial, condescending air, his tendency to find fault where no fault existed, his temperamental outbursts. "As yet," he wrote after a month on the job, "we do not fully understand each other." Welles made this entry in his diary after an especially painful interview with the Secretary.

Bancroft had asked Welles for an opinion on procedures for supplying the African squadron. After researching the matter thoroughly, he sent in his report. On May 25, Bancroft summoned him. As he entered the Secretary's office, Bancroft rose from his desk flourishing Welles' memorandum, and taxed him "in language vehement & almost impertinent . . . about the conditions of things on the coast of Africa & the stores at Port Mahon." Welles could not possibly have known except from the reports, the accounts, and the requisitions of his predecessor about the supply situation of the African squadron. It took some time before he understood what Bancroft wanted—a lapse that did not improve the Secretary's temper. "He seemed to suppose the African squadron unsupplied," wrote Welles after the encounter. "Although not my fault if it was not."

"I believe it is supplied," he said.

"Believe!" said Bancroft, "why don't you *know*? You *must* know & attend to these things."

Despite the provocation, Welles resolved to control himself at all costs.

"The squadron is short of bread," stated Bancroft flatly, "there is not a pound at Port Mahon."

Welles interrupted, declaring that he had complied with the Secretary's orders. "You asked for my opinion, sir, and you have received it early & frankly. If you had asked for my action you should have so expressed yourself & I stand ready to give it."

Bancroft began to contradict but Welles interrupted again to say that the "order is in your hand."

He examined it and said, "this is an improper order, it is not what I intended." He sat down abruptly, seized a pen and scrawled the words "and action" on his endorsement of Welles' memorandum. Returning to the bread question, he again expressed himself sharply that there was a shortage.

"I know the squadron has a pretty full supply. I suppose and believe there is bread at Port Mahon," Welles said.

"Suppose!" replied Bancroft, "this will not do. We can not get along so."

Welles excused himself, went to his office, and returned with the inventory which showed 39,000 pounds of bread at Port Mahon.

"It happened," he recorded, "that I am right on every point."[6]

This was the only heated exchange between the Secretary and his new bureau chief. Bancroft, it would appear, examined carefully all of Welles' reports, which included a dozen or more recommendations that would simplify yet strengthen procurement procedures. Money would be saved, naval stores and transport improved. The analyses were comprehensive, the figures accurate, the estimates based on careful market research and comparisons of contractual performances over long periods of time. The Secretary was impressed, and his attitude changed accordingly. Welles noted, for instance, on June 11 that "the Secretary was particularly respectful in his deportment & studious to please." Though their relationship was improving, Welles continued to have difficulty in securing accurate information about ships and squadron operations which would necessarily affect his duties. After the declaration of war with Mexico on May 13, 1846, he was told the Navy would be enlarged but not given any further information. Faced with making the supply estimates for the next fiscal year, he tried to pin down the Secretary on the subject. He was unsuccessful. Eventually the Secretary came to appreciate Welles' honesty and competence, but their association was never really harmonious.[7]

Bancroft was under pressure from Polk as wartime conditions strained the obsolete military services to the utmost. High-strung and restless, the Secretary was an imaginative rather than a conventional administrator. Uppermost in his mind was a driving impulse to reform what was obviously an inadequate naval arm, even for a second-rate power. But his energies and talents for innovation were constantly being diverted by other duties that imposed heavy drains on his physical and mental resources. He could not neglect omnipresent political chores, nor his Cabinet role of counseling the President on general policy as well as naval affairs. The war with Mexico, of course, magnified all of these responsibilities, while adding immensely to the staff and line obligations of the Navy Department. Since the total department personnel, including copy clerks and messengers, stood at twenty-five, everyone was overworked. No wonder Bancroft's temper, uncertain at best, erupted frequently. Routine matters of naval administration left him frustrated and, at times, bewildered, for his temperament (perhaps his life-long habit of collecting and marshalling data) was such that he was incapable of broadly delegating his authority. That he felt keenly these petty but irksome tasks was evident in his practice of badgering and berating his subordinates over details when he should have trusted their judgment. Compounding the Secretary's dilemma was Polk's conduct of the war. Like Bancroft, the President seemed incapable of delegating powers. Ever distrustful of his administrators, he personally enforced high standards for departmental honesty, efficiency, and economy.[8]

Another problem was that no one in Washington, not even the President, was able to calculate the duration and the demands of the war during that summer of 1846. With most of the powerful Whig minority in Congress opposing the conflict, and with economy a sacred word in both houses, the President remained undecided about the size and needs of the armed forces. When Welles complained, as he did frequently, that there was a lack of system, that he could not secure hard information on which to base his estimates for the next fiscal year, that Bancroft was misleading and evasive, he was merely voicing the traditional complaint of a responsible official trying to execute policy when no firm policy existed.

Other bureau chiefs were in the same quandary, and they, like Welles, were under constant pressure to present plans for reforming their branches of the service. No doubt reform was long overdue, but it would take more than Bancroft's energy and the dedication and ability of the bureau chiefs to repair thirty-five years of neglect by a niggardly Congress. And the twenty-ninth Congress was no more disposed than its predecessors to loosen the purse strings beyond what was absolutely necessary to win the war.

Of all the bureau chiefs, Welles had the most time-consuming and the most politically sensitive job. His associates, except Dr. Harris, the medical chief, worked through the commandants of the various navy yards. Provisions and clothing, however, were obtained exclusively from private contractors. True, there were naval agents in the major ports who were charged with procurement responsibilities. Welles knew that these men—all political appointees—were subject to pressure from interested parties. One of his first reforms was to relieve the naval agents of purchasing, which he centralized under his own control in Washington. He did use the agents for market reports, for the advertising of bids and for preliminary negotiations; but even in these areas he drew up careful guidelines and stipulated that his office would be the final authority for any award. In removing a major opportunity for graft or favoritism from the agents, Welles was fulfilling one of the President's sternest dicta—an honest administration. He was also able to effect economies by hard bargaining and lot purchasing. Inevitably, as he knew, political pressure would be exerted upon him. He was prepared for this and determined to resist it. Bancroft supported his bureau chief, as did his successor, John Y. Mason.[9]

Interferences and pressures of this sort were facts of political life which Welles understood and knew how to manage. Other political problems of a different calibre were not so readily met nor so easily solved. Sharp conflicts of opinion were emerging within the Democratic party over the conduct of the war, the proposed Walker tariff, the eventual settlement with Mexico. In his boardinghouse parlor, Welles listened as Preston King and Niles discussed the sectional implications of probable land acquisitions on a vast scale. Hannibal Hamlin of Maine—then serving his second term in Congress—Senator Fairfield, and Jacob Brinkerhof of Ohio were frequent visitors. The dark, coarse-featured Hamlin seemed most attractive, "with his boyish good humor, his modest demeanour, his decided principles." But Welles reserved his highest praise for Preston King, whom he thought the ablest Democrat in the House—"Few gave him credit for all he [had] accomplished."

Conversation, though free and easy, was always earnest and usually critical of the new administration. An ardent nationalist, Welles speculated that the New Yorkers might be placing partisanship over the true interests of the country. "I will shrink from no just responsibilities," he confided in his diary. ". . . but I shall not, to gratify any man, give an opinion for a change, without fully understanding the whole question." His position on the upcoming tariff bill was more politically astute than that of either the doctrinaire free-traders or the moderate protectionists in the group. He opposed drastic revision because it would reduce revenues when government expenses were rising to meet the costs of the Mexican War. "My chief effort has been," he explained, "to restrain my friends from unwisely committing themselves without reflection in favor of the new law . . . I fear there will be an exhausted Treasury despite loans & all the pretended additional receipts of Walker." He was unsuccessful in convincing the free-traders with his practical arguments. His friend Niles, long a moderate protectionist, likewise rejected the formula, though it would have made his stand more palatable to the organization Democrats of his own state and region.[10]

A manufacturer himself, Niles was not entirely the disinterested advocate he would have others believe; yet he probably would have supported the Walker proposal if he had not decided that it was a sectional measure aimed directly at the manufacturing interests of the North. Behind Walker the Connecticut Senator saw the gaunt figure of Calhoun. As soon as he studied the Secretary's report, he was convinced it was drawn up on behalf of the slave states to hoodwink Northern farmers and arraign them against Northern industry. Southern planters, of course, would be the major beneficiaries. Senator Niles was beginning to see the outlines of a gigantic conspiracy to isolate and ruin Northern industry. The repudiation of Van Buren, his patronage troubles, the problem of Texas, and now the tariff—all were links in the chain of evidence.

For a subtle manipulator, Walker had been quite clear in de-emphasizing the importance of industry to the average American. "If we reduce our tariff," he wrote in his report on the tariff, "the party opposed to the Corn Laws of England would soon prevail and admit all our agricultural products at all times freely into her ports, in exchange for her exports." Walker's statement was all Niles needed to make a stand —to unmask what he believed to be the villainy that had been growing like an insidious plant since 1830. It was in vain that Welles pleaded with him to attack the administration on the safer ground of revenue loss. Niles would not retreat. On July 6 he criticized the Walker proposal in general terms, giving notice that he would make a major address on the tariff after he studied the details.[11]

President Polk was disturbed. He respected Niles' powers of trenchant analysis, his persuasive rhetoric. The day after the Senator's brief remarks, Welles was startled when Secretary Bancroft shattered precedent by appearing personally in his room instead of sending a messenger. Could they have a brief chat at 3 p.m., before he went to the Cabinet meeting? When Welles arrived at the appointed hour, the Secretary immediately came to the point. "He expressed great anxiety at the course of Judge Niles on the tariff," a party measure of the utmost importance to the administration. Welles interjected that "Niles had settled opinions & convictions on the subject & that it would probably be difficult to turn him from them." Bancroft urged him to talk with Niles and added that "he would call and have a conversation with him." That evening at seven Bancroft was announced at Mrs. Scott's. Tense, as usual, the Secretary strove vehemently to enlist Niles' support. Welles, who was present, said nothing. Despite Bancroft's barrage of facts, opinions, and appeals to party loyalty, he could not move his fellow New Englander. At the end of their long conversation, he shifted to another approach. Would Welles and Niles dine with him two evenings hence? It was graciously put and graciously accepted.[12]

The two men found a mellow, relaxed Bancroft when they were ushered into the drawing room before dinner to meet a small group of guests. Their host had prepared his list with some care so that the gathering would be congenial. Included were two of Niles' personal friends—Henry Gilpin, a former colleague in Van Buren's Cabinet, and the genial George Dromgoole, a member of Congress from Virginia. Major Abraham Van Buren completed the party. Eldest son of the ex-President, he added a touch of color to the affair with his bright new uniform and the knowledge, soon imparted, that he was to leave within the week to join General Taylor's army, somewhere in northern Mexico.

The evening was hot and humid, the meal heavy—turtle soup laced with sherry, boiled chicken, baked ham, soft-shell crabs, a variety of game birds, topped off with ice cream and cakes. A half-dozen wines were constantly being passed. Neither this solid repast nor the temperature nor the wines affected the conversation, which Welles described as "sprightly." After dinner they all strolled in the garden. "Bancroft wished to touch Niles," Welles noted with satisfaction, "but knew not how. He accomplished nothing."[13]

Polk was no more successful than his Secretary with the recalcitrant Senator. The austere President went out of his way to be affable and persuasive in a friendly interview at the White House. He urged Niles to vote for the measure, but, if he could not, would he at least refrain from attacking it? His greatest desire, Polk said, was to unite and strengthen the party, "so as to leave it strong & triumphant to his successor." Niles' independent attitude could only lead to more factional strife, of which there was too much already. The Senator would give no such assurance. He stoutly maintained that the tariff was a sectional measure, that it unnecessarily arrayed agriculture against manufactur-

ing and would reduce revenue in wartime just when it was most
needed. Polk recognized a character as inflexible as his own. His steady
gray eyes did not betray the chagrin he must have felt as he bid his
former mess-mate a cordial good evening.[14]

Reluctantly, Welles devoted all of his spare time for the next two
weeks assisting Niles in analyzing Walker's report, a 950-page document
with thousands of items and a complex series of schedules. Once engaged, however, he supplied the Senator with his most telling argument—Walker's *ad valorem* schedules were simply a reversal of Clay's
minimum valuation principle, which, when applied to the iron industry, for example, gave a bounty to British ironmasters and fabri-
cators, at the expense of American labor and capital. In a four-hour
address to an attentive Senate and full gallery, Niles charged that the
tariff was a first step in returning the United States to a colonial status.
As he came to the end of his speech, disheveled, dripping with sweat,
his ruddy face twisted with emotion, he gave full play to his fears of
Southern domination—his paranoid dread that an aggressive, expansionist, slave-plantation system would encircle and eventually destroy
free institutions.

"Sir," he said, looking directly at Calhoun, "it seems to be admitted
that when the Democratic party is in power, its chief strength is in the
South; and hence it is, that the South have assumed not only to direct
its measures but seem determined to define and settle its principles."
He and his Northern colleagues would have been willing to compromise. All sections "should have yielded something of their extreme
pretensions." But no gesture of conciliation had been made, no consideration given for any incidental protection of important industries.
Quite the reverse! "We are a patient people," declared Niles, "we have
borne many things and have not complained: but you must not press
us too hard against the wall; there is a point beyond which we can not
go."

Welles disagreed with the protectionist theme in Niles' argument,
veiled as it was. He did not think it expedient and foresaw difficulties
with the organization at home.[15] He may have recognized that his
friend had distorted the picture, that in the flow of argument he exaggerated the ruinous impact of the Walker schedules on manufacturing
interests. Yet by now he too had succumbed to the overheated, partisan
atmosphere of Washington. He found most disturbing the political
motivation, real or imaginary, behind the tariff bill, not its economic
impact. King and Niles were persuasive men, but both were emotionally unstable. Niles would never fully recover from his breakdown, and

King had spent four months in the Hartford Retreat for temporary insanity some seven years before. Fairfield, who might have balanced the other two, was in such constant pain from his arthritic knees that he could scarcely get about, much less take part in the discussions. When he was not playing cards, for which he had a passion, Hamlin would visit for a talk. A strong party man, he was a moderating influence, except on the slavery issue; but during the summer of 1846 political problems in Maine, where he was a leading candidate for the United States Senate, claimed most of his attention and interest.

Had Welles been exposed to more objective views, he would still have agreed with the Southern conspiracy thesis of Niles and King. His brief residence in the self-contained Washington community had changed his perspective. "With a Southern President, and a Southern press, to direct and form public sentiment, is it to be wondered at," asked Niles, "that Southern influence has obtained an ascendancy, greatly exceeding the real merits of the one or the instrinsic strength of the other?" Welles had no doubt that the new tariff bill originated "with the South Carolinians in the days of nullification."[16]

In time he became acclimated to the Washington environment, yet he always remained critical of a culture so alien to his native place. A New Englander and a Puritan at heart, he found little in common with "the Southern Gentry." At a trade fair he visited in May 1846, he did not remember seeing among "the very great variety" of specimens of skill, ingenuity and industry . . . a single article [made] south of the Potomac." The trade fair coincided with racing week, which gave Welles an opportunity to draw an invidious comparison between the vacationing Southerners at the race track—"they own the horses, they make the bets"—and the frugal, industrious Northerners, "busily engaged . . . in examining everything to be seen, hearing everything to be heard, and have brought some specimens of their handiwork to pay the expenses of their journey." Washington hotels, he observed acidly, were filled with Southerners who were paying "from one & a half to three dollars a day . . . & over their wine, swearing about Yankees who are plundering the South." In contrast, the busy, acquisitive "northern artizans," he noted with approval, were paying less than a dollar a day for room and board. No wine, no horses, no bets for them, apparently, as they moved among the nutmeg graters, the shingle-splitting machines, the Colt patent revolvers, and mused about better corkscrews or mousetraps or cast-iron coffee mills.[17]

Beyond the material differences in the two cultures, beyond the city's bias against Yankees (a kind of discrimination that Welles felt

keenly), was the different image of politics and of political organization one perceived through the broad lens of official Washington.
Welles had long complained that the party powers never understood
local situations, that advice from the states went unheeded, that communications were distorted. Yet he too was being influenced by the
notion that politics in Washington was an end in itself.

For years he had been an ardent expansionist. As early as 1827 he
was writing diatribes against John Quincy Adams for sacrificing
American claims in Texas. Sam Houston and the Texas War for
Independence stirred his imagination. Manifest Destiny appealed to a
contentious nationalism bred into the very fiber of his being since boyhood days. On the slavery issue, he took the moderate stand of most
Northern Democrats. The Constitution protected slavery when established in a state by the will of the people. Those who would interfere
with slavery were threatening the Union. It was purely a state concern,
a local issue. Though he deplored slavery, he placed abolitionists and
nullifiers in the same category—dangerous, unruly minorities who
menaced the integrity of the nation, the sanctity of the Constitution.
"Much as Northerners may deprecate slavery," he wrote in 1833, "they
do not wish to interfere with Southern institutions."

When Prudence Crandall, an abolitionist school teacher, with the
assistance of William Lloyd Garrison defied the town of Canterbury,
Connecticut, and set up a school for out-of-state Negro girls, Welles
sustained the action of the town in prosecuting her. "No one, we
presume, even in these days of black philanthropy," he editorialized,
"will wish an influx of Negroes from abroad. . . ." Two years later,
in a letter to William Leggett, whom he admired as an editor and a reformer, Welles complained "that you occupy so much space with the
abolition question." But unlike many of the most vocal abolitionists,
he was consistent on civil rights and racial equality. "Until I am persuaded to admit the Negroes to be companions & associates," he wrote
Leggett, "I shall not be likely to advocate their emancipation. Until I
can be satisfied that they are capable of enjoying and maintaining
civil rights, I shall be opposed to their having & exercising in this
country the privileges of freemen."[18]

So long as the slavery question did not promote sectionalism, Welles
was content to let the institution alone; indeed, he hoped that statesmanship would provide for westward expansion without further agitation on the subject. If any serious contest should arise, if slavery should
act as a ligature that would bind states into a threatening sectional
combination, the fault would lie with the South. Northern abolitionists

were noisy, their creed unconstitutional and therefore reprehensible, but they were a tiny lunatic fringe, not a real danger. He envisaged no combination of free states arising from their propaganda. "Slavery . . . is an absorbing question at the South," he wrote in 1836, "and is drawing a line of distinction that ought not to exist . . . it is causing an alienation among us, and will as certainly draw the cords of affinity closer between the South and Texas."[19]

Feeling as he did about slavery and the Negro, and cherishing the expansionist view that westward lay the course of empire, early in 1845 Welles did not understand why his New York friends were opposing the admission of Texas. He, like they, had been distressed by Van Buren's defeat at Baltimore, but Polk's election closed up that political division in Welles' mind. From distant Hartford he thought the Barnburners, or radical New York Democrats, in Congress were taking an exclusive position against Texas merely to settle scores, that they were placing narrow partisan interests and ideas of revenge over the greater interests of the nation. He had not appreciated the dilemma of many Northern Democrats. Niles explained that "we want Texas, but we do not want it at the expense of the Constitution." His Northern colleagues were willing, he said, to admit Texas with slavery, but its territorial claims were matters of graver concern. "To admit a state larger than all the territory north west of the Ohio & to give it the power of retaining its limits, or of carving out of them four states; and this to guarantee slavery, in advance in the whole country whether the people, who may settle it, desire it or not, is asking a little too much." Without comprehending all of the political and sectional crosscurrents in Washington, Welles reminded Van Buren that "the Texas question" was emphatically a national one. Why then should New York play South Carolina's game merely, as he put it, "because the general government would not assume to prescribe the local organization of the territory, so as to influence some abstract notions of a balance of power?"[20]

After his arrival in Washington he began to rethink the entire question of the territories. He listened to King and Niles talk of Southern influence over the administration. The Calhoun clique, they declared, was giving away free territory in Oregon to expand the slave empire from Texas to the Pacific. The Walker tariff bill was another aspect of the Southern political thrust which was to weaken the free states in preparation for the final takeover. Niles, King, and other radical Democrats from the free states who dropped in from time to time gave Welles the impression that the North, if it did not look after its own interests, would be encircled by slave states: manufacturing, free labor, and small farmers would be absorbed into an Africanized continent. The territories already gained or anticipated were central to the Southern grab for power—they must be made central to the Northern defense of its free institutions.

There was a good deal of excited speculation before Mrs. Scott's smoky hearth. Much of it the practical Welles discounted privately as emotional or hypothetical, but he was concerned. He had a high opinion of King—"frank, blunt and ardent"—and of other radical New Yorkers—"men of remarkable intellect & character." He was, of course, susceptible to their line of argument. Conspiracies, counterplots, intrigue had been part of his natural environment for years. The notion of state sovereignty, when confined only to South Carolina, could be dealt with on Jacksonian terms. But if, as Niles and the Barnburners maintained, it was a device to isolate and circumscribe the free states, then the situation was far more serious. "I should have preferred a different course," he wrote in his diary, but now he agreed that this was impossible. "The North are [sic] beginning to feel their wrongs & are disposed, if not to resent them, certainly not permit their continuation."[21]

Exciting times would be ahead; new questions of deep significance would be debated; there would be alignments of party and of party leadership. Welles sensed the opportunity and the dangers to him personally. Interest and purpose kindled his ambition, but caution moulded his action, for he was uniquely vulnerable. Niles was an old man, without the responsibilities of a growing family; Preston King was a bachelor, and his district was far more radical than any comparable district in Connecticut. Hamlin, Brinkerhoff, and other Democrats of close acquaintance were not officeholders, their freedom of action not so limited as his. Somehow he had to explain basic political shifts to the people at home whom he himself had drilled in loyalty to organization. Somehow, he had to keep his job, for family and professional reasons. Were he to have any future in politics, he would have to remain in Washington. Only here could he form proper assessments of national issues; only here could he know when and where and with whom he would make his stand. So he had rationalized, though not without some struggle of conscience, during which time he thought of resigning. The course he outlined for himself could not, in the nature of things, be an open and manly one. He would be working against the administration, but he would be concealing his purpose as much as possible. In a letter to Van Buren, Niles explained why: "The slave power rules as tyrannically here as it can in Louisiana, that is made the test & tie of fealty to the administration. . . ."[22]

The first move in Welles' devious, delicate operation was to coax the *Hartford Times* away from its steadfast support of the administration. Next to Niles, Alfred E. Burr, the *Times* editor, was Welles' closest personal friend. He was thirteen years younger than Welles—a small-eyed, generous-featured man, rather Emersonian in appearance but certainly not in personality. An excellent printer—the best in Hartford —Burr was methodical, accurate, and industrious. As an editorial writer, he commanded a flowing style, not unlike Welles', but lacking in his flair for vigorous probing prose. In politics he was a fierce partisan, a Democrat who worshipped at the shrine of organization. Principle and party were so fused in his mind that it was difficult for him to grasp new issues if they seemed to threaten the Democracy. Warm-hearted, generous, a good friend and companion, he could be narrow, perverse, and stubborn in his editorial chair.

When Welles had left for Washington he had entrusted his political future to Burr. At the time he did not realize the extent of the power struggle at the summit of the party. As he began slowly and cautiously to move away from the national organization, he sought to bring Burr and the *Times* along with him. He might have succeeded if there had been more time and if he had been able to make his physical presence felt in state party circles. The rapid political and sectional shifts during the early stages of the war were complex and baffling, difficult enough to explain by letter, doubly difficult if the recipient was such an ortho-dox party man as Burr. Niles' stand on the tariff seemed outrageous to Burr, and to Democrats generally in the state. It violated party doc-trine, and it attacked a Democratic administration which, after some initial hesitancy, had been more than generous in distributing patron-age to the state. Burr immediately took issue with Niles in the *Times* and committed the paper to full support of the tariff, though he con-fessed it "was the most painful article that I ever penned." He was con-vinced, he said, "that had the *Times* taken sides with Judge Niles' speech, the Democratic party would have been in complete tatters." Welles replied calmly to the outburst. He pointed out that Niles had always favored a revenue tariff which, incidentally, protected "Ameri-can labor and American interests."[23] He constantly hammered on his theme that reduction of revenue during wartime would result in defi-cit spending and inflation.

The tariff bill passed, and the uproar at home faded away, only to be renewed more vehemently when Niles rose up during the second session of the twenty-ninth Congress to defend the Wilmot Proviso. The occasion was a heated debate over Polk's request for a $3 million appropriation to underwrite extraordinary wartime expenses. The origins of the war, said Niles, were "somewhat unfavorable to the character of the country." He refused to "recognize the right of this government to interfere with the domestic concerns of any people . . . especially to impose slavery on a conquered foreign country." How, he asked the slave state Senators, could "the interests of a neighboring state endanger the institution of slavery? There must be a boundary somewhere. They could not have the whole world made subject to slavery to avoid contact with freedom." When the bill for organizing the Oregon Territory came up in the thirtieth Congress, Niles made his greatest effort on the slavery question. As on all other significant issues, he leaned heavily on Welles for advice and for the actual drafting of his remarks.

Debate centered again on the Wilmot Proviso, which was lodged in the twelfth section of the bill. Senators Bagby of Alabama and Calhoun urged the section be stricken, declaring that the Constitution protected property, hence slavery, in the territories. Democrats of less extreme views voiced the popular sovereignty principle, which was then coming to the fore. Niles attacked both positions. Calhoun interrupted his discourse to assert that all territories belonged to the states, which were co-equal, and therefore "no discrimination can exist between those who hold and those who do not hold slaves." Protection of property was a state concern, Niles replied, subject to local police power; it was not uniform. Slaves were not recognized as property in many states, or, as he put it, turning Calhoun's position on himself, "what is property in one state is not property in another." If the Constitution protected slavery in the territories, it would make the federal government "the propagandist and supporter of slavery," a new question, connecting "this government with slavery—it makes slavery a Federal right—an institution not established by an act of Congress indeed, but which is a part of the Constitution itself." Popular sovereignty, he remarked, was "not so extravagant, but would have the same end." "In the one case, we are called upon to incorporate the principle of slavery; in the other, to permit it to be done—to leave it to introduce itself if it can, either with or against the will of the people of the territory." His final effort on the Oregon bill (a speech that lasted all night) was in many ways prophetic. He dissected Calhoun's position and foretold its fatal consequences. Unerringly, he penetrated the weakness and the dangers of popular sovereignty, summarizing all that had been said by such radical Democrats and freesoil Whigs as John P. Hale, Hannibal Hamlin, and his neighbor in Hartford, Representative James Dixon, whose speech on the Wilmot Proviso in an earlier session Abraham Lincoln thought the best he had ever heard on the subject. The Bleeding Kansas of the future, the Dred Scott decision, the ultimate demand for a national slave code could all be extrapolated from the Senator's remarks. In them, too, could be seen the fears of the North, of the free states being forced step by step along the road to slavery unless and until they drew the line. Niles' rhetorical display lent strength to the faint-hearted; it set up a rationale for confused Northern Democrats and wavering Northern Whigs. Without his mighty effort, Oregon might not have been organized as a free territory.[24]

Welles bore the major burden of trying to explain the Senator's position to the New England Democracy. It was uphill work all the way. When he thought he had them committed to the principle, he would receive word from Burr that "anyone who sticks to Wilmot will be alone with the Whigs & Abolitionists." His patient argument finally did make an impression, however. Burr and others condemned the Proviso as needlessly provocative, but they accepted it in principle—a breakthrough that was canceled out when Silas Wright of New York, Welles' candidate for the party's presidential nomination, died suddenly in August 1847. Welles, and, indeed, all of the Proviso Democrats of the North, had been united behind the New York statesman. Welles had just maneuvered the *Hartford Times* into supporting Wright, a move calculated to start the campaign in New England.[25]

Stunned at the loss of their leader, free-soil Democrats for some months did nothing to bring forward another candidate, nor did they devise any convention strategy. Not so the administration Democrats, who by the year's end had proposed Lewis Cass of Michigan, James Buchanan, and Levi Woodbury—all opponents of the Proviso. Their negative stand on an issue so vital to the interests of the free states seemed deplorable to Welles. Woodbury, especially, raised his ire. "Cold, selfish, and heartless, and faithless," he wrote of the New Hampshire politician, "subservient to the South, an ingrate to the North."[26]

Speculating on the probable conquest of Mexican territory, Welles reduced the political and legal consequences to their essentials. Slavery had been abolished throughout Mexico. Mexican laws and institutions, including abolition, would stay in force until American legislation altered or repealed them. Slavery, then, could not be extended except

by statute. "Congress must permit or it must exclude slavery and politicians will be compelled to act," he concluded.[27] The territorial settlement had to be an issue in the forthcoming campaign. He was counting on his New York friends to make it an issue—whether this meant
defeat for the party or not—to make a stand on the Proviso, and to
nominate a free-soil candidate at their state convention in Utica. Cass,
Buchanan, and Woodbury might cancel each other out, he reasoned,
permitting the organization men headed by R. J. Walker to foist another Southern candidate on the convention. Somehow, someone must
energize the Barnburners, a nominee possibly who would at the proper
time throw all of his support to Van Buren. He envisaged a similar
deadlock among the Whigs between the supporters of Clay and Zachary Taylor. If both parties split and four candidates were in the field,
Welles assumed that Van Buren's national reputation would ensure
him the election and a victory for free soil. A stalking horse was needed,
and what better man to perform this function than his friend Niles,
one of the most ardent and outspoken defenders of the Proviso in the
Senate, yet a warm supporter of the war effort? Since he was not embroiled personally in the bitter feud between the New York factions, he
might gain the support of both.

Welles' suggestion met with no encouragement from either Preston
King or Azariah Flagg—one of the few remaining senior members of
the old Albany Regency after Wright's death and Marcy's defection to
the Hunkers. They wanted none of their leading men engaged in the
"profligate scramble" at Baltimore. "We would not wrong so pure a
man as he [Niles] is by placing his name among the political prostitutes
in the democratic party who are bidding for votes," wrote Flagg. Failing in his attempt at high political strategy, Welles did take some comfort from Flagg's apparent determination. "When the political jockeys
have worked us into the minority," Flagg had said, "we can perhaps
build up a return to the principles of the ancient Democrats." Despite
this ringing assertion, Welles thought it sheer folly for the Barnburners
to go into the convention armed only with resolutions. What politician, however honorable his intent, would place his career and his
livelihood on the block for his principles alone? Welles wanted the free-
soilers to have some convention votes for bargaining power.[28]

By the spring of 1848 signs had multiplied that Lewis Cass would be
the Democratic party's nominee. Popular sovereignty, an idea that Niles
and Calhoun both denounced vehemently during the Oregon debates,
was now the Michigan Senator's formula for settlement of the terri-

torial dispute. It was commanding such broad support from conservatives and moderates that he had far outdistanced his competitors. The Barnburners had been right in dismissing Welles' wishful assumptions of a convention deadlock.

Late in May almost all the members of the New York Hunker delegation to the National Convention visited Washington, where they began a series of conferences with Cass partisans and administration men such as Robert J. Walker, Marcy, and Thomas Ritchie, editor of Polk's organ, the *Washington Union*. Prominent among them was the trim, sharp-featured editor of the *Albany Argus*, Edwin Crosswell, who was also a defector from the old Regency organization. Welles had grave suspicions that a deal was about to be made when he learned that Crosswell, "prowling around here like a cat," had visited both Thomas Hart Benton and John A. Dix for several lengthy conversations. John Dickinson, the Hunker Senator from New York, let it be known that there would be no trouble. "It was whispered," said Welles to Van Buren, that "there was to be an arrangement."

On May 22, a day or so after the arrival of the Hunkers, Welles was delighted when he met the stout, perspiring Preston King on the street near the Navy Department. King accompanied him home, where, after dinner, they talked far into the evening. He was relieved when King told him that the Barnburners would accept no compromise and were for "a distinct organization & a new nomination, if . . . they were excluded or presented with an unacceptable candidate."[29] Yet he felt it necessary to caution the New Yorker that "in raising the standard, many will falter, some would desert and there were innumerable obstacles." Welles feared that the Barnburners would back down under the lash of patronage. "Have our New York friends the firmness to meet the crisis?" he asked Van Buren after Cass's nomination at Baltimore. The answer came dramatically, not from Kinderhook, but from Utica, where the Barnburners, meeting in convention, seceded from the Democracy and set up their own organization. Nominating Van Buren for President and Henry Dodge, a Wisconsin Democrat, for Vice President, they launched the Free-Soil party. Welles maintained his correct official deportment, but he was secretly delighted at the independent action of his New York friends. Gleefully, he wrote Van Buren on June 23: "This movement was wholly unexpected & has fallen like a thunderbolt in Washington." Two weeks later a similar "thunderbolt" fell on Welles, an unexpected result of the Van Buren nomination which would tax his discretion to the utmost.[30]

A committee of New York free-soil Democrats headed by John Cochrane, a Tammany Democrat, invited Welles to address a mass meeting for Van Buren—"free soil and free labor"—to be held on July 18 in New York City. Acutely embarrassed, Welles wrote four drafts of his letter before he was satisfied that in declining the invitation he had not cast any doubts on his belief in the cause. He knew that the honorable course would be to resign his position and become an open partisan, yet, again, personal considerations prompted him to follow the devious path he originally charted. Obviously, he could not remain a federal officeholder and electioneer for a man and a platform opposed by his administration and presumably his party. This he stated in his final letter to the committee, which he marked confidential. He was explicit, however, in his personal endorsement of Van Buren and was "utterly opposed to the extension of slavery into territory now free by any action or authority of the general government."

For someone who had been prodding the New York radicals over the months to take a firm stand, Welles betrayed a lamentable want of firmness himself. Yet none of the active free-soil Democrats saw anything weak or furtive in his position. Discussing the proscription of Proviso officeholders with Van Buren some months earlier, Niles had said, "Mr. Welles is perhaps the only exception, & he of course has to be very cautious with whom he expresses his real opinions."[31] Not long after Welles mailed his letter to Cochrane, the Utica men raised their sights and aimed for free-soil Whig support. A new convention was scheduled for Buffalo in mid-August, where the schismatic Democrats hoped to broaden their appeal and extend their organization. Welles was decidedly skeptical about the new strategy. He admitted that there would be some of the very best men in both parties—"men of high moral courage and resolute purpose." But he also foresaw in attendance "many who are dissatisfied politicians—disappointed men—and ultra & impracticable themselves, who cannot conform their ideas or actions to attainable ends. . . ."[32]

The Buffalo convention, however, exceeded his expectations and engaged his warm, though, as usual, private, support for its free-soil plank. He had some doubts about the expediency of nominating Van Buren on a fusion ticket. The ex-President's political career, he thought, was too controversial for many Whigs to stomach. Other planks that committed the party to Whig doctrine—internal improvements at public expense or the Western idea of free homesteads—he would not support. He had come to the conclusion that the old parties had never been parties in any real sense of ideological clash, but factions that were rotten to the core—ripe for dissolution. He thought this could be best accomplished by a return to state nominations on the free-soil issue alone, a move that would bring about the "more general disruption of old organizations & after the breaking up there would have been a stronger more efficient reconstruction & on a better basis."[33] Welles saw clearly that the place to strike at the national organizations—their weakest spot—was at the state and local level from whence they derived their power. If a groundswell of local opinion could be cultivated, then organization men—Cass, Woodbury, and Buchanan on the Democratic side, Clay, Seward, and Taylor on the Whig—would find their party strength fragmented, at least in the North. He was still the idealist, the independent (albeit the careful one), the proselyte who would purge the evils of the national party system by a return to the older forms where individual expression would be unfettered, where the better angels of human nature could reassert themselves. Presumably, after destruction and reconstruction, a new organization would emerge which in time would undergo the same process, and so on. There was not a little of John Randolph's or Nathaniel Macon's old republican philosophy in his thinking; nor was Welles' position devoid of his passionate contempt for all Whiggery, a mere deviant in a one-party system. For exactly opposite ends, his views came perilously close to those of the Southern ultras.

As the campaign moved into its final stages, pressure increased on Northern officeholders. Having successfully avoided the stigma of free-soilism, Welles was suspected of guilt by association—of being, if not an open advocate of the dangerous doctrine, at least a fellow traveler. "I find myself an object of distrust & suspicion," he remarked, ". . . many are evidently fearful of associating too intimately with me lest they should be suspected. I shall not be surprised at any day," he continued, "to find myself designated for removal."[34] He managed to survive without compromising his principles, though several traps were prepared for him. When pressed for an explanation of his political views, he admitted that his opinions "did not square with the Administration & especially not on that pertaining to freedom or slavery in the territories." In an argument with Mason on the subject, Welles explained that he opposed abolitionists, but neither he nor any other Northern Democrat had taken upon himself "the responsibility of defending the morality of slavery . . . in supporting the rights of the slave states, we [do] it on constitutional and not abstract principles." Sensing that Mason did not believe him, Welles suggested they call upon Marcy for an opinion. At the War Department, the beetle-browed old Hunker listened carefully to the points at issue, then delivered his verdict in measured phrases. Politically, he told Mason, "I can fight your battles so long as you make the Constitution your fortress. But if you go to the Bible or make it a question of ethics, you must not expect me or any respectable member in the free states to be with you."[35]

# CHAPTER 14

# Independent Democrat

PRESIDENT ZACHARY TAYLOR REMOVED Welles from office on June 16, 1849, termination effective at the end of the month. Mary was expecting another child and could not safely be moved, so the Welles family lingered on in Washington until the birth of John Arthur a month later. On August 1 Mary Welles had recovered sufficiently for him to move the entire family, including the Scottish maid, Agnes, and Mary Curtin, a companion for his invalid daughter, into Mrs. Daniel's boardinghouse while he supervised the breaking up of the household. He intended to remain there until fall, when their Hartford house would be vacant, but Anna Jane caught the mumps. Since the other children had not been exposed, Welles moved the entire family to Grandmother Hale's roomy home in Lewiston. By mid-October they were settled again in Hartford at their old home—Number Eight Welles Avenue.[1]

It was good to be back among family friends and familiar scenes, though Hartford seemed rather dull after the excitement of Washington. Welles thought the city had improved socially during his three-year absence. "There is a better and more catholic spirit prevailing," he decided, "a relaxation of that stiffness and austerity which once existed." Perhaps it was the material change in the little city that led him to make this comment. Hartford did show evidence of progress, even in the short period of time he had been absent. The shabby, wooden railroad depot that spanned the Park River was gone, and workmen were putting the finishing touches on an elaborate, brownstone station on Asylum Street, near the center of town. Sidewalks now bordered all the major streets, and flood drains were being installed. Many of the stately trees, Welles noted sadly, had fallen victim to these improvements; but the Charter Oak—old in the days of Sir Edmund Andros—continued to defy the forces of nature and the hand of man. Gas lights, the most spectacular improvement, were replacing the immemorial oil lamps. Welles had been home about one month when the new system went into operation. From his parlor window of an evening he could catch a glimpse of the smoky glow on the lamp posts along Main, one block east of Welles Avenue.[2]

Despite what he chose to regard as a mellowing of Hartford society, Welles found that his reception in party circles was distinctly chilly. Prepared for some difficulty, he had a long talk with Niles before he visited any of his old associates. His heart was touched at his old friend's appearance and state of mind. Niles looked old and feeble. He had just lost his second wife and had resumed his careless dress and his slovenly ways. He gave a grim account of the New England Democracy, with special reference to Connecticut. The organization he and Welles had founded was in alien hands. The masses of the Democracy, he believed, were well-intentioned but purposely misled by a small clique in Hartford and New Haven. Bereft of sound principles, these placemen were determined to maintain their control. There would be no room for Welles, as there had been no room for him in party councils. Niles gave no sign that he would give up the struggle. At sixty years of age, his health uncertain, he was as full of fight as a gamecock, denouncing in colorful language the Democracy that had cast him into the outer darkness.

Welles was more realistic than the impulsive ex-Senator. Privately, he felt that Niles had permitted himself to be trapped into an independent position, that if he had been more discreet he might have maintained his party influence without sacrificing his stand on the Wilmot Proviso. Certain that time was on the side of the Free-Soilers, he believed that sooner or later, perhaps in the next Congress, the Southern ultras of the Democratic party would precipitate a crisis. Politically, the situation did not seem so desperate in the state. The Free-Soilers had shown surprising vitality. In three of the four congressional races, a fusion of Free-Soilers and Democrats elected their candidates, among them Welles' old associate, ex-Governor Chauncey F. Cleveland. And they were strong enough in the General Assembly to deny Colonel Thomas H. Seymour the governorship—no mean feat, for the handsome, personable Seymour, Connecticut's only Mexican War hero, was the most popular candidate the Democrats had ever nominated.[3]

Welles did not expect to be welcomed by such men as Isaac Toucey,

Seymour, or the Ingersolls in New Haven. But he believed them to be, above all, men of expedience, practical politicians who would not ignore the obvious changes that had come about in public opinion. In this he made a grave miscalculation. He failed to evaluate the ambition and the commitment of Isaac Toucey, who had assumed party leadership. In one of his rare political blunders, Welles had given Toucey the opportunity he had been seeking for twenty years—a voice in the national councils of the party.

After serving two terms in Congress, Toucey had been elected Governor in 1846. With both Welles and Niles in Washington, he saw his chance to combine with the Ingersolls and capture the party. The suave lawyer moved fast, creating havoc in the nicely balanced machine Welles had left behind. In their dilemma, those party leaders who opposed Toucey beseeched Welles to find a federal office of sufficient status for him to accept so he would leave the state. The times were propitious. Ralph Ingersoll, Minister to Russia, and Attorney General Nathan Clifford had just resigned their posts, leaving Connecticut without a senior office and New England without a representative in the Cabinet. Welles rounded up support for Toucey as Attorney General from party notables in the New England states. Polk was favorably disposed. At Welles' suggestion, Toucey hurried to Washington for a visit to the White House. The President had already canvassed his Cabinet, suggesting several names for the Attorney Generalship, among them Toucey's. The only suggestion made—and it was unanimous—was that the nominee be opposed to the Wilmot Proviso. The cautious Polk must have determined Toucey's stand on the Proviso when he talked with him in mid-May. Toucey was nominated and confirmed without debate on June 18, 1848.[4]

Though profuse in his expressions of gratitude to Welles, the new Attorney General quickly began to undercut him at Washington and at home. He gained the confidence of Secretary of State James Buchanan, who marked him down as a valuable assistant in furthering his own presidential ambitions. Under Buchanan's expert tutelage Toucey was quick to recognize the tangible benefits of Southern support in return for Northern appeasement on the slavery issue. The Union, he rationalized, could only be maintained by conservative men, North and South, crushing the free-soil issue once and for all. After more than twenty years of trimming in politics, Toucey had found a cause. That it suited his conventional notions about the nature of the Union and placed him squarely in the mainstream of the Democracy made him all the more dogmatic about its validity. His term of office was necessarily brief—only nine months—but with Buchanan's powerful support he improved every advantage that came his way. When the Polk administration ended on March 4, 1849, Toucey had risen from the ranks of obscure Connecticut politicians to be one of the leading organization Democrats in New England.

Welles had grossly underestimated Toucey's political acumen, his unquenchable thirst for prestige and influence. He seems also to have been unaware of the Attorney General's decided opposition to the free-soil movement. Toucey's reticence he attributed to his proverbial caution about "new and strongly contested questions."[5] He quickly discovered his error when he visited the *Times* office for a chat with Burr the day after his return to Hartford. Welles found the editor alone, scratching away on a piece of foolscap, his table piled with newspaper cuttings, old proof sheets, empty ink bottles, and glue pots. Burr was delighted when he saw the familiar erect figure at the door of his room. There was much to talk about—deaths, births, escapades, prosperity for some, financial ruin for others, all the trivia of life in a small town, and, inevitably, politics.

When Welles asked about Burr's views on party affairs, the editor plumped squarely for popular sovereignty. Welles was taken aback when his friend dismissed the Free-Soil party's successes of the previous year as a political fluke. How could Burr be so blind to the great moral issue in the making? Anyone who ignored the Free-Soilers in Connecticut politics was bound to be in trouble. "We can not and we should not close our eyes to the existing state of things and to approaching troubles because we desire things to be different," Welles warned. But he was unable to convince the *Times* editor then or on any other occasion during the closing months of 1849. Party associates, many of whom were neighbors or personal friends, began avoiding discussion of political topics when Welles was present. It was a trying time for such a sensitive man. Emotional ties bound him to the party which he had helped father and whose fortunes had been bound up with his for almost a quarter of a century. He did not want to risk old friendships by defying the organization, as Niles had done, yet he would not recant on the Proviso. "I think their views erroneous," he wrote a confidential friend, "and they undoubtedly think mine so. With them I want no controversy, nor they with me." He would steer a neutral course within the party and remain in the background for the time being. Eventually, he hoped, he would be able to regain his leadership through the country delegates and commit the organization to free soil.[6]

Welles had assumed that the threatening state of affairs in Washington would assist the free-soil movement. What he did not foresee was the wave of fear that swept through the North when the debate in Congress over the status of the Mexican cession reached tempest proportions. Never before had the South acted with such unity and determination. Moderate men in both major parties recoiled from taking any provocative steps that might fragment the nation. Profoundly disappointed, Welles began to doubt his "own capacity & judgment." Seymour gained the party's nomination for the governorship on a popular sovereignty platform. The Whigs, exhibiting little more stamina, nominated the relatively unknown Lafayette Foster of Norwich, a moderate on the territorial question.

Both campaigns were conducted in the midst of the great Compromise debate. With the outcome uncertain, Connecticut voters clung to party lines, the result again being no majority for Seymour, the Free-Soilers holding the balance of power in the legislature. When the Assembly met in May, however, President Taylor's stubborn refusal to accept any Compromise measure brought the gravest crisis of all. Frightened by a possible disruption of the Union that the Southern ultras were threatening, sufficient free-soil-inclining Democratic members, in a gesture for solidarity, swung over to Seymour and elected him. Welles and Niles did not bestir themselves to prevent this, for they were bending every effort toward a more important object—the defeat of Toucey in his second bid for a Senate seat. Rather a deadlock with no election than Toucey. The twenty-five Free-Soil members of the legislature pledged themselves to divide their vote between Niles and Cleveland and hold to the end. If the ninety-four Whigs stood firmly by Roger S. Baldwin, the Whig incumbent—and there was every reason to believe they would—Toucey could not be elected. One other element entered the strategy. Welles still had some firm friends in the regular organization, and many others who were under obligation for past favors. If enough rallied around their former leader to carry a part of the organization with them, Niles and Cleveland stood ready to release the Free-Soil vote to him. There might be just enough votes to elect him.

Welles had been indifferent toward the regular organization, "contented to float on the current, asking nothing, expecting nothing, and doing nothing."[7] But behind the scenes he worked for a large fusion vote on the first ballot. The thought of returning to Washington clothed in the dignity and importance of a Senator goaded him to feverish but carefully masked activity. After all, he was the only man of stature in the party who was acceptable to the Free-Soilers. Welles' notion of his own availability would have been reasonable if the party leaders had been open to reason. They were not. The Wilmot Proviso was anathema to all regulars—a political heresy that threatened their party and their nation. Anyone who differed from this view, however slight the difference, was suspected of evil intent.

When the legislature went into joint session to elect a Senator, the Whigs and the Free-Soilers stood firm for their candidates, Toucey losing steadily as each vote was taken. After the tenth ballot, it was obvious that he could not win, yet a hard core of his supporters refused to yield. The time had come for Welles' name to be suggested. When a country delegate asked the Democratic caucus to express an opinion on Welles, there was a "dead silence" from the Hartford members. Finally, William J. Hammersley, a prosperous book dealer said, "Gid is a personal friend of mine but gentlemen he can not be elected," a statement that went unchallenged. Fifteen ballots were taken over a three-week period before the General Assembly adjourned with no election. Welles did not receive a single vote on any ballot.[8] Angry and despondent by turns, he had to face the fact that his influence was not worth a rush among the party leaders of his own county, so long the stronghold of his personal power.

The strain and disappointment of the senatorial contest undermined Welles' sturdy constitution. During most of the summer he was unwell, suffering from repeated headaches and other minor complaints which left him weak and dispirited. Rarely did he visit his old haunts—the *Times* office, Hammersley's bookstore, the City Hall. Though he could not bring himself to break with Burr, he saw him only on infrequent occasions. "It pains me," he wrote in his diary, "to find strange doctrines urged, good men decried and bad men extolled in the paper with which I was so long connected." What he had always dreaded was materializing: political differences were separating him from his personal friends and depriving him of a major diversion, the public expression of his views on political subjects.[9] Well-meaning friends, worried about his state of mind, offered him the presidency of the newly incorporated Charter Oak Insurance Company, but at first he was reluctant to accept responsibility for a business that was completely new to him.

Excluded from the councils of his own party, he could see no future in the Free-Soil party organization, many of whose leading spirits he thought captious and bigoted. The great Compromise measures of the thirty-first Congress had also sapped Free-Soil strength, bringing a deceptive calm to the political scene. With that sense of perspective which Welles invariably viewed events, he believed that the Compromise could not bridge over the widening gap between the slave states and the free states. For a time the cry of "Union" would dampen the basic issues involved, but the smoldering embers of the territorial question could not be quenched so long as the Fugitive Slave Law remained on the statute books and "that mischievous doctrine of popular sovereignty" blew up swirls of political sparks.

He decided to take the insurance post because he needed some active employment, or as he put it, "a pretext for employment, a place to resort," outside of the family circle. No sooner had he accepted than the Hartford town meeting elected him to be a member of the Board of Assessors, an unpaid, thankless job that made more enemies than friends. Though he could ill afford the time, and the duties would be irksome, he felt obligated to undertake the additional task. Welles was never more self-righteous than when he penned these lines in his diary: "It has disgusted me to witness on the part of too many of our citizens a wish and anxiety to get distinguished offices, but who always shun and evade the humble but necessary situations."

He had been president of the Charter Oak company only a few weeks when he was asked to approve bills that an array of lobbyists had submitted. His refusal was prompt, and it was followed by a stern lecture on business ethics to the Board of Directors. "If such payments were allowed by the company," he informed the board, "then they must dispense with his services," for "he could not be associated with such infamous practices." The directors found other sources of funds to settle their prior obligations, but relations between them and Welles grew increasingly strained. He found fault with "the reckless competition that exists," with "bad and unprincipled agents." "That 'hazardous schemes' should be connected with purposes of a social and benevolent character . . . makes the whole seem shocking to me." Clearly, his connection with Charter Oak was drawing to a close. "I do not intend to preside," said Welles, "over a company of speculators." Shortly afterwards he resigned.[10]

Until he had satisfied himself that the board of the Charter Oak company did not meet his standards of probity, Welles worked hard to master a business which he found tiresome and exacting. Outwardly professing indifference to politics, he yearned to regain his former influence in party affairs. Niles went abroad during the summer of 1851, further narrowing Welles' social and political activities. Life seemed one dreary round of arguments over risks with insurance agents he did not trust, wearisome debates over policy with his fellow directors, and cranky complaints from property owners over their assessments. His diary provided an anodyne of sorts, but anything like a closely reasoned article for publication was too demanding in his present state of mind. "Am listless and sad," he reflected, ". . . can feel very little interest in passing events. I write but little for I am unable to compose my mind to it and seldom take up my pen at home."[11] Once only during the early summer did he cast off his lethargy to take a brief but important role on a public issue.

The Fugitive Slave Law was beginning to arouse some public resentment in the North as its harsh provisions became more widely known. William H. Seward's powerful speech denouncing the law and appealing to a law higher than the Constitution had created a sensation in New England. Following Seward's course, the New York *Independent*, a leading Congregational newspaper, attacked the law in forceful terms. Leonard Bacon, one of the *Independent*'s editors, was the most prominent Congregationalist minister in New Haven and a mighty power in the denomination. In Hartford, Horace Bushnell, the nation's most gifted theologian and the conscience of that city's business community, made pointed references in his sermons to the injustice of the law, its violation of basic human rights. Privately his remarks were less restrained. "As it is," he wrote his friend Dr. Bartol, "I must and will say . . . that there are things required in this abominable Fugitive Slave Law that I will not do—no, not even to save the Union. . . ."[12]

Connecticut's conservative Whigs and Democrats, fearful for the Union, joined forces behind the organization men to whom party and Union were one and inseparable. More as a defensive measure against restive elements, a majority of the faithful in both parties stood ready to support a General Assembly resolution declaring that the state would abide by the Compromise measures. The minority (frustrated fusionists and regular Free-Soilers) turned to Welles for assistance while the resolution was still in committee. Casting off temporarily his acute depression, he wrote out in one evening a set of resolutions that would expose, as he put it, "the outrageous and palpably unconstitutional" character of the Fugitive Slave Law. Welles used Madison's Virginia Resolution of 1798, which he copied verbatim to provide the main context for his argument. From it he derived two additional resolutions specifically condemning the Fugitive Slave Law. If one accepted Jeffersonian doctrine, the constitutional position was clear. The Fugitive slave provision in the United States Constitution was a solemn compact between the states, and neither Congress nor any other instrumentality of the federal government was mentioned in the provision. The power, then, lay solely with the states, which, Welles admitted, were enjoined to render up fugitives. But the states themselves, as sovereign entities, were the judges of who were fugitives and who were not—their laws and their courts were the deciding factors. Federal agents who entered free states to seize alleged fugitives were invading the states' jurisdictions. The law, in Welles' words, was "an assumption of undelegated power" that set state laws aside and gave judicial powers to a commissioner who might not necessarily be a judge and whose decree was final without appeal. It "permits a citizen to be deprived of his liberty through *ex parte* evidence taken at a distance and without confronting the witnesses against him"—no trial by jury, no protection of habeas corpus, no time permitted for the accused to secure witnesses in his own behalf.

Welles' resolutions were a powerful indictment, one of the most cogent and persuasive constitutional arguments he would ever make. Locally, they served their purpose in squelching the pro-Compromise resolution. But their significance as an educational document went far beyond state boundaries. Bryant devoted an editorial to them in the *Evening Post*. The *New-York Tribune* published the resolutions with favorable comment. They were picked up and reprinted by scores of antislavery papers in the Northeast and the Old Northwest. Welles sent Van Buren a copy, together with a long letter amplifying his argument and citing historical as well as constitutional precedents. The ex-President thought them admirable, though he was depressed that political principles were so little understood as to require restatement of old republican doctrine.

Except for this one excursion, Welles studiously refrained from any active participation in public affairs. Parties continued in their confused state, with conservative Democrats about equally balanced with conservative Whigs, and Free-Soil elements holding the balance of power. Neither of the old-line organizations was willing to make the concessions demanded for Free-Soil support. Isaac Toucey, to Welles' satisfaction, again failed in his bid for the Senate.[13] Toucey's insistence on being the undisputed master of the party had brought him into collision with other ambitious claimants and threatened the Hartford-New Haven axis.

Overshadowing the factionalism—which beset the Whigs as much as the Democrats—was the gathering uproar over the Fugitive Slave Law. Welles' resolutions could not have been more timely. Carriage-makers in New Haven, worrying about their Southern trade, backed up the regular organizations. The rising insurance industry of Hartford wanted no political disturbances that would staunch the rich flow of premiums on cotton risk accounts, but, beyond these special interests, businessmen as a group were divided on the territorial and the slavery questions. Many of Welles' most radical friends were dry goods merchants or manufacturers, such as Albert and Calvin Day and John M. Niles. Politics was still a personal affair, the organization an end in itself, the issues more a matter of ritual and rhetoric than of ideology. Even the muffled rumblings of class conflict during Jackson's administration had been more fanciful than real. The Compromise of 1850 was destroying the Whig's national organization and with it the two-party system, but the state organizations held fast.

Although the territorial question began with the Wilmot Proviso, the issues were not understood in Connecticut, nor in much of the Northeast, for that matter. The press was largely responsible for this state of public ignorance. Supported in part by federal and state patronage, partisan editors did not print information they considered disruptive. The acrimonious debates over the slavery question which claimed major attention during the twenty-ninth and thirtieth Congresses were deliberately not reported or were glossed over by the *Hartford Times*, for example. When Welles complained about the blackout of congressional news, Burr replied that there was "so much infamous stuff, so much quarreling . . . I feared if we published full reports our friends would in some measure partake of the spirit" and jeopardize the state election. Welles' concern about partisan censorship seemed amply justified during an extensive tour he made through the Northeast in the late summer of 1848. "Neither the democratic nor Whig presses," he wrote Van Buren, "have published in the free States the powerful arguments made in Congress against the extension of slavery. Devotion to organization forbids them from speaking the truth."

Popular sovereignty had thrown a smoke screen over the territorial question, deluding partisan editors and organization leaders as well as the average voter. Finespun arguments over whether a territory possessed sovereignty made little impression on the public. Burr, for instance, could see no practical difference between free-soilers and popular sovereignty men in the North, and he had given the subject careful attention. "We are all free-soil here," he exclaimed heatedly after continued prodding from Welles, and then went on to expound the popular sovereignty view.[14] California's admission to the Union as a free state at the express desire of her people was a triumph for the partisan editors. It took much of the force from the arguments of the free-soilers, who had stoutly maintained that popular sovereignty was a cloak under which slavery would be smuggled into the territories. The Fugitive Slave Law was another matter. What Welles saw as a patent violation of human rights and the rights of the states was striking through to the masses in the north, even forcing a change in the tone of the controlled press. Burr read Welles' resolutions with care and found much to commend in them.

By happy coincidence, the editor had finally decided that Toucey's insistence on again being the party's choice for Senator was endangering the organization. Perhaps Welles was right after all. Others in the state organization who had grown restive under the whip of Toucey and his managers, but who adamantly opposed free-soil agitation, saw Welles' position in a new light. "Their prejudice . . . does not extend to me," Welles wrote, "and my known hostility to the compromise, they are satisfied, is founded in reason and honest conviction. . . ."[15] The *Times* editor proposed they renew their old political-editorial partnership, an offer that Welles gratefully accepted. Reconciliation put his vast store of knowledge, his experience, and his powerful connections again behind the chief Democratic paper in the state.[16] It also eased tensions that might have split the Democrats into opposing camps. Toucey and his clique continued their personal opposition to Welles and worked for Buchanan. They also brought pressure on Burr, who for once did not flinch when they threatened disciplinary action. Unprepared to make a test, Toucey backed off, keeping Buchanan's name discreetly before the public in the columns of the *New Haven Register*. An uneasy truce prevailed. By now Welles was working with "Conscience" Whigs as well as free-soil Democrats. Charles Sumner of Massachusetts had been added to his list of correspondents and political allies.[17]

Welles, Burr, and Cleveland (who had been triumphantly re-elected to Congress on a fusion ticket in the spring election of 1852) acted as a team against the Buchanan forces—and the Stephen A. Douglas forces—in the state. But their efforts, Welles insisted, should not be merely defensive in character, nor should they be local in application. Connecticut influence must be exerted nationally. From his Washington experience, he knew the dangers of premature presidential booms, yet he wanted to test the old method of state nominations as a first step in abolishing the national convention system. The candidate had to be chosen with care, preferably a Southerner, one who would be acceptable to the thousands of Free-Soilers in precarious alliance with party regulars. Expediency dictated that Welles restrain his deep-felt convictions on the Fugitive Slave Law—his firm belief that it was *the* vital issue of the times. No Democrat could be nominated, much less elected, who opposed the law openly. His personal choice was Sam Houston, a Southerner who, he felt, could deal effectively with Southern extremists, a man of national stature, of independent convictions, and, above all, a staunch Unionist in the Jackson sense. Houston's name had bobbed up from time to time in the political gossip relayed by the Washington letter writers, but few of the party's leading managers had taken him seriously as a candidate, which made him all the more appealing to Welles. No one symbolized manifest destiny better than Houston; no one in Welles' eyes combined more effectively popular appeal with sound political doctrine. Although Houston had voted for the Fugitive Slave Law, Welles thought him shrewd enough to handle that explosive issue tactfully—not force it on the North, and, recognizing its violation of states' rights, work for repeal.

Before anything could be done, careful soundings had to be made. At the moment the warring factions in New York were trying to patch up their differences. For Houston to be a formidable candidate, he would have to have strong support from the Empire State. Writing Preston King in early September, Welles gave the portly New Yorker the impression that Houston was the popular choice of Connecticut Democrats—scarcely an accurate appraisal of a party that divided between Douglas, whom the New Haven clique were favoring, and Buchanan, Toucey's choice. Douglas was probably the most popular among the masses of the party; Houston was merely a gleam in Welles' eye. Yet the gleam brightened perceptibly when he elicited a favorable response from Francis Preston Blair, Sr., one of the kingmakers in the party and a leader of its radical wing. With this assurance, the *Hartford Times* floated Houston's name in a series of carefully written articles from Welles' pen. Half a dozen country papers, from Maine to North Carolina, responded with favorable comment. The boomlet, for it was nothing more at this point, got added impetus when Houston's senatorial colleague, Thomas Jefferson Rusk, began to coordinate efforts for his fellow Texan in Washington. His activities and those of Welles had enough impact on Edmund Burke, who was quietly surveying the political scene in New England, to mark Houston as one of the three leading candidates. Burke, whom Welles had known for years, was a wire-puller of some renown. He was currently seeking the vice presidential nomination for Franklin Pierce. From John A. Dix came word that the radicals might rally behind Houston, but he declared frankly, "I consider the whole game a doubtful one, the multiplicity of candidates may give us a good man. In the meantime if you can carry Connecticut for Houston . . . it will be a point gained." Preston King finally answered Welles' inquiry in early December. He mentioned a new possibility, William L. Marcy, whom he personally opposed but had to admit "many of our friends" support.[18]

With all this conflicting information before him, Welles decided that a Washington trip was a matter of some urgency. He wanted to talk with Houston and Rusk, who were being assisted now by several clerks Welles had installed in the Navy Department when he was bureau chief. He persuaded Burr to join him. The company would be pleasant, but more than that, he thought it wise for the editor to be more closely identified with the radical leaders of the party. Welles, it would seem, was taking no chances that the *Times* might slip back under the thumb of Toucey and his conservative associates, or Hunkers, as the radicals called them, borrowing the term from their New York friends, the Barnburners.

At the National Hotel they met with Sam Houston and Rusk, and the four had a long conversation in which politics vied with anecdotes. The bearded Houston, in picturesque military garb of his own design, was genial and expansive—now recalling an incident of the Texan war, now speaking in reverential tones of Andrew Jackson, now praising extravagantly or damning eternally personalities living or dead. Welles had observed him in action on the floor of the Senate. He had heard all the rumor and legend that had grown up about the man, but he had never enjoyed the opportunity of an informal, intimate conversation, of being with Houston when he was relaxing with friends. It was a thoroughly delightful occasion. Welles decided that the Senator was one of the most independent men he had ever met, that he would never be managed by any designing clique. To the carefully controlled New Englander, Houston seemed tactless in his remarks, his judgments more intuitive than reasoned, yet his comments on politics revealed a depth and a shrewdness that more than compensated for his other weaknesses. Clearly a man of action and of transparent honesty, the Texan knew the devious ways of the jobbers, the fixers, the calculating operators who infested the capital. Journalists Welles and Burr saw Houston as splendid copy—controversial, of course, but all the better for that.

Exhilarated by Houston, they were brought back to reality when they dined with Preston King and Blair. The dinner was elegant, for the sharp-eyed, sharp-tongued Jacksonian editor, grown rich on the profits of the *Congressional Globe*, lived sumptuously at Silver Spring, his rambling country estate. Welles spoke glowingly of Houston, but Blair doubted whether the Texan was acceptable to the South, which was currently leaning toward Buchanan and Douglas. He and Benton were still supporting William O. Butler of Kentucky, a well-known Indian fighter who looked like Andrew Jackson, though they were quite willing to back Houston if he could develop any strength in the slave states—an unlikely prospect. Blair added that most of Douglas' legion of enemies were partial to Butler. Preston King agreed, doubtless mentioning the fact that Hannibal Hamlin and "Prince" John Van Buren, the ex-President's gifted son, were trying, with Marcy, to arrange a solid New York delegation for Butler. Welles was bound to respect these comments, since Benton, Blair, and King were among the most knowledgeable politicians in the party. He still thought Houston "the strongest candidate we can bring out," but he was not as confident about his chances for the nomination after the Blair dinner. Typically, he gave vent to his feelings in his diary: "There is uncertainty and worthlessness in the party's organization . . . intrigues that are disgusting . . . the compromise measures and the union movements have deranged parties and broken down principles. . . ."[19]

No sooner had Welles returned to Hartford than Butler was accused of making a deal with the free-soil faction of the Democratic party. Though he denied the allegation, the Kentucky legislature forced him to state publicly that Congress had no power over slavery in the territories. This declaration took him effectively out of the running. Free-soil Democrats on the verge of joining their Hunker brethren drew back, making it plain they could not support anyone who would permit slavery in the territories north of the Missouri Compromise line.

After the collapse of the Butler boom, Welles saw his chance to push Houston into the breach. In Washington the opinionated Free-Soil Senator Charles Sumner came to the same conclusion on Houston that Welles had five months earlier. "I am won very much by Houston's conversation," he wrote John Bigelow, "with him the Anti-Slavery interest would stand better than with any man who seems now among the possibilities; he is really against slavery, and has no prejudices against Free Soilers. . . ." On Welles' invitation, Houston visited Connecticut to see and be seen. It was hoped that the state convention about to meet would declare for him and that Houston men would be chosen as delegates from the various districts. The flamboyant Texan made an excellent popular impression, but his marked cordiality to Welles and Burr aroused the usual jealousy and fears of the conservative managers of the party. "Houston's name will be urged as a sort of compromise," wrote Congressman Colin M. Ingersoll from New Haven. "We of this quarter can not go for it—even if we have to break with them." As a result, the convention refused to endorse any of the candidates, and the delegates were uninstructed. Had a poll been taken of the rank and file Democrats, it probably would have shown Houston to be more popular than Douglas or Buchanan, but, as Welles remarked scornfully, "as things are now constituted, there is very little independence in political action." Noting the chaos that was reigning within the Whig party among the "silver grays," the Seward radicals, and the pro-slavery Whigs of the South, he decided "it would be a blessing to the country to have the democrats also unable to unite." He wanted a clean sweep of the old party organizations, "the corrupt and pernicious combinations which have become chronic . . . a thorough shaking up would do us good, and I should rejoice to see at least a half a dozen candidates."[20]

Welles' outlook was not improved by Toucey's election to the Senate on his fourth try. The Whig party in the state, now showing unmistakable signs of disintegration, could not muster enough strength to check him even with Free-Soil support. Welles still cherished a forlorn hope that Douglas, Cass, Buchanan, and Marcy would use each other up and Houston would break the impasse. The Connecticut delegates, Burr complained from the Democratic convention in Baltimore, "are very uncertain . . . you can not draw out of them with a corkscrew a word as to who they will vote for . . . if we only had six right men here, they could do a great deal."[21] Even if united and skillfully led, the Connecticut delegation could not have done much for Houston in a convention so tightly controlled by the Buchanan, Cass, and Douglas managers. During the forty-eight roll calls before the final rush to Franklin Pierce on the forty-ninth, Houston's vote never rose above ten.

Welles was astonished when news of Pierce's nomination reached Hartford. He had met the nominee on several occasions and thought him pleasant—indeed, charming—though scarcely a man of presidential timber. In former years closely associated with Levi Woodbury—a dubious recommendation in Welles' eyes—Pierce was known as an orthodox Jacksonian of the strictest type. Only on the slavery question—the most vital of all, to men of Welles' stamp—did there seem a certain ambiguity; yet even on this politically delicate subject Pierce had declared himself—he had once criticized the Fugitive Slave Law before a public meeting in New Hampshire. Since then he had preserved a discreet silence in public—beyond his enthusiastic acceptance of the Democratic platform, including its specific pledge not to repeal or change the law "so as to destroy or impair its efficiency." Preston King voiced the uneasiness of the free-soil Democrats when he wrote Welles that "the platform is mischievous in its present and future consequences." What, he queried, *would be* Pierce's policy" on the controversial act if he were elected?

Many radical Democrats, finding themselves in a similar dilemma, turned to Welles and Niles for the answer, because few had had any contact with Pierce. King, who made it his business to know everyone of consequence in party circles, was not personally acquainted with the candidate. Blair and Benton had vague impressions of his being a hardworking Senator on the insignificant committee on pensions. Information was especially sought from Niles, who had been a friend of Pierce before he had resigned abruptly from the Senate in 1842.

Welles and Niles found themselves in an awkward position. Their original ambivalence about the nominee was not dispelled after they learned more about the convention proceedings. Welles was troubled by the prominent part that two Boston Hunkers, Caleb Cushing and B. F. Hallet, had played in the nomination. All the traits he detested in practical politics—rampant ambition, shiftiness, secret maneuvers, sudden betrayals—were personified in the careers of these "comorants," as Niles described them. Cushing, an able lawyer, accomplished linguist, and fine essayist, approached politics with a devious cynicism unparalleled among the partisan freebooters of the day. He had started his career in the Whig party, became one of the Tyler apostates, and, when they were cast adrift, eased into Democratic ranks, where he soon became the leading Massachusetts Hunker. Old John Quincy Adams had known him as a man of no moral principles—"a Prodicus or a Gorgias in the days of Socrates."[22] Hallet, his partner, or rather, junior partner, among the conservative Democrats of the Bay State, bore similar stains of blatant opportunism. Should such men be in Pierce's confidence, as Welles half suspected, a bleak future lay in store for the free-soil Democrats of New England.

Viewing the situation realistically, Welles and Niles had no alternative but to hope that Pierce, in the interests of harmony and of his own future, would not be guided by men of such easy political virtue. They were well aware that their friends in other states were eager to resolve factional strife, to share in the promised spoils of a Democratic victory. With what knowledge they had of Pierce's character, they hoped that he, as a New Englander and a life-long Jacksonian, would resist further expansion of slavery and leave enforcement of the Fugitive Slave Law to the states, where they felt it properly belonged. Niles wrote to William Petit, an intimate friend of Van Buren, and to Preston King that Pierce's stand on the platform ought to be accepted as a matter of expediency. Welles took a different line: assuring other troubled Democrats of his acquaintance that the candidate would do, he stressed the importance of having moderate men from both North and South in the Cabinet. For the crucial post of Secretary of State, his choice was John A. Dix, a New York Barnburner or Van Buren Democrat but certainly not of the radical free-soil faction. Twice Welles recommended Dix in the strongest possible terms to King, who forwarded the letters to Pierce. Through Petit and King, Blair, Van Buren, and Benton were apprised of their ideas on the nominee and his potential Cabinet.[23]

At home the Hunkers were more at sea than the free-soil faction in the party was. Since none of them had worked for the Pierce nomination, they had no choice but to bury their differences. For the first time in four years the Democrats presented a united front, and they carried the state easily for Pierce in November. Niles and Welles wrote long letters to the President-elect, proffering their advice and suggesting Cabinet members, among them most prominently John A. Dix. Welles made bold to warn Pierce that Caleb Cushing was not acceptable to the free-soil Democrats "of this quarter." "If . . . all the leading Democrats in and about Boston were to leave at once for Oregon," he had no doubt that "the democracy of Massachusetts would be benefitted." Welles closed his letter with a wise injunction which, if it had been followed, might have spared the Pierce administration many of its disastrous blunders: "Past differences and rivalries are not to be conciliated in the way of appointments. To recognize these differences is to perpetuate them."[24]

Pierce first bent one way, then the other; and finally, in an effort to placate all factions, pleased none. His selection of Marcy for the State Department in place of Dix was acceptable to Welles and his friends, but Cabinet posts for Jefferson Davis and Caleb Cushing seemed a most outrageous pandering to Southern extremists and their Northern allies. Cushing's appointment could only give aid and comfort to Welles' political enemies in New England. Typical of his opponents' vengeful attitude was the clamor they had raised when Dix was being mentioned prominently for the State Department. "In my judgment," wrote Toucey to Governor Seymour, "it [Dix's appointment] would be attended by the most disastrous consequences, that the Northern Democracy should be represented in the cabinet by a gentleman who was a free-soiler and went against us in 1848."[25]

The original hopes of the free-soil Democracy, that it would have a controlling influence over Pierce, were neither raised nor completely dashed by his Cabinet appointments. Welles' posture of watchful waiting seems indicative of their general outlook. Whatever his doubts regarding the new President, there was some evidence that Pierce would curb the sectional pretensions of the South and in the distribution of patronage do justice to the thousands of free-soil Democrats who had voted for him. His immediate popularity must also be taken into account. Welles was too much of the political realist to waste his substance on the desert air. Senator Toucey and Governor Seymour were in an accommodating mood, willing to accept his advice on patronage matters and to assist him in securing posts for deserving Democrats. Seymour, who had fought with Pierce in Mexico, recommended Welles' brother-in-law, Reuben Hale, for the collectorship of the Port of Philadelphia, a post he subsequently received. When Toucey visited Washington in mid-March, he worked unsuccessfully to secure a foreign mission for another of Welles' friends. Pierce was ineffably charming and apparently agreeable to tactful suggestions from Welles on local appointments. After his last visit, Welles came away from the White House with the distinct impression that the President might just reconstitute the party—cut the cords that bound the Southern sectionalists to the northern Hunkers and, by strongly asserting states' rights, rally the Jacksonians of the slave states against those who would distort its true meaning. Four weeks later, when he was again in Washington, charged with a variety of political chores, he sensed a change in the Pierce mystique, "a credulity regarding appointments" that he had not suspected earlier.[26]

Welles had had enough of Washington for the time being, and enough of politics, for that matter. The Hunkers were again in full sway at home after a sweeping victory at the polls over the Whigs, who had lost a good third of their strength to the Free-Soilers. In other times and under other conditions he might have been tempted by this display of third party strength, but prohibitionists and abolitionists had gained a decided influence over the disaffected Whigs that made up the bulk of the Free-Soil membership. The amalgam of old Whig doctrine, abolition, and prohibition struck at two basic concepts dear to Welles' heart—the rights of states to preserve their integrity against encroachments of the national government, and the rights of individuals to manage their own private affairs without the interference of the state. Much as he was dissatisfied with the condition of the Democratic party, he would not countenance either abolition of slavery where protected by the Constitution or sumptuary laws that interfered with the individual's right to do as he pleased with his own life. He remained a Democrat, but his doubts about the character and the judgment of the new President increased.

The administration's policy on patronage was already signalling disaster in the pivotal states of New York and Massachusetts, where armies of Hunkers and free-soil Democrats clashed with relentless fury. Commenting on the vicious role Cushing had played in the Massachusetts conflict, Welles said that, if Pierce "does not prove a Tyler, I shall be thankful. . . . No wise man or sound Democrat would have taken to his bosom Caleb Cushing."[27]

When the first session of the thirty-third Congress was scarcely six weeks old, Welles was sure that Pierce would prove worse than Tyler, not just in his appointment policy, but in statesmanship. He had read all the texts of a new bill introduced by Senator Stephen A. Douglas that would create the new territory of Kansas out of the Nebraska territory and organize it under popular sovereignty. As reported on January 23, 1854, a section had been added that explicitly repealed the Compromise of 1820. Welles recognized at once the sweeping implications of the bill. In principle, popular sovereignty was broadened to include all remaining lands of the Union. If the bill became law, a precedent would be set that would permit slaveholders free access to the entire public domain. Alleged geographical limitations seemed now the only deterrent to a slave-state-dominated continent that Welles and Niles had feared was in the making during the early years of the Polk administration. At that time both men had scoffed at the notion that slavery was constrained by any physical boundaries of climate or soil or growing seasons. Slavery had once existed in the free states; it was currently flourishing in Missouri. Why should it not be profitable in Kansas, Nebraska, and other unsettled areas north of the Compromise line?

The almost casual move for repeal of a solemn and venerable compact with thirty-four years of history and tradition behind it, one of the few landmarks in the heritage of the young Republic, dramatically confirmed the point Welles had been trying to make for some years. Popular sovereignty was a delusion that deprived the federal government of any political control over its own territories. A decision made in a scattering of rude frontier settlements where law and order was likely to be a meaningless phrase would determine the future of the American empire. Crucial issues of domestic policy would not be determined in Washington, but on the prairies of Kansas and Nebraska. "Senator Douglas," wrote Welles in February 1854, "has committed a great and for himself an inextricable error. . . . Some of our Southern friends . . . should recollect that the vibrations of the popular pendulums are to extremes. One extreme follows another as they will find. . . ."[28]

# CHAPTER 15

# Free Soil and
# Frémont

ON MAY 31, 1854, President Pierce signed the Kansas-Nebraska Act.
Two days later one Anthony Burns, a Negro slave who had fled to
Massachusetts, was returned to his master over the angry but non-
violent protest of Boston's citizens. Anticipating trouble, the authorities thought it necessary to make a display of armed might, so Anthony
Burns was escorted to the ship that would carry him South by a company of federal troops—over 100 armed deputies and marshals and
1000 state militiamen.[1]

It had been a bad week for freedom, for free soil, and for states'
rights. To Gideon Welles, who had followed the dispatches being telegraphed from Boston, the events of those first days of June stamped
out whatever lingering hopes he may have had that right would prevail. In his despair, he lashed out at the great betrayal in Washington,
at the feckless President guided by his "vicious advisors." The two-
party system was dead, if indeed it had ever existed. Perhaps it had all
been delusion, a conjuring trick, conceived and manipulated by designing men out for power and office. The activities of "fixers" such as
Robert J. Walker, Caleb Cushing, and James Buchanan during the
preceding three presidential campaigns had convinced Welles that national nominating conventions were painted sets behind which small
cliques pulled the wires and levers of party machinery.

Welles had finally decided that any organization which forbade individual comment, whose leaders arrogated to themselves the right to
determine what men and what measures would govern the nation, was
flouting public opinion and holding democracy up to contempt. Never
before had he felt so strongly that the major parties had outlived their

usefulness, that for the preceding four years, at any rate, it had been impossible to distinguish anything but the "remnants of old organizations . . . founded on past associations and antagonisms." "Where," he asked, "are the lines and landmarks . . . that separate the democrats and the Whigs?" Since the passage of the Compromise measures in 1850, the Democrats had lost their principles and the Whigs their identity. "Old issues had become obsolete, new ones avoided or suppressed." Centralism, he charged, "controls democrats and Whigs alike." If anyone doubted the allegation let him look to Washington, where Pierce had, as Welles put it, just "nationalized" slavery, or to Boston, where 1200 armed men and a cannon loaded with cannister had "invaded" Massachusetts under federal mandate to seize a man without due process of law and with utter disregard for the rights of a sovereign state.[2]

But anguish rather than rage guided Welles' pen as he indicted parties and party leadership in article after article. His memory went back to 1846 and the Walker tariff, the debates over the Wilmot Proviso, the time when Niles and Preston King had talked of an Africanized continent. Since then two more successful attacks had been mounted on free institutions. The options of the North and of states' rights, as Welles understood them, seemed to be dwindling away. Southern extremists and their Northern toadies (present-minded speculators and placemen) had gone far beyond Alexander Hamilton in asserting the power of the federal government over the local institution of slavery. The Fugitive Slave Law had been a monstrous perversion of Jeffersonian Democracy. Now the Kansas-Nebraska Act, this "adopted bantling of Northern political aspirants," was it not reserving the national domain for slaveholders? And if it was, when would the federal government force slavery upon the free states? The more he thought and wrote about contemporary events, the more he was convinced that he was witnessing the death throes of the great Republic. The Democratic party, which had claimed his most productive years, had degenerated into an alien thing, an instrument of subversion. Late at night and alone he questioned the meaning of his own life, the drifting into politics, the decision to make it a career. Had he squandered his youth and his energy and his talents for nothing? He was fifty-two years old, a politician without a party, a public man who lacked a public, and, for all he knew, an editorial writer without an audience. At times like these his own sense of personal failure was deepened by his private grief, for within the year he had lost a son, Herbert, and his only daughter, Anna Jane.

Herbert's death, in August 1853, had been sudden and heart-wrenching, but for the sake of the family Welles had controlled his feelings. The death of his eighteen-year-old daughter in April 1854, however, was almost more than he could bear. Welles had always been more deeply attached to his daughter (whose large brown eyes and heavy dark brown hair were so like his mother's) than to any of his other children. His heart ached at her suffering. Whenever he saw a group of healthy, active boys and girls sleighing or skating or walking carefree through the streets on a pleasant day he "thought much and sadly of dear Anna Jane, whose early youth has been so overcast with pain and illness and in so many deprivations of what makes life at her age gladsome and joyous." When she was fifteen her right arm became paralyzed, and he taught her to write with her left hand. He always spent a part of each day at her bedside, reading to her, planning what they would do together when she was well. Though it became increasingly obvious that she would not recover, he and his wife grasped at every straw, every hope that somehow she would be cured or that someone would hit upon the appropriate remedy. They consulted half a dozen physicians, including the celebrated Dr. Marshall Hall of London, a world authority on the nervous system, who was visiting New York gathering material for his book on American slavery. Hall, who was not well himself at the time, was brought to Hartford at great expense. He raised Welles' spirits temporarily when he confidently pronounced that she would recover and prescribed new medications. Yet her condition deteriorated. In their desperation the anguished couple employed clairvoyants and dangerous drugs like chloroform. There would be short-term remissions when Welles dared hope she was improving, only to be followed by a steeper decline. In December of 1853 the young woman's suffering became so intense that only Welles, his wife, and a full-time nurse entered the sick room. Finally, toward the end, his iron resolve was broken down completely by the intense suffering of his beloved daughter. He found he could not bear to visit her for whatever comfort he might give. "Coward, shrinking wretch that I am," he accused himself, "I can not attend the bedside of that suffering child. It would . . . with all my efforts and resolutions, unman me." In his depression everything seemed futile. "If one so pure and good as our dear daughter is so tortured and distressed, what inducement is there to live and do? The ways of God are past finding out." Anna Jane died a few months after he made this entry, on April 10, 1854.[3]

The passing of his daughter had a curious effect on Welles. To be sure, in a sentimental man who idolized his family the sorrow was deep

and lasting. Years later, amid all the cares and responsibilities of a
Cabinet post in wartime, he would remember her birthday and indulge a moment of silent grief. Until he left for Washington in 1861,
he and his wife paid a visit at least once a month to the family burial
plot in Spring Grove Cemetery where Anna Jane, her baby sister, and
her three baby brothers were buried. But apart from his private grief,
Anna Jane's lingering illness and agonizing death seems to have quickened Welles' interest in political affairs.

Previously, when family tragedy had befallen him, Welles had re-
treated within himself, betraying a lack of confidence which was evident in the style and in the substance of his writings. For a time he
would curtail his political activities, or, indeed, anything that might
bring him into contact with people. Then slowly he would grope his
way back from the depths of melancholia. His writing would improve,
his interest would quicken, and he would be again in public.

Though more stricken than ever before, Welles did not follow his
usual pattern of retreat and exclusion. His daughter's death in some
ways strengthened his will, not just to work and to mingle in society
but to work vigorously and well. Some of his more trenchant pieces on
public affairs were completed during the spring and summer of 1854.

The party might still be redeemed, he thought, as he watched with
satisfaction the hurricane of protest from the free states when the Kansas-Nebraska bill was unveiled. Leonard Bacon, nestor of New England
Congregationalism, besought Senator Toucey "in the name of millions" to vote against the measure, "as he would answer to his fel-
lowmen and to his God." Toucey refused to be moved by Bacon's letter, which appeared in the New York *Independent*. Nor was he deterred
when he was burned in effigy from one end of the state to the other,
nor when the legislature elected the abolitionist Francis Gillette to be
his colleague and a "Conscience Whig," Lafayette Foster, to be his
successor.[4] Isolated in the Washington community, Toucey had misjudged the sentiment at home, believing it to be the work of a few disappointed politicians like Welles, Niles, and Chauncey Cleveland. Yet
many organization Democrats at home were just as unaffected. Daniel
Seymour, writing his cousin Thomas, the ex-governor, then Minister
to Russia, spoke harshly of the *Hartford Times*, which Welles had
swung behind the anti-Nebraska Democrats. "The fact is, Tom," he
wrote, "that paper must give less heed to Gid Welles & his clique or it
can not much longer be the mouthpiece of Democracy."[5]

In all of these stirring events Welles involved himself. "I have been
denounced by some as a free-soiler," he wrote, "though I never gave a

free-soil vote." But he had opposed the extension of the Missouri Compromise line to the Pacific in 1848, and he opposed it now. If the original Compromise of 1820 were before the country, he would be against it, as he would be against all efforts to establish slavery in the territories under federal auspices.[6] Welles' position had really not changed since 1846, though he was becoming more directly involved with antislavery Democrats and Whigs. Elected a trustee of the Emigrant Aid Company which had just been formed in New York by Eli Thayer and Horace Greeley to settle free-soil whites in Kansas, Welles attended his first meeting at the St. Nicholas Hotel on August 1, 1854.[7]

As he moved deeper into the mainstream of the radical New York Democracy, he renewed some friendships of years past and his circle of acquaintances widened. He met for the first time John Bigelow, Bryant's partner in the editing of the New York *Evening Post*. Each had known the other by reputation and by correspondence. Bigelow had long admired the lucid style and the clarity of Welles' editorial work, as had Bryant, who had been publishing Welles' letters and editorials in the *Post* for six years. At this time Welles, through Bigelow, had as much influence on the editorial policy of the *Post* as any other politician in the country did. His old Jacksonian views and his free-soil inclinations coincided almost exactly with those of the *Post* editors, neither of whom would associate himself with the Free-Soil party. Though opposed to further extension of slavery into the territories, he did not approve of anything else the Free-Soil party espoused: protective tariff, internal improvements, prohibition, abolition. While a chance existed that their views on the territorial question might capture the Democratic party organization in the free states, they would keep clear of any splinter groups.[8]

Since 1848, when Welles had written a vigorous attack on national conventions (which the *Post* had published), his small but influential group of independent Democrats—all newspapermen—continued to flirt with the idea of nominating presidential candidates in a select number of journals and running them through an availability contest. Blair, Bigelow, and King were receptive to the idea. During 1854 the *Post* experimented with the technique. Welles suggested Houston again. The Texas Senator had electrified the free-soil Democrats with his fiery denunciation of the Kansas-Nebraska Bill. "What say you to Houston . . . ," he wrote Blair in mid-summer of 1854, "and a movement at once." Blair was receptive, and so was King. Bigelow of the *Post* and Burr of the *Times* stood ready to float Houston's name. Then Welles learned that his candidate was suspected of being a

Know-Nothing. He immediately shied off. His long acquaintance with nativism in many forms convinced him that it was a class of bigotry unworthy of any free and enlightened citizen, much less a presidential candidate.[9]

The Know-Nothing party, newest and hardiest manifestation of nativism, had appeared as a formidable political force during the debates over the Nebraska bill. In New England, nativism had been a sporadic political issue since the mid-1830's. Directed mainly against Roman Catholics, and fanned by such blatant forgeries as *The Confessions of Maria Monk*, it had the same intolerance and emotional fervor as the Anti-Masonic movement.[10] But unlike the Anti-Masonic movement, nativism had never developed beyond a purely local organization.

The heavy influx of Irish and German immigrants during the 1840's and early 1850's created social disorder and economic imbalance, especially in the cities and towns of New England and the Middle Atlantic states. In 1830 Connecticut had the most homogeneous population of any state in the Union, its people almost entirely of English stock. Twenty years later, one out of every five citizens was foreign-born. Perhaps half the population of the major cities and towns were recent immigrants. Slum areas had sprung up like poisonous growths along the railroad lines where the factories were. Dirty, rat-infested, crime-ridden, the immigrant ghettos not only disfigured the appearance of the cities, but they also created social ills that could not be confined to any one district.

To be sure, it was the rapid industrialization of southern New England in the 1850's that was really responsible for the slums. The railroads, for instance, were the prime carriers of the blight, but no enterprise could have been less concerned about its social obligations. The Hartford and New Haven's engine houses, repair shops, and water tanks stood right in the center of Hartford. Bounded on one side by the city dump, where the filth lapped up to the edges of Asylum Street and the portico of the new Park Street Church, the railroad terminus gave way on the west to an odoriferous soap works and a row of ramshackle tenements with outhouses projecting over the east and northeast bank of the Park River. A disgusted Horace Bushnell, in a moment of ironic whimsy, had the river "saying, as it were to the coming ornament, 'We give you such help as we can.'"[11] Yet the sober Yankee could and did blame intemperance, crime, vice, dirt, disease, and in fact almost everything disagreeable upon the immigrants. As the Whig party began to break up after 1852, local party leaders, anxious to preserve their political careers and sensitively attuned to a promising issue, began entering the Know-Nothing movement with the express notion of converting it into a new party. The movement, which had been organized into secret lodges, continued to veil its proceedings even after being heavily infiltrated by Whig politicians.

The Democracy may have fallen on evil ways, but it had never given in to nativist bigotry, however tempting it might have been as a political issue. The Whigs had frequently—and truthfully—charged the Democratic party with the soliciting of votes from the illiterate (and presumably immoral) immigrant community.[12] Among the old Jeffersonian tenets that kept men like Welles and Bryant within the Democratic organization must be counted the clear stand of the party against nativism under any guise.

By early 1854 Welles recognized the unmistakable signs of political organization and action from the Know-Nothing lodges. Chauncey Jerome, the rich clock manufacturer, was elected mayor of New Haven on a straight-out Know-Nothing ticket. In the fall elections the new party captured forty-eight towns, most of which had been Whig strongholds.[13] Observing its activities and weighing its probable impact, Welles assumed it would help "derange, dislocate and utterly demoralize old party organizations." What he failed to recognize was the outline of a procrustean bed the Know-Nothings were preparing for anti-Nebraska Democrats as well. The movement struck him "as a miserable piece of machinery . . . repugnant to intelligence and common sense and wholly inconsistent with our institutions."[14] Yet he acknowledged that "the order has gathered in great numbers" and could be useful if managed by men of "right principles."

The success of the Know-Nothings and the fusion movements in over half of the Northern states during the summer and fall offered an impressive argument that a new party might be organized on the territorial issue alone. Events in Kansas pointed even more forcibly to a political convulsion of major proportions. Eli Thayer's free-state companies and the proslavery Missourians had already made a powder keg of the eastern section of the territory. Clashes between the two forces were expected at any time. Welles was beginning to doubt that the Democracy could or should survive, and as he took his soundings of the state of the nation he reinforced his ties with sympathetic Whigs such as Truman Smith, who had moved to New York City, and James Babcock, editor of the *New Haven Palladium*.[15] Through King and Bigelow, Welles was brought into closer contact with new party enthusiasts, most of whom, though radical antislavery men, agreed that the Free-Soil party was not worth saving. Dr. Gamaliel Bailey, abolitionist editor of Washington's only Free-Soil paper, Senator Charles Sumner, Congressman Joshua Giddings, and Governor Salmon P. Chase of Ohio exchanged views with Welles. All moved cautiously in the political arena, despite their spirited rhetoric on the subject of slavery in the territories.[16]

Like many anti-Nebraska Democrats, Welles was not quite ready to abandon the party of his youth. Sound practical reasons reinforced his sentimental attachments. The various state fusion movements, he felt, must prove that they could work in harmony, that former political enemies could really cast aside the discipline acquired from twenty years of electioneering. He was enough of a cynic in matters political to wait and see. The emotional side of his nature, too, made any open break with the party a painful, personal affair. While there still seemed a reasonable chance that the Northern Democracy might purge itself of the Kansas-Nebraska folly and take the lead in banning slavery from the territories, he would continue to remain aloof from all new party movements. His friend Burr was still defying the administration, still refusing to be intimidated by Toucey and his coterie. So long as the *Times* and the *Evening Post* maintained what Welles felt were true Jacksonian principles, he saw some hope for the party.

But the administration Democrats had already regrouped their forces and, with the active assistance of President Pierce, were counterattacking. By mid-summer of 1855 the pressure on Burr was so intense that he feared he would face financial ruin. He had neither the courage of his convictions nor the means to hold on during a protracted struggle which he knew would rend the party.[17] Welles found again that his articles were not welcome in the columns of the *Times,* and he turned to other journals, as he had before.[18]

In March of 1855 he had composed but not published an elaborate piece attacking the Fugitive Slave Law, the Kansas-Nebraska Act, and the "alleged" two-party system. For the first time he aired his views locally in a paper other than the *Times*—the *New Haven Palladium,* foremost Whig organ of the state. Denying vigorously that he was now, or had ever been, a free-soiler, Welles admitted that in some respects he "most cordially concurr[ed] with that party," but he emphatically rejected the two major parties—"mere hulks in the channel of progress." As he drew upon constitutional argument and upon the history of the Republic, he declared solemnly, "men and organizations may change, but principles never change." Fundamentally, it was a question of centralism as opposed to states' rights. From Hamilton's and Jefferson's time to the current crisis in Kansas, one or the other view of government's role determined the issues and the party contests. For fifteen years, under the constant thrust of partisanship and sectionalism, the traditional notion of states' rights had been gradually distorted. The parties, now meaningless, "are both to be brushed aside, for the honest instincts . . . of all the free states are right on the fugitive slave law, [and] freedom in the territories. . . . These are the living rising questions of the period, and on them a struggle is to be had. . . ."[19]

It had taken no inconsiderable amount of tortured reflection before he decided on the break. He knew he would meet with a chaos of conflicting ideas, a strange mixture of political backgrounds, prejudices, and suspicions, in any new organization. Could he associate freely and openly with men who, to use his own expression, had "dipped [themselves] to the eyelids in the froth, scum and virulence of the hard cider campaign"? What of the abolitionists and the Know-Nothings? Boldly, he had proclaimed these sectarian political groups to be names only, that the principles behind them "were all that mattered." Could he honestly subordinate his own prejudices for the greater good?[20]

For some time he and Niles had planned a leisurely trip West, where they could test the political climate, inform and be informed. Welles' own personal fears about his political course on new and unchartered waters were apparent in his diary entry for May 26, 1855, written four days before his departure. "Why leave home & a happy family, & assume fatigue, expense & some risk? I feel that I am rusting, that age is bringing on me timidity & inertia." His spirits had improved considerably by the time he reached Ohio. The garrulous Niles, as always, was an agreeable companion, with a quizzical eye for the passing scene and many a word to describe it.

Welles made it a point to visit political leaders of all persuasions, but through habit and acquaintance most of his visits in the West were with Democrats, and conservative ones at that. He did enjoy the particular attention of Salmon P. Chase, who gave him and Niles a drive around Cincinnati. Chase's enthusiasm for the new Republican party and his certainty that it would prevail in Ohio confirmed some judgments Welles had already made. The day before, in Columbus, he had visited with Samuel Medary, the power among administration Democrats of Ohio and editor of the *Ohio Statesman*. Medary, a vehement supporter of the Kansas-Nebraska Act, was well aware that his visitors were sharply critical of the measure and of its sponsor, his close friend Stephen A. Douglas. Yet that did not interfere with his cordial greeting, nor with his flow of conversation on pertinent subjects, which he delivered like round shot from his desk while he scribbled editorial copy furiously on page after page of foolscap.

For a practicing Quaker, Medary had very decided, even pugnacious views on the propriety and the constitutionality of the Fugitive State Law and the repeal of the Missouri Compromise. If any trouble occurred in Kansas it would be the fault of Eli Thayer and Horace Greeley's "Plan for Freedom." Public opinion, he admitted, was in a curious state of flux, but the newly organized Republican party was opposed by both the Whig organization and the administration Democrats. The Know-Nothing party had not committed itself to any fusion movement with the Republicans. Medary rather admired Chase, not for his radical antislavery views, but because of his stump-speaking ability, his intelligence, and his energy. If anyone could rally all the various shades of antislavery opinion in Ohio, he thought Chase was the man. Welles spoke very little, as the white-bearded editor, by the very vehemence of his opposition, acknowledged a far more cohesive free-soil movement in Ohio and a much stronger Republican organization than Welles had suspected.[21]

Except for his talks with Medary and Chase, Welles gathered most of his political intelligence and his understanding of public opinion from the local newspapers, and more especially, from close attention to the small talk of his fellow passengers on the Western trains. But on his return trip, while passing through Detroit, he gleaned some valuable information about the state of the Democratic party from the venerable Lewis Cass. He found the stout old politician "living in unostentatious ease and luxury" in his mansion on Fort Street, near the center of Detroit. Cass was deeply concerned about the future of the Union. "Fanaticism at the south and fanaticism at the north," he told Welles, "are equally unanswerable. Neither will compromise or make concessions." To emphasize his point he spoke of Senator Atchison of Missouri, whom he said had toured the Southern states during the past winter "concerting measures with the governors and leading men at the south to make Kansas a slave state." For President Pierce Cass had only contempt. He had "begged the President not to identify the administration with it [the Kansas-Nebraska bill]," and had been assured by Pierce that the bill was wholly unacceptable to him. Then, with a deep sigh, that veteran of many a political contest said, "the next man he saw had probably different views from mine and the President doubtless agreed with him also."[22]

From Detroit Welles and Niles rode by train to Buffalo and Albany. They reached New York on July 2. Tired, his clothes rumpled from a month of hard traveling, Welles spent the night at the Metropolitan Hotel. After breakfast he went directly to the dingy building that housed the *Evening Post* on the corner of Nassau and Pine Streets. He found Bigelow almost buried under editorial and business chores (Henderson, the business manager, and Bryant were out of town) and trying rather unsuccessfully to edge that talkative Jeffersonian Abijah Mann out of the office. Welles cut short his visit, but not before he gave Bigelow a condensed version of public opinion and political parties in the West. The popular appeal of the administration party was eroding away. Though Douglas still retained a vast personal following—in fact, he stood alone as the most powerful politician in the Northwest —he too was losing ground. Welles was optimistic that Ohio, Indiana, and Michigan would repudiate the Democracy with fusion tickets. Illinois, he thought, would remain with the old organization because of Douglas' personal influence. It was time, he advised Bigelow, to go ahead with plans for a new party organization based on broad enough principles to harmonize most of the independent antislavery factions.[23]

That evening he was home again, studying the mail and the newspapers that had accumulated in his absence. The Know-Nothing tide, he noticed, was still running strong; but even stronger ran the anti-Nebraska sentiment. Connecticut already had a personal liberty law on its statute books to prevent the execution of the Fugitive Slave Law. While he and Niles were in the West, Know-Nothing Governor William T. Minor had condemned the Kansas-Nebraska Act in unsparing terms, calling upon the General Assembly to "protect the just rights of the state." All to the good for men of Welles' outlook, but the shortsighted Know-Nothings had darkened their image among independent Democrats, Whigs, and Free-Soilers by transplanting their nativism into discriminatory legislation that made it more difficult for immigrants to vote and disbanded the various Irish militia companies.

Welles realized that no national party could ever be organized, much less win an election, with that kind of philosophy and leadership. The German vote, so important in the Old Northwest and in the Border states, would surely be alienated by Know-Nothing planks, even if the platform opposed slavery in the territories. Nor could those independent Democrats and Whigs who were steeped in Jeffersonian ideas of religious tolerance and the equality of individuals accept this mockery of the Declaration of Independence. "I have no faith in its reported principles," he wrote Preston King, "and detest a secret political organization. A proscription of men on account of birth is as odious certainly as that of color."[24]

Clearly, it was time to organize a new party, but what of the Know-Nothings, an organization that Welles recognized was "an embarrassment in itself, and perplexes the contest of Fifty-Six"? Any new party would have a hard fight on its hands with the entrenched leadership of the Know-Nothings, though Welles never doubted that the new party would prevail. On the national scene, the Know-Nothings had already broken over the slavery issue into Northern and Southern wings. With no future as a national organization, and strongly opposed by independent Democrats, Whigs, and Free-Soilers in the North, they would have to give way. Thus he had reasoned. And as he began actively to organize a new party in the state, he opened a blistering attack against the Know-Nothing party, "this monstrous . . . intrigue," charging that its leaders were crass political adventurers "with whom one cannot counsel or act without feeling himself defiled and degraded."[25]

While he was working hard to build a new organization in the state, he was also very much a part of the planning that was going forward to create a new national party. "I presume you are aware that some of our friends are discussing Frémont's availability," wrote Bigelow in late December of 1855. Welles had heard mention of Frémont and thought well of him but did not know much about his political views beyond the fact that "he has a general reputation and is obnoxious to none." Welles made it plain to Bigelow that something more than a name was needed when he pleaded ignorance of Frémont's judgment and administrative abilities.[26]

The day before Bigelow wrote Welles about Frémont—Christmas Day, in fact—Francis Preston Blair, Sr., entertained a select group of influential antislavery men. Blair's guest list had been shrewdly conceived, representing as it did leading personalities among all the antislavery factions. His object was a discussion of plans for a new antislavery party and of presidential candidates who might lead it. The guest of honor was Congressman Nathaniel P. Banks of Massachusetts, whom the antislavery factions had finally agreed to support for Speaker of the House. At the time he was far in the lead of all candidates, but could not command a majority. A suave, theatrically handsome man in his late thirties, Banks was a charming dinner companion. If for no other reason than his romantic good looks and his soft, musical voice, any hostess—even the bluff Mrs. Blair—would count herself lucky to entertain this apparent man of destiny. For that matter, most women would have been attracted to the tall stately Senator from Massachusetts, Charles Sumner, and the equally tall and stately Governor of

Ohio, Salmon P. Chase—the one a bachelor, the other a widower. Fat, jolly Preston King, and Dr. Bailey, the consumptive editor of the *New Era*, completed the group. These latter two could not match the impressive dignity of Sumner and Chase or the studied charm of Banks, but each in his own right lent a special virtue that the other lacked— King had transparent sincerity, and Bailey, matchless enthusiasm.

Sumner and Banks, though both from the same state, were as ill-paired as any two politicians in the country. Banks, a politician's politician, a man of expedience rather than principle, had been first a Democrat, then a Free-Soiler, and was currently an antislavery Know-Nothing. Sumner was Free-Soiler, a passionate antislavery man, who never deviated from his course though men like Welles thought he wore his principles on his sleeve. Salmon P. Chase, the Republican Governor of Ohio, was very nearly as radical on the slavery issue as Sumner, but a much more pliable politician. In the teeth of the Democratic and Whig organizations, he had launched a new party which elected him to the governorship by a solid majority in its first campaign. Almost single-handed, Chase had destroyed the old-line organizations in Ohio and made that state a stronghold for the new Republican party. With anti-Nebraska New York Democrat King, New England Free-Soiler Sumner, antislavery Know-Nothing Banks, abolitionist Bailey, and Blair himself an independent Democrat from a Border state, the dinner at Silver Spring was broadly representative of all sections and antislavery persuasions.

Surprisingly, in one evening's discussion all of Blair's objectives were attained. At Chase's suggestion, the group agreed that, after Banks won the speakership, "deemed an indispensable antecedent," a preliminary meeting should be held at Pittsburgh "some time in March" which would float candidates for the presidency and determine whether fusion were practical. If it were, the meeting would organize a new party and plan for a convention to be held in Cincinnati. There was some talk of Welles' notion to imitate Jackson's "spontaneous" nomination in 1828, but this was discarded as impractical. "Much as we are opposed to national conventions," explained King, "our friends here and at Washington think there is no other way in which we can agree upon a candidate." Having decided upon this mode of action, the group discussed informally the question of candidates. By common consent Benton was ruled "out of the question." Blair suggested Frémont, who seemed a good choice. No one present was particularly confident that the new party, if it could be organized in time, had the remotest chance of winning a presidential election. At least Preston

King shared this negative attitude, as did William H. Seward, who had been invited to the dinner but had declined when he learned its purpose. In all likelihood, those present were looking ahead to 1860, and no one, not even the intensely ambitious Chase, was willing at this point to gamble with his political career. "Nothing definite will be reached," wrote Preston King to Welles one week after the dinner, "until the House is organized and our position there more clearly settled."[27]

Welles remained cool to Frémont, preferring Chase or Blair if a new party were organized. He was less receptive, in fact downright hostile, to Blair's idea that a prominent Know-Nothing, such as Banks, should be on the ticket. He distrusted the supple politician from Massachusetts, and by now he was bending all of his efforts to break up the Know-Nothing organization in Connecticut. So vehement was Welles on the subject that King and Bigelow made a flying trip to Hartford to convince him that the Know-Nothings would not be the leading component in the new party.[28]

On February 2 that "indispensable antecedent" was accomplished; Banks was finally elected Speaker on the one hundred and thirty-third ballot. Welles had already made known the tentative plans of the Silver Spring group to his friends and associates, old and new, in Hartford. Characteristically, he remained in the background, delegating the chore of calling a preliminary organization meeting to a young lawyer, Joseph R. Hawley, a new acquaintance who was co-editor of Hartford's only abolitionist newspaper, appropriately named the *Republican*. Hawley wasted no time. On February 4, 1855, Welles, Niles, and a dozen or so independent Democrats, conscience Whigs, and Free-Soilers met in Hawley's law office on Main Street. Three decisions of major import were agreed upon: a new party would be organized immediately; it would be called the Republican party; it would accept but not solicit support from the Know-Nothings. Arrangements had already been made to secure Union Hall for the official organization meeting on February 11, one week later. Hawley had prepared the call, which was approved and ordered printed; then Niles brought up the question of establishing a party newspaper more broadly defined than the *Republican*—not a new subject by any means among the independent Democrats present.[29]

From time to time, for a year and a half, one or another of Welles' associates had registered a strong protest about the policy of the *Times* on the slavery question. Inevitably there had been talk about establishing a rival paper, a topic that had become more pointed after the

*Courant* went over to the Know-Nothings. Each time Welles had squelched the idea, pleading that the time was not right, even though he knew by late 1854 that his argument had little foundation and that it was causing some "dissatisfaction to friends in consequence." During the winter of 1854-55, some months after he had been "virtually excluded from the *Times,*" the question was again raised. Welles refused to associate himself with the project but said that, if a paper were established that was not Whig and not Know-Nothing, he would write for it. The concession was not enough. Welles' experience was deemed absolutely essential for success. The project languished.[30]

When Niles renewed the proposal in Hawley's law office, repeating what was common knowledge—that no political party could be organized without its own press—everyone turned to Welles. With some reluctance, he agreed that he would take upon himself the responsibility of setting up the editorial office and of supervising the editorial page for a time. He even had a name for the paper, not original, but serviceable—the *Evening Press.* Niles volunteered to raise the funds needed to start a daily, which he estimated would be in the range of $10,000. He had no difficulty in securing pledges of $100 each from 100 Hartford citizens, among them himself and Welles. A prospectus for the *Evening Press* was prepared for the mass meeting, which went off as scheduled on February 11.

Over two hundred of the city's leading citizens crowded into Union Hall, along with the idle, the curious, and those who came to spy out the proceedings for the opposing parties. Only three items were presented to the body: endorsement of the *Press,* election of a committee of seven to organize a mass convention, and consideration of a series of resolutions which set forth the basic philosophy of the new party. Welles had prepared the resolutions that consigned the old parties to the scrap heap and arraigned the federal government for "unauthorized assumption of powers" in "nationalizing" slavery. They were accepted with enthusiasm, as was the prospectus for the *Evening Press.* Hawley and Welles were elected to the organizing committee.

While Welles attended to all the details of setting up the *Press,* he also acted as a one-man committee of correspondence. For a business manager, he called in William Faxon, who was more than happy to give up his struggling *Weekly Express* in Amherst, Massachusetts, and come home to Hartford. Welles had known Faxon for some years as the able, industrious, and methodical young man in the *Courant* office, one of the best journeymen printers in Harford. For editor, he chose Edwin Pierce, the talented and experienced son of an old friend, but behind the scenes Welles himself would carry a major share of the burden until he was sure Pierce could manage the delicate job of expressing party sentiment. Quarters were secured at 66 State Street, between the Hartford and the Exchange banks. On February 27, 1856, the first issue came off the press. It bore the unmistakable imprint of Jefferson, Jackson, and Gideon Welles, but more significant than its style or content was the fact that it announced the formation of the Republican party.[31]

Occupied as he was with launching a new party and a new daily newspaper, Welles could not attend the Republican organization meeting in Pittsburgh. Niles declined also, because of failing health, so James M. Bunce, a rich merchant and a close friend of both men, agreed to represent Connecticut at the meeting. Under the circumstances, Bunce was a wise choice. Not well enough known to be included among those who were organizing the meeting, he was spared the factional bickering that marred the preliminary discussions. Had Welles attended, he would surely have been asked and just as surely would have decided that an all-inclusive antislavery party was impossible to organize.[32]

In laying down the strategy for the party, Welles recognized that its objectives had to be limited at this stage in its development. But on one point he was adamant: the party must preserve its separate identity. "It is not expected nor is it desirable," he wrote Babcock, the *Palladium* editor whom he was using as a communication link with Know-Nothing leaders, "that the two parties opposed to the Administration should amalgamate, but they should cooperate. Let each preserve its own identity, but act in harmony and good faith against a common antagonist." If the Know-Nothings did not have a majority in the legislature, he wanted it agreed that they would vote with the Republicans against the administration Democrats in the election of a Governor and, particularly, of a United States Senator. For Toucey was again the candidate of the Democrats, and Welles deemed it imperative that he be defeated.

So much was at stake, and yet there was so little time to organize the new party against a highly disciplined foe. Welles knew what he was up against because he himself had been the major influence in fashioning the tight organization of the Democratic party. He also was well aware that most of the Know-Nothing leaders were seasoned Whig politicians before anything else.[33] February was half gone before the first Republican meeting. The first issue of the *Press* appeared at the end of the month, well after the major parties had held their conventions and had started their campaigns. If the Republicans were to agree on a ticket for state officers and members of the General Assembly, they had to bypass the usual machinery of town, then district, meetings for the election of convention delegates. With a mass convention the only alternative, every possible effort was made to have it broadly representative of all sections of the state. Accordingly, in the first number of the new *Press* a call went out for a convention to be held at Hartford on March 12. Assuming they could nominate a slate and agree on a platform, the Republicans would have exactly three weeks for their campaign before election day on April 2. The most any Republican leader could possibly hope for was a good turnout at Hartford, followed by some slight show of strength in the election.

More than two hundred men crowded into the second floor of Gilman's saloon, which, with a fine disdain for the sensibilities of the prohibitionists, had been chosen for the convention. As expected, the Know-Nothings who had infiltrated the convention tried to control it. The first item of business was an informal ballot for the nomination of state officers. When Know-Nothing Governor William Minor led Republican Chauncey Cleveland in the first informal ballot for Governor but did not gain a majority, several of Welles' old friends made vigorous speeches on the importance of maintaining a Republican party identity and program. While the verbal exchanges were being traded on the floor, Niles, Cleveland, Hawley, and a half a dozen other independent Whigs and Democrats insisted that Welles was the only man of sufficient stature to parry the Know-Nothing onslaught. Welles allowed himself to be persuaded. He could not disavow the sentiments that he had expressed in his letters and conversations on the subject, nor was his attitude all that self-sacrificing. As head of the ticket, he automatically became chairman of the state committee that was being organized, a key post that would control the party's direction. He would also be assured of replacing Niles on the national committee.

Influenced by an array of forceful arguments against amalgamation, the convention enthusiastically nominated Welles for the governorship on the first formal ballot. An immediate reward for his "sacrifice" was the platform, which condemned the further extension of slavery and excoriated Know-Nothing intolerance. The election results, though they went heavily against the Republicans, rather pleased Welles. He polled almost 7000 votes, about one-fourth of those received by the Democratic and the Know-Nothing candidates, a better than respectable showing for a party that had been in the field less than a month.

The campaign had been followed closely by the Republican press in New England and New York. Welles got major exposure and favorable publicity that carried his name into the thousands of cities, towns, and villages where the Boston *Daily Telegraph,* the Washington, D.C., *National Era,* the New York *Evening Post,* and the *New-York Tribune* circulated. Rising politicians, some old veterans, and a good many ordinary citizens who had never heard of Welles were learning about his desperate struggle against fearful odds for the principles of all liberty-loving men. Welles, the insider, the introspective wire-puller whose name only politicians conjured with, was emerging as a national figure in the antislavery North.[34]

Neither the Democratic nor the Know-Nothing ticket commanded a majority, so the gubernatorial election had to be decided by the legislature, where the Republicans held the balance of power. Welles counseled the Republicans, only three of whom were former Democrats, to support Minor, the Know-Nothing candidate—to cooperate but to resist amalgamation. In return he sought a voice in the selection of a Senator. Brushing Republican claims aside after Minor's election, the Know-Nothings nominated an ex-Whig Congressman from Hartford, James Dixon. From a Republican standpoint the nomination was not a strong one. Dixon, a tall, wiry man with a bulbous forehead and a full beard, looked the inoffensive retiring scholar, but his well-earned reputation for clandestine intrigue belied his otherworldly appearance. Irresolute in public affairs, he was a dangerous antagonist in the private arena of political cut and slash. James D. Baldwin of the Worcester *Spy,* who knew Dixon well, drew a harsh though accurate portrait: "Altogether too timid, too sly, and treacherous in his dealings," wrote that clear-headed editor, "and too much of a 'Miss Nancy' to make a good leader."[35] Welles had long since taken Dixon's measure, and he resolved that his little group of Republicans should put up a show of opposition. He knew that they could not prevail, but he believed that a display of strength was in order. The Know-Nothing leaders must be made aware of the Republican party and their obligation to it. Acting on Welles' advice, enough Republicans held out against Dixon to deadlock the General Assembly. After ten ballots with no election Welles felt that they had made their point and that further opposition would be considered factious. Dixon was elected on June 4.[36]

Meanwhile, Welles was being drawn more deeply into the national organization of the party. The Pittsburgh meeting had elected Niles to the Republican party's executive committee, but he was never able to perform any duties or to participate in committee deliberations.[37] Worried about Niles' health and his deteriorating mental condition,

Welles persuaded his old friend to take up temporary residence in New York City, where he could be looked after better than in Hartford. Niles had developed cancer of the jaw and was relapsing into acute melancholia. Toward the end, wracked with pain, he refused both food and medicine. He died on Sunday, May 31, 1856.

The old Jacksonian left an estate of over $60,000. Among the beneficiaries were the city of Hartford, which received $20,000 to be invested as "a fund for the poor," and "my friends Gideon Welles and Calvin Day." Niles directed that each receive the sum of $15 "to purchase a cane as a memorial of my friendship and esteem." When Welles, who was named the executor, read the simple moving document, he turned his face to the wall in the *Press* office until he could control his emotions and write his friend's obituary. Despite his very real sense of loss, Welles would in time experience a sense of relief similar to that which he had felt after his father died. Hartford would never be quite the same for him without Niles, but he was his own master now.[38]

Several months before Niles' death the executive committee of the Republican party was looking to Welles for advice and for campaign material. "We need your good counsel," wrote Edwin D. Morgan from New York, ". . . we ought to know soon who should in reality be adopted as our standard bearer." In his reply, Welles ruled out Judge McLean, whom Morgan had mentioned, as "an old trimmer," and came out strongly for Frémont. Frémont's letter to "Governor" Charles Robinson of the "Kansas free state" had dispelled Welles' initial doubts. He though it frank, manly, and clear on the territorial issue. The party must come out unequivocally for Frémont, he advised Morgan, but, like others of the more radical anti-Nebraska men, he wanted assurance that Frémont could "be depended upon in the great issues." By now he had met the "Pathfinder" and his vivacious wife, Jessie, at their New York home on Ninth Street. While everyone was attracted to Jessie's charm and quick intelligence, the explorer seemed a little slow, a trifle fuzzy on delicate political issues that needed sharp delineation. Welles' friend William Chace of Providence, secretary of the Republican national committee, summed up the general attitude of the party leaders when he told Salmon P. Chase that he had the day before met Frémont "and rather liked him. His election if it takes place will be through the direction and management of superior men to himself."[39]

Welles was not a party to the complex transactions of the North American Convention in New York City that virtually assured Frémont the support of the antislavery Know-Nothings. Kept informed of the general strategy by Morgan, he could only deduce that Banks, who emerged as the nominee, and then withdrew, had played the vital role. With all his heavy responsibilities, he simply did not have the time to involve himself directly in such matters. He always responded to Morgan's frequent pleas for advice, though rarely did he initiate policy or question it except in the broadest context. Welles did not lack for able assistance from Hawley, Calvin Day, Pierce, Faxon, and James Babcock in New Haven. But somehow all matters of crucial import eventually gravitated to him. His most vexing problem, as it was for the national committee, was the Know-Nothings, who, by their disruptive tactics in the towns and in the congressional districts, made it doubly difficult to organize a new party.[40] No member of the Republican state committee dared risk district meetings for the election of delegates to the national convention at Philadelphia. The committee chose two delegates at large and sixteen other delegates purporting to represent the congressional districts. Gideon Welles listed himself as a delegate from the Third District, New London County; his brother Thaddeus would represent Hartford.[41]

The tone of the new party, so dull and lackluster in February, had become noticeably brighter by August. Although the conservative nativists had nominated Millard Fillmore on an American ticket, they were expected to obtain most of their votes in the slave states, where the Republicans were weakest. Yet experienced Republican politicians underestimated the Know-Nothings' capacity for making mischief. As the date for the Philadelphia convention approached, men such as Seward and Chase, who had been wary of the infant organization, discovered that they had had a deep interest in its welfare all along. Civil strife had broken out in Kansas. There had been enough death and destruction for Horace Greeley to coin the phrase, "Bleeding Kansas," which gave the Republicans an emotionally charged campaign issue. The new party had just been presented with its martyr in the person of Charles Sumner, savagely beaten at his desk in the Senate by the South Carolinian, Preston Brooks.

With so many problems behind him, Welles could afford to be unusually cheerful when he arrived at Philadelphia's Musical Fund Hall to attend the first Republican convention. A well-seasoned campaigner, he had quickly sensed the hopeful, good-natured mood of 3000 enthusiastic delegates and spectators. Elected to the national committee in Niles' place, he was also the unanimous choice of the Connecticut delegation for membership on the platform committee. At a private suite of rooms in the Girard House, where the platform committee met, he did the most important and for him congenial work. Of the twenty-two members on the committee, only two had gained national stature for their editorial ability—Francis Preston Blair, Sr., and Welles. Preston King of New York, Joshua Giddings of Ohio, and David Wilmot of Pennsylvania were able writers, but their reputations rested more on their political work and their oratory. None of them had engaged in any public letter writing or editorial work for some years.

These five men easily dominated the work of the committee, yet it is safe to say that Welles and Blair were the principal authors of the working drafts. The language of two highly significant resolutions—one emphasizing states' rights within the context of the Union, the other denying the authority of any political body or individual to establish slavery in any of the territories—so closely resembled Welles' writings since 1850 that, if he did not draft them, he certainly contributed significantly to their style and substance.

Proud of his part in what he must have known would be an historic document, Welles was caught up in the storm of enthusiasm that greeted David Wilmot, the committee chairman, as he read each resolution, then waited for applause to cease before he read the next. Welles knew the platform by heart, but he was strangely stirred as Wilmot's strong, full voice floated over the hushed throng.[42] And what old Jeffersonian would not have been moved when he heard the arraignment of Franklin Pierce—and "his advisors, agents, supporters, apologists and accessories before and after the fact." The "crime against Kansas" had evolved into a conspiracy against freedom, or as the great Declaration had put it: "A history of repeated injuries and usurpations, all having in direct object the establishment of an absolute Tyranny over these States." Pierce was surely no George the Third; Caleb Cushing bore little resemblance to Lord North; the platform, despite its extravagant phraseology, was no resounding manifesto for universal freedom or even national emancipation. But to the excited delegates, Welles among them, those magic phrases of Thomas Jefferson were again being invoked against a tyranny—this time a tyranny of section and of special interest that was riding booted and spurred over the rights of states and the rights of man. After a bitter struggle behind the scenes with the nativist-leaning John McLean, Frémont was nominated on the first ballot. William L. Dayton, a free-soil Whig from New Jersey, received the vice presidential nomination.

From the excitement and the drama of the convention, Welles was brought back to the hard reality of the Connecticut campaign. In a letter to Morgan he described the materials he had to work with as "undisciplined . . . filled with jealousies and narrow prejudices." The national chairman was encountering similar problems, though on a larger scale. A resourceful merchant and banker with a flair for calculating risks, Morgan was a big, handsome man who never seemed to know exactly "how to sustain his role."[43] He had seen enough of the political world, however, to realize that he needed Welles' expertise and sense of perspective. The Morgans and the Welleses had been neighbors and friends for a score of years in Hartford. Morgan's cousin and partner, George, was married to Mary Welles' sister, Caroline. The Morgan firm handled Welles' investments.

To the national chairman, Welles seemed always cool, deliberative, and canny, but behind the public face—now almost concealed by a full white beard—was the same insecure, hesitant moralist he had always been. Morgan, a man who could act impetuously, mistook Welles' caution for strength; his cynicism not as a sign of weakness, but of shrewd, realistic appraisal.

Welles' assessment of a special political situation was acute when he cautioned the members of the national committee about the peculiarly narrow-minded quality of the average voter. "Missionary labor seems essential before the speakers can be effective," he wrote Morgan early in the campaign, "and as to speakers . . . until the enthusiasm is fully aroused, the people will be jealous of speakers from abroad." "The Frémont cause," he continued, "embraces every variety of party, sect, creed and people. The speakers then should . . . forget old party appeals. We are inaugurating a new, young, vigorous and healthy movement. . . ."[44] But his fretful attitude about spending money, even in the critical states of Maine and Pennsylvania, his fears about its accountability, and his concern for system in the management of the national headquarters, all of which reflected the other side of Welles' character, were not especially productive at this stage of the desperate campaign. His complaints that some pennies might go astray compare unfavorably with his advice that "men will work more zealously if they are told we will succeed. More than this there are a thousand who want to vote for a winner." Welles knew that winners were not made by faith alone. As the campaign progressed the instruments of mass persuasion—all of which cost money—had the most astonishing impact on the public Welles had ever seen. "The Frémont and Jessie" campaign, as it came to be known, brought so many people into Hartford that a "Frémont Camp" (more money) was built on a vacant lot on the corner of Asylum and High Streets. It was a rough wooden building with unplaned wooden benches, but it held 2000 people, and it was filled to capacity when some well-known figure such as Joshua Giddings spoke. Paradoxically, Welles grumbled about expenses to the very end of the campaign.[45]

When the vice presidential question became so embarrassing that it threatened to split the party, Welles performed invaluable services that justified Morgan's respect for his tact. The final surrender of the North Americans, their agreement to back Dayton, was in no small measure effected by Welles' consummate management of the joint North American and Republican convention that met in Hartford on August 6. Despite the opposition of their leaders, the North Americans and the Republicans adopted the same electoral slate—Frémont and Dayton. Connecticut now seemed safe for Frémont, but far more important than the event was the timing of it. It caught the North American national committee at just the right psychological moment, when it could have decided either way. The committee gave in to Republican demands and backed Dayton as the vice presidential candidate. Chairman Morgan was grateful to Welles for "the business so well-done at Hartford." He could afford to say now that "there is no immediate matter pressing upon us."[46]

Morgan's admission that all was under control at national headquarters was welcome news. Welles would continue to give his "good counsel," but for the time being he would not have to disrupt his life and squander his energy in flying trips every week to national headquarters at the Trinity Building in New York City. Although the campaign was exciting—indeed, exhilarating—to Welles, he was glad when it was all over. Frémont's sweep of New England, New York, and Ohio had proven that the slapdash Republican organization was stronger than anyone had supposed. Welles firmly believed that if the Republicans had had another thirty days for their campaign, they would have won. "I have never seen a defeated party so full of vigor and enthusiasm, so resolute and determined," he said, "here, we are ready for the campaign of 1860."[47]

CHAPTER 16

# Chicago: 1860

ALL WAS FUNCTIONING efficiently and the *Press* was prospering and claiming less of Welles' time; the state committee presided over a party organization that almost ran itself.[1] It was one of the rare times in his long career that Welles ventured to prophesy victory. Despite his optimism and that of other seasoned politicians, however, the party was still the "piebald, ringnecked" creature it had been at its birth nine months before.[2]

Leading figures among the old Whigs and the independent Democrats, the bones and sinews of the Republican party, were acting as one against the extension of slavery. But the two factions were beginning to differ sharply over the means of keeping the territories free and white, a difference that reflected their former political beliefs and their mutual suspicion of each other's intent. To a certain extent, Welles was prepared for the partisan clashes that were bound to take place in a fusion movement. With his notion of recurring theme in the development of political institutions, he had always thought of the parties as merely defensive agents, organized from time to time to protect the federal system from the interest-oriented tyrannies of transient groups that happened to gain control of the government. His belief in states' rights remained as narrow and doctrinaire as that of the most extreme republican of the old Virginia school. Yet in his case such an intense political conservatism, such an unyielding devotion to pristine Jeffersonian ideals, could and did lead him down radical paths during the political confusion of the 1850's. It was a conservatism that made him and Preston King and the Blairs and William Cullen Bryant all Republicans.

There was something too abstract about their stand, something rather cool and remote in their efforts to explain the slavery issue as primarily a constitutional question. Though Welles was not entirely devoid of humanitarian ideals, at the same time he was not especially concerned with the human aspects of the slavery problem, which would, he thought, be dealt with effectively if the states were left free to cope with it. The territories were jointly owned by all of the states and by the people. Congress, which represented both, must legislate on the subject of slavery in territories, but it must legislate according to principle and precedent that had been laid down by Jefferson in the framing of the Northwest Ordinance—or, as Welles and his friends preferred to call it, the "Ordinance of Freedom." An article he wrote for the *Evening Post* in December of 1858 best explains his position and that of most independent Democrats.

Welles drew an analogy between the bank question of the early 1830's and the slavery question of the 1850's. Both, he argued, involved the same set of principles, and in both special interest groups sought to undermine the federal system for their own advantage. Proponents of the Bank of the United States had tried to nationalize banking, to legislate a monopoly and thus deprive the states and the people of equality of opportunity. Similarly, proponents of slavery were trying to nationalize that institution and thus deprive free labor and free states of their rights to compete on equal terms in the territories. Welles' argument was open to attack on many grounds. Even his history was askew. He, of all people, should have remembered that the masses had gone against the Bank because they thought it an aristocratic institution, a royal remnant which somehow had survived the Revolution and was threatening the very essence of democracy. On slavery, too, Welles had misjudged the swing of public opinion in the North. Most of the rank and file Republicans, Senator Dixon reminded him, "oppose the course of the government . . . not because of their objections to centralization, but on humanitarian grounds. They are willing to centralize if only it can be against slavery and not for it." To Welles and other fastidious states' rights Democrats, Dixon's comments reflected typical Whig carelessness about the division of powers. Still, they had to admit that most Republicans were not moved by disquisitions on government. What did move them was a curious blend of humanitarianism, racism, and economic determinism, expressed in demogogic terms. "Ours is the White Man's party for the interests of FREE WHITES," blared the *Hartford Courant*, "the Democrats are fighting for more niggers [sic] and slavery."[3]

Welles could never feel comfortable with crude appeals to racial and sectional prejudice. Means were just as important to him as ends, and though he could bend for the sake of expediency, there were definite limits beyond which he would not go. Questioning the lack of any fixed political convictions among his Whig colleagues, he became increasingly critical of their motives as well. The North Americans had fallen prey to factionalism, that blight of all new and controversial organizations. A younger element among them, more alert, vigorous, and open-minded, wanted to foster the spirit and the thrust of Anglo-Saxon ethnic pride within the ranks of the Republican party. "Americanism" to these younger men was "an instinct of nationality . . . a lineal descendant of John Bull." It could not be reasoned away, they said, "for the essential principle thereof is right."[4] Welles dismissed such contentions, preferring to see in them evidence of a power struggle between the younger men and the older, more experienced Know-Nothing leaders. He was gratified at the more tolerant outlook of the "young" Americans, but, as far as he was concerned, they too were crypto-Whigs, motivated by expediency rather than principle. Both sets of Americans backed the "Union" movement in the spring of 1857—the younger group asserting its Republicanism, but insisting that fusion rather than a straight-line organization was essential for success. Some of Welles' closest associates agreed with them—for instance, William Faxon, the co-proprietor of the *Evening Press*.

Under Edwin Pierce the *Press* had hewn closely to the Democratic-Republican line, but the labors of putting out a daily and of reporting accurately through its editorial columns the views sometimes conflicting) of the opinionated men who made up the Republican leadership broke down Pierce's frail constitution. He was forced to relinquish his editorial post, though not without a parting shot or two at the fusionists and at his own partner, Faxon.[5]

Joseph Roswell Hawley, who succeeded Pierce, was Welles' personal choice. The thirty-year-old Hawley was not the ideal candidate in Welles' opinion, but he was the best man available. Energetic, forceful, ambitious, he had the debating skills, the literary ability, and the practical experience to present the party's case effectively on the editorial page. Steady, unassuming Faxon, upon whose shoulders the success of the enterprise ultimately rested, was an enthusiastic supporter of Hawley, and his vote of confidence must have carried weight with Welles. Perhaps Faxon's was the determining voice, because Welles had certain reservations about young Hawley. He mistrusted his abolitionist past, his impulsive nature, his close relationship with John

Hooker, the Beechers, the Stowes, and, indeed, all of that abolitionist element which he considered ultra in the Republican party.

Hawley started on what Welles called firm ground when he said that the *Press* would adhere to its position in "the great political contest between free and slave labor," and that the Republican party would receive the paper's unqualified support so long as it remained faithful to the Philadelphia platform.[6] But to Republicans of Democratic background who were acutely sensitive to the slightest shift in direction Hawley soon appeared to have moved his course one or two points toward Americanism. As yet he was not fully attuned to the power struggle within the American party and to the suspicions of the independent Democrats that Americanism was simply a Whig device to encircle and destroy all those who had followed Jackson.

It was embarrassing for Welles to be subjected to Whig intimidation within his own party; and it seemed the height of folly not to go on the offensive and broaden Republican appeal to the thousands of uncommitted Democrats. Welles was in complete agreement with James Dixon, a former Whig who nevertheless recognized the problem of identity. "What we want," wrote Dixon, "is a leaven to work in the Democratic party. The Republican party is thought by many to be only the Whig party abolitionized."[7] Meanwhile, the impressionable Hawley let himself be persuaded by the astute special pleading of young Americans who condemned Know-Nothingism with all its "infinite humbug of grips, signs, passwords, secret councils . . . ," but then subtly praised its nationalism and predicted that the Republican party could not succeed without its support. That support, it was made clear, could be gained only by a coalition, or a "Union party, as it was called,[8] which, at the proper time, "the yet unchristened union child" would be baptized "by the name Republican."[9]

Almost immediately Welles and his friends called the young editor to task. The Union party, they said, was a "cheat and a fraud." In his quiet, courteous way, Welles discussed politics with Hawley, trying to draw him out on his aims and policies but careful not to give offense or to suggest that he was dictating. Welles concluded, after several weeks of tactful questioning, that Hawley was "never able to give any definite answer. If he thinks at all he must be aware he is foundering in the most degrading species of Know-Nothingness." Others of Welles' friends were not so politic. That high-strung dabbler in politics, Mark Howard, a power in the burgeoning insurance industry, refused even to enter the *Press* office, but seeing Hawley on the other side of Main Street one day, he called over rudely that "the Know-Nothings were loading him with filth and that he was busying himself in rubbing in it." Calvin Day was likewise boycotting the *Press* office.[10]

Hawley may have thought of himself as an independent, but he could not with all his strength of purpose stand out against the prestigious independent Democrats who had founded his paper. When he swung around and castigated the Americans, pronouncing the Union movement a sham, Orris S. Ferry, a rising lawyer from Norwalk and a power among the younger Americans, complained that he was being unjust to the Whigs. "Of the 43,000 who voted for Frémont," wrote Ferry, "at least 35,000 were either Whigs or young men of Whig families." Ferry accused the *Press* of too much talk about the old Democracy—"Jackson, Silas Wright . . . and too little of the old Whig Champions." Poor Hawley! Wherever he turned, he was sure to meet with criticism, a telltale sign that the Frémont campaign had but temporarily closed up the deep divisions within the party.[11]

As plans were made for the spring campaign of 1857, the Whig-Republicans refused to slacken their grasp on the party machinery. Welles and his outspoken Hartford friends decided it was time to make a strong show of their independence. Hawley was finally brought round. He demanded in the *Press* that former Democrats be given a just share of the nominations and that the party platform be completely purged of nativist sentiments. His choice for governor was Gideon Welles.

Welles did not receive the nomination, but he piled up enough votes to defeat the American candidate, Governor Holley, and throw the nomination to a businessman from Norwich, William A. Buckingham, a staunch Whig who had kept himself clear of the Americans. Eventually Welles would appreciate the administrative and executive talents of Buckingham, who was elected Governor and served for seven consecutive terms. At the time and for the next two years, however, he and his group of supporters saw Buckingham as another hungry Whig consuming a distinguished office and dictating the party program. "I am mortified to be associated with men so wanting in generosity and tact; judgment and discretion," said Welles, ". . . but as things are—national politics predominating—I see no inducement to support any man who is identified with the administration and its policy." Overriding his personal concerns, his hurt pride, his relegation (as always, it seemed) to the sidelines, was the glaring fact that Whig intransigence had again thrown away thousands of Democratic votes.[12]

For a brief period during the winter and spring of 1858 Welles had a glimmer of hope that the party would be forced to change its policy. Stephen A. Douglas was feuding with the Buchanan administration over the government of Kansas. When the President recommended that Congress approve the Lecompton constitution, permitting slavery in that strife-torn territory, Douglas demanded proof that a majority of the actual settlers had approved the document. Delighted by Douglas' strong stand, Welles accurately foresaw the Senator's ultimate break with the Buchanan administration. He made haste to compliment him on his speech, and, at the same time, he hinted delicately that the Republicans were not indifferent to his welfare. "Rest assured," he wrote, "the popular heart is with you and will sustain you." Douglas could not possibly have missed the implication, especially as it came from a prominent member of the Republican national committee.[13] Republicans in Washington were equally happy about Douglas' new position, and they, like Welles, did not want to overlook any opportunity that might come their way if a full-scale confrontation took place. Senator Dixon drily commented to Welles "that he [Douglas] is honest when we regard his former unscrupulous course." Lest he be misunderstood, Dixon was most positive on not looking too closely into the Illinoisan's motives. "He is right now & if he will but continue so, I am willing to forget the past & cordially act with him & his friends in the future."[14] Preston King, a far more influential Republican and a more talented observer in matters political, was watching Douglas closely, too. In early January of 1858, he thought the Illinois Senator was courting the Republicans. "He will be careful, I think, not to do anything in the Senate offensive to our side."

Whatever the outcome, the Republicans were sure to reap substantial benefits. Buchanan seemed more completely in the hands of Southern extremists than Pierce had been. Lecompton was adequate proof, if proof were required, that they had driven the administration into "nullifying squatter sovereignty." The President was prepared to flesh out the Dred Scott Decision by forcing Lecompton on Kansas. Welles knew that neither Douglas nor his constituency could tolerate such a complete scuttling of his program. Many Washington Republicans, in their eagerness to capture the Douglas Democrats, were asking themselves whether the party was ready "to sustain him for the presidency in 1860, if circumstances were favorable." Everyone recognized that it was the critical time in Douglas' career. Dixon was ready to do anything for him, but, as he wrote Welles, Douglas "does not wish Republicans at present to avow their friendship for him."[15]

Though far more cautious and restrained than Dixon, Welles was clearly thrilled at the prospect of a Jacksonian Democrat leading a grand coalition in 1860. For the first time in years he seemed to feel that "true" principles were about to triumph over expediency. "I have not a doubt there is to be a revolution," he wrote Douglas. "You must go forward in this work & lead the host to battle & to victory. It is your mission & the more trying the ordeal to you personally, the greater will be your reward." Welles was a major force in planning the national organization of the Republican party, but his official standing did not deter him from saying to Douglas: "I write you as an old brother Democrat."[16]

Despite such overtures from prominent Republicans in and out of Congress, the Little Giant seemed strangely hesitant when Welles suggested that he write one or two of his lieutenants in Connecticut and urge them to swing their influence behind the Republican ticket. "Things [were] still in a state of transition at the west," Douglas advised Dixon, "and it would not do for him just now to meddle in any way with our election." Could Douglas in fact disavow popular sovereignty without alienating his only sure source of strength, the Democracy of the Northwest? Possibly, but it would require long and careful preparation. The situation in his own state, for instance, was so complex that he would run a very real risk of subordinating himself to Lincoln and Lyman Trumbull were it known that he had an understanding with the Republicans. His colleague, Senator Trumbull, a sharp-featured, testy, Connecticut Yankee who had moved to Illinois, immediately flared up at any mention of Douglas' availability. Yet Douglas' stock among Republican leaders continued to rise, alarming both Lincoln and Trumbull.[17]

After Douglas' debates with Lincoln, Welles and Preston King wrote him off as a candidate. "Douglas has determined to work out his own destiny," King commented in mid-August, "preferring to make the contest in Illinois turn upon his own personal position and fortune rather than upon the principles and public interests that divide the opinions of the country."[18]

As the bright hope of a Douglas candidacy abruptly faded away, Welles became more and more disillusioned with the Republican party. How anomalous it was that he, who represented the state in the national councils of the party, should be completely disregarded at home. The Whig-American majority, if anything, was more disdainful than ever of the minority Democratic faction. "I confess, I am becoming tired of it," he wrote Senator Foster, "I will go and vote while it avails, which under such management can not be long but I do not feel inclined to labor with much zeal under such circumstances.[19] Yet labor he did on the national committee, if not in local politics.

Scarcely a week went by that a letter did not pass between him and party chairman Morgan. At least once a month he was in New York or Washington conferring with his fellow committee members. With Douglas cleaving to the Democracy, most experienced Republicans believed the Southern ultra wing would disrupt the party rather than accept him as the candidate. The nomination for 1860 looked far more promising now than it had in 1856. If the party could keep its warring factions under control, and if the administration continued with its proslavery policy in Kansas, a Republican was sure to win the presidency.

The astute Thurlow Weed, whom Welles disliked personally and detested politically, had sensed the opportunity and was covertly pushing William H. Seward, his collaborator. Preston King, recently elected to the Senate with Weed's grudging approval, was charged with bringing the Democratic faction behind Seward's candidacy. Though King owed his seat more to Greeley than to anyone else, he was eager to placate the old Whig boss. From mid-summer of 1858 until the Republican convention two years later, he would use every means at his command to persuade Welles and other influential ex-Democrats that Seward was the strongest candidate.[20]

To a conservative Jacksonian like Welles, Seward was everything that was wrong with American politics. The casual little Senator from New York had never thought much of the sacred doctrine of states' rights, and while it must be assumed that he believed in a wise government, he had certainly paid little attention to the Jeffersonian ideal of a frugal one. Since the death of Henry Clay, Seward was the Whig of Whigs in Democratic circles, and not just because of his radical stand on slavery. He was thought to be a spokesman for the "interests," a careless almoner of the public treasure, a man of many expedients but of no conviction. Nor were bitter memories of earlier partisan conflict softened by his highly visible partnership with Thurlow Weed, mysterious master fixer who, to sensitive Democratic nostrils, trailed a faint odor of corruption between his office in Albany and his New York City sanctum at the Astor House.

Even if Welles had not been bedeviled by the Whigs in his own state, he still would have thought Seward a natural enemy. The treatment his faction was receiving from "brass-bound" Whigs made him all the more intractable to King's prodding—and to that of Dixon, Blair, and Bigelow. Mounting pressure for Seward brought out all of Welles' stubborn individualism. He began exerting his own influence among party leaders and publicists against Weed's carefully constructed, well-oiled machine. "It is crowding matters seriously," he remarked to the elder Blair, "to intrude and force upon us the most prominently obnoxious centralist that can be selected."[21]

In late September of 1858 that "obnoxious centralist" committed a major blunder which may have cost him the nomination. Addressing a large audience in Rochester, New York, he chose a felicitous but politically unfortunate phrase—"irrepressible conflict"—to depict the struggle between freedom and slavery. It was a phrase which lent itself to stereotyping and which he would many times regret he had ever uttered. Beyond the words themselves, the tenor of the Rochester speech shook the precarious unity of the Republican party. Seward spoke as a Whig, not as a Republican, and he recklessly and falsely charged that Democrats had always been proslavery. Thomas Jefferson, Andrew Jackson, and James K. Polk had all been all slaveholders; Martin Van Buren had appeased the slave power in his first inaugural. Slavery, Seward implied, had been a source of political division between the Whigs and the Democrats, with the Democrats always upholding the institution.

Welles and a host of Democratic-Republicans were outraged by what they termed Seward's "imperial" stance, his distortion of history for the benefit of the Whigs. Under the pseudonym of "Democratic-Republican," he submitted to the *Evening Post* a long, well-researched attack on the Rochester speech. Like all of his published pieces, the argument was clear and persuasive—the tone restrained, but with a keen edge. His major point was that Seward was confusing the sham Democracy of the Buchanan administration with the real Democracy of Jackson and Van Buren. In rejecting Seward's thesis that slavery was synonymous with Jacksonian Democracy, he observed with some irony that it had been a Whig administration, not a Democratic one, that had forced the Fugitive Slave Law upon the land and acquiesced in popular sovereignty for the New Mexico Territory. Welles' letter to the editor was carried on the front page of the *Evening Post*. On the editorial page, William Cullen Bryant praised the accuracy of Welles' historical account, while warmly applauding his constructive criticism.[22]

The letter set the record straight for all Republicans who had once been Democrats, and Dixon wrote that in Washington it was considered "very able even for Gideon Welles." The effect on Preston King was electric. He decided that there had to be a meeting in New York York at once, and he besought Welles to meet with him, Morgan, and Bryant. The conferees met as King planned, but with one additional member, Senator Seward. If Seward's attendance had been planned to promote some sort of compromise, it failed completely. "Of course we had no particular conversation," said Welles, "and should not have agreed if we had."[23]

More damaging in the long run to the Seward cause was Welles' connection with Dr. Bailey of the *National Era* and other free-soil editors. Beginning in mid-summer of 1858, Welles wrote numerous long articles for the *Era* which identified him in the popular mind as one of the more radical Republicans, yet a radical with a vast store of common sense, a logical debater in print calmly presenting the facts (as he saw them) and avoiding exhortation. One thing the *Era*'s audience got from Welles' articles was a thorough grounding in the principles of federalism and its relation to the slavery problem. D. W. Bartlett, Bailey's associate, was so impressed that he begged for a column-and-a-half article every week. "You and Dr. Bailey agree upon nearly all questions," he wrote, requesting "a piece that would make up, say, three or four installments."[24] Welles' timely attacks on the Buchanan administration, and the data he supplied against Isaac Toucey, the Secretary of the Navy (whose governance was being investigated by the Senate Committee on Naval Affairs), earned him many powerful admirers in Washington. The subtle way he worked against Seward through the *Era* was also appreciated by such ambitious contenders for the nomination as Salmon P. Chase, a frequent visitor of Bailey and Bartlett.

In writing against Seward for what might be termed loosely the far left faction of the party—abolitionists and radical free-soilers of various hues and persuasions—Welles also spoke against him to moderates and conservatives, irrespective of political antecedents. To Francis Preston Blair, Sr., as conservative perhaps as any Republican on current social and economic questions, Welles repeatedly raised serious doubts about the suitability of the New York Senator, and this well before Horace Greeley's campaign against him in the *Tribune*. Welles was also active in opposing Seward with fellow members of the national committee, particularly its most influential New England members, George G. Fogg of New Hampshire and William Chace of Rhode Island. He was not successful in persuading Governor Morgan, though he did apparently raise some doubts in the national chairman's mind. Though Welles was tireless in his anti-Seward campaign, he never descended to personal attacks. He readily admitted that the New York Senator had statesmanlike qualities and that there was no disagreement between them on the slavery question. But he could and did raise serious doubts about his loose political and fiscal habits, which he maintained would alienate a majority of the old Democratic faction.[25]

Welles was effective also with old Hartford friends who had moved elsewhere in New England and had become influential Republicans. Most were journalists whom he had known during Niles' brief flurry with the Free-Soil party, most were radical if not abolitionist on the slavery question, and most mistakenly took Welles to be as radical as they. His preference for President, Salmon P. Chase, coincided exactly with theirs; his skillful marriage of old Jeffersonian Democracy with antislavery sentiment, perhaps his greatest contribution to the campaign of 1860, appealed to their inherited political bias and their humanitarian ideals.[26] Among the radical fringe, the able John Dennison Baldwin, formerly editor of the *Boston Telegraph* and now of the Worcester *Spy*, praised him for just this reason. A Democrat before he became a radical Free-Soiler, he believed Welles to be "wise, judicious and far seeing . . . one of our greatest men."[27]

Baldwin had the heavy frame and broad features associated with the English yeoman stock from which he sprang. Well over six feet in height, heavy-boned and heavy-muscled, he looked like a farmer rather than an editor, writer of romantic, melancholy verse, and amateur archeologist. It would have been even more surprising to those who did not know Baldwin to hear that the energetic, hard-hitting journalist was also an ordained Congregational minister who had left his congregation in Branford, Connecticut, to establish Hartford's first Free-Soil paper, the *Charter Oak*.

Welles had met Baldwin when he returned home from Washington in 1849. With such a mutuality of interests, the two men became close friends, and, though Welles was not as outspoken as Baldwin on the territorial issue, he agreed substantially with the editor's views. In 1852 Baldwin sold the *Charter Oak*. He moved to Boston, where he became part owner and principal editor of the *Boston Commonwealth*. He soon made that struggling weekly a major force in developing free-soil opinion throughout Massachusetts. Charles Sumner, Theodore Parker, and Henry Wilson were attracted to this blunt, yet curiously sensitive journalist, whose simple, direct prose was an admirable vehicle for conveying his and their sense of rising moral indignation. The friendship and patronage of this group added to the *Commonwealth*'s circulation, and to its influence. Renamed the *Telegraph* in the middle 1850's and thereafter published as a daily, it carried several of Welles' articles on the centralizing features of the Pierce and Buchanan administrations, the unconstitutionality of the Fugitive

Slave Law, the strife in Kansas. Obviously, it was not because of Seward's alleged radicalism that Baldwin in the *Telegraph*—and in the *Spy* when he took over that paper in 1859—was cool to his candidacy.[28]

In the midst of his activity against Seward, Welles met and talked at some length with Abraham Lincoln. He had known the Illinois politician by reputation for several years, remembering well how the unknown Lincoln had almost edged out William L. Dayton for the party's vice presidential nomination in 1856. More recently he had read Lincoln's debates with Douglas. The Illinois Republican's stance on popular sovereignty, the wealth of historical knowledge he displayed, his cogent interpretation of the Constitution, were as an impressive display of statesmanlike utterances on the political implications of slavery as any Welles had ever seen. He could not have agreed more completely with Lincoln's Cooper Union address and with the speeches he delivered in New England.

Unquestionably this Midwesterner, little known even to professionals, whetted Welles' curiosity. He had come from nowhere to challenge the redoubtable Stephen A. Douglas. He had held his own in debate against a man who was conceded by all to be the most resourceful debater in the nation, and in fact he had almost defeated Douglas for the Senate in an election where the legislators who voted for him represented more popular votes than did those who voted for the idol of the Northwestern Democracy. Welles' interest must also have been quickened by mounting evidence that Lincoln would play an important role in the 1860 convention, possibly even be a contender for the presidential nomination. If he did, he might weaken Seward's chances, a prospect that Welles found worth cultivating. To be sure, Lincoln, like Seward, was a Whig, but, judging from his public addresses and from what he was told about his politics, Welles concluded that the Illinois lawyer was far more scrupulous about the constitutional implications of slavery and states' rights than Seward was.

The Connecticut campaign of 1860, during which Lincoln spoke throughout the state, had more than its share of excitement. John Brown's raid and his execution in December of 1859 had had a mighty impact on public opinion; the specter of civil strife, the continuing depression, and the persistence of factionalism within the Republican party all pointed to a Democratic victory.[29] Had it not been for a temporary closing of ranks against the greater enemy and the spontaneous invention of a marvelously effective campaign device in the "Wide Awakes," the Republicans would have lost the election. As it was, their ticket won by a margin of only 541 votes. The "Wide

Awakes," who organized and drilled on military lines, served the double purpose of injecting color and fervor into the campaign and protecting Republican marchers from the brickbats of Democratic bystanders, many of whom had been hired by the central committee to break up the rallies and processions. They were a striking group, these "Wide Awakes," young men with glazed cloth capes and caps, their kerosene torches mounted on stout wooden staffs—good for lighting, and for fighting if necessary.[30]

With his full white beard streaming in the gusty winds of early March, his gray wig (already the subject of editorial merriment in the opposition press) askew when he lifted his flat, broad-trimmed hat to acknowledge the salute of a bystander, Gideon Welles marched in the front ranks of the torchlight processions with friends and close political associates. Always offered a place in Mayor Allyn's carriage, which carried the speaker of the evening, Welles preferred to be in the procession, where he could savor at first hand the excitement generated by a thousand tramping men. In his fifty-eighth year, looking every inch the patriarch, he was recapturing for a moment the long-lost magic of his youth, those times which he once described nostalgically: "I know of nothing better than a smart, warmly contested political contest . . . the hopes, the disappointments—the joy and the indignation—the satisfaction and the vexation. . . ."[31]

He did not ride with Abraham Lincoln to the City Hall, where the tall, homely and by now weary and travel-stained Westerner was to address a mass meeting of Hartford citizens. But he was in the escort with Hawley, Calvin Day, Mark Howard, and his near neighbor—the parade's marshall—George Bissell, who was swinging the same white hat he had swung so vigorously in the Frémont campaign.[32]

As a member of the Republican national committee and one of the party's leading ex-Democrats, Welles did sit on the dais, where he was able to observe the speaker closely as well as hear him clearly in the densely packed chamber. Lincoln spoke extemporaneously, glancing from time to time at the dozen or so words and phrases he had written out on two little scraps of paper. Welles must have soon realized that the orator had nothing startlingly new to present, that most of his material had already been used before in New York and in other New England cities. Yet somehow, despite the awkward gestures, the shrill voice, the gaunt appearance, Lincoln invested the well-worn expressions and the country humor with new meaning. Welles was on his feet joining with the rest of the wildly applauding audience when Lincoln, paraphrasing his Cooper Union conclusion, closed his two-hour address with the ringing phrase: "Eternal right makes might. As we understand our duty, let us do it."

That afternoon Welles had had a long talk with Lincoln at Brown and Gross's bookstore on the corner of Main and Asylum Streets. Their conversation was interrupted frequently by customers, the idlers, and the curious, who recognized Welles and guessed that his companion was the Illinois "giant killer" all the papers were talking about. For Hartford was still a small town and the word traveled fast. Welles probably made more of an impression on Lincoln than Lincoln did upon Welles, though the *Evening Press* would later praise the Illinoisan's speech as "earnest, strong, honest, simple in style and clear as crystal in his logic." The editorial analysis may have been written by Welles or by Hawley. Whoever authored the piece, the compliments were unusually generous from what was now a decidedly Democratic-Republican paper. Lincoln's estimate of Welles was further strengthened when the two men met again at the *Press* office, where they conversed for about an hour, this time with no interruptions.[33] On the following day Lincoln spoke in New Haven, where he was an overnight guest of the *Palladium* editor, James F. Babcock. It would have been strange indeed if he had not asked his host about political affairs in Connecticut and New England—and about the work and reputation of Welles.[34] It would have been equally strange if Babcock had not given him a glowing testimony to Welles' character, his political abilities, and his standing among the Democrats, inside the party and outside it. Even without Babcock as a spokesman, Welles would have been of special interest to Lincoln, because he was chairman of the Connecticut delegation to the Chicago convention. Babcock knew of Welles' antipathy toward Seward, the leading candidate of the Republican party. The New Haven editor may well have told his house guest that Welles was for Chase but that the delegation was uncommitted.

Connecticut's more radical Republicans, of whom Welles was the acknowledged chief, had feared that the leaders of the defunct American party, working with old-line Whigs, would control the convention and select delegates committed to conservative candidates such as Edward Bates of Missouri ("Madame Bates" in the parlance of the New York *Herald*) or even John Bell of Tennessee.[35] Their fears proved groundless when A. N. Clarke, editor of the *Courant*, foremost Know-Nothing journal in the state, presented Welles at the Republican state convention as "the nearly" unanimous choice of the First District (Hartford County) for delegate. Further, he said, with what must be considered a graceful distortion of Welles' presumed stand but close to the truth of the matter, that "the conservative spirit of the state would be honestly represented through him." Clark then nominated Welles as a delegate-at-large and chairman. He was elected by a large majority on the first ballot. Welles now held two important posts—influential member of the national committee and now chairman of the Connecticut delegation—and his preference for a candidate was the subject of speculation among the party leaders. He immediately became a high-priority target for the managers of potential nominees.[36]

Welles' attitude was shared by most New England Republicans, who, for one reason or another, were opposed to the New York Senator. Seward had connections with corrupt men; Seward was hated by the Know-Nothings, and therefore could not carry the key states of Pennsylvania and New Jersey; Seward was radical on the slavery issue. Yet, as Bigelow wrote William Cullen Bryant, "Circumstances, his enemies, the Devil if you please, have made Seward the representative man of the Republican party."[37] Even Welles had to agree, though he was unwilling to abandon his campaign until there was absolutely no prospect of success.[38] Seward was not to have the nomination by default, but who could step into the shoes of the Senator from New York? Who had the stature and the prominence? Who, in fact, could satisfy even a minority of the vociferous factions in the party? Orris S. Ferry, now a Congressman from Connecticut's Fourth District, posed some of the formidable questions that any successful candidate had to face. "Very little Republican principle in Pennsylvania and New Jersey," he wrote Welles, "while the great foreign element of the Northwest is ultra in all its views. . . . Between the two lies our danger. Without the German vote we lose the North West. If we accommodate to the wishes of this wing of the party, there is danger in the middle states."[39]

Meanwhile, agents of Simon Cameron, whose unsavory political career in Pennsylvania was not unlike that of Weed's in New York, were plying Welles with letters that proclaimed Cameron's availability and fitness for the presidency.[40] They were wasting their time. Welles had met Cameron in 1827 and had followed his political career both through the newspapers and, more intimately, through correspondence with his Pennsylvania relatives. He had only contempt for the Pennsylvania spoilsman whom everyone knew had purchased his senatorship from a corrupt legislature. Though Welles doubted the sincerity of Cameron's bid for the nomination, regarding it only as power play that would gain him a Cabinet post, he did fear that, if a general scramble occurred, in the confusion Cameron might make off with the prize.[41] Nor would Welles be convinced by the arguments of his friends the Blairs, or of Horace Greeley at the *Tribune*, that Edward Bates, an old-line Missouri Whig, was the ideal candidate. Why, the man was not even a Republican—and he was still a slaveholder, despite his opposition to slavery in the territories. As much as he opposed Seward, Welles agreed with Hawley that the New York Senator was infinitely preferable to Bates. Chase continued to be his first choice and would remain so.[42]

The man from Illinois may have impressed Welles, but certainly not enough to make him change his mind. James F. Babcock, who was now committed to Lincoln and openly advocating his nomination in the *Palladium*, drew neither aid nor comfort from Hartford. When Norman Judd, one of Lincoln's managers, a former Democrat, and a fellow member of the national committee, wrote Welles about accommodations in the Tremont House for the Connecticut delegation, he made no mention of Lincoln. The tone of his letter was formal, correct, and cold. One would never have suspected that Welles had come to know Judd quite well over the preceding four years, nor that he had any knowledge of Judd's candidate for the presidential nomination.[43] Lincoln did have two supporters among the Connecticut delegates, Edward Noble and Edgar Tweedy, both of the Fourth District and both converted by Babcock. Babcock's fine hand can be seen in a letter Noble wrote Welles the day of Lincoln's speech in Hartford, suggesting that he call the delegation together so that there would be "some concert of action . . . unless it is to be understood that every man goes on his 'own hook.' "[44]

Welles acted on Noble's suggestion. He fixed Tuesday, March 13, as the date for a meeting at the Allyn House in Hartford. Most of the delegates attended. Though Welles and ex-Governor Chauncey F. Cleveland were the only ex-Democrats there, they were able to scotch all Seward sentiment. Both men had hoped to commit the delegation to Chase, but they were unsuccessful. Cleveland voiced the same complaint to Chase that Welles had been making for several years. "If we had less whiggery," he wrote, "and more Republicanism here we should not have to struggle so hard."[45] More realistic than Cleveland, Welles was content that the delegation would not support Seward.

The disruption of the Democratic party at its Charleston convention had made possible the selection of a more radical Republican and had boosted Seward's stock in Chicago. The startling split in the Democratic party had absolutely no impact on the Connecticut group, a typical display of phlegmatic conservatism which, for once, Welles approved. Party sentiment was overwhelmingly pro-Seward, as Welles

was all too keenly aware. He must have been grateful that his delegation at least was so unyielding in its stand against the magnetic New
Yorker and his persuasive chief manager, Thurlow Weed.

Welles and his son Edgar boarded the "New England special" in
Detroit for the day's ride to Chicago. The train was jammed with delegates, reporters, and politicians, with aimless pleasure-seekers and with
professional noisemakers (among them Gilmore's brass band from
Boston). A twelve-and-a-half-hour trip over the parched plains was tiresome and uncomfortable. The hot dry winds off the Michigan prairies
sifted fine dust through the sills of the bolted windows and the open
doors at the ends of each car. Many of the passengers sought refuge in
whiskey, which added a measure of the coarse boisterousness that
Welles always found annoying.[46]

Although the rates for the "special" were a bargain and Welles was
nothing if not prudent about expenses, he had not planned his boarding of the train at Detroit to save money, but to sound out his fellow
New Englanders just before they were exposed to the heated partisan
atmosphere of Chicago. It was a wise decision. He was able to talk
with such friends as Edward L. Pierce, confidant of both Sumner and
Chase; John Dennison Baldwin of the Worcester *Spy*, a member of the
Massachusetts delegation; and George G. Fogg of the Concord *Independent Democrat*, New Hampshire's member of the national committee. Young Joseph Hawley, who was aboard as a reporter for the
*Evening Press*, probably sat in on the conversations. And either here
on the narrow seats of the dust-choked swaying cars, or later at the
Tremont House, Welles conferred with the elderly Senator James J.
Simmons, chairman of the Rhode Island delegation. That their discussions bore fruit would soon be evident when Rhode Island cast no
votes for Seward on any ballot, even though the state had been claimed
for him up to the day before the convention began.

From Baldwin and Pierce Welles was happy to learn that the Massachusetts delegation was not as solidly for Seward as he and the rest of
the country had thought. New Hampshire and Vermont were divided
too. As for Maine, all the delegates at large, the chairman, and a majority of the delegation were "firm" supporters of the New York Senator—how "firm" was anybody's guess.[47] The situation in Maine
resembled that in Massachusetts, but there were many ex-Democrats
among the Maine delegates who, in Welles' judgment, would not take
much coaxing to back another candidate. The crucial Maine delegation
reflected the divergent interests of its Senators, William Pitt Fessenden,

ex-Whig, and Hannibal Hamlin, ex-Democrat. Fessenden, thin, acerbic, and dyspeptic, was an intensely loyal supporter of Seward. His colleague, the more genial ex-Democrat Hamlin, had for some time believed that it would be unwise to nominate Seward when, as he expressed it, "we can elect another while we might fail with him." Yet his was a cautious opposition.

Old Jefferson-Jackson principles were as much a part of Hamlin's political character as they were of Welles', and his antagonism, while it was couched in terms of availability, betrayed a reaction against Seward's Whiggishness as displayed through Fessenden's power base at home. But Hamlin, above all, wanted harmony. He shied away from any move that might disturb his sensitive, politically potent colleague. When asked for advice by several of his supporters on the Maine delegation, he had sidestepped the question. Before the New England "Special" pulled into Chicago on Monday night, Welles had been able to form a reasonably accurate picture of Seward's strength in New England.[48]

The colorful greeting that the citizens of Chicago gave the New Englanders more than made up for the rigors of the journey. All of the avenues leading to the depot, and all the side streets in its vicinity, were brilliantly illuminated. Rockets soared up into the clear sky of early evening. A brace of nine-pounders rumbled out a welcome that reverberated over the placid surface of Lake Michigan. On hand were the city's "Wide Awakes," armed with their flickering kerosene torches, to escort the New Englanders to their quarters; on hand also was a goodly share of Chicago's expatriate Yankees, some to greet friends and relatives, others just to hear the old twang and for a brief moment be with their own. Welles and his son Edgar were met by the Sons of Connecticut and by his host, William H. Brown, a rich Chicagoan who had arrived with his carriage to accommodate the tired, travel-stained pair.

Brown's mansion on Michigan Avenue was some distance from the depot and from the Richmond House, which Thurlow Weed had converted into a Seward headquarters. But Welles' rest was disturbed by the pandemonium that greeted the arrival of the New Yorkers early in the morning of Tuesday, May 15. Their train of thirteen cars was jammed with "bully boys" and "bravos" and "blood tubs"—wire-pullers from upstate and ward heelers from Manhattan and Brooklyn, all calling themselves the "irrepressibles," most of them drunk, if Murat Halstead, who traveled with them, has given us an accurate report. Although excursion rates were cheap, Thurlow Weed, it was whispered, was paying at least a part of their expenses out of a huge slush fund he had at his command.

Early the next morning Welles managed to squeeze through the packed corridors of the Tremont House, unofficial party headquarters. He left Edgar in one of the parlors and began the laborious, though stimulating, business of moving among the delegates, greeting those he knew, introducing himself and being introduced. He conferred with the Blairs—Montgomery, Old Frank, and Young Frank—with Preston King, and with Morgan. He seems to have avoided the Lincoln men— ponderous Judge Davis, punctilious Norman Judd, and polished Leonard Swett.

Any politician of experience and insight would have decided after a few hours at the Tremont that Seward would be nominated—probably on the first and most certainly on the second ballot. New York, of course, was solid; Pennsylvania was said to be committed after a complimentary vote for Cameron.[49] With his record of steady opposition to the Know-Nothings, Seward was the acknowledged favorite of the Germans outside of Missouri, where Bates had the edge because of Young Frank Blair's influence, and Illinois, where steady Gustave Koerner was managing just barely to hold his countrymen in line behind Lincoln. Both states were restive, however, and could easily bolt for Seward. Carl Schurz, an attractive and romantic figure not only to the German immigrants but to the youth of the party, had been campaigning for Seward over the preceding six months. What young man had not heard of Schurz's exploits in the European revolutions of 1848, of his daring rescue of Professor Kinkel from the gloomy Prussian prison of Spandau? Schurz had brought in line his own state of Wisconsin and neighboring Minnesota. German delegates scattered among other Western states were strong for Seward.[50]

Thurlow Weed—"My Lord Thurlow," as he was known to his multitude of friends and enemies—had set up what amounted to a personal court at the Richmond House. There he received delegates, dispensed hospitality, and dispatched orders. A tall, cheerful man, Weed cultivated a persuasive manner and a soft voice, almost a whisper, that made a new acquaintance feel as if he were a confidential friend of long standing. He strengthened the wavering, won new converts, and inspired confidence among delegations already committed to Seward; nor did he shrink from using the power of money as a material token of his regard for the honesty and sagacity of a doubting Thomas —be he German, Irish, or native American. Horace Greeley, an object of curiosity and respect to many, of fear and hatred to some, and of amusement to others, stated flatly that Lord Thurlow "was ready" to spend almost any amount of money to purchase the Pennsylvania delegation. And Greeley was certain that Weed had already bought "some of the small frontier and border states," as he rather contemptuously described them. The apple-cheeked editor of the *Tribune*, whose peculiar dress, eccentric manner, and singular appearance belied his political skill and his personal power, was attending the convention as a delegate from Oregon, having been excluded from New York by the Weed-directed New York machine. The most dangerous of Seward's foes and the most malevolent of Weed's enemies, the politically ambitious Greeley had made the first of many canvasses he would make before the convention. He was not hopeful. As he telegraphed his Washington correspondent and political confidant, James Pike, "Your Maine delegation was a poor affair . . . Massachusetts also was right in Weed's hands contrary to all reasonable expectations. I cannot understand this." Vermont, too, now seemed to be in the Seward camp. But Welles had a better grasp of New England sentiment than Greeley, who was likely to jump to conclusions and had little or no patience with the taciturn, indirect discourse Yankee politicians invariably used in public. That able editor had been too long removed from his native New Hampshire, too long associated with the dynamic metropolis of New York, to remember the horse-trading Yankee of his youth. For all his native wit and perception, he had missed the asides, the homely anecdotes, the rustic parables—all those trifling nuances of meaning which the New Englanders habitually employed to mask their motives and their feelings. Thurlow Weed made the same mistake. Though a brilliant politician, an operator with a rare quality of sensing a situation and sensing it accurately, regarding the sentiment of the New England delegates, Weed erred on the positive side as badly as Greeley did on the negative.

Not more than six months earlier, the New York boss had poured money into the desperate campaign the Republicans had waged in New Hampshire. He let it be understood that more sinews of war would be available for their next state campaign. New Hampshire Republicans were under such heavy obligations to him that he relied upon their assurances of support without bothering to follow them up, a serious blunder in view of the fact that George G. Fogg of the *Concord Independent*—and the national committee—was in Chicago. An old Democrat and a valued friend of Welles, Fogg opposed Weed as a matter of principle. Neither past favors nor future expectations had any influence upon him. Quite the contrary, they simply confirmed his suspicions that the "Albany program," as Welles called it, was Whiggism in its most blatantly corrupt form.[51]

On Tuesday, the day before the convention opened, Weed felt certain he had Maine, New Hampshire, Vermont, and Massachusetts in his pocket. With one of his flanks safe, he brought all of his major power to bear on Horace Greeley's doubtful states—Pennsylvania, New Jersey, and Illinois. Of these three, Pennsylvania absorbed most of his attentions. Weed's strategy was sound in the main. Where the Albany generalissimo blundered was in tactics. He concentrated too much of his resources on the center—Pennsylvania and New Jersey—permitting Judge Browning of Quincy, Illinois, a conservative and a recent convert, and David Davis to work for Lincoln on one flank and Welles to work against Seward on the other.

Welles' conversations on the train and at the Tremont House the following day led him to a conclusion which was best expressed by his son Edgar: "Two or three thousand N.Y. men will be here and it looks very much as if Seward would be nominated. In my opinion, however, it looks doubtful and I hardly think he will be." This letter was written hours before the Seward crest had peaked, and it demonstrates that Welles had made a more accurate assessment than Greeley, or Weed, or his friends the Blairs, or the Illinois heavyweight, Judge David Davis.

But there must have been many times during that crucial Tuesday that Welles and his New Englanders despaired of the result. At 10:30 that night, Weed, who was beginning to pay some attention to his flanks, had captured the New Hampshire delegation, despite the best efforts of Fogg and Welles. Earlier in the day Welles had engineered a caucus of the Connecticut and Rhode Island delegations, and, as agreed, Seward did not receive one vote. Later, when Welles learned that New Hampshire had gone for Seward and that Vermont was trembling in the balance, he fought back with every possible weapon, the solid anti-Seward vote of his own state and of Rhode Island, the corrupt image of Thurlow Weed with his fists full of "voluntary" contributions, and always the anti-Whig themes of profligate administration, centralism, plutocracy, and corruption.

It is quite possible, indeed, circumstantial evidence supports the notion, that Welles sent out the distress signal that brought Lincoln's chief managers on the double-quick to the Maine suite and then on to the New Hampshire headquarters. Browning was invited to address both groups, and he harangued them in his florid, Kentucky style, after which both he and Judge Davis moved among the delegates. The Maine men gave them a careful hearing, nothing more, but Browning must have struck just the right note with New Hampshire, since its caucus, which an hour or so before had voted to support Seward, completely reversed itself. Now the New Hampshire men almost unanimously agreed to support Lincoln. Someone, quite probably Welles, acting through John Dennison Baldwin, asked the Lincoln group to address the Massachusetts delegates also. The Bay State men listened intently to Judge Browning but remained noncommittal, though a half-dozen or so delegates, with whom Welles had spent a great deal of time, were already opposed to Seward. Baldwin, their spokesman, like Welles, was a Chase man, which made him especially influential with John A. Andrew, the conceited, dogmatic chairman of the Massachusetts delegation. As a politician, the stout, perspiring Andrew may have wobbled "like an old cart," but he had for some time harbored doubts about Seward.

However felicitous Browning's phrases, however sensible the special pleading of Judge Davis, other factors had been more important in forming Andrew's judgment. The ambitious chairman of the Massachusetts delegation hoped to be nominated for Governor in the fall and needed the support of the influential Worcester *Spy*. He had also heard of the switch in New Hampshire and the seesaw battle in the Vermont suite. He, of course, had been well aware of Connecticut's and Rhode Island's decision not to back Seward. For the time being, Andrew was a tacit convert to the Lincoln cause, though he still preferred Chase and could easily swing back to his original position of support for Seward.[52]

What Welles and a few friends had done that hectic Tuesday was to chip away at Seward's strength in New England. Their biggest chip had been New Hampshire, but they had started some cracks in otherwise solid blocs of Seward strength. Andrew, for instance, would be for Lincoln on the first day of the convention, but more because of Baldwin's influence than because of the Illinois men. Welles knew that he could make no major breakthrough in his own region, but, as he made his weary way through the dense crush of the Tremont's corridors and as he listened and talked in the badly ventilated suites reeking of unwashed bodies, stale with the smoke of cheroots and stogies, where the mantels of Egyptian marble were cluttered with bottles and glasses, the fireplaces and carpets spotted with tobacco juice, Welles thought of the impact his work would have in the electric atmosphere of the convention.[53] As was customary, New England would be called first in the roll of states, Maine leading off. Any significant losses for Seward would be recorded on the tally sheets of thousands of delegates, reporters, and spectators. What was needed was a sufficient weakening to offset the battering-ram of seventy votes that New York would cast immediately following the announcement of the Connecticut vote. Welles was almost certain that he had accomplished his objective.

The exertions of Tuesday had been wearing, and Welles was physically tired when he displayed his credentials at eleven o'clock Wednesday morning to one of the doorkeepers at the Wigwam, the convention hall on the corner of Lake and Market Streets. The size of the building may have impressed him, but not its incongruous appearance. A great barn-like structure, the Wigwam was Chicago's imitation of New York's Crystal Palace. It was knocked together out of unplaned pine sidings and rough, resinous rafters and studding. The tops of three mock bell-towers, perched like lanceheads over the corners, and three fluted elipses tacked onto the outside wall just below the roof line were meant to convey a touch of elegance. Inside the eye was assaulted by a profusion of eclectic decorations on patriotic themes which the ladies of Chicago had had draped, wound, pinned, and plastered on the evergreen embowered uprights that supported roof and galleries. The stage where the delegates would sit, as if on exhibition, was emblazoned with pine boughs and bunting. In front of the stage space was reserved for reporters. Poised above the heads of the delegates, ready to take flight, was a large gilt eagle, wings spread, while just below the stage was a conventional orchestra pit for brass bands and, beyond that, the main floor for alternates and spectators who held special tickets as guests of the delegation. Behind the stage rose the brick wall of the warehouse to which the three-sided building had been attached. Chicago papers, proud of the Wigwam, said it would accommodate 12,000 people; the stage alone had room for 600 grouped around the speaker's rostrum—a slightly elevated dais. In the exuberance of its interior decorations and in the raw, unfinished appearance of its exterior, this odd jumble seemed, as one Easterner observed, "All our extravagance at the bung and all our economy at the spigot."

At 11 a.m., May 16, 1860, Chairman Morgan opened the convention. The atmosphere inside the Wigwam was stifling. Though the building was well-supplied with windows, the sultry weather outside offered no relief to the thousands of spectators who jammed into the galleries, the main floor and—through the generosity of many delegates—the stage itself. His daily routine out of phase, Welles probably dozed through the flamboyant oratory of the first two days. He may have enjoyed a moment of merriment when the temporary chairman, David Wilmot, who had no sense of the ludicrous, appointed Preston King and Carl

Schurz to escort the permanent chairman, George Ashmun, to the podium. King was short and very fat; Schurz was over six feet tall and painfully thin. As Schurz recalled it, the image of Don Quixote and Sancho Panza was so complete that both he and King could not resist a broad grin, and "a titter ran over the convention which might have broken into a general guffaw" had not Ashmun been inducted quickly.

Anxiety among Seward's opponents reached a high point late in the evening after the second day of the convention. Greeley was just one of many who decided that the opposition could not concentrate on one man; he telegraphed the *Tribune* at 11:40 p.m. that Seward would be nominated. In contrast, Welles seemed cool, unconcerned, and cautiously optimistic, but even he could not escape the Seward ambiance which seemed to permeate the very air one breathed. Having done as much damage to Weed's well-laid plans as he could on the first ballot, he and Baldwin and Fogg were now working hard for a much more dramatic switch on the second. While Greeley was giving vent to his despair, the state of Vermont was showing signs that it would give its entire vote on the second ballot to one of Seward's competitors. If Welles was not one of those who were working so successfully with the Vermont delegation, Weed certainly thought he was, and Lord Thurlow was not one to make mistakes in these matters.[54] Thus it came as a distinct shock to Welles when the first ballot was taken that Seward's "supporters were more numerous and better prepared and disciplined than others." As he had assumed, the anti-Seward votes of the New England states, which had been considered strongholds of Whiggism, had stiffened waverers in other states. Lincoln emerged as Seward's strongest competitor, but his 102 votes, as Welles knew, could melt away if he did not sustain momentum on the second ballot. Welles expected that Cameron's votes would be cast for someone else, but probably not Lincoln. Vermont's vote could be of crucial importance, especially if the bulk of New Jersey votes clung to Dayton, as seemed likely. Welles still preferred Chase and thought he had a chance. He was not adverse to Lincoln, though.

Voting began on the second ballot: Maine, no change; New Hampshire, Lincoln, nine, Seward, one—a gain of two votes for the candidate from Illinois. The chairman called Vermont. Peter B. Washburn, a lawyer whom Welles knew slightly, stood up and, in a clear voice that reached out to the farthest gallery, cast the state's entire vote for Abraham Lincoln. Had George Ashmun not been quick with his gavel and his cry for order, the balloting would surely have been interrupted by the swarms of Lincoln men whom Jesse Fell and David Davis and

Norman Judd had packed into the hall. As it was, the New Yorkers started "as if an Orsini bomb had exploded." Massachusetts voted next —no change—then Welles arose and, controlling his nervous stammer, gave two more Connecticut votes for Lincoln. He and Cleveland were still holding out for Chase; there were four votes now for Lincoln; the rest of the delegation was for Bates. On the second ballot, Seward gained eleven votes and Lincoln seventy-nine. When Pennsylvania, which for two days had been causing some merriment and much speculation by calling caucuses when important votes were being taken, threw all of its Cameron votes to Lincoln, Welles knew that the necessary momentum had been sustained. On the third ballot, Ohio switched four votes from Chase to Lincoln, giving the Illinoisan a majority. The delegates rose to their feet as one man to cheer and applaud. Thousands of hats and handkerchiefs cascaded from the balconies or erupted from the floor. Welles was on his feet cheering with the multitude; yet when it came his turn to announce a change in the Connecticut vote—a mere compliment—he and Cleveland remained true to Salmon P. Chase. Though Welles admired Lincoln and knew him better than he did Chase, he was acting according to his principles. Chase was the better man, he thought, and it was a duty, indeed, a trust, imposed upon him by his friends and neighbors back home not to be swayed by emotion or to engage in empty gestures, especially after the primary goal of defeating Seward had been achieved.[55]

Curiously, the vice presidential nomination which followed had more immediate and direct import for Welles than the nomination of Lincoln. The successful Illinois managers, before the convention adjourned for dinner, had decided that New York should have the privilege of naming the candidate. It did not take a very discerning politician to recognize that Seward and his crestfallen friends ought to be placated. Nor was it an especially astute conclusion that if possible the candidate ought to be an Easterner, a former Democrat, and a man acceptable to the New York Senator. Preston King was the obvious choice. No northern Democrat and few Whigs—Joshua Giddings being a notable exception—had such a distinguished antislavery record. King, not Wilmot, was the nimble parliamentarian who, perceptively and with the best of good humor, had attached the Wilmot Proviso to whatever legislation would ensure a maximum of debate during the late 1840's. But King, no doubt remembering Silas Wright's refusal of second place in 1844, would not accept. At the caucus of delegation chairman held during the dinner recess, William Evarts declined in positive terms for New York.

King had been Welles' first choice too. Accompanied by Baldwin, Welles had visited with King prior to the caucus, and they canvassed the situation. All three men were opposed to Cameron, who was being touted by Lincoln's managers on the floor of the Wigwam before the caucus. When Baldwin, in an off-hand manner, suggested Hannibal Hamlin, Welles strongly seconded the suggestion, for Hamlin's nomination made sense from both a geographical and a political point of view. Lincoln was a Western Whig, Hamlin an Eastern Democrat. That he was also a personal friend of Seward and of King convinced them, and, later, the party leaders at the caucus, that his nomination possibly would sooth injured feelings in the Empire State.[56]

There remained only one more function, and that merely the ceremonial one of informing Lincoln of his nomination. Welles was among the distinguished group of Republicans who were made members of the delegation. He made light of his decision to visit Springfield, implying that he was taking the trip because he thought it would be "a good time for Edgar." But he would never have missed the opportunity of witnessing what he knew would be an historic occasion—and of renewing his acquaintance with the nominee. He was curious also about Lincoln's family, his style of living, and whether his manner had in any way been affected by his sudden elevation to national responsibilities of a most compelling order.

Welles was reasonably certain that he would be congratulating the future President of the United States. Apart from his more lofty motives, he shared at least one of the baser instincts that had prompted a flock of politicians to crowd aboard the special train the Illinois Central provided. During the months, as Republican prospects brightened, the possibility of the long-coveted, long-deferred Cabinet post was never far from his mind. He had done important work at the convention, not directly for Lincoln, but against Seward, work that played a significant role in the final result. At the age of fifty-eight, it was now or never. Welles would leave no business undone, would pull every string, tie every knot, to achieve his lifelong goal. Conscious of his official importance as a member not only of the national committee but of its executive arm, he would make the most of his mission, inconspicuously present, but in the front rank with George Ashmun, F. P. Blair, Sr., and Governors Morgan of New York, Ramsey of Minnesota, and Boutwell of Massachusetts.

Everything went off pleasantly. The trip down, which took all day, was as comfortable as the management of the Illinois Central could make it. Lincoln's rather modest home must have reminded Welles of

his old residence on Welles Avenue where he and Mary had established their first household. Springfield, a typical, treeless Western
town with wooden sidewalks, its main street dwindling off into feature-
less prairie, was much as he remembered numberless new towns and
cities on his travels through that raw, unfinished country. The nominee's response to Ashmun's remarks was simple, straightforward, and
mercifully brief, but dignified and eminently appropriate to the occasion. After the ceremony, Lincoln greeted each member warmly, shaking hands in his odd pump-handle way. Did he grip Welles' hand a bit
more firmly than the others? Was his apparent delight at seeing him
again and recalling their meeting in Hartford a sincere expression of
regard? Or had it some deeper meaning? These were some of the questions that Welles pondered as he lay in his berth on the return trip to
Chicago that night. He had been favored with one of the few beds provided, "and slept about as well as on board a steamboat."[57]

# CHAPTER 17

# New England's Representative Man

FEW OF THE CONGREGATION of Washington's Epiphany Episcopal Church realized that the elderly man who accompanied Judge Samuel H. Huntington to Sunday services was the new Secretary of the Navy, Gideon Welles. Many of the parishioners must have been curious about the stranger, for his appearance was striking enough to warrant more than a second glance. Very full, snow-white whiskers covered most of the face, though his upper lip was shaved clean; and from his head a cascade of gray curls tumbled nearly to his shoulders. His appearance was bizarre even for those days of spectacular masculine display.[1] Welles was fortunate that he did not attract more attention, for he had reached that stage of weariness where his control over his emotions was very thin indeed.

He and his family had attended Epiphany from 1846 to 1849, when he was a bureau chief in the Navy Department. Now, as he went through the forms of worship, he could not help but reflect upon past sorrows and present burdens. "I bore up very well," he wrote his wife, "until the choir began to sing, when I found the tears involuntarily betraying my weakness."[2] He had arrived, he was well aware, at the goal toward which he had been striving for more than thirty years and which, in his darker moments, he had never expected to reach. Heavy responsibilities would be his as a Cabinet officer, for he was serving at a time of national crisis, the gravest crisis the nation had ever faced. He was quite sure that this new administration, with its tall, ungainly leader, a man he scarcely knew, would make a history of its own, as

significant perhaps as the history made by the Revolutionary generation.

He was also acutely conscious of his official burdens, of the fact that
his performance would be measured not only by his chief, his party,
and his section but by the cruelest and ficklest of tests—public opinion.
Something of an expert in that field, he could only anticipate the
vicious jibes of the irresponsible journalist, the crude japes of the
vulgar cartoonist.

Fearful and expectant by turns, he had been alert to the mounting
tensions in Washington since Lincoln's inauguration. Though deeply
disturbed by the tragic condition of the divided nation, Welles was
enough of a romantic to relish the excitement of the hour, enough of
an egotist to revel in the prestige and the perquisites of his new office.
As the service at Epiphany fell into its accustomed pattern, Welles'
thoughts drifted away to the "memory of the old days . . . daughter—
the past and the present . . . exciting affairs . . . the living moving
throng and great events impending." After the service, in the privacy of
his room at Willard's, while he worked on Saturday's pile of official
and personal mail, his mind wandered back over the progression of
events that had brought him to his present position.[3]

Most vividly did he recollect the Chicago convention and its aftermath. As he mused about the campaign—the party's for Lincoln and
Hamlin, his own for a Cabinet post—the images of William H. Seward
and Thurlow Weed must have been uppermost in his mind. The
jaunty little Secretary of State had already raised Welles' ire at his
pretentious assumption that he spoke for the President. As for Weed,
he could not help but suspect that the casual policies of the administration on patronage were traceable to Albany influence. Welles had never
trusted Seward's politics or his motives, and though he respected Weed
for his mastery of the political arts and crafts, he firmly believed him
to be a spoilsman of the worst order. His distrust of "the Albany
Clique" was shared by most radicals, especially those of Democratic
background. So worried had they been about patronage that until
almost the last moment they had tried to convince Lincoln that Welles
should be given the Post Office rather than the Navy Department. They
shuddered at the thought of such a mighty dispenser of jobs as the
Post Office coming under the Weed-Seward grasp. Welles had been
quite willing to accept either department, and in fact he was not sure
whether he was to be Postmaster General or Secretary of the Navy until
Lincoln sent his nomination to the Senate.[4]

After the election the question of who was to advise, if not control, the new administration had been the chief topic of conversation among knowledgeable Republicans. The Weed-Seward faction—and it packed a heavy punch—stepped up its pressure. Welles was early marked for exclusion as a troublesome radical Democrat who somehow had been a major force in preventing Seward's nomination.[5]

Evidence of Weed's personal hostility toward Welles and of his first stealthy approach to Lincoln came through a chance encounter of the two Easterners on a Mississippi steamboat three days after the Chicago convention. As he still had some business affairs to settle in southern Illinois, Welles left Chicago on May 21, for Rock Island, where he hoped to catch the steam packet to Quincy. He missed the regular boat but in the evening was fortunate to book passage on an unscheduled vessel which, he was warned, had "very indifferent accommodations." To his astonishment, the first person he met as he went aboard "in the confusion and dusk of evening" was Thurlow Weed, who, according to the newspapers, was supposed to be traveling in Minnesota. "I saw at once," Welles said with considerable relish, "that the meeting was not only unexpected but that it afforded him no gratification." Weed was not even civil. He turned on his heel and strode rapidly to his quarters on the boat, where he remained during the trip to Rock Island. The realization that Springfield was the obvious destination of the New York boss laid to rest any wishful thinking Welles may have had that Lincoln would keep the "Albany lobby" at arms' length.[6]

As a member of the party's executive committee, Welles watched from within the activities of Lincoln and Weed, both master politicians.[7] He quickly learned that David Davis and Leonard Swett had been responsible for Weed's secret trip to Springfield.[8] The gist of the meeting was also relayed on to him. Weed, he was told, "was somewhat presuming and officious, yet was treated with considerable courtesy"— but Lincoln, it was said, could not be drawn out. Davis and Swett "were more free in their communications, promises and concessions. . . ." Welles believed that Weed, dissatisfied with Lincoln's noncommittal attitude, had struck an alliance with Simon Cameron, and sought to bring the nominee to heel by doing little or nothing in support of the campaign while at the same time sending dire reports off to Springfield. This "apparent holding off," as Welles phrased it, did bring Davis and Swett on the double to a late summer meeting at Saratoga. Lincoln's emissaries, who, Welles chose to believe, were acting on their own, met with "the Albany Clique" and with two Pennsylvanians, Simon Cameron and one of his lieutenants.[9] All agreed, said Welles, that Seward "should in the event of the election of Mr. Lincoln of which there was little doubt, receive as was generally expected the appointment of Secretary of State and Simon Cameron of Pennsylvania that of Secretary of the Treasury . . . this arrangement, though for the time apparently acquiesced in, or not emphatically repelled, was never ratified and carried into effect by President Lincoln."[10]

Then and for the next several months Welles thought Lincoln to be an honest, well-intentioned person who was way out of his depth when dealing with such hardened, scheming professionals as Weed and Cameron. On the whole, he agreed with Senator Dixon, who had served with the nominee in Congress, that Lincoln was "a man of more than average talents—and as honest as the light of day . . . rather credulous & unsuspecting and may possibly be exposed to the crafty and cunning men, who professing honesty, may take advantage of him."[11] Though resigned to the probability that Seward would be offered one of the top Cabinet posts if Lincoln were elected, Welles, as he had done before Chicago, worked to neutralize what he chose to call the "Albany policy." In pursuit of this goal he became one of the rallying points for all radical Republicans who might accept Seward but who would never trust Weed and who held Cameron in total contempt.

Welles watched with professional interest as the smoldering feud between Greeley and Seward that had been fanned into flame by the editor's activities at the convention became public knowledge and then went beyond the bounds of any possible reconciliation. Yet Welles knew that Seward still maintained a firm hold on a majority of leading Republicans.[12] That he had been deeply hurt by his failure at Chicago even his inveterate enemies admitted; that he had subsequently come out vigorously for Lincoln and had campaigned for him through New England and on into the Middle West evoked admiration from many erstwhile detractors. His tour was a resounding success both for the party and for his own personal fortunes. After the Republican victory in November, Edward L. Pierce, the Massachusetts radical and a friend of Welles, Chase, and Sumner, wrote "there is only one man in the country to whom in fact & in popular estimation any place is due as a debt—and that is Mr. Seward."[13] Welles was careful in his correspondence to avoid any criticism of Seward and to steer clear of Greeley. Weed and Cameron were fair game, however.

Meanwhile, his energies, skills, and interests were being diverted by the ominous moves of the Southern ultras. Exactly one week after the election, the news from South Carolina had seemed so alarming to Bryant and Bigelow that they asked Welles for a series of lead articles on the Nullification crisis during Jackson's day. Their obvious intent was to strengthen the resolve of the Buchanan administration in the hope that the President would emulate his vigorous predecessor and take stern measures if necessary. Welles did not disappoint them.[14] His long historical essay, published in two installments took up half the front page of the *Evening Post* on December 1 and December 7, 1860.

Jackson's handling of South Carolina in 1832 was held up as the proper course for the Buchanan administration. On constitutional points Welles distinguished between states' rights and state sovereignty, using basically the same argument that James Madison had advanced in 1829.[15] That the Union was a limited government he freely admitted; the states and the people possessed all reserve powers not delegated to the federal government; but the power of Congress to enact tariff legislation was clearly a delegated power, not a reserved one. Calhoun, in rejecting a fundamental division of powers, had rejected the Constitution. If state sovereignty was a subversive doctrine in 1832, one must conclude that it was no less subversive in 1860. Southerners who read the *Post*, and who knew it to be one of the most prominent of Republican papers, properly concluded from Welles' articles that the new administration would not accept secession in any form. Lincoln may have been silent, but his very silence argues forcefully that he approved of the principles Welles set forth and the means that the Old Hero had employed to assert them almost thirty years before.

Congressman Orris S. Ferry wrote that both Connecticut Senators, Foster and Dixon, were caving in to Southern demands. "Better civil war for ten years," cried the excitable Ferry, "than a division of the Confederacy or a Federal sanction of slavery."[16] Welles could discount much of Ferry's alarming news, because he knew of the Congressman's emotional nature and relentless ambition. What really alarmed him about events in Washington was word from Preston King, who was emotional too, but a far more reliable source. Buchanan, King charged, was "undoubtedly under the influence of traitors. It is believed that Foster, though looking with fear on the approaching storm will be firm in his votes. Dixon is more disturbed & it is difficult to say what he will do."[17] On December 22, Welles heard directly from Dixon, who personally bore witness to his lack of stamina when he said, "the ship is drifting on the rocks and we ought to buy time with conciliatory measures."[18]

If Welles had not been convinced of Dixon's timidity before, he was now. He also had to assume that many other Republican Congressmen shared the Senator's opinion. Two weeks earlier, when he received his first intimation of concessions in the face of strident Southern demands, he had written Dixon one of his calmly persuasive letters, which he hoped would stiffen some backbones yet not slam the door on conciliation. He was glad, he said, that members of Congress generally favored a policy that would harmonize differences. "If we have done anything wrong let us make haste to correct it. . . ." "But," he continued, "I am not aware that the Republicans have done anything, or that they propose to do anything that disturbs the rights of others, or will suspend the Constitution or imperil public liberty." "Let us then be cautious," he enjoined Dixon, "that we do not weaken our own cause and that of justice and right, by surrendering to improper demands, privileges and principles which [it] is our duty to maintain." But Dixon and those Republicans who listened to him would not heed this sensible advice.[19]

When Welles received Dixon's apparent capitulation, South Carolina had already seceded from the Union. Buchanan had done nothing. Welles would have been surprised if he had. For more than a year, in at least a dozen articles, he had excoriated the President. Timid, treacherous, wretched, unprincipled, corrupt, vacillating, vindictive, venomous were some of the pejoratives he used to fill the editorial columns of the *Press*. Welles coupled his genuine contempt for the man with a forlorn hope that savage indictments carried by the Republican press would compel the President to act—if only to preserve his self-respect and the prestige of his office. For Welles had long believed Buchanan was devoid of any statesmanlike qualities, a mere partisan chief who had surrounded himself with courtiers like Toucey or corrupt disunionists like John B. Floyd, his Secretary of War. No appeal to reason was likely to move him, nor had indictments from the Northern press and the pulpit been any more persuasive.

As the new year opened, all Buchanan seemed willing or able to do was ask the nation to pray for deliverance, in Welles' eyes, a public confession of his complete mental and moral collapse. It now dawned on the Republicans that for the next three months, while the nation drifted toward destruction, there would be no Executive head. Vexed beyond measure, Welles wrote of the lame-duck President in his diary: "Wretched man! most of our public troubles are to be attributed to his weakness and wilful perversity."[20] Yet leadership of some sort had to be maintained at all costs until Lincoln was inaugurated. Welles and men like him looked to the President-elect in Springfield and to the Republicans in Congress for guidance. They found to their dismay

muel Welles, father of Gideon Welles. Died
34. Ivory miniature. Courtesy of Mrs. Jesse A.
Brainard, owner.

John M. Niles. Courtesy of Connecticut Historical
Society.

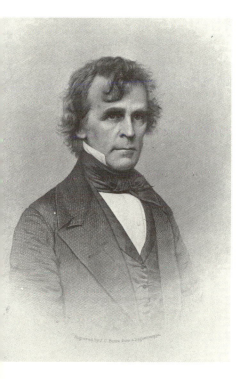

ator Isaac Toucey. Courtesy of Connecticut
Historical Society.

Postmaster General Amos Kendall. Library of
Congress.

Mary Jane Hale Welles at forty-one. Matthew Wilson painting. Courtesy of Mrs. Jesse A. Brainard, owner.

Gideon Welles at fifty-seven. Matthew Wilson painting. Courtesy of Mrs. Jesse A. Brainard, owner.

Edgar Thaddeus Welles. Courtesy of Thomas W. Brainard, owner.

Thomas G. Welles as a midshipman, c. 186 Courtesy of Thomas W. Brainard, owner.

na Jane Welles. Ivory miniature by M. Parrott. Courtesy of Thomas W. Brainard, owner.

Hubert Welles, c. 1862. Brady photo. Courtesy of Thomas W. Brainard, owner.

ohn A. Welles, c. 1856. Courtesy of Thomas W. Brainard, owner.

Mary Juniata Welles, d. 1858. Prescott-White photo, Hartford. Courtesy of Thomas W. Brainard, owner.

John Lenthall, Chief, Bureau of Construction and Repair. National Archives.

Guatavus Vasa Fox, Assistant Secretary of the Navy, 1862–1866. Courtesy of Lloyd Ostendorf.

Commander John A. Dahlgren. U. S. Navy.

Admiral David Glascow Farragut. Brady-Handy Collection, Library of Congress.

Rear Admiral Samuel F. Du Pont.

John Ericsson

U.S.S. *Monitor*. Library of Congress.

Secretary of War Edwin M. Stanton. Library of Congress.

Secretary of State William H. Seward. Library of Congress.

"The First Reading of the Emancipation Proclamation." Seated (left to right): Secretary of War Edwin M. Stanton, President Lincoln, Secretary of the Navy Gideon Welles, Secretary of State William H. Seward, Attorney General Edward Bates, Standing (left to right): Secretary of the Treasury Salmon Chase, Secretary of the Interior Caleb Smith, Postmaster General Montgomery Blair. Library of Congress.

Francis Preston Blair, Sr. Library of Congress.

Senator Charles Sumner. Brady-Handy Collection, Library of Congress.

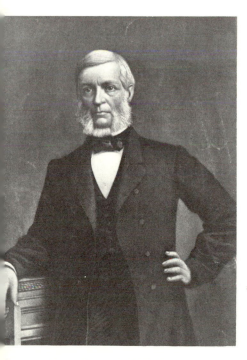

George Bancroft. U. S. Navy.

Henry Winter Davis. Brady photo. Library of Congress.

Gideon Welles in the mid-1860's. Courtesy of Connecticut Historical Society.

U.S.S. *New Ironsides.* Smithsonian Institution.

that they could take little comfort in the actions of either.[21] With the future of the Union apparently at stake, most Northerners, Welles among them, were in a resolute state of mind that concealed the apprehension they really felt, their desperate yearning for a strong hand. The emotional outbursts of Congressman Ferry, who saw treason everywhere, were not calculated to accomplish anything constructive. On the other side, the quavering notes of Dixon, Foster, and other appeasers were scarcely reassuring. Lincoln was quietly communicating a tentative policy to a few chosen lieutenants, but his policies were not generally known. Had Welles been apprised of the President-elect's views as he related them to Lyman Trumbull, for instance, he would have been much relieved. As it was, most of the information he received about the intentions of the new administration was shrouded with ambiguities.

Unable to form any opinion on the facts as they were developing in Washington, the public of the Northern states had to depend for its information on the press, which took its cue from the inflammatory and irresponsible reporting of the great New York dailies. The *New-York Tribune* saw either appeasement or treason in every effort to compose differences between the two sections. Bennett's *Herald* and Bryant and Bigelow's *Post* were scarcely more responsible, the one calling for conciliation at any price, the other demanding Jacksonian measures. Seward, chief spokesman for the Republicans in the Senate, was the prime object of popular attention. His stand opposing the Crittenden resolutions, which would have applied the Missouri Compromise line to the territories, was generally applauded, but his equivocation on a Border state proposal that New Mexico come in as a slave state brought suspicion and scorn from the articulate militants. When Charles Francis Adams, then in the House, offered the New Mexico resolution and secured its adoption in committee, both he and Seward were accused of collusion and of truckling to the South. Edward L. Pierce, who had been a warm supporter of Adams and had urged him for the Cabinet, was now muttering, "We cannot understand Mr. Adams' course here."[22] Seward's political reputation with the radicals suffered another setback when Thurlow Weed began lobbying for his own compromise plan—extension of the Missouri Compromise line to the Pacific. Though Weed was acting alone, the public concluded that he was speaking also for his long-time associate. Welles could only benefit from these events in Washington, for by this time he was widely regarded as one of the more prominent Cabinet contenders.

He had been quietly campaigning for himself since the Chicago convention. So tactful had been his maneuvers, so disinterested had his pose seemed, that his earliest backers had no inkling they were being manipulated. He selected his supporters with great care, as is evidenced by his first choice, George G. Fogg, secretary of the Republican national committee. Welles had known Fogg, a competent editor and a former Democrat, since the Frémont campaign. Industrious, quick, and penetrating in his analysis of political crosscurrents, this earnest yet affable journalist had early proved his worth to the national committee. But it was not Fogg's personal qualities that commended him to Welles at this time; it was his strategic position. As secretary he had coordinated the campaign with the Republican executive committee, the nominee, and the state organizations. Always on the move, he quickly established a working relationship with Lincoln, for whom he acted as a major channel of communication with the Eastern Republicans. To have Fogg as a backer was to have strength where it counted.

Other early supporters were John Dennison Baldwin of the Worcester *Spy*, Edward L. Pierce, and Senator Henry Wilson, all from Massachusetts and all identified with the radical wing of the Republican party. Senator James Dixon, a conservative but an old freesoil Whig who had also served in Congress with Lincoln, owed Welles a substantial political debt which he was anxious to repay. His was the first letter Lincoln received suggesting Welles for the Cabinet. It was borne to Springfield by Mark Howard, who had a special letter of introduction from the Connecticut Senator. Bryant and Bigelow and Greeley of the anti-Seward faction in New York could be counted upon when needed. Preston King of the pro-Seward faction would do anything in his power for his close friend of twenty years' standing. After Fogg, King turned out to be the most important factor in Welles' campaign, even though he had never met Lincoln. King had recommended Hamlin for the vice presidential nomination and had thereby earned an obligation of sorts.

When Lincoln asked Hamlin to visit with him at Chicago in late November, he surprised the Vice President-elect by "promising him" the New England appointment. But before Hamlin had much chance to speculate about this unprecedented compliment, Lincoln restricted his choice by suggesting they discuss a list of candidates he had prepared for the Navy Department. Hamlin later recalled that the list was quickly narrowed down to three: Charles Francis Adams, Nathaniel P. Banks—who had just completed his third term as Governor of Massachusetts—and Welles. Lincoln had asked that Hamlin be absolutely frank in his estimate of the various candidates. And though Lincoln spoke in glowing terms of Banks' prominence and administrative experience, he listened carefully when the Maine Senator said bluntly that Banks was a "trimmer in politics," distrusted and disliked by many in New England. Hamlin's recollections up to this point ring true, but he errs in stating that his personal objections removed Banks from the list. The ex-Governor of the Bay State and ex-Speaker of the United States House of Representatives was far too prominent a politician to be dismissed so lightly. Banks would remain a formidable candidate almost to the very end, and in all likelihood he was Lincoln's first choice for New England.

Lincoln spoke also of the Cabinet in general terms, indicating his desire to balance sectional interests with political antecedents, conservative and radical elements, and personal ambition. What he was suggesting was a coalition government designed not only to meet the impending constitutional crisis, but to cope with the realities of the Republican party—young, unstable, faction-ridden. It was an ingenious policy and must have appeared so to Hamlin, but it would require able management. Lincoln concluded their interview by asking Hamlin to carry out two important missions. The first dealt with William II. Seward and would lead to his appointment as Secretary of State; the second concerned the New England representative for the Cabinet. Was it to be Adams, Banks, Welles, or possibly another not on Lincoln's original list? The President-elect had only one condition. Every member of his Cabinet must agree that he would uphold the laws of the land, including the obnoxious Fugitive Slave Law. Intimations of Welles' radicalism had reached Lincoln's ears. What was his position on this controversial legislation? Hamlin believed that Welles was opposed to the Fugitive Slave Law, but that as a responsible citizen he would uphold it until it was repealed.

When the Vice President-elect reached Washington, the first person he sounded on Seward's availability was Preston King, who suggested he "confer directly with the governor." Hamlin also spoke of Welles in a guarded way as a possibility for the Cabinet, and King gave him a warm endorsement. King, it would appear, confirmed Hamlin's opinion as expressed to Lincoln, that Welles would support the Fugitive Slave Law, though he would actively seek its repeal. Reassured but still not absolutely certain, the busy presidential emissary found time to confer personally with Dixon. Hamlin came directly to the point.

"What are the views of Mr. Welles with regard to . . . the intent and meaning of the clause in the Constitution for the rendition of fugitives from service?" Should "Congress or the states . . . provide for their delivery to the claimant?"

Dixon thought that Welles "agreed with Mr. Webster's opinion . . . the duty should be performed by the states."

"That was always my opinion as an original question," said Hamlin, "but as the other doctrine was held by the framers of the Constitution . . . and has been acquiesced in I have adopted it."

Alluding to the Fugitive Slave Law of 1793 and Justice Story's opinion in the Prigg case, Hamlin wondered whether Welles would be bound by Webster's construction "if called upon to execute the present law?"

Dixon thought his opinion was merely theoretical and that he would yield it in practice, "if acting under official responsibility."

Though Dixon had known from the first question that Welles was being considered for the Cabinet, he did not expect the candor of the statement that followed.

"Mr. Lincoln and I," said Hamlin, "agree that the Fugitive Slave Laws must be executed in good faith." He added that Lincoln had mentioned Welles' name for a post in his Cabinet and that he "was very favorably impressed. . . ." It was "indispensable," however, that Welles agree with Lincoln's views on the Fugitive Slave Laws.

The interview over, Hamlin, his dark, seamed face set in an authoritative cast, looked directly at Dixon. He spoke slowly, giving weight to each word: "this must be emphatically confidential and known to no human being but the three of us." If Welles desired to be a candidate, he should write out his opinions on the Laws and post them to Dixon. The letter would be forwarded to Springfield.[23]

At this time Welles had no inkling that his quiet campaign had made such an impression at the summit. He had first noticed his name (misspelled) mentioned as a Cabinet possibility by the Springfield correspondent of the New York *Herald* on November 24. But this was so obviously an idle rumor inserted as space filler that he gave it little more than a passing glance. From then until December 5, his name did not appear on any of the changing Cabinet slates being carried almost daily by the New York press.

The Dixon letter, which he received in the evening mail of December 5, must have shaken him considerably. He was, of course, aware that Hamlin had visited Lincoln in Chicago and suspected his mission had dealt with the Cabinet. There was no reason, however, for him to imagine that his own name was discussed. None of his special friends had been near Lincoln. His slight acquaintance with Hamlin went back to Mexican War days. Unknown to him was the favorable impression he had made on the President-elect in Hartford some ten months earlier. His important work at Chicago had not gone unnoticed. And Hamlin really knew him better by reputation than Welles had any reason to suspect.

Despite the obvious coaching from both Dixon and Hamlin, Welles had in mind exactly what he wanted to say. Though painfully aware that this letter might well prove the most important single document he would ever write, he completed it in one sitting with but few minor changes on his rough draft. He might have edited more carefully his concluding statement expressing an opinion that the return of fugitive slaves was a matter for state jurisdiction. Almost ten years before, he had written for the *Evening Post* and the *New Haven Palladium* a forceful constitutional argument on the fugitive slave provision of the Constitution. Then he had taken ground against Story, arguing that the provision was merely a compact among the states, that it had nothing to do with federal power. Obviously, his reference to state jurisdiction in his letter to Dixon rested on the same constitutional interpretation—comity among the states. But such a doctrine, as he well knew, amounted to the practical nullification of any federal fugitive slave enactment, barred as it was from execution by the personal liberty laws of the various free states, his own included.

Without knowing Welles' entire argument, Lincoln might have been bothered by the notion that the federal government should relinquish "to the states the power of rendition" and demand of them its execution under the constitutional requirements. How could the federal government demand compliance if it had no power over state action? But more difficult than any legal technicality or constitutional interpretation was Welles' idea of states' rights, which would have further inflamed the lower South. Otherwise, the letter conformed admirably with the views of Lincoln and Hamlin. Nor could they have disagreed with his private opinion of the law: "Unnecessarily harsh and offensive . . . framed to beget animosity and hatred . . . calculated, if not designed, to promote ill blood and unkind feelings . . . fruitful source of sectional bias. . . ." Welles as a Cabinet officer would perform his duty under the law but would work for its repeal.[24]

Hamlin was still traveling east toward Washington when George Fogg arrived to spend Thanksgiving in Springfield and to discuss party problems with Lincoln. Fogg had found himself in a rather delicate position regarding the Cabinet member from New England. His per-

sonal preference was decidedly for Welles, whom he admired as a political writer and a former Democrat of intelligence and integrity. But
before he visited Springfield, he had been approached by Amos Tuck,
also a good friend and ex-Democrat—and a citizen of his own state.
The handsome Tuck, whose youthful, regular features contrasted strikingly with his flowing mane of white hair, had been chairman of the
New Hampshire delegation, which had played a key role in the nomination at Chicago. Tuck, however, had not provided conspicuous leadership in bringing the New Hampshire vote over to Lincoln. In Fogg's
estimation, Welles' services had been far more significant—and not just
in one New England state, but in the entire region. Yet he deemed it
his duty to recommend Tuck. Luckily for Welles' candidacy, Tuck had
early indicated that he would be satisfied with the lucrative customs
house in Boston. Even so, Lincoln added Tuck's name to the list of
possibles. A much more formidable—indeed, Welles' most serious—rival
continued to be Nathaniel P. Banks, who had just accepted the presidency of the Illinois Central Railroad.

In the early hours of November 7, after he was certain of his election, the sleepless Lincoln pondered, among other things, the composition of his Cabinet. As he would relate to Welles some years later, the
Cabinet slate that he devised on that occasion was "essentially the
same" that he would recommend to the Senate on March 5, 1861. Lincoln's recollection was clear. Where Welles went astray was in his interpretation of "essentially." He chose to assume that he was one of the
original slate, but the weight of evidence does not support such a conclusion. Three days before the Hamlin meeting, David Davis had written Lincoln, ". . . if you prefer Governor Banks to anyone else I have
little doubt that he would gladly accept." The portly jurist did not like
Banks, as he pointed out to Lincoln, though he spoke highly of his
"fine administrative abilities" and of his strong following among "the
original Democratic side of the House." From then on the Banks movement gained rapid impetus.

On December 8 Lincoln wrote Hamlin that he thought Banks
"would accept a place in the cabinet." He wanted an opinion, but
the phrasing of his letter in the light of his previous interest in Banks
left little doubt about his personal inclinations. Hamlin chose not to
be influenced by the broad hint: he replied that either Charles Francis
Adams or Welles would be preferred by New England. "Mr. B.," he
wrote, "is a man of decided ability but he *is* wonderfully cold and selfish." Ten days later Lincoln vetoed Adams, Hamlin's first choice. He
needed "a man of Democratic antecedents from New England," he

said. "I can not get a fair share of that element in without." Banks, Welles, or Tuck, he put to Hamlin, "which of them do the New England delegation prefer? Or shall I decide myself."[25]

As Welles had assumed after he learned of the Saratoga conference, the prairie lawyer had already stumbled in his dealings with Cameron and Weed. Whether he wanted Seward in his Cabinet or not, the President-elect had been maneuvered into a position where he had to offer his chief party rival first place. Weed's gentle manner, his pungent remarks, and his political expertise seem to have disarmed Lincoln as they had disarmed many another discerning man through the years. Arriving in Springfield on December 20, Weed closeted himself with Lincoln for a talk that lasted the better part of the day. Despite Weed's reputation, Lincoln chose to be frank and open on Cabinet matters as well as on the secession of South Carolina, news of which had just been received in Springfield.

Naturally these stirring events in the deep South claimed precedence, and then, as Weed remembered, "after this subject had been talked up and over and out," Lincoln shifted discussion to the Cabinet. The Whig chieftain was deeply gratified when Lincoln said he intended to offer Seward the State Department. He could not have been pleased, however, by Lincoln's next remark, that Chase would be invited to take the Treasury Department, and he was especially disturbed when Welles was named as the probable candidate from New England. Several other men from that section, he was certain, would be much more acceptable. Except for Cameron, nominally an ex-Democrat, on whose appointment he assumed a guarded position, the mastermind of the "Albany Clique" made it clear that he interpreted the nomination and election as a Whig triumph, and he pressed for an all-Whig Cabinet. But his animus toward Welles transcended partisanship. As he was leaving Lincoln's house, he made one of those playful comments with which he had consigned to political oblivion scores of ambitious office-seekers. If the President-elect stopped long enough in New York, Baltimore, or Washington "to select an attractive figure-head, to be adorned with an elaborate wig and luxuriant whiskers and transfer[ed] it from the prow of a ship to the entrance of the Navy Department," Weed thought that he would have just as serviceable a Secretary at much less expense. "Oh," Lincoln replied quietly, in the same ironic vein, "wooden midshipmen answer very well in novels, but we must have a live secretary of the navy."

A few days after Weed's departure, Seward accepted the State Department. Lincoln knew this appointment would raise a clamor from the New Yorker's many enemies, the Democratic element particularly. Quite obviously, he had been preparing for such an event when he ruled out Adams, an ex-Whig deemed close to the Seward faction. Given the choice between Banks, Tuck, and Welles, Hamlin made a very positive endorsement of Welles, as did George Fogg, who advised Lincoln that, while he himself must stand by Tuck, "Welles had some valuable qualities in a much higher degree. . . ."

When these letters arrived in Springfield, Lincoln was under mounting pressure from the Seward faction, which included that craggy-visaged, small-eyed opportunist, Simon Cameron. This master of the untrodden way had come and gone with a Cabinet invitation that he was supposed to refuse in due course. Lincoln was more wary with Cameron than he had been with Weed, but again he was outwitted. The visits set afloat rumors that were skillfully used by the "Albany Clique" in the press to promote Seward and Cameron as indispensable men in the crisis. By implication, Seward would dominate the new administration. It was to be his choice, not Lincoln's, that would govern Cabinet appointments.

Weed and Cameron for once overplayed their hands. They grossly underestimated Lincoln, whom they wrote off as a local and purely accidental phenomenon, at best a second-rate Zachary Taylor. They seem not to have anticipated the furious opposition their campaign would arouse among the radical Democrats of the party. Connecticut-born Henry B. Stanton, lawyer, wit, and reformer, spoke for the Republican Barnburners of New York when he flatly stated that the administration would be a failure if Seward, Weed, and Cameron prevailed. "For you," he wrote Welles, "to occupy a place in the counsel of Mr. Lincoln will give confidence to the radical democracy of New York now in the Republican party, the men who adopt our principles because they are Jeffersonian. . . ." Chase and Welles were the bright hopes of the radicals.

As George Fogg remarked, a great effort was being made for Seward (which he thought would succeed), but its success would improve Welles' chances because the "Seward program" included Charles Francis Adams for New England.[26] Fogg admitted that the situation was an extremely fluid one, even intimating that it might be beyond Lincoln's control—so great were the forces begotten by the mutual anxieties and aspirations and animosities of the contending factions. The Massachusetts congressional delegation unanimously recommended Adams in a strongly worded statement, but privately Henry Wilson was not enthusiastic, as he explained in a follow-up letter to Lincoln. He had deferred, he said, to the wishes of his colleagues and to the Massachusetts central committee. If Welles were appointed from New England, he would be just as pleased. "I know them both well," he said, "and I can truly say that they are able, pure and true men. Mr. Welles is . . . no speaker, but one of the best writers in our section of the country." Lincoln's sometimes fumbling troubleshooter, Leonard Swett, who was in Washington at this time, added the weight of his counsel to that of Wilson. He had not thought much of Welles before his visit to the capital. Now he was certain that Welles would be a good appointment, and that he had broad support in New England. The indefatigable Fogg, who not only kept Welles posted but, in shuttling between New Hampshire, Boston, Washington, and Springfield, gathered and reported high political moves, saw to it that Governor John A. Andrew and other Massachusetts radicals wrote letters to Springfield, supporting Welles and Chase and denouncing Banks and Adams. A worried Henry B. Stanton and an irate Edward L. Pierce harped on the dangers of the Weed-Seward drive and the necessity of having radical Democrats in the Cabinet.[27]

From Washington Fogg wrote Welles that he was going again to Springfield as "bearer of dispatches" to prevent if possible the "success of Weed's scheme to control and ruin Mr. Lincoln's administration." He found Lincoln "cool, self possessed and true." Upon asking him what he intended to do for New England, he replied, "My present impression is the same as yours—if I were obliged to make a selection today it would be Mr. Welles." Lincoln was still hedging his bets. Though Fogg talked "very frankly" with him about Banks and concluded that the Governor did not have a chance, he was being unduly optimistic. The business and financial community of Boston stood solidly behind Banks and was more than willing to supply whatever funds might be required to place him in the Cabinet. And State Street was not his only means of support. That old Websterian, George Ashmun, who had presided over the Chicago Convention, was pulling every lever at his command for Banks. The *Springfield Republican* stood at the head of numerous influential country papers in demanding his inclusion as the "Democratic" member from New England. If Adams could not go in, Weed wanted Banks for New England. When he realized, rather tardily, that his first choice was unacceptable, he threw the solid resources of his well-knit organization into the drive. But the strident voices of William Cullen Bryant and Pierce, coupled with the deeper warnings of Stanton, Fogg, Hamlin, Henry Wilson, Charles Sumner, and Massachusetts' new Governor, John A. Andrew,

effectively blanketed the Banks' partisans. All in one way or another
supported Welles, more to stop Banks than for any other reason.[28]

Still pursuing his discreet course, Welles joined in the criticism of
the appointments already announced—Seward for State, Bates for Attorney General. Typically, he made no direct approach, but in communicating his fears of Whig dominance to Fogg, he felt reasonably
certain his views would reach Springfield. And in fact it could have
been Lincoln himself speaking when Fogg admitted that the Cabinet
"does look like a Whig concern now. Yet Mr. Lincoln does not mean it
[to be so] . . . he delays further action in order to get out of an unfortunate dilemma"—an obvious reference to the Cameron promise.[29]

Besides overplaying his political hand, Weed was losing his gamble
to put together a coalition in Congress that would hold the Border
states in the Union. By the first week in February six more slave states
had followed South Carolina's example. A provisional government had
been established in Montgomery, Alabama. Conservative and moderate Republicans, most of the old Whig school, were frantic in their efforts to make some sort of adjustment.

The Crittenden compromise had failed, but not without further tarnishing the reputations of both Seward and Adams in the eyes of the
radicals, who thought, as Welles did, that it was the work of "an old
Whig compromiser who took the Breckenridge platform and wants to
adopt it as a compromise." Dixon, reacting to the chorus of radical
criticism, had decided that any kind of moderate course was now impossible. In a despairing mood he wrote: "I see no solution but war!
folly rules the house on both sides . . . the New York *Tribune* is most
pestilential in its influence . . . see how they denounce C. F. Adams
for his scheme of conciliation." Far from the superheated atmosphere
of Washington, Welles found Dixon's attitude as incomprehensible as
that of the Southerners and most Northern Democrats. When South
Carolina batteries fired on the *Star of the West* as she tried to provision
Fort Sumter, Welles scribbled in his diary: "Am disgusted at the conduct of almost the whole of the people in the slave states, and mortified
to see so many here at home . . . rejoicing over the madness and folly
of the secessionists. Wretched must be that people when party malig-
nity can triumph over patriotism and country."[30]

Fundamentally an insecure person, Welles had early in life worked
out positions on public and private questions that acted as sanctuaries
for him in times of stress and uncertainty. Though he cultivated the
pose of a calm, cautious, deliberate man of affairs, he was underneath
it all highly emotional, a self-conscious pessimist who steeled himself

for the worst in any given situation so that he would be mentally and morally prepared for disappointment or sorrow. Such an attitude intensified his innate skepticism about the motives of men. But if he was always on guard in his dealings with his fellow Americans, testing always whether this one or that measured up to his own moral certainties, Welles never for a moment doubted the worth of his nationalism as embodied in the Union. He was as horrified at news relayed by Dixon about Sumner's great fear that the Union would *not* be divided as he was at the partisan glee of the Breckenridge Democrats in his own state, who felt that the Republicans had brought disunion on themselves.

When he learned that Governor John A. Letcher of Virginia had proposed a convention of the states to promote peace and union, he saw a sinister plot where no plot existed. Yet in response to Governor Buckingham's telegram of February 2 asking him whether the state should send delegates, he wired back: "It will be well to have the state represented." Acting on Welles' advice, the Governor did send a prestigious group to Washington but gave them instructions which left little room for compromise. While the ill-fated conference was in session, Buckingham wrote Welles again, explaining that he had received no official invitation to appoint commissioners.

Ever suspicious, Welles concluded that the Governor had had a devious purpose in mind. Certain that the conference would fail, and, like other Northerners, failing to grasp the extent of the political crisis, he confided to his diary that, if he had been told no official invitation had been sent, he would have acted differently. The fact that Welles, a man of clear vision and of long experience in evaluating public affairs, should have been so misled by the trend of events as to accuse the Virginians of political blackmail shows how far mutual distrust had corroded the concept of Union. In another sense, too, Welles, along with many Northerners, simply refused to believe that the provisional Confederacy would amount to anything. Once Lincoln was inaugurated, a cool, deliberative policy, firm yet tactful, would solve the current dilemma.

Republican party leaders both in and out of Congress seemed as much concerned about Seward, and whether he would or would not control the new administration, as they were about the secession crisis. At a time when statesmanship was so crucial, too many of them were engaging in politics as usual. George Fogg, for instance, seemed obsessed by the notion that the "Albany Clique" was bent on destroying the Republican party at its moment of triumph. "Seward and Weed have done everything to debauch us; and if we escape we can thank our lucky stars," he wrote Welles a few weeks before the inauguration.[31] To Lincoln he was even more explicit. Optimistic about the growth of Union sentiment in Virginia and Maryland, he rejected as pure nonsense the idea that any effort would be made to disrupt the inauguration. But he said darkly, "there is another danger, if not a conspiracy, which is more formidable—to demoralize and ultimately destroy the noble party . . . leaders in this conspiracy are Thurlow Weed, Simon Cameron and their affiliated associates. Knowingly or unknowingly Mr. Seward is playing the leading part in the drama. . . ."[32]

In mid-February Lincoln entrained for Washington. His leisurely progress from Springfield—he made over thirty stops in Ohio alone—took on the appearance of a political junket. Welles and his radical associates did little else but speculate about the wire-pullers and the office-seekers who surrounded the President-elect. When the special train left Buffalo for Albany, he was certain that there was "intrigue and strife as to who shall have his custody and ear at the latter place. . . ." Weed's coterie was much in evidence. The master himself talked with Lincoln at the Delavan House in Albany, and unquestionably he made one last push for Banks or Adams.[33]

Welles was not without spokesmen, however. Mark Howard, who had met with Lincoln shortly after the election, nominated himself as Welles' chief manager and set up headquarters at Willard's in Washington. He, too, became so engrossed in the battle of the factions for the "possession" of the President that he paid scant attention to the national crisis. If one were to believe Howard, the nation was lost if Seward prevailed. "The voice for you," he wrote Welles in one of his daily bulletins, "is general and *potent*. I have seen and set in motion all our leading friends, including all the members of our delegation. Hamlin is very firm and decided and outspoken for you and all consider him more than a match for Mr. Seward in this matter." Lincoln had not changed his mind, though, as Hamlin explained, he was very much embarrassed by Cameron, who had not yet withdrawn. Even with the wily Pennsylvanian out of the way, there could still be heavy opposition to Chase and Welles. So much so, thought Howard and Hamlin, that Lincoln might be driven to take Adams for the Post Office or the Navy and Senator Simmons of Rhode Island for the Treasury.

All of these fears proved groundless, but the conflicts they inspired made heavy inroads on the time and energy of the Republican leadership, whether pro- or anti-Seward.[34] Spared the tumult and the crush and the importunities that beset Lincoln, Seward, and Hamlin, Welles was nevertheless in an agony of suspense during that last week in February. He was receiving an average of a dozen letters in each mail from Washington, all optimistic but none wholly positive. He was scanning the editorial pages and the telegraphic dispatches of a dozen daily newspapers; all carried his name on their slates, but always with some reservation and some with mention of other possibilities. His expectations dashed so many times before, he did not rule out his being overlooked again. Reacting somberly to Edgar Welles' enthusiasm, he said, "It is by no means certain my son, that I shall go . . . I have as yet nothing from Washington, except assurances from friends. . . ."

The long-awaited summons came the very next evening in a telegram from Hannibal Hamlin: "I desire to see you here forthwith." Skeptical to the last, Welles had done no packing. His personal affairs were not in order, and within minutes, so it seemed, after receiving the telegram, friends and neighbors began dropping in to congratulate him or to offer assistance. He had to be hospitable and courteous, though well-meaning visitors kept him from performing necessary chores. When he took the train for New York the next day he found he had left his razor, razor strop, and brushes behind.

Welles was lucky to get a seat on the Washington cars. He had asked no favors of the railroad and was sharing the discomfort of a thousand fellow passengers in "a double" train of ten cars each. Just as the train was crossing the Susquehanna, however, he had his first taste of the special privileges which went with a Cabinet post. An amiable stranger had worked his way through the car until he came to Welles, who was sitting with a Hartford friend. He introduced himself as William S. Wood, the railroad man who had arranged Lincoln's trip to Washington, and breezily commented that he knew Welles "had been sent for and was on the train." A private car was waiting at Baltimore for his use—the same car, in fact, that had carried the Lincolns.

Welles would have preferred not to accept such grand accommodations or any special treatment, and was embarrassed at the thought of his reception in Washington. Assuming that Wood had been assigned by higher authority (as indeed he had), Welles acquiesced, traveling the last fifty miles to Washington in carpeted, paneled, and armchaired elegance. Once at the depot, he did refuse all favors pressed upon him by many friends and some strangers. He accepted only the offer of a lift to Willard's, where to his chagrin he was unable to find a room and had to accept Mark Howard's suite—an uncomfortable but expensive parlor and sitting room on the second floor.[35]

The "crowd and crush" at the hotel were greater than he could ever remember. Worse yet, the jam in the corridors held up the arrival of his trunks so that he had no change of clothes. Should he present himself to the President-elect still wearing his "old rig?" Surely a prospective Cabinet officer ought not to make his first appearance before his Chief in dirty, disheveled attire. Recalling the word "forthwith" in the Hamlin telegram, and with only forty-eight hours remaining before the inauguration, Welles decided to pay his respects anyway. Much to his relief, Lincoln had gone out to dinner. He left his card and went off in search of his trunk, which was finally delivered around midnight.

At an early hour the following morning, John G. Nicolay, Lincoln's private secretary, appeared at Welles' room with a note requesting him to visit the President-elect in his suite on the same floor. Lincoln's greeting was cordial, but he obviously had little time to spare, and he was in something of a quandary. As Welles related it to his son, "there is a strong desire on the part of most of our political friends that I should go into the Postoffice. For my own part, I feel very indifferent." Lincoln preferred Welles in the Navy Department, where he could "assist him in a responsible station in a period of some difficulty." Then, apologizing for his indecision, he said he might have to nominate Welles for Postmaster General. Just the day before, Lincoln had squelched yet another attempt to drive Chase and Welles from the Cabinet.[36]

This last flare-up of factionalism had touched Welles personally. "I can't step into the halls which are crowded, or the street," he complained, "that I do not find myself stared at & criticized—all of which is to me, you know, annoying and I shall be glad as soon as this novelty is over."[37] The "novelty" of his position would not end, as he implied it would, after his nomination as Secretary of the Navy on March 5 and his confirmation by the Senate.

No stranger to the pressures of patronage, Welles still found them to be far more trying than he had ever expected.[38] During the first week, he felt as if he had been buried alive under masses of correspondence and a seemingly endless procession of visitors, few of whom could be turned away without political risk. "Today," reported the *Herald*'s Washington correspondent, "the jam of place-seekers in the different departments was greater than on any previous day. All the secretarys manifest a great deal of caution and care in the selection of material for clerical and other positions, although Congressmen and other distinguished bores do not show any great delicacy in their recommendations."[39] Welles early resolved he would try to satisfy partisan demands where possible, but never at the expense of proven ability and long experience. There would be no political tests in the Navy yards or in the Department itself—except loyalty to the Union. On this score he was adamant. But no sooner had his predecessor, Isaac Toucey, turned over the keys to his office than he was presented with a loyalty problem that was imperiling the entire naval organization.

# CHAPTER 18

# Conflict

"A STRANGE STATE OF THINGS existed at that time in Washington," said Welles, recalling the sense of perpetual crisis that gripped the new government during its first month in office. Members of the Cabinet, who had access to more information than the general public, saw treason everywhere. To the worried Secretary of the Navy, new in his office and perhaps overly conscious of his responsibilities, his own department seemed a hotbed of disloyalty.

Welles had been harshly critical of Isaac Toucey for meekly accepting the resignations of naval officers from the seceded states. Dismissal from the service, or even arrest and court-martial, should, he had thought, be meted out to those who would desert their country under cover of resignation. Now that the problem was his, he found it to be far more complex than he had anticipated. Although many naval officers "were of questionable fidelity," how was he to determine the degree of loyalty without recourse to star-chamber proceedings, an arbitrary move from which he shrank instinctively? He would not perform an unjust act, the dismissal of an officer, for instance, simply because his Southern birth laid him open to suspicion or to the malicious gossip of interested parties. Nor, as he realized, could the Union afford the indiscriminate loss of talent and command experience. The resignations of sixty-eight officers had already seriously undermined the basic structure of the Navy.[1]

Welles needed advice, and he needed it fast. With the President's consent, he appointed Silas Stringham, a senior officer whom he had known for years, to be his assistant for detailing officers. Stringham would not only advise him about their fitness for duty, but would vouch for their loyalty to the Union. The appointment (and the new post, which Congress would not legitimatize for two years) met with approval even from that fastidious naval officer, Samuel F. Du Pont, whose initial impression of the new Secretary was far from flattering.[2] In making this move Welles was reacting to the secession crisis, though he recognized that the Department needed a personnel chief if it was to establish effective control over highly competitive officers, most of whom had well-developed political connections. He did not at the time realize that the appointment of a detailing officer would have ramifications beyond purely naval affairs—that it would become another instrument in William H. Seward's impromptu policy of appeasing the South. In fact, he created the office and appointed Stringham before he grasped the full implications of the secession crisis, before he knew how desperate the situation really was.

On March 6, 1861, General Winfield Scott briefed Welles and Simon Cameron, the new Secretary of War. For the first time Welles was apprised of the condition of Forts Sumter and Pickens. He was astounded when Scott said emphatically that Major Anderson's small garrison at Sumter would be starved out in about six weeks. Welles and Cameron both insisted that prompt measures be taken "to relieve and reinforce the garrison." The old General, grizzled, gouty, dropsical, but still a magnificent figure, turned to Welles and said grimly that the Army could do nothing. He thought any attempt to reinforce by sea would be a failure, "the question was one, however, for naval authorities to decide."

The next day Welles and Stringham met with Scott, his aged adviser General Joseph B. Totten (another relic of the War of 1812), Cameron, Seward, and the President at the White House. Scott had not changed his opinion, nor had Welles. Relying on the advice of Stringham and his fellow townsman Commander James H. Ward, a courageous, highly intelligent professional, Welles asserted that the fort could and should be supplied by a fleet of tugs. Secretary Seward vehemently opposed any relief attempt, and the President was especially anxious to avoid belligerent measures, or indeed any action at all, even political removals, that might disturb public opinion in the still loyal slave states. Welles was not pressed for any conclusion, but he left the meeting fully conscious that he would have to make the case for relieving not just Sumter but Fort Pickens, off Pensacola, Florida, the only other important military post in the deep South that flew the Stars and Stripes.[3]

Over the next two weeks, as Welles sought both political and professional advice, listened to Cabinet deliberations, and followed public opinion, his initial reactions under went a complete change. Seward, with Lincoln's concurrence, had argued at Cabinet meetings that any attempt to relieve Sumter by force would precipitate hostilities and surely cause Virginia to secede. When Lincoln polled the Cabinet on March 15, Welles thought that Sumter should be evacuated, an opinion shared by four of his Cabinet colleagues. Montgomery Blair, the new Postmaster General, insisted that an effort be made to hold it. Chase hesitantly supported him.

Although he was prepared to oppose anything Seward might offer by way of policy as a matter of general principle, Welles found himself more in agreement than otherwise as the Border state problem came into stark relief. In Virginia, where a state convention was then in session, Unionist and secessionist elements were so delicately balanced that any overt act could tip the scales toward secession. Welles agreed with Seward that, if Virginia seceded, some, possibly all, of the Border states would go out. Washington would be cut off from the North. Immense human and matériel resources would revert to the new Confederacy. He was also aware of Seward's desperate efforts to hold Virgina, and, in the main, he approved of almost any concession that would strengthen the Unionists in that state. Like Lincoln, Welles would not now risk war and the probable loss of the Border states for Fort Sumter. The Northern press, he felt, had prepared the public for evacuation of the fort. "The shock . . . has done its work," he advised Lincoln. "The public mind is becoming tranquillized under it and will become fully reconciled to it when the cause[s] . . . shall have been made public and rightly understood." At no time, however, in Cabinet or in Department discussion, had there been any doubt about the ability of the Army and Navy to hold Fort Pickens.[4]

But when "an excited" President announced to his Cabinet on March 28 that General Scott strongly urged Pickens be evacuated too and for the same reason as Sumter—military necessity—Welles' attitude changed again abruptly. Lincoln's statement astonished most of the Cabinet, all of whom knew, or thought they knew, that Pickens had recently been reinforced by regular army troops and was well protected by strong elements of the home squadron. Welles, for one, decided that Scott was offering political advice under the guise of his military expertise. There was a direct connection between Seward's policy of appeasement and Scott's hesitant, defensive doctrine. Welles was quick to believe that the supple Seward was using the old General as a front behind which he was playing fast and loose with the security of the nation and the integrity of the Republican party.[5] Public opinion in the

North, Welles judged, would reluctantly accept the evacuation of Sumter on the grounds of military necessity, but never the abandonment of Fort Pickens. The national flag must be kept waving somewhere in the Confederacy. As Mark Howard wrote Welles on March 19, "the telegraphic rumors . . . that Fort Pickens also was to be abandoned almost crushed the spirits of our best Republicans. . . . We are oppressed with the feeling that Seward's policy will . . . demoralize the North without securing any substantial benefit in return."

By the third week in March, Welles was ready to believe the worst of Seward's mysterious maneuvers and to doubt the wisdom of what the newspapers were calling Lincoln's "masterly inactivity." From what he could learn, the waiting game Seward was playing with the Confederate commissioners, who were then seeking recognition of their government, seemed perilously close to compromising the administration. The very presence of the commissioners in Washington disgusted Welles. Daily association with the belligerent Montgomery Blair, who thought a Jacksonian stand on Sumter would rally the Border states to the Union, was hardening his attitude, making him more receptive to some action—any action—rather than this intolerable suspense and delay. The President's announcement about Fort Pickens removed all lingering doubts. When asked again for an opinion on whether Sumter should be relieved or abandoned, Welles lined up with his colleagues Blair and Chase in urging that an effort be made to provision the fort. Shortly after Welles filed his opinion, Lincoln directed the Navy Department to fit out a relief expedition along the outlines of a plan worked out many weeks earlier by Gustavus Vasa Fox, a former naval officer and manager of the Bay State Woolen Company's mill at Lawrence, Massachusetts. His ideas, similar to those proposed by Commander Ward, gained a ready audience from Lincoln because they had the backing of Fox's brother-in-law, Montgomery Blair—not only because of his family's political influence, but because he had been educated at West Point and was thus regarded as something of military expert. The expedition should be ready to sail by April 6, 1861.[6]

Fox's plan was based on the simple premise that, given the factors of surprise, speed, low visibility, or any combination of these, the Confederate batteries could be run with acceptable risks. Depending on circumstances, he would use either fast, heavily armed, shallow-draft tugs or iron whaleboats. A small fleet of warships would lend support just outside the shoal waters that surrounded the narrow ship channel leading into Charleston. Once within the harbor, the small boats would be covered by the guns of Sumter. If it were feasible, elements of the supporting fleet might enter the channel and join in the bombardment of Charleston's defenses or cope with any hostile warships. From the first, Welles had been attracted to Fox, a magnetic man "of undoubted ability and courage," though he considered his plan "hazardous" and warned Lincoln that "failure would be attended with untold disaster." Yet he raised no objection to Lincoln's request that Fox, a civilian, should command the transports under War Department orders. Unknown to Welles, however, the President had still not made up his mind. He summoned Fox to Washington on March 30 and told him to prepare the expedition. But, enjoined Lincoln, "make no binding engagements!"[7]

The first inkling that Lincoln might have reversed the new aggressive policy on Sumter came to Welles while he was dining at Willard's in the early evening of April 1. John G. Nicolay, one of the President's private secretaries, interrupted him at the table and handed him a package of documents from the White House. That the package had been personally delivered at such an hour by Nicolay and not by one of the White House messengers placed a special priority upon the documents it contained. Obviously the President, a considerate man, wanted his Secretary of the Navy to examine these papers at once, or he would not have sent them when he knew Welles, along with the rest of Washington, would be dining. Nor would he have chosen his overworked senior secretary to act as an errand boy on a routine assignment. While his unfinished meal grew cold, Welles read carefully and with increasing amazement a series of instructions from Lincoln involving naval matters that would normally be the direct responsibility of the Secretary. Even more startling, the papers displayed an intimate knowledge of naval affairs which he knew the President did not have. All of the documents in one way or another reflected upon his authority as Secretary—in sum, they betrayed a lack of confidence in his ability.

One paper was of such an extraordinary character that Welles could not believe the President had been aware of its implications when he signed it. The Secretary was directed to have the home squadron, which comprised most of the nation's available naval forces, remain off Vera Cruz, Mexico, because of "important complications in our foreign relations." Captain Stringham, Welles' invaluable confidential assistant for personnel affairs, was detached and ordered to command the fleet units off Pensacola, Florida. If these orders were not damaging enough, Captain Samuel Barron, a Virginian, whose loyalty to the Union Welles doubted, would relieve Stringham. Welles saw at once that the handwriting of the order differed from an officious postscript which told the Secretary what to include in Barron's orders. The condescending tone of the postscript was so unlike any previous communications he had had with Lincoln, as was the tone of all of the documents in the package, that he suspected they were Seward's work. Yet Nicolay had delivered the package, and Lincoln had signed each document. They must be presumed to reflect his policies and opinion. Welles wondered if, after all, he had been misled by the President, whom he had marked down as an able man, but too generous and kindly for his own good, too deferential to his meddlesome Secretary of State.

Welles and other Cabinet members resented Seward's pretensions to being the controlling influence, the "premier" of the administration. They objected to the notes they received from him, or his son Frederick, the Assistant Secretary of State, at odd hours, summoning them to meetings with the President for the discussion of affairs concerning their own departments. The garrulous little Secretary was always present, but, as Welles and others observed caustically, they were never invited when foreign policy was to be the subject of discussion. Salmon P. Chase, overly-conscious of his own status (he too had been a governor of an important state, he too had been a United States Senator), acted as a spokesman for his colleagues. He suggested to the President that at stipulated times every week regular Cabinet sessions be held. Lincoln readily agreed. But Seward continued to send his little notes and to monopolize Lincoln's time and attention. Now, just as Welles was in the midst of organizing the naval part of the Fox expedition, he received these conflicting instructions from the White House, all of which seemed to bear Seward's imprint.

"Without a moment's delay," said Welles, "I went to the President with the package in my hand." Lincoln was alone in his office, seated at a table writing, when he looked up and saw Welles bearing down on him with such an anxious look that he impulsively blurted out, *"What have I done wrong?"* The worried Secretary wanted an explanation of all the orders and instructions which Lincoln had sent him, for they involved administrative matters of more immediate concern to his office than to that of the President. As a sample he read the Barron order to the President, emphasizing the intrusive tone of the postscript. Lincoln professed great surprise that he had signed the order, adding promptly that Welles should pay no attention to it. He explained that Secretary Seward and two or three young men had been in his office all that day working out the details for a project which Seward had been

developing for some time. Lincoln said nothing more about the project
beyond murmuring that he had left all the details to Seward and had
signed batches of papers, many of which he had not read, "for he had
not time and if he could not trust the Secretary of State he knew not
whom he could trust." Welles asked the identity of the "young men"
who had assisted Seward and learned that they were Captain Montgomery Meigs of the Army, a brilliant engineering officer then in
charge of constructing the Capitol, and Lieutenant David Dixon Porter of the Navy, one of the social lions of the capital who was known
to have been a close friend of Jefferson Davis and other Southern
Congressmen.

Welles must have been most curious about Seward's project, but,
since the President did not volunteer an explanation, he did not press
for one. However, he did complain about his being bypassed in the selection of a subordinate with whom he would have to maintain confidential relations, especially a subordinate whose loyalty was in question. He told the President frankly that he suspected Barron of
secessionist sympathies. Under the circumstances, Barron's appointment to such a sensitive position would be, he thought, taking much
too great a risk. Lincoln reiterated that Welles was master in his own
house, that he must disregard the Barron orders along with all other
orders and instructions in the package.

Relieved that he still had the President's confidence, Welles left the
White House pondering the many unanswered questions raised by this
curious set of circumstances. He had never trusted Seward in politics,
but he did not for one instant doubt his loyalty to the Union. The
Secretary of State, he concluded, had been made the victim of an artful
intrigue by promoters of the secession movement in Virginia. Porter
seemed the prime architect of the conspiracy, which Welles decided
must involve other senior naval officers as well.[8]

Yet both the President and the Secretary of State were more deeply
implicated than Welles knew at the time. The states of Virginia and
Maryland were at the crux of the problem. Seward had persuaded Lincoln that nothing should be done which might strengthen secessionist
opinion in these sensitive Border states. Unsure of himself as the crisis
thickened about him, the inexperienced President accepted gratefully
the advice of the only Cabinet member he really admired, his self-
assured, buoyant Secretary of State. Seward and Lincoln both wanted
time, which they felt would eventually ease tensions and pave the way
toward reunion.

The Barron intrigue, as Welles called it, was not originally a product of Porter's fertile imagination, though Porter suggested the urbane Virginian as new Chief of the Bureau of Detail. Courtly and suave, known as the "naval diplomat," Barron was perhaps the most influential naval officer in Washington. Seward presumed that he, as chief of officer personnel in the Navy Department, would exert yet another strong force for Unionism, through the professional military, upon the public men and politicians of Virginia and Maryland. Neither Seward, nor Porter and Miegs, nor the President, for that matter, seem to have speculated on the possibility that he might use his position to strengthen secession in his home state of Virginia.

Only consummate pretension on Seward's part and woeful carelessness on the part of the President can explain why the word of a mere Lieutenant should have been accepted and acted upon in a matter involving the status of a Cabinet officer. Seward evidently had such a low opinion of Welles that he assumed he would accept Barron without question if ordered to do so by the President. Had Welles not responded as he did, the morale, not to mention the efficiency, of the Navy would have been more gravely impaired than it already had been by the wave of resignations. Welles had been right in his judgment of Barron, whom he would dismiss from the service just three weeks later.[9]

The entire episode was characteristic of the fumbling policy Lincoln and Seward had developed to further their hopeless quest for peace and union. If Welles had been aware of other moves, other orders that had been drafted under Seward's supervision, he would not have been so charitable to his colleague as he was when he left the White House on April 1. Urged on by Seward, Lincoln finally formulated a policy that gave him maximum flexibility. Organization of the Sumter relief expedition would go forward and be ready by the specified time if needed—need being determined by Northern public opinion, by any actions of the provisional Confederacy, and by the Virginia convention. Word that the Fox expedition was being outfitted in New York had already leaked to the metropolitan press, but there had been nothing definite about its destination. Should everything go according to plan, the small task force being assembled to relieve Fort Sumter would never sail.

The President may have been pursuing a Buchanan-like policy, as many Border state politicians and editors had already discerned, but he saw clearly enough that some symbol of national authority had to be maintained in the Confederacy. If not, as he would say at a later date, "it would discourage the friends of the Union, embolden its

adversaries . . . it would be our national destruction consummated."
He had come to the conclusion that Sumter could not be supplied
with the forces at hand, and he shrank from the consequences of a
humiliating and bloody reverse. On April 1, Major Anderson still had
at least two weeks of supplies on hand. Lincoln calculated that this
would give him just enough time to make Pickens impregnable without risking certain war and probable defeat in the action. Relief of
Fort Pickens, as Lincoln explained to Congress with an unusual degree
of candor, "would be a clear indication of *policy,* and would better
enable the country to accept the evacuation of Fort Sumter as a *military necessity.*[10]

Seward's project that Lincoln had mentioned to Welles but would
not elaborate upon was a dramatic strengthening of Pickens as a prelude to the evacuation of Sumter. Preparations for the demonstration
at Pickens, unlike those for Sumter, were top secret. While everyone,
including the Confederate government, was assuming Charleston to
be the objective of Fox's task force, its most powerful unit would suddenly appear before Fort Pickens. Behind the mantle of this positive
move, the Fox expedition would be on hand to evacuate Sumter on
the grounds of military necessity without overly straining the credibility of the administration. Thus, on that April 1, Lincoln also signed
an order giving Lieutenant Porter command of the heavily armed
*Powhatan,* which had just arrived at the Brooklyn Navy Yard and
which Fox had earmarked for his project.

In giving the *Powhatan* to Porter, even for a temporary assignment,
the President was acting with utter disregard for seniority. Porter, a
Lieutenant, would be relieving Samuel Mercer, a full Captain. More
embarrassing still, Lincoln ordered Andrew H. Foote, the Acting
Commandant of the Navy Yard, in the most positive terms not to inform Welles' office that the *Powhatan* was being readied for sea. The
consensus has been that Seward was wholly responsible for all the
orders, that the President was so busy he knew little or nothing of
either the Sumter or Pickens relief expedition. But along with a mass
of circumstantial evidence one fact stands out: Lincoln personally
handed Porter orders to take command of the *Powhatan.*[11]

When Acting Commandant Foote read these orders, the crew and
officers of the *Powhatan* were on leave and the ship itself was undergoing repairs.[12] Foote, a schoolmate of Welles from Cheshire days and
a cantankerous sea dog, was a stickler for procedure. Anything so irregular as direct orders to him from the President borne by the high-
strung Porter, who burst in upon him on April 2, was to be viewed

with deep suspicion. Foote had kept in touch with events in Washington and knew of Porter's association with many of the Southern officers who had resigned. "How do I know you are not a traitor?" he demanded peremptorily. "Who ever heard of such orders as these emanating from the President? I must telegraph to Mr. Welles before I do anything, and ask for further instruction."[13] Just the day before he had received two almost identical telegrams, the first from Welles ordering him to fit out the *Powhatan* for sea duty "at the earliest possible moment" and the second from Lincoln, twenty minutes later, ordering him to do the same thing. This had been unsettling enough. Now Porter was demanding that he disregard departmental orders and accept the President's directive as coming from the Commander in Chief. According to Porter (whose recollections are more vivid than reliable, but seem to ring true in this case), it took three hours of discussion before he convinced Foote that Lincoln's orders were not the work of Southern forgers, a clever plot to steal the *Powhatan*.

Fox, who could have cleared up the mystery, was in Manhattan, a whirlwind of energy, arranging for the charter of tugs, seeing to provisions, recruiting personnel. But he never visited the Navy Yard. Secretary Welles was handling the Navy part of the expedition, why should he enquire? Thus, it was Welles himself who learned that something was amiss in New York. His informant was Acting Commandant Foote. Whatever Porter and Meigs might have believed about the magic of the President's orders, Foote had to cover himself and do it without seeming insubordinate to the White House through any breach of security. He wrote a letter to Welles on April 4, explaining that he was preparing vessels for sea, but that the orders did "not come direct." On the next day, Foote telegraphed the Secretary that he was "executing orders received from the government through "the Navy officer as well as from the Army officer." If Foote's letter had not alerted Welles, his telegram certainly did, for no Army officer was associated with the expedition. Welles immediately ordered a delay in the *Powhatan*'s sailing. Puzzled about a situation which was developing mysterious aspects, Welles took the precaution of reading his orders for the *Powhatan* to the President, who approved them without comment.

Meanwhile, in New York, the worried Foote sent Welles' telegram on to Meigs and Porter, who were staying at the Astor House while they completed their arrangements for the relief of Fort Pickens. Porter replied caustically, suggesting that Secretary Welles' telegram was bogus. "Would he think you dare to countermand an order [written order] of the President?" Porter asked. Still, he and Meigs would telegraph Seward, and they would "stay over tonight to keep telegraph-ing."

Despite their bravado, Meigs and Porter were now as much con-cerned as Foote about the contradictions emanating from Washington. Had Welles learned of the Pickens' expedition? And if so, had he con-vinced the President that the *Powhatan* was needed for Sumter? Was the demonstration of federal strength at Pensacola to be abandoned? One thing was certain, someone had to clear the channels of communi-cation. A telegram went off to Seward, who realized from its urgent language that he must settle the matter with Welles at once.

Seward had nothing but contempt for Welles, whom he regarded, disdainfully, as a petty politician from Connecticut, a cypher whom chance had placed in a position far beyond his abilities.[14] Taking his son Frederick with him, he stalked into Welles' rooms at Willard's between eleven o'clock and midnight on June 5. He had a telegram from Captain Meigs, he told Welles, which stated that orders from the Navy Department were in conflict with other orders and a source of obstruction as well as embarrassment. The self-assured Seward calmly but firmly demanded their retraction. Welles was completely taken aback. What orders? What activity could they possibly embarrass? As if he were dealing with an inferior who was being importunate about affairs of state, Seward "supposed it related to the *Powhatan* and Porter's command." Bridling at his manner, Welles remarked sharply that there must be some mistake. Porter had no command! The *Pow-hatan* was the flagship of the Sumter expedition. Discussion grew heated, with Welles admitting "some excitement on my part," Seward cooly standing his ground, even after Captain Stringham, who was called in, supported his chief's contention. Finally Welles insisted that they should call on the President, though it was nearly midnight. On their way to the White House, Seward decided that he had misunder-stood Welles and had better make an effort to mollify his angry col-league. He conceded that he might have been wrong; that, "old as he was, he had learned a lesson from this affair . . . he had better attend to his own business and confine his labors to his own Department."

Lincoln was still at work when the two Sewards, Welles, and String-ham arrived, all showing signs of strain. He may have looked sur-prised, as Welles remembered his appearance at the time, but he surely knew that this untimely visit dealt with Seward's project. He was quickly briefed about the conflict in orders and shown Meigs' tele-gram to Seward asking for clarification. Seemingly bewildered, he looked first at Welles, then at Seward, finally suggesting that Welles might be mistaken about the *Powhatan*. Was not some other vessel the flagship of the Sumter expedition? Welles gave an emphatic negative which was backed up by Stringham, but to prove his case beyond any doubt he excused himself and hurried off to his office in the Navy Department, next to the White House, where he got a copy of his orders to Captain Samuel Mercer of the *Powhatan*.

One can reconstruct the scene—Seward, tense and tired, but alert, lounging carelessly on a sofa; young Frederick Seward and Captain Stringham in the background; Lincoln, weary beyond belief, his table cluttered with documents, possibly annoyed by Welles' sudden departure for proof, yet anxious that there be harmonious relations among the members of his Cabinet. As yet he had not decided about Sumter. He would not come to a final decision for another twenty hours, after a unique set of circumstances had made the Fox expedition an imperative. No doubt the President did what he could to encourage small talk while Welles was absent, but Seward must not have been his usual jocund self. The Secretary of State was about to play his last card with the Confederate commissioners, and now, despite all of his desperate maneuvering for time, this unexpected *contretemps* with Welles threatened all he had been trying to do over the past three weeks of dodging and weaving, as he sought to stabilize a deteriorating situation.

Welles read his orders to Captain Mercer, reminding Lincoln that he had read them to him on April 1. Lincoln now remembered the instructions and his approval of them. Without any explanation he turned to Seward and said, "The *Powhatan* must be restored to Mercer . . . on no account must the Sumter expedition fail or be interfered with." Though uncomfortable, for once his composure ruffled, Seward was not quite ready to give up. He argued that Pickens was more important. When Lincoln said it could wait, Seward doubted whether a message could be got through to the Navy Yard in time. The President insisted. Seward bowed to the inevitable, but the telegram which he sent to Foote over his own signature was not transmitted until 2:30 the following afternoon. And instead of stating that the action to be taken was by the direction of the President, he simply ordered Porter to "Give up the Powhatan to Captain Mercer."[15]

Foote received this message at 3:00 p.m. about thirty minutes after the *Powhatan* had sailed. During the morning Porter had quashed all of his objections by reminding him again that Lincoln's orders were

explicit. Both Seward and Welles had been informed but had not replied. Having cleared himself with superior authority, Foote saw no
reason why he should retain the vessel and every reason why he should
release her under presidential order. Seward's message, however,
aroused again all of his latent doubts. He ordered one of his staff officers to charter the fastest steamer in the city in an effort to overtake
the *Powhatan.* Despite her headstart, she was overhauled at the Narrows. Seward's telegram was handed to Porter, who had taken over
command.

Resolute, audacious, and heedless of consequences, Porter wrote
out a one-line telegram to Seward and a brief note to Foote, both of
which he entrusted to Foote's staff officer. To Seward he said, "I received my orders from the President and shall proceed and execute
them." To Foote, Porter explained his dilemma, adding a bit of information that proves Lincoln had not been exactly straightforward
with Welles. "The telegram you sent me," wrote Porter, "afforded me
no comfort; on the contrary burdened me. Still the President said
nothing and I must obey his orders; they are too explicit to be misunderstood. I got them from his own hand. He has not recalled them.
. . . . This is an unpleasant position to be in, but I will work out of
it."[16]

Porter would work out of it, although Lincoln never could bring
himself to trust a man who had so mercilessly exposed his administrative shortcomings at a time when important businessmen and politicians were grumbling about his lack of any well-defined policy. Seward's reputation for statesmanship was also damaged, at least in the
New York business community, which soon became aware of his devious role in the Sumter-Pickens imbroglio. Paradoxically, however, the
detachment of the *Powhatan* spared the administration what would
have been a bloody reverse in Charleston Harbor. Had such a powerful steamer been available to Fox, he probably would have tried to
come to Sumter's aid when he observed the fort under bombardment.
On April 12 the *Powhatan,* as well as supporting fleet units, would
have been blown out of the water by the heavy Confederate batteries,
which had the exact range of each point in the main channel approach
to Sumter.[17]

At the time, however, it must have seemed a gross tactical error to
deprive the Sumter expedition of its most powerful fleet unit. For on
the very day, almost to the hour, Porter made off with the *Powhatan,*
Welles was interrupted by a travel-stained naval officer who had come
directly from Captain Adams, commanding the fleet off Pensacola. He

had secret communications for the Navy Department. Welles was horrified when he read them, one dated March 18, the other April 1.

In his earlier dispatch Captain Adams painted a gloomy picture of fleet readiness due to lack of supplies, especially water. Welles must have smarted under the implied criticism that he had neglected the Pensacola squadron. Adams had not received a word from the Navy Department since he had taken over command of the squadron on February 6. All of his information about fleet movements he had gleaned from the New York papers. Tardily, Welles had ordered the store ship *Supply* to Fort Pickens without informing Adams. She left from New York bound for Pensacola on March 14. The *Supply* should have been dispatched as soon as Welles took over, because Captain Adams' readiness report of February 19 was lying on his desk, and so was a draft of Toucey's letter ordering the *Supply* to sail for Pensacola and provision the fleet as soon as possible. On that date the squadron had stores and water for thirty days. It would take three weeks at the very least for any of the store ships to make the trip.

The supply problem was serious, but other information from Adams portended disaster. A shipload of troops that had been sent in the steamer *Brooklyn* under orders from General Scott to reinforce the 100-man garrison at Pickens had not been landed because Captain Adams had refused to accept an Army order. He explained to Welles that the Buchanan administration had arranged a truce so long as the status quo was maintained. He required a direct order from the Navy Department before he would shoulder the responsibility of an act which he felt would surely touch off civil war.

The frustrated and frightened Welles immediately went to the White House, where he told Lincoln that Pickens, which everyone had thought safe, might now be in deadly danger. As Welles recalled the incident, "we both deemed it absolutely essential that a special messenger should be forthwith sent overland with orders to immediately land troops." Fortunately, a brave and capable officer, John Worden (who later commanded the *Monitor* in its famous duel with the *Merrimack*), was in town. Welles' administrative actions had been sluggish since he had taken office, but he acted with decision at this juncture. After satisfying himself that Worden, whom he did not know, was loyal, he sent for him and quickly outlined the mission, explaining its dangers, the probability of being searched, and imprisoned, if he were caught bearing dispatches to Captain Adams. Yet Welles also stressed the importance of the mission, which if successful would save Fort Pickens for the Union. Speed was essential. Should the Confederates move on Pickens, they would do so when Adams weakened his squadron by sending fleet units after stores, as he had indicated might be necessary if he were not provisioned before April 1.[18]

Worden promptly accepted the assignment. After making hasty preparations, he returned to the Navy Department, where Welles read him the department's orders to Adams, which he handed over unsealed, at the same time cautioning the officer to memorize them and destroy them if in danger of capture. Should such a contingency arise, he was to deliver the orders orally, explaining the reasons for their destruction and certifying that they were a true copy. He was not to mention his assignment to anyone, not even his wife, and was to leave on the mail train for Richmond. Worden's mission was successful, though he was stopped several times and had a narrow escape in Atlanta, where he destroyed the orders just before he was searched.[19]

With Pickens in jeopardy and its fate unknown in Washington, the Sumter expedition, still outfitting in New York, took on new and vital dimensions of political importance. Lincoln must now have made his final decision that Fox had to sail at once. There was to be no more of the "delay, indecision, obstacles" about which Fox had complained darkly three days earlier. "My expedition is ordered to be got ready but I doubt if we shall get off," he had told his brother-in-law Dr. Lowery. "War will commence at Pensacola. There the government is making a stand and if they fire upon reinforcements already ordered to land, Fort Pickens and the ships will open upon the whole party."

Fox had not received his orders until late at night on April 4. The next day he was in New York, but, as the President was aware, he needed three days to charter, prepare, and provision his tugs and transports.[20] Lincoln still had seventy-two hours during which he could stop or postpone the expedition, which had already been deprived of its most powerful warship, the *Powhatan*.

The President's decision to force the issue at Sumter is revealed in his note of April 6 to Governor Pickens of South Carolina, stating that the federal government would attempt to supply Sumter "with provisions only; and that if such an attempt be not resisted, no effort to throw in men, arms or ammunition will be made." That order, over Cameron's signature, went out by special messenger at 6 p.m., several hours after the President had learned that Fort Pickens might be in grave jeopardy. Those few hours must have been among the most trying of his stormy presidency, for he knew that war would probably result from his efforts to provision Fort Sumter—a war that would be started in the wrong place at the wrong time.

Washington learned that the Fox expedition had sailed on April 8, and on receipt of the news Lincoln sent a message to Governor Andrew Curtin of Pennsylvania: the "necessity of being ready increases. Look to it."[21] The President and those members of his Cabinet who knew about the tiny Sumter task force could not have been hopeful that they would ever see Fox and his brave volunteers again. Yet in a sense Lincoln rationalized that their sacrifice, if it should come to that, would be justified, however painful the decision. Should the Charleston batteries smash Fox's little catch-all force after Confederate authorities had been told that it carried only provisions, then they would have the burden of starting hostilities, and under the most unfavorable light. "I told the Major [Anderson]," said Fox to Montgomery Blair, after Sumter surrendered, "how anxious the Prest was that they (S.C.) should stand before the civilized world as having fired on bread, yet they had made the case worse for themselves as they knew the Major would leave the 15th at noon for want of provisions. . . ."

As it turned out, Fox's force was of no use except to provide transportation home for Anderson and his garrison. Porter in the *Powhatan,* with her 300 sailors and her boats, was nearing Pensacola. The tugs which had been chartered in New York never arrived; the sea was so rough that Fox would have been powerless to render any effective assistance.[22]

Lincoln still hoped that Virginia would cleave to the Union even after the surrender of Sumter and his call upon the states for 75,000 militiamen to suppress rebellion. For almost a month Welles had felt the President's restraining hand when he brought up the subject of reinforcing the Navy Yard at Norfolk. On two or three occasions he had tried in vain to secure troops that could be sent to Norfolk for the defense of the yard if Virginia seceded, and at least once he had gone over General Scott's head and appealed to the President. To no avail. Lincoln agreed with Scott that no troops could be spared. Again he cautioned Welles that any unusual activity at Norfolk would tend to promote uneasiness in Virginia about the government's intentions.[23]

Hobbled by a lack of troops and by the President's go-slow policy, Welles made only routine moves to prepare for any assault upon the largest and best equipped of all the Navy's shipyards. Its mighty granite graving dock and its huge cranes, or "shears," as they were called, were unique, replaceable only at great cost in money and time. Besides these important ship repair and construction facilities, there were machine shops, foundries, rope walks, sail lofts, and ship houses. In the yard and near-by magazine were tons of powder and over 700 naval cannon, many of them of the newest Dahlgren design, as well as valuable naval equipment of all kinds. Berthed at Norfolk were several warships, including the *Cumberland,* flagship of Commodore Garrett Pendergrast, and the *Merrimack,* one of the newest and most powerful steam vessels in the Navy, though out of commission at the time.

Among the routine moves the Navy Department made for the protection of the yard was the recruitment of 250 enlisted men, but these had been diverted to the Sumter and Pickens expeditions. It was not until April 11, with Fox's fleet nearing Charleston, that Welles ordered the recruitment of another 200 men for Norfolk and the chartering of a vessel to transport them there. Though enlistment was invariably slow in the peacetime Navy, Welles had had enough time to recruit two or three times the number of men he needed. Knowing what he did about the gravity of the crisis and the probable demands on existing manpower, he should have been much more prompt and energetic than he was. In other respects, however, he acted as vigorously as he could within the limits imposed; and after the fall of Sumter, he took a fearful risk at the eleventh hour when he stripped the Washington Navy Yard—one of the key defenses of the capital—of its marines and sailors in a vain effort to save Norfolk.

Welles began to react forcefully to events at Norfolk when he received a letter from the Commandant of the yard, the venerable Commodore Charles S. McCauley, in response to an enquiry of his regarding the *Merrimack.* He had written McCauley on April 10, 1861, reminding him that in view of the "peculiar condition of the country" he must be especially vigilant and instructing him to prepare the *Merrimack* for removal to Philadelphia without giving "needless alarm." In another dispatch he asked the Commodore how much time he thought it would take to ready the *Merrimack* for sea. His answer— one month—received the following day, staggered the Secretary. He had already been told by his competent Engineer in Chief, Benjamin Isherwood, who knew the condition of the *Merrimack*'s engines, that it would take at the most a week for her power plant to be put in a state of readiness.[24]

Welles had no reason to doubt McCauley's patriotism or his ability, and despite his age (he was sixty-eight) the Commodore seemed just the right man for the difficult and delicate situation at Norfolk. His naval career, during which he had performed successfully a number of important missions that required tact and steadiness, was marked by dependable rather than showy qualities. As a young man, McCauley had also displayed leadership in several sharp naval actions against the British during the 1812 war. Senior officers still talked of his refusing the princely sum of $10,000 a year in 1825 from a Boston shipping firm to command its flagship.

Had Welles probed deeper into McCauley's career, however, he would have noted that the Commodore, except for a brief diplomatic mission in 1855, had for twenty years been an administrator rather than a sailor. During the Mexican War, when men such as Shubrick and Stockton were at sea, McCauley was Commandant of the Washington Navy Yard. Years of shore duty in the tight, tidy world of Washington and Norfolk, where routine and formality reigned supreme, had ill prepared him for the unfamiliar and the unexpected.

While Lincoln was pursuing an appeasement policy toward Virginia, McCauley was the ideal officer for command of such a politically sensitive post. There would be no precipitous action, no meddling with the patronage, no sensational items from the Commandant's office for the Norfolk press while he was in charge. On the other hand, a perceptive administrator should have been alert to the possibility that McCauley's virtues might well prove to be serious defects if he were confronted with a dramatic change of events or of policy. Welles sensed a latent weakness in McCauley when he read the Commodore's comment on the availability of the *Merrimack*. And he acted promptly. He sent Engineer in Chief Isherwood and Commander James Alden to Norfolk with orders to sail the *Merrimack* to Philadelphia. Though he impressed on these two officers that not a moment should be lost in shifting her, he also warned them not to create "a sensation." Still uneasy about the situation, he ordered Captain Hiram Paulding to Norfolk the following day with a long communication for McCauley. Paulding's orders were oral, but they conferred plenary powers. If Paulding had any doubts about the safety of the yard, he was to act for the Secretary.

Unfortunately, the letter Welles sent by Paulding to McCauley was not so explicit. In what seems an excessive sense of propriety, he did not insist that the old Commodore advise "freely and fully with Paulding." This letter and others Welles sent the Commandant during the critical period between April 10 and April 16 betray an ambivalence which contributed to McCauley's indecision. He was advised, for instance, on April 10, "that great vigilance should be exercised in guarding and protecting the public interest." But in the same letter he was urged to prepare for evacuating the *Merrimack* and most of the other ships at Norfolk. Should McCauley be ready to fight or to flee? Welles did not offer any opinion then, nor in the much longer letter that Paulding delivered. The *Merrimack* must not leave "unless there is immediate danger impending," but Norfolk must be defended "at any hazard, repelling force by force if necessary. . . ."

With three commodores, his competent Engineer in Chief Isherwood, and a senior commander in the person of James Alden all at Norfolk, Welles felt reasonably secure about the situation despite the secession of Virginia, which he read about in the telegraphic dispatches of the *Evening Star* on April 17. He would have been appalled, however, had he known what was happening in Norfolk, where all was confusion, indecision, and despair. Not one of the three commodores thought to either destroy or transport some 2800 barrels of gunpowder that were in the magazines at old Fort Norfolk.[25] Only Isherwood showed imagination and leadership qualities.

Within four days' time, working with men that he personally recruited in Norfolk, Isherwood had the *Merrimack*'s machinery in working order, hired a black gang, and coaled the vessel. But when he and Alden reported that steam was up in the *Merrimack,* McCauley was at a loss what to do. He was worried about the obstructions that he heard the state of Virginia was sinking in the channel. He wondered whether he would need the *Merrimack*'s heavy batteries to assist the *Cumberland* in defending the yard. Alden disposed of his first objection by informing the fretful old man that he had already sounded the channel and charted a course between the obstructions wide enough and deep enough for the *Merrimack.* Following up his advantage, Alden called attention to the peremptory nature of the department's orders, having no knowledge, of course, that McCauley had just received from Paulding Welles' equivocal orders that *"perhaps"* it would be better not to move the ship unless danger was imminent.

Yet Alden's comments seem to have had their effect. Turning to Paulding and to Pendergrast of the *Cumberland,* McCauley asked their advice. When both agreed that an effort should be made to take out the *Merrimack* with the sloop of war *Germantown* in tow, he told Alden to prepare the vessels for departure and report back. Much to Alden's chagrin, and to the despair of Isherwood, after all preparations were made, the ships winded, and the *Merrimack*'s wheel turning at the dock, he changed his mind. "Draw the fires in the *Merrimack*!" he ordered.

In view of his ambiguous instructions from Welles, one might sympathize with McCauley's dilemma and possibly see some reason for his inaction, though it is hard to excuse his failure to ship the *Merrimack*'s guns and put her in a state of readiness for the defense of the yard. But Paulding, Pendergrast, and even Alden were not as positive and direct as they might have been. None of them chose to question the Commodore's decision. And Paulding, who had the authority from Welles, preferred not to exercise it. He was as guilty as any in accepting without proper investigation the wildly overblown reports that thousands of hostile troops and batteries of artillery would attack the yard if they made any further preparations. That the local population was excited could not be denied. Officers of the yard whose families lived in town provided eyewitness testimony to this. But they could give no specific information about troops or artillery.

Paulding spent only one day at Norfolk, returning to Washington on April 18. He reported to Welles that McCauley was competent and loyal and that he had the situation under control, and he added further, if Welles' recollections are at all clear, that while some of the officers attached to the yard were Virginians who wanted to be relieved, he thought they would stand by the flag until they could be replaced. He had the same opinion of the workmen. However, Isherwood and Alden, who arrived in Washington at about the same time, flatly contradicted him. They spoke of indecision, confusion, and disloyalty in high quarters. Alden exonerated McCauley, though clearly he was upset at not being able to carry out the department's orders. Isherwood was not so forgiving. He harshly charged the Commodore with drunkenness and senility. In view of these conflicting statements, it is not surprising that Welles should, as he put it, "have greatly regretted" Paulding's return. He now had deep misgivings about McCauley's fitness. Virginia had seceded the day before, and, with presidential constraints finally removed, Welles bent every effort to reinforce the 470 sailors and marines who were defending the yard.

With Lincoln's support, he managed to wring out of General Scott a regiment of Massachusetts volunteers that were helping to garrison Fort Monroe. He stripped the Washington Navy Yard of its marines, leaving that key post completely defenseless. To the commandants at New York, Philadelphia, and the commanding officer of the receiving ship at Baltimore he sent urgent telegrams to dispatch all naval recruits by chartered vessels to Norfolk.[26] In case the yard had to be destroyed and the ships scuttled, Welles ordered the Acting Commandant of the Washington Navy Yard, Commander John A. Dahlgren, to ship the necessary combustibles and other equipment aboard the tug *Ana-*

*costia,* which happened to be available.[27] It was a commendable display of energy on Welles' part, but it was marred by two major blunders that were to defeat all of his plans.

His first mistake was in giving command of the relief expedition to Captain Paulding. Paulding, who had relieved Stringham as chief of personnel, had been working long hours and was run down physically as well as mentally. In his sixty-fourth year, he was too old, too set in his ways, for such a dizzying procession of difficult and unfamiliar assignments.[28]

But a more serious mistake than Welles' choice of commander—indeed, an unforgivable error—was his failure to notify McCauley promptly that the expedition was on the way. The Navy Yard was only eighteen miles by water from Fort Monroe, with which Washington was in easy communication. Had the old Commodore known he was to be reinforced, and approximately when, he probably would have stood firm.[29] As it was, he fell prey to the explosive atmosphere of rebellion outside the gates of the yard and disloyalty within. While Paulding in the *Pawnee* was steaming to his assistance, the bewildered and hapless McCauley had under his direct command only three loyal officers and sixty marines. Pendergrast on the *Cumberland* had 350 officers and men, and there were about 60 sailors on the old *Pennsylvania*—in all McCauley could call upon 470 officers and men to defend the yard against what he believed were 3000 troops. Convinced that more and more obstructions were being laid across the channel, and with no word about reenforcements, he decided to scuttle the vessels in the yard. The order was carried out on Saturday morning, April 20, a scant three hours before Paulding arrived in the *Pawnee* with 600 sailors and marines.[30]

Paulding, who took over immediately, decided after a brief survey that all the vessels in the yard were beyond salvage. Had he brought a complement of divers (another essential detail overlooked by the department), he could have had the leaks stopped and the ships afloat and seaworthy within seventy-two hours. Even without the ships, of which only the *Merrimack* was of real value, the yard was of great military and strategic importance. And Paulding had ample means to defend it— about 1000 well-armed, well-disciplined sailors and marines.

Without consulting any of his officers, he decided on the spot to destroy the yard and fire the sinking vessels. He, too, it seems, feared the channel obstructions and an assault by overwhelming forces on the yard. Like McCauley before him, he grossly overestimated the strength of the Virginia militia. Had he gathered some reliable intelligence before acting so precipitously, he would have learned that the Virginia forces, not his own, were in deadly peril. With what he had, Paulding could have swept all before him, captured Norfolk and neighboring Portsmouth, opened up communication with Fort Monroe, raised the vessels, and held that vital area of Virginia securely in Union hands for the rest of the war. A great opportunity had been presented to him and to the Navy, but he failed to appreciate it.[31]

The destruction of the yard itself was another example of bad judgment and faulty execution. Precious time was spent firing the easily replaceable wooden ship houses and obsolete sailing vessels, the *Germantown, Pennsylvania, Plymouth,* and *Dolphin.* But the graving dock, which was of inestimable value to the Confederacy, was undamaged. Other facilities, the ordnance building, smith's shops and sheds, timber shops, brazing shops, foundries and machine shops, all of which could have been thoroughly and systematically razed, were so little harmed that all were capable of full operation within a few days.[32] Paulding's demolition did provide a spectacular fireworks display for the surrounding countryside and aroused the ire of Virginia's General William B. Talliaferro, who commanded the state militia in the area.[33]

Welles was upset when he learned about the destruction of the Norfolk Navy Yard, but it was not until he read the reports of the officers of the expedition that he realized the full extent of the mismanagement. He knew at once that there would be a congressional investigation which might reflect unfavorably on himself and on the service. "McCauley and Pendergrast committed a most lamentable mistake," he wrote, unaccountably excusing Paulding. Yet, with his accustomed sense of perspective, he could see how they acted as they did: "They were not partisan politicians and could not believe that so wanton, causeless, and extensive conspiracy existed, and when the crisis came, they were confounded and not prepared to act. When they did act, it was in bewilderment and error."[34] This assessment was more revealing about government policy in those hectic days as the Union drifted toward war than Welles would have cared to admit, either then or at a later date, after all the facts were in. If it applied to the commodores, it applied with equal force to Welles himself, the President, and Secretary Seward.

# CHAPTER 19

# The Executive Touch

THE WEEK OF OCTOBER 20, 1861, had been a time when nothing seemed to have gone right, when an accumulation of problems, great and small, immediate and portending, personal and political and public, all met in a discouraging array to bear down upon the overworked Secretary of the Navy. The more he labored, the less he seemed able to accomplish. Mistakes he had made months before, as the nation plunged into civil war, were now being subjected to public scrutiny. He had always known that they would be, but why should they obtrude themselves at this time, just when the greatest operation ever planned by the Navy was about to be launched?

He had just received word that the Confederates had blockaded the lower Potomac, cutting off Washington's access to the sea. Without the cooperation of the Army, which was not forthcoming, the Navy was helpless in its aim to silence the heavy enemy batteries that overlooked the river. Welles was particularly irked because the household funiture he was having shipped by sea from Hartford would have to be re-routed and carried by rail—more delay, more expense, more inconvenience. After seven months of hotel living, he was looking forward to the comfort of his own establishment. In August he had leased, for four years, at $1500 a year, the residence of George A. Magruder, former Chief of Naval Ordnance, on the corner of Lafayette Square and Sixteenth Street. Although it was not as large a house as those Chase and Cameron were renting, it had a better location; it was just across Pennsylvania Avenue from the White House.[1] Mary Welles had brought some servants from Hartford and engaged others in Washington, but redecoration was slower than anticipated. Welles was forced to board the servants and his family in hotels—more expense, more inconvenience, more delay.[2]

His Assistant Secretary, stocky, bearded Gustavus Vasa Fox, had been absent most of the week, and Welles was doing Fox's work as well as his own. The duties of the Assistant Secretary, largely in the professional sphere, dealt with impending operations. Welles was uncertain whether his decisions on specific vessels and specific personnel were in fact correct ones, whether, for instance, the Port Royal expedition should be delayed until Charles O. Boutelle, a civilian hydrographer and pilot, could join Commodore Samuel F. Du Pont, the Flag Officer in charge. Welles knew that Boutelle, who had charted the approaches to Port Royal, South Carolina, for the Coast Survey, was important to the success of the expedition. But was he indispensable? Only Fox would know. Welles did not trust his own judgment, nor did he completely trust Du Pont in the matter. For the new Flag Officer seemed overcautious, bent on postponing the operation until he had provided for every possible contingency.

After his recent experience with the delaying tactics of Captain Silas Stringham, Welles had grown impatient with the demands of his squadron commanders. Stringham may have been a special case, but he literally had to be forced into assaulting the Hatteras forts, an action that gave the Navy its first victory while tightening the blockade of the northern approaches to the Confederacy. Nor would he follow up his victory and clear the undefended sounds south of Hatteras. No amount of persuasion, not even direct orders, could budge Stringham from his moorings off Old Point Comfort. Out of patience, Welles replaced him with the huge, terrible-tempered Louis M. Goldsborough, who, together with General Ambrose E. Burnside, was now organizing a joint operation to accomplish what Stringham could have managed alone had he pressed his advantage.[3]

However critics might disparage the administration of the Navy Department, Welles knew that he and Fox had built up a respectable fleet in less than six months' time. Over 100 well-armed, well-manned vessels, most of them steam powered, stood poised to seize bases on the southern Atlantic and Gulf coasts, an essential precondition to an effective blockade. And more, many more, were joining the fleet every day. He could remember how appalled he was when Lincoln had proclaimed a blockade over more than 3500 miles of southern coastline, much of it double coastline of inner sounds and outer shores. The United States Navy had less than fifty vessels available for this gigantic task. Welles realized that if the government failed to have a sizable fleet on station in short order, the European powers might treat the blockade for what it really was—a mere manifesto with no means of backing it up.[4] He and Fox immediately set in motion a massive naval building program. But new construction took time, and in Welles' judgment there was little time to spare. Only the mercantile community of the North could furnish ships rapidly and in quantity. The guns of Sumter had not been silent a week when naval officers were purchasing vessels in the New York and Boston market for hasty conversion to blockade duty.

Despite these achievements, Welles was being belabored in Congress and in the press. In his list of grievances for the week of October 20, he wrote that John P. Hale, Chairman of the Senate Committee on Naval Affairs, had given formal notice that he would conduct a full investigation of the Norfolk disaster. Congressman Charles H. Van Wyck of New York had earlier indicated a similar intention on the part of the House committee. So there would be two congressional inquiries about Norfolk. For some time he had expected that Hale would make such a move, but coming as it did on top of these other problems, he found the notice irritating and alarming at the same time.[5]

In his gloomy mood, Welles felt much put upon by irresponsible Congressmen. Where were they, he asked himself, when the question of peace and war hung in the balance? Where were they when secessionists in Maryland cut off Washington from the North. To Welles' jaundiced eye, the answer to these questions had come months earlier in the form of two letters John P. Hale had mailed from his haven in New Hampshire. Hale wanted Navy contracts for clients in Boston and Portsmouth. When the capital was deemed safe from capture, Welles contemptuously noted, Hale had appeared personally, seeking special favors for the same parties. He rebuffed the Senator, albeit politely.[6]

The chairmen of Senate committees had been invited to confer with appropriate Cabinet heads in early June, 1861, so that essential legislation would be ready for the special session on July 4.[7] Hale appeared, but he refused to visit the Navy Department or to have anything to do with Welles and Fox. Welles was satisfied at the time that he could expect no help from him—that, on the contrary, the self-seeking Senator from New Hampshire would use his position to attack the department unless he was appeased with contracts for his clients. Welles absolutely refused to give in, let the consequences be what they may. Here before him lay the consequences—congressional investigation. He would be lucky, he thought, if he escaped censure for the Norfolk disaster, let alone what damage his reputation could suffer when his procurement policies came under scrutiny. There were too many disappointed contractors with political influence for him to quash an enquiry. He must start at once to prepare a defense, despite the more compelling needs of overseeing the Navy's role in the war effort, the urgent demands of counseling the President on matters of politics and of state.[8]

Still, it was obvious to the least discerning eye that the Navy Department had accomplished much since the hectic days after Sumter. Welles could remember the time in early March when he first climbed the narrow stairs to his second-floor office. The same oil paintings of Hull and Decatur and McDonough and Perry still hung on the walls of the corridor, as they had when he was a bureau chief. Some of the clerks he had known in 1846 rushed up to greet him.[9] Captain Joseph Smith, looking a little older, to be sure, was still Chief of Yards and Docks, and still in the same office he had occupied fifteen years before. The other bureau chiefs—Horatio Bridge, in Welles' old post of Provisions and Clothing; John Lenthall of Construction, Equipment and Repair; Dr. William Whelan of Medicine and Surgery; and Captain George Magruder of Ordnance—were relative newcomers, though not exactly new faces to Welles. On the infrequent trips he had made to Washington during the Pierce and Buchanan administrations, he had always found time to drop in on the department. His friend John Williams, who had stayed on as a clerk, had kept him posted on department affairs.

He knew all of the bureau chiefs were conscientious, hard-working professionals, practical, conservative in outlook, and honest. Only John Lenthall could claim more than a local reputation. The department's naval architect, he had designed most of the new steam-powered warships. These vessels, sturdy, screw-driven, heavily armed frigates, were like Lenthall himself—dependable rather than innovative, slow, formidable ships of deep draft. They were not highly maneuverable, but they were seaworthy; none as yet had foundered, even when riding out gales of hurricane force. Lenthall was not an amiable man. Nor were his ships amiable ships. They were not meant to be. Their mission was coast defense, which demanded that they sustain the heavy pounding of Atlantic storms as well as the shot and shell of potential aggressors. For this role they were as admirably designed and as admirably equipped as any wooden war vessel of the day.

Lenthall's great fault, apart from his bearish personality, was his professional conservatism. A fine architect of wooden ships, he looked with contempt upon any innovation that intruded upon his vision of stately sailing steamers with well-seasoned white oak hulls and double-braced hackamatack framing. Welles, a cautious man himself, was struck with Lenthall's integrity. And, innocent that he was in matters of marine technology, he rated the architect's professional qualities high.

He was quick to learn, however, that John Lenthall could be the despair of naval officers, inventors, and politicians alike.[10]

Even if Welles had lacked confidence in any of his bureau chiefs, he could not have removed them until they had completed their terms of office, which were prescribed by law. The President, of course, could remove them, but well-established custom decreed that he exercise his power only for due cause. When Welles took over from Toucey, there was only one professional vacancy which he could fill—that of Engineer in Chief, the principal subordinate of the Chief of Construction, Equipment and Repair. To this important post, Welles appointed Benjamin F. Isherwood, a young naval engineer who, like Lenthall, enjoyed something of an international reputation. His treatise, *Engineering Precedents,* a vast, two-volume collection of test data on marine boilers, had attracted notice abroad.

Isherwood, who happened to be in Washington on duty, had heard that the post was open and lost no time in advancing his case. But his reputation as a careful, if somewhat controversial engineer, his good naval record, and the fact that Lenthall had confidence in him were the deciding factors in Welles' mind. By the very nature of his duties, he would be working closely with Lenthall. The relationship had to be a harmonious one.

Welles would learn in due course that Isherwood was more demanding and dogmatic than his chief, that he too spurned the theoretical and the abstract in favor of the empirical and the practical. Yet these qualities would simply confirm Welles in his judgment that he had made the right decision. For above all, as he and Fox struggled to improvise a Navy, they needed the proven rather than the experimental. In Lenthall and Isherwood he may have received over-much reliability, but he would be spared the costly mistakes that might well have occurred had more creative minds been overseeing new construction.[11]

Commodore Joseph Smith, Lenthall, and Isherwood acted as a steadying influence on the department, which was rapidly becoming demoralized. Captain George Magruder, the Ordnance Chief, and all of his clerks, resigned when Virginia seceded. Captain Franklin Buchanan, Commandant of the Washington Navy Yard, followed Magruder's example some days later, believing that Maryland, his native state, would join the Confederacy also. Fortunately, Commander John A. Dahlgren was stationed at the yard. There, for many years, he had conducted trials of his own and other ordnance systems. An experienced naval officer and an expert in ballistics, he was familiar with the administration of the yard. Welles made him Acting Commandant until he could select a replacement for Buchanan. On Welles' advice, Lincoln appointed Captain Andrew Harwood, who had a substantial background in naval ordnance, to replace Magruder.

Quite apart from resignations, low morale, and an inadequate staff of draftsmen, clerks, and messengers, which at full strength numbered seventy-four, including the Secretary himself, Welles inherited a department notorious for red tape and inefficiency. Weakened by years of congressional neglect, it was, in Du Pont's words, "the most rickety and stupid" of all the departments.[12]

Although Welles was acquainted with most of the clerks and bureau chiefs, he needed a confidential assistant whom he could trust. He was quite certain that war would erupt soon, if not at Pickens or at Sumter, then at some other border point along the line that divided the United States and the provisional Confederacy. Toucey had bequeathed to him a pitifully small Navy, most of which was obsolete, its best units scattered all over the world. Reorganization, expansion, and modernization were urgent, even if this crisis were overcome without conflict. Welles had to have not only a loyal, hardworking deputy but a man of vision, of intelligence, of proven ability, and of some political acumen.

The office of Chief Clerk was within his power of appointment. It was currently being held by Hobart Berrien, a department veteran of many years. Welles appointed him on a temporary basis until he decided on a permanent clerk. His mind turned increasingly to William Faxon, business manager of the Hartford *Press*. Welles had known Faxon for many years. He admired his managerial skills, his talent for business affairs, his discretion. Besides, Faxon was on terms of intimate friendship with important members of Welles' Hartford circle, men such as Mark Howard, Calvin Day, and Joseph R. Hawley. Though Welles was as yet unsure whether he wanted Faxon as his Chief Clerk, he did want him in the department. He had an immediate vacancy for a clerk of the second class. Implying that he would soon have a more senior position at his disposal, he asked Faxon if he would come to Washington. A widower with two children to support, Faxon found the $1200-a-year position a good deal more attractive than his share of the *Press*'s profits. The post would be secure for four years, something that could not be said about the *Press*'s operations, dependent as they were on the ever-changing fortunes of politics. An added inducement was the prospect of receiving $2200 a year if Welles made him Chief Clerk. Faxon accepted, assuming his duties on March 15.

Within two weeks Welles was certain that Faxon was the man he wanted. Heavily bearded, with a grim set to his jaw, Faxon presented a forbidding face to the world. In reality, he was a kindly, highly emotional man who, like Welles, had learned to exercise an iron control over his feelings.[13] His work was meticulous; his relations with his fellow clerks were easy, following a brief period of hesitancy on both sides.

After Sumter, Southern sympathizers resigned, leaving vacant two chief clerkships of bureaus. Acting Chief Clerk Hobart Berrien handed in his resignation, too, but for a better post in the Treasury Department. When Faxon applied for the chief clerkship of the department, he was both surprised and hurt to receive a noncommittal reply. Welles had to be vague because the senior Blair and his son, Montgomery, Welles' Cabinet colleague, were demanding that Gustavus Vasa Fox be appointed Chief Clerk.

Welles liked the ebullient Fox, so forceful, so energetic, yet so genial. His credentials, both political and professional, were impressive. A successful businessman but formerly a fine professional naval officer he had also, while on detached duty before retiring from the service, commanded the *Ohio* and the *George Law* for the United States Mail Steamship Company. Through his family relationship with Montgomery Blair he had direct access to the President. More persuasive perhaps than all these credentials in Welles' mind was that the President thought highly of Fox and felt under strong obligation to him for undertaking the ill-fated Sumter expedition.

Knowing all this, Welles still tried to reserve the Chief Clerk's post for Faxon. He mentioned to Lincoln that he would have Fox reinstated to his former rank of Lieutenant in the Navy if he wished. A suitable command at sea was his for the asking. Lincoln warmly seconded Welles' course as the least a grateful government could do for a brave and resourceful man. With what he thought was a presidential mandate, Welles went ahead and told Faxon to take over as Chief Clerk on May 8.[14] He had not reckoned with the Blairs, however, nor had he imagined that the President would gratify them at his expense.

When Lincoln told Montgomery Blair of Welles' plans for Fox, he was treated to an earnest, well-reasoned argument that Fox's professional expertise was desperately needed in the Navy Department. His talents would be lost if he were buried on blockade duty. Lincoln was as easily persuaded by Blair as he had been a few hours earlier by Welles. Though he was reluctant to interfere with the internal affairs of the departments, he casually broached Fox's appointment to Welles. Taken by surprise, Welles raised various objections. Obviously, he resented the intrusion. Lincoln did not press the issue. Later, either he or Montgomery Blair suggested a way out of the difficulty. When Congress met in special session on July 4, the administration would ask it to create the position of Assistant Secretary—a post now urgently needed for the expanded role of a wartime navy. Fox would be named Assistant Secretary and Faxon could then be made Chief Clerk, a compromise which made sense. The responsibilities of the Secretary's office would be divided between those best qualified to discharge them. Faxon, a landlubber like Welles, but a capable administrator, would supervise office management, official correspondence, and routine administration, and would coordinate all matters of budget and finance including contracts among the various bureau chiefs. Fox would have primary responsibility for professional matters—operational planning, communication with squadron commanders, direct supervision of fleet movements, and the blockade. In short, he would act as civilian Chief of Naval Operations. Faxon would serve as Welles' Chief of Staff, or, as Fox saw it: "When Faxon and I were together there were really two Ass't. Sec'ys. a civil and a naval one."

Had Welles been a Chase or a Seward, he might have taken a firm stand against Executive interference. He was neither. He was not as arrogant as they—and, it should be said, not as important to Lincoln, politically or personally. The newspapers were holding Welles responsible for Norfolk; they were describing the Navy Department as a nest of red tape, a natural habitat for old fogys like Welles. Another reason for Welles' capitulation was his long friendship with the Blairs. As much as his heart might have been with Faxon, prudence demanded that he not alienate this powerful family which had always been so helpful to him. Nor could he dismiss Fox's experience. Faxon had his talents, and there was a place for him in the department. In any ordinary peacetime situation, he would have been a capable assistant, relying upon the bureau chiefs to advise the Secretary on professional matters. But these were no ordinary times. Someone was needed who could command the respect as well as the cooperation of the bureau chiefs and the squadron commanders. Fox was a godsend to Welles. After an all-day session with him on May 8, Welles was quick to recognize that his own personal pique, his sense of obligation to Faxon, were small things compared to the greater needs of the service and the Union. As Lincoln had said, "He is a live man whose services we cannot dispense with."

After Congress created the post of Assistant Secretary the organization worked smoothly. But Welles' initial resentment had been sufficiently manifest for Lincoln to take direct action. In a rather peremptory note, which Fox handed to Welles, he said, "My wish, and advice is, that you do not allow any ordinary obstacle prevent his [Fox's] appointment." Welles gave in to the Executive dictate without a murmur.[15]

Dealing with Faxon was a painful matter, however. After reading him the President's note, Welles asked his frank opinion. "I told him promptly," said Faxon, "that I desired him to suit himself without reference to me—that I should feel that I had been degraded in the eyes of my fellow clerks, the thing having gone so far." "I will take care of you," replied Welles. "But I don't see where the place is," Faxon insisted. "I'll find one—I'll make one," said Welles. After some hesitation, Faxon agreed to continue. In July, Congress sanctioned the new post of Assistant Secretary. Lincoln appointed Fox. As soon as the Senate confirmed him, Welles gave Faxon the Chief Clerk's desk.[16]

Once he had appointed Fox, he studied the man carefully, maintaining a certain aloofness until he was satisfied that his new deputy was as competent as represented. They were as unlike as any two men could be. Welles was reserved, cautious, soft-voiced, tactful, and abstemious, a skillful politician. Fox was vocal, outgoing, brusque at times, impatient; he enjoyed good company, good food, good wines. Even such a *bon vivant* as young John Hay, the President's junior secretary, deferred to Fox when it came to exotic beverages or unusual dishes. Seward, a kindred spirit, delighted in entertaining Fox because he was so sincerely appreciative of the fine cuisine which always graced the Secretary's table. In a social setting, Fox was a delightful companion who fairly charmed the Lincolns.

But if Fox advanced the cause of the Navy at the White House and among a select group of Cabinet members and Congressmen, he was too strong a personality, too positive in his opinions, too lacking in discretion not to attract enemies in the service and in the government. Impatient Congressmen may have written off Welles many times, but he had few real enemies. In fact, those who clamored for his removal usually had a kind word for him, praising his loyalty, saying that he meant well, that he was simply too old for his vast responsibilities. With Fox it was a different matter. Thought to be the brains and the guiding force of the department, he was quite unfairly charged on many occasions with decisions that his chief had made or errors that were the Secretary's responsibility. Yet he was intensely loyal, never complaining if unjustly accused—a quality that Welles prized above all his other capabilities.[17]

Curiously, these two men, so different in most ways, had married women of similar tastes and temperaments. And both adored their wives to the point of idolatry. Mary Jane Welles and Virginia Woodbury

Fox were intelligent, intense beings, both of whom enjoyed ill health. Virginia Fox made fragility an art. Her more or less chronic state of ill-health, whether real or imagined, forbade children and made for an unusual marital relationship. Denied a normal family life, Fox seems to have sublimated his emotions in the furious energy he expended on his job. Welles had an enormous capacity for work, too, but Fox outpaced him. With his extensive social life added to his increasing labors, Fox's health was none too good, despite his robust appearance. Welles' health was uncertain, too, but after his family arrived in November, 1861 he began to feel better almost at once. Although Mary Welles had her frivolous side, she was a good manager who made an orderly, comfortable home for her husband.

Welles took great pride in his three boys, especially his oldest son, Edgar, who was at Yale during most of the war. A demanding father, he set high standards of achievement for all of his sons, treating them to frequent discourses on the excellence of moral virtue. Yet always he sought to build up their confidence in themselves. He asked Edgar's advice on various important matters and shared with him many of his views on affairs of state.

Welles' second son, John, a quiet, studious young man, seems to have been taken for granted by his parents. Not so his youngest son, Tom, a mischievous, high-spirited adolescent who caused his father endless worry. Tom's pranks, his inattention to school work, his thoughtlessness, and his unsettled habits were not really serious faults, but to Welles, who was always striving for perfection, they loomed larger than they deserved.[18] Welles' family furnished him with a sense of well-being, of release from the awful tensions of his office. Poor Fox was childless and had to contend with a wife who offered him little domestic comfort. Faxon, a widower, boarded his two children with relatives in Hartford. Neither Fox nor Faxon had much of a refuge from work or much of a reason to reduce the killing regimen.

With two such able subordinates working ten to twelve hours a day and offering a strict example for the bureau chiefs and clerks, Welles began to see definite progress in overcoming what had seemed insurmountable problems two months before. Samuel F. Du Pont was amazed at the new "executive" touch in the department. "It has vitality and energy never seen there before," he said. "Now I am not so well satisfied with the Navy itself as with the Department."[19]

Du Pont made this comment just as a special board of which he was a member was completing a project of great strategic significance—comprehensive plans to implement the blockade of the Confederate coast.

Initially, Welles had objected to Lincoln's proclaiming a blockade over more than 3000 miles of Southern coastline. In the emergency Cabinet meeting of April 14, 1861, Welles argued that the government was engaged in putting down an insurrection, not a foreign war, that the coastline to be blockaded was not foreign territory, but an integral part of the Union. If a blockade were proclaimed, foreign powers would, he predicted, extend belligerent rights to the Confederacy. He called his colleagues' attention to the fact that under international law one of the criteria of a blockade was that it be effective. Of the ninety ships in the tiny, largely obsolete Navy, Welles had less than fifty available to interdict commerce with the Confederacy. European powers knew that any blockade the United States Navy might establish could not possibly be effective for some time. Consistent with their national interests, Britain or France could flaunt the blockade. The Navy simply was not prepared to accept any challenge.

The best course, Welles suggested, was to close the ports in the seceded states. Any vessel under American or foreign registry trying to enter a closed port could then be seized in direct violation of municipal law, its crew subject to criminal prosecution as smugglers. In making his argument Welles overstated the case, as he no doubt meant to do. He had been reading Wheaton, Theodore Dwight Woolsey, and other contemporary authorities on international law. He was well aware that his argument of effectiveness was not a particularly strong one. No blockade in history had ever been more than partially effective. Most had been paper blockades at first, gradually becoming more effective as more blockading ships were built and went into service. Yet the earnestness of his argument, the appeal he made to the sense and to the emotions of his colleagues that it would be a rash as well as ludicrous act for a nation to proclaim a blockade of its own ports, impressed a majority of the Cabinet. Seward answered Welles, but he was not well prepared for this unexpected onslaught. Cameron and Smith deferred to Seward's judgment. Chase, Blair, and Bates supported Welles' position. Lincoln decided that the subject of a blockade needed further study, so he deleted the section dealing with it in his proclamation announcing that a state of insurrection existed.

The Cabinet met again the following day and was presented with a separate draft proclamation announcing a blockade of the entire Confederate coast south of North Carolina. The document adroitly disposed of Welles' argument of effectiveness by its wording—the government "deemed it advisable to set on foot a blockade of the ports"—which meant that, as means became available, the blockade would become tighter, a phraseology that conformed with British precedents in the Napoleonic Wars. Obviously, Seward, and probably Lincoln, had consulted various treatises on international law, too. Seward had chatted informally with Lord Lyons, the British Minister.[20] In the end, however, the native shrewdness of the two men compelled them to dismiss Welles' argument as not being realistic. They would have to resign themselves to the certainty that the European powers would accord belligerency status to the Confederacy. But in return they could reasonably expect these same powers to proclaim their neutrality in accordance with international law. Lincoln issued his Blockade Proclamation on April 19 and on April 27 extended the blockade to Virginia and North Carolina. As expected, Britain, France, and other powers proclaimed their neutrality, though their nationals were free to trade with either belligerent at their own risk.[21]

When the special session of Congress met in July, one of its first acts was to give the President discretionary power to close the ports in rebellious territory. Seward promptly informed the European powers of the congressional action, claiming the principle that an insurrection existed, even though the United States had conceded, through its blockade proclamation, that the insurrection was also a war. Welles stoutly maintained to the end of his life that the closing of the ports was the proper path to follow, that the government should never have trifled with its territorial integrity, but his position had been impractical and potentially dangerous from the start. By taking the course they did, Seward and Lincoln were able to avoid complications that would inevitably have arisen had the United States tried to maintain abroad the fiction that it was not waging war.[22]

The policy settled, Welles had no choice but to convert the blockade from a formality to a reality. Lincoln had specifically directed him "to take such means as might seem to me necessary in the emergency to maintain the national authority." The President added that he "would share with me or take upon himself the responsibility of such orders as I in my discretion should issue."[23] Where should he begin? Fortunately, he did not have to cast about for temporary expedients. A very talented bureaucrat, Alexander Dallas Bache, Superintendent of the Coast Survey, came up with an answer that Welles gratefully accepted. Bache proposed a board, or "committee of conference," as he called it, to draw upon hydrographic and meteorological materials in the file of the Coast Survey office and topographical information from the archives of the Army Engineers so that a comprehensive strategy could be developed to implement the blockade.

Bache, who gave every appearance of being a kindly, otherworldly academic, was not so disinterested as he seemed. The government's first civilian scientist of any stature, this great-grandson of Benjamin Franklin was a first-rate promoter of technical and scientific projects, his own Coast Survey being a prime example. For years he had managed to wring enough funds from a skeptical Congress not only to keep the Survey in being, but to expand its functions.

The Survey, of particular interest to Bache and his major source of income, could have become a casualty of the war had he not seen the opportunity of using it to devise blockade strategy. His offer came at precisely the right time. Personnel of specialized skills were available to make up the board. Commander Charles H. Davis, long an associate of Bache and the compiler of the *Nautical Almanac,* was serving in the department as Assistant Detailing Officer. Captain Samuel F. Du Pont, considered one of the most capable senior officers in the Navy, was Commandant of the Philadelphia Navy Yard. His able assistant, Percival Drayton, could take over for the two or three weeks it was thought would be required to correlate all the pertinent information and draw up systematic plans. Either General Joseph G. Totten or his assistant, Major John G. Barnard, was on hand to represent the Army and furnish topographical data. Bache would act as chairman, Davis as secretary. The enthusiastic Fox alerted the principals, during the third week in May, that the department was about to establish a blockade board.

At this point the project might have languished, a victim of Welles' "avalanche" of confusing and critical problems, had he not received in early June, through Old Frank Blair, an ominous letter from John C. Frémont, then in London preparing for his departure home. Frémont had written that Confederate agents "are very active here. The last steamer brought them an accession of credit and they completed yesterday the purchase of two screw steamers and are contracting for more." Fox reminded Welles of the Bache proposal, and by June 27 the board had assembled. Charged with the selection of two ports to be seized, one in South Carolina, the other in Georgia or Florida, the board was to report on their feasibility as coaling and supply depots for the maintenance of the blockade along the South Atlantic coast. The department's instructions were brief, but Bache, with his eye on larger things and his Coast Survey ever in mind, decided from the outset that the board would develop a comprehensive "manual for blockading." Despite his kindly nature and engaging manners, he was a harsh taskmaster. "All days are working days here now," wrote Du Pont. By July 25, not quite a month after their first meeting, the board had submitted four reports, or "memoirs," and a recommendation that the Atlantic blockading squadron be divided into two commands, one responsible for the Virginia and North Carolina coasts, the other for South Carolina, Georgia, and Florida.[24]

Lodgements on the rebel coast were also recommended, so that the blockade could close the Carolina sounds and establish bases for future military and naval operations. The reports themselves were brief, but they provided all necessary information for the civilian planners to make intelligent decisions. They were accompanied with a wealth of charts and other technical data that would be invaluable for the actual implementation of the blockade, not only on the Atlantic coast, but also the Gulf coast and the Mississippi River. Welles and Fox studied the documents carefully. Delighted with the firm, logical line the reports took—a close blockade and the systematic capture of enemy ports as means became available—Welles presented the reports to the President and Cabinet, who were impressed by them, too. Fox seized the opportunity to exploit the advantage.[25] He told the President that the seizure of the depots recommended in the reports—Fernandina, Florida, and Bulls Bay or Port Royal on the South Carolina coast—would require a large naval expedition and an adequate army force to defend them after capture. Welles kept in the background. Fully agreeing with Fox, he deferred to his subordinate's personal influence with Lincoln, his flair for advocating plans that gripped the President's imagination. Anxious for the armed forces to make some positive move after the Bull Run defeat, Lincoln needed little persuasion. A fortnight after the Bache committee had presented its recommendations to the department, they were accepted and put into operation. General Thomas W. Sherman, a testy West Pointer, was selected to command the Army part of the amphibious expedition. His force would consist of 10,000 men. Du Pont was chosen to head up the Navy side.[26]

Meanwhile the department had been working feverishly to build and purchase, a blockading fleet, and man it. Acting under Lincoln's blanket authority, Welles and Fox had Lenthall and Isherwood design a class of gunboats for blockade duty. Wooden vessels of comparatively shallow draft, they were to be strong enough to mount heavy guns, yet sufficiently maneuverable and fast to intercept blockade-runners. Within a matter of weeks, designs for a class of single-screw gunboats had been conceived, plans drafted, specifications written, and bids issued for the construction of twenty-three such vessels.[27]

Before these gunboats were on the stocks, Lenthall and Isherwood were designing another new class of light draft gunboats for close-in blockade duty—the unique double enders. Narrow of beam, these ships were equipped with two sets of engines that were installed amidships but worked in opposite directions; a rudder was attached at each end. Designed to dash up streams and inlets too narrow for them to turn around in, they would simply use the other engine and rudder for the return trip. Unfortunately, their paddlewheels and machinery were exposed to artillery fire in the close quarters where they would operate. Besides being vulnerable, they were so difficult to handle in a seaway that Du Pont found them about as useful as a Chinese junk.[28]

Within the four months of Sumter's fall, forty-seven frigate, sloop and gunboat hulls, ranging from 500 to more than 2000 tons, were on the stocks in Northern shipyards. Thousands of workmen in a score of plants and foundries were manufacturing marine boilers and engines, deck gear and ordnance. But new construction took time. And Welles judged there was none to spare, if the blockade was to pass muster with European powers. Before the Bureau of Construction had begun drawing up plans, he had ordered the purchase of merchant ships suitable for conversion to blockade duty.[29]

# CHAPTER 20

# Trials and Triumphs

NEW CONSTRUCTION UNDER department contract to the design and specifications of Lenthall and Isherwood, burdened the line officers and engineers who were detailed to supervise the work. But the duties were familiar—inspection of materials and workmanship, ensuring that the contractors were abiding by the specifications, that the work progress kept up with stipulated completion dates. Only three classes of vessels were involved; variations in power plant and armament were minor. The task was arduous, though well within the professional competence of the officers involved. Purchase of merchant shipping was another matter. Here they were dealing with dozens of different hulls and power plants, from large steamships to small tugboats, and a hundred or more owners, all accustomed to making the best bargain possible, adept at concealing weaknesses. In the nature of the business, the department could not furnish contract guidelines. Each purchase or lease had to be made on an individual basis in a market where profit was the sole incentive.

Driven hard by the sudden increase of their responsibilities, and unskilled in the demanding art of ship brokerage, the naval officers' initial efforts left much to be desired. New York merchants whom Welles or Fox knew personally wrote the department that the naval officers were being bilked by shipowners. They were paying as much as double the price then prevailing on the market. And in many instances, it was claimed, they were being fobbed off with obsolete vessels from which all valuable gear had been removed prior to sale; yet they were still paying for the gear.

Samuel R. Pook, the senior naval constructor in New York, was an excellent naval architect, but he proved to be an execrable purchasing agent. After analyzing Pook's transactions from data George D. Morgan, Welles' brother-in-law, and William Aspinwall, both New York merchants, supplied him, Welles concluded that "a palpable and gross" fraud had been perpetrated on the department.[1] Yet it was not until he received similar reports from Boston that Welles decided naval officers could not cope with the hungry merchants. He needed, he felt, trusted businessmen who had had years of practical experience in dealing with the shipowners. Forbes and Morgan had suggested such a course, but it was Morgan who made the clinching argument, and it secured for him a highly lucrative brokerage business. He had skillfully blended the personal with the political in convincing Welles that ship purchases in New York could best be handled by one man. That man should be George D. Morgan.

"Can you not give me something," Morgan had pleaded only two weeks after Sumter. "My business is gone & I should like to be employed here by you." A week later he charged that Moses Grinnell and Simeon Draper, two of Thurlow Weed's trusted lieutenants, were making exorbitant profits at the Navy's expense through their control of Samuel Breeze, Commandant of the Brooklyn Navy Yard. Welles was alarmed that Breeze should be trafficking with any of Weed's men, but he moved cautiously. Already under heavy attack in the New York *Herald* because he had rebuffed a direct approach from W. O. Bartlett, Cornelius Vanderbilt's agent and a writer for the *Herald*, he was sensitive to the power and the prejudices of the New York commercial interests.

After weighing the risks, Welles made the only decision he felt lay open to him if he was to extemporize an effective blockade fleet rapidly without excessive costs. In early June he gave Morgan and Aspinwall the agency for making charters, but it was not until Pook broke under the strain that he made Morgan the agent for purchasing as well. John Murray Forbes, owner of shipping lines and railroads, shrewd but scrupulously honest, received the same authority at the same time in Boston. In appointing the two men, Welles' instructions were that the purchases be suitable for conversion to blockade duty. Only once did he feel it necessary to furnish any direction. Fox had mentioned that Morgan might buy one or two of Vanderbilt's large steamers. "It should not be thought of for the moment," he wrote, "we can get a couple of propellors for supply boats—we don't want the old Big [Vanderbilt] Boats." Welles trusted Morgan and Forbes so completely that he did not stipulate any conditions of employment in his letters of authorization.[2]

The two agents for the department had an embarrassment of riches to draw upon. The United States was second only to England as a maritime power. Over four million tons of shipping, 98 per cent of it owned by Northerners, plied the seas under American registry.[3] War had completely disrupted the extensive cotton-carrying trade to the North and to Europe, while it had dampened all maritime activity in the North. When the Confederate government issued letters of reprisal, rumors swept over Northern commercial communities that the privateers were being purchased in Europe. Marine risks soared. Shipowners cut back drastically on their sailings. Temporarily at least, there was a buyers' market for ships that could be converted to naval use as transports, supply vessels, armed tugs, colliers, blockaders, even cruisers.

From the beginning the New York agency was more important than that in Boston, and George D. Morgan proved a good choice for agent. But in driving hard bargains with New York shipowners he incurred the wrath of the city's shipping magnates, who had been unloading vessels on the government at exorbitant prices. While Morgan put an end to their dreams of sudden wealth, at the same time he opened himself to attack by charging a 2.5 per cent commission which was paid by the seller, but which, of course, was passed on to the government. If Forbes was compensated for his services, it did not appear in any of his transactions. On October 20, Welles received a letter from his nemesis, Senator John P. Hale of New Hampshire, warning that "folks would censure the employment of my brother-in-law." The charge of nepotism could not be dismissed lightly. On the same day he also received a sharp letter from Governor E. D. Morgan, George Morgan's cousin and partner, demanding that the Navy clear out of their New York office. "E. D. M[organ]," Welles noted in his list of grievances for that week, "joins enemies—wishes the government agency to leave the premises with which he is connected."

From August 1, 1861, when Morgan became sole agent for both charter and purchase in New York, until he ceased purchasing in December of that year, he bought eighty-nine vessels, of all types and sizes, ranging from a paddlewheel steamer costing $200,000 to a tug worth $5000. In all he spent $3,500,000, about $900,000 less than the total asking price. For his services he received approximately $70,000 in commissions, a large sum for less than six months' work "considering," as the indignant *Tribune* charged, "that the times are very hard and that the last summer was an exceedingly dull one for trade." That Forbes had not asked a commission for his services (which were not one-tenth the volume of Morgan's) was cited as additional proof that Welles, in collusion with his brother-in-law, had placed profit above patriotism.

Welles, of course, had fair warning that Morgan's agency would become a public issue. Weed's faction, which he had so unceremoniously pushed aside, early took the offensive in the Albany *Evening Journal* and the *New York Times*. W. O. Bartlett kept up a withering fire on behalf of the Vanderbilt interests in the *Herald*. The *Tribune* soon joined the fray because it believed favoritism was being practiced and because Greeley decided that Cameron and Welles were corrupt and incompetent. Welles had not liked Morgan's commission arrangement, but he was assured that it was accepted practice in the ship brokerage business. He needed the vessels urgently. Knowing and trusting Morgan, he was willing to risk the inevitable criticism in the interest of national security.[4]

Welles had shown commendable energy in the rapid buildup of a blockade fleet, but he lagged far behind Stephen R. Mallory, the Confederate Secretary of the Navy, in grasping the implications of ironclads. Mallory had recognized at once that the Confederacy could never match the shipbuilding potential of the Union. Only a revolutionary weapon like the ironclad warship might redress the balance. He had the wit to make the gamble.

Unlike Welles, the Confederate Secretary had had considerable experience in naval affairs, having served as Chairman of the Senate's naval affairs committee from 1853 until 1861. Thoroughly familiar with the industrial might of the North, he was much better versed in the state of naval architecture than his Union counterpart. While Welles had been composing political editorials and helping to organize the Republican party, Mallory had been studying British and French experiments with ironclads.

When the Confederacy came into possession of the Navy Yard at Norfolk, Mallory's first concern was raising the partly burned *Merrimack*. On May 8, just three weeks after the secession of Virginia, he recommended to the Confederate Congress that "not a moment should be lost" in constructing an ironclad. In his letter, a copy of which found its way to Welles and Fox, he presented convincing arguments that ironclads would destroy the Union's wooden fleet. Two days later the Confederate Congress accepted his recommendations.[5]

The day before Mallory got his authorization, Welles wrote Abram S. Hewitt, the Trenton, New Jersey ironmaster, that the department was not planning to build any iron vessels. But during the next month word kept coming into the department that the Confederates were working on ironclad designs. This information was solid enough to be taken seriously. Welles and Fox acquainted themselves with the literature on armor-plated vessels. They sought advice from John Lenthall and from high-ranking naval officers such as Joseph Smith and Charles H. Davis. All were skeptical, especially Lenthall, whose opinion, as one of the nation's leading naval architects, they were bound to respect. And Lenthall considered ironclads to be a "humbug." Nevertheless, Welles and Fox felt they should be prepared for any contingency. Still, in deference to the experts' opinion, Welles decided to leave the matter until the special session of Congress met on July 4. Even then he moved with deliberation, merely calling Congress' attention to the need for an ironclad building program.

New in his dealings with Congress, he had assumed that his recommendation would result in prompt action, that the chairman of the House and Senate naval affairs committees would meet with the department and hammer out the necessary legislation. When more time than he judged he could afford went by without any call from Charles B. Sedgewick, Chairman of the House committee, or John P. Hale, his counterpart in the Senate, Welles himself drafted a bill asking that he be given authority to appoint an ironclad board. Should the Congress' report be favorable, he wanted an appropriation of $1,500,000 for the design and construction of three experimental vessels. To forestall criticism, professional and political, he stressed the experimental nature of the project. Then, instead of approaching the committees directly, he asked an old associate, Cornelius S. Bushnell, a New Haven businessman, to present the bill. Bushnell, a clever speculator, railroad promoter, and resourceful lobbyist, enlisted the aid of the Democratic Congressman from his district, James E. English. Together they secured the support of Sedgewick. After many days of "untiring effort," with Bushnell lobbying Congressmen and Senators and English and Sedgewick working on their committee colleagues, especially those in the Senate, the bill was reported favorably and carried in both houses on its first reading. Lincoln approved the legislation on the same day, August 4, 1861.[6]

Welles immediately appointed Joseph Smith, Hiram Paulding, and Commander Charles H. Davis, whose technical reputation had been enhanced by his service on the blockade board. All three openly confessed their ignorance of ironclads. (In the meantime, in Norfolk, Mallory had approved the design for the *Merrimack* a month before. Workmen had already cut down her hull and were beginning to install her plating when Welles' ironclad board was still advertising for designs.) The board spent one month in examining some fifteen proposals. Only two seemed to have any merit—a conventional gunboat and an equally conventional frigate. Bushnell, the resourceful New Haven grocer, was responsible for the gunboat plan. Scenting profits, and relying on his inside information, he had Samuel Pook design a partially ironclad gunboat. Merrick and Sons of Philadelphia submitted the design for the frigate. But the board cast doubts on the stability and the positive buoyancy of both vessels, loaded down as they were with masses of armor plate above the waterline.[7]

In Washington, on the steps of Willard's Hotel, Bushnell chanced upon the New York marine machinery builder and iron founder, Cornelius H. Delemater, to whom he confided the board's concern about the stability of Pook's design. Delemater advised him to consult John Ericsson of New York, the Swedish-born inventor and engineer. Ericsson, he assured the worried Bushnell, would give him an exact calculation in a matter of hours. On his way home from Washington, Bushnell stopped in New York, where he went to 95 Franklin Street, home and office of John Ericsson. The brilliant but controversial engineer, after examining the plans and the data, set Bushnell's mind at rest. "She will easily carry the load and stand a six inch shot at a respectable distance," he said. Then Ericsson asked if Bushnell would care to examine a plan of "a floating battery absolutely impregnable to the heaviest shot and shell." Always on the lookout for anything potentially profitable, Bushnell was all eagerness. Ericsson took from a dusty box the model and plans of a flat-bottomed, self-propelled battery with an ironclad, steam-powered, rotating turret and ironclad deck and sides mounted on a smaller wooden hull, the armor projecting over the propeller and external shafting at the stern and over the anchor well at the bow. Armament consisted of two heavy-caliber guns, shielded by eight inches of laminated wrought-iron plate and backed up by thirty inches of seasoned white oak. The deck and sides were designed to have a five-inch armature made up of one-inch plates, like the turret. The vessel—or rather raft, for that was its general characteristic—would be conned from a tiny pilot house, made of heavy iron beams, forward of the turret.

Bushnell was captivated as much by the novel design as by the inventor himself. Erricsson was articulate, his presentation profoundly impressive. Bushnell may have been a wholesale grocer, a railroad promoter, and a speculator, but he had more than his share of Yankee ingenuity. He had never met anyone so persuasive. He knew that Gideon

Welles was then in Connecticut, closing up his affairs in Hartford and moving his family to Washington. Bushnell asked if he could present the plan to Welles. Ericsson was more than happy to oblige. He provided him with a set of plans and a pasteboard model that illustrated the rotation of the turret. Without stopping at his home, the unwearied promoter hurried through to Hartford.[8] Welles was also struck by the ingenuity of the design. Unaware of the troubles Ericsson had had in the past with the Navy Department, he thought Bushnell should present the design to the board immediately. But the shrewd New Haven speculator had just had his own trials with the department. He judged that he needed more than Welles' support, as influential as it was, to clinch the deal. From Hartford he journeyed to Troy, New York, where he met with John A. Griswold and John F. Winslow, iron manufacturers who had devised the tongue-and-groove system of plating for his own partially armored gunboat. The canny Bushnell knew that both men were friends, and Griswold in fact a political ally, of Secretary Seward. He explained Ericsson's plans, showed them the model, and offered them a partnership if the board accepted the battery. They supplied him with strong testimonials to Seward. Off to Washington by the next train, he made straight for the State Department, where the Secretary obligingly gave him a letter of introduction to Lincoln. Like Welles and Bushnell himself, the President had a strong interest in the mechanical arts. The unique plan so interested him that he agreed to be present when Bushnell made his presentation to the board.

The next day, September 13, at 11 o'clock in the morning, with Lincoln, Fox, Smith, and Paulding as his audience, Bushnell explained the salient features of the battery—its revolving turret, low freeboard, heavy guns, and light draft. He produced the model and illustrated the turret mechanism. The professionals present were all taken by surprise. Fox was enthusiastic; Paulding and Smith had a good many objections. Then all turned to Lincoln, who, as usual, illustrated his point with a joke. "All I have to say," he remarked, "is what the girl said when she stuck her foot into the stocking. It strikes me there's something in it." His interest fell far short of endorsement.[9] And after Bushnell repeated his presentation for the full board, he "found that the air had been so thick with croakings that the Department was about to father another Ericsson failure."

Undismayed, the indefatigable Bushnell finally managed to persuade Smith and Paulding to support the project, on the condition that Charles Davis, who had been present at the later briefing, approve. When Bushnell sat down with Davis and tried to make his case, he failed. "Take the little thing home and worship it," said Davis scornfully, "as it would not be idolatry, because it was in the image of nothing in the heaven above or on the earth beneath or in the waters under the earth."[10]

When Welles arrived that evening, Bushnell was waiting for him with a mournful account of his day's work. The only way to save the battery, he thought, was to have the magnetic Ericsson argue his own case. Welles agreed. Bushnell was off on the night train to New York, where he met Ericsson the following morning. The tired but still spirited promoter did not scruple to twist the facts when Ericsson asked him what the board thought. He assured the temperamental inventor that all members were favorable but that Davis wanted a few details explained further, adding that Welles wanted him to clarify these points on the morrow. "Well, I'll go tonight," said Ericsson.[11]

Meanwhile Welles had spoken to Commodore Smith, whom he found favorable to the battery. By now he had learned how sensitive Ericsson was to wrongs he had suffered from the Navy years back. He was also aware of Lenthall's and Isherwood's decided opposition to anything Ericsson might bring forward. Davis, too, had been free in his criticism. But Fox liked the idea. Commodores Smith and Paulding were willing to take a chance if all liability for failure was underwritten by the contractors. The battery, as Bushnell described it, was remarkably inexpensive and, even more important, could be completed, so he understood, in three months' time, while the other ironclads would require from six months to a year to complete. Work on the *Merrimack* was well advanced. As Mallory had felt he must gamble on ironclads, so Welles felt he must gamble on Ericsson. He asked Commodore Smith, the Chairman of the Board, to treat Ericsson "tenderly, to give him a full and deliberate hearing."[12]

After an all-night train ride which frayed a temper uncertain at best, Ericsson was prepared for a few perfunctory questions. He mistook the board's businesslike posture as hostility to him personally and to his design. Indignant at such treatment, he was about to leave but then decided that he ought to inquire what the board's objections were, if any. Smith, as kindly as a bluff old commodore could be, said that they were worried whether the craft would be stable in a seaway. Ericsson planned to make a brief reply but, warming to his subject, gave an eloquent lecture on the stability of his battery. Even Davis was impressed, though he was certain that Ericsson's vessel would have excessive stability (as indeed it did). Smith conferred briefly with his colleagues, then asked Ericsson to return that afternoon for a further conference in the Secretary's office.

When the touchy inventor appeared at the time appointed, Welles asked if he would repeat his presentation. Ericsson complied, giving a more vivid performance than he had that morning. He closed his remarks by saying that he would complete the vessel in ninety days.

"How much will she cost?" asked Welles.

"Two hundred and seventy-five thousand dollars," was the prompt reply.

Welles turned to the board and polled them individually. All agreed that Ericsson should be awarded a contract. Enjoining the inventor to begin work immediately, Welles said that the contract would be forwarded to him.

Ericsson took him at his word. With funds advanced by Bushnell, Griswold, and Winslow, he ordered the plating from Abbot and Company of Baltimore, the largest rolling mill in the country. Thomas F. Rowland, whose shipyard was at Greenpoint, Long Island, across the East River from Manhattan, would construct the hull. Turret, turret machinery, and main engines Ericsson entrusted to his old associate Cornelius Delemater of the Novelty Iron Works. The keel of the vessel he named the *Monitor*—because it would constantly admonish Confederate leaders of Union strength—was laid on October 25, 1861. She was launched January 30, 1862, and turned over to the Navy on February 19.[13]

If Ericsson had not had to contend with the changes Commodore Smith demanded, he might have made his construction target date. What with Smith's changes, various accidents to her machinery, building errors, essential adjustments made after trial runs, laggard progress payments, and no additional funds for overtime, the *Monitor* was not finally commissioned until March 4—and she was still only five weeks late. She left New York under tow two days later, and on March 9 she engaged the *Merrimack*. The *Galena*, Bushnell's lightly armored gunboat, would not be ready for another month, while Merrick and Sons' 3500-ton ironclad, the *New Ironsides,* would not be commissioned until late August. To the indignation of Ericsson and his suppliers, the government did not pay for the *Monitor* in full until after she had proven herself in combat with the *Merrimack*. Years later, the inventor-designer still bristled at this lack of faith in his vessel. "The *Monitor* was private property on going into the battle at Hampton Roads," he wrote, "the Government had however a lien on the vessel, having advanced a certain part of the contract amount."[14]

While the department was considering ironclads, the more immediate concern of implementing the reports of the blockade board claimed major attention. Welles and Fox were planning a series of amphibious blows from Cape Hatteras to the coast of northern Florida. They had gained presidential approval, and the War Department was cooperating. But in the ever-shifting sands of military priorities, Welles could never be sure about Army support. George B. McClellan had succeeded Scott as Army Chief. Welles, like the rest of Washington, admired the young general, though he had already detected his reluctance to release troops for any operation he did not control directly.[15]

As trifling as the Cape Hatteras victory was, it earned plaudits for the Navy, fed the ambition of Fox for more and greater displays, and inspired Lincoln to more extensive operations along the Confederate coast. Grumbling, crusty Adam Gurowski wrote of Welles after Stringham's victory, "only two members of the Cabinet drive together, Blair and Welles and both on the right side, both true men impatient for action."[16] Where the more deliberate Welles, wiser in the ways of government than his ambitious assistant, kept calm amidst the chaos of conflicting demands, bureaucratic intrigues, and emerging interservice rivalries, the impatient Fox met these obstacles head on. He had already decided the "navy department was quite hopeless," that "a private concern would be ruined by conducting business as it is carried on here." In his drive to place the Navy in the forefront he would frequently create the very problems of which he so bitterly complained. "One of his characteristics," said Du Pont of Fox at this time, "is that he prefers planning and project to execution—so you are always afraid that he is going to propose a change."[17] Yet Fox could not be blamed for a lamentable breakdown in communication which very nearly beached the Du Pont-Sherman expedition before it got underway.

Someone in high authority—Lincoln, Seward, or McClellan—had, quite independently of the Navy, arranged for an amphibious assault, under the command of General Ambrose Burnside, on the North Carolina coast, south of Hatteras. Fox was crestfallen when he first got wind of this new operation. McClellan was already showing signs of reluctance to part with Sherman's troops. It appeared likely that, if they went anywhere, they would go to Burnside. Compounding the problem for the department was the fact that Fox and Welles had tied up so much commercial shipping that delay or cancellation of the Port Royal expedition would be ruinously expensive, not to mention the injury that would be done to the morale of the Navy itself.

The original plan of the Du Pont-Sherman operation was to capture Fernadina or Bulls Bay, both weakly defended—a modest affair. Port Royal, South Carolina, which Bache's committee conceded would be a

far more valuable objective than the other ports, was thought too formidable. The committee's caution had not deterred Fox, who opted for
an attack on Port Royal as soon as he studied the reports. Situated
midway between Charleston and Savannah, Port Royal could lead to
greater things. But its capture meant the use of more naval power.
Welles and Fox intensified their pressure on Morgan and on the
contractors.[18]

Now, after all the work, all the exhortations to contractors, all the
coaxing of the military, now, when an armada of seventy ships was
being assembled in New York, Lincoln and the War Department
seemed about to shelve the Port Royal operation. When Burnside applied to the department for a naval aide to assist him in his expedition,
Fox was determined to clear the air. With Welles' approval, he asked
for a conference with Lincoln on the Du Pont-Sherman expedition.
The meeting was set for the evening of October 1 at Secretary Seward's
home.

As Fox was preparing to leave for Seward's, Du Pont appeared at the
Department. Hurriedly explaining what he knew about the Burnside
expedition, Fox asked him to come along. The two men found Lincoln and Seward sitting together on a sofa in the upstairs parlor.
Lincoln looked quizzically at Du Pont. He had to be reminded that
the Flag Officer was the commander of the naval expedition. Seward
was smoking furiously, talking rapidly, and gesturing with his cigar
to emphasize a point. Fox, who was also smoking a cigar, sat down on
the sofa next to Lincoln. Du Pont watched, horrified, as Fox carelessly
blew smoke in the President's eyes. No one had bothered to inform
Cameron, McClellan, or Sherman about the meeting. Seward dispatched his son Frederick and Assistant Secretary of War Tom Scott to
track them down. Finally Cameron appeared, soon followed by a
dishevelled Sherman, who had gone to bed (he had refused to be disturbed until he learned Lincoln wanted him). McClellan could not be
found anywhere, so the discussion opened without him.

Fox asked about the Burnside expedition, which he understood was
a presidential project, but which, he explained, cut directly across the
joint Army-Navy expedition that had been in preparation several
months. Lincoln, irritated at the lack of planning for the conference,
flared up. He denied categorically that he had any knowledge of a
competing operation. Cameron slyly hinted that Seward must be the
culprit because he "regulated all the business of all the departments."
Scott in the meantime had located an Army staff memorandum that
outlined the Burnside expedition. Everyone present denied that he had

even heard about such a memorandum. Lincoln, still simmering, said that he would go back to Illinois if his memory was "so treacherous." Du Pont quietly suggested "that as we had been two months discussing another expedition, it would be wise to handle one at a time." Cameron agreed. The original operation would go forward as planned. At this point, McClellan appeared, and the President, in an amazing about-face, declared that the joint operation would have to be given up. "It would cost so much money," he said. "I said nothing," wrote Du Pont to his wife, "but thought of all the work this summer—and of all the fixed determination of the Cabinet." Fox would not surrender that easily. The argument went back and forth until McClellan reluctantly acquiesced in a postponement of his own amphibious operation. Sherman could have 14,000 men. Once a consensus had been reached, "then came the haste of ignorance," as Du Pont described it; "we must go in four days!"[19]

Neither Welles, nor Fox, nor Du Pont, for that matter, dared give Lincoln and McClellan any more time to change their minds. At New York, where Du Pont had gone to supervise the last details of fleet organization, Fox planted the idea of Port Royal in the Flag Officer's mind. Welles was careful to include Port Royal in the instructions he issued Du Pont on October 12, but the decision was still left in the Flag Officer's hands. On October 16 the fleet left New York for Hampton Roads, where it would rendezvous with the transports and auxiliary vessels. While at sea, Du Pont had almost convinced himself that Port Royal should be the objective. Fox banished all doubts when the fleet arrived at Hampton Roads on October 23. He insisted upon Port Royal. Six days later the largest and certainly the most heterogeneous fleet ever organized by the United States sailed out of Hampton Roads —course south southeast.[20]

Welles steeled himself to await the outcome of the expedition with his accustomed fatalism, until he awoke on November 2 to a screaming gale of wind and rain out of the southwest. At the department he was told that the storm was general at least as far south as Cape Hatteras. He seemed as composed as ever at the news, but he confessed to his son Edgar that it "was very trying to me and may have made sad havoc with my summer and autumn labors . . . may prove calamitous to the country." He could only hope that the fleet was beyond the worst part of the storm, which at times reached hurricane force. If not, he despaired for the frail New York ferryboats, the overloaded transports, the untried gunboats. What if most of them foundered off the treacherous shoals of Hatteras? The loss of life could reach into the thousands.

In his darker moments he doubted if the administration could survive such a catastrophe.

He had to live with his fears for another week before he began to receive glimmers of information, from Confederate newspapers, that an attack had been made on Port Royal. It was not until Charles Steedman, Captain of the armed transport *Bienville*, brought dispatches from Du Pont on November 13 that he learned what a brilliant success had been achieved six days earlier. The fleet had survived the dangerous storm off Hatteras with the loss of only twenty men and two fragile transports. After a few hours' bombardment, Du Pont's heavy vessels, moving in a circular formation within Port Royal harbor, drove the Confederates out of the forts, at the cost of only thirty-five casualties. It had been a Navy operation entirely. While the soldiers in the transports looked on, sailors hoisted the Stars and Stripes over Forts Walker and Beauregard. The magnificent harbor of Port Royal was securely in Union hands. No less important strategically, the Navy now commanded the inland waterways between Charleston and Savannah, strengthening the blockade immeasurably. But the public was more interested in the victory itself, the novel tactics employed, the fact that South Carolina, widely regarded as the sole cause of the war, had been successfully invaded.[21]

Stringham's and Du Pont's successes stilled for a brief time the clamor that was being raised against inefficiency and corruption in the administration's conduct of the war. The victories certainly helped Welles, who had been under steady attack in the metropolitan press from the beginning of his tenure. His physical appearance, his refusal to make himself available to the press, his reluctance to award contracts on a partisan basis or to staff the Navy Yards with ward politicians, all inspired criticism and undermined the public's confidence in him. Months before Port Royal, Welles was being labeled as a sleepy Father Neptune, Washington's Rip Van Winkle. The Northern public chuckled when clever publicists had him designing Noah's Arks, being substituted for a dying sailor's grandmother, being pictured as the old man of the sea astride "Sinbad" Lincoln's shoulders. When Cameron left the Cabinet in early 1862, it was confidently believed that Welles would soon follow him. Van Wyck's select committee, which had begun investigating all government purchases in July, had revealed shocking irregularities in Army procurement. Cameron's War Department was exposed as an incredible example of maladministration, a warren of intrigue, favoritism, graft, and waste. But the Navy Department had not been spared. Pages of testimony on naval contracts called into question certain procurement practices. It was revealed that Welles had dispensed with sealed competitive bidding for the purchase of merchant ships and that Morgan had profited immensely from his change in traditional policy. Cornelius S. Bushnell, the busy promoter of the *Monitor*, had profited largely through his personal relationship with the Secretary. The Committee had found no evidence of outright corruption, as it had in the War Department accounts, but Bushnell's practices had been far from ethical. As for Morgan, it was clear that he had made a small fortune and equally clear to anyone who studied the testimony carefully that the government, not the shipowners, had made it possible for him to do so.[22]

John P. Hale had been one of those careful readers. As Chairman of the Senate Committee on Naval Affairs, he had known about the Morgan agency from the beginning. He had had Morgan in mind when he offered a resolution of inquiry into Navy purchasing just after Vice President Hamlin called the special session to order on July 4, 1861.[23] Nothing came of the resolution because Hale did not push it. One of the laziest of the Senators, he was quite content to have the House select committee do his work. Hale's apparent inaction also worked to his advantage. Traditionally, the Senate committees were the spokesmen for the various departments, not their critics. Had Hale made an immediate and direct frontal assault on Welles, he would have risked the displeasure of his colleagues, even his post as chairman. But if a committee in the other house unearthed material that reflected on the administration of the Navy, he could never be accused of breaking an unwritten rule. In fact, it was incumbent upon his committee to assess the evidence, to recommend changes—which he interpreted as the resignation under fire of Gideon Welles.

Hale's tactics were sound, his sense of timing superb. His attack was launched at Welles' most vulnerable point—nepotism. He waited until the newspapers had thoroughly raked over the War Department disclosures before he had the Senate instruct his committee to investigate Navy contracts.

The newspaper campaign against Welles, which had never really ceased, picked up momentum after it was learned that Hale would investigate the Navy Department.[24] On January 11, 1862, the day Lincoln accepted Cameron's resignation, the Senate directed Welles to make a full report on the Morgan purchases. Anticipating its action, he had been shaping his defense for a month. He was ready with a complete report on all the Morgan transactions.

Welles staked his case on the emergency that had confronted the unprepared administration. No time could be lost, he asserted, in acquiring a fleet that could enforce the blockade. This meant large-scale purchases of privately owned vessels and their conversion to government service. Honesty and economy were both equally essential, Welles reminded the Senators. Naval officers were not only unfamiliar with commercial brokerage, but unable to supervise new construction and make purchases as well. Sealed bids, too, were not appropriate for the purchase of older vessels. Owners merely bid up the costs of merchant vessels which had to be purchased individually on the basis of particular need. The only way he could ensure speed of purchase, economy, and reliability, he explained, was to centralize all such ship purchases in the hands of a trusted individual. That trusted individual had been George D. Morgan, a successful businessman whom he had known intimately for over twenty-five years and whose ability and integrity he could personally guarantee. In no instance had Morgan charged sellers more than the customary rate for ship brokerage in New York—2.5 per cent of the purchase price.

Welles had put the strongest face he could on the matter. He concealed nothing, denied most emphatically that he had played favorites, argued that Morgan was as entitled as any ship broker to his commission. He presented proof that his agent had driven hard bargains, saving as much as twenty times the amount of his commission. He made a strongly worded, well-argued defense, which, however, could not conceal the fact that he had blundered.

Shrewdly, Hale refused to judge the worth of the transactions, but concentrated his attack on the commissions. Carried away by his own rhetoric, he accused Welles of corruption, and in a final outburst on the Senate floor, he implied that the entire administration was riddled with graft and waste. Hale's remarks made good newspaper copy. For several weeks editorials in the newspapers and cartoons in the illustrated weeklies pilloried Welles. Conscious that any retreat on his or Morgan's part would reflect upon his probity as well as his judgment, Welles refused to recognize that any wrong had been committed. Nor did he lack for defenders in influential quarters.[25]

Welles may have been reticent in his personal relations with the press, but he of all men knew the value of good publicity. He had not neglected this vital area of public communication. In New York City, the chartmakers G. and W. Blunt were valuable spokesmen for the department. When asked, John Ericsson would always take time out of his busy schedule to write eloquent public letters or to appear before interested groups defending the department and explaining its actions.

Mark Howard and James Dixon were especially diligent in having any favorable newspaper comment reprinted in the Boston and New York papers. Howard, a private citizen with extensive political connections, and Dixon, a Senator, lobbied for the Navy in Congress and among New England merchants. The exacting Senator James W. Grimes of Iowa, one of Hale's colleagues on the naval affairs committee, was a staunch ally as much out of his contempt for the self-important, indolent Hale as for his friendship with Fox. Donald McKay, the great clipper ship designer, and John Murray Forbes could be counted on for cogent pieces generally favorable to the Navy and its administration.

After Hale's attack, Welles' volunteer public relations men went into action. Forbes sent an open letter to George Ripley of the *Tribune* which was a remarkably effective defense of the Department's ship purchases. He admitted that Welles had erred in permitting Morgan such high commissions and "M[organ] deserves some scorching for not disgorging the surplus . . . , but still as a whole the thing which might have been better done was well done; to blame it too severely is to put a premium upon routine."[26]

The Department's defenders helped with favorable publicity, but the timely victory of Flag Officer Foote in capturing Fort Henry on February 6, 1862, helped more. News of this brilliant exploit, again an all-Navy affair, blunted Hale's onslaught. More important to Welles' continued tenure was the attitude of the President. Lincoln knew that the Navy Department was not the sleepy place the newspapers pictured it. From the onset of hostilities Welles, and then Welles and Fox in a team arrangement, had displayed remarkable energy and foresight. Dozens of warships were being built. Foote's ironclad fleet in the West had been constructed almost overnight, it seemed. Yards that had never built anything but flimsy, light-draft riverboats were fabricating heavy, if unhandy, gunboats, using house carpenters, plumbers, and blacksmiths in place of the traditional ship-building trades. Everything in their construction, except ordnance, was being manufactured in the West—marine engines strong enough to drive the unwieldy vessels against the Mississippi current, $2\frac{1}{2}$-inch ironplate for the casemates and machinery armor, iron paddlewheels, stacks, fittings. Three experimental but formidable ironclads were on the ways at Mystic, Connecticut, New York City, and Philadelphia. Lenthall's gunboats and double enders were being launched at the rate of eight a month. Three naval victories had been won so far, and two more naval operations had reached the advanced planning stage. The blockade was steadily becoming more effective.[27]

Welles had made a mistake in the Morgan affair, and he had showed poor judgment in his dealings with Bushnell, but for the time being Lincoln felt that his presence in the Cabinet was imperative. An uproar was rising in Congress and in the country over McClellan's inert posture, his daily communiques of "all quiet on the Potomac." The President could ill afford to admit further weaknesses in his administration. He could not, without seeming to compromise his leadership, bow to the will of John P. Hale and the commercial community of New York and Boston. Nor would he risk certain disruption in the Navy Department while it was planning a spectacular blow at the Confederacy—the capture of New Orleans. As Welles wrote his son Edgar, "the President & the Cabinet and most of Congress I believe, to be very firm and decided friends of mine." On February 14, 1862, a week after Hale's demand that Welles be censured, the Senate by a vote of 31 to 5 rejected his resolution.

While the Senate roll call was being taken, Flag Officer Andrew H. Foote was attacking Fort Donelson, a much heavier work than Fort Henry and just ten miles due east, on the Cumberland River. Goldsborough was preparing a joint assault with Burnside upon New Berne, North Carolina, and had two expeditions at sea ravaging the coastline and the sounds of that state. Du Pont was preparing to seal off Savannah. Newly appointed Flag Officer David Glasgow Farragut was at Key West, Florida. Within the week he would be at Ship Island, thirty miles off the Louisiana coast, the staging area for his attack upon New Orleans. An aggressive naval strategy was in operation not just along the 3500 mile coastline of the Confederacy, but also along the vast interior river system south of the Mason-Dixon line, an additional 3000 miles of watercourse to be blockaded and eventually, it was planned, to be cleared of the enemy.[28]

The department had embarked on a stupendous task whose range and scope would have overwhelmed lesser men than Welles and Fox. Yet now, in early 1862, with rapidly mounting responsibilities, and, it seemed, steadily mounting criticism from all quarters, they were more confident than ever before. Welles had proved to himself that he could withstand the unrelenting pressures of high office. With this assurance he had developed a measure of professional competence. But equally important to his state of mind was the emergence of a clearly defined mission, a strategic framework within which he could function effectively. Though he had not realized it fully at the time, he had been presented with the two basic imperatives for a naval strategy within two weeks of Sumter—the blockade proclamations and a plan of action for blockading the Mississippi. He had set to work at once implementing the coastal blockade. Operations on the Mississippi, however, were less familiar. Further, they were complicated by a matter of jurisdiction between the Army and Navy. Which service would build, man, and direct the river gunboats, or "floating batteries," as the Army men called them? And, ultimately, should river operations be defensive, as General Scott maintained, or should they be offensive?

The problem of naval strategy in the West solved itself. Initially, Welles had favored Eastern operations for a variety of reasons: the Army's claim of exclusive jurisdiction in the West, vested state and local interests, pressure for coastal blockade. Nevertheless, he sent two exceptionally able naval commanders West—first John Rodgers, then Andrew Hull Foote. They managed to build a fleet of wooden and ironclad gunboats with Army funds and man it largely with troops and river men whom they trained. Then they proved that their motley array of gunboats was indispensable to military movements. Foote, who succeeded Rodgers in December 1861, finally demonstrated that the river flotillas could be more effective if free of direct Army control. The joint Army and Navy successes at Forts Henry and Donelson, which had opened up river highways into the Confederacy, signalized a change from a purely defensive war in the West to an offensive war in which the Army and Navy would strike South and East, clearing the Mississippi and the Tennessee rivers and eventually taking New Orleans.[29]

Preoccupied by the immense problem of the Atlantic and Gulf blockade, Welles had been deaf to the constant pleas of Rodgers and Foote. He did authorize the shipment of naval ordnance, and he did permit an occasional draft of sailors and marines to be sent West. But he was more apt to reprove Rodgers for exceeding his authority in contracting for ships without first clearing with the Army than to help him meet his matériel needs out of naval supplies and appropriations. Foote fared better because he was more diplomatic, and because the department could spare more resources now that the war effort was speeding up. Welles and Fox had also managed, in August 1861, to have Congress authorize the permanent rank of Flag Officer—equivalent to Major-General in the Army—which cleared up much of the command confusion in the West. But Foote was still largely dependent upon the Army quartermaster corps for most of his needs. His forces were still at the beck of the Army theater commander. "Flag Officer Foote," said a Cairo, Illinois, newspaper, "has been laboring here under the most trying circumstances. It appears that neither the army nor navy will claim this service as a branch of theirs, so it stands alone in the centre reaping no assistance from either, except what has been fairly forced from the heads of the Departments."

Foote quite literally worked and fretted himself to death trying to direct his ambiguous command. A conscientious officer, he was as much a casualty of inter-service bickering as he was of the wounds he received at Fort Donelson and the diseases he contracted from the unhealthy river service. It was not until Foote had been relieved at his own request, with his fatal illness already upon him, that the department gained control over the river squadron. Even then, the Army clung to the ram fleet it had constructed and would not give it up until Welles convinced Lincoln, after a warm debate with the new Secretary of War, Edwin M. Stanton, that confusion, inefficiency, and additional expense would result from a divided command.[30]

All the efforts of John Rodgers and Foote, of McClellan, Frémont, and Halleck, had been aimed at first securing a line north of the Ohio River and then, through combined operations, moving south and east down the Mississippi, the Tennessee, and the Cumberland rivers. As early as August 2, 1861, McClellan had outlined his strategy in a memorandum he submitted at Lincoln's request. The President accepted McClellan's logic. But so did the Confederate government, which moved as quickly and vigorously as its scant resources would permit to block the offensive.

In the Navy Department, Welles and Fox were finding it increasingly difficult and wasteful in scarce men and ships to maintain even a loose blockade of the many entrances and passes through delta of the Mississippi. The escape of the Confederate raider *Sumter* from New Orleans in June served as a specific target for captious editors. A cacophony of press complaints greeted the news that three heavy blockaders were driven out of the delta by a makeshift force of light Confederate riverboats.[31] Although inured to the continuous attacks in the metropolitan press, Welles was worried about the Gulf blockade. The report that the Confederates were building several powerful ironclads in New Orleans added to his anxiety. This unpleasant news meant that a larger and stronger Gulf squadron would have to be concentrated in one area, leaving the screen woefully thin in others.

Fox had been considering the possibility of a naval attack on New Orleans ever since the successful capture of the Hatteras forts. He was familiar with the city and with the peculiarities of piloting vessels from the Gulf to the port. The steamers he had commanded in the merchant service had called at New Orleans on their way to Panama from New York. He also was familiar with Forts Jackson and St. Philip, which guarded the winding channel below the city—just familiar enough, in fact, to be ignorant of their real strength. Du Pont's success at Port Royal, coming as it did right after the fiasco in the Mississippi delta, crystallized Fox's musings about a naval attack on New Orleans. Now he was convinced that warships could pass the forts with relative impunity. If Du Pont and Stringham had succeeded in daylight, a night passage of the more formidable New Orleans forts would be accomplished with acceptable risk. Fox had always favored night actions, staking much on surprise, low visibility, and moving targets.

New Orleans was a special case, he pointed out to Welles. The forts were constructed on marshy ground, their guns so close to the water's edge when the Mississippi was in flood that the squadron's batteries would overlook them. Any barriers that the Confederates might use to obstruct the channel could not, he believed, last a week against the Mississippi's current. Once above the forts, the fleet would have New Orleans at its mercy and would cut all communication between the city and its defenses. Except for the two forts, all of the land defenses of the city had been positioned to guard against attack from the north. Even Jackson and St. Philip had not been strengthened as they should have been because the defenders of the city had discounted any attack from the south. What commander would be so reckless as to march an army through the swamps of the delta, considered impenetrable to any large military force that had heavy baggage trains, artillery parks, cavalry units?

A joint attack would leapfrog an army force over the swamps, cut off the defenders south of the city, and secure its position against any counterattack with the guns of the fleet. Fox admitted that the Confederate river flotilla was most to be feared, especially the powerful ironclads under construction. But this was all the more reason for haste. Once the ironclads were completed and ready for action, the opportunity wauld be lost. Fox's presentation was arresting. To Welles it seemed tactically good, the very boldness of the stroke intriguing. A naval capture of New Orleans would be a tremendous achievement that would deal a crippling blow to Confederate forces in the West. Nor was Welles indifferent to the personal acclaim he could expect from such a successful stroke. In the heady aftermath of Du Pont's victory, he was susceptible to the lure of another and infinitely more glamorous operation.

What had started as merely a quest for some means to strengthen the

Gulf blockade had, through a singular logic of events, ended as a proposal for a daring new strategy which, if successful, would alter the entire war effort in the West. Welles was a cautious, frugal administrator, but he was also a romantic; he invariably fell in with Fox's bold plans. All that was needed to clinch the proposition in his mind was fresher information than Fox, or Bache's Coast Survey, had on the delta, on the various ship channels, the river's depth at high and low water, the state of Confederate defenses, the power of the enemy's river fleet—in short, an expert opinion on the feasibility of the operation.

By accident or by design, Lieutenant David Dixon Porter happened to be in town after six months on blockade duty with the Gulf squadron. He had the intimate knowledge that Welles required. The only problem with Porter, and that a serious one, was whether he would give an objective appraisal. Welles had not forgotten how he had acted with Seward in bypassing the department's role in the Sumter expedition. He cherished a latent distrust of any officer who trifled, as Porter had done, with the chain of command. Fox dispelled all doubts about Porter's reliability, assuring Welles that he would give accurate, first-hand information free of personal bias.

Welles probably did not take too much convincing. He knew that Porter had a fine record, that he was a courageous, intelligent, if somewhat unorthodox officer, the only authentic naval hero to come out of the Mexican War. He also relied heavily on Fox's judgment, and Fox had nothing but praise for Porter, whom he had known for years. Black-bearded, commanding, articulate, Porter did not disappoint Fox. His answers to the questions about the delta and the approaches to New Orleans revealed an observant, inquiring mind. More than that, in appearance and deportment he projected that quality of nervous energy and imagination that Welles associated with dynamic leadership. Welles and Fox soon took him into their confidence and presented him with the plan for taking New Orleans by a naval attack. As Fox had anticipated, Porter instantly became a zealous convert, though he insisted that a mortar bombardment of the forts was an essential precondition for success. Obviously this would eliminate one of Fox's key factors—surprise. He vigorously disputed Porter's contention that mortars would make both forts untenable in forty-eight hours. Welles, however, decided that Porter should be allowed to make his case at the proper time.

On November 14, 1861, after their discussion with Porter, Welles and Fox hurried to the White House. They waited until Lincoln was alone, asked that the interview be private, and then outlined their plan. The President was astonished. He had always thought in terms of moving south down the Mississippi. His military advisers and the politically potent governors of the Western states had reinforced this strategic notion. But Fox's reasoning, which had convinced Welles, was equally attractive to Lincoln. In fact he was carried away with the idea and, as usual, wanted immediate action. Why not hold a meeting that very night at General McClellan's house? He had to be consulted anyway. If they met at the White House, as Welles suggested, there would surely be constant interruptions. Before leaving, Welles stressed the need for secrecy, citing the recent leaks that alerted the Southerners to the destination of the Du Pont expedition. Lincoln readily agreed. But, to Welles' chagrin, the President brought Seward to the conference that evening.

McClellan paid close attention to the proposal. His line of questioning, when the department rested its case, betrayed his skepticism, however. He thought that a force of 50,000 men with heavy seige equipment would be needed. The Army could not spare such a large force. When reminded that it was to be purely a naval operation, that only a small force of troops—say 10,000 men—were needed to occupy the city, McClellan agreed to cooperate. Porter then advanced his scheme for a mortar bombardment, which the General promptly and strongly endorsed. That settled the question. McClellan was not only General in Chief; he was considered the nation's leading expert on the use of heavy artillery. To Fox, the mortar decision came as a bitter disappointment. Construction, organization, and deployment of a mortar flotilla would delay his private timetable as much as four months— four precious months during which the Confederates would not be idle in strengthening the defenses of the city.

However passionately he felt he was right, Fox was not the kind of person to slacken his efforts because he had been overruled. The more the risk, the harder he would work to lessen it and the greater the resources he would throw into the contest. Porter was deputized to oversee the purchase and conversion of coastwise schooners for mortar vessels. Andrew A. Harwood, the Ordnance Chief, and his assistant, Henry A Wise, were directed to spare no expense in contracting for the earliest possible delivery of heavy mortars, mortar beds, and shells.[32]

Paradoxically, the selection of a commander was not the subject of intense investigation and evaluation. To be sure, Welles set Nelsonian standards as guidelines. But there was not an officer in the Navy whose record could meet these exalted tests. The most likely candidates— Du Pont, Goldsborough, and Wilkes—all had important assignments from which they could not be spared. If strict seniority were to be followed, the commander had to be drawn from the captains on the active list. Only one captain remained on the active list who was not disqualified by age or record—David Glasgow Farragut.[33] "He had a good but not conspicuous record," said Welles. "All who knew him gave him credit of being a good officer, of good sense and good habits. . . ." He might have added that Farragut was sixty years old—a year older than himself—that he had been passed over three times for squadron command, that he was nearsighted, but refused to wear spectacles. In all his fifty years of service, with over twenty years at sea, Farragut's greatest accomplishment had been the establishment of the Mare Island Navy Yard in San Francisco—scarcely the strongest recommendation for command of a complex and hazardous expedition. If he had no enemies in the service, he did not have any staunch advocates. Welles remembered Farragut from the days of the Mexican War.

Porter, whose father, the old Commodore, had raised Farragut as a foster son, thought him the best of his rank in the Navy. Upon Fox's recommendation, Welles decided that Porter should have the command of the mortar flotilla; thus, Porter's opinion carried weight. Both men seem to have overlooked the likelihood that Porter's special relationship with Farragut might have colored the testimony of one so ambitious. Others whom Welles consulted gave favorable reports. But Commodore Joseph Smith, the only one who thought Farragut bold, courageous and energetic, would not commit himself on whether he could handle a squadron. The fact that he was a Southerner, a native of Tennessee and resident of Virginia until she seceded, was a factor against him at the time. Later Welles and Fox would claim that in abandoning his home, his possessions, and his lifelong friends for an uncertain future in the North he had made a favorable impression on them. Such may have been the case, but Welles rarely permitted sentiment to influence what he knew to be political reality. Should the expedition fail, John P. Hale and men like him would be quick to exploit the anti-Southern feeling in the North if by doing so they could hurt Welles.[34]

What probably made Welles fall back on strict seniority was that Dahlgren was being urged for the command. At the conclusion of the conference at McClellan's house, the President had proposed a short river trip the following day to visit the converted gunboat *Pocahontas*. En route, Lincoln said to Welles, "I will make a captain of Dahlgren as soon as you say there is a place." And at a Cabinet meeting a day or so later Lincoln again urged the promotion. Knowing the President's

high regard for Dahlgren, Welles could not dismiss these recommendations lightly. Nor could he fail to connect them with the New Orleans
command. Dahlgren was perhaps the most ambitious officer in the
Navy. The timing was too close. If he were forced to take Dahlgren, a
junior commander who had not been to sea since the Mexican War,
Welles knew that the morale of the naval officer corps would be damaged severely. He may have had doubts about Farragut, but he was infinitely preferable to Dahlgren, and on paper at least he was far better
qualified.

Farragut's selection did raise questions within the small group that
knew of the New Orleans expedition. Lincoln, doubtless chagrined
that the Department had ignored his broad hints about Dahlgren's
fitness, made it plain that he had never heard of Farragut. Even Montgomery Blair, who had been brought into the selection process, questioned whether Farragut was the right man. While the matter was still
under consideration, Farragut met Blair and Fox for breakfast, where
he was presented with the department's plan. His unrestrained enthusiasm, his conviction that he could pass the forts and capture New Orleans with two-thirds of the vessels proposed, struck Blair as vaporous
posturing. But he deferred to Fox's unqualified approval of Farragut.
Seward was skeptical too. Would not Du Pont be a better choice?
Welles thought not, though neither he nor Fox was entirely satisfied
with their selection. Farragut, on assuming his command of the Gulf
squadron, did not dispel their fears when he began to bombard the department with requests for more ships, more men, more supplies, and
more equipment of all kinds.[35]

Farragut was in desperate need. He was particularly short of coal
and ordnance stores. He was also concerned about the state of the
blockade off the Louisiana, Mississippi, and Florida coasts. He needed
light draft vessels to work close in shore. But to Welles and Fox, thousands of miles away, Farragut's incessant demands seemed unrealistic.
They were concerned about his request for light draft vessels, assuming,
wrongly, that Farragut had altered the department's plan and would
not use his heavy vessels for the attack. As Welles explained departmental policy on an impending operation, "I never left it for the officers to decide whether they thought it best. Admiral Farragut did not
know that we intended to capture New Orleans and Forts Jackson and
St. Philip till the matter was decided upon and he was notified of his
appointment, told what was required of him to do."[36]

Thus, the worried Fox had some grounds for disregarding sound
practice in a military organization when he wrote Porter that "I trust

we have made no mistake in our man but his dispatches are very discouraging. It is not too late to rectify our mistake. You must frankly give me your views from Ship Island." Porter's reply could not have set Fox's mind at ease. He said that it was too late for a change, adding that "men of his age in a seafaring life are not fit for important enterprises, they lack the vigor of youth. . . . I have great hopes of the mortars if all else fails." This would be the pattern of Porter's private correspondence with the department even after New Orleans was taken. He would undercut Farragut and his captains, especially the sturdy, reliable H. H. Bell, in such a way that Welles and Fox never had clear grounds for a reshuffling of the command. Yet in every instance he covered himself should Farragut fail, while slyly advancing his own cause should he succeed.[37]

Though increasingly doubtful about Farragut and almost sick with worry about the expedition, Welles and Fox spared no effort to supply him with what he requested. They sent seventeen of the twenty-three new eleven-inch gunboats to augment Farragut's heavy frigates and sloops of war. Porter's mortar flotilla with armament, crews and escorts sailed into Ship Island a week after Farragut's arrival there. Only in supplying that precious commodity, coal, was the department dilatory, and this was beyond its control. Unrest in the coal fields had slowed down contractors' deliveries. Sufficient quantities of coal would not arrive in the Gulf until several days after Farragut had dragged the last of his heavy ships over the mud banks and into the deep water of South West Pass.[38] Well before that, General Benjamin F. Butler, commanding a force of 18,000 men, had arrived in a fleet of transports. Altogether, the squadron that assembled at the delta of the Mississippi dwarfed that of Du Pont's at Port Royal in tonnage of vessels and in the fire power of its 200 heavy guns.[39]

The sense of fatalism that had sustained Welles while awaiting the results of the Port Royal expedition failed him at this hour. In an agony of suspense, he awaited the verdict, his faith in Farragut severely shaken by Porter's insidious campaign and Farragut's own stream of complaints. He poured out his troubles to Captain Charles H. Davis, whom Du Pont had sent north with reports. "Oh, if you and Du Pont were only there I should have no fears about the result,—Du Pont and Foote and yourself enjoy our perfect confidence."[40] Welles could hardly believe his eyes when he read the first telegraphic dispatches from New Orleans in the Richmond papers. Farragut had not only passed the forts; in the process he had sunk most of the enemy fleet guarding the city. The Richmond *Examiner* and the Petersburg *Express* both gave relatively full reports on April 26, and they were reprinted in the *New-York Tribune*. On April 27 rumors were thick in Washington that New Orleans had fallen. Dahlgren hurried to the White House for confirmation. Lincoln said simply, "there's the dispatch, read it."[41]

Welles had to wait until May 8 before he received full details of the battle. It had been a night action, fought under the eerie light of a rising moon. The flashes of the heavy guns from the big ships and the answering fire from the forts and the Confederate navy's river fleet cut through the dense smoke, picking out the fire rafts and blazing cotton bales that the city's defenders sent downstream against Farragut's vessels. At one point in the confusing battle, a Confederate fire raft had collided with Farragut's flagship, the U.S.S. *Hartford*, instantly setting her aflame. But the sailors soon quenched the fire and the doughty admiral pushed on with the attack, his fleet pouring broadsides into the forts, engaging and sinking all but two vessels in the Confederate fleet at the loss of but one of his own. That morning, April 25, the Union fleet of twelve ships steamed slowly up the river, silenced the Chalmette battery near English Turn, just below the city, and anchored off the blazing wharfs and warehouses. After a brief parley, New Orleans surrendered to the Navy. Later, with Marines guarding the streets, squads of bluejackets, ignoring the curses and the menacing gestures of the hostile crowd, ran up the Stars and Stripes over the lofty Customs House, the City Hall, and the Mint. Forts Jackson and St. Philip had by this time surrendered to Porter. The Navy had carried off the entire operation, even accepting the surrender of a cavalry regiment. On May 1, 1862, Farragut presented New Orleans to General Butler and his occupying troops.

At first Farragut's grand accomplishment had been marred by an erroneous report from his courier, Captain Theodorus Bailey. No one in Washington knew where Farragut was. His frequent changes of mind as to whether he should attack the port of Mobile, Alabama, or proceed up the Mississippi to meet Foote and Halleck, were perplexing to Welles and Fox, though they themselves were in part responsible by not being more specific in their instructions. Welles had ordered Farragut to reduce the forts, capture New Orleans, and, taking advantage of the panic, push up the river and seize Mobile in addition. He had not included any order of priority beyond the capture of New Orleans. But he obviously meant that a quick thrust upstream was to take precedence over Mobile, and he thought he had made this clear to Farragut.[42] When Bailey was asked how many ships Farragut had sent up the river to meet Foote coming down, he replied, "none"—a true statement of the situation at the time he left, but not so when he made his report. Eventually the lapses in communication straightened themselves out. The President and the department finally realized that their near-sighted Flag Officer was a great fighting admiral, an authentic naval hero.

Eighteen months after these stirring events, Lincoln, brooding about Meade's failure to pursue Lee after Gettysburg, told Welles that "there had not been, take it all in all, so good an appointment in either branch of the service as Farragut. . . ." Compared to the selection of senior officers in the Army, the Navy had a far superior record in choosing the right men for the right job. "Perhaps," the President said, "naval training was more uniform and equal than the military."

"I thought not," said Welles, truthfully enough, "we had our troubles but they were less conspicuous."[43]

# CHAPTER 21

# Neptune and Mars

At a few minutes before eleven in the morning of January 1, 1863, Gideon Welles walked across Lafayette Square to the White House. In the East Room he found the President looking haggard but smiling broadly as each Cabinet member shook his hand and wished him a Happy New Year. The day was beautiful, "bright and brilliant," which would mean a larger crowd than usual for the customary afternoon receptions. Welles felt sorry for Lincoln and for his other Cabinet colleagues, who could expect an even greater crush than usual when the public came to pay its respects. He at least would be spared the ordeal. His youngest child, Hubert, a cheerful little boy of three, had died suddenly of diphtheria six weeks before. The crepe on his front door was a somber warning to the multitude that the Welleses were not receiving. At half past eleven, senior Army and Navy officers in full dress arrived at the East Room of the White House to pay their compliments. Welles introduced each naval officer to Lincoln, exchanged a final handshake, and left before noon. He returned directly home, where he remained the rest of the day, making no calls on friends or colleagues. Later in the afternoon, he read the Emancipation Proclamation in the *Evening Star*. As he scanned the legalistic phrases, he pondered the consequences of what he was certain would be "a landmark in history."

Everyone, he thought, must now be aware that the character of the nation was undergoing a radical change. "I am content," he mused, "to await the results of events, deep as they may plough their furrows in our once happy land."[1] He may have actually believed that he could await future events calmly, though there would be, as he phrased it, "tares and weeds" among the fruit. Yet not twenty-four hours before, one of his most cherished convictions had been violated when Lincoln signed the Act dividing Virginia, the "ancient commonwealth" of his youth, with all its memories of Washington and Jefferson and Madison. Forty of Virginia's western counties, Unionist in sentiment and securely in federal hands, would henceforth be the sovereign state of West Virginia. Lincoln had asked the Cabinet for written opinions on two points: "Is the act constitutional? Is the said act expedient?" Welles lined up with Blair and Bates in opposing the bill on both grounds. He refused to admit that a part of a state, "a fragment," as he called it, could represent the entire state within the meaning of the Constitution. Nor did he think it expedient to take such a drastic step during times of domestic turmoil. Virginia—loyal Virginia—was represented in Congress. Its Senators and Representatives, all but one of whom resided in its western counties, should continue to represent the entire state. The loyal government of Virginia, Welles admitted, was a provisional one, but in view of the war it was the best that could be framed to keep the federal system intact. "An observance of the rights of the states," he had written, "is conducive to the Union of the states." Lincoln thought otherwise, and in the same *Evening Star* that carried the Emancipation Proclamation Welles read that the dissenters, himself included, had lost the argument. He was not troubled enough, however, to make any specific comment about it in his diary. Emancipation claimed all of his attention, as well it might.[2]

He had joined his more radical colleague, Chase, in criticizing Lincoln's draft of the Proclamation, because it explicitly exempted areas formerly within the Confederate states but now under Union Army control. Believing as he did that the doctrine of states' rights was the organizing principle of the federal Union, he wanted no boundaries that were not the traditional boundaries of the states—no separation, either physical or emotional, that might subvert the loyalties of the citizens to the nation. He had opposed General Scott's "Anaconda" plan, that would rely on river and coastal blockade to strangle the Confederacy primarily on political grounds, because he thought it presupposed a territorial boundary between warring states.[3] In a similar vein he had vehemently opposed Lincoln's formal proclamation blockading the Southern ports, for by so doing, he declared, the United States was recognizing the Confederacy as a distinct nation. Neither Lincoln nor Seward nor, fortunately, the European powers held this extreme position, and even Welles himself realized that, technically, the Confederates had to be accorded belligerent rights. But he never changed his mind on the principle of states in the nation, nation in the states.

It was therefore quite in keeping with Welles' style of nationalism that he should see a danger to the integrity of the Union in those areas which Lincoln specifically exempted from the Emancipation Proclamation. Constitutionally, he could follow Lincoln's reasoning to a certain point. Emancipation was a justified war measure and, he thought, "safely within the President's war powers." Slave labor was important to the war-making potential of the Confederacy. As Commander in Chief, Lincoln had an obligation to weaken and eventually destroy that potential. Further, Welles agreed with the President that, since slaves were considered property within the Confederacy, and, indeed, within the Union too, it was perfectly legitimate to confiscate by emancipation enemy property that was being used against the United States. What he did not accept was Lincoln's perfectly logical argument that slaves in loyal states or in any area under control of Union arms could not be supporting the rebellion. The exemptions Welles felt were irrelevant and inconsistent. How incongruous that slavery should be protected where Union arms had prevailed and banned where they had not! Exemptions admitted boundaries where none should exist. He was looking ahead to a restoration of the Union and feared that this war measure, like the creation of West Virginia, would undermine the federal system. Freeing parts of states and not freeing others would bring about "a clashing between central and local authorities."[4] Had Lincoln accepted Welles' advice, the Proclamation might have avoided certain jurisdictional difficulties. That he did not shows an understandable preoccupation with conservative opinion, with Constitutional restraints, and with property rights in the Border slave states.

After all, the Army of the Potomac two weeks earlier had suffered bloody repulses at Fredericksburg. Only a few days earlier a senatorial cabal had tried unsuccessfully to dictate the membership of the President's Cabinet councilors. Public morale was at a low ebb, as Welles recognized. Yet this condition had been more or less chronic over the past two years. He remembered well the chorus of complaints about the conduct of the war during the fall of 1861.

In November of 1861 the Navy had won a brilliant victory at Port Royal, South Carolina, and had made substantial progress in blockading the Southern coastline after its capture of the Hatteras forts. But Welles recalled vividly the more or less constant attack he had endured from the mercantile community of Boston and of New York. He was prepared then, as he had been throughout his long career in politics, to expect the worst, to accept the fact that the President might be forced to ask for his resignation. Four months had passed since Bull Run. A nation that lacked a military tradition had bent every effort to recruit, equip, and train an army. It had staked its faith in General George B. McClellan, "the young Napoleon," who had speedily whipped the raw volunteers into a semblance of soldiers, the disordered regiments into the semblance of an army.

When, asked impatient politicians and newspaper editors, would the General make an attack with his splendid army? Had he deigned to make a reply, he would have said, emphatically, not until he was ready —which meant ready down "to the last gaitor button." Lincoln, deferring to McClellan's professional expertise, had not pushed him, had not even asked McClellan for his plans of operation. And that arrogant officer, made more arrogant by his sudden rise to fame and power, had not seen fit to communicate with the President, let alone with his bumbling Secretary of War, Simon Cameron. McClellan's inaction, a product jointly of his own limitations and of Lincoln's lack of firmness, seemed a national scandal to impatient Northerners. Much of their spleen was being vented on the hapless Cameron during the fall of 1861. If this were not damaging enough to Cameron personally, stories of maladministration, and of unparalleled corruption in war contracts, came from Washington and from General John C. Frémont's former command at St. Louis, Missouri. Businessmen, public men, and private citizens who visited the Secretary came away appalled at the lack of order in the War Department. The disgusted William Cullen Bryant, for instance, was expostulating that "Mr. Lincoln must know, I think, that Cameron is worse than nothing in the Cabinet."[5] His pockets bulging with notes to himself, his desks piled high with unsigned requisitions, Cameron seemed utterly bewildered by the enormity of his job, which next to the presidency had suddenly become the most important in the nation.[6]

Lincoln had been aware of Cameron's shortcomings since September 1861. Yet he waited, sharing the fears of thoughtful men that any hasty action might have serious political repercussions while at the same time bring a worse man than Cameron into the Cabinet.[7] By early December he decided he had to risk it. Cameron must go. In making up his mind the President was unquestionably influenced by William H. Seward. The meddlesome Secretary of State had been an original supporter of Cameron, and to Welles' disgust had been instrumental in having that Pennsylvania wire-puller appointed Secretary of War. But as the lines of force began to polarize within the Cabinet, Cameron had come to rely more on Salmon P. Chase than upon Seward. The responsibilities of his department threw him into a close working relationship with the nation's chief financial officer. Ideologically, too, Cameron found Chase's radical views on slavery more congenial than those of the conservative Seward. It was Cameron's stance upon this sensitive issue that finally moved Lincoln to take action.

Welles, of course, read the papers and listened to the gossip. Not a member of the inner circle, and under attack himself, he had until recently paid little attention to Cameron's administrative shortcomings. When the Secretary of War made an impassioned demand for arming fugitive slaves at a Cabinet meeting on November 15, Welles did mark Lincoln's obvious displeasure. He had taken no part in the discussions, nor had Montgomery Blair, whom he knew opposed Cameron's position. Seward, usually so garrulous, was silent also, though Welles thought he spoke through his "creature," Caleb Smith, the Secretary of the Interior, who took Cameron to task, as did Edward Bates. Had Welles been asked, he would have supported Cameron, because the Navy was actually doing what was merely claimed for the Army.[8] Almost a month before, Welles had written Mark Howard that "my own action has been much in the spirit of Frémont's proclamation. That is, I have returned no persons fleeing from Virginia unless they were secessionists, whatever was their condition or color." When Lincoln attacked Cameron, he was also attacking Welles, and not just his convictions but his actions.[9]

A prudent and loyal councilor would have modified then and there his instructions to the blockading squadrons. This Welles did not do, although Lincoln had made his position unmistakably clear. Nor did Welles change his policy even after Cameron restated his radical views in public at a boisterous party given by John W. Forney, formerly a close associate of ex-President Buchanan and the editor of the Philadelphia *Press* and the Washington *Sunday Morning Chronicle*. A power in Pennsylvania politics, Forney was one of those mercenary editors whom Welles despised. Among other traits that made him anathema to the frosty Connecticut Yankee, Forney was a notable toss-pot, as steady in his consumption of potables as he was unsteady in his politics. Now a conservative Republican, he had been rewarded for his rapid conversion by being made, at Lincoln's insistence, Secretary of the Senate.[10] Arriving in Washington several weeks before Congress convened, he had made his rooms at Mrs. Mill's large home near the Capitol a center for free liquor and freer talk. One evening, a few days after the explosive Cabinet meeting, Caleb Smith and Cameron delighted Forney and his guests, among whom were several newspaper-men, by staging a repeat performance of their debate in Cabinet over the arming of fugitive slaves. Both men had been drinking heavily, which added color and belligerence to their argument. The press, hun-gry for sensational items, further magnified the dispute and, with a casual disregard for the facts, portrayed a Cabinet rent with dissension.[11]

Welles read about the party, paying special attention to the con-servative editorials that condemned Cameron. He had just completed his own annual report, together with an abstract of it for the Presi-dent. Boldly, perhaps recklessly, he let both documents stand as writ-ten. He had instructed naval commanders to shelter any fugitive slaves who sought the protection of a naval vessel. "They should be cared for and employed in some useful manner," he said, "and might be en-listed to serve in our public vessels or in our navy yards, receiving wages for their labor."[12] Specifically, he authorized captains of block-ading vessels to sign them on as "boys" and to pay them the regular wages for such unrated men—ten dollars a month and one ration, the equivalent of a private's pay in the Army.

Moral as well as practical concerns had prompted Welles to take the stand he did. Like Cameron, he hated slavery and believed it to be one of the major causes of the war. As a public officer, he would not be a conscious agent in returning fugitives, though he knew he would not be where he was if he had taken such a stand when he was being con-sidered for the Cabinet. Of course, there had been no armed rebellion then, and at that time he could—and did—say in all good faith that it was the undoubted legal responsibility of any federal official to ex-ecute the Fugitive Slave Law. But Welles had a ready reason for non-compliance now, a reason which he carefully inserted in his instruc-tions to naval commanders. Fugitives who voluntarily sought refuge from insurgent masters were not fugitive slaves within the meaning of the law. Their masters, in rebelling against the lawful authority of the nation, had forfeited, as individuals, the equal protection of its laws. Obviously, the Fugitive Slave Law, an act of the United States, did not apply to those who rejected the sovereignty of the United States.

An equally compelling reason in Welles' mind was that slaves were being used for the aid and comfort of the enemy. Through their forced labor, they were furthering the Confederate war effort. Welles and Cameron were in complete agreement on this point, and so were the more radical members of Congress, those who had opposed the Con-fiscation Act of August 6, 1861, as a half-hearted measure, because it applied only to slaves employed directly in aid of the rebellion. Most radicals felt the Act tended to keep the Southern blacks at home, where their labor helped feed the Confederate Army.[13] Besides, the Navy needed men. The Navy did not enjoy the state and federal bounties which went to Army volunteers, and squadrons were badly under-manned. Fugitive blacks could perform many tasks on shipboard that were being performed by whites. As that inciteful naval officer, Percival Drayton, himself a South Carolinian born and bred, wrote, "for the present we have nothing to do better than to weaken their masters and strengthen ourselves by holding on to all we can lay our hands on and for this, I for one have no scruples in doing, obeying as I am the most positive directions of the Secretary of the Navy."[14]

After sending his abstract to the White House, Welles read a copy of Cameron's report, studying carefully the portion that dealt with fugitive slaves. Cast in speculative terms, the pertinent paragraphs seemed rather tactless intrusions on a sensitive political issue. Yet Cameron only claimed that it might "become the duty of the government" to aid slaves, should the exigencies of war demand it. It was hardly an inflammatory statement—it was far less radical than Frémont's unilateral emancipation proclamation in Missouri, which Lincoln had recently disavowed. Welles decided that his colleague had either been blowing off steam when he made his informal pronouncements or was fishing for radical support without committing himself officially.

Welles' own remarks on the subject were much more explicit, and when he received word from the White House that Lincoln wanted his entire report, he must have suspected that he too would be disciplined. The Cabinet was to meet several days hence to hear the President read his message. Assuming that his comments had displeased Lincoln, Welles prepared himself for Cameron's role of devil's advocate. He would defend his report against his chief and against his closest associates in the Cabinet, Montgomery Blair and Edward Bates. However distasteful, indeed, almost physically sickening, he found the prospect, he braced himself for the ordeal, believing himself right—morally, logically, and legally.

It was a tense Secretary of the Navy who took his usual place on the sofa in the Cabinet room on Friday morning, November 29. When all were seated, Lincoln remarked that his own report was still unfinished, and then stated flatly that the War Department's policy on fugitive slaves was contrary to administration policy. All references to this subject must be stricken before the report was made public. Though Lincoln's peremptory demand may have nettled Cameron, it did not perturb him. If his comments on fugitive slaves had ventured on forbidden ground, which he denied, what of the Secretary of the Navy's report? Cameron insisted that Welles' position on that question was just as objectionable.

This was the moment that Welles dreaded most. Surely Lincoln would agree that his report had taken similar ground on fugitive slaves, and just as surely the President would require him to edit his report. Should he be overruled, as now seemed inevitable, Welles was prepared to defend his actions even to the point of resignation. But, strangely enough, Lincoln brushed off Cameron's allusion to the Navy, insisting that only the Army must conform. When Cameron told him that copies of his report were already in the hands of postmasters all over the country, the angry President directed Montgomery Blair to get in touch with them and have the reports returned. Blair did his best, and he tied up all the telegraph lines of the country for the next twenty-four hours. But some postmasters never got his message, so some of the unofficial versions got into the hands of the editors, who gleefully published them without official sanction.

Welles could only conclude that the President was using Cameron's statement as a pretext to force his resignation from the Cabinet, an aspect of the power struggle between Chase and Seward, and one where the Secretary of State had prevailed. He was but partly right. In his haste to impute sinister motives to his more influential colleagues, he overlooked Cameron's proven incompetence, and, for once, he neglected to apprise Lincoln's actions as those of an eminently practical politician.[15]

The Army was a physical presence in the Border states; the Navy was not. Lincoln could not risk alienating conservative opinion in such states as Kentucky, Missouri, and Maryland, where slavery was legal and where Confederate armies were close by, waiting for an opportunity to strike. Nor would he aggravate a substantial and rapidly growing radical opinion on slavery in the free states. By letting Welles' report stand uncorrected he was signifying that his policy on fugitive slaves was a flexible one. The time had not yet come for the enlistment of black soldiers, but it had arrived for utilizing black sailors. The fact that the Navy was smaller and less conspicuous than the Army, that it occupied no territory, and that it was organized on national and not state lines made it an ideal means for the administration to present a radical face to the public. In another way too, the President was saying that the Seward-Weed influence had not gained the upper hand, that there was still a balance between radicals and conservatives in the Cabinet. The public still thought of Welles as a Chase man, a general impression not lost on the President. Welles' few lines on fugitive slaves were meant to show the radicals of the North that Lincoln had not abandoned them.[16]

Unintentionally, Welles had made himself a significant factor in hastening Cameron's departure from the Cabinet. After the Cabinet meeting on November 29, there had been no doubt in his mind that Cameron would resign soon, an opinion he shared with Montgomery Blair. But who would succeed him? Blair talked of Benjamin Wade, the rough, outspoken Senator from Ohio who had been taking McClellan to task before a newly formed Committee on the Conduct of the War. Welles paid Blair the compliment of nominating him, citing his military training, his political insight, and his eminence in the legal profession as prime requisites for coping successfully with the burdens of the war office. Lincoln did not seek Welles' advice, though he did at one time favor Blair for the post. Whether William H. Seward was consulted or did the consulting is not known and is of no particular moment. What is known is that he and Chase were responsible for persuading a rather reluctant President to nominate Edwin M. Stanton, the former Attorney General, who was a Democrat, a prominent Washington lawyer, and a caustic critic of the administration's war effort.

Seward's and Stanton's relationship went back a year or more, to a time when it appeared to many that the Buchanan administration would have collapsed had it not been sustained by three new Cabinet officers—Attorney General Stanton; Joseph Holt, the Secretary of War; and John A. Dix, the Secretary of the Treasury. It had not been for statesmanlike qualities that Seward found Stanton invaluable at the time; it was for the confidential information the Attorney General was supplying him about administration policy. This role of go-between, while scarcely honorable to his chief, can be justified in the light of the crisis. Seward, at any rate, wasted precious little time in assessing Stanton's character or his motives. The information he received almost on a day-to-day basis he deemed of importance to his own personal aspirations. He might not have considered either Stanton or the information so impressive had he known that Senators Charles Sumner and Salmon P. Chase were also receiving confidential reports from the same source.[17]

As it was, both Chase and Seward thought the information exclusive, and neither was a man to forget services rendered; nor would they disregard Stanton's professions of friendship and personal loyalty.[18] That Bates and Blair disliked Stanton probably had some bearing on Chase's and Seward's urging his nomination; that he was a Democrat, not simply a man of Democratic antecedents, probably counted more with

Chase because his party credentials would carry weight with Lincoln, who always sought balance in his administration. All in all, he seemed an ideal choice, and he was available, a most compelling reason. Chase and Seward had to work quickly or the President might appoint Montgomery Blair, who was not only fiercely independent and as fond of intrigue as they, but a bitter political opponent. They were not about to let Blair prejudice their influence with the President.

The appointment of Stanton surprised Welles, who saw only the imprint of Seward's workmanship. He did not know Stanton personally, but from what he had heard about him he had formed a bad impression of his character. He deplored Stanton's contemptuous remarks about Lincoln and his biting comments about administration shortcomings, which went the rounds of Washington, and he was disgusted at his obsequious courting of General McClellan. Welles also remembered the occasion, months before, when Montgomery Blair impeached Stanton's integrity before the entire Cabinet. Blair may have been in error, but Stanton had been a Cabinet officer in the Buchanan administration, which Welles regarded as the most corrupt the nation had ever endured.[19]

Despite his many doubts about Stanton, he greeted his new colleague cordially when Lincoln introduced them at the regular Cabinet meeting on January 20.[20] The warmth was not reciprocated. Correct rather than cordial, Stanton bowed deeply with "very formal courtesy," a studied pose not lost on Welles. The Navy Department had been under fierce attack from Congress since early December. Stanton believed Welles' tenure was drawing to a close. Disappointed contractors and shipowners were thronging the lobbies of Congress, bent on forcing a complete overhaul of key personnel in the Navy Department. The vindictive John P. Hale, one of Stanton's intimates and Chairman of the Senate Committee on Naval Affairs, was investigating the Norfolk Navy Yard disaster and the Morgan purchases in New York. Northern newspapers, mirroring the mood of some Congressmen, were demanding a change, charging that Welles lacked force and decision. Even his colleague Edward Bates thought him a marked man.[21] To such a sensitive person as Welles, Stanton's manner at once aroused deep feelings of personal hostility.

It was easy to dislike Stanton. He could be rude and overbearing. He did not suffer fools or bores gladly, but he could be charming and courtly, and he could be embarrassingly deferential if it served his purposes. Energetic, forceful, personally honest, a prodigious worker and a master of detail, Stanton was supremely confident of his own ability to cope with any problem. Was he not one of the most successful law-yers in the land, whose fees were averaging $50,000 a year? Had not his tenure in the Buchanan Cabinet, however brief, proved that he could manage affairs of state as easily as he could dominate a courtroom? Stanton's physical appearance, curiously enough, projected his charac-ter, even the devious streak, which Welles soon detected. He had a broad, mobile face and a long, flowing beard. Short and compact of build, he walked rapidly with a slight limp from an old accident. If he were engaged in conversation, he gestured vigorously to make his points, and when he began to talk he would brook no interruptions, not even from the President himself. Nearsighted, he habitually wore spectacles that gave him an owlish appearance but at the same time lent a piercing quality to his large, bright grey eyes. There was no denying that he had a commanding presence. Power and energy seemed to flow from this humorless, irrascible, dextrous, yet curiously sinister individual.

Welles, though incensed at Stanton's demeanor when they first met, did attribute it correctly to the campaign that was being waged against himself in Congress and in the press. Stanton was not only well aware of this, but had been deep in the councils of Welles' enemies, both in-side Congress and out. He had come to the Cabinet as much preju-diced against Welles as Welles was against him.

More important than any personal bias was the fact that Stanton did not know Lincoln's attitude toward the current administration of the Navy. Whatever Chase or Seward or any of his other informants may have told him, Stanton would take no chances until he had satisfied himself that there would be a change.[22] He felt peculiarly vulnerable without a distinct political following. Over a period of twenty years or more he had been a dabbler rather than a professional in politics, de-voting himself in the main to his law practice.[23] As a Cabinet officer, he felt this deficiency keenly and, characteristically, was already taking steps to rectify it.

Stanton had been close to Cameron, had in fact drafted those para-graphs on fugitive slaves that Lincoln found so objectionable.[24] And thanks to the care and consummate tact with which Seward and Chase handled his appointment, Cameron continued on a friendly basis with Stanton. Stanton had, in addition, attached himself to McClellan, who looked to him for advice on political affairs as well as on matters of state in which the General was directly concerned. He was careful to maintain his cordial relationship with Seward and Chase in the ad-ministration and with powerful members of Congress like Charles

Sumner and Benjamin Wade, even though they were Republicans and he a Democrat. He had watched carefully the organization and the growing influence of the Committee on the Conduct of the War (John Hay's Jacobin Club) under its chairman, Benjamin Wade.[25]

During the fortnight preceding Stanton's appointment, the committee had met with Lincoln twice. On both occasions various members had been outspokenly critical of his leadership. At the second meeting, which Lincoln called himself, Welles was present, along with the rest of the Cabinet. Wade acted as spokesman, badgering President and Cabinet on the administration of the war effort. McClellan, who had been stricken with typhoid fever on December 20, was still confined to his bed. Under Wade's relentless probing Lincoln finally admitted that his knowledge of McClellan's plans was vague and partial at best. The committee, quite rightly, took this faltering explanation to mean that there had been little or no specific communication between the President and his General in Chief. It had been holding hearings for a month. On the basis of the testimony and evidence compiled, a majority of the committee believed that McClellan was incompetent, perhaps disloyal. Of course Wade and his colleagues had political axes to grind. They had handled the hearings in such a way that McClellan would be exposed as an inept commander, while Lincoln himself might be compelled to accept committee direction in the conduct of the war. The committee was not at this early date seeking to make the Executive subservient; in its impatience at the lack of any significant progress, it was reflecting the mercurial temperament of the Northern public, its lack of confidence in Lincoln and his advisers, its deep-seated suspicion of the professional military men. The politics of frustration were motivating committee members, who were anything but modest about publicizing their belief that Lincoln should be made responsible.

Despite the fulminations of the Committee on the Conduct of the War, McClellan retained Lincoln's confidence. When Chase reported to Stanton that the President was holding strategy sessions with some of McClellan's subordinate commanders, he dashed off a note to the General, warning him that he was about to be superseded—a reasonable inference, but one completely devoid of truth. No member of the administration, least of all the President, had the slightest intention of dismissing McClellan. Smarting under Wade's inquisition, and deeply concerned about the low state of Northern morale and Union finances, Lincoln did want closer communication with the military commanders. And he had resolved one thing: that the nation demanded a spring campaign. With the Committee on the Conduct of the War pressing him, he could no longer defer to the superior military genius, as he thought, of his General in Chief.[26]

Had McClellan been more reflective, he would have realized that Lincoln would surely not penalize him for being sick. Heeding Stanton's warning, he unexpectedly appeared at the fourth planning session, on January 13. Under the impression that he was the victim of a conspiracy, the headstrong General made the worst possible impression. He refused to divulge his plans and he tactlessly snubbed Secretary Chase, who had staunchly defended him just a week before, when he was being denounced by Wade. Chase was not a forgiving man. McClellan had made yet another enemy who would use all the power of his office, all of his political skill and influence, against him.

Although Stanton was kept informed of these developments, he continued to keep friends in all camps. Possibly he hoped to mediate between McClellan and his enemies, because he visited the General on the evening of January 14, just after Lincoln had offered him the post of Secretary of War. What did McClellan think? Should he accept the post? You must accept, was the prompt reply! And accept he did, after sounding two or three close friends—all Democrats—the following day. With assurances from Seward, from Chase, and from Senator William P. Fessenden of Maine, a leading moderate Republican, that he was loyal, confirmation was a matter of course.[27]

Stanton's first day in office was a busy one. In the morning he took the oath of office, then he visited McClellan, with whom he remained closeted until he had to leave for the regular Friday Cabinet meeting, where he first met Welles and was chillingly formal. That evening he spent several hours with the Committee on the Conduct of the War. His confidence in McClellan, already shaken by Chase, must have been further weakened when he heard the unrestrained comments of committee members, who had become "morbidly sensitive . . . practically incapable of doing General McClellan justice." After listening to the allegations, Stanton concurred fully with the committee, apparently jettisoning on the spot the assurances so recently given McClellan of his friendship and his complete support. "We were delighted with him [Stanton]," said Congressman George W. Julian, speaking for the committee, "and had perfect confidence in his integrity, sagacity and strong will."[28] There would be many more secret meetings with Stanton, who had found one of the sources of power in the slack, fragmented politics of wartime Washington.

With no state organization behind him, no personal following that was beholden to him for past favors, Stanton had few alternatives. A prominent Democrat, he had somehow to rid himself of the Buchanan incubus, yet hold onto his party associates until he solidified his position. And he saw immediately, as Welles observed, that he must put a curb on McClellan's vast powers as Commander of all the armies. Chase had already spoken to him about reorganizing the Army of the Potomac into corps and had advised that McClellan be relieved of over-all command.[29]

But it was not just the radicals in Congress or Secretary Chase who determined Stanton's course; it was also the character of the relationship between himself and McClellan. Each was forming the wrong impression of the other. "McClellan had expected a cordial supporter in Stanton as secretary," said Welles, "and Stanton had supposed he would have an earnest and efficient friend and officer in McClellan. . . ." If Stanton could bend McClellan to his will, he could not only silence but command the Committee on the Conduct of the War. The General thought differently, and he retained the confidence of Lincoln. To be sure, it was a vexed, distracted, harried Lincoln who clung to McClellan, yet a Lincoln who refused to risk a change in command. Precipitous action, such as Wade was demanding and Stanton insinuating, could well result in another Bull Run, this time with no McClellan to gather up the remnants and restore order. The Army, none too stable at best, might dissolve or degenerate into warring factions of ambitious generals. Stanton had no alternative but to put up with McClellan's arrogance (which soon became manifest) and accept the role of a subordinate, the role of a Cameron or a Scott—a bitter draught for a proud, self-confident man.

The President did respond to pressure from Welles and Stanton that something be done about lifting the blockade of the Potomac. Unable to budge McClellan or to learn more about his plans, and unwilling to remove him, the President issued on January 27, 1862, his General War order No. 1. On February 22, Washington's Birthday, there was to be a concerted invasion of the Confederacy by all of the armed forces.[30] Lincoln's order, mainly for political consumption, was also meant to force out of McClellan a plan of operations, which it accomplished. The plan, however, was not the simple, direct, overland attack Lincoln envisaged, but a highly complex maneuver that would transport the Army of the Potomac by water to a point opposite Richmond or, depending upon the reaction of the enemy, to Fort Monroe, at the tip of a peninsula bounded by the York River and the James. Richmond, the prize of the expedition, lay on the James, about 75 miles northwest of Fort Monroe. McClellan's plan would leave Washington with only a thin screen of troops and would involve the creation of a new system of supply by water. Lincoln and Stanton were frankly skeptical, but they bowed to McClellan, who was backed up by a majority of his commanders.

Typically, the Navy Department, whose mission would be of crucial importance in any operation that depended upon waterways for supply and support, was not consulted during the early stages of planning. Stanton could be just as arrogant as McClellan. Though he had been War Secretary for only two months, he had already consigned Welles and the Navy to a lowly place in his personal hierarchy.[31] The Navy might just as well have been on another planet. Stanton spent most of his time at the War Department, seldom visiting the White House, and then usually for brief whispered conversations with Lincoln or Seward, with whom he was clearly on intimate terms. Welles carefully concealed his personal dislike of Stanton, his jealousy of Stanton's influence with Lincoln, his bitterness at being excluded from high-level discussions. But he retaliated in his own way. He, too, would keep his own council. He would communicate with the War Department only by letter, being as coldly formal with Stanton as Stanton was with him. Naval affairs and even those operations that were of immediate concern to the Army Welles took up directly with Lincoln. Ever wary, discreet, and tactful, Welles put his years of experience in the jungle politics of the old Democracy behind every approach to the President. As a courtier, he stood second only to Seward, but his style was entirely different. Where Seward was an outgoing, genial man, whose company Lincoln found enjoyable, Welles was soft-spoken and shy—a man of few jokes, but a good listener who was so courteous that he never gave offense, however heated the temper of discussion. Lincoln found his company interesting rather than relaxing. He was quick to recognize that Welles generally gave good counsel, whatever the issue, that above all, he was trustworthy and completely loyal.

Where Welles was deficient in the easy camaderie that Lincoln prized, he more than made up for his failings by having two capable practitioners of the art at court—Assistant Secretary Gustavus Vasa Fox and John A. Dahlgren, Commandant of the Washington Navy Yard. In the ever-shifting game of internal diplomacy, these two men were experts by taste and by training. Both were particular favorites of the President, and both were dedicated Navy men. Lincoln's friendship for the vigorous, capable Fox went back to pre-Sumter days, when he had impressed the President with his willingness to face the heavy batteries of Charleston Harbor with his little makeshift force of longboats and tugs. Fox, like Seward, was always full of the plans, the stories, and the political gossip that Lincoln relished. Responding to his attractive personality, the President would confide closely held secrets, which were promptly relayed on to Welles. Dahlgren, more somber than Fox, was Lincoln's ideal of what an officer should be. Urbane, dependable, polished, he impressed Lincoln as a real genius. And though the mechanically minded President overrated Dahlgren's technical accomplishments, there was no denying that he was one of the nation's leading authorities on ordnance. Assuming, naïvely, that a professional officer so gifted in matters of technology would be equally well versed in matters of strategy, Lincoln also gave Dahlgren important information about Army planning which got back to Welles. The interests of the Navy were well protected at the White House through the rather specialized personal qualities of these extraordinary men.[32]

As long as Stanton maintained his aloof, condescending attitude, Welles saw to it that relations between the two departments remained on a routine level. Indeed, so secretive was he that he called Fox on the carpet when he learned that his ebullient assistant had told Stanton of the New Orleans expedition, which the Navy had been organizing for four months. Stanton was instantly captivated by the notion of a joint attack on the South's largest city and greatest port. Though Welles had been irritated by Fox's indiscretion—if it could be called that—Stanton became a powerful moving force in helping him clear many obstacles. Later Welles would admit as much when he said that Stanton's cooperation was "the more acceptable because General McClellan, who had known our object and was acting with us by express direction of President Lincoln, appeared indifferent."[33]

Stanton's reaction when he learned of the expedition may have been "gushing," as Fox remembered it, but he made no effort to improve his relations with Welles. Then on Sunday, March 9, 1862, Stanton made Welles feel that he was personally responsible for a naval setback that he exaggerated out of all proportion. The incident, which brought the secretaries into open antagonism, fortunately had a beneficial result, but it would be some months before anything like normal relations were restored between them. In Welles' eyes, Stanton's behavior was so bizarre, his conduct so reprehensible, that he found it very difficult for a time even to be civil in his presence. Years later, those two days—March 9 and 10, 1862—were still painfully and deeply etched upon his memory.[34]

# CHAPTER 22

# Confusion of Purposes

EARLY SUNDAY MORNING, March 9, 1862, Welles received a terse message from the White House stating that the Confederate ironclad ram, *Merrimack*, had steamed out of Norfolk and was destroying the Federal fleet at Hampton Roads. The *Cumberland* had already been sunk; the *Congress*, a burned-out wreck, had struck her flag; the *Minnesota* was stranded and badly damaged. Lincoln wanted Welles at once. Stunned—not at the news of the *Merrimack*, because he had been expecting her appearance for some weeks, but at the destruction she had wreaked—Welles wondered why he had received no word from Navy men on the scene, among whom were his Assistant Secretary, Gustavus Fox, and his new ordnance chief, Henry A. Wise. But as he prepared to obey the President's summons, he remembered Joseph B. Smith was Commanding Officer of the *Cumberland*. Smith's father, Commodore Joseph Smith, Chief of the Bureau of Yards and Docks, would be attending services at Saint John's next door. However grave the crisis, Smith should know of it. Welles went into the church and whispered the information to the Commodore. The old man listened carefully and said, "Then Joe is dead"—an accurate conclusion.[1]

Deeply affected, Welles left the church and hurried over to the White House, where he found Stanton with Lincoln. Other members of the Cabinet began arriving soon after. Everyone was visibly excited and apprehensive except Welles, who, feeling the responsibility keenly, was determined to set an example of calmness. Stanton seemed almost manic as he paced up and down the President's office. Lincoln himself was shaken by the fragmentary reports he had received because the telegraph line to Fort Monroe, never especially reliable, had chosen this moment to break down. Five brief telegrams and a highly colored report from one of the *New-York Tribune*'s correspondents were all the information anyone had. Welles' composure was reassuring to the distracted President. But he insisted on a professional opinion from Dahlgren. He would go himself.

Sweeping up Senator Orville H. Browning, who had just arrived to pay a social call, Lincoln drove off to the Navy Yard. At 10:30 A.M. the marine orderly at the Commandant's office announced that the President was at the door. Dahlgren went out to greet him and was asked to accompany Lincoln and Browning to the White House. "Poor gentleman," thought Dahlgren as he entered the carriage, "how thin and wasted he is." As the carriage sped north on Seventh Street, Lincoln said, "I have frightful news," and he related what he knew of the *Merrimack*'s rampage at Hampton Roads. He did not rule out the possibility of the *Merrimack* appearing before Washington and shelling the city. Dahlgren was not reassuring—"such a thing might be prevented," he said. "If the *Merrimack* entered the river, it must be blockaded . . . all which could be done at the present."[2]

When they arrived at the White House, Browning left and Dahlgren followed the President into his office. Quartermaster General Montgomery Meigs, Assistant Secretary of War Peter Watson, and General McClellan had arrived in the meantime. Meigs was silent, despondent; McClellan was worrying out loud about the safety of his troops at Newport News. But the main center of attention as Lincoln and Dahlgren appeared was a heated dialogue between a frantic Stanton and an icy Welles. With his eyes fixed on Welles, Stanton pictured the *Merrimack* sinking every vessel in the Union fleet, capturing Fort Monroe, coming up the Potomac and bombarding Washington, then steaming north along the seaboard to New York and Boston, bent on its mission of destruction. What did the Navy propose to do about it? Welles replied tartly that the *Merrimack* "could not come to Washington and go to New York at the same time." He would welcome her appearance in the Potomac, because the Navy would then have the means to bottle her up and destroy her. As for McClellan's troops, the *Merrimack* drew so much water that she could not come within miles of their encampment at Newport News.

Welles then alluded to Ericsson's ironclad, the *Monitor,* which he knew was in Hampton Roads. He was confident she would prove more than a match for the *Merrimack,* adding that she would have been there sooner and prevented the disaster, had her contractors met their stipulated deadlines. What is her armament, asked Stanton abruptly?

Two guns, answered Welles. Stanton was incredulous: Bitingly he asked if the Navy's only defense was a single, untested craft with only two guns. Lincoln and the others, who were listening intently, became more alarmed while Stanton cross-examined Welles as if he were a hostile witness, utilizing the bluster, the irony, the sneering harshness that made him famous as a trial lawyer. Unassisted by naval experts save Dahlgren, whose advice was that they should block up the Potomac, Welles stood his ground, maintaining his composure under the most extreme provocation.

As he recalled those anxious moments with all eyes upon him, he found Stanton's manner "unexpressibly ludicrous . . . the wild frantic talk, action and rage . . . as he ran from room to room—sat down and jumped up after writing a few words—swung his arms, scolded and raved." Refusing to be intimidated or confused, Welles gave a report on the *Merrimack:* her speed, her lack of maneuverability, the great depth of water she drew. His information was reassuring to everyone but Stanton, who seemed obsessed with the image of the great ironclad monster belching black smoke as she headed for the Washington Navy Yard. After Welles left the meeting, Lincoln decided that the Potomac had better be blocked. He directed Dahlgren, McClellan, and Meigs to undertake the job. Under Stanton's authority Dahlgren was ordered to requisition canal boats, load them with stone, and sink them in the shallow reaches of the Potomac some miles below Washington.

It was nearly two in the afternoon before Dahlgren reached the Navy Yard to begin preparations for this assignment. Meanwhile, Welles and Stanton carried on intermittent exchanges at the White House and at the War Department, where the military telegraph was now set up. Finally, at 6:45 p.m., with communications restored to Fort Monroe, Fox sent Welles the first account of the battle between the two ironclads. He had left for Hampton Roads the day before when reliable information had been received that the *Merrimack* was ready to come out of Norfolk. The *Monitor,* on which Welles pinned all his hopes, had sailed from the Brooklyn Navy Yard on March 6, and word that she was at Fort Monroe had been received just before the telegraph had gone out of commission.

With no information for almost eight hours, Welles' anxiety became almost unbearable. Fox telegraphed that there had been a four-hour engagement between the two ironclads that morning. He gave few details, but enough to convince Welles that the *Monitor* had proven her worth. While the *Merrimack* was still formidable, she had been driven back to Norfolk. Both vessels, said Fox, fought "part of the time touching each other, the *Monitor* is uninjured." Stanton was not present when this information came through. He and Seward were in a tug on the Potomac returning to Washington after Dahlgren had shown them where the *Merrimack* could be most effectively blocked. In the course of the trip, Stanton gave Dahlgren blanket authority, under the President's verbal orders, to close up the channel. Working at top speed, the ordnance expert was able to inform Lincoln by 9 p.m. that he had collected enough canal boats and was loading them with stone. About the same time the ever-wary Dahlgren telegraphed the same information to Welles and asked if he was acting in conformity with department policy. He received an emphatic negative.

After what he had witnessed during the day, Dahlgren decided he had better obey his service chief. Loading operations were suspended until he had a clear line of authority. The next morning he hurried over to the Navy Department, where he found that Welles had not changed his mind. Accompanied by Dahlgren and by Meigs, who still thought the river should be blocked, Welles went directly to the White House. There he found, as he had the day before, a very angry Stanton, though, he was happy to note, a more relaxed Lincoln. His voice trembling with emotion, Stanton asked Welles if he had ordered work on the canal boats stopped. "I replied," said Welles, "that I had given no orders to prepare and load any boats nor did I intend to." Rudely, Stanton interrupted to say that he had directed the work be done and that he had done so with the full approval of the President to whom he turned for verification. Lincoln agreed that Stanton was correct. He had seen no harm in the project. Dahlgren, Meigs, and Stanton had thought it necessary for the security of the city. He had bowed to their collective opinion. After Stanton's tirades of yesterday, Welles was in no mood to surrender without a protest. Now he had proof that the *Merrimack* was not a threat, and could afford a more positive stance for what he thought was right. The passages with Stanton "were sharp and pungent," as Welles remembered them. "I stated," he said, "that I was very sorry to hear it—that for five or six months we had labored with General McClellan . . . to get this important avenue open to unrestricted navigation and that the Rebels having left we were now to shut ourselves off." Since Lincoln directed it, Welles would do his duty and with a last reproachful look at Stanton, he left the room.

The loading of the canal boats was completed at War Department expense—Welles had stipulated this—but Lincoln, impressed by Welles' comment that the administration would be blockading Washington just when the *Merrimack* seemed to be checked, ordered that the sinking not take place. Some weeks later, when the President was cruising down the Potomac, he was asked about the canal boats that lined the shore at Kettlebottom Shoals—"Oh," said Lincoln playfully, "that is Mr. Stanton's navy. That is, the fleet concerning which he and Mr. Welles became so excited in my room. Welles was incensed and opposed to the scheme, and it seems Neptune was right. Stanton's navy is as useless as the paps of a man to a sucking child. There may be some show to amuse the child, but they are good for nothing for service."[3]

Shortly after the *Merrimack* excitement, Welles had another opportunity to rap both Stanton's and McClellan's knuckles. He took full advantage of it. Stanton had sent Welles a dispatch from McClellan. The Army wanted certain ships detached from the blockading squadrons and sent to Fort Monroe, where they would presumably act under Army direction. Neither McClellan nor Stanton in his note of transmittal mentioned why the ships were wanted. The Peninsular Campaign was about to begin, as Welles knew directly from the President and from information that Fox and Dahlgren had picked up in casual conversations with Army men, including General McClellan himself. The Navy, however, had never been consulted at any level of planning, nor had it ever been advised officially about the details of the operation or even what its mission, if any, might be. The Army command had simply consigned the Navy to a supporting role. It would be told at the proper time what it was expected to do, nothing more.

Stanton's note and McClellan's dispatch seemed a heaven-sent opportunity to put the Navy in the picture and at the same time reprimand the management of the Army. After his recent troubles with both McClellan and Stanton, Welles could not resist the fling. Feigning complete ignorance of the Peninsular operation, he courteously but firmly refused to weaken the blockade by detaching the ships requested unless, as he remarked innocently, Norfolk was to be the objective. In that case the Navy would cooperate to the fullest limits of its power. The overburdened Stanton, strained almost to the breaking point as he labored to meet McClellan's incessant demands, was infuriated by Welles' reply. He read it to the President, no doubt emphasizing its uncooperative tone and probably questioning Welles' fitness for his position. Lincoln was annoyed. He himself had told Welles about the operation and had supposed that the Army and Navy had been working together closely. Now, on the eve of a vast new joint expedition, another open clash between his two service secretaries seemed imminent. Was Welles endangering national security simply to make what the President, blissfully ignorant of interservice rivalries, must have considered a minor point? Everyone knew that McClellan was extremely secretive about his plans.

Anticipating just such a reaction, Welles brought up the subject with Lincoln at the first opportunity. Alluding to McClellan's notorious slowness in perfecting his plans, he pointed out that it would be a great blunder to tie up a major portion of the blockading fleet at Fort Monroe waiting for the Army to move. When McClellan was ready, Welles assured the President, the Navy would be ready with gunboats on the James and the York to guard the flanks of the Army and to lend close, inshore support. Lincoln soon forgot the matter, but not Stanton, who would long remember the rebuff and how cleverly it had been accomplished. He would never again question Welles' talent for administrative infighting. At a later date, both Lincoln and Stanton, said Welles, "gave me credit for an earlier insight and understanding of McClellan's *true* character than they [had] possessed."

Yet the War Department continued to ignore the Navy even after Henry W. Halleck had been brought from the West to become General in Chief, leaving McClellan in command of only the Army of the Potomac. Halleck, paunchy and middle-aged, with a fringe of scraggly white beard that encircled his smooth-shaven, round face, looked anything but a military man. Indeed, what reputation he enjoyed before the war was not as a professional officer, but as a scholar of military science. He had published his *Elements of Military Art and Science,* a volume that enjoyed considerable reputation as a manual of strategy in the United States and abroad, in 1846. His multi-volume translation of Jomini's *Life of Napoleon* followed, enhancing his reputation. And just before the war, he published a second edition of his *Elements,* updating them to include the lessons of the Mexican and the Crimean Wars. Although fifty-seven years old when Welles first met him, he had long since earned the sobriquet of "Old Brains."

Halleck had replaced Frémont as chief commander in the West, and he soon restored order in that chaotic department. Chiefly through the campaigns of his subordinates Grant, John Pope, and Don Carlos Buell, Halleck had gained an undeserved military reputation to go along with his proven organizational skills. Stanton, Chase, and Lincoln, who had brought him to Washington, must not have really understood the situation in Tennessee, or they would never have chosen him as General in Chief. No more cautious, not to say timid, field commander ever lived. McClellan's labored operations seem almost Napoleonic when compared with Halleck's one-mile-a-day advance on the Confederate stronghold of Corinth, Tennessee. The testy Flag Officer

Andrew H. Foote, who had captured Fort Henry and fought well with
Pope at Island Number Ten, thought Halleck "was a military imbecile, though he might make a good clerk."[4] Probably influenced by
Foote's candid remarks, Welles was not quite the objective observer he
thought he was. "The Army has no head," he exclaimed in a moment
of exasperation with Halleck's indecisiveness, and on another occasion
he found Halleck's mind "heavy and irresolute."

Meanwhile McClellan had inched his large army up the Peninsula.
He had almost reached the outskirts of Richmond when the Confederates struck back and, in a series of heavy battles, defeated him, forcing him to abandon his campaign. Welles knew only by rumor and by
newspaper gossip that the army was evacuating the Peninsula. His first
official word came from Commodore Charles Wilkes, who was commanding the cooperating naval forces on the James. In a long telegram
Wilkes explained that, since the Army had left, he needed further instructions. The nettled Welles called on Halleck, only to discover that
the General in Chief had forgotten that there was a naval squadron
cooperating with McClellan, but now that Welles reminded him of the
fact, he thought there would be no further need for the Navy. Welles
raised two questions: could not the flotilla of Navy gunboats on station
close to Richmond support a small army detachment with little or no
risk? Would not such a joint force menace the city and force General
Robert E. Lee, the Confederate Commander, to divert a part of his
army for the defense of Richmond? Halleck "rubbed his elbow first,
as if that were the seat of his thought," said Welles, "and then his
eyes." Perhaps the Navy ought to remain a little longer, but there
could be no army detachment. All troops had been ordered to evacuate the Peninsula.[5]

Welles had been at odds with Army management almost from the
beginning of the war. While his more radical colleague, Chase, and his
more conservative colleague, Montgomery Blair, were still praising
young General McClellan in November 1861, Welles was chastising
him in his quiet way for not assisting the Navy in raising the Potomac
blockade. Before the President and the Cabinet, Welles had spelled out
in detail a sorry sequence of "broken promises and frivolous and unsatisfactory answers" to his insistent requests for Army support. Openly
and candidly he told the group around the Cabinet table that he had
stopped communicating with McClellan, as it was to no avail. Welles'
remarks went completely unheeded, even by Chase, with whom he had
had a private conversation in December of 1861, then expressing as
forcibly as he could how disappointed he was in McClellan, how deep

his misgivings that the man would ever measure up to his responsibilities.[6] But Welles resigned himself to higher authority, and when McClellan finally completed the massive and intricate movement of his troops to the Peninsula, he had a powerful squadron of gunboats, under Charles Wilkes, ready to lend its support.

He still remained critical of McClellan's generalship and just as critical of the armchair strategists in Washington, whom he felt more often than not were thinking as much of their political reputations as McClellan was of his military prestige. Stanton and Chase were now unsparing in their denunciation of McClellan. Of course, Welles did not have the benefit of day-to-day communication with the General. If he had, he might not have been so critical of his colleagues. As it was, he believed that Stanton and Chase were engaged in a politically inspired personal duel with McClellan.[7] Skeptical of their motives and more than a little skeptical of their tactics, he feared that, if they succeeded, they might well injure Army morale and thus endanger the Union cause. Knowing what he did about Stanton's almost pathological hatred of McClellan, Welles wondered about the panic in the War Department after Stonewall Jackson's foray in the Shenandoah Valley. Unwilling to accept the notion that Washington was in danger, he disapproved of Lincoln's order recalling McDowell's corps from McClellan. But no one asked his advice. Nor was he privy to the telegraph campaign of Lincoln, Stanton, and Chase as they tried to bag Jackson by coordinating three Union armies in the valley.[8]

Yet Welles' stature had increased perceptibly with Stanton and with Chase. Even his personal, if not his political and official, relations with Seward had improved, as each had taken more accurately the other's measure. And during the calamitous last week of August 1862 he alone of the Cabinet (Seward was absent) seems to have kept his head, possibly saving the government from collapse at a most critical juncture, certainly rescuing his colleagues from grave embarrassment. McClellan had withdrawn his army from the Peninsula and was slowly reinforcing General John Pope from his new base at Alexandria, Virginia. Pope, with his new Army of Virginia, had been caught by Lee and Jackson at Manassas, on the old Bull Run battlefield. For two days, during which the hard-pressed and blundering Pope called repeatedly upon McClellan for supplies and men, the Confederates broke up his Army of Virginia and drove its disorganized remnants back upon the defenses of Washington. Ugly comments immediately began to circulate in the panic-stricken capital that McClellan had purposefully withheld support from Pope, that his one corps commander to reach the battlefield in time—Fritz-John Porter—had given only token attention to Pope's orders. McClellan had made no bones about his contempt for Pope. Though he had not actively sought Pope's defeat, as was freely charged at the time, he had done precious little to stave it off. And his childish rejoinder to Lincoln, suggesting that Pope get out of his own scrape, laid him open to the charge that he placed his sense of injured pride above his duty to the nation.

Welles had been so occupied in disbanding the James River flotilla and in concentrating a naval force in the Potomac to assist Pope's army that he had not kept as close touch as he might have with the military situation. He was aware, however, of the increasing tension between McClellan and the War Department. Late in the afternoon of Saturday, August 30, Welles had an unexpected visitor—Secretary of the Treasury Chase. He gave Welles a paper in Stanton's bold, slanted script that accused McClellan of grave crimes against the security of the Union. The charges, which were unsupported, held him unfit for command and demanded his immediate dismissal.[9] The document, addressed to the President, bore Stanton's and Chase's signatures. Smith had seen it and would sign, said Chase, but Welles came next in order of seniority. His signature should precede Smith's. Chase's excited manner and the import of the document took Welles aback, but his native prudence did not desert him. He had "long been averse to McClellan," he told Chase, but he was not prepared to make a judgment on his military fitness. He deplored McClellan's arrogance, his insubordination, his sluggishness as an army commander. He would be quite ready to express such an opinion to the President if he were asked.

Chase wanted stronger measures. "The Cabinet must act with energy and promptitude," he said, "for either the government or McClellan must go down."

Have "the Attorney-General and Postmaster-General . . . seen the paper or been consulted?" asked Welles.

"Not yet," replied Chase.

Welles enjoyed a cordial relationship with Chase. He was loath to jeopardize it, but there was something about the procedure which he disliked, something in it of an importunate nature. What would be the impact of such a paper upon the President, if most of the Cabinet made such a formal demand? Was it not an ultimatum to force the President's hand? What of Seward; where did he stand? There were too many imponderables. Welles refused to sign, though he hastened to assert that he was for McClellan's removal and would declare himself "at the proper time and place and in what I considered the right way."

At that moment Blair appeared. Chase, who had retrieved the paper, made it plain to Welles that they should drop the subject for the time being. Blair remained only for a short time. As soon as he left, Welles asked Chase if he should not be called back for consultation. "No, not now," said Chase emphatically, "it is best he should know nothing of it." Welles thought differently, arguing that Blair had a military background and would give, he thought, sound advice. Chase disagreed. Before he left he specifically asked that nothing be said to Blair. Chase's formal request confirmed Welles in his decision to bide his time. He suspected that McClellan was not the only one to be purged, that Blair was being attacked also—an intolerable and unwarranted interference, he felt, with the President's prerogative.

In the evening he went to the War Department for news. There he found Stanton uneasy about the situation at Manassas but with undiminished confidence in Pope and unrestrained fury at McClellan.[10] Although he was alone in his office, Stanton lowered his voice as if he were imparting confidential information. "He understood from Chase," Welles recorded, "that I declined to sign the protest which he had drawn up." Stanton wanted to know where Welles stood on the matter. There were ample grounds, said Welles, for McClellan's dismissal, but any written manifesto from the Cabinet "was discourteous and disrespectful to the President." Stanton, quick to anger, immediately retorted that he was under no obligation to Lincoln, who had saddled him with burdens no man should be called upon to bear. Welles listened patiently while his colleague raged on, agreeing with him in the main and asserting, as he had before, that he would vote for McClellan's dismissal in Cabinet council.

Welles went to bed that night believing that Pope had won a victory despite the calculated obstruction of McClellan and many of his generals. On Sunday morning, August 31, he awoke to the news that Pope's army had fallen back on Centreville, an almost certain portent of defeat. When the Army began seizing churches and private dwellings for conversion to hospitals, panic became widespread among the public. The despondent Halleck told Welles that he feared for the safety of the city, that the War Department had underestimated enemy strength. Though he was a good deal more disturbed than he would admit, Welles was not yet ready to accept the notion that the capital was in danger. Loose talk of military dictatorships, which was rife at the time,

Welles dismissed as the fantasy of weak minds, or the stratagems of the cunningly ambitious. "We need better generals," he said bravely, "but can have no better army."

He would not have been so confident if he had been as close to the situation as Halleck, Stanton, and Lincoln were. The organization of Pope's army had broken down completely. On Monday, September 1, over 20,000 undisciplined, battle-shocked stragglers were on the road between Centreville and Washington. If Lee were able to strike as heavy a blow again, he would have an excellent chance of capturing most of Pope's army. The armies of Virginia and of the Potomac were both demoralized. Desertion was rife, and more than half of both forces were missing or unaccounted for.[11] When Lincoln gave him the facts a week later, Welles was appalled. "Where there is such rottenness, is there not reason to fear for the country?" he asked himself.

On September 1, he had refused for a second time to sign an anti-McClellan circular. Stubborn loyalty to the President and distrust of his colleagues' motives prompted his stand. As before, Chase was the emissary, but the document he bore was much briefer, less harsh in tone, and, to Welles' amazement, had been drafted by Edward Bates, who had signed it, as had Stanton, Chase, and Smith. Welles, who was particular about such things, must have noted that the signatures were not in order of precedence. Stanton's was first, followed by those of Chase and Smith. Bates' was last, and there was a space and room enough for Welles and Blair to sign above Bates' name. Seward was still out of town and not expected for some days. Welles thought this draft an improvement over the previous one, but he would not sign it. He would join no movement against the President. Chase denied vehemently that there was any Cabinet combination against Lincoln or that the paper showed disrespect for the Executive office. He did, however, admit, as Welles had originally suspected, that it threatened the breakup of the administration if McClellan were not relieved of his command. Dismissing Welles' renewed suggestion of a Cabinet conference with the President, Chase angrily said that it would accomplish nothing, it would be "like throwing water on a duck's back . . . the course was unusual, but the case was unusual."[12]

Welles would not budge. As the chagrined Chase prepared to leave, he said that he had not consulted Blair and would not consult him until he had spoken with the others. Now Welles was sure that he had penetrated the scheme. Stanton and Chase would, as he put it, "get their associates committed *seriatim* . . . by a skillful *ex parte* movement without general conversation." He may have seen deviousness where none existed, but considering the past political behavior and the present ambitions of both men, it was a logical inference.[13] And in fact Stanton's catalogue of woes had already captured old Edward Bates, a well-seasoned lawyer who should have known better. "Indignation," wrote Bates in Stantonian language to Francis Lieber, "is a fine moral tonic & sustains me wonderfully . . . against a criminal tendency, a fatuous apathy, a captious, bickering rivalry among our commanders. . . . They, in grotesque egotism, have so much reputation to take care of, that they dare not risk it."[14]

Welles shared these sentiments, but, unlike Bates, he recognized that in the crisis Lincoln had to have a free hand. He had to lead the way, and the Cabinet had to sustain him. On the very next day the wisdom of his refusal to sign the anti-McClellan document became strikingly clear. At the regular Cabinet meeting even Stanton and Chase had to admit that Pope had mismanaged his army, yet all present felt that he had not been supported adequately by McClellan and several of his corps commanders. While the discussion was going on, the President was called out for a moment. No sooner had Lincoln left the room than Stanton said that McClellan had taken command of the Washington defenses. Everyone was astonished—even Montgomery Blair, who had been a steadfast supporter of the General. Chase and Stanton dominated the conversation, denouncing the decision in unmeasured terms. Lincoln, returning, heard at least a part of these heated remarks. Immediately he accepted full responsibility for the decision, adding, however, that General Halleck concurred with him. Pope and McDowell, for whatever reason, had discredited themselves with the Army. McClellan, he believed, still retained its confidence. He knew the ground. He was a good engineer, a good organizer who would gather up the stragglers and restore discipline. And, Lincoln pointed out, he would perform creditably on the defensive, a proven ability which just now was imperative. That McClellan had "the slows," that he "did not have the dynamic, aggressive qualities of a great commander," he acknowledged, but no other general officer could be trusted with the security of the Army and of Washington. The members of the Cabinet, including Welles, did not conceal their anguish and gloom from Lincoln. "Earnestly and emphatically," Chase "stated his conviction that it [McClellan's appointment] would prove a national calamity."[15] Lincoln, gravely distressed at the Cabinet's almost unanimous denunciation of his decision, still made it evident that he would not rescind it. Firmly, he addressed himself to Stanton and Chase, whom he regarded —and rightly so—as indispensable, politically and administratively.

Both men were prepared to resign, as Lincoln no doubt sensed, but after a long discussion he managed to gain from them a grudging acceptance of his move.

When Welles wrote of that tense meeting, over ten years later, his admiration for Lincoln's courage stood out in bold relief. "Every person present," recalled Welles with pardonable exaggeration, "felt that he was truly the chief, and every one knew his decision, though mildly expressed, was as fixed and unalterable as if given out with the imperious command and determined will of Andrew Jackson."[16]

For the next several days, while McClellan brought order out of chaos, Welles pondered the implications of the Chase-Stanton move and his own role in derailing it. Skillfully using what firm evidence he had, he analyzed the Pope and Halleck appointments, the retention of McClellan, the political motivations surrounding these events. All this, of course, he did in private, jotting it down in his diary late at night when, alone with his thoughts, he could cast the villains and the dupes in the tragedy without jeopardy to himself or to the cause. Yet an innate sense of fairness and perspective forced him to soften the indictment of Chase and Stanton, for in many respects he was as opposed to McClellan as anyone else. He found it painful in the extreme that the fate of the country should rest in the hands of such an inept commander. Not that he was a traitor, as Chase so freely charged, not that he was the ringleader in a plot to overthrow the government and set up a military dictatorship, as Senator Henry Wilson and Secretary Caleb Smith had both reported on good authority, but because he was not a commander, because he let the strength of his army "wilt away in lame delays and criminal inaction" and, since his return from the Peninsula had done nothing to ease an undoubted crisis in the military situation.[17]

The more Welles thought about Lincoln's decision, the more he thought it was the only one that could have been made. And as Lee invaded Maryland, he was certain that he had been right in withholding his signature from the proposed Cabinet manifesto. Surely with Lee rampaging in Maryland, no responsible Executive would dare to entrust a disaffected army to a new, untried commander. As he suspected, Chase was far too intelligent, far too resilient, to let a temporary setback in his political fortunes permanently cloud his judgment. The very next morning, in fact, he grudgingly conceded that "it might have been hazardous at this juncture to have dismissed him." "I assured him," said Welles, "I had seen no moment yet when I regretted my decision and my opinion of McClellan had undergone no change."[18]

Welles and his son Edgar, out for their evening walk the night before, had by chance met General McClellan and his staff clattering up Pennsylvania Avenue near H Street. Recognizing Welles, McClellan reigned in his horse, dismounted, shook hands with both men and said goodbye, in an unusual display of graciousness. Welles asked where he was going.

North, McClellan replied, to take charge in Maryland.

"Well onward General is now the word," said Welles—"the Country will expect you to go forward."

"That," he said, "is my object."

"Success to you General with all my heart."

Welles was never more sincere, and, knowing that McClellan would be on the defensive, he agreed with Lincoln that he would perform adequately.[19]

But more was needed than the checking of Lee's invasion. Even if the Confederate army could not be smashed, some sort of victory must be gained to strengthen the Union cause at home and abroad. Welles knew that Lincoln had decided on a momentous change in policy—the emancipation of the slaves—and was merely waiting for a favorable turn in the fortunes of the Union. He had known this for over two months when, on a Sunday morning in mid-July, the presidential carriage, bearing Lincoln, Seward, and Seward's daughter-in-law, rolled up to his door. Welles and his youngest son, Tom, were about to leave for the Navy Department, but when Lincoln said they were en route to the funeral of Stanton's infant son and invited him to accompany them, he immediately changed his plans. "It was a duty . . . and I could not refuse."[20] No sooner had the carriage started than an earnest Lincoln broached the subject of emancipation, to the surprise of both Seward and Welles. He had given it much thought, he said, and he admitted that it was a delicate subject involving grave political, social, and moral issues. "We must free the slaves," Lincoln remarked emphatically, "or be ourselves subdued."[21] What did they think? Seward played it safe, stalling for time. He was inclined to agree with the President, that emancipation was both "expedient and necessary," yet it was a grave question, fraught with many difficulties. He would have to consider it further before he could give an intelligent opinion. Welles replied in much the same vein. Two or three times during the trip to Stanton's summer residence, which lay several miles beyond Georgetown, Lincoln returned to the subject, and, just before dropping off his passengers after their return to Washington, he asked them to give it their most mature deliberation.

Pondering the events of the day at home that afternoon, Welles first concluded that the President was embarking on an entirely new course. He was about to make a move which would profoundly change the direction of the war, the lives of the people North and South, the future development of the nation. Welles did not doubt that emancipation would prove the most crucial decision of Lincoln's presidency, much more significant than his reinstatement of McClellan to top command in the east against a majority opinion of the Cabinet, the party, and the public. As he turned over in his mind the events of the day, he wondered why he, of all the Cabinet members, should have been selected for the initial discussion of policy at the summit. It was quite in order that Lincoln should ask Seward. But why should he be paired with Seward; why not Chase or Blair or Stanton? Welles had noticed that Blair and Smith were the only Cabinet members who did not attend the funeral. What did this mean? As he wrote his wife after his return, "I scarcely know what to make of it."[22]

During the weeks that followed, however, he began to understand why he had been brought in at the beginning. For many months Stanton had been exerting indirect pressure to emancipate all fugitive blacks and to enlist blacks as soldiers. He had permitted, if not encouraged, General David Hunter, who was commanding Union forces along the coasts of South Carolina and Georgia, to organize black regiments. Lincoln had overruled Hunter, but not before embarrassing questions had been asked by congressional conservatives—questions which Stanton dodged.[23] Lincoln was well aware of the fact that Stanton and Chase were most intimate with those radicals in Congress who were demanding emancipation. He knew where both men stood. It is reasonable to infer that he consulted Welles and Seward first because both were spokesmen for moderate opinion; neither man was as conservative as Blair, Smith, and Bates, nor as radical as Chase and Stanton. Emboldened by what he took to be their affirmative replies, Lincoln went ahead, and, during the next two weeks he drafted what he called an "order" that would free the slaves in rebellious states.[24]

On July 22 Lincoln presented his draft for a preliminary emancipation proclamation to the Cabinet. Much had happened during the nine days since he had discussed emancipation with Welles and Seward. The military situation had taken a turn for the worse in the West, where Confederate General Braxton Bragg, based in Chattanooga, seemed poised to invade Kentucky. Congress had just passed the Second Confiscation Act, declaring slaves captured from rebellious owners to be free and authorizing the President to employ them in any capacity. Of equal importance to the immediate issue of emancipation, Seward had given it his mature deliberation and had decided that the times were not propitious. Thurlow Weed, who had been let in on the secret, was waiting in Washington, ready to lend his formidable powers of persuasion against emancipation.

Welles presumably had discussed the proclamation with the President, though nowhere does he mention it. And presumably he had offered no objections. For well over a year black fugitives from rebellious masters had been serving in the Navy. As recently as May 1862, Welles, in an official circular to Flag Officers, had urged them to enlist fugitive Negroes, particularly to man ships' boats.[25] If the Confederacy was using slave labor to sustain its war effort, why should not the Union employ the labor of fugitives? Enlistment of fugitives in the Navy had to be voluntary, of course, but it was actively encouraged by the department and the administration. Though cautious, and aware of the political and social pitfalls in any premature emancipation, Welles would have been an insensitive executive if he had not desired the freedom of loyal blacks who wore the uniform. If they were declared free, then all those held to bondage in the rebellious states ought to be free also—on the ground of military necessity, if no other.

Lincoln's draft proclamation of July 22 was far more sweeping than any Cabinet member had anticipated. They had assumed he would clarify the Second Confiscation Act and its implications for the rebellious states. They had assumed, further, that he would propose a gradual, compensated emancipation, and that he might even favor enlisting the Negroes in the Army for combat duty. All of these subjects had been discussed at a Cabinet meeting the day before. What did surprise them was a separate order, proclaiming emancipation of all slaves in the Confederacy which was to take effect on January 1, 1863.

Even Stanton, who urged the immediate promulgation of this order, was startled at its scope. "The measure goes beyond anything I have recommended," he jotted down hastily on a piece of note paper. Attorney General Bates, whose inveterate conservatism sometimes took unusual turns, was the only Cabinet member who supported Stanton. Welles remained silent. Chase favored arming the Negroes, but he thought emancipation could be accomplished more efficiently, more quietly, and more safely by delegating it to the various theater commanders. Seward surprised everyone by vehemently opposing the issuance of any proclamation at that time. Stanton recorded Seward's argument in his memorandum of the meeting. "Seward," he wrote, "argues that foreign nations will intervene to prevent the abolition of

slavery for the sake of cotton—argues in a long speech against its immediate promulgation—wants to wait for troops. Wants Halleck here.
Wants drum & fife & public spirit. We break up our relations with foreign nations and the production of cotton for sixty years." Seward's
alarming remarks and Chase's timidity prompted Lincoln to say that
he would postpone the proclamation. But apparently he was still undecided, because Thurlow Weed visited him that night for one of his
confidential chats. Weed thought that emancipation by Executive fiat
would stir up hatred and bring about "serious disaffection in the
border states; that it could work no good and probably would do us
much harm." Though his politics had been Whig, Lincoln was anything but Whiggish where the Constitution was concerned. Unless
driven by harsh necessity, he was as tender as any Jacksonian Democrat
to the reserved rights of states. Welles drew a faithful picture when he
characterized him as "always cautious and habitually but inquiringly
reticent on controversial and unsettled questions."[26] Lincoln filed his
draft in one of the pigeonholes of his lofty desk—to wait, as Weed had
urged, the logic of events.

Seward and Weed were right, despite the storm of criticism heaped
upon the President's head by the radicals in Congress and out. Exactly
one month later, with the beaten McClellan withdrawing from the
Peninsula, Horace Greeley, in a rasping editorial, berated Lincoln for
not freeing the slaves of rebel masters. In his eloquent reply Lincoln
re-emphasized that the war was being fought to save the Union, not
to free the slaves. There followed an avalanche of conservative and
moderate opinion in the North, burying, for the time being, Greeley
and other critics. Pope's disaster at Bull Run, which took place within
a week of the Greeley-Lincoln exchange, again justified his course. But
the pressure for emancipation was increasing.[27] The military gain was
obvious. Relations with Britain and France, despite Seward's fears
about cotton, would improve if the nation were fighting for freedom
as well as Union. There was a better than even chance that emancipation would, in time, raise Northern morale. Many Democrats, of
course, would see that it would close all doors to compromise, that the
South would never willingly give up slavery. Citizens of the Border
states, specifically exempted from emancipation, would nevertheless
wonder how they could maintain slavery when a Union victory abolished it everywhere else. Lee's invasion of Maryland, or at least the
part of Maryland that was staunchly Union, provided a series of crucial alternatives. If Lee were not thrown back, if the theater of war
were shifted to the North, the Lincoln administration might have to

agree to Southern independence. If he were crushed and forced to surrender, the Confederacy might collapse and the war end as abruptly as it began. If he were thrown back and the North were secured militarily, then Lincoln could risk emancipation in the rebellious states as a justifiable war measure.

Ever since the abortive meeting of July 22, Welles had known that Lincoln was waiting for an opportunity to issue his order. And he knew from his own experience as a service chief how much the order would weaken the enemy. He was much relieved when McClellan reported victory at Antietam, Maryland, after fourteen hours of savage fighting. Like Lincoln, however, he deplored McClellan's not following up his gain and letting Lee escape into Virginia. Yet the Union was safe; a victory of sorts had been gained. Would Lincoln use it to issue his long-deferred order on emancipation? He had not long to wait for the answer. On the morning of September 22, a State Department messenger appeared in his office with a note from Seward, requesting his presence at a special Cabinet meeting to be held at noon.

Stanton, who was the last member of the Cabinet to arrive, found Lincoln reading a little book. At his left sat Welles, then Smith; Seward was at his right at the other end of the table, lounging carelessly in a chair and facing the President. Behind him stood Blair and Chase. No one was speaking, apparently not wishing to disturb Lincoln, who seemed deeply absorbed, though an occasional broad grin creased his face. Lincoln barely noticed Stanton when he sat down next to Seward. After a moment or two, Lincoln looked up and said, "Gentlemen, did you ever read anything from Artemas Ward? Let me read you a chapter that is very funny." In a solemn manner he read a short piece entitled, "High Handed Outrage in Uticky." Concluding, he laughed heartily and was joined by everyone except Stanton and Chase, neither of whom had a sense of humor. Then, Lincoln threw the book down and said abruptly that he had made up his mind to proclaim emancipation in the rebellious states. As everyone present was aware, he had been determined for some time to take this action, but he had delayed until the military situation improved. "I think the time has come now," he said, "I wish it were a better time. I wish that we were in a better condition. The action of the army against the rebels has not been quite what I should have best liked. But they have been driven out of Maryland, and Pennsylvania is no longer in danger of invasion." He would welcome changes that might improve the style and the legal force of the manuscript draft which he produced, but the substance of the document must stand—"the act and the consequences were his," his

alone the responsibility. To a hushed group, Lincoln read the proclamation. As he came to various key phrases, he paused and commented
on them, demonstrating to all, in Chase's view, that "he had fully considered the whole subject, in all the lights under which it had been
presented to him." The proclamation was not to take effect until January 1, 1863, and would not take effect at all if the seceded states re-
joined the Union before that date. Seward proposed two minor changes
in language, which Lincoln accepted; Blair fretted about Border state
opinion, but the President brushed his quibbles aside. Handing the
draft to Seward, he asked him to have it published the next day.[28]

# CHAPTER 23

# Monitor Mania

To President Lincoln and members of his Cabinet, the military situation in the early months of 1863 looked black. After Burnside's Fredericksburg disaster, the despairing Lincoln, with Chase and the radicals demanding the change of command, turned with much hesitation to Joseph Hooker. Hooker had distinguished himself as a fighting corps commander under McClellan and Burnside. But General Halleck and others who knew of his loose personal habits questioned his steadiness and mistrusted his judgment.

Whatever doubts Lincoln may have had about Hooker as Commander of the Army of the Potomac (and he had many), it would take several months before the new commander adjusted himself to his heavy responsibilities. He had to reequip and reorganize the Army, restore its confidence in itself, enlist its confidence in him, devise a plan of operations. The Western armies faced similar problems. Everything meant delay—delay that would be interpreted as further evidence of a feeble administration. Could the Navy steal a show from the temporarily immobilized Army and capture the imagination of the country? Could the Navy buy the time Hooker and Grant and Rosecrans needed? If Charleston, "the nursery of the rebellion," could be seized as Farragut had seized New Orleans, the political benefits for the administration would be substantial. Welles and Fox had been aware of those benefits before they assumed major importance in Lincoln's mind. Since the Army's failure to capitalize on Du Pont's victory at Port Royal in the fall of 1861, the notion of a joint expedition against Charleston had met with little favor from the Navy Department. Fox had been the earliest and most vigorous exponent of a purely naval operation, but Welles was eager too. Soon the President became a convert.

Mobile, Alabama, and Wilmington, North Carolina, were difficult to blockade. Strategically, the capture of either or both ports should have received a higher priority. But Charleston, the city of Calhoun and of secession, of Sumter and of Southern ultras, had a special emotional significance. Wilmington and Mobile, though major ports of entry for supplies to the Confederacy from abroad, were little more than place names in a gazetteer to the Northern public. Charleston was another matter.

The much-heralded duel between the *Monitor* and the *Merrimack* had produced a veritable monitor craze throughout the North. Few had succumbed so readily as Assistant Secretary Fox. A scant eleven days after the historic encounter, he appeared before the Joint Committee on the Conduct of the War aglow with enthusiasm for the *Monitor*. "Absolutely invulnerable," he boasted to Senator Wade, "as soon as the *Monitor* sank the *Merrimack* the Department would send her directly into Charleston Harbor."[1] Congress obliged by speedily appropriating millions of dollars for ironclad monitors. With Welles behind him, Fox overrode all objections in the Department, and through John Ericsson he immediately contracted for nine more vessels. These ironclads would be improvements on the original *Monitor*, larger and more heavily armored, reflecting experience gained from the *Merrimack* fight. The pilot house, which on the original *Monitor* was a small iron projection on the deck forward of the turret, would now be mounted on the turret for greater safety and better visibility. The redoubtable Ericsson had worked out a gearing system whereby the pilot house remained stationary while the turret revolved beneath it. Where the original *Monitor* had two eleven-inch Dahlgren guns, the new *Passaic* class would pair a monstrous fifteen-inch Rodman with an eleven-inch Dahlgren.

For a hardheaded ex-businessman and deepwater sailor, Fox showed a singular lack of judgment when it came to the ironclad *Monitor*. As wedded to the design as Ericsson himself, he was blind even to its most obvious defects, deaf to its proven weaknesses in performance. In these newer vessels he was certain that the Navy would have the ultimate weapon. Fox was so self-assured, so anxious to gain fresh renown for the Navy (and, it must be added, so overworked), that he brushed aside all questions that were raised about the unique difficulties involved in an attack on Charleston. After Norfolk fell and the *Merrimack* was

blown up by the retreating Confederates in May 1862, Fox actually suggested to Du Pont that the *Monitor* and the little ironclad gunboat
*Galena* were enough to capture Charleston. "Port Royal and New
Orleans suit me," said Fox expansively. The two vessels would simply
run the forts and batteries that ringed the harbor and force Charleston
to surrender. Admiral Du Pont was troubled when he read this note,
dashed off in Fox's angular scribble.[2] He was given little chance to
ponder whether Fox was merely asking an opinion or directing him to
make the trial. For in the very next mail, he was appalled to receive
an official letter from Welles instructing him to make the attempt as
soon as the *Galena* and the *Monitor* could be spared from duty in the
James River.[3] A cautious, methodical commander, the only comparison
he could see between New Orleans and Charleston was that they were
both ports. For six months he had probed every approach to the city,
and he was convinced that it would be risky to make a purely naval
assault even if he had all of the new monitors at his disposal.

Du Pont was vastly relieved when, a fortnight after receiving Fox's
note and Welles' instructions, he learned that the *Galena* and the
*Monitor* had been unable to silence the batteries at Fort Darling,
which stood on a bluff overlooking the James River, about six miles
from Richmond. The *Galena* had been badly damaged by the plunging
shot of the Fort. Direct hits had shaken the *Monitor* itself several
times.[4] Admiral Du Pont, who knew next to nothing about the capabilities of the *Monitor*, concluded that the Fort Darling episode must
surely have chilled Fox's ardor for an immediate descent upon Charleston. "Think coolly and dispassionately on the *main object*," he advised
Fox, "remember there is no running the gauntlet, night or day—no
bombardment of a week to fatigue and demoralize—the defenses of the
Mississippi [are] the merest shams in comparison. . . ." He reminded
Fox that Charleston was a cul de sac, ringed with heavy ordnance,
while the broad Mississippi flowed above and below New Orleans. Nor
could the armament in the small forts guarding the spacious harbor of
Port Royal be compared with the 200 heavy guns posted around
Charleston. To his wife the Admiral used more vivid language: "The
truth is the harbor is a good deal like a porcupine's hide . . . quills
turned outside in and sewed up at one end."[5]

Du Pont's argument and the repulse at Fort Darling slowed down
Fox's timetable but did not dampen his enthusiasm. There simply had
to be more ironclads than he originally anticipated. The assault would
be deferred until the shipyards completed two or three of the new *Pas-*

*saic*-class monitors. The large, unwieldly ironclad cruiser *New Ironsides* was almost ready for trials. Three monitors and *New Ironsides* ought to be more than sufficient force to run the forts.

Over the next several months, Du Pont wrote numerous low-key warnings to Fox, saying that only a well-supported joint operation had any real chance of success. A trusted officer, Captain Percival Drayton, who was then in New York supervising ironclad construction for the Navy, had kept the Admiral informed of weaknesses in the monitors. Even without Drayton's information, Du Pont doubted whether the Charleston batteries could be run with the volume of fire he could mount from his ironclad fleet. The two-gun monitors might be shot-proof, but one round from each ship every five minutes made them woefully deficient in assault capability.

Du Pont's admonitions went for naught. Sublimely indifferent to the navigational hazards of the sinuous, narrow, and shoal-ridden approaches to the harbor, sublimely optimistic about the power of the new ironclads, Fox replied that the original *Monitor* "can go all over the harbor and return with impunity. She is absolutely impregnable." It was left for Du Pont to determine how he could capture Charleston with two or three monitors and *New Ironsides*.

Fox was not being reasonable either about the capabilities of his new weapon, which was largely untested, or the defensive power of the Charleston forts and harbor obstructions. He was as impatient and as cavalier about the problems facing Du Pont as Senators Ben Wade and Zachariah Chandler were impatient and cavalier about the problems facing army commanders with raw troops. But Wade and Chandler, and their colleagues of the congressional Committee on the Conduct of the War, were civilians, not professionals. Fox was a professional. He should have known better. A superb administrator and a prodigious worker, he was nevertheless an incurable romantic, given to dreams of glory in which feats of valor were performed by valiant men in iron ships. He was fiercely competitive and absolutely dedicated to the Navy, though at times his enthusiasm must have seemed puerile to the stately Du Pont. "I feel that my duties are two fold," Fox wrote him in June, 1862, "first to beat our Southern friends; second to beat the Army." With Fox, one was never quite sure which was the enemy. Nor was one ever quite certain he was dealing with the Assistant Secretary of the Navy or with a junior officer training midshipmen in gunnery exercises.[6]

By early October 1862, Fox was exerting such heavy pressure that the worried Du Pont decided a series of personal interviews were in order.

On October 2, he made a flying visit to Washington, where he conferred with Welles for an hour or so. The stalwart Admiral exerted all of his old-world charm in an effort to impress the Secretary. He succeeded only in putting Welles on his guard. What lay behind these courtly manners, this fine address? Welles had already sensed a Du Pont clique in the Navy. At this meeting, and subsequently, he would strive to be fair to Du Pont, but the prejudice was there, not just a prejudice against his style, but rather the time-honored old Jacksonian bias against aristocracy. For Du Pont, wealthy in his own right, was the grandson of a French Marquis, and also the grandson of a world-renowned *philosophe*. He was too urbane, and too protective of himself, however, to offer any unsolicited opinion of the Charleston operation. Welles understood that Fox had this in hand, and, rather ill at ease with this imposing senior officer, he contented himself with listening to a recital of army blunders along the South Carolina–Georgia coastline.[7] The interview was pleasant, but unfortunately productive of misinterpretation on both sides. Each thought he knew the other's views on the impending operation, and each gained the wrong impression from the other. Two weeks later Du Pont returned to the capital. Refurbishing his social and political ties after more than a year's absence, he visited Lincoln, Stanton, Chase, Seward, and Halleck. Fox took him to dinner at Montgomery Blair's. Curiously, Du Pont did not seek another interview with Welles, nor did the Secretary invite him to dine.

With Lincoln, who did most of the talking, Du Pont stressed the moral importance of holding the Southern coasts. With others, he confined himself to anecdotes and polite generalizations. Even the inquisitive Seward could not draw out of him any expressions of fact or opinion regarding future operations.[8] Before leaving Washington, Du Pont had an opportunity to inspect the *Monitor* and observe the fire of a fifteen-inch Rodman, one of the huge guns which would be mounted on the new monitors. He was impressed, yet, remembering Fox's boast that the *Monitor* alone would take Charleston, he feared that he would be rushed into the operation with insufficient resources.[9] Du Pont faced a cruel dilemma. He had his reputation as a fighting Admiral to consider. He admired Fox and enjoyed a cordial relationship with him. Welles, too, though more distant, had always advanced his interests.

Fox and Ericsson might be right. Du Pont recognized that he had to defer to them, that he had to give the monitors a trial, and, if at all possible, present Charleston to the Navy Department. Haunted by a lack of firepower, he felt he had to have more ironclads than the Department was prepared to furnish. If at all possible he wanted a joint expedition, which would, he hoped, capture some of the forts guarding the entrances and thus reduce the heavy concentration of fire on his ships as they slowly steamed up one of the three channels. Fox vetoed the idea. Charleston must be entirely a Navy show. "My friend," said the Admiral gravely, "this is all well, and undivided glory is very pleasant to contemplate, but our country is in a position where certainty of success . . . is of far more importance. . . ." "Oh, yes indeed," Fox replied, "the success must be paramount," but the Navy would achieve it. He was adamant, as rigid and impenetrable as any of his ironclads. All that Fox would promise were additional new monitors as they became available, numbers unspecified. "Curious man," mused Du Pont, "but very smart and smarter every day."[10]

Fox had expected to have four of the new monitors in Du Pont's hands by the end of November 1862. By mid-December they were still not ready, despite pleas, demands, orders, personal visits. The contractors had not been paid their promised advances for several months. They were plagued by strikes, shortages of materials, and constant interference from Ericsson's office. In early January Fox wrote Du Pont that *New Ironsides* and four new monitors would join him within a few days. The original *Monitor* had been on her way to Port Royal when she foundered and sank in a storm off Cape Hatteras on the night of December 30-31, 1862.[11]

On January 6 Welles sent a second set of instructions which defined the operation as purely a naval one. He explained that General David Hunter would be reassigned to Port Royal with a force of about 10,000 men but was not to participate in the actual assault.[12] In acknowledging this order, Du Pont asked for more ironclads. He pointed out how important the operation would be and hinted at failure if he were not more powerfully supported. Hunter's force, which had arrived in the meantime, was, in Du Pont's opinion, not "ready even for the limited cooperation it can give. . . ." As for his estimate of Charleston's defenses, Du Pont said that he had informed the department "through private letters to the Assistant Secretary."[13]

Until now Welles had delegated the Charleston operation to Fox, who had always supported Du Pont and whose confidence in the monitors remained unshaken. Du Pont's letter was totally unexpected. It had never been brought to Welles' attention that Du Pont considered his forces too weak for the assault. Had not the department strained its resources to provide everything required? What were these references to private correspondence with Fox? Was he being misled about the difficulties of a naval attack on Charleston? Were Du Pont's demands reasonable, and could they be met within a reasonable length of time? Although no record exists whether he asked Fox for answers to these questions, he most probably did, for in Welles' reply to Du Pont he made references to harbor obstructions that could only have come from Fox. In fact, it would appear that Fox made available his file of private correspondence and that Welles for the first time realized there had been a difference of opinion between his Assistant Secretary and his squadron commander. At any rate, Welles' direct intervention brought about a compromise that stilled some of Du Pont's qualms, preserved Fox's pride, and satisfied the public demand of "on to Charleston."

"The Department," wrote Welles on January 31, "does not desire to urge an attack upon Charleston with inadequate means; and if, after careful examination you deem the number of ironclads insufficient to render the capture of the port reasonably certain, it must be abandoned." Alluding to the Confederate raiders *Florida* and *Alabama*, then on the high seas capturing dozens of Northern merchant ships, Welles reminded Du Pont that the blockade had been seriously weakened by the detachment of many of the Navy's fastest cruisers to pursue them. "This . . . renders the capture of Charleston and Mobile imperative," he continued, and in an unusual phrase that the proud, inordinately touchy Du Pont was bound to find offensive, he declared that the department would "share the responsibility imposed upon the commanders who made the attempt."[14]

Altogether, it had been a bad month for the Navy. Early in the morning of January 1, 1863, two Confederate river boats, mounting only three small guns and protected by cotton bales, utterly routed a part of Farragut's fleet blockading the Texas coast off Galveston. The frail Confederate "cottonclads" captured the *Harriet Lane*, drove the powerful gunboat *Westfield* aground, where she was blown up by her commander, and captured three coalers. Confused, the captains of the new Navy gunboats, *Clifton, Sachem,* and *Owasco,* steamed out of the harbor under forced draft. The Confederate troops, which had acted in concert with their impromptu naval task force, easily captured Galveston and its small garrison of union troops. The blockade had been breached, if only temporarily—an event that Confederate propagandists trumpeted to the world. Press and public opinion subjected the Navy to scathing criticism, not so much for the capture of Galveston as for the obvious fact that five powerful vessels of the Union fleet mounting twenty-five heavy guns should have been defeated by two river boats mounting three light guns.[15]

On the night of January 15-16, the Confederate-manned, British-built cruiser *Florida* slipped through the blockade at Mobile and began her career of destruction. Again the politicians and the editors heaped abuse upon the department. When it became known that the *Florida* easily outstripped the fastest Union cruiser in the Gulf squadron, Welles was villified in editorials and cartoons, the department castigated as a nest of red tape and old-fogyism.[16] If this were not enough, on the very day Welles wrote his second set of instructions to Du Pont agreeing to share responsibility with him if the Charleston attack failed, the blockade was breached again. Two lightly armed Confederate rams ("paper ships," Du Pont called them), the *Palmetto State* and the *Chicora*, took advantage of an early morning fog and moved slowly out of Charleston Harbor. Their fire damaged four of the blockading gunboats before a half-dozen Union vessels weighed anchor and went to the rescue. Having created destruction and confusion enough for one day, the rams avoided interception and anchored well inside the bar under the guns of Sumter and Moultrie. General Beauregard, in command at Charleston, backed up by the British consul and the captain of a British war vessel in port there, proclaimed that the blockade had been raised.[17] When the excited Seward called on Welles with a batch of newspaper accounts, asking if these statements were true, Welles dismissed them as Confederate bombast—journalistic flummery, "unworthy of a moment's consideration."[18]

Du Pont had his failings, but Welles knew that he maintained a tight blockade. Still he was seriously concerned, not because of newspaper jibes and partisan speeches, but because he feared that morale in the Navy was not what it ought to be. The keen cutlass that had sliced Port Royal, New Orleans, and Memphis out of the Confederacy seemed to have lost its edge. Surely recent responses had been dull and flawed. Welles had every confidence in the efficiency of the blockade, but the uninformed, which meant most of Congress and the people, did not. Every blockade-runner that got through was the subject of intense criticism in the press, while the ten that were sunk, beached, or taken as prizes received little mention. That vaunted Navy, whose capture of Charleston was to raise public morale and buy time for the Army, was again a prime target for the editors. It was no longer a question simply of diverting attention from Army shortcomings, but, to

Welles' mind, the larger question of restoring the Navy's prestige. If Du Pont needed more monitors, he should have them.

By early March of 1863, two more *Passaic* class monitors and a fixed-turret experimental ironclad, the *Keokuk*, were ordered to Port Royal. Du Pont now had seven improved monitors, each mounting an eleven-inch Dahlgren and a fifteen-inch Rodman; the mighty *New Ironsides*, with its fourteen eleven-inch Dahlgrens and two 100-pounder Parrott guns mounted in broadside; the experimental *Keokuk*, for good measure; and two ingenious devices Ericsson had designed to sweep the channel clean of torpedoes and obstructions. The Navy Department had strained its resources to provide Du Pont with a powerful striking force of ironclads. But Welles was plagued with doubts. Were the monitors invulnerable, as Fox and Ericsson claimed? Was Du Pont a fit commander to lead the attack? His confidence in the Admiral had been shaken by the demands for more ships, more men, more supplies. A petulant tone reminiscent of McClellan had crept into Du Pont's dispatches.[19] Then, in mid-February, General J. G. Foster appeared in Washington to protest Hunter's assumption of over-all command in South Carolina and Georgia. Foster spoke of laying seige to the Charleston batteries, with the Navy protecting his forces.

Stanton, Halleck, Fox, and Lincoln listened intently as the General recounted how he and Du Pont had discussed plans for a methodical reduction of the forts, with the army taking prime responsibility. Lincoln was so annoyed at this apparent change in plans (a change that Du Pont would later deny) that he thought Fox ought to leave immediately for Port Royal and discuss it with the Admiral. The two men walked over to the Navy Department to talk over such a visit with Welles, who immediately objected. It would, he said, "touch Du Pont's pride, which is great, and do perhaps more harm than good."[20] Lincoln saw the point and agreed, Welles, who had pinned great hopes on a smashing, all-Navy success, was "disappointed but not wholly surprised." Turning over in his mind Foster's disclosure, he came very close to understanding Du Pont's dilemma. "This indicates," he wrote, "what I have lately feared, that Du Pont shrinks from responsibility, dreads the conflict he has sought; yet is unwilling that any other should undertake it, is afraid the reputation of Du Pont will suffer."

Du Pont indeed was worried about his reputation, but Welles was doing him an injustice when he charged that his motives were purely personal. By now he had had an opportunity to examine the new monitors as well as talk with their captains. He had already discovered that

*New Ironsides* was almost unmanageable in any kind of sea or current.[21] Above all, he was disturbed by the fact that he would have at his command only 32 guns, against nearly 200 of the enemy's. Ericsson's torpedo rafts, built to clear obstruction, in actual practice reduced speed and maneuverability. What if his fleet were driven into the shoal waters on either side of the channel and sunk, to be later raised and repaired by the Confederates? Should this happen, these formidable ships would smash his wooden blockading fleet as the *Merrimack* had smashed the *Congress* and the *Cumberland*.

Du Pont revealed some of these thoughts when he wrote Fox on February 25 that "the *Experiment* for it is nothing else (the trying of 200 guns with twenty) is too momentous to be trifled with."[22] By that time he had tested his monitors against Fort McAllister, a seven-gun earthwork guarding the Ogeechee River to the south of Savannah. The defensive power of the monitors impressed him, but more than ever he was convinced that their slowness of fire and of speed made them weak offensive weapons.[23] Unquestionably, he was exercising sound judgment when he tested the monitors against McAllister, but Welles did not see it that way. "Du Pont," he remarked sourly, "has attacked Fort McAllister and satisfied himself that the turret vessels are strong and capable . . . but at the same time he doubtless made the Rebels aware of these facts."[24]

Experienced naval engineers at Port Royal, among whom was Alban Stimers, who had distinguished himself on the original *Monitor* and who, more than any other naval officer, enjoyed Ericsson's confidence, witnessed the attack and inspected the damage sustained by the attacking vessels. Du Pont was relieved when Stimers, "Ericsson's high priest," agreed with him that more vessels were needed and that more iron plating should be added to the decks.[25] Shrewdly, Du Pont ordered him North to see about the extra plating and to explain why the attack must be postponed until additional changes were made.

Welles, Fox, and Lincoln were deeply distressed by Stimers' report, especially so when he described a council of senior Army and Navy officers held on Du Pont's flagship, U.S.S. *Wabash*.[26] As Stimers remembered the sense of the meeting, it reaffirmed Du Pont's original idea of a joint operation. Welles was the first to speak. Du Pont was disregarding the will of the department. "Positive orders [must be] given," said the President angrily, "how to make the attack . . . the Peninsula over again; the enemy . . . getting stronger every day." Welles added that there had been too much talk about unknown factors, such as obstructions and torpedoes. Delay until April would mean no move until May.

Practically, the Navy would do nothing to screen Hooker's campaign, then in the planning stage. What would the public say? Through Fox and Ericsson and what was known as the "Monitor Lobby," a loose combine of ironmasters, shipbuilders, and engine manufacturers, the Northern press had been oversold on the merits of the ironclads. Welles was responding to this artificially generated opinion when he said, "The attack must be made whether successful or not, the people would not stand it and would turn us all out." Lincoln agreed.[27]

Before Stimers' return, Du Pont was demanding every monitor coming into service. "I think it right to say," he wrote Fox, "that the limit of my wants in the way of ironclads is the capacity of the Department to supply them."[28] Fox, who had been receiving a constant stream of damage and repair reports, was doing his utmost to satisfy him.[29] But he dared not keep any potentially damaging information, unofficial or even private, from the eyes of Welles and Lincoln. Quite likely he glossed over the technical problems that Du Pont was having in trying to correct faulty workmanship, errors in design and arrangement, weaknesses in armor plate and structural forgings that he found in all of the ironclads. Under inflationary pressures, the contractors had cut corners. They had purchased poor materials, had driven the hardest bargains they could make with subcontractors, and had held down labor costs by using unskilled and semiskilled labor whenever possible. Ill-informed about the design, construction, and performance of these novel craft, Lincoln jumped to the conclusion that he had another McClellan in Du Pont, a conclusion Welles did nothing to dispel.[30]

As for the harassed Admiral, he had by now assumed a fatalistic attitude. He would make the attack as ordered, without any appreciable support from the Army.[31] Though Du Pont regarded his mission as a "forlorn hope," he set about grimly making final preparations for an assault that would take advantage of the full tide between April 7 and 10. Ever mindful of a reverse, he took the precaution of setting forth the situation as he saw it to his close friend, the radical politician Henry Winter Davis. He also sent his wife a running journal of letters detailing the Department's increasing pressure for an attack, the faults of the monitors, the risks, and the responsibilities entailed. For months the Admiral had been working up his defense, hardly the stance of an aggressive commander or, indeed, of a man who would be candid with his superiors.[32]

On April 7, 1863, Du Pont made his move on Charleston. After forty minutes of intense bombardment from the harbor defense guns, he ordered his ships to withdraw. His most powerful vessel, U.S.S. *New*

*Ironsides*, which mounted more guns than all of the monitors combined, twice became unmanageable and scarcely saw any action. The fire of the monitors was slow; they seemed to be making little or no impression on the rate of counter battery fire. From what he could see through the heavy smoke as he peered through the observation slits on *New Ironsides*, the monitors were not getting through the obstructions. He would renew the attack, he decided, the next day, after he had heard the reports of his commanders. When he learned, however, that seven of his nine monitors were damaged, one, *Keokuk*, so seriously that she was in a sinking condition, he dared not risk it. Du Pont admitted defeat.[33]

In Washington, Welles felt oppressed and anxious. Recalling the Peninsular Campaign, he wondered whether all such complex efforts were not, by their very nature, doomed to failure. Lincoln shared Welles' apprehension. Du Pont's constant demands for more ironclads, his tentative probes, his experiments, his delays, all reminded him of McClellan. Yet the Admiral's caution had made a subtle impression on both men. Although Welles would never admit the influence, he was certainly more dubious about the monitors than he had been a few months earlier. He doubted if they would remain unscathed under the hail of heavy metal they must endure at close range. For he was certain that a desperate stand would be made at Charleston and equally certain that the city could not be taken without casualties or at the first trial. Only Fox remained confident, encouraging Welles and the President to go ahead when both were ready to call it all off. In fact, it took all of Fox's powers of persuasion, bolstered by his professional knowledge and his long practical experience with naval affairs, to restrain Lincoln from ordering all of Du Pont's monitors to Farragut, who desperately needed them. The time when the capture of Charleston would have raised Union morale had long since passed. Hooker was almost ready to march. In the West, Rosecrans had fought the Confederates to a draw at Stone River and was maneuvering Bragg out of Tennessee. Political considerations that had seemed so important two months before were less significant now. In the President's mind the clearing of the Mississippi ranked equally with the maintenance of the Atlantic blockade. He and Welles had always felt so, but Fox had tempted them with Charleston when the administration needed a breathing spell.[34]

To satisfy the President yet still make the attempt at Charleston, Welles had written out another set of orders to Du Pont on April 2. After the attack, Du Pont was to keep only two ironclads and send all those fit for sea to New Orleans. John Hay, the President's sprightly junior secretary, acted as the courier. His appearance at Port Royal would lend presidential weight to the orders he carried. Hay arrived on Thursday, April 9, two days after the defeat. While Du Pont was reading the dispatches, Hay chatted with C. R. P. Rodgers, Fleet Captain of the squadron. Rodgers said that if the monitors had spent another twenty minutes under the fire of the Charleston forts all of them would have been sunk. What was only a failure would then have been a disaster. Du Pont interjected: "After a fight of forty minutes we had lost the use of seven guns. I might have pushed some of the vessels past Fort Sumter, but in that case we ran the enormous risk of giving them to the enemy and thus losing control of the coast. I could not answer for that to my conscience."[35]

Du Pont took Welles' order to mean that his course had been vindicated; but, worried about public and political opinion, he made two grave errors. He gave exclusive stories of the battle and special transportation to two reporters who had always slanted the news in his favor—Henry Villard of the *New York Times* and William Swinton of the *Tribune*. By playing favorites he earned the enmity of every other reporter on the scene, the one most irritated being the one he could least afford to offend—Charles C. Fulton of the *Baltimore American*. Fulton's paper was friendly to Montgomery Blair. Had Du Pont been more politically astute, he would have seen to it that all reporters were treated equally.[36] He would have taken pains not to alienate the Blairs, who could be tough, nasty political infighters. They were well aware of Du Pont's friendship with Henry Winter Davis, their deadly enemy in Maryland politics.

Du Pont's other mistake was in sending Commander Alexander C. Rhind to Washington with his preliminary report of the action. Rhind, commanding officer of *Keokuk*, the most damaged of the ironclads, had been a monitor enthusiast before the engagement. Now this impetuous and outspoken officer was the most harshly critical of these vessels among Du Pont's officers. In utilizing Rhind as his advocate, Du Pont overplayed his hand.

On the evening of April 12, Rhind reported to the Navy Department. He handed Du Pont's preliminary report to the anxious Welles. After scanning its few lines, Welles asked the bearded, impassive Rhind if he would care to elaborate. He would, indeed. Words tumbled from his lips so rapidly that Welles knew the officer's nerves were on edge. Yet here was an eyewitness account from a commander whose vessel had been closest to Fort Sumter and had suffered the most damage. Welles

felt that Lincoln should hear Rhind's story. While the nervously voluble officer was describing the action of his ship to the attentive President, Fox and Sumner appeared. When Rhind began a severe indictment of the monitors, Fox interrupted him, stating that they were not
designed to engage in duels with heavy fortifications. Du Pont had been
expected to run his ironclad fleet by them. Rhind said that was impossible because of the obstructions and the torpedoes. Sumner asked
curtly why they had not been removed. "I cannot answer for the
others; I did not remove any simply because I could not," said Rhind.
"Well, Joe Hooker will have to take Charleston," said Sumner contemptuously. "Is he going down in an ironclad?" asked Rhind, his
voice heavy with sarcasm, his temper rising. The distressed Welles
managed to intervene and terminate the discussion, which he felt impolitic and impractical. Throughout Lincoln remained impassive, but
he had reached a decision.

Mindful of Hooker's campaign, which was just getting underway, he
would telegraph Du Pont to keep his squadron within the Charleston
bar and continue to threaten the city. The ironclads would at least tie
down a considerable force of the enemy that might otherwise join Lee.
Right after the meeting, Lincoln sent the dispatch. Du Pont, ever fearful of his reputation, took it as a rebuke and asked to be relieved of his
command. Either Welles or Fox reminded Lincoln that his order conflicted with the Department's instructions of April 2, to send all but
two monitors to the Gulf, and one or the other of the two men suggested to the President that the language of his telegram was unnecessarily peremptory. A more conciliatory private letter was prepared and
addressed to both Hunter and Du Pont. Lincoln hoped that another
attack could be made, but, if not, he wanted "the demonstration kept
up for some time." In case any feelings might have been hurt by his
telegram, he expressly denied that any censure had been intended.[37]
Du Pont did not receive this letter until April 24. By then he had
strained his relations with Welles and Fox to the breaking point and
was becoming entangled in a serious political attack on the administration.

On April 15 a long article appeared in the *Baltimore American* that
virtually accused Du Pont of cowardice for withdrawing his vessels
after a brief encounter with the enemy. The writer, Charles C. Fulton,
charged that the damage to the ironclads was trivial, giving specific examples which only Alban Stimers—"Ericsson's high priest"—could have
supplied. Du Pont was enraged that Stimer, one of his own officers,
should have misrepresented the injuries to the monitors. Fulton had

come to Port Royal at the special request of Montgomery Blair, acting through Fox. The overwrought Admiral assumed that the department was covertly censuring him through the medium of a partisan newspaper. Fulton had boasted that he filed a duplicate of every story he sent to his paper with Fox, who it was understood, would censor the copy if he thought it necessary. Without proper investigation, Du Pont rashly concluded that Fox was trying to save his own skin and that of "the Monitor Lobby" by an invidious attack in the *American*.

Welles himself was shaken when he received Du Pont's detailed report on April 20. He had expected a carefully constructed defense from the Admiral, but he had not anticipated a searching analysis of grave structural and design defects in the monitors from their own captains. Fox was more upset than his chief. He had put all of his influence and all of his reputation on the line. At his insistence the government had spent over $5 million for the *Passaic* class monitors. It was committed to more than twice that sum for newer classes. Du Pont alone he could handle. Du Pont and his captains—the best professional officers in the Navy—were more than he had bargained for. Curiously, Fox's faith in the monitors was as staunch as ever.

Even at this date Fox could have made a strong case for the ships as harbor defense craft, a mission for which they were admirably adapted. He could have justified the expenditure on this ground alone. That he did not choose to do so reflects on his professional and political judgment. Welles, though more objective about the monitors than Fox, steadfastly supported his Assistant Secretary. He blamed Du Pont's lack of faith in them as the major reason for their poor performance at Charleston. He thought the captains themselves must have been influenced by their commander. Hoping to gain evidence, Welles sought an opinion from John Rodgers, whose monitor *Weehawken* had been struck fifty-three times but had sustained only minor damage. The much admired Rodgers, perhaps the Navy's finest deepwater sailor, backed up the Admiral. Later Welles spoke privately with Percival Drayton with the same result.[38]

On April 30 he had received a long complaining letter from the Admiral that alerted him to impending political complications. Du Pont, in effect, charged the Navy Department, specifically Fox, with censuring him indirectly by withholding from the public his official report and, at the same time, permitting his character to be impugned by Stimers and Fulton through the columns of the *American*. After conferring with Fox, who indignantly denied that he had ever seen, much less censored, Fulton's story about the attack, Welles decided that Du

Pont's charge was not worthy of notice. "I fear he can be no longer useful in his present command," he wrote in his diary, "and am mortified and vexed that I did not earlier detect his vanity and weakness."[39]

Writing for the record now, Welles sent two letters to Du Pont a day apart; the first he had prepared many weeks before, but had held back at Fox's request until more information had been received. In a friendly spirit, he said that he was withholding Du Pont's report because it was not in the public interest to advertise weaknesses, if any, in the monitors just now. He was sorry that Du Pont and the department had not understood each other, but he had thought that their personal relations were cordial and frank enough for full and free communication. The second letter, answering Du Pont's charge against Fox and Stimers, was terse to the point of rebuke. Enclosed was a copy of a letter from Fox denying that he had ever read the *American* article and stating that Fulton was not under any obligation to file his stories.[40]

The second letter was clearly meant to set the stage for Du Pont's relief. Taken together, both letters made Welles out to be a thoughtful public servant who could be raised to righteous anger only through the querulous comments of a naval commander who would neither avoid nor accept his responsibilities. Should a political battle develop over the ironclads, a battle that Welles thought likely, these documents would act as a first stage in the department's defense.

Welles must have realized that the whole Charleston operation had been a regretable episode on both sides. The Lincoln administration had overreacted to public and political criticism that it lacked energy and force. Despite Welles' claims to the contrary, Du Pont had gone as far as he had dared to warn Washington about the perils of attacking a heavily defended city with experimental weapons. Lincoln and Welles, in pressing him, seemed not to have thought that they themselves could be charged with being rash by the same group that had scored the administration for being so slow and cautious, so wedded to McClellan. Du Pont and Charleston and costly monitors which did not perform were ready-made subjects for a congressional onslaught upon the Executive branch.

After the Charleston repulse, or "demonstration," as Welles referred to it in the press, Lincoln became wary and not entirely truthful with Du Pont's friends. Early in May, Henry Winter Davis had a long chat with the President. The handsome, highly intelligent, politically unstable Congressman was not a man to be trifled with or to antagonize. Core of the radical opposition in Maryland, he was close to Ben Wade, Zachariah Chandler, and other members of the Committee on the Conduct of the War. Chase and Stanton, both of whom were encouraging opposition to the Blairs wherever it could be found, were much in his company. Lincoln kept himself well-informed about Davis's activities. He knew of Davis's plans to run as an anti-Blair Republican Congressman from Davis' old district, and that he was virtually certain to win both the nomination and election.

Davis glossed rapidly but succinctly over Du Pont's alleged mistreatment. What he really wanted was publication of the Admiral's detailed report, especially those parts where the monitor captains had questioned the feasibility of their vessels for the mission entrusted to them. Du Pont's correspondence with the department, warning of the perils of Charleston, should likewise be spread upon the public record. Lincoln replied blandly that much of this information was new to him. He was beginning "to suspect," he said, "that the enterprise was a Department pet—something which had been kept for the Navy alone." But Welles and Fox, as far as he knew, were friendly. Davis quoted the President to Du Pont as saying that "no one stood higher than you with him and the Department. . . ." Lincoln promised to read Du Pont's report and correspondence with Welles and Fox. The President was stalling for time and did not scruple to mislead Davis with what at best were half-truths. Davis' visit, far from helping his friend, would prove damaging. All he had done was further alert the administration to trouble ahead. Welles immediately began preparing his defense against a searching investigation of the Navy's policy on ironclads.[41]

# CHAPTER 24

# A Blunted Trident

DESPITE THE CONSTANT STRAIN and the heavy work load, Welles' health was astonishingly good for a man of his age and sedentary habits. In May 1862, for the first time in his tenure of office, he took a brief trip for relaxation to eastern Virginia, inviting a large party of colleagues and their wives to accompany him. The excursion was a pleasant affair, but, typically, Welles got little rest. He inspected the gunboats that were cooperating with the Army and visited General McClellan at Cumberland on the Pamunkey River. The party returned on the nineteenth, all feeling refreshed by the outing, none more so than Welles. But the pace was beginning to tell.

Welles was quick to find fault with his clerks and with other subordinates at the department. His family, too, felt the rough edge of his uncertain temper. He was especially annoyed at the behavior of his third son, Tom, who was living with his Uncle Reuben in Philadelphia and attending school there. A sensitive, high-spirited adolescent, Tom had always been difficult. Understanding in so many ways when family problems arose, Welles failed to see how much the family's move to Washington had affected his son. Denied his Hartford home and his boyhood friends, denied also the excitement of wartime Washington, Tom Welles was restless and bored with life in Philadelphia. He dared not defy his father, but he did irritate him with complaining letters. "The boy who would day after day tease a father occupied as I am with letter after letter against my opinion . . . has made but little progress," wrote the angry Welles. "He must have obedience, submission and acquiescence in the decision of his elders in superior position. . . ." Welles, whose mind was so clear about most things, seems not to have remembered his own disturbed adolescence, his own waywardness, his own clashes with parental authority. Against his better judgment, he let Tom return to Hartford, where he would attend his old school—a private academy run by the Reverend Joseph Hull.[1] Mary Welles, hopeful that Tom would heed his older brother's advice, urged Edgar to write him often. "Beg him to attend to Mr. Hull's rules and be good for his dear father's sake, a vexatious letter from Tom always makes him sick."

But Tom had not been in Hartford a month when Hull wrote he could do nothing with him. He had not the time to give the personal attention the boy needed.[2] In late June the contrite Tom was back in Washington, and Welles was worrying about what should be done. His dilemma reached the ears of Secretary Seward, probably through Fox. Seward had a chat with Tom, suggesting a naval career but asking him not to discuss the matter with his father. Next, Seward spoke with Lincoln, who was sympathetic. On July 30, 1862, the President sent Welles an order directing him to appoint Tom a midshipman.

Welles, taken by surprise, was amazed when he found Tom enthusiastic. Perhaps this was the answer. He made the appointment, but at the same time he wrote Captain George Blake, the Commandant of the temporary Naval Academy at Newport, that the appointment had been unsolicited and that Tom should have no special treatment.[3] In mid-September Tom left for Newport. Welles was cautiously hopeful that the routine and the discipline of the Academy would give his restless son a sense of purpose, help him to develop a more mature outlook on life. With Tom at Newport, Edgar at New Haven, Mary Welles, John, and Hubert, his youngest child, at Irvington on the Hudson, where they were staying with the George D. Morgans, Welles was alone in the big house on Lafayette Square. Although he missed his family, he would not permit them to come home until the first frost, which was believed to dissipate the fevers of the disease-ridden capital. The extraordinary precautions that Welles took to guard against illness went for naught. The family had not been in Washington more than a fortnight when Hubert was stricken with diphtheria, and within forty-eight hours he was dead. His parents were stunned. "Well has it been for me," said Welles, "that overwhelming public duties have borne down upon me in these sad days."[4]

Welles' colleagues and their wives tried as best they could to comfort the bereaved family. The Lincolns were particularly affected, remem-

bering the death of their son Willie some nine months before, and
Mary Welles' careful nursing of Tad, who had been desperately ill at
the time.

Mary Lincoln and Mary Welles had quickly become close friends.
Both enjoyed Washington society, the glitter and the limelight, expensive dresses, receptions, and formal dinners. Yet both were devoted to
their families and neither had lost that quality of neighborliness, that
spontaneous generosity of their small-town, frontier backgrounds. Ellen
Stanton was too cool and distant for the excitable, domineering Mary
Lincoln; Julia Bates, though warm and sociable, was of an older generation, as was Frances Seward—a frail, withdrawn, very private person.
The Blair women, perhaps because of their secure position in Washington and Maryland society, were not among Mary Lincoln's small
circle of friends. Nor was the beautiful Kate Chase Sprague, who acted
as her father's hostess and political confidante; she was too much the
rival for the plump, matronly First Lady, who fiercely guarded her social position. Of the Cabinet wives, only Mary Welles posed no threat,
and, while she had a genuine affection for this frequently difficult
woman, she also recognized how much the personal friendship of the
Lincolns counted in the never-ending struggle for influence. Mary
Welles was an ambitious as well as a loving wife. And in all the years
her husband had concerned himself with politics, she had always lent
her charm, her open, friendly manner, to aid him in his career.

When Willie and Tad Lincoln became ill with typhoid in February
1862, Mary Welles moved into the White House for a time to help
nurse the sick boys. Despite her best efforts, and the continuous attendance of the two physicians, Willie Lincoln died on the afternoon
of February 20, 1862. With Tad remaining dangerously ill, and Mary
Lincoln showing signs of imminent collapse, Lincoln realized he could
not depend solely on Mrs. Gurney, whose husband was the pastor of
the Presbyterian Church the Lincolns attended, Mary Welles, and
"Aunt" Mary, an old Negro nurse who had been one of Jefferson
Davis' slaves. In the emergency, he turned to Dorothea Dix, supervisor
of women hospital nurses. She brought in a competent, motherly, army
nurse, Mrs. Rebecca Pomeroy, to take charge at the White House.[5]
The exhausted Mary Welles went home for a much needed rest. The
next morning a pathetic note arrived from the President: "Mr. and
Mrs. Welles please call and see us."[6]

Some time after their return from the White House, where they had
tried to console the grief-stricken Lincolns, Mary Welles received a
message from Dr. Robert Kingston, one of the physicians attending

Tad. Mary Lincoln had become hysterical, and she was confined to her bed under sedation. Mrs. Gurley had been at Tad's bedside for days and was worn out. With both Tad and Mary Lincoln requiring constant attention, the doctors thought someone else was needed to help Mrs. Pomeroy. "As in the case of poor little Willie," wrote Dr. Kingston to Mary Welles, "your name was mentioned as one of the family friends and as peculiarly fitted for this charge."[7] Mary Welles went over to the White House immediately. Except for one day, when Attorney-General Bates' wife, Julia, sat up with Tad, she remained with the sick boy, assisting Mrs. Pomeroy, until he was out of danger.

Welles had been upset, as always, by the death of a child. But Lincoln's grief, which was so obvious, touched a personal chord, reminding him of the many occasions over the years when he himself had been similarly afflicted. His family life disrupted, vital business with the President postponed, Welles took what small consolation he could from the fact that Mary Welles and Mary Lincoln had discontinued their weekly receptions, which he loathed but they enjoyed so much.[8]

Gratitude for Mary Welles' services strengthened the bonds of friendship between the two families. Hubert's death, coming nine months after Willie Lincoln's, deeply affected the Lincolns and further strengthened the personal ties between the two families. To Mary Lincoln, this sad event meant the sharing of a common grief. To Lincoln himself it meant something more. For added to his awesome burdens was a nagging worry about his wife's emotional condition, her apparent loneliness amid the splendors of the White House. Lincoln was preoccupied with his problems, so he may not have noticed how his wife's prickly personality, her petulance, her sudden fits of temper, her air of self-importance, drove away many would-be friends. But he seems to have realized that she needed friendship in Washington, and he was profoundly grateful that she enjoyed Mary Welles' company.

Unable or unwilling to seek out new acquaintances, Mary Lincoln clung more tightly to the few firm friends she had been able to make in Washington—only three in all, Mary Welles, Mrs. James H. Orne, and Mrs. Albert White. Mrs. Orne, a Philadelphian whose husband was active in Pennsylvania politics, did not live in Washington, though she visited the capital frequently. Mrs. White, the wife of an Indiana Congressman, was a resident of the District, and the Whites saw much of the Lincolns. But Mary Welles remained Mary Lincoln's closest friend in Washington, a factor that must have influenced in some degree Lincoln's official relationship with Welles.[9]

Before Mary Welles arrived in Washington in November 1861, well-placed rumor had it that Lincoln would make at least one change, and quite probably two, in his Cabinet. Anyone at all knowledgeable about Cabinet affairs believed that Welles was one of the marked men—which he may have been, given Seward's influence and their mutual antipathy. Cameron went, and he was replaced by Stanton, but Welles remained. And he held the President's confidence, despite the fierce attacks upon him in Congress and in the press over his dealings with George D. Morgan.

There was less talk about Welles being dropped from the Cabinet after Willie Lincoln's death, though the campaign to have him removed continued, endangering the President's increasingly delicate relations with Congress. With Lincoln, personal considerations were of course secondary to affairs of state, yet they played a part, sometimes to the disadvantage of his administration. It was fortunate that the President's sense of obligation and of friendship for Welles coincided with the fact that he was a dependable administrator and a sensible counselor. At any rate, the two men maintained something closer than an official relationship through their wives. Welles needed that extra support in the fall of 1862, when his son Hubert died.

He was in the midst of writing his annual report, working closely with Fox to strengthen Du Pont's squadron for a naval attack on Charleston, and trying to analyze the flood of requisitions from David Dixon Porter, who was building a navy yard at Mound City, Illinois. Welles suspected that Porter, his new Acting Rear Admiral in command of the Mississippi squadron, was careless about the expenditure of funds. He was personally watching Porter's accounts. But departmental matters were not the least of Welles' burdens during the fall and winter of 1862–63. He was, as he had been from the beginning of his tenure as Secretary of the Navy, embroiled with the State and Treasury departments over his administration of the blockade.

Since November of 1861, when Commodore Charles Wilkes, in command of the U.S.S. *San Jacinto,* had boarded the British mail packet *Trent* and removed two Confederate commissioners—former U. S. Senators John M. Mason and John Slidell—en route to Europe, Welles and Seward had been at odds over blockade policy. After some hesitation, Welles publicly approved Wilkes' rash act—the removal of persons and papers under the protection of the British flag on a regular mail ship sailing from the neutral port of Havana to the neutral port of Saint Thomas in the Danish-owned Virgin Islands. Although he felt that Wilkes had made a mistake by not adhering strictly to international law—he had not brought the *Trent* into an American port for ajudication before a prize court—he could not ignore public opinion. Overnight Wilkes had become a popular hero. Welles would have been pleased had he known that Edwin M. Stanton, then one of the administration's most prominent gadflies, shared his own belief that Wilkes should have brought the *Trent* in as prize.

Attorney General Bates confidently dismissed any threat of war with England. "There is no danger on that score. The law of nations is clear upon that point," he said. Bates was right in part. Several precedents did favor Wilkes' action, but as many others condemned it. The question was moot. And this was no time to debate fine points of international law or to chide the British on their past behavior. Public opinion in England was touchy about real or fancied insults to the flag. There were too many clever admiralty lawyers in London, too many jingoist editors ready to fault the Lincoln administration and to demand prompt redress. Lord Palmerston headed the British government. If anyone could bend international law to national interest, it was this formidable spokesman for the old school of power diplomacy.

While Seward was rejoicing over the capture and Welles was pondering how he could congratulate Wilkes, Montgomery Blair was urging Lincoln that Mason and Slidell should be given up, along with suitable apologies.[10] Welles soon learned of Blair's advice. His original doubts intensified, he sought counsel from Charles Eames, his consultant on admiralty law, who found ample precedent for Wilkes' action. Still concerned that the *Trent* had not been brought in as a prize, he wrote the Hartford lawyer, John Hooker, whom he knew to be well versed in international law. Hooker answered promptly, urging that Mason and Slidell be given up. Great Britain will demand it, he argued, and "it will be claimed with some plausibility that the right to take contraband from a neutral & to condemn her (for the two go together) applies only where a neutral is going to or from an enemy port."

Realizing the gravity of the situation, knowing also of Lincoln's fears and Blair's counsel, and with John Hooker's temperate letter before him, Welles nevertheless decided he had to make some concession to public opinion. Apparently he did not consult Lincoln when he framed what he thought was a guarded letter of commendation to Wilkes, but his pen moved rather rapidly that day. He could not resist including one tactless phrase that destroyed the cautious effect he had intended. Wilkes' conduct, he said, "has the emphatic approval of the Department." As gently as he could, he then went on to chide Wilkes for not capturing the vessel, concluding that his action "must not be permitted to constitute a precedent hereafter for infraction of neutral obligations."[11] Naturally enough, the Palmerston government judged Welles' "emphatic approval" as the official stand of the Lincoln administration. The unfortunate phrase helped whip up war fever on both sides of the Atlantic, making the task of the diplomats and the peacemakers that much more difficult. On the other hand, Welles' letter gave Seward and Lincoln the clue they needed for acceding to Britain's peremptory demand, yet at the same time satisfying American hotheads. Wilkes had acted without instruction, it was true, but, Welles contended, in boarding the *Trent*, which was obviously carrying contraband persons and papers, he was acting in strict conformity with international law. The *Trent* was a probable prize and should have been taken, along with Mason and Slidell to a prize court for adjudication. In removing the two Confederate envoys and letting the *Trent* proceed to its destination, Wilkes was making a decision that rightfully belonged to the courts. Without the *Trent*, too, Mason and Slidell could not be examined as witnesses or judged contraband of war in a prize court. And since the Confederate rebellion was obviously failing, Seward blandly concluded, Mason and Slidell were of little importance. The government would be happy to release them.

The Cabinet, with Sumner, Chairman of the Senate foreign relations committee, attending, considered Seward's draft on December 25 and again on the following day. All present approved it with only minor changes. The British government waived the demand for an apology, ignored Seward's rhetoric, and agreed to settle the dispute upon the delivery of Mason and Slidell. The *Trent* crisis was over.

Embarrassed at his part in the affair, Welles felt, rather ungenerously, that Seward had forced his hand. He had delayed two weeks before he commended Wilkes—two weeks during which the public was clamoring for the Department's approval of the Captain's act. When he finally complied, Welles had made a slip, yet, in retrospect, he rationalized that this was the least Wilkes and his supporters would accept.

Seward, who knew far more about the diplomatic situation than Welles did, had offered no counsel except to praise Wilkes' actions extravagantly in public. As Welles mulled it over after the fact, he convinced himself that the State Department had pushed him into the untenable position of having to decide whether he should "create discontent and rebuke Wilkes for what the country approved." When Seward recognized that war was a real possibility and reversed his stand, he seemed to have done it in a way that disavowed Welles' statement publicly, while at the same time he helped himself to Welles' way out of the dilemma. Welles should have been satisfied that, if his commendation of Wilkes had deepened the crisis, his statement that Wilkes' action "must not be permitted to constitute a precedent hereafter for infraction of neutral obligation" had also assisted in solving it. But in his petulance, he saw only his own embarrassment, his own irritation that he should have been blamed and used at the same time. Years later, he would grudgingly admit that Seward "should receive credit for the dextrous and skillful dispatch which he prepared on his own change of position. It exhibits his readiness and peculiar tact and talent."[12]

Welles' hesitation in commending Wilkes reflected also an acute awareness that any misstep could have serious repercussions on the efficiency of the blockade itself. It was difficult enough to recruit officers and men for this arduous yet humdrum duty. The ships lay at anchor for months, and the men were tossed around in winter gales, sweltered in the humid summer months, and subsisted on a monotonous diet of salt meat and fish, with only infrequent mails and newspapers from home. The squadrons were always undermanned. There were no bounties, either state or federal, for naval volunteers, and no substitutes either, until late in the war when sailors were finally counted on state quotas. The one big attraction that assured enough officers and men for blockade duty was the prospect of prize money from captured ships and cargo that were condemned and sold at public auction. Any tightening of the rules making the capture of prizes more difficult was going to make it harder for the Navy to keep its volunteer officers—who made up more than 80 per cent of its total complement. Recruitment of enlisted men, never an easy task, would likewise be more difficult.[13]

Responding to the pressures of the commercial community, Welles had already weakened the blockade by keeping a half a dozen cruisers at sea in what seemed to be a vain search for the Confederate commerce raider *Sumter*. While Seward was walking off with the honors in a peaceful and politic settlement of the *Trent* crisis, Welles learned that William Miller and Sons, Liverpool shipbuilders, had almost completed another commerce raider for the Confederates—the *Oreto,* a much more powerful and faster vessel than the *Sumter*. When she put to sea, additional ships and men would have to be detached from blockade duty to hunt her down. It is not surprising that Welles took a firm stand on belligerent rights. Nor is it at all surprising, after the *Trent* affair, that the Palmerston ministry stepped up its insistence on a broader definition of neutral rights. British shipbuilders, merchants, and a host of well-connected adventurers had finally discovered that the war would be a lengthy one, that there were huge profits to be made in running cotton through the blockade for the starving mills of Lancashire. Their chorus of complaints in Parliament about American maritime restrictions could not go unheeded by the government.

British maritime policy, which seemed demanding enough at the end of 1861, developed a harder line during 1862. The indignant Welles saw a concerted effort to take advantage of Union military reverses and extort even more concessions from the administration. He would not—indeed, could not—accede to what he regarded as Seward's policy of appeasement without filing his own protest.

Better informed than his Cabinet colleagues on Britain's industrial and naval strength, he was, paradoxically, far more willing to play the dangerous game of power politics, to flirt with the risk of a war on two fronts, than either Lincoln or Seward was. Apart from his inherited anti-British bias, his strong nationalism, Welles had a long-standing grudge against England for what he regarded as its un-neutral conduct in according belligerency status to the Confederacy. But the most compelling reason for his bristling attitude was that the only way he could defend his own reputation and that of the Navy was through a broad construction of belligerent rights. Neither Seward nor Lincoln, nor even the British shipbuilders, were blamed for the depredations of Confederate cruisers. The newspapers always accused the Navy and Welles of inefficiency in not being able to capture them. When the blockade was breached, as it frequently was, by fast vessels from Havana or Nassau, Welles was belabored as a "Methuselah," a "Jonah." He could and did bear the strictures of the press, the denunciations in Congress, the stereotype image of a sleepy, bumbling, old man. He would not, however, suffer silently for any of Seward's sins. He resented the little Secretary's penchant for meddling in Navy affairs. "He gets behind me," Welles complained, "tampers with my subordinates and interferes injuriously and ignorantly in naval matters."

Seward had maneuvered the Navy Department into a corner where it would be difficult to take a stand that was not against its best interests. The ravages of a new commerce destroyer, the *Alabama*, and the *Oreto*, renamed the *Florida*, reached new heights during the winter and early spring of 1862–63.[14] Northern shipping interests were in a state of panic. Lacking confidence in the Navy's ability to capture these fast, heavily armed raiders, the mercantile community, through the New York Chamber of Commerce and the Boston Board of Trade, urged that the government license privateers to go after them. Secretary Seward immediately saw diplomatic possibilities in having Congress authorize privateering.

Welles believed that Seward was always appeasing the English, but in point of fact the Secretary of State had taken as firm a stand as he could in defense of national interests. To the maritime community of the North and, though Welles would have disputed it, to Secretary Seward, British policy seemed anything but neutral. The threat of unleashing a swarm of privateers upon English commerce could not, Seward felt, be taken lightly by Lord John Russell, Britain's Foreign Minister. Both the *Alabama* and the *Florida* had been built in British yards. The Laird brothers, shipbuilders of Birkenhead, England, were rapidly completing two powerful ironclad rams for the Confederate government. These vessels were designed to be faster and more maneuverable than any ironclad then commissioned in the Union Navy. French shipyards, too, were constructing four fast, partially ironclad cruisers and two ironclad rams that were known to have been ordered by the Confederate government. It seemed obvious to Washington that these ships were being built to break the blockade.

Seward grasped eagerly at the notion that the threat of privateers might act as a deterrent to the British and French governments, might even persuade them to halt construction of the ironclads. Welles was just as deeply concerned as Seward. Indeed, he was about to send John Murray Forbes and William Aspinwall, leading figures in the New York and Boston business community, on a secret mission to Europe, with a credit line of $5 million to buy the rams, if possible.[15] But he objected strenuously to the intrusion of private enterprise in naval affairs. He suspected, and with some reason, that a ring of New Yorkers closely associated with Thurlow Weed were more interested in catching unarmed blockade-runners than they were in fighting Confederate cruisers. Their real intention, he thought, was to wrest a share of the valuable prize captures from the Navy, knowing that they would run little risk and stood to reap large profits. The more vehemently New York shippers insisted that they were only interested in sinking the *Alabama* and the *Florida*, the more certain Welles became that they had other motives. Despite the Navy's opposition, the commercial community, backed up by Seward, had its way. Congress, on March 3, 1863, authorized the President to issue letters of marque and reprisal.

To Welles' dismay, at the first Cabinet discussion of the new legislation Chase warmly seconded Seward on the necessity of licensing privateers. Welles doubted whether any privateer would go after such a heavily armed cruiser as the *Alabama*, even if a large bounty were of-

fered. The investment of capital funds alone for such a venture, he
thought, would approach a million dollars, a large sum for a high-risk
enterprise. He did not deny at this meeting or at subsequent meetings
that the maritime community favored privateering. The seizures made
by the *Alabama* and the *Florida* had driven insurance rates so high
that most of the North's merchant fleet stayed in port. Yet, without admitting any inconsistency, Welles now became the appeaser. Privateers
could involve us in a foreign war, which the nation was in no condition to fight. "To clothe private armed vessels with governmental
power and authority, including the belligerent right of search," he
warned, "will be likely to beget trouble." Though he was not yet fully
recovered from a serious illness, he drafted a long letter on the subject
to Seward.

Then, after reading what he had written, he was torn by doubts. He
had just returned from a Cabinet meeting at which Seward had read
two notes from Lord John Russell to Minister Adams, both declaring
emphatically that the British government would not interfere with the
Laird rams. Welles concluded that British shipping interests were determined to sweep the commerce of the United States from the seas.
Shaken at this new evidence of British intentions, he decided to have
his letter copied anyhow. It was lying on his table ready for his signature late on the afternoon of April 2, when Senator Sumner came into
his office.

Welles and Sumner were both opposed to privateering.[16] They were
in general agreement that if it were permitted, reckless, unrestrained
men, lured only by profit, would surely involve the nation in serious
incidents. Yet something had to be done to modify the policy of the
British government, to restrain British shipbuilders from constructing
commerce raiders and armored rams for the Confederate government.
Sumner had been at the State Department and had read the dispatches
from England. Had Welles seen them? He had, and he was so upset
that he was not sure he would send to Seward an official letter he had
prepared opposing the employment of privateers. When Sumner asked
if he could read the letter, Welles handed it to him.

Like most of his official correspondence dealing with matters of high
policy, this letter was a closely reasoned piece. It would take a discerning eye to discover that he was pleading any special interest. Welles
expressed a very real concern over entrusting belligerent powers to private individuals without proper, clearly defined roles and responsibilities. This line of argument was so well developed that it masked his
equally genuine concern over maintaining the Navy's exclusive right

to take prizes. Sumner complimented Welles on his statement and urged him to send it. He hesitated no longer. Signing the ten-page letter, he directed that it be sent to the State Department at once.[16]

That evening, Lincoln called upon Welles. He explained that Sumner had warmly praised Welles' letter on privateering. The President was curious about the letter, which Sumner said conformed to his own views. Welles apologized for not having a clear copy as yet, assuring the President that he would send one over to the White House in the morning.

Sensing that Lincoln wanted to discuss the matter further, Welles eagerly grasped the opportunity of presenting his case, unhampered by the formal constraints of a Cabinet meeting. He declared flatly that the issuance of letters of marque would probably mean "a war with England," which "would be a serious calamity to us but not less serious to her." The British colonial system was vulnerable. Regular navy ships and privateers would interrupt communications between the home islands and the colonies, "on which she is as dependent for prosperity as they on her." As Lincoln knew, he had opposed privateering from the beginning of the conflict. He had not changed his views. But the recent letters of Lord John Russell on the Laird rams, and the concerted effort, as he viewed it, to break the blockade, were scarcely the acts of a friendly government. The British ought to be warned that there were limits to the forebearance of the United States. Welles would favor using the letters of marque as a bargaining counter against England, but would not invoke them except under the gravest of provocations. Lincoln listened carefully and seemed in general accord with what he said. Some days later, Sumner remarked to Welles that Lincoln had read his letter to Seward and had praised it in the most complimentary terms.

Seward did produce one applicant for a letter of marque. But when the President learned that the candidate was not prepared to go after the *Alabama* or the *Florida,* he lost whatever enthusiasm he had once had for the employment of privateers. Through diplomatic channels, however, Seward did bring the matter of privateers to the attention of Lord John Russell. The veiled threat may have had some influence on the British government's refusal to let the Laird rams go to sea.

Privateering had been only one aspect in a series of disputes between the State and Navy departments that involved the maintenance of the blockade. To the British, Seward often seemed overly pugnacious, even reckless, in his bold assertion of maritime rights that favored the North. But compared to Welles, he was quite moderate. With all his bluster, Seward would always yield a point if pressed hard. Welles, on the other hand, pursued an undeviating line in giving the broadest possible scope to belligerent rights.

As early as November 1861, Welles had dispatched instructions to William K. McKean, his squadron commander blockading the west Gulf coast, that cast the Secretary as a champion of belligerent rights. McKean had asked what he should do about the heavy traffic of small vessels, most of which were sailing under British colors from Havana to Matamoros, a Mexican port on the Rio Grande opposite Browns-ville, Texas. Their papers were in order, but they were loaded with contraband. McKean had no doubt that their cargoes were destined for the Confederacy. "You will not be deterred from preventing such commerce . . . ," Welles replied to McKean, "by any abuse of the English or any other flag." It soon became apparent that the Mata-moros trade was too complex for any naval commander to deal with under these general instructions. Matamoros was some forty miles up-river, and Mexico was a neutral power. Any assessment of cargo des-tination was difficult to make without visible proof of transshipment, a practical impossibility in most cases of contraband. In April 1862, Welles sent further instructions, which not only enlarged upon his pre-vious declaration of belligerent rights in the waters off the mouth of the Rio Grande, but specified where and how they were to be exercised.[17]

Armed with these new instructions, Admiral Farragut, commanding the blockade fleet in the Gulf, was able to step up his rate of seizures. By the summer of 1862 the annoying trade from the West Indies to Matamoros had been pruned back sharply, a development that had not gone unchallenged in the British press and in Parliament. *The Times* and the compulsively conservative *Saturday Review* accused the Palmerston government of truckling under to the boisterous Yankees. Confederate sympathizers asked embarrassing questions in Parliament about alleged insults to the British flag. Reacting to this criticism, the British government instructed Lord Lyons, its Minister to the United States, to protest the seizures and to demand that United States naval commanders be instructed to show more discretion in their interpre-tation of neutral rights. The tone of the note was stiff enough to alarm both Seward and Lincoln, who wanted no repetition of the *Trent* crisis. Seward, in Lincoln's name, directed Welles to issue new instruc-tions that would modify considerably the belligerent rights he had claimed and had enforced for the past several months. The wily Secre-tary of State held back his formal request until he had acquainted

Welles in general terms with the British attitude; by this he hoped to soften Welles' position and avoid any Cabinet confrontation. Welles noted on August 11 that the State Department was worried about the conduct of United States naval officers toward ships under British colors that approached the blockade. "We are not, it is true," he admitted, "in a condition for a war with Great Britain just at this time, but Britain is in scarcely a better condition for war with us."

When he reached his office, the next day, Welles found Seward's note of August 8. After digesting its contents, he decided that the State Department was surrendering American rights that were clearly upheld by international law. He was particularly incensed at the requirement that American naval officers, in searching a suspected blockader, be forbidden to impound papers covered by foreign seals. These were not to be sent to the prize court, as formerly, but to the appropriate foreign officers, there to be opened. If these officials found evidence of contraband they were to forward it to the prize court. That a consul or any other foreign officer was more competent than a United States District Court Judge to evaluate captured documents Welles denied as a matter of fact and of law. Practically, he feared that these officials, having a duty to protect the citizens of their governments, would not be as objective in their opinions as a duly constituted prize court, operating under international guidelines and American admiralty law, would be. He feared this request was the beginning of a diplomatic assault to weaken the blockade.[18]

Welles' mood had been uncertain at best. The weather was unseasonably hot, even for Washington in August. He was in the midst of reorganizing the department, and Faxon, who was responsible for all clerical details, was sick. Welles and Admiral Andrew H. Foote, who had just taken charge of the Bureau of Equipment and Recruiting, had had a misunderstanding about the appointment of clerks. Welles was also worried about his son Tom, and even more worried about the alarming number of United States merchant vessels that were being seized by the Confederate raiders *Florida* and *Alabama*. The commercial community of the North was on a rampage. Another vicious press campaign was under way against Welles for not tracking the raiders down. Privateering was in the air again.

Thus it was an angry Welles who marched over to the State Department, determined not to give way. He soon realized, however, that, whatever the merits of his case, Seward had committed himself to Lord Lyons. The Secretary of State could not change his position without humiliating himself. Nor did Welles think that he could fare any better if he appealed to the President, whom he correctly judged was so "alarmed with the bugaboo of a foreign war" that he would support Seward. He had to content himself with reading Seward a lecture on international law, underscoring the fact that no blockade-runner ever cleared for its real destination, but always for a neutral port. The force of his argument did have some effect on Seward, who professed ignorance of the law. He suggested that Welles modify those points where the State Department had been too yielding, but he thought that the matter of sealed papers could not be substantially altered and still be acceptable to the British. Welles reshaped the State Department draft so that its tone of concession was not so evident, deleted some minor points of procedure that he felt were illegal, and asserted with some vigor that the United States was not relinquishing any of its belligerent rights. In an adroit though unfortunately misleading phrase, he concealed his defeat at the hands of Seward by instructing naval officers "that we should exercise great forbearance with great firmness."[19] Welles had backed down as gracefully as he could on the issue of sealed papers, yet he had given fair notice to Seward and to the British that he had not changed his stand on belligerent rights.[20]

In the spring of 1862, Seward and Lyons had negotiated a long overdue treaty between the United States and Great Britain to suppress the African slave trade more effectively. When Seward brought the treaty to Welles' attention on September 17, 1862, and asked for a list of cruisers to be employed in executing the treaty, Welles detected another sinister plot to weaken the blockade. The regular blockade service was acting as an effective deterrent, he argued. Detaching vessels for this special purpose would restrict their activities and weaken unquestioned belligerent rights. In the exercise of regular search and seizure, Welles assured Seward, the boarding party will not hesitate "to seize slavers or other piratical craft . . . ," but this was not to be construed as "the only object of the search."[21]

The British government did not press for a literal interpretation of the slave trade treaty, though it had by no means given up its policy to curtail what it regarded as Welles' extravagant claims. Six weeks later, on October 31, 1862, Welles received another of Seward's notes. So much in character, he thought, so officious. Seward had taken it upon himself to advise Welles that he should issue yet another set of instructions to all naval officers on sea duty. The subject was a delicate one— the handling of the mails found on suspected blockade-runners. Welles had stipulated that mails were to be sent to prize courts for whatever disposition the judge might order. Seward now asked that they be forwarded with their seals intact as rapidly as possible to their destination. At the time Welles was extremely busy, working with Fox to organize a flying squadron that he hoped would trap the Confederate raiders yet not weaken the blockade. During September and October of 1862, the *Alabama* alone had captured a dozen whalers and eighteen cargo and grain vessels—thirty ships in thirty days. Welles had neither the time nor the inclination to concern himself over Seward's note. He simply told him when they met a day or so later that he would not do what was asked regarding the mails, that in his opinion it was contrary to American and to international law. He never even bothered to make a formal reply in writing.

What Welles did not know at the time was that the agile Secretary of State was sparring with the British, trying to block the mounting offensive of Whitehall. In the absence of Lord Lyons, Seward had given William Stuart, the chargé, a copy of his letter to Welles. Stuart promptly sent it on to Lord John Russell, who assumed that it represented the policy of the Lincoln administration, not just Seward's opinion. He read the letter in Parliament.[22]

Russell's interpretation of Seward's letter was good news to would-be blockade-runners. In determining whether a cargo bound for a neutral port such as Matamoros was in fact contraband, the best evidence, the real manifest—bills of lading and other pertinent papers—could be sealed up in the mails, which now had to be forwarded untouched to their addressees. Certain British shippers interested in the cotton trade were quick to act under the "new" rules. A blockade-runner, the *Peterhof*, which had just brought in a cargo of cotton from Charleston, was quickly fitted out for a return voyage to Matamoros. Confederate agents purchased her cargo, and she slipped out of Liverpool in early February 1863, though not before the American consul in London had discovered a document showing her cargo to be contraband. As soon as this information was received in Washington, the Navy Department alerted Charles Wilkes, of *Trent* notoriety, then commanding the West Indies squadron, that the *Peterhof* was a probable carrier of contraband. On February 25, one of Wilkes' cruisers stopped the *Peterhof* off St. Thomas. The boarding officer deemed her papers to be of a suspicious character.

Deeply concerned about the Charleston expedition, Welles ignored the *Peterhof*, which he knew to be in the custody of the Federal District Court in New York. But on April 11, 1863, the ship and her cargo were abruptly brought to his attention when Seward paid him an unexpected visit. Seward explained that Judge Betts of the New York District had ordered Prize Commissioner Henry H. Elliott to have the *Peterhof's* mail bags opened in the presence of E. M. Archibald, the British Consul. Archibald was asked to examine their contents and remove those letters bearing upon the *Peterhof's* cargo, its consignee, or any Confederate correspondence. These were to be turned over to the Federal District Court as evidence in determining whether the ship and her cargo were lawful prize. All other mail was to be forwarded promptly. Archibald refused and immediately referred the matter to Lord Lyons.

Seward had brought with him Lyons' letter of protest, together with copies of Archibald's dispatches describing the incident and his actions. Welles read the correspondence, noting with astonishment Lyons' remark that "all these proceedings seem to be so contrary to the spirit of your letter to the Secretary of the Navy of the 31st of October that I cannot help hoping you will send orders by telegraph to stop them." Looking directly at Seward, he asked if he had sent the telegram requested. Seward replied that he had not done so, because, he said, it was a matter of naval rather than foreign policy concern. Judge Betts would be more likely to accept Welles' advice than his. Would Welles telegraph him to have all the mails sent directly to their destination unopened? Welles would not! Seward's instructions to which Lord Lyons referred were without authority, were not instructions at all.

The mail, said Welles, "was properly in the custody of the Court and beyond Executive control."

"But," said Seward, "mails are sacred—they are an institution."

"That would do for peace but not for war," Welles replied. "The most that could be conceded," he added, "would be to mails on regular recognized neutral packets and not to blockade runners and irregular vessels with contraband like the *Peterhof*."

On April 13, 1863, Welles wrote Seward an official letter that took the Secretary to task in no uncertain terms for exceeding his authority and compromising avowed national rights. Privately, his feelings were much stronger. Seward's note had been "supercilious and offensive, the concession disreputable and unwarrantable, the surrender of our indisputable rights disgraceful and the whole thing unstatesmanlike and illegal, unjust to the Navy and the country, and discourteous to the Secretary of the Navy and the President (who were not) consulted." However vigorously Welles protested in his official letter to Seward, however freely he might have displayed his feelings in his diary, he must have known that he would be forced to give way again.

Lyons remained adamant, British opinion sustaining his stand. The

British press and the government seemed almost as belligerent about the *Peterhof* and the seizure of the mails she carried as they had been about the *Trent*. Seward was alarmed and embarrassed at the same time. Caught between Lyons' intransigence and Welles' stubbornness, he risked a possible diplomatic rupture on the one hand and what was sure to be an unpleasant Cabinet confrontation on the other. In a last effort to avoid airing the problem before his colleagues, he tried once more to have Welles reverse himself. He wrote him another official letter saying that he had discussed the *Peterhof* case with Lincoln, who supported his position, that the mails must be surrendered. "This was not the time for the Navy," he said, "to raise new questions or pretensions under the belligerent right of search."

Welles would not back down without a fight, and in the open if possible. In his reply to Seward, he emphasized that what was asked would be an unconstitutional interference with clearly defined powers of the judiciary at the demand of a foreign power acting illegally under international law. It was a pithy letter, well calculated to give Lincoln pause, with its frequent references to illegal actions on the part of the Executive.

Welles assumed that Seward would appeal again to the President, and that the President, ever fearful of foreign intimidation, would sustain him. He was also quite certain that Lincoln would spare Seward the humiliation of having to explain himself before the Cabinet. But there was a bare possibility he could forestall the Secretary of State. Before sending his reply to Seward, he took it with him to the White House and read it to the President. Lincoln listened with great interest, then read the letter himself. Studying its contents, he said that Welles had raised points of law with which he was unfamiliar. But he understood that any interference with the foreign mails might well bring on hostilities, an event that must be avoided at all costs. The subject needed further study, he thought. Over the weekend Lincoln spoke with Seward about the *Peterhof* mails. Still not completely satisfied, he asked Welles and Seward to remain after a short Cabinet meeting on April 21 and state their cases. Neither man would retreat from his previous position—Seward harping on the grave risk of foreign intervention, Welles arguing that the doctrine of continuous voyage applied to the *Peterhof* and that this doctrine had been firmly established in international law, largely through British precedents. Mails on suspected blockade-runners were not exempt. These vessels were not, like the *Trent*, regular mail packets, but carriers of contraband whose mail bags contained the surest evidence of their character. It would hurt naval morale, and it would weaken the blockade, if the mails on such vessels could not be examined. The Executive had no right to interfere with a regular judicial process.

Undecided over how to proceed, Lincoln asked Welles and Seward to write out their respective positions for him to study. Welles attacked the problem with his accustomed thoroughness, his usual skill in shaping an argument. Letting all other business pile up on his desk, enlisting the aid of Charles Eames, Francis H. Upton, who had just published a valuable treatise on commerce in wartime, and Senator Sumner, Welles spent the entire week from April 20 to April 26, 1863, preparing a 5600-word brief, studded with British and American precedents, which affirmed the doctrine of continuous voyage.

Welles' mighty effort made no impression whatever. On the very day Lincoln had requested his opinion in writing, Seward wrote to Charles Francis Adams, the United States Minister to Britain, that the *Peterhof*'s mails would be surrendered. While Welles, Sumner, Eames, and Upton were searching out precedents, the federal district attorney in New York, at the direction of the President, was asking the court to release the mails. When Welles delivered his lengthy document to Lincoln on April 27, the mails were already on their way to their destination.[23]

Matamoros would remain a weak spot in the blockade until the war's end, though its trade became less vital to the Confederacy after the surrender of Vicksburg and Port Hudson, the last two Confederate strongholds on the Mississippi, in July 1863. Federal gunboats could now cruise freely on the Mississippi and its major tributaries. They maintained a fairly effective river blockade, one that cut deeply into the overland shipment of contraband from Texas.

As the naval blockade on river and coastline became more efficient during 1864, an increasing internal trade between North and South canceled out much of the blockade's effectiveness. In reacting to this state of affairs, Welles became involved with the Treasury. There had always been a certain amount of contraband traffic from the North that found its way South to be exchanged for cotton, naval stores, and tobacco. In May 1862, Lincoln opened the ports of New Orleans, Port Royal, South Carolina, and Beaufort, North Carolina, for all trade except contraband goods and the passage of persons, papers, and information that would assist the enemy. Since there was no clear definition of contraband goods, only such obvious items as guns, munitions, and the like were liable to seizure. Substantial quantities of foodstuffs, woolen cloth, drugs, even army blankets, of direct aid to the Confederate cause, were freely traded through the blockade.[24]

Welles was probably consulted, and he went along, though no doubt reluctantly, with the President's decision. If Lincoln and a majority of the Cabinet thought it expedient to open these ports, he was not the man to stand in their way. But he objected strenuously when General John A. Dix, the Army commander at Norfolk, backed up by Chase, requested authority to issue special licenses for trade into that city and its environs. Chase had based his argument on the fact that civilians were suffering want because of the strict blockade that Admiral S. P. Lee was maintaining along the Virginia coast. Welles remarked that this was not a case of sympathy, but of duty. Until the President opened the port, he would not alter his instructions to Lee. Stanton supported him, saying that Norfolk would become an open avenue of supplies to General Lee's army. When Chase persisted, Welles said: "Then, raise the blockade. Act in good faith with all. Let us have no favoritism. That is my policy. You must not use the blockade for domestic traffic (or to enrich a few)." Lincoln, who had been inclined to grant Chase's request, asked Chase and Seward to examine the question further in the light of the points Welles had raised.

At the time Welles was having troubles enough trying to maintain a close blockade in the face of mounting resistance from Britain and France. Nor had Lincoln made the Navy's job any easier when he opened several ports on the South Atlantic and Gulf coasts. Now Chase was trying to punch another hole in the blockade at Norfolk under circumstances that Welles could only regard as self-seeking—an opportunity to build up patronage at the Navy's expense. As Welles saw it, the ambitious Secretary was trying to cultivate Dix, who was a prominent war Democrat. Welles absolved Dix and Chase of any corrupt financial interest in the matter, but he would not say the same thing about officers on Dix's staff or the Treasury agents who worked for Chase. These "bloodsuckers," as Welles called them, were attempting to use the Navy, a public service, at public expense for their own private benefit. Their activities stirred up memories of the past when he and his fellow Jacksonians had fought the good fight against a similar proposition, the Bank of the United States.

But beyond the immediate issues of graft and special privilege loomed the greater question of trading with the enemy, of providing the Confederates with goods so that they could kill and maim Union soldiers and sailors, so that they could prolong the war. While Welles had Stanton's support, he could fend off Dix and Chase, though he was not particularly candid with either man as to his own position. When Dix came to see him a few days after Chase broached the matter, Welles misled him. He was not, he told Dix, opposed to opening the port, in fact he would be happy to see it done, but Stanton would have to be convinced.[25] Welles did his best to persuade Dix that any system of licensed trade through the blockade must lead to corruption. The General was stubbornly unconvinced. During the next week Army officers and Treasury agents made so much trouble for Admiral Lee that Welles appealed directly to Chase—Norfolk should remain either closed or open, but no special licenses should be given. Chase, he thought, agreed with him. At the regular Cabinet session immediately following their discussion, however, the Secretary of the Treasury remained silent when the subject came up. And Stanton shook Welles' confidence when he remarked that he thought the Navy Department had approved Dix's system of licensing.

The irrepressible Dix would not be put off. After three visits to Washington during early November, he finally persuaded Stanton to withdraw his objections. Making no effort to conceal his aggravation, Welles insisted that he must have a presidential order before he would instruct blockading officers to accept Army or Treasury licensing in the Norfolk area. Chase and Stanton each drafted an order for the President's signature. Lincoln signed Stanton's version on November 11, and the Treasury Department prepared an extensive set of trade regulations. Within a few days dozens of operators, flaunting Dix's licenses and Chase's regulations in the faces of the blockading naval officers, were pouring merchandise of every description except obvious contraband into Norfolk. Bales of cotton were being brought out, not the local products—barrel staves, turpentine, lumber—that Dix had assured Welles would make up return cargoes. As Welles anticipated, abuses and corruption immediately appeared. Yet even he had never thought that they would be on such a grand scale. By May of 1863 he had become so appalled at Dix's "loose and improper management" that he ordered Admiral Lee not to honor "some strange permits . . . wholly unauthorized." When Benjamin F. Butler, a political general who had a talent for exploiting the main chance, succeeded Dix at Norfolk some months later, the management became more scandalous.[26]

Welles had specifically ordered Admiral Lee to watch the coastwise trade carefully and not be deterred in examining cargoes simply because of Treasury licenses or permits from the Army commander in the Norfolk area. But as much as he deplored the traffic, Welles hesitated to antagonize the politically powerful Butler, who had been always cordial to him personally and was a close friend of Fox's. Nor was he willing to challenge Chase and the clamorous cotton manufacturing interests of the North without Stanton's support. Only when two particularly flagrant distortions of the Treasury regulations were brought to his attention in early February of 1864 did he register a strong official protest. Welles might not have done so even then had he not been pressed by family worries.

The previous October he had agreed, with a heavy heart, to let his son Tom resign from the Naval Academy. Welles had hoped that Tom might find himself at Newport, but the young man had been a midshipman scarcely six months when the complaining letters began to arrive. For another six months, father and son sparred through the mails while Tom's record at the Academy declined precipitously. Bowing to the inevitable, Welles accepted Tom's resignation. The young man came home, but, after a few weeks of comparative calm, he became restless, and his frequent outbursts of ill humor soon disturbed the household, no one more than his overworked father. Now Tom wanted to volunteer for the Army. Again Welles opposed what he thought was another example of his son's thoughtlessness. Judging from past experience, Tom would never submit to army discipline. Once enlisted, he could not resign as he had at Newport. Though he would not admit it even to himself, Welles also feared exposing his son to the danger of enemy fire at close hand. The drunkenness and the disorderly behavior of camp life worried him too.

Worn down as much by his extended resistance to Tom's wishes as by his work and responsibilities, Welles was not at his best during the early spring of 1864. When he received yet another note from one of Admiral Lee's commanders, Foxhall Parker, that he was holding two suspicious vessels, the *Princeton* and the *Ann Hamilton*, both of which were operating under Butler's permits, he could not contain himself. Contrary to Treasury regulations, the ships were laden with privately owned goods. One, the *Ann Hamilton*, was also carrying $15,000 in Confederate money and cargo not listed on her manifest. Butler's permits, while specifically referring to Treasury regulations, conferred broad trading privileges, which Welles thought unwarranted. He took the permits to the White House, where for the first time in months he expressed himself freely to the President on the abuses of the Norfolk trade. Lincoln asked him to see Chase, who would know how the vessel had cleared.[27] Welles knew that Chase had delegated all clearances to Treasury agents, just as Stanton had delegated permits to Army officers. He knew also that neither Cabinet officer was supervising the trade and that both would be embarrassed if Lincoln asked for an explanation. With a grim relish he called on the Secretary of the Treasury, knowing that Chase could not provide a satisfactory answer to Lincoln's request.

Chase was not in, so Welles took the more serious step of writing him officially for information about the *Princeton* and the *Ann Hamilton*. His personal worries, his sense of righteous wrath, his frustration over the conduct of the war, all came to a head in his letter to Chase. He did not, as he should have, simply state the facts and say that the President wanted an explanation on the clearances. Instead, adopting a censorious tone, he lectured Chase, blaming the Treasury Department for encouraging a system that fostered graft and favoritism. Salmon P. Chase may have appeared the most composed of men, imperturbable, unruffled, even serene under the most trying provocation. But in reality, he was more temperamental than any member of the Cabinet—"very violent, and occasionally even unjust, while swept by a gale of passion," one of his closest associates described him.

After reading Welles' frosty letter, Chase lost his temper and penned an angry reply. The Secretary of the Treasury was having his own problems too, though they were political, not personal, as Welles' were. He had good reason to suspect Welles and Fox of working against him in his native state of New Hampshire, where he was seeking the presidential candidacy. Welles' letter, wrote Chase, was entirely unacceptable and so personally offensive that he could not believe the Secretary of the Navy had written it. Welles replied promptly, declaring that he had written the letter, but he apologized for offending the Secretary and disclaimed any intention of lecturing him. Chase was somewhat mollified, but he would not drop the imputation Welles had made, that the license system was corrupt and that Chase was responsible for it. Chase had always thought Welles a man of mediocre ability, honest, possessing some skill for argument, but slow, cautious, a mere creature of Lincoln's will. He would never admit before the President, who was receiving copies of all this correspondence, that he might have erred. Confident that he and his staff would overwhelm these feeble contentions of the Navy, he mobilized all of the considerable talent at his disposal in the Treasury Department. The result was an able brief contending that the two vessels were operating within Treasury regulations. A lengthy correspondence followed. Chase wrote all the letters from the Treasury Department. His experienced and capable Assistant Secretary, Maunsell B. Field, thought them exceptionally fine pieces. But he had to admit that those received from the Navy Department were so impressive that "we were even a little overmatched in the controversy." All of the senior people in the Treasury Department assumed Fox was the author.

Later Field learned that Welles had personally drafted the Navy correspondence and that he had not even consulted any of his subordinates or consultants. "This circumstance," he wrote, "greatly raised my estimate of Mr. Welles, and from subsequent intercourse with him I became convinced that he was one of the ablest, and in every respect one of the best of Mr. Lincoln's immediate advisors."[28]

Welles' letter of March 17 did indeed "overmatch" any of Chase's correspondence. It was a careful analysis of the two cases, and it left no doubt the vessels were carrying contraband and that one of them, the *Ann Hamilton*, was not acting under Treasury regulations. In sending this letter, Welles was prepared for Chase to take offense, because he, too, thought he had the better of him when he quoted Chase's own regulations in support of Navy action. Chase, Welles believed, would not stand correction with good grace—unlike Seward, who for all his faults and all his arrogance would always admit an error. When Chase did broach the subject at a Cabinet meeting five days later, on March 22, he was more defensive than angry. Seward, who had seen all the correspondence too, asked Chase jocularly if he had any gold to sell.

Chase, in no mood for banter, replied that if he wanted to make money he needed a permit from Butler and a pass from Welles. The Treasury always accepted military permits at face value.

Welles would not let Chase get off so lightly. "But General Butler explicitly states that this trading permit to a Baltimorean to trade in North Carolina was based on your 52, 53, and 54 trade regulations. . . ."

"Ah," Chase replied, "the permit was before the regulations were promulgated."

"No," Welles said, "they were distinctly and particularly cited as his authority."

As much discomfited by Welles' air of certainty as he was nettled by the trend of the conversation, Chase made a clumsy joke. Seward came to his rescue by opening up another topic.

In both cases under contention Welles was vindicated. The *Ann Hamilton* was adjudged a lawful prize, while the other vessel, the *Princeton*, was not permitted to trade in North Carolina. But the significance of the entire affair was neither Chase's discomfiture nor Welles' triumph. From that time on the Treasury made a serious and, on the whole, successful attempt to enforce its own regulations on trading through the blockade.[29]

Unfortunately, the Treasury Department, much to Welles' disgust, was not so amenable to reform in a far more significant area—the issuance of licenses themselves. He could do nothing except deplore the air of corruption, favoritism, and abuse surrounding the internal cotton trade, which the government was regulating. As the Confederate hold on cotton-growing territory weakened, Lincoln came under increasing pressure from Congress and Northern and European textile manufacturers. Along with the lobbyists came the usual sordid train of opportunists who saw the profits to be made in getting cotton out of the South, if they could do so under special license.

While Dix was pushing for licensed trade through the blockade of the Virginia and the North Carolina coasts, others were securing special permits from Chase, and even from the President himself, to trade in cotton through enemy lines. Welles was more outspoken about these privileges than he had been about the Norfolk trade. He was opposed to any system of trade permits—"these schemes to fight and feed the enemy," borrowing Attorney General Bates' succinct phrase. Yet he also recognized that legitimate commerce between North and South was an essential first step in reconstructing the nation. The problem, of course, lay in what was legitimate and what was not, which necessarily involved the means with the ends. By January 1864, he had come to believe that all of the country west of the Mississippi and north of New Orleans ought to be opened to trade. He so expressed himself in Cabinet, where the President overruled him.

Lincoln himself had submitted a rough draft of a general order that would permit owners of cotton to deposit their bales at New Orleans and Baton Rouge. There the cotton could be purchased with greenbacks only—no gold, no barter of goods. The traffic would be under the supervision of the Treasury Department. Chase drew up the new regulations, which were put into effect on January 26, 1864.[30] Abuses began at once as Treasury agents did a brisk traffic in cotton on their own and sold licenses to cotton speculators. Welles denounced the system unsparingly, not only because he felt it was demoralizing, but also because he was certain that it was becoming a patronage machine for Chase. He saw no special privileges involved, however, when the Navy seized thousands of bales of cotton and shipped them off to prize courts. In the Red River Campaign, Admiral Porter and his officers and men devoted more of their time and their resources to seizing cotton than to their mission of providing support for Banks' army. When

Chase criticized Porter's activities, Welles was quick to defend him. "The naval men," he said, "could capture and retain nothing which the courts do not adjudge a good prize." Whether it was a good prize or not, the Navy's operations in cotton became so flagrant that Congress acted to remove captured enemy property from the jurisdiction of the courts. Ownership was vested in the government. Welles complained about this action in Cabinet, but Lincoln signed the bill into law.[31]

The President overruled his Secretary of the Navy once again, within the next few months—this time under circumstances that scarcely did him credit. Heavy frauds had been discovered in the purchasing of supplies at the Boston, Brooklyn, and Philadelphia navy yards. Welles was appalled. He prided himself on an honest and efficient administration. Now he learned that corruption was tainting the Navy Department. His strictures against lax procedures at War and Treasury, his frequent indictment of most Congressmen as profligate partisans or "lobby-jobbers," must have seemed less than convincing even to himself. He took prompt and vigorous action to prosecute the malefactors, even though most were prominent businessmen with political influence. Those who felt the heavy hand of the department were the Smith brothers, Franklin and Edward, of Boston, who were on cordial terms with Representative Samuel Hooper and Senators Sumner and Hale; Isaac Henderson, the Navy agent in New York, who was co-publisher with William Cullen Bryant of the *Evening Post*; and H. D. Stover of Philadelphia, an associate of George Opdyke, the radical politician and ex-Mayor of New York, Thurlow Weed, and Charles B. Sedgewick, former chief of the House naval affairs committee. The Navy secured convictions against all these fraudulent contractors, though not without Welles being subjected to fierce attack from the *Boston Journal* and the New York *Evening Post*. The politicians were active, too, in condemning Welles for what they charged were the harsh and arbitrary actions of Fox and his detective, Colonel H. L. Olcott. After all the investigations, the lengthy trials, the unfavorable publicity, Lincoln set aside the convictions, giving the unfortunate appearance that the Navy Department had acted wrongly, that Welles, like all weak men, gloried in displaying his power by persecuting defenseless citizens.

Those months were among the most trying for Welles personally of his entire career in government.[32] He had spent many anxious moments worrying about his son Tom, who had gone into the Army of the Potomac, first as an aide to General McCook, then on the staff of General Ord. The carnage of the Wilderness Campaign sickened him.

That his son, and his nephew, Robert G. Welles, a Captain in the Tenth U. S. Infantry, might become casualties was never far from his thoughts.

He found that he could not bear the hectic gaiety of the Washington social season. There was something so inhuman about the rounds of entertainment, the costly wines and confections, the glitter and the idle chatter, while soldiers and sailors were suffering and dying. "Something," he wrote his son Edgar, "sad and desponding almost like making merry at a funeral."[33] And increasingly, he had been thinking of the peace that was to follow. Would it be a Carthaginian peace, with the triumphant radicals sowing salt on the ruins of the Confederacy, forcing its people under a yoke of bayonets? Or was it to be a re-unification on moderate terms—the end of slavery combined with the restoration of citizenship to former rebels through the liberal use of executive clemency? What of Negro suffrage, and what of civil rights for the emancipated blacks, which Sumner and Thaddeus Stevens were demanding in Congress? At the regular Cabinet meeting on Friday, November 25, 1864, Lincoln canvassed opinion on reconstruction, which was to form a major theme in his message to Congress. Welles thought it might be good policy to restore both the rebellious states and the people to the Union. "I would not recognize the Confederate Government," he said, "for that is usurpation, but the states are entities and may be recognized and treated with." Stanton, present for the first time in six weeks, made what Welles described as "very pertinent and in the main, correct and well timed remarks." He advised the President to make no departure from his previously announced policies, but "to hold open the doors of conciliation and invite the people to return to their duty." Welles was gratified that Stanton, whom he believed had been following an ever more radical course for a year and a half, was coming around to a more conservative position.[34] He had always been more than half convinced that the Secretary of War had been instrumental in drafting a radical document that achieved wide currency in the summer of 1863—the Whiting letter.

# CHAPTER 25

# On the Defensive

SINCE CHARLES SUMNER HAD advanced his radical ideas on reconstruction in the early months of the thirty-seventh Congress, that question and the closely related question of slavery had occupied little space in the *Congressional Globe* or in the metropolitan press. By tacit consent, Cabinet members had avoided these issues. In Congress too, there had been scant formal discussion over the future status of slavery and reconstruction, but much scrambling for private schemes at the public expense. Questions of state seemed for the time to have been submerged in the lucrative pursuit of government contracts for interested clients.

Then, in late July 1863, an elaborate letter on reconstruction written to the Union League of Philadelphia made the topic of the postwar settlement a matter of wide and earnest public debate. William Whiting, Solicitor of the War Department, had written the letter. Whiting, an able lawyer with an ingratiating personality, was highly regarded by Stanton and Seward. Lincoln also praised his qualities. Welles thought him sharp rather than profound, "such a man as Stanton would select and Seward use."[1] Whiting's letter supplied almost every argument that would be used to justify radical reconstruction. "Do not allow old (secessionist) states with their constitutions still unaltered," he warned, "to resume state power," for they would gain by fraud what they had lost by fighting. He made no distinction between the Confederate states and their people, between their loyal and disloyal inhabitants. By setting up a government and seeking recognition from foreign powers, the Confederacy was waging a territorial war against the United States. Everyone within its limits ceased to become a personal enemy of the

United States and became a public enemy. States' rights, according to Whiting, rest upon personal rights. When these become forfeit, the states become forfeit. "Can there be a sovereignty without a people," he asked, "or a state without inhabitants?" In direct opposition to Welles' concept of an integral Union, Whiting argued that the fighting line was the boundary line. He capped his argument against states' rights with a telling stroke. Assuming that Union victory would be followed by the readmission of former Confederate states on the same basis as before the war, what security, he asked, would there be for the emancipated slave? Would not these states pass laws that would "render the position of the blacks intolerable; or reduce them all to slavery?"[2] The letter produced a sensation in the North. Democrats denounced it unsparingly. Republican reaction ranged from enthusiastic approval to muted opposition. Significantly, Whiting did not state where responsibility lay for reconstruction. Since he was an officer of the administration, it was assumed he spoke for the Executive branch, not the Congress.

Welles suspected that Stanton had inspired the piece, but he was not surprised when Chase broached the subject three weeks after its initial publication. Self-assured, as always, Chase declared that slavery could not be tolerated in any of the rebellious states.

What of the loyal slave states? asked Welles. "Were all the slave states involved in the rebellion, the case would be different for then all would share alike."

Welles stood by the Emancipation Proclamation, but clearly he was concerned about states' rights, which Whiting had said did not apply to the South. The paradox was troublesome and potentially disruptive to the federal system. Some loyal states would remain slave states, while former enemies that had waged war against the Union to expand slavery would be free states. In his conversation with Chase, Welles was groping for a practical solution. He must have surprised Chase, who had always counted him as leaning toward the radical side in the Cabinet. He may even have surprised himself, as his contradictory statements seem to indicate.

For almost forty years his concept of states' rights had ranged him with the more radical political doctrinaires—Loco-Focos, Free-Soilers, Anti-Nebraska Democrats, Republicans. Welles' style of Jacksonian Democracy had been used effectively to help make the Union safe for the North—safe for its free labor and capital, for its individualistic, acquisitive way of life. The radical Jacksonians had stood Calhoun on his head, as Welles, in a rare moment of insight, realized with striking clarity.[3] Now that the Union was to be secure for the new entrepreneurial ethic, states' rights would have to shift gears if it were to survive as a political force. Though admirably devised as a political and constitutional defense against an expanding, dynamic, slave economy, the states' rights of Jefferson and Jackson could not without drastic change be adapted to the centralizing forces of civil war and industrial revolution.

Welles was not prepared to accept such change. Yet he had to recognize the weight of Solicitor Whiting's argument that a complete restoration of the old Union without adequate safeguards against state power could encourage the defeated Confederate states to gain by partisan maneuver what they had been unable to achieve by force of arms. A radical all of his political life, Welles was facing the dilemma of reconciling an intrinsically conservative political philosophy with the radical demands of revolutionary times. Typically, he sought to rationalize his position, and in doing so he fell back upon a strict construction of the Constitution. After his first talk with Chase, he thought much and deeply about the legal and the constitutional problems posed by reconstruction. Nearly a year before, on June 11, 1862, Senator James Dixon had offered a resolution that the states were indestructible, that they were not responsible for the rebellious acts of their inhabitants. Welles was always a close reader of the *Congressional Globe,* and he was also familiar with the various radical plans for reconstructing the Confederacy under the aegis of Congress, once the Union prevailed in the war. He reread Whiting's letter and, remembering Dixon's resolution, thought he saw a way to a just and safe settlement without abolishing the rights of the states. Those who would convert the rebellious states into conquered provinces were making a common error. They had reasoned that the Union was fighting rebellious states, when in reality it was fighting rebellious people.[4] Radical opinion was silent, he had noticed, on the rights of loyal free states, let alone loyal slave states. If some states of the old Union had forfeited their rights to a national sovereignty, might not the rest of the states have forfeited their rights also? The Constitution could not operate one way in the North and another in the South. If the rights of any state, rebellious or otherwise, were taken away, it must alter the relationship of all states to the central government, reasoned Welles.

Three days after Welles worked out his own solution to reconstruction, Chase called at his house and invited him for a carriage ride.

Suspecting that the Secretary of the Treasury wished to continue their conversation of August 13, Welles was happy to put aside unfinished business and join him.

Chase repeated his earlier comments: peace terms must be based upon immediate and unconditional emancipation. If Lincoln stood firm on his Proclamation, any rebellious state that wanted to surrender would have to abolish slavery before it could resume its political ties with the Union.

"That," said Welles, "brings up other questions . . . where is the authority of Congress, or a fraction of Congress, to exclude a state or to prescribe conditions to one of the original states . . . where is the authority of the President or Congress to dictate her local policy—these conditions being new, not a part of the Federal compact . . . the states must have equal political rights or the government cannot stand on the basis of 1789."

Chase answered with Whiting's and Sumner's arguments that the rebellious states had forfeited their rights by making war on the government. He insisted that the abolition of slavery was an essential precondition to any peace terms.

Welles did not think that reconstruction should begin with harsh assumptions regarding states. "Ought we not to act on individuals," he asked, repeating Dixon's argument, "and through them on the states?"

Chase had been an early enthusiast of the territorial approach to reconstruction, though time and political circumstances had considerably modified his views. He was now quite familiar with Welles' conservative approach, which he opposed. But the presidential election was not far off, and Chase was eager for the Republican nomination. In need of all the support he could get, he would not let ideology stand in the way of his inordinate ambition. He encouraged Welles by reacting favorably to his suggestion.

Seizing the opportunity, Welles elaborated on it, pointing out that he knew of no way to punish a state except through its citizens as individuals. "Besides," he said, "it must be remembered we [are] classing the innocent with the guilty, punishing our true friends who had already suffered greatly in our cause as severely as the worst rebels."

Chase seemed to agree with him, but remained vague on states' rights. He did say that he spoke often with Lincoln on these matters. Could he count on Welles for support? Stanton was reliable, but he was apt to go his own way. Seward and Blair opposed him for personal as well as political reasons. Bates and Secretary of the Interior John B. Usher, who had succeeded Caleb Smith, had no influence with Lincoln.

Flattered that Chase should ask his aid, Welles nevertheless would not commit himself. Later, in the privacy of his library, he decided that "the intrusion of partyism" would prove to be the greatest barrier to an equitable reconstruction of the nation. "Chase I see is warped by this. It is not strange that he should be for he has aspirations which are likely to be affected by these issues."[5] Welles had seen through Chase; he knew that the stately Secretary was seeking to consolidate the various Republican factions and was angling to break the power of the Blairs once and for all.[6] Welles would never forget the constitutional crisis less than nine months before, when a caucus of Republican senators had tried to drive Seward from the Cabinet. Chase had been one of the instigators, Welles thought at the time, because Seward stood in the way of his ambition for the presidency. But he was certain that Stanton and Caleb Smith were implicated too. Each, he felt, had come to resent Seward's pretensions and his undeniable influence with Lincoln. It also seemed plain to Welles that Seward's conservatism on emancipation and on the enlistment of black soldiers had been a devisive factor.[7] Since then Seward and Chase had maintained an uneasy truce, but Montgomery Blair, who had also been marked for purging, carried on his personal quarrel with both Chase and Stanton. Welles admired Blair for his common sense, his complete loyalty to Lincoln, and his acute intelligence. He could not fail to recognize his weaknesses, however. Blair's dislike for Stanton bordered on hatred; his contempt for Chase ran dark and deep. Egotistical, voluble, and indiscreet, he broadcast his opinions of both men in conservative Republican and in Democratic cricles. Each week, and sometimes oftener, Blair dispatched his packet of anti-Chase, anti-Stanton venom to S. L. M. Barlow, a New York lawyer, an arch-conservative, and a pillar of the Democratic party.[8] As much as Welles liked Blair, he deplored his vindictiveness, his habit of judging everything and everyone from a narrowly partisan perspective. Blair, his father, and his younger brother Frank, Jr., thought alike on political questions, cherished the same personal dislikes, and acted as a unit when the family's position was threatened.

Within the next two months, as Chase moved to consolidate his position, the Blair family struck back, and it struck back hard. Reconstruction and slavery were the issues, but personal rancour went beyond mere name-calling.[9] In Missouri, Frank Blair, Jr., launched a vicious attack on Chase, holding him personally responsible for the wholesale cotton profiteering of Treasury agents. On October 4, at Rockville, Maryland, Montgomery Blair lashed out at all Republi-

cans who did not echo his conservative views. In a phillipic as frankly
racist as the most bigoted peace Democrat's, Blair charged that the
radicals or the "ultra-abolitionists" (he made no distinction) were determined to force miscegenation upon the country. Using the same arguments Welles had used with Chase—that individuals, not states,
could be coerced—he ridiculed Sumner's state suicide theory.[10]

Whatever the provocation, and however earnestly he opposed radical solutions to delicate and complex problems, Montgomery Blair
overreached himself.[11] The men he despised and against whom everyone knew he was hurling his sharpest barbs—Henry Winter Davis,
Chase, Stanton—were seen as victims of personal slander.[12] Welles was
as much dismayed as any by the tempest the Rockville speech set off.
"We had better see wherein we agreed than where we disagreed" was his
terse comment upon the speech, a remark that drew warm praise from
Seward.[13]

The open warfare that the Blairs had declared in the name of the
President upon all radicals would surely jeopardize Lincoln's leadership. Might it not also set the stage for a contest between the Executive and the Legislature? Reconstruction was of course the major issue;
Welles thought it would be used by scheming men as a pretext to
break down the administration.

More acutely sensitive to his own place in the administration than
to the troubles stirred up in the party, Welles had seen how easily
Davis smashed Blair's political structure in Maryland. Unquestionably, he would take the offensive when Congress assembled in early
December. Welles felt vulnerable on many scores. His views on reconstruction were remarkably similar to Blair's. Chase would have seen
the resemblance, and, if his past relations with prominent radicals in
Congress were any guide, he would have leaked to them the substance
of his talks with Welles. Fox, Welles' valued associate, was Blair's
brother-in-law and closest personal friend. Du Pont, in sullen retirement, was Davis's closest friend and, if rumor had it right, the mortal
enemy of Fox. Charleston was still in Confederate hands. The ironclads had performed no better in offensive operations under Dahlgren
than they had under Du Pont.[14] Confederate commerce raiders were
ranging over the high seas. In Welles' mind, it was not a question of
whether Davis would strike, but when, how, and where.

He had not long to wait. In the mail on Thursday, October 23, was
an official letter from Du Pont. As he read the well-polished phrases
that accused the department of wilfull wrong and demanded redress,
Welles saw the artful hand of Henry Winter Davis, who would make

a martyr of a naval hero. Welles was in the midst of preparing his annual report, but he dropped everything to pen a reply. "Were I to return his jeremiad," he declared, "it would be published, and his grief [would] excite sympathy." The battle lines were forming. He must do his part to defend the department and to relieve the President of any embarrassment. The result was a 5000-word letter in which Welles, with an eye on the press, deployed his formidable editorial talents skillfully. Restrained, chillingly precise, his reply abounded with eye-catching phrases—"your assaults against editors instead of assaults upon rebel batteries," "unworthy of you as they are unjust to the department." Any close reader would recognize immediately that it was a biased *ex parte* account. But Welles was not aiming at the close reader; his message was designed for the casual reader—the average businessman, the country Congressman, the ward politician.[15]

Meanwhile, Stanton was moving discreetly with Davis and his friends. Robert Schenck, a major general and a radical Republican candidate for Congress from Ohio, was on temporary duty to keep the peace during the Maryland elections. Stanton's version of keeping the peace was to overawe Maryland conservatives by a show of military force if necessary. On November 1, when Schenck, after seeing Lincoln, reported for instructions, Stanton said, "Now take Blair, skin him, turn his hide, pickle it—and stretch it on a barn door to dry!" Chuckling over these crude remarks about a colleague, Henry Winter Davis said, "such are the happy relations of the Cabinet among themselves—respectful deference & courtesy shine through their rough utterances of honest hate."

With two friends inside the Cabinet—Chase and Stanton—Davis raised his sights beyond the Blairs to Lincoln himself. Soon after his election to Congress he had asked the President to exclude Blair from the Maryland patronage. Lincoln refused to intervene in what he said was a personal quarrel. The excitable, egotistical Davis, flushed with his easy victory over Blair's faction and outraged at the President's refusal, bade Lincoln a perfunctory goodbye, turned on his heel, and left. "The President's attitude," he said, "was such as to prevent my holding any further political intercourse with him."[16]

Still smarting under what he chose to regard as a presidential rebuke, Davis examined carefully that part of Lincoln's message to the opening session of the thirty-eighth Congress which dealt with reconstruction. He was well aware that the President's moderate policy on this crucial issue had gained wide support from Republicans, ranging from radicals such as Charles Sumner and Zachariah Chandler to conservatives such as James Dixon and James R. Doolittle of Wisconsin. But Davis, a man of impetuous temperament, believed his radical friends to be in error. Lincoln's views were those of the conservatives. What Blair had claimed in his Rockville speech, then, must be substantially correct. That was why the President would not help him with the patronage in Maryland!

A two-pronged attack, against the administration and against what he called Lincoln's "half and half constitution," began to take shape in Davis' mind. He and General Schenck had a special interest in the Navy Department. Schenck wanted favors for his brother, an undistinguished naval officer. Davis hoped to vindicate Du Pont, root out Blair's influence, and expose the "Monitor Lobby," which he was sure the Navy Department was trying to protect. Recognizing presidential reconstruction as the bedrock issue, Davis sensed that he had a good chance to build a congressional coalition against Lincoln by enlisting the critics of Welles and those of Seward in a common cause. If, as he suspected, he could uncover graft and mismanagement in the procurement of ironclads and trace it from the "Monitor Lobby" in New York through to Fox, he could make the most of the Blair connection and involve his muckraking with reconstruction. Seward's unpopular conduct of foreign affairs, his supposed influence over Lincoln, and his relationship with Thurlow Weed made him a likely target. The end Davis had in mind was no less than the denial of renomination to Lincoln.[17]

Treading warily, Welles treated both Du Pont and Admiral Charles Wilkes—then being court-martialed for insubordination—as gently as he could in his annual report.[18] He was especially careful to spare Du Pont's reputation yet not admit any departmental fault. His report and his forceful letter of November 4 to Du Pont made an impression on the Admiral's wife and his naval friends. All of them counseled Du Pont to break off the battle of words with the department. But Davis, who described Welles' lengthy indictment as a "trap," had already taken Du Pont's case out of the Admiral's hands.

Initially, Schuyler Colfax checked Davis' moves against Welles. An amiable, moderate Republican from Indiana, Colfax had just replaced Galusha Grow as Speaker of the House. Both Schenck and Davis himself sought a place on the House naval affairs committee, for from this vantage point they could move effectively to harrass the department; but Colfax, on his own initiative, consulted the Secretary about the naval appointments. He accepted Welles' veto of the two Congressmen.[19]

Blocked by the Speaker, Davis could have enlisted Senator John P. Hale, who had made a profession of baiting the Navy Department; but he was too skillful at intrigue to be saddled with Hale, despite Hale's position as chairman of the Senate naval affairs committee and his well-known hatred of Fox. He had sized up Hale as a Senator who had few friends and scant influence. Disliked by his colleagues on the naval affairs committee—James W. Grimes of Iowa and Solomon Foot of Vermont—Hale had persisted in his personal and largely irresponsible feud with the department. The constant carping against Welles on the Senate floor and in the lobbies had so tried the patience of most Republican Senators that Hale barely retained his committee chairmanship. When it was confirmed early in the session that Hale had accepted a bribe for using his influence with the War Department, Davis thought Hale had discredited himself completely.

If Davis could not use Hale, he knew he could make no headway with Grimes. This handsome, transplanted New Englander spoke for the department in Congress. Friendly to Fox and a loyal supporter of Welles, he did his best to restrain Hale and for the most part had succeeded over the years. Grimes was a moderate Republican on some issues and a radical on others, but he would have nothing to do with any Henry Winter Davis foray on Welles and Fox. Davis decided to bypass the naval affairs committee entirely. Ben Wade was a natural ally in the Senate. Stanton and Chase had both assisted him in Maryland politics, the former through Schenck, the latter through Treasury patronage. Their common hatred of Montgomery Blair and all he stood for was a powerful binder. While Davis was maturing his plans, Stanton was cautiously helpful. Chase's drive for the presidency, however, led him along byways that Davis found conflicted with his own ambitions. "He wishes like Lincoln," observed the Maryland Congressman, "to keep in with both sides & play his game for power . . . they can't be friends with me & my enemies at once." When he wrote these words, Davis, next to Thaddeus Stevens—the grim, old chairman of the House ways and means committee—was one of the more powerful Republicans in the House. Colfax had more than compensated for keeping Davis off the Committee on Naval Affairs by making him chairman of the foreign affairs committee. The Speaker was persuaded also to appoint Davis chairman of a select committee which would consider and report on reconstruction.[20]

The session was not a week old when Davis drew up a resolution that would require Welles to supply the House with all documents concerning the battle action of armored vessels at Charleston. At his request, Representative Jesse O. Norton of Illinois introduced the resolution on December 16. It was referred to the naval committee, but a new clerk forgot to send it. When Davis learned there would be delay, he gave a copy of his resolution to Wade, who promptly secured its passage in the Senate.

In this opening skirmish, Wade and Davis were acting prematurely. Neither had seen Welles' annual report. They assumed that the department would hold back Du Pont's official account of the action at Charleston. But Welles stole a march on them by publishing almost all of the vital documents. He reasoned that, even though the monitors under Dahlgren had failed to capture Charleston, they were effectively sealing that port. They had remained many months within the gale-swept bar and had sustained heavy fire from the channel forts without severe damage. Welles saw no reason now to suppress Du Pont's report. He did not dwell on the fact that the current operation was a joint one, nor did he state that General Q. A. Gillmore, who had replaced Hunter, had at least twice as many men at his disposal as his predecessor had had. Nor did he comment on how Gillmore was methodically, if unimaginatively, silencing most of the batteries guarding the main ship channel. Welles did include all of the official dispatches between Du Pont and the department, as well as Lincoln's instructions, which—depending on one's interpretation—could be damaging to Du Pont.[21]

Public reaction to Welles' report was highly favorable. Sumner, for one, complimented him on it. Editorials in three New York papers—the *Times*, the *Tribune*, and the *World*—spoke up for Du Pont but praised Welles' literary style, the interesting commentary, the record of achievement. Davis had to content himself with an investigation of the Bureau of Steam Machinery while pushing for the department's response to the resolutions on ironclads. Again, he acted impulsively in what turned out to be a personal quarrel between Bureau Chief Benjamin Isherwood and Edward N. Dickerson, a New York patent attorney and inventor.[22]

Despite congressional pressure, Welles would not be rushed into any premature disclosures.[23] Nor would he confine himself to releasing the specific documents Wade and Davis demanded. Congress would receive all pertinent material on the operations of all armored vessels.

Welles' decision meant that he and his assistants had to go through the painstaking task of collecting, sifting, organizing, and having copied the hundreds of documents that were eventually chosen to present the department's case. All the material selected, enough to make up a volume of 300,000 words, had then to be recopied by hand and proofread before it was sent to the printer—a laborious, time-consuming job.[24] Weeks stretched into months, and still there was no response from Welles. Davis, whose restless mind was always conjuring up plots on the part of the Executive branch to inhibit the Congress, complained to Wade and to other like-minded associates. Just as he was about to move another resolution demanding peremptory compliance, Stanton told him that Welles had asked for Gillmore's correspondence with Du Pont. Without any qualms, apparently, the Secretary advised Davis how he might use this information to advantage against a fellow Cabinet member.

Soon after, Wade went to the Navy Department, determined not to be put off with apologies or excuses. The gruff old Senator from Ohio found Welles, his wig askew, surrounded by piles of papers, pen in hand. Mildly, he explained that he was just finishing his own report to go in with the papers.

Davis had boasted to Du Pont that he was loading a mine he had tunneled under the Department. Hurrying to the Government Printing Office on Friday, April 13, Davis was amazed as he riffled through the more than six hundred pages of fine print in galley proof. He marveled at "the vast agglomeration of everything on Ironclads," noted that DuPont's correspondence seemed complete, and realized that Welles had tripped the "mine" with one of his own. There were documents here he had never seen before, some of which he knew at a glance were important. But what particularly caught his attention was Welles' brief letter of transmittal. Replying to specific points in the original resolution, he charged Du Pont with insubordination for not obeying explicit orders from the President and for failing to cooperate with the Army. Of course the Admiral would have ready explanations, all of which rested upon the exact meaning of the orders and dispatches when taken in proper context and according to naval practice. The public and the Congress, as Davis recognized at once, would never distinguish between "an order to cooperate" which Welles did not send and a "request to afford aid and assistance" which he did send and which was printed among the documents.[25]

The volume itself was not meant to deal specifically with Du Pont, the commander; the thrust of its materials dealt with Du Pont, the critic of ironclads. Although Welles answered the Admiral document by document, he was more concerned with defending the Department's ironclad policy. And his defense was masterly. It would appear that he had been fair in selecting and publishing reports and dispatches critical of ironclad vessels. But the over-all impact of the volume was highly favorable to these vessels, the carefully selected documents making the points Welles wanted made unobtrusively and interestingly. Ironclads had their failings; they were experimental vessels. They had stood up well, however, giving more than they took. This was the theme he chose. As for Du Pont, the department had recognized and rewarded his abilities, had dealt courteously but sternly with his infirmities.

For the next few weeks Davis considered various ways of combating the massive report, but he found no promising leads. Unable at this point to attack Lincoln's conduct of the war through an exposé of the Navy Department, he immersed himself in the politically sensitive issue of reconstruction, where the President seemed increasingly vulnerable.

Opinion was beginning to run against Lincoln in Congress and in high party circles. Public morale had sagged again as the war ground down to a dreary stalemate. For several months now, Chase and his close friends had been conducting a stealthy letter-writing campaign against Lincoln.[26]

Although aware of the gathering opposition, Welles kept up a bold front. He told Charles Sumner, for instance, that he assumed Lincoln would be a candidate and thought "a pretty strong current is setting in his favor." In part he was expressing loyalty to his chief. Yet he had reason to believe that the President still retained a large measure of popular support, despite radical politicians, restless press lords, and raucous Peace Democrats. Welles had some solid evidence that a majority of New Hampshire Republicans were for Lincoln, even though the veteran party leaders of that state were in Chase's camp. John P. Hale (how he loathed the name), Amos Tuck, a one-time rival for his own office, and Mason Tappan, Hale's henchman, were all pushing for an endorsement of Chase at the forthcoming state convention.

New Hampshire party conventions normally met in January for March elections, Connecticut conventions in February for April elections. Considered harbingers of public opinion, any expressions of preference were eagerly awaited by professional politicians and by the partisan press. The New Hampshire convention was doubly significant because it was Chase's native state. The Secretary had been early in the field and had enlisted Hale and his New Hampshire coterie in his behalf. But the administration forces had not been idle either.

The state's principal industries, apart from subsistence farming, were politics and the Portsmouth Navy Yard, which, with dependent shipyards, machine shops, and boiler works, employed several thousand men, bringing well over a million dollars a year into the state.[27] Hale had tried desperately to control this rich source of patronage for his own benefit—without success.

Welles had always stipulated that the good of the service and loyalty to the Union cause should be the principal criteria in navy yard appointments. Thus he held to a minimum those political forays that he considered detrimental to the public interest. He saw nothing inconsistent in defining loyalty to the Union cause as loyalty to the administration, a pious, self-seeking attitude that made politicians like Thurlow Weed, Hale, and Hannibal Hamlin gnash their teeth in frustrated rage.[28]

When Chase began his covert maneuvers in the summer of 1863, administration men looked to the Portsmouth Navy Yard as a base of operations for Lincoln. That John P. Hale was to come up for re-election to the Senate in the spring of 1864, and that he was supporting Chase, was not lost on Welles, Fox, and Montgomery Blair. In early June of 1863 Blair journeyed to New Hampshire, ostensibly for a vacation, but actually to test the political climate. In Concord, the state capital, Blair met and talked with a young Republican politician, William E. Chandler, who had just served his first term as speaker of the house in the New Hampshire legislature. The crafty Blair was not deceived when Chandler boldly avowed his radical sentiment, for at the same time he freely acknowledged that there were many paths to Republicanism. What was necessary, proper, and expedient in New England might not be necessary, proper, and expedient in the Border states.

Blair was familiar enough with New Hampshire politics to understand Chandler's remarks. He was open to a deal. Senator Hale was actively seeking a fourth term, deliberately violating the time-honored custom of "rotation" in New Hampshire politics, where there were never enough jobs to go around. Blair knew also that the Hale–Tuck–Fogg clique had long barred the way for the political advancement of an entire younger generation of New Hampshire Republicans.

Hale's re-election to the Senate would mean that New Hampshire Republicans were backing Chase for the presidency. Any action that might be taken to support Lincoln would weaken the Hale machine by weakening its candidate, Salmon P. Chase. Young Chandler may have been an opportunist, but his ambitions fitted neatly with the plans of Lincoln's managers. Blair relayed this valuable information back to Fox and Welles, both of whom had an interest in the defeat of Hale but were more immediately concerned with the renomination of Lincoln.

During August, Fox took his vacation in Portsmouth, where he talked with the master workmen at the yard and with Thomas Tullock, the Navy agent and party boss in the Portsmouth area. Tullock, who had prospered under Welles' "benign" policy of navy yard patronage, was too closely identified with the administration to expect any mercy at the hands of Hale, should Chase prevail over Lincoln. In September, Welles himself visited all of the yards. He needed a change of scene, for he was not well, but it is questionable that the pomp and ceremony that awaited him at each yard gave him much time for rest. He did have time, however, to survey the local political character of the yards and to have a word or two with the Navy agents. "It was not necessary that I should take an active part against him [Hale]," said Welles, "but I have not hesitated to let N. Hampshire men know the facts in a quiet way when they have enquired for them."[29]

The upshot of all this activity was that Chandler, apparently acting alone but actually working in concert with Tulloch and with firm assurances from Washington, moved a strong endorsement of Lincoln at the precise psychological moment on the floor of the Republican state convention. It carried unanimously. With his native state coming out so enthusiastically for Lincoln, the Chase boom suffered a heavy setback—and so did John P. Hale, who, four months later, to Welles' great satisfaction, was defeated for re-election to the Senate.[30]

The Connecticut Republican-Union convention followed within a month of New Hampshire's. When it instructed all of its convention delegates for Lincoln, Chase's candidacy virtually collapsed. In achieving this result, Welles played a much more direct role than he had in New Hampshire, untangling a bizarre intrigue which, had it succeeded, might well have thrown the entire radical faction behind Chase. The death of the United States Marshall for Connecticut, a Dixon man, in December 1863 had created a vacancy in an important post. Both the radical state faction and the conservative congressional faction put forward candidates. But Senator James Dixon moved more promptly than the radicals, and he managed to have Lincoln put his own man, Henry Hammond, in the coveted spot. The overburdened President neglected to ask Welles' advice when he made the appointment. He had acted on the assumption that Dixon, who claimed he spoke for the entire congressional delegation, was reflecting party opinion in Connecticut. As he had planned, Dixon then invoked senatorial courtesy and secured confirmation over the outraged protests of Governor Buckingham, Mark Howard, and the Union League of the state.

Concerned only about his own affairs, Dixon had early decided that Lincoln would be the Republican nominee and McClellan the Democratic. Still uncertain which candidate he would support, the self-serving Senator saw a chance to strike a deadly blow at his political enemies in Connecticut. Through his network of officeholders and the presses he controlled, Dixon subtly sought to identify the state faction with Chase. The fiery Howard, the more temperate but no less vehement Calvin Day, and the irrepressible editor Charles Dudley Warner of the *Press* needed little urging to espouse Chase. Lincoln was deemed to be either a dupe of the congressional faction or a conservative who was bent on destroying radicalism in the state. Howard lined up the Union League. The *Press* began urging that the state convention keep clear of presidential politics.

Welles read the signs accurately and took immediate action. He warned Howard and Warner what Dixon was trying to do. He explained that the Senator had tricked the President and condemned unsparingly his sinuous intrigue. He exerted all of his personal influence to convince the radicals that Lincoln had their best interests at heart, that the convention should renominate Governor Buckingham and identify his candidacy squarely with that of the President's. A somewhat chastened Howard denied that he had ever thought of Chase over Lincoln. Warner, too, blamed his equivocal editorials on the misrepresentations of the Democrats and Dixon's clique. The radicals restrained themselves at the state convention, even though it was dominated by Dixon. Buckingham was renominated, and the delegates selected for the national convention were instructed to vote for Lincoln, but Welles had not seen the last of Dixon's almost pathological concern with his own welfare.[31]

Although the popular tide was setting strongly against Chase, most of the more radical politicians were slow in sensing it. "Chase's friends are at work hard—very hard," wrote Faxon in early March. And Chase himself moved ponderously ahead, seeking to undermine an administration of which he was an important member. To a friend in New York he wrote, "as far as I am now able to see, the next administration, should Mr. Lincoln succeed himself, will be under the influence of Mr. Weed and Mr. Blair and will be vindictively proscriptive of all whom these gentlemen are pleased to stigmatize as Negro-worshippers. . . ." Nor did Chase slacken his use of Treasury Department patronage against his own chief.[32]

On February 22, 1864, the Republican-Union national committee met in Washington at the residence of its chairman, Senator Edwin D. Morgan. Welles termed the meeting "harmonious," judging that "four fifths" of the committee backed Lincoln's renomination. But William Faxon, who went along with him, had a different impression. "Everyone," he said, "wanted to know what his neighbor thought relative to the Presidential candidates and was rather shy in expressing his own opinion." Welles was not shy, however, in proposing that the committee set the early date of June 7 for the convention. A majority supported him, and the President's campaign got a much needed boost at a time when other candidates were being put forward by various interested parties. Welles had already noted that Frémont's name was appearing with some frequency. Chase was still in the running, despite further setbacks in Pennsylvania and New York. Writing from the field, Hawley, a delegate-at-large to the convention, warned that he himself might "go over to the Chase school, and regarding the instructions as binding shall keep out of the Convention, but attend to work for Chase."[33]

Along with the emergence of new candidates came pressure to postpone the national convention. John Murray Forbes, the Boston capitalist, was one of the first to urge delay on Welles. What if the summer campaigns failed? The Republicans would be saddled with Lincoln, while the Democrats would take McClellan and win. Welles chided Forbes on his lack of confidence in Grant, the new and as yet untried Commander of the Army of the Potomac, adding that "he could not see how any different candidate would help the Union cause." If there were military setbacks, it would be the Democrats who would profit.[34]

Desperate last-ditch efforts by supporters of Chase and of other would-be candidates failed to postpone the convention, which met in an atmosphere of gloom and hesitation. Grant's costly strategy in the Wilderness Campaign had driven home the plain fact that even an unflinching leader could not win battles without great cost. Lnicoln was renominated, without much enthusiasm, on the date originally set by the national committee. The next day the convention nominated Andrew Johnson, War Democrat and Military Governor of Tennessee, for the vice presidency.

Reconstruction had immediately become an issue on the convention floor. In his message to the thirty-eighth Congress in December 1863, Lincoln had proposed a plan for the reconstruction of the rebellious states: whenever 10 per cent of those who had been eligible to vote in the election of 1860 took a loyalty oath to support the Union, then a government would be established under presidential auspices and the state would elect representatives to Congress. By the summer of 1864, Louisiana and Arkansas had complied with Lincoln's requirements. Delegates from the "10 per cent" states were now demanding recognition and full voting participation at the Union (Republican) convention. Thaddeus Stevens led the radicals in an attempt to bar them from the proceedings, but he was unsuccessful. However, the roll-call vote on admitting the delegates from the 10 per cent states revealed that a good third of the convention opposed presidential reconstruction as it was then operating. Henry J. Raymond captured the mood of the delegates in a speech demanding a drastic overhaul of the Cabinet—a sure sign that the Seward-Weed faction was at one with the radicals in wanting to sweep out everyone except Seward and Stanton. But Raymond's obvious target was Montgomery Blair, who made a convenient scapegoat for the ugly temper of the delegates. Forced by circumstances and clever management to take Lincoln, the frustrated convention poured forth its wrath when it virtually read the Postmaster General out of the party.

As if he were challenging the radicals in the convention, Lincoln, on June 30, accepted Chase's resignation. He had not wanted to take this step, because he valued Chase as a man of high intellect and superior talent in coping with the complexities of wartime finance. But Chase had been intractable on a crucial appointment—that of the Assistant Treasurer at New York. In this case the resignation of Chase's able deputy in the city, John J. Cisco, created a situation that brought the Seward-Weed faction into open collision with the Secretary's radical friends. Chase insisted on his choice, Maunsell B. Field, as Cisco's successor, refusing even to consider several compromise candidates who should have been acceptable to both factions.

Lincoln could have bowed to Chase, as he had in the past, but now, in the aftermath of the convention, he grasped the opportunity to move away from the radicals. Welles looked upon Chase's departure as a blessing, both because of his financial measures, which he deplored, and because of his political activities. But he was as much surprised by Lincoln's action as he was mystified at his choice of Governor David Tod of Ohio to be Chase's successor. A strict hard-money man, Tod could be expected to reverse the inflationist policies of his predecessor. Could it be that the President did not know the difference? After all, he had been a Whig, and, as all old Democrats knew, Whigs had no fixed financial principles.

When Tod declined the Treasury portfolio and Lincoln appointed Senator William Pitt Fessenden of Maine, Welles was even more bewildered. Fessenden, who accepted the post, was as much an inflation-ist as Chase. Welles did not comprehend the delicate political game the President was playing. Having tried and failed to placate the radicals, Lincoln was now taking steps to divide them. Fessenden was a highly respected Senator who on occasion voted for radical measures but on the whole followed a moderate course, and, as chairman of the Senate finance committee, he had a firm grasp of fiscal affairs. Nor did Welles realize at the time that while Lincoln was disposing of Chase, a poten-tially dangerous rival with radical tendencies, he had also reserved for himself the option of removing a conservative from his Cabinet to ap-pease the radicals. The President had made up his mind not to accept congressional management of reconstruction.

Unable to delay further Henry Winter Davis' bill on reconstruction, which cleared both houses during the end-of-session rush, Lincoln was forced to show his hand. He pocketed the bill and four days later gave his reasons for not signing it in the form of a proclamation. He said frankly that he would not be bound by one inflexible program. Fur-ther, he doubted Congress' power to abolish slavery, suggesting that it should be done by constitutional amendment.[35]

Lincoln kept his own counsel on how he intended to deal with the various radical factions. Welles took no active part in the campaign, unlike Montgomery Blair, who tried through his Democratic connec-tions to keep McClellan from accepting the Democratic nomination. Saddened by the slaughter in the Wilderness, worried about his son and his nephew, who were in the thick of it, Welles came out of his of-fice only to visit the War Department for news or to attend Cabinet meetings.[36]

Welles did engage in a verbal skirmish with Solicitor William Whit-ing of the War Department, whom he suspected had been sent by Sew-ard or Stanton to draw him out on reconstruction. And he had become involved with patronage problems, too, when Henry J. Ray-mond, Morgan's successor as chairman of the Republican-Union na-tional committee, complained bitterly to Lincoln about Welles' policy of keeping politics out of the navy yards. Raymond demanded that all personnel in the yards, from the Commandant to the day laborers, be required to work actively for Lincoln or be discharged. Welles was amazed "that Raymond could debase himself so far as to submit such a proposition and more that he expects me to enforce it." He refused, gave his reasons, and, to Raymond's chagrin, Lincoln supported him.[37]

Welles' passive attitude changed abruptly on August 6, when he read, in the *New-York Tribune*, the most studied attack on Lincoln he had ever seen in a Republican newspaper. The article was signed by both Ben Wade and Henry Winter Davis, but Welles had no doubt that Davis was the author. At the White House that afternoon he asked Lincoln if he had seen it. The President had not; and if it was as described to him, he did not think he would read it. "Well, let them wriggle," he said. He would have no part of any controversy. Welles said nothing at the time, but he felt strongly that Lincoln should study the document, separating out "what there is really substantial" from the harsh language in which it was couched. "The whole subject of reconstruction," he wrote in his diary, "is beset with difficulty and while the executive has one course and Congress another, a better and different one than either may be ultimately pursued." Lincoln ought to have consulted with his entire Cabinet, thought Welles, before announcing his 10 per cent plan.[38]

The President's offhand remarks on the Wade-Davis letter had deceived Welles. Lincoln would not, as he said, respond to the provocation, but he was prepared to appease the radicals, especially Chase's disgruntled following. Blair, he knew, was a prime source for the continuous bickerings and intrigues within the Cabinet. Stanton had not spoken to Blair for months. Seward distrusted and disliked him. As for Blair, he seized every opportunity to malign both of them, in public and in private. Sooner or later harmony had to be restored, if only to ease the pressure in the administration. Yet Lincoln bided his time.[39]

To the untutored eye the military situation seemed to have steadily worsened. Not a week after publication of the Wade-Davis manifesto, Thurlow Weed told the President plainly that he could not be re-elected. Henry Raymond and Leonard Swett, Lincoln's old friend from Illinois, confirmed Weed's pessimistic view. The manifesto itself proclaimed an impending revolt of the radical faction. Conservative Republicans, whom Lincoln counted as close friends—Orville H. Browning and James Dixon, for instance—were looking to McClellan, who was expected to receive the Democratic nomination. Even Lyman Trumbull, Lincoln's long-time associate in Illinois politics, would not support the President publicly. By the third week in August, Lincoln concluded that he could not be re-elected. Assuming McClellan would be his successor, he drafted a brief memorandum pledging himself and his Cabinet to hold the government together between the election in November and the inauguration in March. Without disclosing its contents, he had every member of his Cabinet sign a blind copy.

By now Welles and Blair were the only members of the Cabinet who were still hopeful that Lincoln would be re-elected. Welles had long since discounted any threat posed by Frémont, who had been nominated on an independent radical Republican ticket before Lincoln was nominated at Baltimore. Talk of other candidates, of Democratic strength, of a popular repudiation of Lincoln he discounted as the idle gossip of malcontents, the bluster and brag of Copperheads. But when Farragut's brilliant victory at Mobile Bay failed to raise the drooping spirits of the North, even Welles began to have serious doubts. Prudently, he asked Mark Howard to look into the availability of houses in Hartford.[40] After he read the Democratic peace platform adopted at Chicago, however, he regained his composure. "The issue is made up," he said, "It is whether a war shall be made against Lincoln to get peace with Jeff Davis."[41] Nor did he change his mind when McClellan, the Democratic nominee, repudiated his party's peace plank. He thought McClellan's letter of acceptance "creditable and patriotic," though totally inconsistent with the platform and with the long-avowed aims of a majority of the Democratic party. Welles had more faith than many of his associates, both conservative and radical, in the common sense of the Northern electorate. To be sure, Sherman's capture of Atlanta, just a week before publication of McClellan's letter, had raised morale dramatically. But many shrewd politicians were still hedging their bets.[42]

Lincoln was pessimistic enough to let himself be bullied into dropping Blair from the Cabinet, ostensibly on the condition that Frémont withdraw from the contest, actually because he felt he could no longer afford such a controversial figure in his administration. For some time he had considered Blair to be expendable; yet he would not have bowed to the dictates of Blair's numerous enemies after Atlanta had he not been worried about McClellan. As he explained to Welles after the event, he "was greatly embarrassed by contentions among his friends, by nominal Republicans, by intense radicals and the strong front of the Democrats." His appointment of Governor William Dennison of Ohio to be Blair's successor was scarcely a move in the radical direction. Stanton, for one, did not think Dennison any more reliable than Blair. "Still," as Henry Winter Davis said, "he is different & a change is relief. It shows bullying may do something & that L. thinks more of himself than of his friends."[43]

No sooner had the news of Blair's "decapitation" reached the public than there was pressure for Welles' resignation too. Weed was anxious to pay off old scores. Radicals of the Henry Winter Davis stripe demanded a clean sweep of the Navy Department. It was well known that

Governor John A. Andrew of Massachusetts wanted the post and would be eminently acceptable to all factions. Henry Raymond, still smarting over Welles' refusal to give him free access to the navy yards for campaign purposes, raised this point with the President. Ought not the uncooperative Welles follow Blair? As Raymond related it, Lincoln said that "he would not do it *then*, it might be misconstrued."[44] Davis was overjoyed. Certain that Welles would go out soon after the election, he and Admiral Du Pont made plans to toast his successor with an old and valuable bottle of wine they had long reserved for the occasion. However Davis and his friends might interpret his equivocal remark, the President had no intention of dispensing with the services of Welles and Fox. Their administration of the Navy had been honest, economical, and, if not overly imaginative, sound—except for its single-minded devotion to monitors. Besides, Welles had quietly identified himself with the anti-Weed conservatives and moderates. Lincoln would not bow again to the demands of the Weed machine on the one side and the Davis radicals on the other, for this would seriously compromise his political independence and upset the delicate sense of balance he deemed essential in his Cabinet. As he had said to Raymond, "it might be misconstrued."

The election itself was anticlimatic after the intrigue, the pessimism, the very real fear that the Union cause would collapse. Lincoln carried all but three states and received a popular majority of 494,567 votes. To Welles, the stirring events that occurred between the election and the inauguration on March 4, 1865, lacked the quality of excitement and peril with which he had lived for four years. Clearly, the Confederacy was collapsing. Even the capture of Fort Fisher and Wilmington, North Carolina, by Admiral Porter and General Terry in January 1865 did not stir his imagination as had the earlier naval victories of Port Royal, New Orleans, and Mobile Bay. The administration was weary, treading water, waiting for the end. Old Edward Bates, Welles' last friend in the Cabinet, resigned right after the election, to be replaced by James Speed, a Kentuckian who had no special talent but was close to the President. Chief Justice Taney died, prompting a scramble for the nomination. Welles did something he had never done before as a Cabinet member. He made a personal appeal to the President for Montgomery Blair as Taney's successor. Lincoln spoke kindly of Blair but remained noncommittal. On December 6 he nominated Chase. While admitting Chase's "mental powers and resources," Welles thought that the new Justice would politicize the bench. "His mind is not I fear so much judicial as ministerial. He will be likely to use the

place for political advancement and thereby endanger confidence in
the Court." But to the tired President, the appointment would afford
a much needed pause in the political turmoil that Chase had been
stirring up for two years.

In other ways Lincoln demonstrated his need for some relief from
the fearful strains he had borne. His annual message to the Congress,
unlike his previous ones, was a lackluster document. No bold new program for reconstruction, no fresh ideas—a cut-and-paste job of department reports, of which Welles' was the most readable. On reconstruction, the President reaffirmed what he had already said on the subject,
renewing his plea for a constitutional amendment abolishing slavery.
Welles was disappointed that Lincoln had not made "a more earnest
appeal to the southern people and to the states respectively to return
to duty." The people of the South, he felt, ought to have been reassured that they would not be treated as outlaws, that their persons and
property, except, of course, in slaves, would be respected. Lincoln
thought otherwise. Perhaps he did not want to stir up the radicals
in Congress by re-emphasizing his one-nation, one-people theory of reconstruction. The constitutional amendment was uppermost in his
mind. He hoped he would get bipartisan support for it in Congress
and in the country, but the Democrats would not make the amendment
a party measure.

Despite the Democrats' lack of cooperation, Lincoln, by wielding his
patronage powers, secured the necessary two-thirds vote in the House
on January 31, 1865. Welles approved. Slavery was "the assignable
cause of the rebellion"—its abolition would help preserve states' rights
in the restored nation. His scruples on states' rights apparently did not
include the fact that representatives from only a part of the Union had
approved a proposal that would alter the fundamental law of the entire nation.

As Lincoln's first administration drew to a close, Welles and Fox
again were being assailed from all sides. Only the Navy's fine performance in the capture of Fort Fisher saved them from having to prepare
another exhaustive defense of the department's policies. Wade had unearthed most of the details about the faulty design, construction, and
performance of a new class of light-draft monitors. The Department
could not conceal the fact that gross mismanagement had wasted millions of dollars in vessels that would barely float, much less fight. Fox
and Alban Stimers, their principal designer, were culpable. Neither
the bureau chiefs nor Ericsson had been consulted. As Wade's report
was being debated on the Senate floor, Henry Winter Davis introduced

a bill in the House which would have set up an admiralty board of senior officers to oversee the Secretary's office. Welles, exerting all of his influence and relying heavily on the favorable publicity that followed the fall of Fort Fisher and the capture of Wilmington—the last major port left to the Confederacy—managed to forestall the moves of Davis and Wade.

Yet the disclosures had been damaging. "Are you not coming to see old Welles exit?" wrote the gleeful Davis to Du Pont, shortly before Lincoln's second inauguration. "Only think of that old bottle of wine and come."[45] Davis had overrated the impact of the monitor exposé, and he had underrated Lincoln, who respected Welles' judgment in most matters and had a personal liking for Fox. Though the rumors spread that Welles and Fox would be compelled to resign, Lincoln, on the eve of his inauguration, asked that all members of the Cabinet, except John P. Usher, the Secretary of the Interior, remain for the present. Hugh McCulloch, a conservative Indiana banker and the first Controller of the Currency, was to be nominated as the Secretary of the Treasury in place of Fessenden, who wanted to re-enter the Senate.[46]

Inauguration day was overcast. Squalls of rain dampened female finery and male plumage but not the people's enthusiasm to witness the simple ceremonies. Moments after the honor guard threw open the main entrance to the Capitol, the galleries of the Senate chamber were jammed with bedraggled onlookers. Shortly before noon, Welles lined up with his colleagues and filed into the chamber, taking his seat between Stanton and Speed in an area reserved for the Cabinet, below and to the left of the rostrum. He had just seated himself when Vice President Hamlin and Andrew Johnson appeared and took their places —Hamlin in the presiding officer's chair, Johnson to his right, in the clerk's chair.

Remarkably similar in appearance and in stature, Hamlin and Johnson were tall, swarthy, generously featured men, dressed in identical full dress black suits and black bow ties. By custom, the outgoing Vice President's valedictory and his successor's inaugural were supposed to be brief. Seven minutes had been allotted to each man before the outgoing Vice President administered the oath. Hamlin's little piece of 250 words was well within the time limit. Then it was Johnson's turn. The Vice President-elect had not spoken more than a dozen sentences before Welles realized that something was the matter with him. His voice was loud and unsteady; repetitious phrases trailed off to incoherence. Over and over again he spoke of the power of the people. He was a servant of the people, the Senators were servants of the people. Turning to the youthful-looking Chief Justice, a majestic figure in his black robe, he said thickly, "you, too got your power from the people whose creature you are." The man was obviously drunk, thought Welles, as to his horror Johnson advanced upon the Cabinet and made the same remark to Seward, addressing him by name. Stanton was next, "You too, Mr. Stanton, Secretary of War, and you too MR. ————" Welles cringed as Johnson eyed him blankly and turning to Forney, the Secretary of the Senate, asked "who is the Secretary of the Navy?" "Welles," whispered Forney. "You too Mr. Welles, Secretary of the Navy." Johnson's speech lasted seventeen minutes. He would have gone on longer had he not stumbled to a long pause. Hamlin seized the opportunity to administer the oath.[47]

But all was not over. The new Vice President turned, faced the packed chamber and tried to repeat the oath, pausing after each phrase to remark, "I can say that with perfect propriety." Welles heard Speed beside him groan, "all this is wretched bad taste, the man is certainly deranged." To Stanton, Welles said, "Johnson's either drunk or crazy." Stanton agreed, "there is evidently something wrong." Johnson mumbled meaningless phrases for another five minutes on the nature of the oath itself before he came to a totally irrelevant conclusion. Lincoln, who was sitting in front of the dais, bowed his head during the performance, obviously humiliated. While being escorted from the chamber to the platform at the side of the east portico for his inaugural address, he whispered emphatically to one of the marshals: "Do not let Johnson speak outside!" Welles felt that Johnson's ludicrous performance had made a mockery of the Republic's most solemn official occasion. He was so disturbed that he did not mention in his diary the President's moving inaugural address, with its eloquent plea for a peace without vengeance.

The exciting events of the next three weeks quickly blotted out memories of an inauguration in which nothing seemed to have gone right. Washington shook to the thunder of hundred-gun salutes that greeted the capture of Petersburg, the fall of Richmond, and, finally, the surrender of Lee's army. Lincoln, who had shown signs of severe mental fatigue as far back as December, was not in the city. He had left Washington on March 22 for the Petersburg front without mentioning his plans to any of the Cabinet. The imminent collapse of Lee's army justified his departure. Although he needed a change, a respite from the pressures of his office, Lincoln deemed it essential that he make his policy felt by his actual presence when the end came. He was absent for

almost three weeks and would have stayed longer had not Seward been
thrown from his carriage and seriously injured. Apart from his personal regard for Seward, Lincoln had been relying on him to manage affairs. It was essential that he return. Welles found him looking
fit and cheerful, sharing the holiday mood that pervaded the capital
after the news of Lee's surrender.

On Tuesday night, April 11, in response to a mass meeting at the
White House, Lincoln gave a prepared address on reconstruction. A
cogent, carefully reasoned defense of his policy, delivered in his best
platform style, his rather lengthy speech disappointed many radicals
because of its position on Negro suffrage. Ever the careful constitution-
alist, Lincoln would leave that question to the states. He was hopeful
that the former Confederate states would make literate blacks and
black veterans voters, but he would not impose this condition.

Welles read the address with approval in the Washington *Evening
Star* and went over various points with Lincoln on two separate visits
to the White House. During their first discussion, Lincoln brought up
the subject of his ordering General Godfrey Weitzel to permit the convening of the Virginia legislature. He stressed the importance of having
the legislature of a former rebel state repeal its own ordinance of secession—it was the fastest and surest way to re-establish a civil government. Stanton and others of the Cabinet, he said, did not agree with
him. What did Welles think? Welles doubted the policy too. He had
"no great faith," he told Lincoln, "in negotiating with large bodies of
men—each would encourage the other in asking and doing what no
one of them would do alone." A better arrangement could be made, he
thought, "with any one—the worst than with all." Welles raised also
the question of recognition. Would not Lincoln be committing the
United States to accept the acts of a rebel legislature? What if they
were hostile acts? Lincoln had no fear of that—"they were too badly
beaten, too much exhausted." Yet Welles had made an impression,
and, now that his entire Cabinet had gone against him, Lincoln decided to reverse himself. Not long after Welles had left his office, he
went over to the War Department, where he telegraphed Weitzel not
to permit the convening of the Virginia legislature.[48]

On April 14, the Cabinet met for its regular session. General Grant
was present and ventured a comment or two on the complex subjects
under discussion—restoration of trade in the defeated South and reconstruction. The meeting was long and tiring, especially so to Welles,
who feared he was coming down with a cold and still had work awaiting him at the Navy Department.

It was well into the evening before he cleared his desk. When he arrived at his house, he found that his wife, who was not well either, had already retired. Resisting an impulse to write down the details of the Cabinet meeting in his diary while they were still fresh in his mind, Welles was in bed himself by 10 P.M. He had just fallen asleep when Mary Welles woke him up. Someone outside was excitedly calling for his son John, whose bedroom was down the hall, over the main entrance. Welles arose, went down to John's room, opened the window, and leaned out. Standing below was his messenger, James Smith, so excited he could scarcely make himself understood. Welles' calm voice reassured him. "Oh Mr. Secretary," Smith blurted out, "Mr. Lincoln is killed & Mr. Seward assassinated & I thought I must come and tell you!" "Why James," said Welles, "Mr. L[incoln] was at the Theatre & Mr. S[eward] is confined to his bed, ill, are you sure of this?" "I have been to Mr. Seward's & know it is true about him." James was speaking clearly and emphatically now. No longer skeptical, Welles was certain that something tragic had happened but hoped that his messenger was exaggerating. "Well, wait & I will be down directly," he said. While he was throwing on his clothes, he exclaimed, "Damn the Rebels, this is their work," a remark that thoroughly alarmed his wife. Fearful that armed assassins were roving the city, she begged her husband not to leave the house. "Be quiet," he said firmly, but not unkindly, "if Mr. Lincoln is in danger my place is beside him." With James Smith as his only companion, he crossed Fifteenth Street and was hurrying toward Seward's house when he saw four or five men in deep conversation on the corner by St. John's Church. He was half way across the street when the group broke up, and almost simultaneously the street lamps went out. For a moment or two Welles was "disconcerted" to find himself in darkness. He stopped in the middle of the street, but then, remembering that it was probably the time the city council set to extinguish the gas lamps, he resumed his rapid pace.

Fifteenth Street was crowded, the throng densest around Seward's mansion. Welles was recognized and way was made for him through the mass into the lower hall, which he found jammed with excited people, many of them foreign diplomats in full dress who had heard the news as they were leaving a dinner party near by. Two frightened servants who were trying to hold back the crowd were relieved to see Welles. Pausing just long enough to learn that both Seward and his son Frederick had been attacked and badly injured, Welles made his way as rapidly as he could to Seward's bedroom. There he found Dr. Verdi, the Seward family physician, attending the Secretary, who was lying on his back unconscious. A cloth covered the upper part of his face, his mouth was open, his lower jaw, that had been fractured in his recent accident, was encased in a wire frame. In the light of the flickering gas lamps, Seward's bed appeared to be "saturated with blood." Stanton came in just behind Welles, and at once he began making urgent inquiries about Seward's condition and about the assault itself, speaking so loudly that Dr. Verdi admonished him to lower his voice. When the physician assured Welles and Stanton that Seward's injuries were not likely to prove fatal, they left the chamber, stopping briefly to look in on Frederick Seward, who was not expected to live.

While descending the stairs, Welles asked Stanton whether he had any reliable news about the President. Stanton replied that he had been shot at Ford's Theatre and had not been moved. "Then let us go immediately there," said Welles. Stanton agreed and, on learning that Welles had walked over, offered him a place in the carriage he had commandeered at Seward's door. As they were leaving, General Montgomery Meigs appeared. Earnestly, he advised against their going to the threater. Welles said that nothing would keep him from going to the President. "We [are] wasting time," he snapped out at Meigs, as he pressed through the crowd to enter the waiting carriage. Stanton and Meigs followed in his wake. As they were about to leave, Major T. T. Eckert, Assistant Chief of Military Telegraph, galloped over to them. He had just come from Ford's Theatre, and he drew an alarming picture of the crowds and confusion there. It would be dangerous for Stanton "to expose himself." Welles again interposed, saying that he "knew not where he would be safe and the duty of both of us was to attend the President immediately." Stanton again concurred. With two armed soldiers as escorts, the carriage got under way, the driver skillfully guiding his vehicle through the crowds that had overflowed the sidewalks and were impeding the streets. Tenth Street itself was packed, but their escort forced a way through.

At the theater they were told that Lincoln had been carried across the street to number 453, the modest home of a German tailor named Wilhelm Petersen. The two secretaries went into the house and were directed through a hall to a small bedroom at the rear. Lincoln was lying diagonally across a bed that was too short for his long frame. Except for his heavy, labored breathing and the presence of six surgeons hovering around the bed, he appeared to be in a deep sleep. "His features were calm and striking," thought Welles. "I had never seen them appear to better advantage." But he quickly learned that there was no hope. A heavy-caliber derringer ball had penetrated the President's brain, behind his left ear. "He might live three hours or perhaps longer," advised one of the doctors. Welles saw an empty rocking chair by the bed, sat down and looked about the room, which was crowded with notables. Senator Sumner, Speaker of the House Schuyler Colfax, and all of his Cabinet colleagues except the stricken Seward were standing about the bed or in the hall. Lincoln, who had been stripped of his clothing, was covered with a sheet which Surgeon General Barnes turned down at regular intervals to check the heart action. During the night Mrs. Lincoln came into the chamber at frequent intervals. She wept by the bed, until, overcome with emotion, she let herself be led away. At one point Welles noticed that Robert Lincoln was leaning on the arm of Senator Sumner, who stood at the headboard looking down on Lincoln's face.

At six in the morning, Welles suddenly felt faint, and he left the oppressive atmosphere of the overcrowded bedroom for a breath of fresh air. He found the sky overcast, the weather chilling and damp. Large numbers of people were standing on the walkways and in the street, not excited and alarmed, as the crowd had been the night before, but quiet, "anxious and solicitous." One of them, recognizing Welles, asked him about the President's condition. Was there any hope? When Welles said that Lincoln was dying, most of those within earshot could not conceal their grief. Many of the blacks, who outnumbered the whites in the vicinity of Petersen's house, wept openly.

Feeling better, he returned to Petersen's house, but instead of going back to the bedroom he found a seat in the parlor, where Stanton and Attorney General Speed were taking testimony on the assassination. Restless, Welles returned to the bedroom, where it was evident that Lincoln's struggle was nearing an end. His breathing had become shallower, at times stopping, only to resume, but fainter than before; then it ceased altogether. Welles looked at his watch. It was 7:22 A.M. Dr. Phineas Gurley, pastor of the Second Presbyterian Church, which the Lincoln family attended, offered a brief prayer. Welles and the rest of the Cabinet returned to the parlor, where they all signed a letter, which Speed had prepared, informing Johnson that he was the new President. Dennison, the Postmaster General, thought that Welles, the only member of the original Cabinet present, should deliver the document. But sensing that Stanton would be offended, Welles suggested that McCulloch, senior member in precedence, deliver it.[49]

Drained emotionally, most of the sorrowing crowd left after Gurley's prayer. Maunsell B. Field, Assistant Secretary of the Treasury, Surgeon General Barnes, and a few others, however, remained in the death chamber. Barnes closed Lincoln's eyes and placed silver coins upon them. With a pocket handkerchief he tied up the President's jaw, which was beginning to fall. The body was placed in a plain pine box that had been secured earlier. Draped with the flag, the temporary casket was borne by a squad of soldiers to an ordinary commercial hearse, which carried it to the White House. While they were removing Lincoln's body, Petersen, the owner of the house, came in, seized the blood-soaked pillows and threw them out of the window.[50]

# CHAPTER 26

# Suffrage Is Crucial

WELLES GRATEFULLY ACCEPTED Attorney General Speed's offer of a ride home from Tenth Street. Shocked at the naked violence of the assassination, he realized that the Cabinet and the new President must reassure the people that the government was not impaired. Before Speed dropped him off at his home, Welles took it upon himself to ask the Attorney General if he would arrange a Cabinet meeting with Johnson at 12 noon that day, in the office of the Secretary of the Treasury. Speed was glad to comply.

Welles scarcely knew Andrew Johnson, and what he did know about him was not encouraging. That he was a War Democrat and an ardent believer in states' rights was reassuring. But he had collaborated with Wade as an original member of the radical-inspired Committee on the Conduct of the War. Welles could not have been hopeful about the future, about his own tenure, about the state of a nation whose new Chief Executive would begin his administration in such troubled times, under such dread auspices.

Promptly at noon on April 15, 1865, the Cabinet met with the new President. Speed, acting as spokesman, announced that Johnson had taken the oath of office and that he wished the government to go on as before. Someone asked about an inauguration. Welles opposed the idea emphatically. He was glad that Johnson, who now spoke for the first time, concurred. His acts would best disclose his policy, Johnson said. The new President's bearing was more impressive than Welles anticipated; his deportment, considering the circumstances, remarkably steady. Neatly dressed in a black broadcloth frock coat, matching waistcoat, and black doeskin trousers, he looked younger than his fifty-seven years. Johnson was just under six feet tall, broad-shouldered, trim, yet sturdy of frame. He had a rather stern appearance, mainly because of his large head, prominent features, and small dark eyes under heavy brows. Yet he could not have been more courteous, more deferential to the Cabinet.

The meeting was too brief for Welles to form any opinion of Johnson. He had said that he would continue Lincoln's program for reconstruction, but this could have meant anything. What did Johnson know of Lincoln's plans? Welles left the Treasury Department in as much of a quandary about the new President as when he had ridden home with Speed some hours earlier. There was to be a Cabinet meeting at ten the next morning, where, it was understood, reconstruction would be discussed. Perhaps then the President would come into sharper focus, would disclose his feelings on this compelling question.[1]

Welles was to be disappointed. The members of the Cabinet met at the Treasury Department, where they waited half an hour for the President to arrive, and then another half an hour for Stanton, who was bringing a revised plan of reconstruction for the states of Virginia and North Carolina. Johnson had been informed of the discussion held at Lincoln's last Cabinet meeting, where Stanton had presented a rough draft of a plan for reconstructing the two states. Stanton's plan, drawn up as an Executive Order, would have combined Virginia and North Carolina into one military district. A provisional military governor with functions similar to those Johnson had performed in Tennessee during the war would assert federal authority and require loyal inhabitants to reestablish state governments. The military governor, acting through provost marshals, would see to it that the citizens of the states were guaranteed a republican form of government. But, other than imposing the authority and the laws of the United States, including emancipation, on the former Confederate states, Stanton's draft contained no provisions for the specific protection of the freedmen. At that meeting, Welles had felt he had to register various objections. He had pointed out that Virginia had a state government, headed by Francis Pierpont, a shadow government to be sure, but one that the United States had recognized and had used as a legal entity to sanction the separation of West Virginia from Virginia. The United States had maintained no such relations with North Carolina. Stanton's plan, Welles had said, should provide for this particular contingency. He had also expressed concern about what appeared to be a plenary grant of military authority that would supersede the individuality of the states and would conflict with traditional American concepts of local self-government. At that time Lincoln had said that some of Welles' points were well taken; they had occurred to him when he first read the draft. He had asked Stanton to prepare distinct plans for the two states.[2]

When the Cabinet met with Johnson on Sunday, April 16, to discuss these matters, Stanton had removed Virginia from his proposal, but he had gone into much greater detail than previously in spelling out how the government should deal with North Carolina. Johnson did not commit himself on the revised plan. He did, however, seem to align himself with a hard-line policy on reconstruction when he stated emphatically that treason was the most odious of crimes. Prompt and severe punishment should be meted out to the former Confederate leaders. Everyone present agreed in principle with Johnson. At the time they all believed that Jefferson Davis and other high officials of the Confederacy were implicated in the assassination. Yet the very ferocity of Johnson's vengeful words must have given some members pause. Had there not been enough bloodshed already? No doubt Welles, for one, would have agreed with Horace Greeley, who asked Montgomery Blair whether "we must have military executions and years of Corsican vendettas? Is there anything in the character of the new President to found a hope?"[3]

That evening, at Stanton's invitation, Welles went to the War Department to discuss business involving their respective departments. After concluding, both men sat by the fire and chatted informally—a rare occasion for Welles, whose relationship with the tempestuous War Secretary had usually been correct but seldom cordial. While they were talking, Senator Sumner, Speaker Colfax, and John Covode, formerly a Representative from Pennsylvania, appeared, followed by H. L. Dawes and D. W. Gooch, Congressmen from Massachusetts. Gooch and Dawes were associates of Sumner; Covode, a crude, self-educated businessman, was a power in Pennsylvania politics.

Welles' relations with all of the men had been good on the whole. Barring a recent clash with the Massachusetts Congressmen over the Smith brothers—Boston merchants who had defrauded the Navy—they had all supported his administration of the Navy. He had serious misgivings about their radical tendencies, but neither they nor Stanton could have known the depth or the extent of his mistrust. Few men in public life were as close-mouthed as he, so guarded, even in Cabinet discussion.[4]

When all were seated, Stanton took a paper from the mass of documents on his desk and began to read it slowly. Welles at once recognized it as the revised draft of his plan for the reconstruction of Vir-

ginia and North Carolina. He sensed, wrongly, that the congressional
delegation had come by special appointment and that Stanton did not
know how to get rid of him. Disturbed at the thought that he might be
an intruder at a private meeting, he was shocked that a Cabinet document, an Executive measure still under discussion—copies of which had
not as yet been furnished to the Cabinet—should be disclosed to a
group of Congressmen.[5]

Stanton read on. He finished the Virginia draft and was half through
the North Carolina draft when Sumner, who was becoming more and
more impatient, interrupted him. Was the black man to be granted
suffrage? He would oppose any measure that did not give the black his
rights. Suffrage was fundamental to any plan for reconstruction. While
not contradicting the opinionated Senator, Stanton responded, mildly,
for him, that there were differences among Republicans on Negro suffrage. He felt this was not the proper time to advance such a controversial subject. Just then Welles received a written message which gave
him an opportunity to leave Stanton's office.

During the next few days he was entirely too busy to ponder the
events of that strange and awkward meeting. When Welles did bring
up reconstruction in the Cabinet on Friday morning, April 21, Stanton
was not responsive; nor was any one else. Welles was quite sure now
that he had been an unwelcome guest at the War Department meeting
of Stanton and the Congressmen. Nothing could have been further
from the truth. Stanton had not planned the meeting. Impetuously,
it would appear, he had read the Cabinet documents to test opinion,
much as Lincoln had done with controversial measures. But Stanton,
after all, was not the President. He should not have taken upon himself the responsibility of disclosure, and not in such a way that it would
appear deliberately planned. After the Cabinet meeting on April 21,
with Welles suspicious of his motives, Stanton made another move that
was equally misleading.[6]

At about 7:30 that evening, Stanton was announced at Welles' house
and shown into the library. There was to be an emergency Cabinet
meeting in a half an hour, where important matters were to be discussed. Notices had gone out to other Cabinet members. His carriage
was waiting, could Welles join him? Welles delayed only long enough
to seize hat and coat. He could not recall any time during the war
when the imperious Stanton had ever delivered a message in person to
him at his own house. Arriving late, they found the President and the
Cabinet, General Grant, and Preston King, an old friend of Welles'
whom he now learned had become a personal adviser to Johnson.

Stanton opened the discussion with a terse announcement that Grant had received and would read important dispatches from General W. T. Sherman. In an atmosphere of gathering tension, Grant read Sherman's account of the surrender agreement he had just concluded with General Joseph E. Johnston, who commanded one of the last organized bodies of Confederate troops. The military aspects of the surrender seemed to be in order, following closely the precedent Grant had established at Appomattox. But the agreement did not stop there. Sherman recognized all existing Confederate state governments once their members had sworn allegiance to the Union. In cases where more than one government existed, the Supreme Court of the United States would determine legitimacy. The two commanders pledged themselves to implement a speedy restoration of federal courts; to secure property rights; and to provide for a general amnesty, which would precede extension of the franchise.

That two generals in the field, one of whom was a rebel commander, should arrogate to themselves the responsibility for concluding a peace treaty was a sweeping intrusion of the military into the realm of political affairs. The President and the Cabinet were shocked. Unanimously, they condemned Sherman's action. Much excited talk followed, some members fearing a military coup, until Welles reminded them that Sherman's army was, after all, "composed of citizens like ourselves, who had homes and wives and children as well as a government that they loved." This brief but incisive remark calmed the atmosphere. The President and Cabinet swiftly came to a decision. Sherman was to be told that his political settlement was disapproved, that military commanders were expressly forbidden to interfere with political and civil affairs. If General Johnston still insisted upon the terms of his agreement with Sherman, hostilities were to resume at once. The next day Welles learned that Grant, instead of telegraphing these orders, had left for Sherman's headquarters to convey them in person. "This was sensible," he thought, "and will ensure the work to be well and satisfactorily done."

Throughout the brief, emotion-ridden interlude, he had been critical of Stanton's role in what he saw as a calculated attempt to stir up imaginary fears that would injure the reputation of a popular and able military commander. The Sunday morning papers carried all of Sherman's dispatches, along with an account of the Cabinet proceedings over Stanton's signature. Sympathetic to Sherman, whom he believed had erred because he misunderstood Lincoln's original purpose, Welles was still glad that the facts were spread before the public. Stanton should have been more judicious, more temperate in his language, but the actions were characteristic of the man.[7]

During the chaotic month following Lincoln's assassination, Welles was almost as dubious about the new President as he was about Stanton. Johnson maintained a reserve with his Cabinet, correct but formal, so different from Lincoln's easy-going style. What little he had to say about reconstruction he expressed in harsh language that troubled Welles, who feared an exacting policy of retribution toward the defeated South. Radical Congressmen of the Wade-Davis faction were everywhere in evidence, declaring openly that Johnson was with them, that Stanton would be the only member of the Cabinet to be retained. Davis himself was jubilant. After a few words with the President at a reception on April 21, he exclaimed that he had gotten more right answers to his questions in ten minutes than he had had from Lincoln in four years. "His assassination was a great crime," said Davis, "but the change is no calamity. I suppose God had punished us enough by his weak rule—& ended it!" Preston King and Wade both assured Davis that the Blairs would have no influence. His only worry about the new administration was Johnson's reliance upon Grant, "of whom he seemed not exactly to stand in awe of but anxious to conciliate rather than resolved to command."[8]

Welles would have been gravely dismayed had he known just how cordial Johnson was being to the radicals. Charles Sumner, after badgering Stanton into adding Negro suffrage to his North Carolina plan, got what he thought was a commitment from the President that he, too, would impose it on the Southern states. How this was to be accomplished was not spelled out, but Sumner and Chief Justice Chase, who was also present at the interview, came away as enthusiastic about Johnson as Davis and Wade were.[9]

If suffrage was the essence of Negro rights to Charles Sumner, it was the cornerstone of states' rights to Welles. Any attempt by the national government to deprive the Southern states of their power to decide who should vote would alter the nature of the Union. The tide of radicalism was beginning to surge in the North. Welles' closest friends, men with whom he had been associated personally and politically most of his adult life, were expressing opinions close to those of Thaddeus Stevens and Ben Wade. But Welles refused to be moved by either the claims of friendship or the entreaties of the editors. In principle, he was not opposed to extending suffrage to the blacks, if the various states approved it. Like many of the old Jacksonians, he felt strongly that a potential voter should have enough education to cast his ballot intelligently. "The Negro can take upon himself the duty about as intelligently and as well for the public interest as a considerable portion of the foreign element which comes amongst us," he wrote, "each will be the tool of demagogues." In most of the free states, the blacks did not have the suffrage. Was it politic, he asked, to give them the vote in the former Confederate states? Was it constitutional?[10]

Formal Cabinet discussion of reconstruction was taken up on May 8, 1865, after Stanton furnished each member with a printed copy of his revised Virginia draft. President Johnson invited discussion, beginning with McCulloch, as senior in Seward's absence. McCulloch had nothing to say, nor did Stanton. Welles followed. Though he had only received his copy that morning, he was ready with several changes, which, if adopted, would make substantive changes in Stanton's new draft. Welles objected to the section that delegated to the War Department exclusive responsibility for organizing the government of Virginia. It was such a complex matter, involving so many diverse factors and of such crucial importance to the future of the nation, he argued, that these powers should not be delegated to any one department but be subject to general Executive supervision. Stanton demurred forcefully, but he did not cling to his views when the rest of the Cabinet supported Welles. The other major point Welles raised concerned the relations between the federal government and the Pierpont government of Virginia. Stanton would have used the Pierpont regime merely as an agent to hold elections for a new state government. To Welles' fastidious eye, this meant the state of Virginia had ceased to exist, that it could only be resurrected by the federal government. The United States should assist state authorities, in this case the Pierpont government, to establish and maintain its control, but only at its request and only to aid it in enforcing its own jurisdiction. Again Stanton was reluctant to concede what must have seemed rather an extreme expression of states' rights on the one hand but a contradiction of them on the other. For the Pierpont government could scarcely claim that it was popularly elected. By strict constitutional definition it was not providing Virginia with a republican form of government. In the end Stanton yielded with a good grace that Welles had not expected.

The next day, President Johnson and the Cabinet considered the North Carolina draft. Welles must have been surprised that the printed copy mentioned extending the suffrage to all "loyal citizens," for he was quick to label the phrase ambiguous. What precisely did Mr. Stanton mean by it? Negro as well as white suffrage, Stanton replied. Another Cabinet member immediately objected, prompting Stanton to suggest that the President waive all prior discussion of the point. Each member would simply express his opinion on whether he was for or against Negro suffrage. Johnson agreed. Stanton, Dennison, and Speed declared themselves for Negro suffrage as an integral part of reconstruction; Welles, McCulloch, and Usher opposed it. In explaining his opinion, Welles said that he thought the question of suffrage had been fixed by Lincoln's proclamation of December 8, 1863. As he remembered it, the policy then set forth restricted suffrage to loyal citizens in the rebellious states who had voted in the election of 1860. Obviously, this would deny suffrage to the blacks. Welles reminded Stanton that he had assumed suffrage to be exclusively a state concern, as had all of the Lincoln Cabinet. With each state prescribing its own unique qualifications for exercising the privilege, how could it be otherwise? "We shall get rid of slavery by constitutional means," he added, "but conferring on the black civil rights is another matter. I know not the authority. . . ."[11]

The moment was crucial. Johnson, a War Democrat, was unfamiliar with the state of the Republican party, with the power and the influence of its various congressional factions. As Military Governor of Tennessee, he had been out of touch with national politics for two years. Stanton and Welles were senior Cabinet members, successful service chiefs, trusted advisers of Abraham Lincoln. Johnson had reason to believe that the stricken Seward, who was slowly recovering, favored limited extension of the suffrage. Had Welles joined Stanton and Dennison, had he taken a more realistic, less rigidly constitutional stand and made a forceful plea for limited Negro suffrage along the lines of Lincoln's last public address, he surely would have made a powerful impression on Johnson. McCulloch, an Indiana banker of no special political or public influence, had joined the Cabinet only a few months before. Usher had already been replaced as Secretary of the Interior and was present by special invitation because James Harlan, his successor, had not been able to take up the duties of his office. Johnson was under heavy pressure from Sumner, Chase, Wade, and Davis. If his Cabinet had voted five to two, he may well have conceded the point.

Welles had stoutly maintained that suffrage was a state right, but so was slavery. If he could support an amendment to abolish slavery, logically he could have supported an amendment to extend the suffrage in such a way that the states still could set conditions for its exercise. But Welles would not take the extra step. A deeply ingrained nationalism blinded him to the plain fact that most Northerners believed a war had been fought, not just an insurrection suppressed. Welles' pristine view of states' rights and his insistence on white supremacy in the South could well cheat the North of its victory. In explaining his vote, Stanton had not made any of these arguments, nor had any of the others who voted for extension of the suffrage. If they had, they would have caught Welles in an inconsistency. The President, who had been listening carefully, made no comment, saying, as he closed the discussion, that he would consider the matter carefully. Later, however, Preston King assured Welles that Johnson would not impose Negro suffrage under federal auspices in the North Carolina plan. Welles may have played the decisive role. At least Sumner thought so when he talked to him about his stand at a later date.

The events and the labors of that month had taken their toll. For some time Welles had been planning a short sea voyage along the Southern coast, but the assassination and problems immediately connected with the end of the war tied him to his desk. Reconstruction had gone beyond the point where his counsel was needed. Department affairs were in good shape. The only other major obligation was a ceremonial one of joining the President and his colleagues in reviewing the armies of the Union on May 23 and 24. Welles was moved to awe at the spectacle, as rank after rank of Union soldiers—150,000 of them —passed down Pennsylvania Avenue in front of the White House. As his gaze moved from the throng of dignitaries and their ladies on the reviewing stand to the seemingly endless ranks of blue-clad veterans before him, he thought of the recent tragic events, the absence of the man who more than anyone else had made this triumph possible. "Abraham Lincoln was not there," he wrote in his diary that night, "all felt this."[12]

The next day, May 25, 1865, Welles, Postmaster General Dennison, Calvin Day, and Mark Howard, and their families left Washington. Their vessel, the *Santiago de Cuba,* was a fast, comfortable steamer of 1400 tons that had been completely refurbished after many months of blockade duty. Welles was glad to get away from Washington, glad to leave behind him the air of suspicion and recrimination that hung heavily over the capital. Of late he had found himself clashing with Stanton on almost every major point—not just on reconstruction, but on the court martial of the Lincoln conspirators, the disposition of Jefferson Davis and other high Confederate officials, Army interference with the telegraphic communication of the Navy. For a man who preferred to do battle with the likes of Stanton privately and comfortably in his diary, these frequent exchanges were distressing.

Under clear skies, the *Santiago de Cuba* swung into the placid Potomac and headed downstream. Washington, with all its perplexing problems—the intrigue, the corruption, the confusion of purposes—faded in the distance as Welles and his friends admired the scenery along the river banks, now in the full bloom of a Southern spring.[13]

While Welles and his party were inspecting the ruins of Charleston, Johnson issued his proclamation on the reconstruction of North Carolina. Though Welles had been assured that the President would continue Lincoln's policy, he remained uncertain until he actually read the document. When he did, he was much relieved that Johnson had made no mention of Negro suffrage. In fact, the President had specifically defined a voter as a resident of the state who had taken an oath of loyalty to the United States and had been qualified to vote "as prescribed by the Constitution and laws of North Carolina before May 20, 1861."

Publication of the North Carolina plan inspired discussion among his guests. Calvin Day and Mark Howard both held strong views on reconstruction. Day was certain that the South hated the North "more cordially today than 2 years since." Southerners must not be permitted to have any power in the government, he maintained stoutly, until they gave absolute assurance they could be trusted not to re-enslave the black or turn the national government to their sectional advantage.[14] Welles listened to their arguments, but he counseled patience. How could anything be done that had not already been done without violating the Constitution? He was content to have the states work out their own destinies. Welles returned to Washington on June 8, much refreshed in health and in spirits, optimistic that reconstruction was on the right course. Johnson may have his faults, he was surely no Lincoln, but he was sound on the Constitution. All would be well.

With the President handling reconstruction himself, the service secretaries were free to concentrate their energies in winding down the war effort. In the case of the Navy, this involved numerous policy decisions and much routine supervision. Welles approached the task with some regret.

He and Fox had built a modern oceangoing steam navy. They had concentrated on steam propulsion, armor, and heavy ordnance almost from the beginning of the conflict. "When I took charge of the Department," he explained to Senator Lot Morrill, "I found no settled policy regarding vessels or the course to be pursued—steamers were not popular—ironclads were not popular—heavy ordnance was not popular —everything was in a transition state and a large portion of the officers clung with tenacity to the old state of things. As I had none of these old prejudices and foresaw that we must accept and make use of improvements my views and conclusions were unsatisfactory with many. . . ."

Worried about European intervention, he ordered the design and construction of a fast, 5000-ton, conventional armored cruiser, the *Dunderberg*, which, if she met her specifications, would outclass the best ironclad vessel in any foreign navy. Both Welles and Fox urged upon Congress the necessity for adequate armor plate facilities and fresh-water dockyards to berth and repair the new ironclad fleet.[15] Although the initial impulse for all this increased naval activity was defensive, it had conjured up dreams of empire in the impressionable Fox. Nor was Welles averse to a big navy that could challenge Great Britain, though he was more cautious than his assistant. James B. Eads, the brilliant, self-taught designer and builder of gunboats and ironclads in the West, had been asked specifically to gather whatever information he could on the physical needs for constructing and maintaining a navy worthy of a great power. In 1864, Welles sent Chief Engineer James King to Europe to examine and report on shipbuilding and dockyard facilities there.

It is questionable whether Congress would have been willing to appropriate the additional millions of dollars necessary to make the nation a major naval power. But the naval construction program, such as it was, alarmed the British and probably had a restraining effect on the policy of the Palmerston ministry toward the United States.[16]

Some months before the war's end, Welles reversed himself on pushing for a large, modern fleet. He had sensed a change in the mood of Congress, but, more personally compelling than that, he feared the nation was heading for economic disaster. A hard-money man all his life, an administrator who looked upon economy and balanced budgets as a sacred trust, Welles had been harshly critical of Chase's and Fessenden's financial policies. He abhorred greenbacks, inflation, and what he believed to be the wild extravagance of Stanton's War Department. Of course, the war had always come first. He had developed a service-connected bias, which together with his blockade responsibilities and his anglophobia had led him down the path of expensive naval construction. With the war coming to an end, however, Welles' ingrained sense of thriftiness reasserted itself. Two months before Lee's surrender he directed all squadron commanders to send North those purchased vessels most in need of repairs. Before he left for his Southern trip, he ordered all blockade squadrons cut in half. After his return and during the remainder of the summer, he and Fox reduced the Navy to a planned level of 100 vessels, less than one-sixth of its wartime strength.

Considering that the North in 1861 had been totally unprepared and only partly industrialized, the naval program had been a mighty, and in the main, successful effort. New construction totaled 141 wooden vessels, 49 of which were paddlewheel steamers built for special purposes, and 92 other ships, which were more modern, more efficient, more secure, screw-propelled vessels. To supplement these, Northern shipyards had turned out 62 ironclad or ironhull vessels. Most of them were monitors, but some were conventional heavyweights like the 3500 ton *New Ironsides* and the 5000 ton *Dunderberg*. In all, the Navy had 210 new vessels with a total weight of 256,000 tons and an ordnance of 1675 guns. At a cost in excess of $18 million, the Department had purchased 418 vessels, of which 318 were steamers.

Despite inflation, the Navy had in service a fleet of over 600 vessels, two-thirds of which were kept operational at cost of $314 million—a mere 9.3 per cent of the government's expenditures during the war.[17] In the naval blockade, 1504 prizes, which Welles estimated to be worth $35 million, were either taken or destroyed. Possibly as many more got through to the Confederacy, but it seems reasonable to state that the naval blockade was more effective than any blockade in any previous war; certainly up to that time it was the most extensive.

Welles was satisfied that his administration of the department had been a successful one, but he was just as determined to dismantle the Navy as efficiently as it had been built up. Under the stern injunction of economy, he drove the department hard, impressing on all that each day a given vessel remained in service meant that much more of the public funds was being spent needlessly. Yet the job required finesse and judgment. Much thought had to be given to the human and material needs of the service, if it were to remain the nucleus of a powerful navy. Which vessels, for instance, were to be laid up, and where? Which were to be sold? What of personnel, of training programs already established? What should be done about the officer corps? Which were to stay, and where were they to be billeted? What of the naval shipyards and the naval bases, temporary and permanent? Nor could Welles neglect the political implications of demobilization.

Details such as these left him little time to concern himself with presidential reconstruction, though he followed Johnson's course closely. The President was not a confiding man. After Cabinet discussion of the Virginia and North Carolina models, Johnson had gone his own way. On June 15, and again on July 4, Senator Sumner gave

Welles an opportunity to make his views known both at the White
House and in the Congress. The first two state proclamations had
deeply distressed the Senator because neither had made any provision
for black suffrage. On June 15 he dashed off a note to Welles unsparing
in its denunciation of the proclamations. "Of course their first effort is
to divide the North and to give the democrats an opportunity to organize," he wrote. Welles did not reply for two weeks, during which
time Johnson issued identical proclamations for Georgia, Texas, Alabama, and South Carolina. Then he composed a carefully phrased letter to Sumner, admitting that Republicans differed widely on suffrage
in the South. He was not sure whether the question could be reconciled, for suffrage was a right clearly reserved to the states. Johnson, he
thought, was privately in favor of extending the suffrage, but never
through the unconstitutional means of federal action.[18] Sumner replied, pleading with him to save Johnson "and thus save the country." He stressed his oft-repeated assertion that the Constitution required the federal government to guarantee each state a republican
government. The Declaration of Independence defined a republican
government as one that represented the natural rights of man rather
than the legal rights of states. These were the principles that lay behind the Constitution—not practice, not precedent, not consistency.

Welles dismissed Sumner's letter as passionate rhetoric, impractical
and unconstitutional. But he did use the correspondence as a pretext
for a talk with Johnson on reconstruction, hoping to prod the President into taking political steps that would draw the lines then and
there. Sumner was "organizing and drilling" kindred spirits on the issue of Negro suffrage, he told the President. The Senator's letters,
which he read to Johnson, were evidences of larger, potentially dangerous combinations that were forming against the administration. Negro suffrage in the South, he thought, was to be the paramount issue.
Johnson listened and said he was aware of the opposition, but he refused to take it seriously.[19]

On July 4, 1865, in Chicago, Henry Winter Davis, much more a
leader of radical party opinion than the impulsive Sumner, made an
unusually candid speech which bore out Welles' contention that Republican extremists were pursuing an exclusively partisan course. Davis
would strip the entire planter class of all civil rights and at the same
time confer those rights on the blacks. "I am no enthusiast. I am very
little of a philanthropist. I have no supreme love of the Negro over
the white, but I know his vote is important . . . ," he said, in a moment of supreme cynicism. "We need the votes of all the colored peo-

ple; it is numbers, not intelligence that counts at the ballot-box; it is right intention not philosophic judgment that casts the vote." Welles made no comment on Davis' remarks at the time. He clipped the speech from the paper, however, and filed it away. He was now certain what the radicals were after. He saw no reason to change his mind on a remark he had made to Johnson a few days earlier. Yet he was making a dangerously bland assumption that Negro suffrage was an artificial question, a fabrication made by Davis, Sumner, and other radicals to embarrass Johnson for electioneering purposes. "As there must and will be parties," he said complacently, "they may as well form on this question as any other."[20]

On July 13, 1865, Johnson completed the first phase of presidential reconstruction when he established a provisional government for Florida. All seemed relatively calm. The *New-York Tribune* and Bryant's *Evening Post*, harbingers of radical opinion, gave the Florida proclamation only passing mention, though both papers continued to push for an extension of the suffrage. Mark Howard, who had spent the previous month traveling in the South, reported general acceptance of Johnson's program. Howard had mingled with all classes in all regions. He found submission, but little real friendship for the government. Paradoxically, in the deep South, the storm center of secession, he saw less open hostility than in the Border states of Tennessee and Kentucky. The commercial classes everywhere, "from interest if from nothing else," said Howard, "will soonest come to the earnest support of the Government."[21]

Howard's reassurances did nothing to allay Welles' apprehension at the rise of what he called "ugly" sentiments in the South. Reports were beginning to flow into Washington that Unionists were being harassed politically and socially. The new Johnson state governments were accepting with ill grace the mild political conditions imposed upon them. "The tone . . . in the South is injudicious and indiscreet in many respects," Welles commented. "I know not if there is any remedy, but if not, other and serious disasters await them, and us also perhaps." The old secession leadership seemed to have gained control of most Southern states. To Welles' chagrin, it was supporting prominent ex-Confederates for state posts, and for Congress as well.[22]

By late August, hostile Northern reaction was on the rise. Welles' protégé, General Joseph R. Hawley, who visited Washington at the end of the month, was strong for extending suffrage to the blacks. In cautioning Hawley on the constitutional and political pitfalls, Welles did not think that the public was prepared to accept universal manhood suffrage. And he questioned the integrity of the radical leaders who would make Negro suffrage the overriding principle of the Republican party. Except for Sumner, whom he felt to be sincere, Welles did not believe one prominent radical—not even Thaddeus Stevens—accepted social equality. Stubbornly, he persisted in considering the suffragists to be narrowly partisan, their objective to control the government so that they could remake the nation in their own image and to their own advantage.[23]

Yet he was no less critical of his old friend Montgomery Blair, who had just made another of his vitriolic personal attacks on Seward and Stanton. Speaking at Clarksville, Maryland, Blair demanded a reorganization and realignment of parties which Welles thought premature. Johnson was far more provoked than Welles at Blair's personal onslaught. On September 2, he called Blair into his office, where he chided him for playing the Copperhead's game. Johnson was reported to have said heatedly that he would not listen to such offensive remarks about members of his own administration. Subsequently, Johnson related his conversation to Seward, who promptly sent it on to Stanton through Major Thomas T. Eckert, assistant chief of the military telegraph. "Mr. Seward feels assured that everything is satisfactory as you could wish," reported Eckert. "He said he would be glad to have you informed of this, but did not wish to write it himself."[24] As Welles had suspected for some months, Stanton and Seward were trying to bring the President around to a moderate policy on reconstruction that would be acceptable to a majority of the party.

Under their influence, Johnson had gone further than Lincoln, though cautiously, in imposing conditions on the defeated states. Welles reluctantly conceded that such conditions were necessary. But any imposition of Negro suffrage on the Southern states, he felt, would make a mockery of the federal system. Now that the insurrection had been put down, its leaders were liable for punishment. The states, however, could not be coerced without the federal government conceding that they had seceded, without the Union punishing the loyal and disloyal citizens alike.

Meanwhile, many Northern radicals were seeking to extend the franchise through state action. In Connecticut, an amendment to strike the word "white" from the state constitution was to be voted upon in a special election on October 2. Welles had hoped to avoid a public stand, but the lines were drawn too sharply. Without consulting him, the Democratic *Hartford Times* declared flatly that he opposed suffrage for the blacks. Charles Dudley Warner of the Hartford *Evening Press* wrote Welles on September 20, enclosing the *Times* article. "I need not say," wrote Warner, "that it will hurt us badly unless at once contradicted by you."[25]

Welles authorized Warner to deny that he had ever said he was opposed to Negro suffrage, yet he refused to be quoted on the issue because he held that mischievous partisans would misconstrue whatever comment he might make. His rather lame excuse was not accepted, at least not by Warner, who telegraphed him on September 26 for a definite expression of opinion. Welles was irked, and he still refused to give a categorical answer. He wrote that he favored intelligence, not color, as the basis for suffrage.

By stipulating intelligence, not race, as the prime qualification for the suffrage, Welles in effect was replying to Sumner and his radical associates who wished to confer the privilege indiscriminately through federal action. "I would not enslave the Negro, but his enfranchisement is another question," Welles said, "and until he is better informed, it is not desirable that he should vote. . . ." He conceded that there would be a time when the black should vote, but he would never accept him as an equal. "I am no advocate of social equality, nor do I labor for political or civil equality with the Negro. I do not want him at my table, nor do I care to have him in the jury box or in the legislative hall, or on the bench."[26]

To Welles' surprise, but not his regret, the Connecticut suffrage amendment was defeated by a substantial majority. Although he would have voted for it, had he been in the state, he rejoiced at the popular rebuke of the radicals. Hopeful that the referendum would serve as an example in other areas, he placidly assumed it would reverse the trend toward centralism. Some of the more practical radicals agreed with him.[27]

In seeking a formula that would make his doctrine of non-interference more palatable to radical opinion on suffrage, Johnson gave his personal views to George Stearns, a Boston millionaire and philanthropist who happened to be in Washington at the time. The President said that as a private citizen of Tennessee he would "try to introduce Negro suffrage gradually." Black veterans would have first priority, but he favored giving the vote to any adult male who could read and write or owned property valued at $200 to $250. If the whites of the eleven ex-Confederate states had only acted on this advice, a majority of the Republicans would have sustained the new governments. But every one of them presented a deaf ear, including Johnson's home state.[28] Still, the President flinched from taking the necessary final step which would have made his reconstruction program a complete success.

He was too much of a Jacksonian Democrat to force Negro suffrage on the Southern states, even though he could have done so under the war powers. As the *New-York Tribune* had repeatedly pointed out, he had already infringed upon the states' corporate rights in establishing his provisional governments. But Johnson had made it clear that he had intervened only to preserve the integrity of the Union. Eradication of slavery was one of the principal means to that end and was therefore justified. Suffrage and other civil rights were of local concern. He would not accept the argument that the extension of suffrage either by Executive or by Legislative fiat was essential to the maintenance and the security of the Union. Quite the contrary, he thought such action would weaken the Union by further weakening the rights of states. The new governments in the former Confederate states recognized the dualism of his reconstruction policy and rashly exploited it. Perhaps 150,000 blacks could have met Johnson's tests—so few and so widely distributed that their votes would never have presented any threat to white-dominated home rule. No one except a handful of extreme radicals seems to have considered that the extension would have been anything more than a symbolic gesture.

Though worried about the attitude of the Southern states, Welles simply would not abandon the political habits of a lifetime. His own experience had taught him that small, tightly organized groups with definite programs could usually lead the uninformed masses. The more extreme the views, the more persuasive the charm. It had been so with secession, where determined extremists such as Rhett and Yancey had imposed their will on the Unionist majority in the South. Now a similar group of irresponsible extremists in the South, thought Welles, were embarrassing the President's generous peace program and playing into the hands of irresponsible extremists in the North—the radical Republicans.[29]

Welles could see a cruel dilemma ahead for men of his temperament and beliefs, whom he believed made up the vast majority of the party. Unless there were a realignment of parties in the old tradition of political change, the administration might lose control of its own party. If that should happen, the only alternative was the Democratic party, an organization Welles had fought passively since 1850, actively since 1854. For the time being this alternative was unthinkable. He held the Democratic leaders to be largely responsible for the war, many, indeed, he believed were tainted with treason. And he feared a fusion between the Southern and Northern Democrats that could dominate the government for evil ends, as it had in the 1850's.

Mark Howard, again traveling in the South, reported a dramatic change of opinion. Writing from Atlanta on November 13, he said that the subdued feeling he had found on his earlier trip to the region had been replaced by a mood of obstinacy and bitterness, especially in South Carolina. "It is astonishing," he remarked, "how lightly the oath is taken. Many have said that since it was forced upon them they did not consider it binding." In early December, Howard was convinced that the white masses in the South were still rebels in spirit. Only the presence of the military has managed to keep them from taking overt action. "Withdraw the troops," he said, "and generally the Union men especially from the North say they will not be able to remain in the country."[30]

# CHAPTER 27

# The Issue Is with Him

HOWEVER MUCH HOWARD'S WARNINGS disturbed Welles, he was infinitely more concerned about the ominous mood of the new Congress. On Saturday, December 2, 1865, congressional Republicans met in caucus, where they raised a joint committee of fifteen to which would be referred everything concerning reconstruction. The caucus refused to recognize Johnson's governments in the South, asserting that Congress must also play a significant role in reconstruction.[1] When the Republicans chose Thaddeus Stevens to present the resolution for the Joint Committee, Welles regarded it as a calculated move against the Executive. At the first opportunity, he spoke with Johnson about these maneuvers. The President was calm, as usual, and confident that he was master of the situation. Convinced that Johnson had either been imposed upon or had misjudged the capacity of the radicals to manipulate their fellow Congressmen, Welles was not surprised when all of the other former Confederate states, including Tennessee, were denied representation.[2]

Johnson's first annual message did nothing to calm the troubled Congress, though it was a powerful state paper. It was ghostwritten by George Bancroft, and the President was so secretive about its preparation that no member of his Cabinet was aware of any author but himself being involved. The *New-York Tribune* had words of praise for the message—"a state paper of signal ability and unusual frankness." It disagreed with Johnson on only one point, but that a crucial one. He had asserted that he could not, without admitting that secession had occurred, impose suffrage on one part of the Union without imposing it everywhere. "The dialectics which prove that no state has been out of the Union," said the *Tribune*, "would as easily demonstrate that no man ever committed burglary or forgery, because none had any right to do aught of the sort."[3]

Two days after Congress had organized and listened to the President's message, Senator Sumner was shown into Welles' office. Without any visible sign of emotion he excoriated Welles and Seward as being "foully, fatally culpable" in supporting Johnson. Welles asked politely if Sumner thought anyone in the Cabinet opposed the President on reconstruction policy. "Stanton does," was the prompt rejoinder. Welles disagreed, though Sumner offered evidence to support his claim. Then he asserted that two other members of the Cabinet also agreed with his radical views. These could only be, thought Welles, James Harlan, who had displaced Usher as Secretary of the Interior in May 1865, and James Speed, the Attorney General.[4]

As the year closed, Welles was cautiously hopeful that the administration would weather the radical assault. He still suspected that Seward and Stanton were playing a double game. Now he believed Harlan and Speed to be untrustworthy. While he approved of McCulloch's conservatism, and his undoubted loyalty to the President, he deplored his lack of political experience and statesmanship. Altogether, the Cabinet did not measure up to his standards, nor did it give the kind of support and advice he thought the President needed.

Welles had come to respect Johnson, whom he felt had integrity and common sense. That they were both old Jacksonian Democrats and strict constructionists made for an harmonious relationship. Whatever differences they may have had on political theory were mere matters of degree. The President was not quite as fastidious about states' rights as Welles was, not quite as elitist on the suffrage question. He was less rigidly moralistic, less judgmental than Welles, more likely to accept the arguments of expediency that Seward and Stanton put forth. In Welles' eyes, Johnson's great weakness was his assessment of politicians and their motives. Over-confident of his ability to control a turbulent party in turbulent times, he seemed unable to distinguish his friends from his foes. The radicals may have been a minority of extremists, but Welles knew that they were men of superior intelligence, and masters of intrigue within Congress, of public relations without.[5]

Johnson's detached attitude toward the radicals Welles incorrectly attributed to "the baleful influence" of Seward and Stanton. Both men were trying to steer the President away from a collision course with Congress. But after eight months in the presidency Johnson saw no reason to compromise his principles by any further concession to party opinion. A reasonable man, as he saw himself, following the reasonable guidelines his predecessor had sketched out, he confidently expected the Congress to behave reasonably. What he had done was restore the rebel states to the Union with the least possible damage to constitutional restraints. The rhetoric of a Sumner, the growls of a Wade, the sarcasm of a Stevens were simply the rantings of a tiny minority. Certain that he, not they, could swing the majority to his conservative, constitutionally correct stand, he was relying on Stanton, Seward, Speed, and Harlan to be his agents in the cause, never dreaming for a moment that some of them were already opposing him.

Although Welles had never served in Congress, he had a more realistic view of its workings and of its leading men than the President did. On December 30, Henry Winter Davis died of pneumonia in Baltimore. Welles believed Davis to have been the most able, the most influential, and also the most unscrupulous of the radical leaders. Yet his loss, while it might temporarily hurt the radicals, was not irreparable. There still remained Thaddeus Stevens, the most skillful party tactician in either House. Welles had known Stevens for thirty years. Since their first meeting at Harrisburg, Pennsylvania, in 1836, he had closely followed the career of this extraordinary man. Stevens, then in his seventy-fourth year, was physically grotesque. His heavy, long, deeply seamed, dead-white face contrasted vividly with his bright dark eyes under heavy black brows, and incongruous brown wig, whose curly locks brushed his shoulders. One of his feet was deformed, so that he walked bent forward, in a slow, lurching gait. But it was his voice, not his appearance, that emphasized the sinister effect—it was flat, devoid of expression, sepuchral. A master of the cutting diatribe, the withering sarcasm, the mordant metaphor, he cut down his opponents verbally with never a change of tone.[6]

Stevens had a vindictive streak in his character which was all too evident in his attitude toward the defeated South. But he could be kindly, and he had a disarming sense of humor. Welles in a way admired him, probably because he shared many of Stevens' humanitarian impulses—opposition to slavery, imprisonment for debt, and capital punishment. Though diametrically opposed in their theories of government and their thinking on civil rights for the blacks, each respected the other. "To the colored race," Welles wrote years after Stevens' death, "he seemed always more attached and tender than to the whites, perhaps because they were enslaved and oppressed."[7]

No radical in the Senate had the political insight or the charisma of Stevens. But Welles also believed Wade to be a dangerous antagonist.

Like Stevens, the blunt Senator from Ohio had traits that made him stand out among his colleagues. He was crude, and incredibly profane, but he radiated a kind of homely sincerity that made him a power among his peers. A sturdy champion of the Legislative branch, he had early come under the influence of Henry Winter Davis. Once a working associate of Johnson's, Wade had nothing but contempt for him now. Prowling the halls of Congress, delivering his scathing remarks in his bluff but honest manner, he impressed lesser men with his views. Unlike the President and some of his Cabinet associates, Welles took Sumner seriously too. He had always made allowances for the Senator's weaknesses—his pedantry, his vanity, his supercilious posturing—for he recognized that Sumner was something of a Northern institution. An impractical, unpredictable idealist, Sumner was not an organization man. But he represented, Welles felt, a strong moral influence in the legislative halls, where self-interest rather than public interest had been the dominant theme for as long as he could remember. What Welles had in mind was summed up in a tart comparison he made between Sumner and Nathaniel P. Banks, who had just received the Republican nomination for Congress from Middlesex County, Massachusetts: "There is no intimacy between Banks and Sumner," he said, "they are unlike. Sumner is honest but impracticable. Banks is precisely the opposite."[8]

Whether potentially corrupt or honest, intelligent or feckless, the Republicans in the thirty-ninth Congress were moderate on the issue of reconstruction. Though most hoped for an arrangement with Johnson, they were sensitive to Northern public opinion and were quick to set in motion the machinery for a much tougher program than the President's. During the first week in January, Lyman Trumbull of Illinois—like Welles, an old Democrat, rather conservative on most issues, but a zealot when it came to the protection of individual rights and privileges—drafted two bills that would help the Southern black in his transition from slavery to freedom. During the closing weeks of the war, a Freedmen's Bureau, with limited tenure and limited powers, had been created to assist Southern blacks and poor whites. One of Trumbull's bills would expand the powers of the bureau so that it could more effectively cope with discrimination against the freedmen. Trumbull's other bill made the freedmen citizens of the United States, while it defined and protected those of their civil rights that were being jeopardized by the "black codes"—vagrancy statutes the former Confederate states enacted which had virtually imposed peonage on the emancipated blacks.

During successive days in late January, spokesmen for the various

moderate factions visited with Johnson in hopes of effecting a compromise on these items of congressional action and the whole range of reconstruction policy. Horace Greeley was one of the first to appear at
the White House. "I begged the President . . . ," said Greeley, "to
take control of the Joint Committee on Reconstruction. . . ." Johnson,
who had been smarting for some months under the attacks of the
*Tribune*, was not disposed to accept the advice of a man he privately
referred to as a "sublime child," an editor whose erratic behavior, he
said, had "nearly bothered Mr. Lincoln's life out of him."[9] Misunderstanding Greeley's intent, and overestimating his own capacity to control Congress, Johnson listened politely to the earnest editor, then
privately wrote off his suggestions.

Yet on Saturday, January 27, he invited Senator James Grimes of
Iowa for a breakfast meeting to educate himself more fully in the
moderate position. Grimes, who was friendly to the administration,
was a sensitive man with strong prejudices. A close friend of Chairman
William P. Fessenden of the Joint Committee on Reconstruction, he
despised Stevens and Sumner. If handled properly, Grimes could be a
potent ally. Fretful lest Johnson ally himself with the Democrats, who
were openly supporting his program, the Iowa Senator said quite
frankly that the President would be the only loyal man in such an
arrangement. Johnson allayed his fears on that score. He seemed also
to sympathize with Grimes' moderate position on reconstruction. The
elated Grimes promptly suggested that the President see Fessenden.
Johnson agreed, asking him to arrange an interview for the next day if
possible. Eager to impress his views and those of the moderate majority
on the President, Fessenden accepted the invitation. The two men remained closeted from ten in the morning until two in the afternoon on
Sunday, January 28, 1866. Fessenden, intelligent, testy, a good hater,
was no man to be trifled with. The leading moderate in the Senate, he
considered most radicals as unreasonable fanatics and, like his associate Grimes, counted many of them among his numerous personal
enemies. Although he genuinely sought a reconciliation between the
President and Congress, he was not averse to its benefits in humbling
some of his own bitter foes. If anyone could isolate the ultra radicals,
Fessenden was the chosen instrument. Somehow in the course of their
conversation Johnson bumbled badly. Fessenden left the White House
believing the President would back several proposals that enjoyed solid
support among the moderate factions: a suffrage amendment to the
Constitution and, pending its ratification, immediate suffrage for quali-

fied blacks in the District of Columbia, the Freedmen's Bureau Bill, and the Civil Rights Bill.[10]

He was amazed to find himself in error when he read in the Monday morning papers that Johnson had not meant this at all, that their four-hour conversation had practically gone for naught. Johnson had talked with James Dixon after Fessenden left his office. Dixon was one of the three conservative Republicans in the Senate who supported Johnson's policies without reservation, and it was Dixon, not Fessenden, who enjoyed the President's confidence.[11] Johnson made it clear to the Connecticut Senator just how far he would go to meet moderate opinion, then personally drafted the gist of his remarks for publication.

Johnson did not favor a constitutional amendment on suffrage; if Congress insisted on one, he thought that the qualified voters in each state should be the basis for its representation in Congress. The states could judge for themselves what qualifications they might require for suffrage, if any. The concession was a modest one, indeed. To the extent that the former Confederate states limited Negro suffrage, they would lose just that much representation in the House and the Electoral College. Johnson's amendment would repeal the old three-fifths clause in the Constitution, whereby blacks were counted for some representation but of course had no vote. If he had made a small concession toward placating the moderates on the amendment issue, he opposed them on giving the vote to qualified blacks in the District of Columbia. It would be, he thought, an ill-timed experiment in race relations, one that would lead to civil strife in the District. Of more immediate chagrin to Grimes and Fessenden, he was silent on the Freedmen's Bureau and the Civil Rights Bill.[12]

Moderates and radicals alike wondered just how Johnson's position squared with his pronouncement of a few months earlier. Then he had been widely quoted as saying that as a private citizen he would support qualified Negro suffrage in his home state of Tennessee. Most agreed with the *Tribune's* Washington correspondent, who asked, "Is he only in favor of the franchise where he is not, and opposed to it where he is?"[13]

To Johnson's dismay, his vigorous stand against conferring suffrage on the blacks in the District drew effusive praise from the Democrats. There was even talk in the papers that he was about to make a wholesale removal of Republican officeholders in favor of Democrats. But he stubbornly clung to his Union party affiliation. He welcomed support from any quarter, though under his leadership and within his party. "I have never appointed a copperhead to office, and so help me God I never will," said the usually reticent Johnson to Rush Sloan, a radical officeholder in Ohio.[14]

Welles was in complete agreement. It had become common knowledge that he was an unswerving supporter of the President. Mary Welles' reception on January 31, 1866, for the first time was crowded with Democrats and with known sympathizers of the Confederacy, all of whom had avoided the Welleses during the war. Welles shrugged off this new popularity, attributing it to the excesses of the radicals. The President was right. If he would only take a statesmanlike stand and couple it with some strategic removals, he would carry Congress and the country with a revitalized Union, not a corrupt Democratic, organization.

On February 19, 1866, Johnson took that stand when he vetoed Trumbull's Freedmen's Bureau Bill. Welles applauded the veto message, which contained many of his own ideas. A week earlier, McCulloch had asked him if he had read the bill. He had not. He had been opposed to federal welfare during the war but had deferred to the feelings of the President and Congress. Now that the war was over, he felt more strongly than ever that welfare was a local, not a national, responsibility. The next day Johnson himself asked for Welles' opinion of the bill. The President had already sought advice from Grimes, Fessenden, and Trumbull, all of whom urged that he sign the bill, and from conservative Senators Edgar Cowan and James R. Doolittle, who opposed it. Seward found the bill objectionable, too. Significantly, Johnson did not consult those of his Cabinet whom Sumner had identified to Welles as sharing his radical opinions—Stanton, Harlan, and Speed. Nor did he speak with Postmaster General Dennison, who in Johnson's presence, had recently voiced his fears about a resurgent Democratic party.[15]

When Welles read the Freedmen's Bill, he was shocked not so much at the system of government-sponsored welfare it provided as at its provisions for enforcement. As he defined it, the bill would bypass all state courts in any actions affecting discrimination against blacks. Special courts would hear the complaints, and they would not conform to fixed rules of law and evidence. There could be no appeal to federal courts. "A terrific engine," he wrote in his diary, "more like a decree emanating from a despotic power than a legislative enactment by republican representatives." He drafted a short paper with several specific objections. He condemned unsparingly the military character of the powers to be conferred under the act. He found the bill "partial and invidious, & will injure and oppress the innocent as well as the guilty." The bill, in depriving a person, black or white, of due process, conflicted with the Fifth Amendment to the Constitution.[16]

Johnson read his veto message to the Cabinet at special session on Monday, February 19. A lengthy document—almost 4000 words—it was a well-reasoned, well-written argument along extreme libertarian lines. The Cabinet spent four hours reading and digesting the message. No one, not even the suspect three—Stanton, Harlan, and Speed—dissented openly, though they regretted that Johnson would not sign the bill. Welles wholeheartedly approved of the veto but was uneasy about the final result. "Until a vote is taken," he said, "the master spirits will have time to intrigue and they will be active as well as cunning." Johnson should be prepared for the worst; he should be ready to act decisively on the patronage front if the Congress went against him. He feared that Johnson had no practical contingency plan but was relying as usual on Seward, and probably still upon Stanton, to muster his supporters.[17]

Welles' apprehensions were not, he was happy to see, justified. Though partisanship was running high, enough Republicans joined with the eighteen Democrats in the Senate to sustain the veto. Welles was beginning to have second thoughts about the Democratic party. "Kindness begets kindness. They treat him [Johnson] respectfully, while the Radical leaders are arrogant, insolent and dictatorial." He had almost come round to the position of Montgomery Blair, who was openly associating with the Democratic party. As Blair wrote his friend Barlow, "it is no longer in Johnson's power to keep out of the Democratic party if he would do so."[18]

The hearings of the Joint Committee on Reconstruction troubled Welles. He was aware that the committee's lengthy recital of atrocities against Negroes and Unionists in the South was exaggerated, and that much of it was fictitious. But even if the testimony were biased, he had to accept the fact that lawless, rebellious bands roamed the area. He was politically astute enough to realize that the hearings were having an unfortunate effect on Northern opinion.[19]

Welles had not counted on the defiance of the defeated rebels, nor had he perceived that they would take advantage of Johnson's good intentions toward them as a sign of weakness. He had now to accept this, to admit that many of the Southern whites "were bad, malignant, foolish to a great extent." But, he asked himself, how could the harsh measures of the radicals make them any better intentioned? Was the nation always to remain disunited? The Southerners had lost almost $3 billion in slave property alone, possibly an equal sum through inflation, confiscation, destruction. They were being compelled to pay in addition a part of the Union's debt incurred in defeating them. They were now being excluded from representation. Was it unreasonable, he asked, that there had been an upsurge of hostility among Southerners when Congress refused to permit them representation in direct violation of the Constitution?

The problem of the Southern black was a perplexing one, Welles admitted, but he had no ready answer. The most he would provide during the transition from slavery to freedom was the protection of the federal courts and the Bill of Rights. Practically, he must have known that a poor, ignorant black would never have the understanding, much less the means—to bring suit in a federal court, that granting him theoretical protection was granting him no protection at all. Yet he would not give up his abstract position, trusting that, eventually, education, training, and mutual dependence would provide a harmony between the races, and that the blacks would gain equality of opportunity. As he explained to Senator Grimes, "the country has a present and future before it . . . we must reunite or diverge still further soon. We cannot remain inactive, must either advance or recede."[20]

Satisfied that the better elements in the South would, if not antagonized, bring social stability to their region, Welles prepared to support Johnson in what he recognized as a power struggle between the Legislative and the Executive branches, between those who would stand by the Constitution, as he understood it, and those who would tear it down. All other issues in his own mind were subordinate to this great political crisis. Yet, even with his new-found conviction, he was embarrassed by Johnson's intemperate remarks on Washington's Birthday to a crowd that gathered before the White House.

The speech was overlong, the personal allusions to Stevens, Sumner, and other leading radicals in bad taste, undignified, and scurrilously abusive. As Welles expected, the radical press pilloried the President. Papers such as John W. Forney's *Washington Chronicle* called him an irresponsible, drunken demagogue. The *New-York Tribune*'s Washington correspondent said that Lee had finally taken Washington.[21] While the press campaign was gathering momentum, Congress passed Lyman Trumbull's Civil Rights Bill with overwhelming majorities. During the interval between Johnson's speech on February 22 and the final passage of the bill in the House on March 18, the administration had lost ground in Congress.

Johnson seemed calm and confident, however. He asked Welles and Seward for written opinions on the Civil Rights bill, just as he had previously consulted them on the Freedmen's Bureau bill. He also requested a draft veto from Henry Stanbery, an able Ohio lawyer who had been brought to his attention by Thomas Ewing, Jr., son of the old Whig warhorse and lobbyist. Trumbull, as before, gave the President a digest of the bill, at the same time arguing forcibly that he sign it. Perhaps because of the tumult in Congress, Johnson decided that other members of the Cabinet should have ample opportunity to study the bill before he took any action. He waited over a week before he discussed his veto message with the Cabinet.

Welles' major objection to the bill was that it attacked the nature of the federal Union. Under the pretext of enforcing the Thirteenth Amendment, the national government was destroying the police power of the states, interfering with the relations between a state and its inhabitants. The basic doctrine of local self-government would be undermined to such an extent that the states would be put upon the road to extinction. "It is absurd," wrote Welles indignantly, "to ask what particular provision of the Constitution is violated by the bill. The whole of it is violated." On March 26, Johnson convened the Cabinet, but, before reading his message, he asked for an opinion of the bill from each member.

Seward, who led off, supported only the first phrase of the bill, which conferred national citizenship on anyone born in the United States. The remainder of the bill, he believed, had many unconstitutional features. The Secretary would have Johnson concede explicitly in his veto message that emancipation carried with it federal citizenship. He would range Johnson squarely against some of the more objectionable features of the Dred Scott decision, yet not have Congress impinge upon state police power or prescribe the qualifications for state citizenship.[22] In this way, the veto might be made more palatable to Congress without upsetting the balance of powers or giving the blacks any real protection. McCulloch, who had been up to that time a staunch supporter of Johnson, and who was more conservative than Welles on some issues, said that he had not read the bill carefully. He said he hoped the President would approve it, then deferred to Stanton.

This time Stanton was better prepared. The bill was imperfect in many respects—it was not one such as he would have drawn—but in the course of a lengthy argument he urged Johnson to accept it on the basis of expediency. All others agreed in general with Stanton, Welles finding himself the only member unequivocally against the entire bill. The fact that an overwhelming majority of the Cabinet advised against veto made little or no impression on Johnson. Confident that his consti-

tutional position was unassailable, he altered not one jot of his message. In doing so, he made a grave political error. Far from accepting
Seward's modest proposal of federal citizenship for the blacks, he went
into considerable detail to explain that citizenship was unnecessary.
Repeatedly, he questioned whether any legislation was constitutional
when eleven of the thirty-six states were not represented in Congress.
Like his previous veto, it was an able presentation in defense of state
police power, but it was also a ringing assertion of white supremacy.
Welles and Seward had each contributed to its arguments, though
Johnson himself and Henry Stanbery were the principal authors.[23]

Congress did not act on the veto until April 5, despite the uproar that
greeted its reception. A major reason for delay was that the Connecticut
election was to take place in just six days. The result might provide a
clue to the state of public opinion.

Welles had tried to keep himself clear of the election campaign, but
inevitably he had been drawn in. Joseph R. Hawley, his friend and
protégé, was the Republican nominee for the governorship. The Democrats, showing more sense than they had for years, had nominated a
New Haven businessman, James E. English, who had served in Congress
during much of the war and had been a loyal supporter of the war
effort. No stigma of Copperheadism attached to his name. But anyone
familiar with Democratic politics in the state could readily discern that
the extreme Peace Democrats, ex-Governor Thomas H. Seymour and
his close associates, were still influential in the party organization. The
Connecticut Republican convention, meeting just before the Freedman's Bureau veto, adopted a platform that endorsed both the President and the Congress. The veto, however, followed closely by Johnson's ill-advised public attack on the radicals, weakened the Republican platform and embarrassed the state ticket. "The usual feeling
here is one of sadness and humiliation," wrote Hawley. "Does he really
mean to leave us?"[24]

Welles was disturbed at the direction the campaign was taking. The
Democrats were supporting the President, but nine-tenths of the Republicans were backing Congress. Almost all of Welles' Hartford
friends, men he had known and admired for thirty years or more, were
opposing Johnson's policies. Should he back Hawley and his equivocal
platform? Or should he admit the bankruptcy of the Union coalition
and go for the Democrats, whose organization was still largely controlled by politicians he had opposed since 1854? It was an ugly choice,
and one that he would postpone as long as he could. He favored

Hawley, but not the platform. Privately, he believed, as he had in the 1850's, that the parties had long since outlived their usefulness. They had been organized upon issues that were no longer relevant. New issues had come to the fore. If the President had only acted promptly and decisively to draw the line, to explain his course in a series of carefully worded proclamations, to weed out radical officeholders and replace them with reliable men, a vigorous Union coalition would never have permitted the ambiguities of the Connecticut election.[25]

Hawley won the election by the narrowest of margins—a result that afforded little aid and less comfort to Johnson's opponents in Congress. Yet they were not deterred from making every effort to override his veto of the Civil Rights bill. A change of one vote in the Senate gave them their much-needed victory on April 6, 1866. Four days later the House went against Johnson by a majority of almost three to one.

The mental turmoil, strains, and labors of the previous two months had undermined Welles' health. He was not sick enough to stay in bed, but he was far from well. Nervous and irritable, he was becoming increasingly critical of the President's apparent inaction. Spurred on by Senator Doolittle, who wanted Stanton and Speed removed from the Cabinet, Welles spoke about these matters with Johnson, breaking his long-time rule of not giving advice unless asked. The President admitted that he was dissatisfied with Harlan and Speed, but a sense of delicacy prevented him from removing them. He had no proof that Stanton was acting with the radicals. In those few instances where Stanton had disagreed on major policy, he had withdrawn his objections. In fact, all three Cabinet members, if they had not sympathized with Johnson's policies, had not directly opposed them. Should he take the initiative, it would be misconstrued. He particularly shied away from any confrontation with Stanton. "His department had been an absorbing one during the war," the President said, "and still was formidable. To have an open rupture with him in the present condition of affairs would be embarrassing certainly."[26]

Welles was dissatisfied with Johnson's response, but he was unwilling to push the President further, despite a firm conviction that every passing day without decisive action was weakening the Union coalition. All he could do now was to debate the merits of presidential reconstruction with any influential Congressman or politician who visited the department. In the battle of words Welles acquitted himself with distinction, even getting the better of Lyman Trumbull, but he made no converts. He did enhance his reputation as a formidable expounder of the Constitution according to the gospel of Jefferson, which was by then a fruitless exercise in semantics.

On May 1, 1866, Welles had an opportunity to display both his constitutional lore and his conservative animus where it might have some effect. The Cabinet had before it a recommendation from the Joint Committee on Reconstruction affirming an amendment to the Constitution along the lines of the Civil Rights Act. Designed specifically to curtail state power over the whole broad spectrum of civil rights, it conferred both state and national citizenship on the Negro. The troubled President asked for individual opinions. Unwilling to wait his turn, Stanton made a brief declaration, saying that he had always supported the policy of the administration. Although he had once favored Negro suffrage, he had since expressed no opinion on it. Seward opposed the amendment; so did McCulloch. Stanton was silent when his turn came up. Welles, who followed, would not let him escape with his opening statement, for it could be construed as favoring Negro suffrage, and therefore favoring the amendment. Portentously, Welles agreed with Johnson that it was appropriate for each member to declare his opinion. Then, he turned to Stanton, awaiting his reply.

Welles' tactic put Stanton in an uncomfortable position. He extricated himself, though with some difficulty. Stanton said promptly that he did not sanction the amendment as drawn. He did think, however, that the administration ought to meet with members of the committee and work out a compromise. This move would not only improve the language of the amendment, but would reconcile many of the differences existing between the President and Congress. Welles disagreed. Still feeling out of sorts, he spoke rather sharply, arousing Stanton's ire, which had been smoldering since he had been forced to declare himself. He interrupted, accusing Welles of demanding an unconditional surrender from Congress, of being an "ironclad on this subject of Reconstruction." Confused as much by Stanton's interruption as by his obvious anger, Welles gave a muddled reply. The brief exchange ended with Stanton declaring that Welles' convictions were exactly the opposite of his own and of Congress', Welles stating that he "could compromise no principle, nor consent to any usurpation." Harlan, the last to speak, agreed with Stanton.[27]

The next day, Welles was delighted to find in the papers a precís of each member's opinion on the amendment. For the most part, the accounts seemed quite accurate, though Stanton, he thought, was made to appear more positive and direct than he actually had been. He had no doubt that Johnson had furnished the information, if not the report itself. "He has shown tact and sagacity in doing it," said Welles, correctly divining that Stanton's radical friends would be shaken.

Stanton had certainly been backed into a corner, if, as he was now beginning to suspect, Johnson would not meet Congress half way. Radicals and moderates had gained the impression from Stanton of a deeply divided Cabinet with a President who might yet strike a truce. The report hurt his credibility. Stanton still hoped that he would not have to make a public statement, but Johnson was determined to smoke him out if he could. After dodging the issue for almost a month, the War Secretary finally realized he would have to speak for the record. In response to a call from a mass meeting of Johnson supporters, he read a carefully prepared statement, reviewing where he had agreed and where he had disagreed with the President. On the crucial Fourteenth Amendment, he objected only to one section—that which would deny for four years all those who voluntarily supported the rebellion from voting for members of the House of Representatives and members of the Electoral College.[28]

Meanwhile, Welles' health did not improve. Aggravations, importunities, and departmental obligations pressed on him more relentlessly than they had since the end of the war. Fox resigned on May 22 to head a special diplomatic mission to Russia. Welles was faced with the problem of trying to fill the place of a man who had been invaluable to him. Faxon became Assistant Secretary, and Welles, following the example of his colleagues Seward and Stanton, made his son Edgar Chief Clerk of the Department. Fox's departure created a void that could never really be filled. Welles did the best he could, taking over many of Fox's duties himself.

As he was coping with these administrative problems, Welles was asked if he would be a candidate for the United States Senate. Assured of Democratic support and of Senator Dixon's machine, he had an excellent chance of being elected. He would accept a draft, he let it be known, but he would not "enter into such means as are too freely used to obtain it." Orris S. Ferry, former Know-Nothing Congressman, former major general, now a radical, won the seat.[29]

If he had been true to his oft-repeated convictions, Welles would have made the effort. Had he won, which was probable, he would have revitalized the faltering Union party in the state. His election would have secured another conservative Senator, and it would have had much more than just local ramifications at a critical period for Johnson. Welles had been concerned about the President's failure to take decisive action, but when the moment came for him to make a decisive step, he had been lacking himself.

He was feeling the weight of his sixty-four years. While his judgment of men and their motives remained caustically acute, his judgment of measures and his counsel on policy were doctrinaire and dogmatic. When pressed he would take refuge in high-minded principles, not seeming to remember what he had so frequently expressed during the war—that revolutionary times brought drastic changes. It would have been the better part of statesmanship to bend before the blast than to stand rigid and risk a break. Stanton had been right when he said that Welles not only had a "fifteen inch gun leveled at Congress, but was for running [his] prow into them." Reports from his home state and elsewhere clearly revealed to him that Johnson Republicans were but a fraction of the party. They also demonstrated, rather conclusively, that the Democrats would not abandon their organization. Yet the bloody riots in Memphis on April 30, and those in New Orleans two months later, did not disturb his composure. He ignored the Memphis riot, in which a mob of poor whites killed and injured 127 Negro men, women, and children. The New Orleans riot, in which some 250 blacks and their white sympathizers were victims of the city's police, called forth a pejorative comment on the radicals that distorted the facts. Stanton was culpable in withholding vital information to embarrass Johnson, but neither he nor any of the radicals in Washington had instigated the riot, as Welles so heatedly charged.[30] Clearly, it would seem that the South was safe for neither politically active blacks nor for loyal whites.

On the day of the New Orleans riot, Welles listened to E. M. Pease give an account of similar dangers in Texas, of harassment and persecution that Union men were encountering. Welles had nothing to offer. Pease, a former Governor of Texas, had been one of Welles' clerks when he was Postmaster of Hartford during the mid-1830's. Welles knew him to be an honest, high-minded man, a nephew of his friend and mentor John M. Niles. Pease told Welles that five-sixths of the Texans hated the federal government. Unionists lived in the state at their peril. Although Welles was distressed, he counseled passive acceptance of an admitted wrong, a patient striving to alter public opinion. Dissatisfied with what he felt was a totally unrealistic approach, Pease declared that federal troops must be stationed in Texas. Military force was the only means to protect the lives and property of blacks and loyal whites.

Welles disputed the point. "Is it wise," he asked, "for one-sixth to come forward and place themselves in direct antagonism to the five-sixths?" . . . "This government is not one of force, it cannot attempt to control the elections in the states, and that by military force." If this were done, it would subvert the nation's system of government. He would maintain the principle of home rule, of states' rights, even if this involved restraint upon freedom of speech and of the press. Welles could not see beyond his own special verities. He had been so involved in political theory for so long that he would sacrifice party, would flaunt public opinion even in the North. Nor was his political acumen as incisive as it once had been. Despite massive evidence to the contrary, he persisted in believing that, if Johnson exerted more leadership, the Democrats would give up their organization, identity, and purpose to be led by a handful of conservative Republicans most of whom were officeholders who had long since forfeited political respect in their own communities.

Only after the Fourteenth Amendment passed the Senate in a form that Johnson found intolerable did he begin to react, and then hesitantly. Under the tutelage of Seward, Fessenden, Trumbull, and Stanton, the Senate had toned down the more drastic provisions of the House version. Unknown to them or to the moderate factions in Congress, no amount of tinkering would have satisfied Johnson. He was now opposed to any change in the Constitution while eleven states were not represented in the ratification process. Welles had helped in crystallizing Johnson's opinion. On several occasions he had underscored this particular point with the President, and he had raised the issue vigorously during his brief debate with Stanton on May 1.[31]

In the four months that followed, Welles did what he could to help Johnson rebuild the Union party and re-establish his leadership. He helped Senator Doolittle set up and publicize the National Union convention, which met in Philadelphia on August 14, 1866. But perhaps his most important service to Johnson was drawing from Stanton a clear statement of his position. Stanton had remarked casually at the end of a Cabinet meeting that the War Department had no bunting to donate for the convention. He suggested that the Navy might have a supply. Seeing his opportunity, Welles moved in for a sharp thrust. His bunting had always been on display. Would Stanton show his?

Surprised at the remark, Stanton reiterated that he had no bunting. "Oh show your flag," said Welles.
"You mean the convention," said Stanton. "I am against it."
"I am sorry to hear that but glad to know your opinion."
"Yes, I am opposed to the convention," Stanton repeated.
"I didn't know it. You did not answer the inquiry."

"No, I did not choose to have Doolittle or any other little fellow draw an answer from me," he said.

Stanton's direct reply cleared the air. Of the four Cabinet members who had disagreed with Johnson over fundamental policy, only Stanton remained. If Johnson had any lingering doubts about his loyalty, Welles' questioning should have removed them.[32]

The resignations of Speed, Dennison, and Harlan had permitted the President to appoint members who accepted his views on reconstruction. Their replacements, however, scarcely added political strength to the administration. Henry Stanbery, who replaced Speed, was the ablest of the new members, but he was a political unknown outside his native Ohio. The new Postmaster General, Alexander Randall, had spent the previous four years as a bureaucrat in Washington. Orville H. Browning, who became Secretary of the Interior, was a courtly politician of the old style. His large-scale lobbying during the war had cost him the close friendship he had once had with Lincoln and had left him with a musty reputation. His conservatism, however, was unimpeachable. He, too, had no following of any consequence. If, in the interest of harmony, Johnson neglected political reality, he was not lacking in political courage. He would take the fight to the people of the North and the Middle West on a 2000-mile speaking tour.

Though Welles shrank from public appearances, he accompanied Johnson, Seward, Randall, General Grant, Admiral Farragut, and other dignitaries in the "swing around the circle," as Johnson defended his policies in the metropolitan centers of the North and the Middle West. Again, Welles feared that the President's occasional intemperate remarks, made when he was goaded by hecklers, would injure his cause, as indeed they did. He observed that in all the cities where the presidential party made stops there was a near total absence of radical leaders and politicians. He also noticed that Grant, while he remained on the tour, and Farragut were major figures of attention from the crowds of curious onlookers. But he was impressed with the crowds—their size and their favorable attitude, and mistakenly took them to be a measure of Johnson's popularity.

The cool reception of the proposed Fourteenth Amendment, he thought, had already shown that public opinion was going against the radicals. Yet he recognized that anti-Johnson Republicans were still in control of the state and local party appartus. Welles blamed Seward and Stanton, even Johnson himself, for this dangerous situation. Had the President acted promptly on his advice when the thirty-ninth Congress had developed its own reconstruction program some eight months earlier, the organization would be in the hands of reliable conservatives. While favoring a closer tie with the Democrats, Welles was dismayed at their narrow-minded partisanship, the fact that they were nominating for office so many men whose actions during the war were unsavory at best. "Such candidates," he said, "can gain no recruits. There is a kinder feeling towards beaten Rebels than towards Copperheads."[33]

As the fall elections approached, Welles became more pessimistic. He was certain that Seward, Weed, and their followers in Congress, led by Henry J. Raymond of the *New York Times,* had blurred the issues. The average voter was given no clear choice on the proposed Fourteenth Amendment, for instance. Discouraged by hints of impending disaster he was receiving from correspondents in Connecticut, Iowa, and Pennsylvania, he hoped the Johnson ticket and the Democrats would hold their own. The patronage ax had been falling for some months, but Welles thought it was being wielded with neither finesse nor discrimination. Still, the new officeholders might just hold the line. His apparent flight from reality amazed Faxon. "How Mr. Welles could believe the administration was to be victorious surpasses my comprehension—and yet he so expressed himself. . . ."

Despite the fact that the fall elections went heavily against the President, Welles refused to recognize that there had been any ideological reason for Johnson's defeat. False issues, hatred of the South, distrust of Southern intentions toward the Negro and toward the Union itself, refusal of the Democrats to place country before party—these had misled the true feelings of the people. "Never," concluded Welles, "was a political campaign so poorly managed." Congressional foes of the administration had spent nine months perfecting their organization, while Johnson, listening to Seward and Stanton, had done nothing. Welles could not agree with Senator Grimes, who correctly analyzed the results. "Now, the question is will the President accept the popular judgment," wrote Grimes. "The issue is with him and if disaster comes to the country it will flow from his act. The party will spring up soon demanding stronger terms than are now proposed and that party will be increased by the President's opposition to the present propositions."[34]

# CHAPTER 28

# The Madness of the Hour

ABOUT SIX O'CLOCK IN THE EVENING, Friday, December 29, 1866, at the old Welles' homestead in Glastonbury, Robert G. Welles, Gideon Welles' nephew, walked into his father's study. He embraced his father, Thaddeus Welles. then moved back, took a pistol from his pocket, and shot himself in the head. He died instantly. Robert Welles was twenty-four years old, reserved, thoughtful, a proven leader of men. He had enlisted in 1861, had been in fourteen major engagements, was badly wounded at Gettysburg. He had been a captain in the regular army.[1]

Welles was fond of all his nephews and nieces, but Robert and his older brother Samuel claimed a special place in his affections. He had used his influence to further the careers of these modest, conscientious young men—Samuel with a post as a naval constructor, Robert with a much coveted regular army commission. Both had more than justified his trust in them. Six months before Robert's suicide, a boiler explosion at the naval shipyard on Mare Island, California, had fatally injured Samuel. His sudden death had been a heavy blow to Robert Welles. The rigors of campaigning had undermined his health, the years of combat had induced a serious battle fatigue. Like so many of the more sensitive veterans, he sought a measure of relief in drinking, which further impaired his mental and physical powers. Just when he seemed to be on the mend, when he had shaken off his reliance upon liquor, came the news of Samuel's death. He resumed his drinking, and he grew distant with his family and friends. Then he shot himself.

On New Year's Eve, 1866, Welles received the news of the tragedy, along with a description of its awful circumstances, in a long letter from his grief-stricken brother. How similar Robert's symptoms of breakdown had been to his own fifty years before, when his mother and his grandparents had died all within the space of a few months! During that gray spring of 1816—the famine year in New England—he, too, had taken the same long, solitary walks in the woods that Robert had taken before his suicide. "We were all at fault," said Welles, "that we did not cheer and encourage him and strive to make him social and merry. . . ."[2]

He would indeed have been unfeeling had he not seen in his own family tragedy a part of the greater tragedy that had befallen the nation—four years of bitter war between a kindred people, a war in which his gifted nephew, Robert, and his chief, Abraham Lincoln, had been among the casualties as surely as if both had perished on the battlefield. How was it to end? Were the Civil Rights Act, a second Freedmen's Bureau Act, passed over the President's veto, and the Fourteenth Amendment, forced upon the South, to provide "everlasting sectional animosity?" Everything seemed a cruel paradox to the old man. "Exclusion has taken the place of secession," he wrote Edward Bates, his former colleague. "We must be disorganized in order to be organized."[3] Yet he would do what he could with a pen that had not lost its cunning, with a gift for debate on constitutional and political points.

Addressing himself to the congressional moderates, Welles strove to present not just the Johnsonian view, but his own view of social change, a view that had guided his political thinking for half a century—the Jeffersonian ideal that the people in their localities knew best how to cope with their own social and economic problems. The nation was huge—its population, its customs, its interests diverse. Centralism, which he feared the radicals were trying to impose, would substitute for natural progress an artificial constraint, a transient conformity that would cripple local self-government, first in the South, but ultimately in the North.

At one time, ownership of property had been an essential requirement for the suffrage in most of the states, but, gradually, a majority of the states had lifted the property restriction for voting. That, he was inclined to think, would be the trend for Negro suffrage. But even if it were not, the federal system was far too valuable and far too delicately balanced to be sacrificed in the heat of popular fears and partisan debate for the "sham" slogan of "equal rights." He had used that slogan himself years before, when, as a Loco-Foco Democrat, he had fought for equality of opportunity against entrenched interests. Equal rights then had meant breaking down the barriers to unrestricted, individual enterprise. Equal rights now he took to mean special government intrusion in favor of one race over another in one part of the country and not the other. "Our government is not a consolidated empire," he admonished Senator Grimes, "but a federal republic. Some of the states may, after experience, become more restricted—some may enlarge still farther, and permit not only the blacks but the women to vote. I do not want the central government to thrust its arms into these questions."[4]

Yet, as he strove to convince moderates like Grimes to stay "the madness of the hour," he questioned the President's grasp of congressional politics. Surely any politician with a modicum of sense must realize by now that there could be no adjustment with the radicals, no compromise; only capitulation. Yet just before he learned of Robert's suicide, Senator Dixon, as much in the President's confidence as anyone, told him that Johnson was still relying upon Stanton. Welles regarded this an act of supreme folly in view of the sentiment fast developing against the administration in the thirty-ninth Congress. For he had never been more certain that Stanton was deceiving Johnson.

Emboldened by the Republican landslide in the November elections, Congress had been turning out a spate of bills and resolutions that bore the stamp of Stevens, Sumner, and Wade. Despite these signs of increasingly radical opinion in the North, the only Southern state to ratify the Fourteenth Amendment had been Tennessee. Johnson had omitted any reference to the Amendment in his second annual message. Privately, he was advising the former Confederate states not to accept the Amendment, even though Congress had made it plain that they must ratify it in order to be readmitted.[5] On January 3, and again on February 7, 1867, Thaddeus Stevens foreshadowed the stance of extreme radicals when he spoke for his military reconstruction bill. The South was unsafe for loyal blacks and Unionists, he charged. These states had illegal governments which must be abolished; the states themselves must revert to territorial status under military rule. They had forfeited any rights they might have had through their recent treason and their current refusal to obey the law of the land.[6]

Several bills were aimed directly at curtailing the President's powers to frustrate the will of Congress. One had been drafted by Stanton himself, who, for the first time in his tenure of office, stood ready to reduce the traditional civilian power over the military. That bill, cleverly attached as a rider to the army appropriation bill, made it unlawful for the President to move army headquarters from Washington. The rider also compelled him to issue all military orders through the General of the Armies—a weakening of his war powers.[7] The authorship of the rider was known only to Colfax, Stevens, Fessenden, and George S. Boutwell, ex-Governor of Massachusetts, who was a first-term Congressman but stood high in the councils of the party. While the bill was pending they kept the secret well.[8] Soon thereafter, Congress passed another bill, this one aimed at protecting Republican officeholders from the long arm of the President. Entitled the Tenure of Office bill, it forbade the President to remove any officeholder whose appointment required the advice and consent of the Senate. In a separate section that dealt with Cabinet officers, the bill seemed to cover only those officers whom Johnson himself had appointed, but this was an arguable point.[9] Congressional action was justifying Welles' oft-repeated and as oft-neglected warnings to Johnson—that during the first year of his administration his opponents in the party were having their own men appointed to office.

Possibly to test Stanton's loyalty, possibly also because he was at a loss to know how to proceed against Stevens' reconstruction bill territorializing the former Confederate states, Johnson asked the Cabinet to give him individual opinions on the Tenure of Office bill. Every member denounced it, Stanton being the most emphatic. Seward said that he had spoken to no one about the Act and that he thought it best not to anticipate an override, "that storms were never so furious as when threatened." His remarks prompted Stanton to explain that he also had been discreet about reconstruction. He had mentioned the subject only once in passing to Sumner, well over a year ago. Either Stanton was a master of duplicity or he had had a change of heart, thought Welles. Whichever, he could not resist an ironic thrust with a self-righteous twist at his colleague's profuse expressions of loyalty. "I confessed," said he, "I had not been as reserved as Seward and Stanton in expressing my opinions."[10] That evening in his study, after writing down the events of the day, he turned his attention to an impeachment resolution offered by Congressman James M. Ashley of Ohio. This resolution had been discussed by the Cabinet, too, though briefly. As he pondered the situation, Welles decided that Ashley's move had been deliberate, not simply an emotional outburst from a radical whom even the *New-York Tribune* labeled an extremist. Recently, the Supreme Court had seemed to strike at the very basis of military reconstruction in the Milligan, Cummings, and Garland decisions. Welles concluded that with the judiciary ranged against the radicals, they would have to modify the jurisdiction of the courts and remove the President or give up their program.

Through the months of January and February, a sorely divided Congress—whose members found it difficult to separate personal animosities from ideological differences—managed to carry on its battle against Executive power, Andrew Johnson, and ten of the eleven ex-Confederate states. Before convening the new Congress on March 4, 1867, one day after the expiration of the thirty-ninth Congress, the radicals had managed to gain two Senators and one Representative: over Johnson's veto, they had passed an Act making the Territory of Nebraska a state. The radicals had hoped to make Colorado a state also, but were unable to muster the necessary votes for an override.[11]

Ultra radicals continued to press for impeachment, while they bickered with the moderates and the conservatives over Steven's military reconstruction bill. Seward, to Welles' disgust, was visiting the halls of Congress almost every day, attempting, he thought mistakenly, to head off the radical onslaught. "He is dancing round Stevens, Sumner, Boutwell, Banks and others," Welles declared, malice sharpening his words. "Runs to the Capitol and seats himself by Stevens in the House and by Sumner in the Senate."[12]

Welles may have been critical of Johnson as a politician, but his observations were mild compared to those of Montgomery Blair, who thought the President an imbecile for clinging to the chimera of the Union party. Stingingly, Blair wrote Barlow how Johnson had spurned his advice, accepting instead the counsels of Seward and Stanton, "whose cowardice and treachery invited his destruction." Yet the Blairs had not completely given up on Johnson. Neither they nor Welles realized that in their constant efforts to keep him resolutely in the conservative camp they were now injuring his cause as much as Stanton and Seward, exerting pressure in the opposite direction, were.[13] These individuals were all men of ready wit, of strong personality, political masters and statesmen whom Johnson, considering his background and his ignorance of Northern politics, was bound to respect. In patronage and in policy he was pulled first one way, then the other, concealing his indecision behind a reticence that was immensely frustrating to them. He would not associate himself with the Democrats, as the Blairs were demanding, nor would he align himself with the moderate majority of the Republican party until it was too late. He seemed always several steps behind public opinion, whether it be expressed in a conservative or in a radical fashion.[14]

Just two days before Montgomery Blair had written so disparagingly of Johnson to Barlow, his father, F. P. Blair, Sr., again sought to rescue the President from his predicament. It was a forlorn hope at best, as old Blair must have known, yet, if it succeeded, Johnson might just ease out of the shackles being slipped on him by the radicals. Blair's plan was drastic—a Jacksonian sweep of the entire Cabinet and its replacement with men who commanded both popular and political support.

For major posts Blair proposed the ablest of the war governors, Oliver P. Morton of Indiana and John A. Andrew of Massachusetts. Horace Greeley and General Grant would replace Seward and Stanton. With such national figures around him, Blair reasoned, Johnson could face down the radicals, reconstruct the Union party on a sound basis, and work to repeal the harsher aspects of congressional reconstruction. Johnson was tempted, but in the end he did not accept Blair's advice. Well over a year later, he mentioned the incident in a letter to one of his secretaries, Benjamin Truman. "It would have been hard," Johnson said, "to put out Seward and Welles who had seemed satisfactory under the greatest man of all."

Blair's letter still lay unanswered on the President's desk when Nathaniel P. Banks, now an anti-administration member of Congress, visited the White House on a similar mission. Banks' proposition was more conservative. He merely aimed at heading off any more collisions between the President and Congress. Speaking for the moderate radicals, he wanted a man in the Cabinet—significantly, not Stanton—who would act as a channel of communication between the Executive and Legislative branches. Horace Greeley as Postmaster General, he thought, would serve the purpose admirably. In discussing Banks' visit with his private secretary, Colonel Moore, at lunch that day, Johnson exhibited a high-minded but very unpolitical posture. He admitted that his Cabinet did not lend any strength to his administration, that he could replace its members with much stronger men and "settle the question in two hours." But he could not bring himself to face the resentments that would inevitably follow from some members nor the hurt feelings of those whom he liked personally, who had been loyal to him, and who had performed great public service under the "martyred Lincoln."[15]

On February 15, while Johnson was still mulling over Blair's startling proposal and Banks' suggestion, Welles at least proved his worth as a shrewd counselor. He alerted the President to the dangers of submitting to Congress under his name a mass of unverified materials that would have gone a long way toward proving that he was not executing the Civil Rights Act. Congress had asked the Executive branch for a report on civil rights in the South. All of the Cabinet members except Stanton had treated the request as a matter of routine. The War Sec-

retary had asked Grant to have General O. O. Howard, Commissioner
of the Freedmen's Bureau, collect and forward evidence bearing on the
state of civil rights in the South. Bureau agents compiled all sorts of
testimony, depositions, newspaper clippings, and interviews that displayed a picture of grave civil disorder in the South, directed mainly
against blacks and white loyalists. Howard's report, which contained
440 separate documents, was raw information. True accounts were
mixed with falsehood, gossip, and exaggeration. After glancing through
its pages, Stanbery, incredulous, spoke out of turn, condemning the report unsparingly.

As Stanbery had remembered the congressional resolution, it had
asked for whatever information had come before Johnson regarding
the faulty execution of the law. None of this material had ever reached
Stanbery, the chief law officer, much less the President. Stanton disagreed emphatically, claiming that the information Grant had forwarded him was pertinent to the resolution. Seward and Randall both
backed Stanton, Randall making a clever suggestion that the President
send in the report with a covering letter in which he declared that he
had known nothing of these alleged crimes and disorders when he received the resolution. Now that they had come to his attention, he was
having the Attorney General conduct a full investigation. Stanton
seized eagerly upon Randall's idea and began to alter the draft letter
of transmittal on the spot.

At this point Welles interrupted. The material was inflammatory,
and much, if not most, of it had been culled by partisans with a partisan end in mind. If Johnson made such an official communication, it
"would be said at once by mischievous persons, that here was information of which Grant complained but of which the President took no
notice." Stanton, adopting a grave stance, said that he and Grant both
thought the material valuable and appropriate. But in his zeal to have
Randall's suggestion carried, he blundered badly. He was quite certain,
he said, that copies were already in the hands of certain Congressmen.
Would it not be better to follow Randall's suggestion than to have it
imputed that the President was concealing evidence? Johnson, who
made no comment, concluded that his Secretary of War had, on his
own responsibility, supplied copies of an Executive document to outsiders before the President or the Cabinet had seen it, with the express
purpose of injuring him.[16]

At that one stroke, Stanton lost much of the confidence he had built
up with the President. He may have acted in good faith, but it was
plain that he had not thought out the full implications of his action.

Possibly, he was too proud to admit such a gross error when he attempted to push his report through with an assist from Randall and Seward. Welles thought otherwise. He readily convinced McCulloch, Stanbery, and Browning that the radicals in Congress had in fact designed the report to hurt Johnson, perhaps to aid in building up momentum for impeachment. They accepted Welles' devil theory that Stanton was playing the ringleader in a conspiracy against the President. The mild-mannered Browning, though he had said nothing during Cabinet discussion, was incensed at Stanton's conduct. "It was a mean, malicious thing," he wrote in his diary. "Stanton was very persistent and manifestly wanted to do the President an injury. I have no faith in him. He has no sincerity of character but is hypocritical and malicious."[17]

So disturbed was Welles after a day of mulling over this and other intrigues in which he thought Stanton had figured, that he walked to the White House through a downpour to impress his views on the President. He was particularly concerned that General Grant, whom he had already marked as a political *naïf*, was being manipulated. Johnson listened quietly to his catalogue of suspicions, agreeing with him that Stanton might be culpable. If it were not raining so hard he would send for Grant and ask for an explanation. Welles simply could not rouse Johnson to any sense of alarm about Stanton, about Grant, about the military reconstruction bill, about other pending legislation, all aimed at the Executive office. He went away as dampened and chilled in spirit as he was in body, muttering to himself that Johnson "still hesitates, fails to act." What he did not know was that the President was deeply concerned. But other than having an interview with Banks, he had taken no positive moves either to modify the legislation before Congress or to ask for Stanton's resignation.[18]

During the following week, after much personal bickering and disagreement between the two houses, Congress passed the Military Reconstruction bill and the Tenure of Office bill. Neither measure would have been accepted in such extreme form had it not been for the Democratic minority, which voted steadily with the extreme radicals in a misguided and totally unrealistic effort to split the Republicans. Welles had only contempt for their partisan tactics and reserved his sharpest barb for their leader, Reverdy Johnson, the Senator from Maryland.

When President Johnson laid the Military Reconstruction bill before the Cabinet, Stanton was the only member who advised him to sign it. But four days later, on February 25, 1867, with the Tenure of Office bill up for discussion, no member was so vehement in urging a

veto than he.[19] Either encouraged by Stanton's forthright support or
seeking his involvement on the administration side, the President asked
Stanton to prepare the veto message.

Stanton had expressed his true feelings about the Tenure of Office
bill. As a lawyer, he was well aware that it was patently unconstitutional, even through the most tortured interpretation. It was a matter
of plain fact that any President must have confidence in his subordinates, for he relied upon them to assist him both in the administration
and the execution of the laws. Yet Congress was insisting that he could
not remove his own assistants without the advice and consent of the
Senate. Through long and arduous experience, Stanton, the great War
Secretary, was more keenly aware of these matters than any member of
the Cabinet, not excepting Welles and Seward.[20]

Opinion was one thing, openly identifying oneself with the President in drafting a veto message was something else. Despite the fact
that many moderates in the Congress had thought the bill unwise, they
had voted for it. And the radicals had considered it indispensable to
their entire reconstruction program. Stanton tried to beg off. He said
he was overwhelmed with work, which was true enough. He complained that rheumatism in his arms made it difficult for him to write,
a lame excuse. Everyone present knew that Stanton could easily dictate
a draft, as he had done so many times before. Stanbery, Johnson's principal ghost-writer, also pleaded to be excused because of overwork. The
President turned to Seward, who likewise was not enthusiastic but who
agreed, if Stanton would help out. As the meeting was breaking up,
Johnson whispered to Welles that he ought to prepare a draft, too.
Welles demurred as politely as he could, sensing that here was a rare
opportunity to associate Seward and Stanton with the administration.
Feigning innocence he said, "I would have no objection to contributing to the document, but it had gone into hands that seemed willing
to grapple with it, and I thought would do it justice." Apart from asking him where might be found a copy of Daniel Webster's speech on
removals, to which Welles had alluded in Cabinet discussion, Stanton
and Seward did not consult him on the draft. For once he approved
heartily of being ignored on an important matter of state.

Nor was he asked to help with the veto of the Military Reconstruction bill, though he had given unsolicited advice on the subject to the
President. In this case, he did feel slighted, especially after he learned
that Jeremiah S. Black was assisting in drafting the message. While
Black was a good lawyer, he had remained a partisan Democrat whose
political views Welles deplored.[21]

Johnson could have pocket-vetoed both the Military Reconstruction bill and the Tenure of Office bill, but, standing on principle, and exhibiting courage, if not sense, he refused to take the course of political expedience. The fortieth Congress, which was to convene immediately after the expiration of the thirty-ninth, would have repassed the Reconstruction bill, though in a more moderate form, if Johnson had displayed any political finesse. The Tenure of Office bill, opposed by such influential moderates as Fessenden and Sherman, would probably not have been resurrected. Secure in his sense of principle, Johnson chose defiance. He sent in his vetoes to both bills, which Congress promptly overrode.[22]

On March 4, the President went to the Capitol to consider end-of-session measures. He took with him unsigned the army appropriation bill, the second section of which, written by Stanton, curtailed the President's war powers. At 9:30 in the morning, Welles joined him in the President's room, and, at 10:00, when all of the Cabinet had assembled, Johnson asked their advice about the army bill. Browning had prepared a veto which all except Stanton and Seward approved. Both of them argued convincingly that, if Johnson vetoed the bill, the army would be thrown into disarray at a critical time in the nation's affairs. Reluctantly, the President signed the bill, on condition that a protest be sent in with the Act. Then he asked for an opinion from each member on the protest, which Stanbery had prepared in the meantime. When he came to Stanton, the War Secretary said, "I make no objection to it." "But," said Johnson, "I wish to know whether you approve of a protest." "I approve your taking whatever course you may think best," said Stanton.[23] At the time, the House judiciary committee was seeking evidence on which to impeach the President. Welles had no doubt about the outcome of its investigation, or about Stanton's role. To his deeply suspicious, almost morbidly critical mind, Stanton was the marplot of impeachment, staying where he was so that he could use all the power of his office to influence General Grant and bring the Army under the secure control of Congress. Welles was mystified by Johnson's forebearance and Stanton's effrontery.

Welles and his colleagues were so perplexed at the onward rush of events that they badgered Johnson, hoping he would take some action, any action, that would at least head off impeachment and preserve the structure of the government. On May 8, Johnson let slip his iron self-control after McCulloch had again urged him to approve a slate of military governors immediately, under the provisions of the Reconstruction Act. To the surprise of all present, he roundly cursed the radicals. "They might impeach and be damned," he concluded passionately, "I will do nothing to check impeachment, if there is any wish to press it. . . . God almighty knows I will not turn aside from public duties to attend to these contemptible assaults. . . . Let the House go forward and bury themselves in the matter if they wish."[24]

Yet it would seem that his display of fury came more from his own frustration, his own sense of insecurity, his own fancied humiliation in front of his Cabinet, than from any firm resolve. For he soon asked Grant to provide him with a list of military governors and at the close of the Cabinet meeting on March 12 took Stanton aside for a fifteen-minute whispered conference. In an agony of curiosity, Welles had to content himself with speculating about the conversation. He had no doubt that Johnson had told Stanton the names of the military commanders. When they finished their talk, the normally glum Secretary of War was in high spirits. He even told McCulloch a joke, permitting himself a hearty laugh. Welles assumed that Johnson was again bowing to Stanton. Since Thurlow Weed was in town, Seward must be involved, too. "These two men," he wrote angrily, after the appointments were announced, "have sacrified the President—made his Administration impotent."[25]

Confronted with Southern resistance to registration of black voters, Congress passed a supplementary Reconstruction bill, which removed all electoral procedures from the local civil authorities and specifically gave them to the military commanders. Welles was so disgruntled that he did not even mention this legislation in his diary. Nor did he write anything about General Sheridan's peremptory removal of the mayor of New Orleans, several municipal officials, and the attorney general of Louisiana. Although Sheridan's action was widely publicized, the President remained strangely silent. Neither Sheridan's action nor the supplemental Reconstruction Act that was passed over Johnson's veto were discussed in Cabinet.

Tension eased somewhat within the administration when Congress adjourned on March 30.[26] But everyone knew that there would be difficult times ahead, as most of the generals, who were without experience in politics and knew nothing of the intricacies and compromises of civil administration, sought to govern the South.

Welles had taken some small comfort when the Democrats won in Connecticut, where they captured the governorship and three of the state's four congressional seats. The fact that most of his lifelong friends had supported the Republican candidate—Hawley, his former protégé—did not trouble him or stay his rigid and unrealistic stand on abstract principle. Rather, he condemned his old friends as "narrow minded party men of Calvinistic notions in politics and religion" who accepted without question *a priori* judgments on the South and saw no need for further investigation. He made no effort to understand that the passions the war had unleashed were not then capable of rational analysis, much less cool and sober judgment. Welles had been in Washington too long, and his identification with the Executive branch was too complete. A total absorption with the war had further conditioned his mind, which had never been flexible on broad issues. He was no social philosopher who could grapple with sudden change and understand its implications. Nor was he the pliable politician interested only in the election returns. While he had understood Lincoln, he misunderstood Johnson, a man who was totally out of his depth.

Welles did, however, recognize the charismatic qualities Seward and Stanton brought to bear upon the President. Seward's counsel he thought deplorable, "politically worse than worthless . . . full of tricks and expedients which accomplish nothing, while they beget distrust." If Seward was weak, at least he was loyal to the President. Stanton, on the other hand, was "wicked," treacherous, arrogant, bent on destroying Johnson to serve his own greed for personal power. In making these remorseless judgments, Welles never realized that he was indicting Johnson also, for there were many sides to the emotion-laden questions of the hour.[27] Welles was expressing his own frustration, the fact that he was not being asked his opinion on how the President might execute the Reconstruction acts. He believed that Seward and Stanton were counseling Johnson, when in fact they were as much in the dark as he.

Congress had adjourned without passing any further legislation clarifying the execution of the Reconstruction acts. Confiding only in Stanbery, the President saw a way to water down the intent of the two Reconstruction acts through the instructions he would send the district commanders, who were already asking for guidance, from Grant. On April 3, 1867, a week after Sheridan's abrupt interference with the civil authorities in Louisiana, Johnson asked Stanbery to prepare an opinion with an eye to as strict a construction of the acts as possible. He was particularly anxious that the sweeping disenfranchisement of former Confederates under the first Reconstruction Act be modified through a loose interpretation of Congress' ironclad oath.

On May 14, after more than a month of suspense, Stanbery read the first installment of an elaborate opinion on the execution of the acts. Welles now knew that Seward and Stanton had not been consulted.

Stanbery, in direct contradiction to the intent of Congress, had restored the suffrage to practically all of the Southern whites who had been disenfranchised. Stanton reacted sharply, charging that the Attorney General was deliberately misinterpreting the acts. Welles said nothing. Relieved that the President had not let himself become, as he had thought, "a creature of Stanton," he considered Stanbery's elaborate opinion of little value—an exercise in the absurd. A second installment was read on May 23, and a second debate developed between Stanton and Stanbery. After listening carefully, Welles' attitude softened a trifle. He felt Stanbery had done as good a job as possible in trying "to make sense out of a nonsense, law out of illegality." "Why," he asked himself, "strive to solve an insoluble problem?"[28] On June 12 Stanbery read his last installment, an exceedingly elaborate, and, to Welles, tedious argument. Johnson, imperturbable as ever, summed up: the military was a police force, subordinate to the civil authorities.

With all except Browning present at the regular Cabinet meeting on June 18, Welles again listened to the verbal clashes between the Secretary of War and the Attorney General. And for the next three days of special meetings on the subject, Stanton doggedly stood his ground, as Johnson and Stanbery went from argument to catechism. Stanton denied that the President could judge for himself how the reconstruction laws were to be executed. Again and again he insisted that the district commanders were responsible only to Congress, that the President could not remove them save for "willful neglect or wanton abuse" of their authority. "I would advise," said he, "that no instructions be issued except to send them a copy of the acts of Congress and direct them to execute according to their own judgment."[29] Johnson was invariably courteous to his embattled Secretary of War, ever anxious to conciliate him, to win him over. But the sessions were an exhausting and an emotionally harrowing experience to these deadly serious men. All feared the collapse of civil government, renewed rebellion, the specter of anarchy.

His nerves taut after four days of bitter and, to his mind, senseless debate, Welles finally declared that the President had been put in an anomalous position. He had sworn to support the Constitution and faithfully execute the laws. The Reconstruction acts made these two obligations incompatible. Quite appropriately, Johnson had referred the acts to the Attorney General for an opinion. How else would he be in a position to enforce them? Uniformity of action among the commanders was necessary too; there would have to be a general code of enforcement that among other things would resolve inter-district conflict and maintain order through established guidelines. But these instructions, he declared, should go out merely as an opinion of the Attorney General for the commanders to follow if they saw fit. He agreed with Stanton that Stanbery's elaborate brief was an opinion, nothing more. The laws in question were defective, unconstitutional, impractical. They had to be put into operation, however, "You, Mr. President may attempt it," he said gravely, "but you cannot succeed." Congress would never accept any Executive interference with martial law in the South or any attempt to modify its intent through execution. In a bitter statement that betrayed all his pent-up emotions, he recommended that Johnson do nothing, disassociate himself from Stanbery's opinion, under no circumstances send it out as an Executive Order. He would thrust the whole question of military reconstruction back into the hands of Congress, where it had originated. "It is legitimate for them to execute as to enact such laws," he said, implying that the Constitution, with its distribution of powers, was a dead letter. Stanbery replied that the President had to act. Welles was quick to deny that he proposed any evasion of responsibility. The Attorney General's opinion was sufficient until Congress reassembled, but, if Johnson sent out instructions under his own signature, it would signify that he sanctioned the legislation. For once everyone agreed. Both Stanton and Stanbery drafted preambles, Stanton's draft being preferred after some minor editing. In this form advisory instructions were sent out to the district commanders through the Adjutant General. Grant wrote the district commanders that "Stanbery's opinion had no force of orders." As he said to Sheridan, "I would not be controlled by them farther than I might be convinced by the argument."[30]

The next day, when Welles opened his *National Intelligencer*, he was disturbed to find a record of the exhaustive Cabinet debate. As far as he could see, the report was reasonably accurate, his votes on the various propositions correct. But he felt that publication of the Cabinet proceedings had weakened Johnson in the public eye because it would be inferred that he dared not move without Cabinet support. If the President thought that Stanton's lonely dissents, now spread before the country, had been damaging to the Secretary, he had made a grave error. The Secretary of War, it would be said, was the sole champion of congressional rights and Northern power against a President who was conspiring with Southern traitors and Northern Copperheads to re-enslave the blacks and to control the Union Army and use its power for his own benefit.[31]

# CHAPTER 29

# Drama and Melodrama

CONGRESS REASSEMBLED ON July 3, 1867. There were the usual divisions among the moderates and the radicals, but in relatively short order both houses approved a third reconstruction bill. In dealing with Stanbery's opinion, Congress gave sweeping powers of government to the district commanders, subject only to the control of Grant and the Congress. Presumably, the President could still remove a commander, but only for cause. The bill also clarified the intent of the preceding Reconstruction acts by ordering the commanders to construe them liberally. As in the two previous acts, Johnson did not consult Welles in the preparation of his veto message. Again Welles seethed with jealousy and hurt feelings. Certain that Stanbery was the author, he spitefully attacked him in his diary—a sharp lawyer, no statesman. As for the veto, he thought it too long and polemical, understanding that Congress's judgment was predetermined, but failing to understand that Johnson was seeking an audience larger than Congress—the people of the North and South.[1]

Congress adjourned on July 20, the day after it had overridden Johnson's veto. But the House judiciary committee and an *ad hoc* "assassination committee," of which Benjamin Butler and James M. Ashley of Ohio were the most prominent members, remained in town, taking testimony and attempting to gather evidence that would furnish grounds for the impeachment of the President.[2]

Ashley, the most zealous of the congressional investigators, impulsive and visionary, was so determined to convict the President that he would not scruple to fabricate evidence. A blunderer even in this role, he left evidence of his own complicity that found its way to Johnson. Ashley had tried to suborn Sanford Conover, alias C. A. Dunham, a convicted perjurer, to testify that Johnson was implicated in the assassination plot against Lincoln.

Welles was disgusted when he learned of the transaction. It confirmed for him that the radicals would stoop to any means, however tainted, to remove the President. He was not surprised that Ashley should have had dealings with Conover. Joseph Holt, the Judge Advocate General and close confidant of Stanton, had used Conover as a witness for the prosecution in the trial of the Lincoln conspirators. At that time he had given false testimony that Jefferson Davis was implicated in the plot. His perjury discovered, Conover had been convicted and was currently in the old Capitol prison, where Ashley had talked with him. Among the papers that Johnson presented to the Cabinet was a pardon petition for Conover signed by Holt, Ashley, and Albert Gallatin Riddle, former War Department counsel. Carelessly, Ashley had left four personal notes among the pardon papers which linked him directly with Conover.[3]

What had begun as a difference of opinion was ending in an onslaught upon the Executive branch itself; for the Third Reconstruction Act had virtually stripped the President of any power to interfere with congressional reconstruction. But extreme radicals like Butler and Ashley were also partisans who needed a villain to set against the heroic stand of Congress. Johnson's unpopular position, his tactless tenacity, his Southern origins, his apparent plans to rob the North of a just peace made impeachment seem a political imperative to them.[4]

The Ashley-Conover connection had both farcical and dangerous aspects. When Welles examined the Conover papers with Randall, Browning, and McCulloch in the President's library, he instantly saw the hand of Stanton. The signatures of Holt and Riddle on Conover's application for pardon, and Conover's allegation that Ashley, Riddle, Holt, and Butler had conspired to suborn him, clinched the case for Welles. He made no accusation, but he planted a doubt in Johnson's mind when he said obliquely that there must be "spies in his household." The President knew, as did Welles, that Holt and Riddle were among Stanton's closest associates.[5]

Whether Welles' insinuation had any bearing on Johnson's decision to ask for Stanton's resignation, two other events which took place in close succession surely did. Johnson discovered that Stanton had actually drafted the Third Reconstruction Act. And a few days later, he was shocked to learn he had never seen a clemency petition for Mrs. Surratt, who had been hanged as a conspirator in the assassination of

Lincoln. John Surratt, the son of the executed woman and a fugitive for more than two years, was being tried for his alleged complicity in the plot. His defense counsel forced the government to produce the clemency petition, which had been signed by five of the nine officers who had found her guilty. Judge Advocate General Joseph Holt had taken Mrs. Surratt's death warrant to the White House for Johnson's signature, but he had so arranged the papers that the President who was sick at the time signed it without seeing the petition.

On July 31, before this disclosure in the Surratt trial, Johnson had had a long talk with General Grant. He wanted to reassign General Sheridan, who, as military chief of the Gulf District, had just removed the Governor of Texas without consulting him. Johnson had also decided to request Stanton's resignation and wanted Grant's advice and support. The General demurred. Sheridan was too popular. If he were reassigned, Johnson would injure himself with the people and with Congress. Nor did he think it politic, or lawful under the Tenure of Office Act, to remove Stanton while Congress was not in session.[6]

Grant's attitude gave Johnson pause. He said nothing to the Cabinet about Stanton but did ask its opinion on the removal of Sheridan. Not one member, not even Welles, advised him to take the step. With opinion so united against him, the President held the matter in abeyance. Two days later, at the urgent request of McCulloch, Welles, at a private interview, reluctantly asked Johnson not to remove Sheridan, on the grounds of political expediency. The President grew rather heated in his remarks about the extreme radicals, but then agreed that Sheridan was really a secondary figure. He showed Welles Grant's letter advising that no action be taken against Sheridan and Stanton. Until then, Welles had no inkling that the President might request Stanton's resignation.

"Grant is going over," was Welles' first comment.

"Yes I am aware of it. I have no doubt that most of these offensive measures had emanated from the War Department," said Johnson. Welles saw that he feared to act without Grant's support. "It would be most unpleasant," he said, "to make the attempt and not succeed."

Welles could barely conceal his satisfaction that Johnson was nerving himself to get rid of Stanton. But, thoughtfully, he weighed the risks and advised the President to make the move.

Then, on August 3, came the evidence of Holt's perfidy in the Surratt petition. Johnson demanded and received the documents from the War Department. On examining them, he jumped to the conclusion that Stanton was responsible, as he technically was, for Holt's action. Then and there he dictated a note to Stanton, saying that his resignation would be accepted.[7] On August 6, before the regular Cabinet meeting, Johnson asked Welles to step into the library, where he mentioned that Stanton had refused to resign. Would he advise bringing the correspondence before the Cabinet?

"By all means," said Welles, scarcely believing what he had heard.

Stanbery, and, of course, Stanton were absent. The other members of the Cabinet were as startled as Welles had been. Browning had no doubt that the President could suspend Stanton under the Tenure of Office Act. All agreed with him, but, acting on Seward's advice, the tense President decided to take no action until he had an opinion from Stanbery.[8]

Later he told his secretary, Colonel Moore, that he would "leave Mr. Stanton hanging on the sharp hooks of uncertainty and then suspend him." His defiant words, it would seem, were an obvious attempt to conceal his own "sharp hooks of uncertainty" from his faithful secretary, who was well aware of Stanton's insolent rejection of his chief's request.[9] Twice during the next five days, Welles urged Johnson to remove Stanton, and Holt, too, for good measure, without any reference to the Tenure of Office Act. When the President asked whom he should nominate to replace Stanton, Welles promptly named one of the Blairs—a sound recommendation if Johnson wanted to make a constitutional test. For Frank or Montgomery Blair, Johnson knew, would stand by him and accept arrest for defying the law, thus forcing the matter before the courts. Johnson was dubious about the Blairs, about their Democratic affiliations, about the widespread prejudice that existed against them. But he was sufficiently impressed to ask: "Where is Frank at this time?" Welles did not know. Montgomery Blair had recently returned from Virginia. He would know. With Johnson's approval, Welles hurried over to Blair's house, found him at home, and said that the President wanted to see him.[10] Montgomery Blair found Johnson "very unhappy & in a very helpless pitiable condition." After a pointless conversation which lasted an hour, he advised him to send for Grant.[11]

Blair's suggestion made much more sense than Welles' to the President, who was desperate to restore his stature with the people. Grant was the most popular figure in the land. To the distracted nation he represented an image of strength and conviction. If he would consent to having Stanton replaced, Johnson might yet hold the radicals in

check. With Grant's support he might even recoup his own political
fortunes. The appointment of Frank Blair would merely add to his numerous enemies. Grant might even give Johnson a second chance to
unify the nation on his own terms, to become its political leader in his
own right, not through an assassin's bullet.

He wasted no time in contacting the General. Adroitly playing upon
Grant's well-known sense of responsibility for the welfare of the Army,
Johnson asked him if he would accept the post of Acting Secretary of
War. Grant said that, since the decision had already been made, he
would obey orders. Then Johnson asked if he harbored any personal
resentments, as had been rumored. Grant emphatically denied the rumors, though he did make it clear that he differed with Johnson on reconstruction, an admission that did not concern the President. Quite
the contrary, after Grant left, the President's spirits soared. Pugna-
ciously, he said to Colonel Moore that he might well rephrase the draft
order suspending Stanton so that it would include the word "removed"
as well. Seward arrived before the President could make any rash decision, and took him off to church. The order that Colonel Moore delivered to Stanton the next day was in strict conformance with the
Tenure of Office Act.[12]

His suspension and the appointment of Grant as his temporary replacement came as a heavy blow to Stanton. He had never thought the
President would have the courage to remove him. Even if he did, the
Senate would reinstate him when it met in December. The proffer of
the post to Grant and his ready acceptance put a different light on the
matter, exciting all of Stanton's suspicions and decidedly weakening
his political position. A fifteen-minute meeting between the two men,
at which Grant tried to explain his reasons for accepting the War office, only contributed to mutual misunderstandings. Under great stress,
Stanton acceded to Johnson's order, but not before making a public
issue of it in the press and in the Congress.

In his reply to the President, Stanton denied the legality of the suspension and, in an ingenious phrase, made it appear that Johnson was
using military force to oust a civilian Secretary. Welles was shown
Stanton's letter, which he dismissed as mere "blustering." He had
overlooked entirely the martyr role Stanton had cast for himself, his
subtle appeal to Congress, his hint to the American people that a military coup might be in the offing, his fears that Grant might even be the
agent, or perhaps the man on horseback. For the language Stanton had
chosen could justify any or all of these interpretations.[13]

Unquestionably, there were grounds for Stanton's suspicions. He and the commanding general were too dissimilar in personality and outlook ever to be close friends. Grant, like most general officers, had had his brushes with Stanton during the war. He, too, had experienced the edge of his temper in their official correspondence. Both Sherman and Grant at one time or another felt that Stanton had dealt unfairly with them. Even after the war, when Grant was a popular hero, the truculent Secretary continued to issue his peremptory orders, treating him no differently than he treated other general officers. Gradually, over eighteen months, relations had improved between the two. Stanton had made a mighty effort to curb his impatience and his arrogance, his jealousy of Grant's immense prestige.

Under the best of circumstances, this would have been difficult. Grant was so reticent that only a few intimate friends knew what he was thinking about at any given moment. It was hard for the great Secretary to unbend, particularly with such an illustrious subordinate. Yet he had no alternative.

Democratic and Republican politicians, recognizing Grant's political worth, had been cultivating him since Lincoln's death. A military man, Grant was like so many of his kind—politically innocent. In the beginning, he had associated himself with Johnson and had fallen under the expert tutelage of the Blair family.[14] He had accompanied Johnson in his "swing around the circle," thus identifying himself with the President's cause. It was then, for the first time, that he realized from the crowd response at the various stops how popular he really was, how unpopular were the President and his policies.

Uninformed about the complexities of the federal system, he wasted little time on the abstract question of whether there had been a war or an insurrection. To Grant it had been a war, and the Peace Democrats in the North who had opposed the government were little better than traitors. Along with a large majority of his fellow citizens, he soon came to believe that Johnson was making a coalition possible between these unpatriotic, treacherous Northern men and the ex-Confederates, to rule the nation as if no war had been fought, no victory won. The reconstruction program of the congressional moderates would defeat such an enterprise. Astute Republican politicians drove home this simple idea when they tempted Grant with the presidency.

As the strife between the President and Congress increased, Grant became concerned over the Army, which was necessarily involved in carrying out the Reconstruction acts. Initially, he was reluctant to become acting head of the War Department. Why associate oneself with an administration in which most of the public lacked confidence, and whose policies he himself opposed? He finally bowed to Johnson's request because he wanted to keep the Army clear of administration harassment until Congress reassembled in December.[15]

Welles' memory of Grant went back to early March of 1864, when he had first seen the short, deeply tanned officer talking with President Lincoln. He had been introduced to him then and had attended the brief meeting the following day, at which Lincoln had presented Grant with his commission as commanding general.[16] During the early months of Johnson's administration, Grant attended numerous Cabinet meetings, where he said little, but spoke to the point. In November 1865, Johnson had Grant make a tour of the Southern states to report on their condition and the loyalty of their inhabitants. His report, in which he wrote that conditions were better than he had expected, looked to a speedy restoration of the Union. Welles thought highly of Grant, of his views and of the modest way he presented them. That he was not friendly with Stanton made him all the more attractive. Welles knew that Stanton and Halleck had mistrusted Grant for his bouts of drunkenness. But it was not until Johnson's "swing around the circle" that Welles actually saw him inebriated. Grant and Surgeon General Barnes had become so drunk in Cleveland that Edgar Welles and an attendant named Crouse had had to help carry them aboard a special boat for Detroit, where they would rejoin the presidential party.[17] Though abstemious himself, Welles had seen enough hard drinking among public men not to be bothered by the incident. What did concern him was a rather sudden change in Grant's political convictions that his sensitive antennae picked up about half way through the trip. Yet it was not until January 1867 that he finally realized Grant was moving away from the administration on reconstruction.[18] And even then, he was reluctant to give up on the General, believing that he was a simple but honest soldier whom devious men were manipulating.[19] When he read Grant's reply to Johnson of August 1, advising strongly against the removal of Stanton and Sheridan, he began to wonder whether the game had been lost.

Welles made no comment when Johnson told him of his second conversation with Grant, which had taken place on August 10. As the President explained it, the General had agreed to serve as temporary Secretary of War. "Grant will be likely to exercise some common sense which will modify action," Welles thought. More important, the war office would cease to become a center of intrigue, as he believed it had been under Stanton. Yet, some weeks later, after an hour's conversation with Grant on the condition of the country, Welles found him more ignorant of constitutional restraints than he had supposed.

Whatever lingering doubts Welles may have had about Grant's understanding of political questions were removed when the Cabinet discussed an arbitrary act of General Daniel E. Sickles, military governor of the Carolinas. Sickles had suspended all judicial processes and judgments, including those of the federal courts in his military district. He gave as his reason that the courts would rule the Reconstruction acts as unconstitutional. At first Grant had ordered Sickles not to obstruct the proceedings of federal courts, but then, feeling that there must be two sides to the question, he countermanded his order. Welles was shocked when Grant casually said that "Congress had put in his hands the execution of this law, and he intended to see it was executed." Grant agreed, however, to telegraph Sickles that he was not to interfere with the judicial process of the federal courts. "I advised the President to make short work of King Sickles," said Welles, as the meeting broke up.[20]

Some days later Grant sought to spar with the President over his orders to relieve Sickles and Sheridan, but he soon found himself floundering in both the technical and the substantive points at issue. He asked the icy President if he could be excused from further Cabinet meetings, for he "preferred not to be mixed up in political questions." Without a change in his demeanor, Johnson said he could do as he wished. Grant returned to the War Department, where he wrote a long and contradictory letter. He repeated what he had said in Cabinet, that he wanted only to carry out his official duties, avoiding Cabinet meetings where political topics came up for discussion. After pleading incompetence in this area, Grant foolishly devoted several pages to subjects of a purely political nature, and then, even more foolishly, he leaked the letter to Forney's *Washington Chronicle*, where it was worked up into an editorial indictment of Johnson.

The President could have answered Grant and published the correspondence. Wisely, he sent for the General. Mincing no words, he exposed the weaknesses of the letter, in particular the assertions by which Grant had arrogated to himself complete Executive powers over the Southern military districts. Realizing that he had blundered badly, Grant asked if he could retract his Cabinet statement and his letter. Johnson offered no objection.[21]

Through the entire month of September, while the radical press raged over the removals of Sickles and Sheridan, Welles was engaged in a running argument with Stanbery over writs of habeus corpus issued by state judges on behalf of newly enlisted naval personnel, to remove these men from naval jurisdiction. Welles contended that the writ did not affect enlistment, which was a contract with the government, while Stanbery maintained that naval authorities must obey the writ and produce the "body" in court. In the end Welles lost the argument, but he consoled himself with the biting comment that Stanbery's opinion was "a mere lawyer's brief not a statesman's views." He kept a weather eye on political developments, however.

In early October he learned that the President had sent for General Sherman, in the hope that he would agree to replace Grant, or to act as a conservative influence on him. Welles, far more perceptive than Johnson, doubted that he would perform either role. Privately assessing both generals, Welles thought Sherman the more intelligent, but at the same time the more unstable. Their characters and personalities were complementary, each supplying something the other lacked, thus laying the basis for their mutual trust. But in any major difference of opinion between the two men Welles felt sure that Grant would prevail.[22]

On October 8, and again on October 10, Welles warned the President against asking Sherman to replace Grant, whom Johnson believed had become a radical. Heartened by sweeping Democratic victories in Ohio and Pennsylvania, Welles sensed that Grant would be more responsive than before. He advised Johnson not to lose a minute in having a long talk with Grant, who might yet be detached from the radicals. Welles added that without the General Congress could do nothing. Admitting that Grant was poorly informed on governmental and political matters, Welles still believed him to be "at heart honest, patriotic and desirous of doing right."

Johnson listened intently. As Welles and other members of the Cabinet were taking seriously the threat not only of impeachment, but of attempted arrest before trial, his advice to consult directly with Grant, not through Sherman, was eminently a sound one. Johnson acted upon it, visiting Grant at the War Department on October 12, 1867. Their conversation was friendly but direct. The President wanted to know what Grant would do if Congress tried to depose him before impeachment. Grant said that he would obey orders. If he should change his mind he would inform the President. Johnson reported to Welles that Grant seemed to understand the problems involved. He thought the General could be relied upon.

Welles agreed. "Grant will make good his word, and act, I have no doubt, in good faith."

Yet, clearly, there was room for misunderstanding, even in the President's mind. Later that week, in a private conversation, Johnson suddenly offered Sherman the War Department. Sherman declined. As for Grant, he still reserved his freedom to decide whose orders he would obey, and under what circumstances.[23]

What did seem evident was that the issue had now gone well beyond reconstruction. It could involve the very existence of the Republic itself. As Welles had said earlier, "Grant would be a tower of strength." After the presidency, he held "the most important post in the country." Welles was wrong in only one respect, and that a crucial one. It was not the President, not the Congress, but Grant who held the reins of power, if he chose to wield them.

Constant anxiety about the state of the nation, long nerve-wracking sessions that seemed to get nowhere, and lack of exercise and proper rest had again weakened Welles' none too robust constitution. He had been more or less unwell for some time, suffering a series of painful carbuncles and frequent digestive upsets. On November 1, after the regular Cabinet meeting, he collapsed. For several days he was barely conscious, so sick that an old friend from New Haven, who visited briefly, thought he would die. Under the careful ministrations of Mary Welles and the able medical care of Dr. Phineas J. Horwitz, who had replaced Dr. Whelan as Chief of the Navy Bureau of Medicine and Surgery, Welles began a slow recovery. Although the President was being more bitterly assailed than ever by Congress, which was now in session, he and his daughter, Mrs. Patterson, visited Welles' sickroom sometimes twice a day. His other Cabinet colleagues, including Grant, all paid him at least one visit. It was not until November 30 that Welles was able to attend a Cabinet meeting.[24]

Weak and tremulous of voice, he nevertheless gave an incisive opinion on four questions Johnson laid before the Cabinet at a special meeting on that day. The judiciary committee of the House had just reported a resolution to impeach the President on purely political grounds. For months the committee members, spurred on by Butler and Ashley, had been trying to find evidence against Johnson. They had quizzed members of his personal household, even examined his bank account, but had found nothing of an incriminating nature.[25] The President, whatever he may have felt about this harassment, gave no sign even of annoyance to his Cabinet. He was concerned that a majority of the House committee would vote for impeachment, but he was more disturbed by various bills before the House that aimed to depose or suspend him before impeachment and conviction, though this would be patently unconstitutional.

The extreme radicals were surpassing all their previous efforts in incredibly vituperative speeches against Johnson and the South. So extravagant were their harangues that even Horace Greeley became concerned for the party and for the nation. "If Congress will ever adjourn without inflicting upon us any new nostrums, we can have a chance to carry your state [Connecticut]," he wrote Joseph R. Hawley, "but the daily demonstrations of Stevens, Butler, Sumner, Wade, etc., their evident desire to make conditions so repulsive the South will not . . . , reconstruct herself. . . ."[26] With leading members of Congress making such irresponsible statements and offering so many provocative bills that their actions concerned Greeley, it is no wonder that Johnson should ask the Cabinet for opinions on what his course should be if the threats became realities. He was also anxious to learn Grant's position in the event of a direct confrontation. Every member of the Cabinet said any law deposing him would be unconstitutional and must be resisted. Grant noted that such a law could not apply to Johnson, because it would be *ex post facto*. The President must keep his post until the courts decided its constitutionality. Welles agreed but argued, for Grant's benefit, that the Executive was a coordinate branch of the government whose powers could not be weakened by the Congress acting under "the mere party caprice" of a transient majority.[27]

For the next six weeks, while Welles gradually regained his health, Johnson maneuvered to enlist Grant's support against the probable reinstatement of Stanton. Welles was not involved, nor was he informed of what was going on. The Senate had not yet acted on the Stanton case, but everyone expected it would do so on Monday, January 13, or, at the latest, on Tuesday, January 14, 1868. Welles could only guess that Johnson had some kind of arrangement with Grant, who, he was quite sure, was acting in concert with Stanton and the radicals. He so expressed himself to the President on Saturday, January 11. Johnson refused to believe him. He had already prepared a letter dismissing Stanton, after having a long conversation with Grant earlier that very day.[28] Johnson wanted his Acting Secretary to hold the War Department if the Senate reinstated Stanton. Shrewdly, he calculated that Congress would not dare force Stanton upon Grant, that it would rescind its action and leave him in undisputed control. But the General had begun to appreciate the hazards of his position, caught as he was between the Congress and the President. And on that Saturday morning he visited the President with every intention of bowing out. He told Johnson that he was not willing to hold the office in defiance of Congress, that he would not subject himself to the possibility of fine and imprisonment. Upset at the sudden collapse of his plans, Johnson made a melodramatic offer to accept full responsibility, stand trial, and, if adjudged guilty, pay the fine and serve the prison term. Unable to persuade Grant, he fell back on his next best line of defense, one that Henry Stanbery had probably outlined. If Grant felt that he could not remain in office, he should return his post to the President before the Senate acted. Then at least Johnson would hold the office, which would aid him immeasurably in bringing the Tenure of Office Act before the courts. Grant seems to have agreed. Perhaps he did so, perhaps he did not resign at once, because of Johnson's commanding personality, perhaps because of a habitual deference to his superior officer. What does seem evident is that he and General Sherman, who was again in Washington, wanted Stanton out of the way. Sherman's father-in-law, Thomas Ewing, and Senator Reverdy Johnson of Maryland, both conservatives and friendly to Johnson, acted as their political councilors.

On Monday, January 3, at different times, Sherman and Reverdy Johnson called at the White House, where they urged the President to nominate ex-Governor Jacob D. Cox of Ohio as Secretary of War. Cox, a moderate, was acceptable to most Republican factions, and he stood a good chance of Senate approval. Some three months before, Sherman had mentioned Cox's name to Browning as an ideal replacement for Stanton, "who," he said, "ought not to be reinstated."[29] Grant knew of Sherman's and Reverdy Johnson's errands. He approved them, if he did not actually instigate them.

Though the President gave no direct answer to either man, they each left the White House expecting that Cox or someone else would be nominated. Despite Grant's unequivocal statement that he would not risk arrest, despite the visits of General Sherman and Reverdy Johnson, whose role as Grant's emissaries must have been unmistakable, Johnson expected the General either to hold the office or to appear and place it in his hands, as he thought they had agreed. Grant, on his side, waited hourly for the President to nominate someone in his place, preferably Governor Cox. The nomination never came, nor did a summons from the White House. The Senate, in the meantime, reinstated Stanton. Grant did as he said he would do. The Tenure of Office Act was a law until judged unconstitutional. He would obey that law rather than risk arrest. Locking up the office of the Secretary, he turned the keys over to the Adjutant General. The following morning he sent a note and a copy of the law to Johnson, stating that he had relinquished his post. It is fair to assume that in a bungling way he and

Sherman had tried to help Johnson get rid of Stanton, whom both disliked and distrusted, but at the same time keep clear of the contest between the Congress and the President. Johnson did not see it that way at all. Believing, sincerely enough, that Grant had broken his word, he was determined to expose him. That his chances to test the Tenure of Office Act in the courts had been weakened lent the fury of despair to his long pent-up frustration.[30]

No member of the Cabinet was aware of these happenings when the regular meeting convened on Tuesday, January 14. All they knew was that the Senate had reinstated Stanton. When they saw Grant in his usual place at the council table, they must have concluded that he had thrown in his lot with the President. Grant soon dispelled any such notion. His turn in the regular order came up, and Johnson asked if he wished to offer any topic for discussion. Grant said that he was present only at the special request of the President. He was no longer a member of the Cabinet, having relinquished the War Department the night before as soon as he had learned of the Senate's action. Maintaining his self-control with difficulty, Johnson asked Grant a series of questions which aired their understanding, or misunderstanding. Hard pressed, Grant acknowledged that he had agreed to release the War Department to the President if the Senate reinstated Stanton.

"Did not Mr. [Reverdy] Johnson come to see you?" asked Grant. "I sent General Sherman yesterday after talking the matter over. Didn't you see Sherman?"

The President said that he had seen both men, but could not see what bearing their visits had on the understanding he had with Grant.

"Why did you give up the keys to Mr. Stanton and leave the Department?" he demanded.

Grant apologized. He had intended to call but had been so busy that he had not found time. Painfully embarrassed, he asked to be excused.

That night, Browning met Sherman at a reception given by Postmaster General Randall. Sherman "spoke bitterly of Stanton's restoration," said Browning, "and seemed to think the President blameable for not nominating Cox."[31]

Johnson was technically in the right, but he was woefully in the wrong when he did not explore the Cox appointment further with Grant himself. In the passion of the moment he would now commit a more serious blunder. The exchange between Johnson and Grant had been so unusual that Welles wrote out his recollections fully, while everything was fresh in his mind. "My intention and wish," he said as he finished the commentary in his diary, "is to do injustice to neither, but fairly present what took place and the remarks of both." Browning, too, wrote down a full account in his journal that same day. Both accounts were in substantial agreement. Both had Grant admitting that he had agreed to see Johnson on Monday.

At the White House, Johnson, furious at what he regarded as a deception and even more furious at the collapse of his plans, gave an account of the meeting to a reporter for the *National Intelligencer* which cast Grant in a bad light. The article appeared on January 15, 1868.[32] Welles thought the account was an accurate reporting, but Grant and Sherman, unaware that there were two faithful diarists in the Cabinet, disputed the statement. Grant had learned the elementary political lesson that, when no record is kept, statements can be disputed and meanings denied. He visited Johnson and complained that his remarks had been misrepresented, that some statements were simply untrue. Johnson said that until he had read the *Intelligencer* he could not comment. Grant, and Sherman, who accompanied him, left the White House, hoping that the President would correct the record in such a way as to remove any stigma upon Grant's integrity.[33]

After they left, Johnson had Colonel Moore read the article to him from his scrapbook. He thought it a fairly stated case. And at the regular Cabinet session on Friday, January 17, he had Moore read them the *Intelligencer* article. When he finished, Johnson asked those present—Seward had left—if the account was a fair one. Everyone agreed that it was, Browning and Welles volunteering that each had made lengthy memoranda on the subject.

At this date it would have been infinitely more expedient for the President to have pursued a tactful course with the General. Johnson could have bypassed Stanton and issued his orders through Grant, a procedure Grant would have preferred and one that would have quickly made Stanton's position intolerable. But the stubborn President, availing himself of Cabinet support, would not take the road of expediency. He began what became an extended and acrimonious debate with Grant in the public press in which he caught Grant in a lie. The break was now irreparable. Johnson had two powerful enemies in the War Department. He could easily have had none. One can understand why he acted as he did. No public official, much less a President, had been so personally abused on the floor of Congress, in the press, on the streets. No President had been so often deceived by those whom he had trusted. Johnson was so weary, so overworked, that he may have misunderstood Grant's overture through Sherman and Reverdy Johnson. But, above all, he was in fundamental disagreement with Grant over the execution of the reconstruction laws.[34] After he had disposed of Stanton, he had meant to manage Grant. For this he needed a Secretary of War who more nearly shared his views, certainly not Governor Cox, who was too radical; General Sherman if he would accept, and if he refused, which seemed likely, perhaps Johnson would act as his own Secretary should the Senate refuse to confirm his candidate.[35]

The Cabinet debate, the disclosures, and the acrimonious correspondence that followed made as profound a personal impact on Welles as it had made on Johnson. To the end of his life Welles would hold Grant beneath contempt, a faithless liar, a drunkard, a man utterly devoid of talent in civil affairs. His hatred of Grant would become an obsession, his judgment of Grant's character warped. In his diary, as in his correspondence with trusted friends, he castigated the General. For in Welles' eyes Grant had committed the two greatest of all sins: a betrayal of public trust and a breach of personal loyalty. Even Stanton, whom Welles now hated too, and for much the same reasons, commanded a respect which Welles would never accord Grant. With all his long-developed skill in assessing men and motives, Welles failed utterly in his evaluation of Grant. The only aspect of Grant's complex nature that he appreciated at all was his fatalism, perhaps because he had that personality trait himself. "Like most men who have had extraordinary good luck," he wrote Montgomery Blair, "he is a fatalist, and, having reached his personal position without much merit, he knows not what further is in store for him, but waits events patiently and watches and takes advantage quietly and with a good deal of sagacity and shrewdness. . . ."[36]

The public dispute between Johnson and Grant quickly died out, and the President wrapped himself in a strange silence, except for talking with newspapermen, a penchant Welles deplored. For the third time, the House had refused to impeach the President. The halls of Congress were relatively quiet. But without consulting anyone, Johnson was preparing a final showdown. The order dismissing Stanton that had been drafted on January 7 was known only to the President and Colonel Moore.[37] After Stanton was reinstated, the only reason Johnson did not move was because he was trying to find a suitable replacement. General Sherman made it plain that he would not serve, nor would he accept even a military assignment in Washington. Similarly the Chief Clerk of the War Department, John Potts, declined an acting appointment. In none of these extemporised maneuvers did Johnson consult his Cabinet. He did pick up eagerly Welles' suggestion that he needed a man he could trust as Adjutant General because all the orders went through that office. The incumbent, Acting Adjutant General E. D. Townsend, was a good man but completely under Stanton's domination. Casually, Welles mentioned that Lorenzo Thomas, who had been Adjutant General, was at odds with Stanton.

The next day, February 14, the Cabinet had its first hint that Johnson was about to take action. "Who is Secretary of War?" Welles asked. Johnson replied "that matter will be disposed of in one or two days." But the Cabinet was kept in suspense for another week. When Welles learned on February 21, that the President had nominated General Lorenzo Thomas as Acting Secretary, he was amazed. Thomas was no friend of Stanton, that he knew, but he was a hard-drinking, garrulous, old dandy, fit for the routine of the Adjutant General's office, but scarcely a proper choice for such a delicate assignment.[38]

As expected, Johnson's impulsive action of defiance threw Congress into an uproar. John Covode, now a radical Congressman from Pennsylvania, immediately introduced a resolution of impeachment in the House, and it was referred to Thaddeus Stevens' Committee on Reconstruction. The Senate went into executive session which lasted far into the night. After fierce debate, the Senate, by a strict party vote, resolved that Johnson had acted unlawfully.

Wild rumors swept the city throughout the day. Edgar Welles, who was attending an afternoon party where a good many officers of the Washington garrison were present, brought back alarming information to his father. At about 4 o'clock an orderly had appeared from General W. H. Emory, the garrison commander. All officers of the Fifth Cavalry were ordered to headquarters. Shortly afterward, a second orderly brought word that any additional officers attached to Emory's command should report for duty. Fearing some kind of military action, Welles, who was not well at the time, sent Edgar to the White House, but Johnson was at a state dinner and had asked not to be disturbed. Early the next morning, Welles found the President in his office with Stanbery, and he imparted Edgar's information. Johnson, puzzled, said that he had given no orders for troop movements.

"Someone has," said Welles, "Who is it, and what does it indicate? While you Mr. President are resorting to no extreme measures, the radical conspirators have their spies—have command of the troops."[39]

After Welles left, Johnson sent for Emory. The mysterious order, he learned, had come from Grant, who had decided, in view of the excitement, that the garrison should be at its post.

On February 23, Stevens' committee reported favorably on Covode's resolution. The House immediately acted to impeach the President. From then until the Senate's final acquittal of Johnson by one vote on May 26, 1868, Welles was more of a spectator than a participant. Appalled at the President's failure to ask the advice of his Cabinet during most of this critical period, the despairing Welles was even "tempted to listen to the accusation of his enemies that he deserved and courted impeachment." Welles sharply criticized Johnson's predeliction for being reticent with his friends while holding free and open conversations with newsmen.[40]

The Cabinet did consult with Johnson in the choice of counsel. But Welles let his distrust of Seward lead him to oppose William M. Evarts, who was considered to be the finest legal mind in the country. In what was a mere quibble, he admitted Evarts' abilities, yet argued that, since the trial would be a political affair, Johnson should have politically attuned lawyers who could meet the impeachment managers on their own ground. Still, Welles' were the most forceful of the Cabinet arguments against Johnson's appearing before the Senate in person. The President's counsel had the decisive voice in convincing the stubborn Johnson that he would demean the stature of the Executive if he attended the trial. Doubtless they shuddered at the possibility that he would be baited into making a spectacle of himself. Welles had helped them make their case to Johnson.

Welles gave a good account of himself during the brief time he was permitted on the witness stand. But his most important, indeed, vital, service to the President's defense did not lie in his verbal testimony. Much of the President's case was supported by a wealth of material Welles supplied from his diary—dates, gist of conversation on important points, the positions of Cabinet members, such as Stanton, on the Tenure of Office Act. Browning's diary was also valuable to the President's counsel, but it was Welles' fuller and richer account, with its careful attention to slight differences of opinion, that was used to telling advantage by the defense.[41]

Welles was at the White House when the dramatic first vote was taken on the eleventh impeachment article. This was the article on which Johnson was most likely to be convicted, because it was the most sweeping in its indictment. He was specifically accused of declaring that the thirty-ninth Congress was not a legal body; that he had sought to circumvent the law requiring him to issue all orders on reconstruction through General Grant; that he had tried to avoid executing the Military Reconstruction Act of March 2, 1867, in the manner

Congress intended; and, finally, that he had attempted to violate the Tenure of Office Act.

Welles was also present the following week when the impeachment managers sought conviction on articles two and three, which simply accused him of unlawfully appointing General Thomas as Secretary of War *ad interim,* without the advice and consent of the Senate. The second vote was more suspenseful than the first. Extreme radicals had brought unrelenting pressure to bear on two of the seven Republican senators who had voted for acquittal; they were considered the most likely to reverse themselves.

It was regular Cabinet day, Friday, May 26, when the second vote was taken. A corps of messengers at Willard's Hotel speeded telegrams from the Capitol to the White House, reporting each motion and each vote as the Senate prepared for the final test. Welles marveled at Johnson's composure during the preliminaries, and during the final test, when he was again acquitted by one vote. What he did not know was that the President believed the issue had never been in doubt.[42] Senator James W. Grimes, before he was felled by a stroke, had acted as an intermediary between Republican Senators and the White House. Chief Justice Chase, too, made no secret of his opposition, not only to the impeachment but to military rule in the South. He made his influence felt.[43] Johnson had assurance that he could count on at least two additional Republican Senators—Morgan of New York and Nye of Nevada—who for party reasons preferred not to display the courage of their convictions.[44]

After the Senate adjourned its trial of impeachment, all else was anti-climax. Welles viewed with approval the departure of his old enemy Stanton, who relinquished the War Department as soon as he learned of the Senate's adjournment after failing to convict. General John M. Schofield, who was acceptable to both Johnson and the Senate, replaced him. He served as Secretary of War until the end of the term.

Five days after Johnson was acquitted of high crimes and misdemeanors on the eleventh article, the Republican Convention in Chicago nominated Grant for President and Schuyler Colfax, Speaker of the House, for Vice President. Welles was not impressed. "Grant has lost his moral strength by untruthfulness," he said, "and Colfax is very weak and superficial." Nor was he enthusiastic about the Democratic nominations, Horatio Seymour of New York for President, Frank Blair, Jr., of Missouri for Vice President. "Seymour has intellect but not courage. His nomination has been effected by duplicity, deceit, cunning management and sharp scheming." He was more partial to Frank Blair, Jr., Seymour's running mate, but was well aware of his weaknesses, his bellicose personality, his intemperance. What struck him as the supreme folly of the Democrats, however, was that they should have teamed a colorless politician whose conduct during the war was not above reproach with a strong Union party man like Blair. The mixture was not compatible. "They have put in jeopardy an election which they might have made certain," he said.[45]

After the trial and the strenuous campaign, after the ranting and the raving and the constant tension of three years, Washington relapsed into an unusual calm. Enough reconstructed Southern states voted for the Fourteenth Amendment to give a requisite majority for ratification in July 1868. Grant prevailed over Seymour, as Welles had expected. With a sense of relief, Welles prepared his last annual report as Secretary of the Navy.

Welles permitted himself a final tribute to the Navy's service during the war, tactfully reminding his countrymen of his successful administration. On March 3, 1869, accompanied by chiefs of bureaus and the senior officers, he attended Johnson's last reception for the departments. Old Admiral Joseph Smith, who, more than eight years before, had gone with him to Lincoln's first reception, was again by his side. Welles remembered Smith saying to the tall, gaunt President, "we will perform our duty, and expect you to do yours." Before introducing Smith, who now, as then, was the senior naval officer present, Welles said that "these are the men who, in war and peace, have stood fast by the government and union." Johnson greeted everyone warmly, and the simple ceremony was over. Upon his return to his office, Welles bade farewell to the department staff. It was after four o'clock in the afternoon when he finally finished all of his tasks. As he prepared to leave the room he had occupied for eight years, he mused briefly upon the heavy responsibilities he had carried, the criticism and abuse he had suffered. But there had been "many pleasant and happy hours," and as he left he thought chiefly of these, of the victories at Port Royal, Fort Henry, New Orleans, Mobile Bay, and Fort Fisher; of his pleasant associates; of Abraham Lincoln, who would drop in at any hour of the day or night for news or a chat. In twenty hours he would be a private citizen again. His public life had ended.[46]

# CHAPTER 30

# Old and Full of Days

WELLES FELT A GREAT sense of relief now that the cares and responsibilities of high office were over—no more carping criticisms in the papers, no more Congressmen seeking favors and threatening reprisals if they were turned away, no more agonizing over the merits of this ambitious officer or that. He missed the daily routine, the brisk walk to the department in the morning, the return at night, the neat piles of orders, dispatches, and requisitions that had been referred to him by the bureau chiefs, some for information, some with request for guidance, some for his own action.

During the first two weeks of his retirement, a constant stream of visitors occupied his attention. Primarily senior officers or bureau chiefs, they spoke of the changes being made in the department. Grant had appointed a little-known, wealthy Philadelphia merchant, Adolph Borie, to be his Secretary of the Navy. Borie himself was as astonished as the old Washington hands were at his appointment; he had no qualifications, not even political ones, and no desire to educate himself in the responsibilities the office entailed. The new President had a ready answer for his reluctant Secretary. He would provide him with expert assistance in the person of Vice Admiral David Dixon Porter. Borie would function as Secretary in name only, while Porter, as Grant's special deputy, would run the department.[1]

Porter lost no time, not only in implementing his ideas, but in settling some personal scores. Since the election, he had been counting on his friendship with Grant to permit him a decisive role in naval affairs. For many months, while he awaited the summons, he had drafted

regulations so comprehensive that they even specified uniforms for enlisted men and officers alike. An opinionated man, Porter had his own
ideas on how the Navy should operate. Some were progressive, many
were reactionary, but all were predicated on naval officers rather than
civilians formulating policy in the department. His plan, similar to the
old Board of Admiralty concept that had been proposed so many times
during the war, would have made a nullity of the Secretary's office.[2]

As soon as Porter took charge, the clerks in the department were
set to working as hard as they had in wartime copying and dispatching
scores of general orders. There were changes in personnel, too. Isherwood was the most important victim of Porter's vengeance, and his
removal signified a general assault on all staff officers. During his eight
years as Secretary, Welles had steadfastly supported and even encouraged the aspirations of the staff officers, especially the engineers. Steam,
he believed firmly, was the motive power of the future, and engineering
officers were as important in naval operations as officers of the line.[3] In
March 1863, he had secured an opinion from Attorney General Bates
which he used as authority to raise the relative rank of the staff. Then,
with Lincoln's approval, he issued a departmental regulation embodying Bates' opinion. He had never thought the regulation would stand
a legal test and had urged at various times that staff officers, through
their friends in Congress, make the regulation a law. But the staff officers, as cliquish and self-interested as the line officers, were not content with the mere raise in rank which the department had accorded
them. They would regret that they had not taken Welles' advice.
Among the many changes Porter secured was an opinion from the new
Attorney General, E. Rockwood Hoar, that reversed the Bates' ruling.
Armed with this judgment, and with Grant's approval, the Vice Admiral reduced the rank and perquisites of the entire staff to what they
had been prior to 1863.[4] Lenthall, Isherwood, Smith, and Bridge kept
Welles posted on the tornado raging in the department. Edgar and
Faxon related how Borie was simply a front for Porter. Faxon, who had
remained in office for a few days to brief the new Secretary, told how
all was confusion at the White House, how Grant was unaware of elementary facts—for example, that commissions could not be issued without his signature.[5]

Although the Navy Department claimed his prime interest, Welles
could not have possibly ignored Grant's other Cabinet appointments.
They simply confirmed his belief that Grant was totally unfit for the
presidency. When Admiral Farragut told him that the President had
nominated Elihu B. Washburne as Secretary of State, simply to com-

pliment a loyal supporter, Welles said disparagingly, "Grant considers the places his, not the country's."[6]

As interesting as the Washington scene was to such a seasoned political observer, the onset of spring reminded Welles that he must make plans for his retirement. For family and personal reasons, he would return to Hartford. Yet in many ways he was loath to leave this fascinating city where he had so many friends, where he had experienced notable success along with failure and disappointment. Hugh McCulloch and Montgomery Blair both urged him to stay, reminding him that after eight years' separation, "his ties with Hartford had been weakened, friends had died or moved away, many familiar landmarks would be gone or altered beyond recognition." Welles had to agree. But his feelings about his "native place" were stronger than his fear of change. Mary Welles, too, was eager to leave. She had experienced to the full the pleasures of Washington's social whirl. Now a new administration held the government, and with it a new society was forming in the capital, a society of which the Welleses were not a part. She wanted also to be near the graves of her children, perhaps recapture, if she could, some of the simple joys of her early married life.

The decision made, Welles had to find accommodations for his family. Mary Welles wanted to live in the fashionable southern section of the city. Faxon, who had resigned on March 9 and had left for home the next day, did some preliminary prospecting. Welles was depressed at his report on Hartford real estate. There were plenty of suitable homes for sale, but the prices seemed very high, more than he thought he could afford.[7] Welles' salary, $8000 a year, had just barely covered his living expenses. The style of living expected of a Cabinet member, made more costly by wartime, inflation, had left no surplus for savings, and he had not been able to spare the time from his demanding post to manage his investments properly. His income as a result had declined in real purchasing power. Uncertain about the future, he thought seriously about renting a house, but then he would have to face the problem of his furnishings and his voluminous papers. To store them involved additional expense and much inconvenience. If he rented for a season he would have to move again, with all its unsettling aspects, all of its confusion.[8]

Finally, he decided he would have to buy. Prudently, he would board the family at the Allyn House in Hartford while he made a careful search himself. Though Admiral Porter must have known that Welles had a low opinion of his policies and his politics, he placed at Welles' disposal the Navy dispatch boat, *Tallapoosa*, to transport his household effects. Finally, on April 27, he left the spacious three-story Slidell mansion which had been his home for eight turbulent years. Most of the family furnishings had been packed and were already on board the *Tallapoosa*. The remainder were being auctioned that day. Edgar stayed behind to close up the house and return the keys to its owner. After a day's rest at his brother-in-law's home in New York, Welles and his family reached Hartford.

On Monday morning he began the arduous and frustrating task of looking for a home. As he had expected, everything did seem strange and different. Acquaintances he met on the street were polite but distant by Washington standards. He had forgotten how restrained New Englanders could be in casual encounters. The Monday papers had announced his arrival, and when only two of his old friends came to call, he felt hurt. Although he had not wanted any public applause, he did feel that eight years of service in the highest circles of government merited some recognition, the offer of some few friends, at least, to help him in locating a suitable house. "I come almost as a stranger . . . ," he lamented. During the week, however, more friends called. Some had been out of town, others had been indisposed or simply had not noticed the brief announcement in the papers. Welles had been too ready with his criticism, as he now recognized. "The prompt cordiality of Washington is not characteristic of Hartford," he said.

By now Edgar had arrived. Welles and his three sons spent the entire week examining real estate. Appalled at the prices, Welles nevertheless decided he would have to make a quick purchase. The furniture would be arriving any day. It would be to everyone's convenience if he could have it moved in directly from the boat. Besides, he rationalized, real estate was a sound investment, "in consequence of the unsettled and uncertain condition of the currency." He purchased for $29,200 a roomy house and two lots of land on Charter Oak Place, a secluded area in the south of the city. The property, which belonged to J. Woodbridge White, he felt, was "too expensive for his income, but the best he could obtain anywhere in Hartford."

On Tuesday, May 18, before the Whites vacated the premises, Welles' household effects arrived from Washington. He lost no time in having the furniture placed in the house, and wondered why the Whites were not more affable. Typically, Welles blamed Mrs. White, "who has a questionable companion and prompter in a man named Fuller." There followed several days of confusion and physical labor, which told on Welles, who was nearly sixty-seven. Two hundred and twenty-four boxes came from Washington, along with six wagon loads of furniture from Glastonbury, and other things that had been stored with friends. In the midst of this domestic upheaval, Mary Welles fell, injuring herself so severely that she had to remain in bed.[9] Despite this mishap, despite problems with new servants, Welles and his three sons had everything in place by the end of the week. He was now free to work on his investments, arrange his papers, and resume his critical analysis of the Grant administration.

One of his first moves was to strengthen his finances. Mark Howard and Calvin Day offered valuable counsel. He also continued his relationship with E. D. Morgan's banking firm, but he was now relying more heavily on his wartime friend, James B. Eads of St. Louis, Missouri. This brilliant self-taught engineer, marine designer, banker, and railroad owner was engaged in the design and construction of the first steel bridge in the nation. Welles acted on his advice in Western railroad investments. He retained Robert Lincoln to look after his real estate holdings in Chicago.[10]

These arrangements made, Welles began to sort out his papers and to sketch out various historical projects. A political history of the Jacksonian period seems to have claimed major interest,[11] but he could not resist the temptations of journalism. As of old, he supplied articles to the *Hartford Times* on local and national politics. A special target, of course, was the Grant administration, which was beginning to flounder in a mass of inept appointments where spoils rather than public service were too often the criteria of office. Welles did not as yet command a national audience for his opinion. But he soon would.

Six weeks before Welles left the Navy Department, Henry J. Raymond, the founder and editor of the *New York Times,* a Weed-Seward paper, had collapsed and died of apoplexy on the doorstep of his own house after visiting his current mistress, Rose Eytinge. Welles, who had detested him for years and thought of him as "an unscrupulous soldier of fortune," would have accepted as truth what Henry Ward Beecher told John Bigelow about Raymond's character. In one of the more amusing outrageous remarks of the Gilded Age, Beecher had said, "Raymond died of women not of hard work at all." That worthy divine was even then carrying on an affair with the wife of Theodore Tilton, his closest friend and the editor of the religious daily, the New York *Independent.* Shortly he would be exposed as the most pious adulterer of the century. Whether Welles knew of Raymond's escapades or not, the editor's death gave him much needed entrée to the metropolitan press, for John Bigelow took over Raymond's post on the *Times,* whose columns had always been closed to Welles. Bigelow was hospitable to Welles' writings, and on September 23, 1869, his first editorial appeared in the *Times*. Many others followed.[12]

Welles continued to toy with a major work until the summer of 1870, when he discovered his metier—the historical essay. For some time, it had been common knowledge that Thurlow Weed was working on his memoirs. In the June 1870 edition of *The Galaxy,* Welles read with growing irritation a chapter from Weed's autobiography covering March and April of 1861. Weed made himself appear *the* moving force of the Lincoln administration. Through his friend Seward, the indomitable old Whig boss had been able to keep a steady hand on the helm. Other Cabinet members—Chase, Welles, Blair—were, by implication, unfit for the great responsibilities that had been so suddenly thrust upon them. Weed was particularly critical of the Norfolk Navy Yard disaster, for which he held "Father" Welles responsible.

Nettled by Weed's distortion of the truth, stung by the allegation that he had been unfit for his job, Welles at once began a rebuttal, drawing upon his own papers.[13] The result was an argument that demolished Weed's position and cast grave doubt on Weed's memory, if not his veracity. But Welles' essay was more than just a polemic, well-anchored in fact; it was also an interesting narrative that placed in perspective events, situations, and decisions as "the secession crisis came to a head." His article, which appeared in the July edition of *The Galaxy,* was commented on widely and favorably in the press, and many papers ran long excerpts of it. Thus stimulated, Welles prepared another article, a narrative on the attempt to relieve Fort Sumter.[14] At regular intervals—as if they were chapters of a book—articles appeared in which Welles described and evaluated incidents of the war and reconstruction: Fort Pickens, the capture of New Orleans, emancipation, reconstruction under Lincoln and Johnson.

All of the essays had certain points to make. It had been the Navy, not the Army, that had captured New Orleans; Admiral Farragut, not Admiral Porter, had won the victory. Seward was cast as a devious meddler, Stanton as a disloyal intriguer who lusted after personal power. Throughout, Lincoln was seen as a great President—strong, perceptive, humane, his own master. Welles had to draw on correspondence and memory for the first three articles—those on Sumter and Pickens. But his diary formed the core of the rest and lent them their authoritative cast.

In the midst of organizing and cross-referencing his personal papers, Welles had laid aside this congenial labor to plunge again into editorial combat. The case at issue was the 1869 annual report of the

Secretary of the Navy. Borie had resigned after serving not quite four months. His successor, George Robeson of Camden, New Jersey, was, like Borie, unknown to the public or to the leading politicians. Grant made the appointment as casually as he had Borie's—on the advice of a staunch supporter in the Senate, Alexander G. Cattell of Pennsylvania. Robeson was a pleasant man with a taste for good wines and fast horses.[15] An excellent trial lawyer, he had just enough experience in local politics to appreciate how lucrative public office could be if one were careful with the accounts. Unfortunately for the genial Robeson, Gideon Welles had not lost his sharp eye for figures; nor did he lack sources of information within the Department.[16]

In his first annual report Robeson made the mistake of relying on slapdash material Porter had provided to justify his reforms at the expense of Welles' administration.[17] Acutely sensitive about his record, deeply disturbed at the havoc the Vice Admiral was creating in the department—re-rigging steamers for sail, driving the staff officers to the wall, diverting large sums for whimsical schemes such as changing the uniforms of the enlisted men—Welles replied at length in an open letter to Robeson. Published first in the *Hartford Courant*, it was republished or digested in most of the major newspapers. Welles ridiculed Robeson's pretensions to economy, exposing Porter's unfounded and unchecked assertions with fact, with simple logic, and with arithmetic. Writing from Lowell, Massachusetts, Fox praised Welles' letter in typical fashion. "The blow you gave them was like a XX inch. Everyone can see that their whole establishment is crooked from top to bottom."[18]

When he wrote his open letter, Welles was concerned chiefly with a defense of his own actions. But he seized the opportunity of exposing what he felt was a wasteful, extravagant administration. He had not looked for any corrupt practices. When Admiral Smith, nearing the end of his career in the department, mentioned that Robeson had blended two parts of two fiscal years, Welles could only have agreed with him that there had been an effort to deceive, to hide certain costs. Welles' letter stirred up a brief controversy in Congress, where Sumner's close friend, Henry L. Dawes of Massachusetts, was crusading for economy in government.[19]

Some careful footwork and some bluster on the part of Benjamin Butler, who was now currying favor with Grant, sidetracked any investigation. Robeson went on being Washington's most eligible bachelor, entertaining at "brilliant affairs" where Grant was frequently the honored guest.[20] Those who knew the ruddy, rotund Secretary, whose care-

fully trimmed white sideburns and garish dress gave him the appearance of a "sporting man," wondered how he could afford his lavish
style of living. In the fall of 1871, the Chief of the Bureau of Construction and Repair, "Honest John Lenthall," as Welles always called him,
was dismissed from his post. His replacement was a naval constructor
of dubious repute, Isaiah Hanscom, whose brother, Simon P. Hanscom,
was an office broker who had worked closely with Nathaniel P. Banks.[21]

Lenthall may have been of retirement age, but he resented being
shunted aside, as Isherwood had been, to make a place for a man who,
if not personally dishonest, would not stand up to the contractors.
Robeson had already forced Lenthall to pay out a substantial wartime
claim to the shipbuilder T. F. Secors, a claim that had been disallowed
by Welles and by three successive Navy boards. Over Lenthall's protest, a fast steamer, the *Tennessee,* had her new Ericsson engines removed, along with two of her four boilers. Other engines were ordered,
and the *Tennessee* was reconverted into an old-fashioned ship-rigged
frigate, her small steam plant capable of furnishing auxiliary power
only. A new set of Isherwood engines that had been bought for her,
engines like those which had driven her sister ship, the *Wampanoag,*
faster than any comparable ships in any of the world's navies, was left
unused at the Washington Navy Yard. The *Tennessee*'s Ericsson engines, which had cost the government $700,000, were sold to John
Roach, a New York shipbuilder, for $35,000, as junk.[22] Lenthall
wrote Welles of this transaction and provided him with information
on the Secors claims. From other sources Welles learned that there were
irregularities in the purchase of coal and of brick. The fact that a
claims broker and contract jobber of long experience, Simeon Johnson,
was haunting Robeson's office confirmed for Welles the fact that the
Navy Department had become a sink of corruption. He made a copy of
Lenthall's letter available to Charles A. Dana of the *Sun,* though after
Lenthall himself and Isherwood, among other disgruntled staff officers,
had given Dana the information.[23] Welles had not been on particularly
good terms with Dana during the war, when the bearded, balding
*Tribune* editor, as Assistant Secretary of War, had been Stanton's
right arm. His dislike of Dana had been professional only, the same
bias he and Fox had against all senior people in the War Department.
Dana was an able, if opinionated, editor, and, as far as Welles knew,
he was honest. Welles regularly read the *Sun,* which Dana had purchased three years before. Though Dana was a bit radical in politics
for his taste, Welles shared the editor's contempt for the Grant administration. Scarcely a day had gone by since the inauguration that there

was not some biting comment on that "intellectual colossus," Dana's ironic epithet for the President.[24]

On February 17, 1872, the *Sun* opened its assault on the Navy Department with a lead article entitled "The Good Fortune of John Roach & Son of New York." Welles read it with satisfaction, noting that Dana had used most of the material on the *Tennessee* which he had supplied. Two days later came "The Robberies of Robeson," and on the February 21 Dana published a comprehensive article charging Robeson with specific instances of graft in the Secors claim, the *Tennessee* conversion, and the supply of coal to the Navy, through a single agent, A. G. Cattell and Company. A day later Welles received a guarded note from Dana with a clipping of this article. Welles replied in the same guarded way that he could personally substantiate some of the allegations, while he had only heard about others.[25] With what information he had, Dana now felt secure enough to expand upon his charges. When he finally ended the series on February 29, he had impeached Robeson, Senator Cattell, and Joan Roach of collusion and rampant graft before the bar of public opinion. One week later, Austin Blair, a member of the House from Michigan and an old acquaintance of Welles, asked for a special committee to investigate the charges of the *Sun*. The House approved, Speaker James G. Blaine appointing Blair chairman. Hearings got under way at once, with Dana demanding and receiving the unusual power of examining and cross-examining witnesses himself. Robeson also broke precedent when he asked the committee if he could conduct his own defense. Obviously, he was relying on his redoubtable skill as a trial lawyer to confuse the witnesses against him.[26] The committee had no option after granting Dana extraordinary privileges. It allowed Robeson's request.

Welles, Edgar, and Faxon were subpoenaed as witnesses. They were to appear on Monday, April 15. They left Hartford on the morning of the thirteenth, reaching Washington in early evening. Welles was tired from the long day's journey, yet he had scarcely finished dinner at Willard's when a sergeant-at-arms was at his elbow with an urgent summons that he appear immediately before the committee. Suspecting a Robeson trick, fatigue gave way to suppressed anger. As he made his way to the committee room, he was determined that no small-time Camden lawyer would get the better of him.[27]

Members of the committee began the questioning, but after a half an hour or so, the Secretary himself took over. Robeson, the picture of ease and of deceptive courtesy, was anxious to justify the Secors claim. Time and again he pressed Welles to admit that claims could be reopened at any time, even if closed up by a previous administration. Robeson's line of questioning was clear to Welles. In his carefully phrased answers, he managed to enter on the record that the Secors claim had been disallowed by three separate boards of experts before the case had been closed. Tartly, he reminded the Secretary that if contract decisions could be set aside by succeeding administrations, he could visualize opening up the accounts for the building of the *Constitution* and making readjustments to the heirs of the contractors that would reflect such intangibles as inflation since 1795. The entire administration of the government would break down if the various Executive departments could not settle their accounts.[28]

Brushing aside the irony, the lecture in elementary public administration, Robeson sought details from Welles on the actions of the various contract boards. Patiently, keeping the irritation he felt out of his voice, he explained that he never went into such details. These were the province of the bureau chiefs. Still trying desperately to wring some sort of damaging admission out of the old man, Robeson kept coming back to specific board recommendations and departmental action upon them. In a firm voice, Welles answered: "I began by saying to you at once that I had but a general recollection . . . now as to going to details, to know whether I recollect that which was green or that a nail was driven here or driven there, I can not do so. I did not attend to matters of that kind."[29] During one of these exchanges, Admiral Porter whispered to Faxon, "the fool—he had better let that old gentleman alone."[30]

The persistent Robeson tried other lines of inquiry, but they were no more fruitful. Nor did the brief examinations of Faxon and Edgar Welles help his case. Robeson could not prevail against Dana, who brought out the fact that the Secretary had paid over $166,000 in claims that the Welles administration had disallowed and closed up. Other evidence Dana gave proved beyond question that the Secretary was not fit for the post he held. But Dana was unable to demonstrate actual graft. The committee decided not to pursue the matter any farther.

Robeson's image was untarnished in Grant's eyes. He remained as Secretary of the Navy, continuing to give his lavish parties and acquiring expensive Washington real estate. Perhaps emboldened by the whitewash, he became more deeply involved with the Cattells. When he was finally brought to book by a thorough investigation in 1876, the amount of graft he had received in the form of kickbacks on supplies for the Navy was startling, even to the hard-bitten buccaneers of the

Gilded Age. Yet the jovial rogue not only managed to escape impeachment, he actually served two terms in Congress during the 1880's. Although Welles, Edgar, and Faxon testified again in the 1876 hearings, they added little to the sordid record of plunder and maladministration that the House Committee on Naval Affairs uncovered.[31]

These two trips, and one to the Centennial Exposition in Philadelphia, were the only journeys Welles made south of New York City. He was now finding travel fatiguing, and only because of his wife's urgent plea could he be persuaded to spend a few weeks at Newport, Rhode Island, each summer.[32] Still, for a man of his age, he remained extraordinarily active and alert. His major interest continued to be the history of the Lincoln and Johnson administrations, and he wrote essays on them; yet he concerned himself with state affairs. He drafted resolutions for the legislature that would make Hartford the sole capital of the state. He wrote a series of powerful articles in the Hartford papers urging a revision of the Constitution of 1818, which his father had helped draft.[33]

Inevitably, he was drawn into national politics as the liberal Republican movement began to gather momentum during the fall of 1871. The passions and the animosities that reconstruction had stirred up were fading fast among the Republicans. Welles now was on friendly terms with such "radicals" as Carl Schurz and Jacob D. Cox. He was invited to attend a meeting of liberal Republicans at the Fifth Avenue Hotel in New York, where it was hoped that Horace Greeley, who had been nominated, could be induced to withdraw.[34] Welles—whose candidate, B. Gratz Brown, had been passed over in favor of Greeley—believed that the contest was hopeless and did not attend the meeting. He refrained from any active participation in the campaign. Instead, he devoted his time to completing his articles on reconstruction for *The Galaxy* and in writing editorials on local affairs.

Resigned to another four years of Grant, he was disgusted, though not surprised, at the low state of public and private morals. For several months after the election, Welles did little or nothing except carry on his correspondence with old colleagues such as Montgomery Blair and O. H. Browning. Then in April 1873, Charles Francis Adams delivered a eulogy on William H. Seward, who had died the previous October. Adams had thought, along with so many of his contemporaries, that Seward was the mastermind of the Lincoln administration. Even close observers had cast Lincoln as a shrewd politician, but no statesman—weak, indecisive, undignified, a pleasant joke-maker. The tragedy of his assassination had reminded the articulate public that he had been a good man, humane, kindly, endearing in his ugly, awkward way. But few would consider that he possessed more than ordinary abilities. Seward and Chase were the stars, Lincoln the background, the comic relief. Adams shared these sentiments more than most because he had been indebted to Seward for many favors, not the least of which was his ambassadorship to England.[35]

When Welles read Adams' eulogy, he resolved then and there that justice must be done to Lincoln, that Seward must not have the last word. The result was two more essays that formed the basis of Welles' only book, *Lincoln and Seward,* a modest little volume of slightly over two hundred pages. He drew, of course, on his diary and his voluminous correspondence, but he also asked for impressions of key events from Blair and from Chase.[36]

Welles began *Lincoln and Seward* in much the same manner he started his first article in *The Galaxy* that had corrected Thurlow Weed's account of the Norfolk Navy Yard disaster. He specifically rebutted Adams, as he had Weed, and in doing so gave a polemical tone to the book. But his sense of history was better developed than it had been in his earlier work. He allotted only a few pages to Adams' argument, moving easily into a narrative that brought out, as he saw them, the qualities of Lincoln and Seward. The nation learned something of Seward's political style and got an inside, though by no means complete, look at the maneuvers that resulted in Lincoln's nomination. He discussed foreign policy during the war, showing with documents and with closely reasoned discussion how large a part Lincoln had played in what everyone had thought was Seward's exclusive domain. In the course of this discussion Welles did not fail to place himself in the best possible light. But through it all, Lincoln emerges as a towering figure, coping admirably with herculean tasks. Welles made the most of his adroit quashing of Chase's intrigue that had almost forced Seward from the Cabinet. He described succinctly the abortive attempt to have the Cabinet control Lincoln after Pope's defeat at Second Bull Run. Lincoln, for the first time, was presented as a great President, easily the peer of Washington, Jefferson, or Jackson. Welles insisted that Seward, too, had remarkable qualities, a "versatile and prolific mind," but that in no way was he a man of Lincoln's stature. Seward was "less persistent and reliable, less capable of establishing and enforcing policy, less capable of grasping great questions and successfully wielding the highest functions of government."[37]

The reception accorded *Lincoln and Seward* was most favorable.[38] Republican politicians, and a host of writers, both popular and serious, on the Civil War, would now grasp more perfectly the many facets of that unique man, Abraham Lincoln. Perhaps without realizing it, Welles had supplied a significant rationale in his effort to bring out the truth. He was the first promoter of the Lincoln legend. Nor did Welles stop with his publication of *Lincoln and Seward*, though he had several bouts of serious illness in 1874 and again in 1875. During 1876 and 1877 he composed nine essays that, taken together, make a political history of the Lincoln administration from the election in November 1860 through the fall of 1864. These last essays are more objective, more comprehensive, less litigous than any of his previous work.[39]

Welles took a certain amount of pride in his essays. Yet they fell far short of his original ambition to write a history of the nineteenth century, as George Bancroft had done for the eighteenth. Even his own role in the history of the Civil War and reconstruction was barely touched upon in his published writings. When packing up and arranging his papers just before leaving Washington in mid-April of 1869, he made one of those gloomy, fatalistic comments that appear with such frequency in his diary. He had an awareness of having served his country to the best of his ability during exciting and perilous times. His ambition had been gratified. The part he had played in the successful conclusion of the war was its own reward. Though he had hoped he could recount those Washington years as well as all the years before —the party contests of the Jackson era, the Whigs and the Democrats, the great free-soil contest—he realized this task was beyond him now. Old and full of years, he had experienced trials, misfortunes, tragedies. What he personally had accomplished, not only as Secretary of the Navy but as a lifelong observer and practitioner of politics on all levels, "will soon pass in a degree," he remarked sadly, "or be only slightly recollected."

Would his place in casting the history of his times rest upon the slender stack of essays he had written? There was always the diary, which he had neglected during the first year and a half of the Lincoln administration. He made haste to repair that omission by writing up key episodes while his memory remained clear, drawing also on letters and documents he had brought from Washington. At that time he probably was still planning a major work that would cover the war and reconstruction and would be based largely on his diary. His setting up of an alphabetical file on his papers and writings, which could easily be cross-referenced with his vastly larger chronological file, suggests that the war and reconstruction would be but a part of a larger work.

At any rate, he edited his diary thoroughly, excising some material that he thought might be in poor taste or would excite personal controversy. He may have devoted some thought to its publication as memoirs, following the example of Thomas Hart Benton. Or, given his gift of describing and analyzing politicians and statesmen of the past, he may have wanted to write a life of Lincoln, imitating Boswell's *Life of Johnson,* which he had had Edgar purchase for him in 1870.[40] But there was so much material and so little time that he never completed the many major projects he had sketched out. The diary kept during the Lincoln and Johnson administrations remained in its original manuscript, the political history of the Jacksonian era, in bits and pieces in his alphabetical file. This huge collection of diaries, documents, and reminiscences—one of the great collections of primary source material for the political and social history of the United States during the nineteenth century—would remain relatively untouched until forty-five years after Welles' death, when it became available to scholars. Welles had failed to write the great works he had projected. It had not been until retirement that he realized what a heavy toll the war and reconstruction had taken upon his mental and physical resources.

The diary, several thousands of manuscript pages, had been a faithful companion, especially so in Washington. That it was a valuable historical document, Welles believed. But he seems never to have regarded it as more than a source for the kind of history which he wrote of the first eighteen months of the war, when he had not kept a diary. Yet, as interesting and as vivid as that brief account is, the diary proper, which he began writing on August 10, 1862, and continued with few interruptions until June 6, 1869, is far more impressive than any more formal history that Welles might have written. His essays, his *Lincoln and Seward,* pale before the vigorous, uninhibited, and frequently unpolished but always simple prose of the diary. And through his work—for it is not just a diary, but opinion, description, biographical sketch, commentary on the social, political and economic scenes— Welles' character and personality come through with startling clarity. It is all there: his sanctimonious moralizing, his bitter, often mean, caricatures of his contemporaries, his honesty in public affairs, his jealousies, ambitions, fears. Error, gossip put forth as fact, even distortion of events for personal gratification, vie with the unvarnished truth, the perceptive analysis, the devastatingly accurate phrase that consigns some venial place-hunter or petty spoilsman to the trash heap where he belongs. Seward, Stanton, and Chase were all remarkable men; each had more influence in shaping national events than Welles did. An insecure man, Welles resented their popularity, their strength, their arrogance, and, while he generally shrank from any open encounter with them, he got his revenge by cutting them down in his diary. While this essentially furtive exercise relieved Welles' frustration and vented his anger in a vicarious manner, it is of value to the biographer but can mislead the historian.

Welles himself found virtue in Thaddeus Stevens when he wrote his history of the Lincoln administration, years after Stevens' death; the diary flays Stevens at every opportunity. Yet it is just this perverse quality which makes the diary such a human document on such a grand scale. One need not accept Welles' strictures upon Stevens and Stanton and Seward, but one sees them as they actually were, in part how they appeared to many of their contemporaries. Welles creates a scene, one-sided to be sure, but with a spontaneity and a freshness that makes the reader also a spectator. Like William Byrd of Westover and the two Adamses, Welles kept one of the nation's great diaries. That his colors are more often blacks and grays than crimsons and yellows, that his irony often smothers his wit, should not detract from these volumes as works of art as well as historical sources. While he tinkered with the hundreds of pages of manuscript, adding, deleting, punctuating, polishing, Welles must have relived the stirring scenes in which he had been both observer and participant. But by now he knew that the history would never be done, that the diaries would, if they escaped destruction, be used by others. It seems doubtful that he recognized to any significant extent their literary quality. And it seems probable that his inability to utilize them for the history he could not write cast a pall over his declining years. As he apologized to his son Edgar in February 1875, "I am getting old and somewhat indifferent to praise, and disposed to avoid controversy. I feel my infirmity, and as Professor Henry said, without some companion to assist me shall do but little."[41]

Mindful of his waning physical powers, Welles dared not venture out on cold winter days.[42] But when the weather was fine, he always took a daily stroll down Main Street, a striking old man with white flowing beard and a wide-brimmed felt or straw hat, depending on the season. One by one, colleagues, friends, and opponents died. Each passing left yet another gap in his memory of the past. His friend and colleague, Edward Bates, and his adversary and colleague, Stanton, died in 1869; the agile Seward, who had so often gotten behind him, and Seward's rival, Salmon P. Chase—whom Welles once described as "clumsy but strong"—both died in 1873.[43] Sumner followed in 1874,

Andrew Johnson in 1875, and his own dear brother Thaddeus in 1876. He, who had been the weakest physically of Samuel Welles' four sons, had survived them all.

In the late fall of 1877, friends and family noticed that Welles had become unsteady in his walk, that he was gradually losing weight. Yet he seemed to improve in December and was seen walking as erect as ever on Main Street.[44] He had just completed another long article on the Lincoln administration for the *Atlantic Monthly* and was correcting the proof in February 1878 when a carbuncle suddenly developed behind his right ear. Twice before he had suffered from these painful streptococcous infections and recovered. This time the infection would not respond to lancing and poultices, the standard remedies. On Saturday night, February 9, Welles knew that he was going to die. The infection had spread to his throat. He could not swallow; his breathing became difficult. His condition became rapidly worse on Sunday. Now he could no longer speak, but his mind remained clear. He managed with feeble gestures to indicate that he wished to be baptized in the Episcopal Church. After suffering unspeakable agonies for three days, the pain seemed to ease on Monday, but it was obvious to those by his bedside—Mary, his sons John and Tom—that the end was near. At 6:45 p.m., a little after the winter night had settled over the city, Gideon Welles slipped away.[45]

# ABBREVIATIONS USED
# IN THE NOTES

BLP    Blair-Lee papers, Firestone Library, Princeton
ChHS    Chicago Historical Society, Chicago, Ill.
CHS    Connecticut Historical Society, Hartford, Conn.
CSL    Connecticut State Library
EML    Eleutherian Mills Library, Wilmington, Del.
HL    Huntington Library
IHS    Illinois Historical Society, Springfield, Ill.
LC    Library of Congress, Washington, D.C.
LWP    Levi Woodbury papers, Library of Congress
NA    National Archives, Washington, D.C.
NHHS    New Hampshire Historical Society, Concord, N.H.
NYHS    New York Historical Society, NYC
NYPL    New York Public Library, NYC
NYSL    New York State Library, Albany, N.Y.
VBP    Van Buren papers, Library of Congress
WP    Welles papers

# NOTES

## CHAPTER 1

1. *The Farmer's Almanac,* Boston, 1847, p. 2.

2. Welles, MS Diary, May 23, 1846, WP-HL; Francis H. Curtis, "Glastonbury," p. 37, pamphlet, Glastonbury, 1928, Sterling Library, Yale. Leonard W. Labaree (comp.), *The Public Records of the State of Connecticut for the Years 1783 and 1784,* Hartford, 1943, pp. 252, 429. Richard S. West, Jr., *Gideon Welles, Lincoln's Navy Department,* Indianapolis and New York, 1943, pp. 15-17.

3. H. B. Learned, "Manuscript Sketch of Gideon Welles," p. 3, H. B. Learned Collection of Papers Relating to Gideon Welles, LC.

4. Welles to John M. Niles, Nov. 13, 1834, WP-LC. *Roll of the State Officers and General Assembly of Connecticut, 1776-1881,* Hartford, 1881, pp. 117, 132ff.

5. *Record of Service of Connecticut Men in the War of the Revolution, War of 1812, Mexican War,* Adjutant General's Office, Hartford, 1889, pp. 277, 396, 628, 548, 651; John C. Pease and John M. Niles, *A Gazetteer of the States of Connecticut and Rhode Island,* Hartford, 1819, p. 13.

6. Welles, "Address of the State Convention to the Democrats of Connecticut, 1835," pamphlet, Sterling Library, Yale.

7. Welles, MS, "Reminiscences of Glastonbury," p. 7, Learned Coll.

8. Welles to Samuel Welles, Sept. 22, 1819, Lincoln Shrine, Redlands, Calif.; Welles, "Reminiscences of a Boyhood," Learned Coll. (This manuscript reminiscence must be used with care, for it contains some misstatements. For example, Samuel Welles did not accompany his son to Cheshire.)

9. West, *Welles,* p. 20.

10. Welles to Samuel Welles, Oct. 12, 1818, Lincoln Shrine, Redlands, Calif.; A. H. Foote to Welles, Dec. 18, 1823, WP-LC.

11. Howard K. Beale (ed.), *Diary of Gideon Welles* (3 vols.), New York, 1960, Vol. II, p. 269. Hereafter cited as Welles, *Diary.*

12. Welles, "Reminiscences of a Boyhood," p. 8, Learned Coll.

13. Welles to Samuel Welles, Sept. 22, 1819; Lincoln Shrine, Redlands, Calif.; Welles, "Reminiscences of a Boyhood," p. 11, Learned Coll.

14. *Ibid.,* p. 12.

15. E. E. Beardsley, "An Address Delivered in St. Peter's Church, Cheshire, Oct. 1, 1844, On the Occasion of the Fiftieth Anniversary of the Episcopal Academy in Connecticut," p. 24, pamphlet, Sterling Library, Yale, E. D. Woodbury to H. B. Learned, Aug. 10, 1906, Learned Coll.

16. Welles, "Reminiscences of a Boyhood," p. 9, Learned Coll.; Glenn Weaver, "America's First 'Junior College': The Episcopal Academy of Connecticut," Connecticut Historical Society *Bulletin,* Vol. 27, No. I, Jan. 1962, pp. 20, 21.

17. Welles, "Reminiscences of a Boyhood," pp. 10ff, Learned Coll.

18. A. H. Foote to Welles, Dec. 18, 1823, WP-LC; William Beardsley (comp.), *Officers, Teachers, and Alumni of the Episcopal Academy of Connecticut, 1796-1916,* New Haven, 1916, p. 63; West, *Welles,* pp. 20, 21.

19. See, for instance, his harsh comments on Cheshire, scribbled on a page of his copy of Virgil's *Aeneid;* see also J. P. Nichols to Welles, Apr. 25, 1822; W. Patten to Welles, 1820; Welles to Samuel Welles, Sept. 27, 1820, WP-LC.

20. Agreement between Welles and Ransome Tomlinson, Jan. 28, 1822, Thomas G. Welles Collection, Coventry, Conn.; West, *Welles,* pp. 24, 25; C. F. Manchester to Welles, Aug. 7, 1824; Samuel Welles to John G. Tomlinson, May 13, 1828, WP-LC; Ransome Tomlinson to Welles, Feb. 27, 1833, WP-CHS.

21. Welles to Amasa Jackson, May 22, 1822, WP-HL.

22. Gideon Welles, "Memorandum of a Journey to the Interior of New York and Northern Pennsylvania in the Autumn of 1822," WP-HL.

23. C. F. Heverly, *History of the Towandas, 1776-1886* (Towanda, Pa., 1886), Ch. 1.

24. Welles, "Memorandum," WP-HL.

25. Heverly, *History,* pp. 47, 48, 171, 169.

26. Welles, "Memorandum," WP-HL; Franklin Ellis (ed.), *History of That Part of the Susquehanna and Juniata Valleys Embraced in the Counties of Mifflin, Juniata, Perry, Union and Snyder in the Commonwealth of Pennsylvania . . .* (2 vols.), Philadelphia, 1886, Vol. I, p. 466.

27. Welles, "Memorandum," WP-HL.

28. *New York Mirror and Ladies' Literary Gazette,* Vol. I, Sept. 13, 1823.

29. *Ibid.,* Jan. 24, 1824; Feb. 7, Mar. 27, May 29, 1824.

30. For a sketch of the *New York Mirror,* see F. L. Mott, *A History of American Magazines* (3 vols.), New York, 1930-38, Vol. I, pp. 320-30.

31. Amasa Jackson to Welles, Sept. 15, 1822, WP-LC.

32. Welles to B. L. Raynor, Apr. 8, 1824; *Catalogue of the Officers and Cadets Together with the Prospectus and Internal Regulations of the American Literary, Scientific and Military Academy at Middletown, Connecticut,* Middletown, 1825, *passim.*

33. C. F. Manchester to Welles, Aug. 7, 1824; Amasa Jackson to Welles, Nov. 4, 1824, WP-LC.

34. See sample letters that describe the academy and its routine in François Peyre-Ferry and Alden Partridge, *The Art of Epistolary Composition and a Discourse on Education, Middletown,* 1826, pp. 216, 247.

35. M. E. Goddard and H. V. Partridge, *A History of Norwich,* Hanover, N.H., 1905, p. 233.

36. Welles fared the same as all entering cadets. The procedure is outlined in Peyre-Ferry and Partridge, *Art of Epistolary Composition,* p. 216.

37. *Ibid.,* p. 255; Sidney Forman, *West Point: A History of the United States Military Academy,* New York, 1950, pp. 39-41, 43-45, 62-64.

38. Catalogue, American Literary, Scientific and Military Academy, 1821, Norwich, Vt., Middletown, Conn., 1825.

39. William A. Ellis (ed.), *Norwich University 1819-1911, Her History, Her Graduates, Her Roll of Honor* (2 vols.), Montpelier, Vt., 1911, Vol. I, pp. 6-7.

40. Homer White, *The Norwich Cadets: A Tale of the Rebellion,* St. Albans, Vt., 1873, p. 30.

41. Ellis (ed.), *Norwich University,* Vol. I, pp. 16-17.


## CHAPTER 2

1. Thomas S. Weaver, *Historical Sketch of the Police Service of Hartford,* Hartford, 1901, pp. 27, 28.

2. Welles to Southworth, Aug. 1826, WP-LC.

3. W. W. Ellsworth to Welles, Jan. 18, 1830, WP-LC. J. Hammond Trumbull (ed.), *Memorial History of Hartford County, 1633-1884* (2 vols.), Boston, 1886, Vol. II, pp. 526, 527; Vol. I, 114, 115.

4. S. G. Goodrich, *Recollections of a Lifetime* (2 vols.), New York and Auburn, 1857, Vol. I, p. 436.

5. Pease and Niles, *Gazetteer*, pp. 13, 45.

6. Trumbull (ed.), *Hartford*, Vol. I, pp. 554, 598, 602.

7. *Ibid.*, pp. 593, 594.

8. Welles, MS, "Reminiscences of Hartford," WP-LC.

9. Gordon S. Haight, *Mrs. Lydia Huntley Sigourney, the Sweet Singer of Hartford*, New Haven, 1930, pp. 34-40.

10. Welles to Mitchell, Aug. 1825, WP-LC.

11. Assignment of Bowles and Francis to John Francis and John M. Niles, July 1, 1824, WP-CHS; Trumbull (ed.), *Hartford*, Vol. I, pp. 616, 617. Welles contributed some financial support to prevent it, as Welles wrote later, "from passing into the hands of those who were friendly to the new [Adams] administration." *Hartford Times*, Mar. 23, 1835.

12. Gurdon W. Russell, *Up Neck in 1825*, Hartford, 1890, p. 37; Welles entry in H. R. Stiles, *Genealogies and Biographies of Ancient Windsor Connecticut, 1635-1891* (2 vols.), Hartford, 1892, Vol. II, pp. 534, 535.

13. Caroline Robbins, *The Eighteenth-Century Commonwealthman*, Cambridge, Mass., 1959, pp. 115-25; Clinton Rossiter, *The Seed Time of the Republic*, New York, 1953, p. 141; John M. Niles (ed.), "Preface," in John Trenchard and Richard Gordon, *The Independent Whig*, Hartford, 1816.

14. J. M. Niles, MS Address before the Bay State Association, Boston, Mass., n.d., WP-CHS.

15. Stiles, *Genealogies*, p. 535; Pease and Niles, *Gazetteer*, pp. 13-16, 109.

16. Edward C. Kirkland, *Men, Cities and Transportation, A Study in New England History, 1820-1900* (2 vols.), New York, 1968, Vol. I, pp. 22, 12; Robert G. Albion, *The Rise of New York Port*, New York, 1939, p. 250.

17. Henry B. Stanton, *Random Recollections*, New York, 1887, pp. 9, 10.

18. Henry A. Mitchell to Welles, Feb. 10, 1825, WP-CHS.

19. Welles to Gideon Tomlinson, Jan. 1826; Welles to Samuel A. Foot, Jan. 23, 1826; Tomlinson to Welles, Jan. 14, 1826; Foot to Welles, Jan. 25, 1826; Welles to Foot, Feb. 1826, WP-LC; Welles to Henry Clay, May 12, 1826, WP-NYHS.

20. Welles to Mitchell, Mar. 1826, WP-LC.

21. Mary B. Cheney, *Life and Letters of Horace Bushnell*, New York, 1905, p. 13.

22. Frances M. Caulkins, *History of New London, Connecticut, from the First Survey of the Coast in 1612 to 1852*, Hartford, 1852, pp. 596, 597; John Hooker, *Reminiscences*, Hartford, 1899, pp. 185, 186.

23. Carlos Martyr, *William E. Dodge: The Christian Merchant*, New York, 1890, p. 32.

24. Charles C. Sellers, *Lorenzo Dow, the Bearer of the Word*, New York, 1928, p. 218; Thomas Jefferson to W. Short, 1820, in Saul K. Padover (ed.), *Thomas Jefferson on Democracy*, New York, 1946, pp. 119, 120.

25. Bernard Bailyn, *Education in the Forming of American Society*, Chapel Hill, 1950, p. 41; Sidney E. Mead, "Denominational: The Shape of Protestantism in America," *Church History*, Vol. 23 (1954), pp. 312-18.

26. William Tudor, *Letters on the Eastern States*, Boston, 1821, p. 393.

27. Michel Chevalier, *Society, Manners and Politics in the United States: Being a Series of Letters on North America*, Boston, 1839, pp. 317-19.

28. J. P. Mayer (ed.), *Alexis de Tocqueville, Journey to America*, New Haven, 1960, p. 150.

29. See, for example, Welles, MS fragment of an editorial for the *Hartford Times*, May 1826, WP-LC.

## CHAPTER 3

1. Welles to J. B. Horton, Feb. 15, 1828, WP-LC.

2. Frederic Hudson, *Journalism in the United States from 1690-1782*, New York, 1873, pp. 323, 325; Bayard Taylor, *Critical Essays*, New York, 1880, pp. 314-18.

3. Welles to Mitchell, Jan. 16, 1827, WP-LC; Robert V. Remini, *The Election of Andrew Jackson*, New York, 1963, p. 41. Donald B. Cole, *Jacksonian Democracy in New Hampshire, 1800-1851*, Cambridge, Mass., 1970, p. 67.

4. Welles, MS, "Historical Sketch of Political Parties in Connecticut," pp. 4-5, Learned Coll.

5. B. H. Norton to Welles, May 28, 1825, May 15, 1826; N. A. Phelps to Welles, May 21, 1826, WP-LC.

6. Alan W. Brownsword, "Connecticut Political Patterns, 1817-1826," unpublished doctoral dissertation, Univ. of Wisconsin, 1961, pp. 246-48.

7. *New York Times*, Aug. 27, 1872.

8. *Ibid.*

9. Welles, "Political Parties," p. 18, Learned Coll.

10. *Ibid.*, p. 19.

11. Joseph Barber to Welles, May 31, 1827, WP-LC.

12. *Ibid.*

13. David Plant to Welles, Dec. 22, 1826, Jan. 12, 1827; Orange Merwin to Welles, Dec. 13, Dec. 18, 1826; Jan. 7, 1827; Samuel Church to Welles, Feb. 5, 1827, WP-LC.

14. Welles to "My Dear Sir," Nov. 21, 1826, WP-LC.

15. Brownsword, "Connecticut Political Patterns," p. 252.

16. *American Mercury*, Feb. 27, 1827.

17. Two of the twelve senators elected were the caucus candidates, but two of the ten caucus candidates had also received county convention nominations. Brownsword, "Connecticut Political Patterns," p. 280.

18. *Hartford Times*, Apr. 16, 23, 1827.

19. Newton C. Brainard, *The Hartford State House of 1796*, Hartford, 1964, pp. 23, 48, 49; Tudor, *Letters on the Eastern States*, p. 393.

20. Joseph Barber to Welles, May 31, 1827, WP-LC.

21. Welles to Mitchell, June 26, 1827; Welles to B. H. Norton, Oct. 8, 1827; Samuel Simons to Welles, Dec. 8, 1828; Welles to Barber, June 1827; Obediah Beardsley to Welles, June 14, 1827, WP-LC.

22. Andrew Judson to Welles, July 9, 1827, WP-LC.

23. *Connecticut Courant*, July 23, 1827.

24. Welles to Mitchell, Feb. 11, Jan. 16, 1827, Welles, MS Diary, May 21-Aug. 8, 1827, WP-LC.

25. *Ibid.*, pp. 2, 5, 8, 10, 15. Samuel Colt, then living in Paterson, New Jersey, was one of the six.

26. Welles to James A. Jones, Aug. 20, 1827, WP-LC.

27. He may have sympathized with Carey, who had been driven from the convention by an intrigue of Charles Jared Ingersoll. Jonathan Roberts, "Memoirs of a Senator from Pennsylvania," *Pennsylvania Magazine of History and Biography*, Vol. 62, No. 4, Oct. 1938, p. 508; Welles, MS Diary, n.d. (1827), p. 14, WP-LC.

28. N. Starr to Welles, Nov. 30, 1827; William Vandeusen to Welles, Dec. 7, 22, 1827; Abiel Loomis to Welles, Jan. 4, 11, 1828, WP-LC.

29. Welles to Church, Dec. 13, 1827, WP-LC.

30. *American Mercury*, Mar. 2, 1828.

31. Welles to George Merrick, Mar. 5, 1828, WP-LC; *Connecticut Courant*, Mar. 4, 11, 1828; Andrew Judson to Welles, Mar. 27, 1828, WP-LC.

32. *American Sentinel*, Apr. 16, 1828; Orange Merwin to Welles, Apr. 8, 1828, WP-LC.

## CHAPTER 4

1. Welles to Mitchell, May 6, 1828; I. W. Crawford to Welles, Apr. 14, 1828, WP-LC.

2. Possibly also Niles was a link because he supported William H. Crawford, Van Buren's candidate for President in 1824; Welles, "Historical Sketch," pp. 17, 18, Learned Coll.

3. Robert Fairchild to Welles, June 23, 1828, WP-LC.

4. Andrew Judson to Welles, June 14, 1828, WP-LC; Brownsword, "Connecticut Political Patterns," pp. 322, 325; *New England Weekly Review*, Oct. 12, 1829.

5. *Ibid.*, H. L. Ellsworth to Welles, Jan. 11, 1832, June 30, 1829, WP-LC.

6. R. R. Hinman to Welles, July 1, 1828, WP-LC.

7. *American Mercury*, Sept. 2, Oct. 21, 28, 1828; Feb. 3, 1829; Brownsword, "Connecticut Political Patterns," pp. 331, 332.

8. The amendment was approved by the people, but the vote was much closer than that of the presidential race. It carried by a majority of only 1600 votes. Brownsword, "Connecticut Political Patterns," p. 334.

9. Welles to Overton, July 7, 1827, WP-LC; *American Mercury*, Nov. 8, 1830.

10. Niles to Welles, Feb. 12, 1829, Feb. 17, 1829; John Russell to Welles, Feb. 17, 1829, WP-LC.

11. *New England Weekly Review*, Oct. 12, 1829.

12. Everett S. Stackpole, *History of New Hampshire* (4 vols.), New York, 1917, Vol. III, p. 95; John W. Moore (comp.), *Printers, Printing, Publishing and Editing*, Concord, N.H., 1886, p. 103; Hudson, *Journalism in the United States*, p. 272; Cyrus P. Bradley, *Biography of Isaac Hill of New Hampshire*, Concord, N.H., 1835, pp. 8, 9, 16; James Parton, *Life of Andrew Jackson* (3 vols.), 2nd ed. New York, 1861, Vol. III, p. 181; *New-York Tribune*, Mar. 24, 1851; V. J. Capowski, "The Making of a Jacksonian Democrat: Levi Woodbury, 1789-1831," unpublished doctoral dissertation, Fordham Univ., 1966, pp. 5-16, 21-24, 29, 30; "The Era of Good Feelings in New Hampshire: Gubernatorial Campaigns of Levi Woodbury, 1823-1824," *Historical New Hampshire*, Vol. XXI, No. 4, Winter 1966, pp. 5, 15, 24, 29; Welles, *Diary*, Vol. III, p. 304; Cole, *Jacksonian Democracy*, pp. 3-5, Ch. III, *passim*.

13. Parton, *Life of Andrew Jackson*, Vol. III, p. 182.

14. Connecticut *Mirror*, Feb. 7, 1829; Samuel Simons to Welles, Mar. 7, 1831; I. W. Crawford to Niles, July 5, 1832, WP-LC; Niles to Timothy Pitkin, July 20, 1828, WP-HL.

15. Welles to Stiles Nichols, Dec 10, 1828, WP-LC.

16. Welles to Erastus Smith, Dec. 16, 1828; William Boardman to Welles, Dec. 25, 1828; Robert Fairchild to Welles, Dec. 26, 1828; Welles to Boardman, Jan. 1, 1829, WP-LC.

17. *New London Gazette*, Mar. 18, 1829; *American Mercury*, Aug. 16, 1830, Jan. 27, 1829.

18. *American Mercury*, Jan. 27, 1829.

19. Welles to Boardman, Jan. 1, 1829, WP-LC.

20. *Middletown Gazette*, Jan. 14, 1829.

21. Norton to Welles, Jan. 19, 1829, WP-NYPL; Norton to Welles, Jan. 10, 1829, WP-LC.

22. ["Perley"] Poore, *Perley's Reminiscences of Sixty Years in the National Metropolis* (2 vols.), Philadelphia, 1886, Vol. I, p. 41; Harriet Martineau, *Retrospect of Western Travel* (3 vols.), London, 1838, Vol. I, p. 237; Welles, MS Diary, June 20, 1846, WP-HL.

23. Welles to Niles, Feb. 12, 1829; Isaac Hill to Niles, Jan. 29, 1829, WP-LC.

24. Martineau, *Retrospect*, Vol. I, p. 258.

25. Welles to Niles, Feb. 9, 1829, WP-LC; E. A. Cohen and Co., *A Full Directory*

*for Washington City, Georgetown and Alexandria,* Washington, D.C., 1834, p. 4; Constance Green, *Washington Village and Capital, 1800-1878,* Princeton, N.J., 1962, p. 102; William Stickney (ed.), *Autobiography of Amos Kendall,* New York, 1872, pp. 287-88.

26. Welles to Niles, Feb. 9, 1829, WP-LC.
27. *Ibid.*
28. *Ibid.*
29. *Ibid.,* Feb. 10, 1829; Niles to Welles, Feb. 6, 10, 12, 25, 1829, WP-LC.
30. *National Intelligencer,* Feb. 17, 1829; Stickney (ed.), *Amos Kendall,* p. 288.
31. Welles to Niles, Feb. 12, 1829, WP-LC.
32. *Ibid.,* Feb. 20, 1829; Welles to "Dear Sir," Feb. 1829, WP-LC.
33. Niles to Welles, Mar. 3, 1829; Welles to Niles, Mar. 5, 1829, WP-LC.
34. *Ibid.,* Mar. 5, 1829.
35. Welles to Isaac Hill, Mar. 25, 1829, Isaac Hill papers, NHHS.
36. Niles to Welles, Mar. 3, 1829, WP-LC.
37. George Goodwin to David Daggett, Apr. 15, 1829, Daggett papers, Sterling Library, Yale; *Connecticut Courant,* Apr. 28, 1829.
38. David Henshaw, Nathaniel Greene, and others to Jackson, Mar. 12, 1829, WP-LC.
39. Despite letters from Ellis and others pleading with them to watch over Connecticut appointments. Ellis to Welles, Apr. 14, 1829, WP-LC.
40. Isaac Hill to Niles, May 9, 1829, WP-LC.
41. H. L. Ellsworth to Niles, Apr. 20, 1829, WP-LC; *Connecticut Mirror,* Apr. 24, 1829; *American Mercury,* Apr. 28, 1829; Duff Green came to Norton's aid, however, by securing him an appointment in the Boston Customs House. There, he soon became a member of David Henshaw's clique and for the next year boosted Calhoun's stock. Hudson, *Journalism in the United States,* p. 308.
42. George Goodwin to David Daggett, Apr. 29, 1829, Daggett papers, Sterling Library, Yale; William H. Ellis to Welles, Apr. 27, 1829; B. L. Rayner to Welles, May 8, 1830, WP-LC.

CHAPTER 5

1. *Hartford Times,* Oct. 26, 1829; *New England Weekly Review,* Oct. 19, Dec. 29, 1829; *New Haven Palladium,* Dec. 5, 1829; *American Sentinel,* Mar. 10, 1820.
2. Stiles Nichols to Welles, Dec. 23, 1829, WP-LC.
3. William Ellis to Welles, Jan. 2, 1830, WP-LC.
4. Niles to Welles, Nov. 8, 14, 1829, WP-LC.
5. Welles to Hill, Apr. 24, 1830, WP-LC; Green asked Welles to sound out Van Buren on this proposition. *Hartford Times,* Apr. 18, 1831.
6. William L. Storrs to R. S. Baldwin, Dec. 30, 31, 1829, Baldwin Family papers, Sterling Library, Yale.
7. Welles to Duff Green, Jan. 6, 1830, in *Connecticut Courant,* June 21, 1831.
8. John Spencer Bassett (ed.), *Correspondence of Andrew Jackson* (7 vols), Washington, D.C., 1926-35, Vol. IV, 1829-32, pp. 235, 236.
9. Isaac Hill to Welles, Apr. 20, 1830; Welles to Hill, Apr. 24, 1830, WP-LC.
10. Isaac Hill to Welles, May 7, 1830, WP-LC. Hill suggested that if Welles needed corroboration, he write Senators Rowan and Grundy, Representative Hubbard of New Hampshire, and Colonel David Brodhead of Boston.
11. *Ibid.,* Niles to Welles, May 24, 1830, WP-LC.
12. *Hartford Times,* June 1, 1830.
13. Stickney (ed.), *Amos Kendall,* pp. 371, 372; Welles to Kendall, n.d. (1831), WP-CHS.
14. William Ellis to Welles, Jan. 20, 1830, WP-LC.
15. Welles to Van Buren, Dec. 27, 1830, VBP-LC; Van Buren underlined Welles' exressions of support, and his account of the Green conversation.

16. Welles to Phelps, n.d. (1831), WP-LC; Welles to "Dear Sir," Jan. 1831, H. B. Learned Coll. This is an undated draft of the letter which acknowledges receipt of Kendall's letter of Jan. 24, 1831; Amos Kendall to Welles, Jan. 24, 1831, WP-LC; Welles to Kendall, Feb. 3, 1831; Kendall to Welles, Mar. 10, 1831, WP-CHS.

17. Kendall to Welles, Feb. 21, 26, 1831, WP-LC.

18. *United States Telegraph,* Feb. 25, 1831; *Connecticut Herald,* Mar. 8, 1831.

19. Jonathan Harvey to Welles, Mar. 6, 1831, WP-CHS; Kendall to Welles, Mar. 8, 10, 14, 19, 1831, WP-LC.

20. Kendall to Welles, Mar. 10, 14, 19, 1831, WP-LC.

21. *Washington Globe,* Apr. 6, 1831; Duff Green to Welles, Apr. 6, 1831, WP-LC.

22. It is possible that Kendall did not know of this decision. At any rate, he thought the course "questionable," fearing that Branch, Berrien, and Ingham, Calhoun's supporters in the Cabinet, would do more damage outside the administration than within it. Kendall to Welles, Apr. 23, 1831, WP-LC.

23. William B. Lewis to Welles, Apr. 7, 1831; Kendall to Welles, Apr. 8, 1831, WP-LC.

24. Kendall to Niles, Apr. 10, 1831, WP-LC.

25. Welles to Duff Green, Apr. 13, 1831, Mar. 31, 1830, WP-LC. *United States Telegraph,* Apr. 14, 1831.

26. Kendall to Welles, Apr. 15, 1831, WP-LC; Jackson to John Coffee, Apr. 24, 1831, in Bassett (ed.), *Correspondence of Andrew Jackson,* Vol. IV, pp. 263, 264; Welles to Noah Phelps, n.d. (1831); Noah Phelps to Welles, Apr. 16, 1831, WP-LC; *Hartford Times,* Apr. 18, 1831.

27. Possibly the Cabinet resignation had been delayed until Jackson and Van Buren were satisfied that the Welles-Green affair would not reveal Calhoun in a martyr's role. Eaton's letter of resignation had been dated April 7, Van Buren's April 11; The President replied to Eaton's resignation on April 8, but asked that his departure be deferred until a successor could be obtained. He replied to Van Buren on April 12, again requesting he stay in office until a successor was appointed. Berrien resigned on April 15, Ingham on April 19, Branch on April 22. Parton, *Life of Andrew Jackson,* Vol. III, pp. 347-58. The *Globe* made the initial announcement on Apr. 20, 1831; Kendall to Welles, Apr. 23, 1831, WP-LC.

28. *New England Weekly Review,* Apr. 25, 1831.

29. See for example, editorial comment on Welles, *New York Courier,* Apr. 22, 1831; "Richmond Whig" in *National Intelligencer,* May 2, 1831. Almost every paper in the country reprinted the articles in the *Globe* and the *Telegraph* in which Welles was prominently mentioned and quoted.


CHAPTER 6

1. William A. Smith, *Secondary Education in the United States,* New York, 1932, pp. 26, 27; see also Bernard C. Steiner, *The History of Education in Connecticut,* Bureau of Education Circular, No. 2, Washington, D.C., 1893, pp. 48-50. The district schools were in a state of neglect. Since the state had acquired a school fund from its sale of lands in the Western Reserve, towns had come to depend on the income from this capital for the support of common schools, rather than taxing themselves. *New England Weekly Review,* Apr. 13, 1829; Elihu Burritt, *Thoughts and Things at Home and Abroad . . . with a Memoir by Mary Howitt,* Boston and New York, 1854, pp. XIV, XVIII.

2. Lorain T. Pease to Niles, Dec. 28, 1835, WP-LC; Randall Stewart (ed.), *Nathaniel Hawthorne, the American Notebooks,* New Haven, 1932, p. 71.

3. Members of the old Federalist party would have agreed. Writing to David Daggett in early 1835, Theodore Frelinghuysen said, "I have no doubt my dear sir that you have traced the mischief to its origin. Mr. Jefferson did, by his writing and conduct debauch the moral sentiment of the nation and we are groaning now under the

dreadful influence of his philosophy—as false in politics as it was then in morals."
Frelinghuysen to Daggett, Jan. 2, 1835, Daggett papers, Sterling Library, Yale.

4. *Hartford Times,* Oct. 20, 1834; Russell, *Up Neck,* p. 37.

5. See, for example, the career of Theodore Nelson Parmelee, a native of Branford,
Connecticut, two years younger than Welles, editor of the National-Republican, then
Whig journal *Middlesex County Gazette,* later Washington correspondent for James
Gordon Bennett's New York *Herald,* office-holder during the Tyler administration.
Parmelee to Woodbury, Dec. 1834, June 1835, LWP-LC; Parmelee to Van Buren,
Feb. 7, 1835, VBP-LC; Parmelee to Welles, Jan. 29, Feb. 6, 1835, WP-LC; Parmelee,
"Recollections of an Old Stager," *Harper's Magazine,* Aug. 1872-June 1874, *passim.*

6. In 1790 there were 75 post offices in the United States and 1875 miles of post
roads. In 1835 there were 10,770 post offices and 112,774 miles of postal routes. Hartford *Patriot and Democrat,* Dec. 3, 1836.

7. Samuel Kellogg to Niles, Dec. 15, 1835, WP-LC.

8. Mayer (ed.), *Alexis de Tocqueville, Journey to America,* p. 69; Niles to Welles,
Jan. 2, 1832, WP-LC.

9. J. J. Crittenden to David Daggett, Jan. 31, 1836, Daggett papers, Sterling Library,
Yale.

10. Welles, "Miscellaneous Sketches," p. 57, WP-CHS. During the so-called "panic"
session of the legislature, May 1834, the Whig majority removed 4 sheriffs, 10 county
judges, 22 probate judges, and 256 justices of the peace. *Hartford Times,* June 30,
1834.

11. Chevalier, *Society, Manners and Politics,* p. 317. R. I. Hinman, a Jacksonian
party man of Salem Bridge, wanted from $100 to $500 in the new gold coinage to be
circulated in Waterbury. "The Whigs say," he wrote Welles, "gold will never circulate and all that is said abroad by the Democrats is all nonsense." Hinman to Welles,
Aug. 28, 1834, WP-LC.

12. Jeremy Cross to Leffingwell, Feb. 18, 1828, Miscellaneous Connecticut papers,
NYPL.

13. William Ellis to Welles, Mar. 7, 1830; Welles to Niles, Feb. 16, 1829; Niles to
Welles, Jan. 4, 1830, WP-LC; *Hartford Times,* May 9, 1831; *American Mercury,* Jan.
23, 1832. William W. Andrews (ed.), *The Correspondence and Miscellanies of the
Hon. John Cotton Smith,* New York, 1847, p. 98.

14. Welles to Phelps, Apr. 1831. He also wrote a similar letter to Dr. Samuel
Simons. Welles to Simons, Apr. 3, 1831; Noah Phelps to Welles, Apr. 27, 1831,
WP-LC.

15. *Hartford Times,* May 9, 1831.

16. See, for example, "General Chauncey Whittlesey's Renunciation of Free Masonry and Appeal to the Public," pamphlet No. 3, Connecticut Anti-Masonic Tract
Association, Hartford, 1834, NYPL.

17. Bridgeport *Republican Farmer,* Nov. 3, 1830; Noah Phelps to Welles, Apr. 27,
1831; William Ellis to Welles, Mar. 20, 1830, WP-LC. Even Welles, who was not a
religious man in the accepted formal sense, recognized the sectarian bias of the
movement. Welles to Niles, Feb. 16, 1829, WP-LC. Commenting on the nomination
of William Wirt for President by the Anti-Masonic party, Welles asked in the
*Times:* "with equal propriety and justice might one expect an anti-Presbyterian, or
an anti-Methodist, or any other anti-nomination?" *Hartford Times,* Oct. 24, 1831.

18. It is probable that a bargain was struck to ensure Anti-Masonic support for
Clay. Nathan Smith, the Anti-Masonic candidate for U. S. Senator, was elected
largely by National Republican votes. Samuel Foot, an avowed Clay man and a candidate for re-election, received only 24 votes in the House to Smith's 123 on the
final ballot. *Hartford Times,* May 2, 1832. H. L. Ellsworth to Van Buren, Mar. 10,
1831, VBP-LC; *Hartford Times,* Aug. 20, 1832; "Proceedings of the State Convention
of the National Republican Young Men, Hartford, 1832," pamphlet, Sterling Library, Yale. The convention was held on Oct. 17, 18, 1832.

19. Niles had written Van Buren in February that "our cause is advancing slowly but surely . . . we have a tolerable prospect of success." Niles to Van Buren, Feb. 2, 1832, VBP-LC. In March he predicted "a good fight against the Claymen." Niles to Ingoldsby W. Crawford, Mar. 19, 1832, Crawford papers, Connecticut College; Niles to Welles, May 8, 1832, WP-LC.

20. *Middletown Gazette*, Nov. 28, 1832; the Jacksonians polled 11,001 votes in Connecticut, 12,824 votes in Massachusetts. *Connecticut Courant*, Nov. 15, 1832.

21. William S. Holabird to Welles, Nov. 28, 1832; Noah Phelps to Welles, Dec. 8, 1832; *Hartford Times*, Dec. 31, 1832; Niles to Welles, Jan. 31, 1832, Feb. 11, 1833; Zalmon Wildman to Welles, Mar. 28, 1833, WP-LC.

22. P. T. Barnum, *The Life of P. T. Barnum Written by Himself*, New York, 1855, p. 2.

23. Ellis wrote from New Haven that leading politicians were complaining secretly of "Hartford influence and *Times* dictation." Ellis to Welles, Jan. 1833. Noah Phelps, in Middletown, let it be known that he was displeased with the proposed congressional ticket, though he made no specific comments. Welles' partial draft of an article on Connecticut politics in 1833. Andrew Judson echoed the same sentiments from the eastern counties. Ellis to Welles, Jan. 12, 1833; Judson to Welles, Jan. 21, 1833; Niles to Welles, Jan. 31, 1832, WP-LC.

24. For Ellsworth's loss, see *House Exec. Doc.* 308, No. I, 22nd Cong., 1st sess., p. 977; *Connecticut Courant*, Oct. 29, 1827, Apr. 1, 1837.

25. Welles to the Democratic Delegates representing Districts No. 1, No. 2, and No. 3, Feb. 7, 1833; Noah Phelps to Welles, Feb. 8, 11, 1833, WP-LC; *Columbian Register*, Feb. 9, 1833; *Hartford Times*, Feb. 18, 25, 1833; *Middletown Gazette*, Feb. 27, 1833; *New Hampshire Patriot*, Feb. 25, 1833.

26. William Holland to Welles, Feb. 20, 1833, WP-NYPL.

27. Niles to Welles, Mar. 1, 1833. Welles was not surprised to learn, on March 16, that the Clay Democrats in New Haven would not support him either. William Ellis to Welles, Mar. 16, 1833, WP-LC; *Columbian Register*, Mar. 16, 1833. Welles lost to his old law mentor, William W. Ellsworth, by almost 3000 votes out of about 16,000 cast. He ran well only in Hartford County. *Connecticut Courant*. Apr. 23, 1833.

## CHAPTER 7

1. Nathaniel Hawthorne, *Passages from the American Notebooks*, Vol. XVIII, *Works* (22 vols.), Boston and New York, 1900, p. 272.

2. "William Leggett," *United States Magazine and Democratic Review*, Vol. VII, No. 25, Jan. 1840, pp. 6, 8, 16; William Cullen Bryant, "William Leggett," *ibid.*, July 1839, Vol. VI, No. 19, p. 22; Fitzwilliam Byrdsall, *History of the Loco-Foco or Equal Rights Party*, New York, 1842, pp. 15, 16, 98.

3. H. L. Ellsworth reported in 1832 that 10,841 men, women, and children were employed in factories. These and their dependents amounted to perhaps 15 per cent of the state's population. *House Exec. Doc.* 308, No. 1, 22nd Cong., 1st sess., p. 892.

4. John R. Commons *et al.* (eds.), *Documentary History of American Industrial Society* (10 vols.), Cleveland, Ohio, 1910-11, Vol. V, pp. 141-45, 176, 177. Richard Leopold, *Robert Dale Owen*, Boston, 1940, pp. 65-70. William Ellis to Welles, Nov. 25, 1830, WP-LC; *New London Gazette*, Dec. 8, 1830; A. M. Schlesinger, Jr., *The Age of Jackson*, Boston, 1945, pp. 151, 170.

5. *Connecticut Sentinel*, Apr. 14, 1830; William Ellis to Welles, Nov. 25, 1830; Thomas Mussey to Welles, Jan. 25, 1831; *American Mercury*, Dec. 27, 1830; Niles to Welles, Dec. 10, 22, 1830, WP-LC.

6. Niles to Welles, Dec. 22, 1830; Cole, *New Hampshire*, pp. 95, 96; Jonathan Harvey to Welles, Feb. 1, 1831, WP-LC.

7. Welles to Niles, Nov. 13, 1834; WP-LC; "Address of the State Convention, Mid-

dletown, Jan. 28, 1835, to the Democrats of Connecticut," pamphlet, New Haven, 1835, Sterling Library, Yale.

8. *Hartford Times,* Jan. 30, 1832, Oct. 21, 1833.

9. See, for example, Kendall to Welles, Sept. 13, 1830, WP-LC. Ellsworth also corresponded directly with Van Buren and Woodbury on the bank's policy of protecting its stockholders from state taxation. H. L. Ellsworth to Van Buren, Dec. 18, 1831, VBP-LC; H. L. Ellsworth to Woodbury, Nov. 16, 1831, LWP-LC; *Columbian Register,* Sept. 28, 1833.

10. Abraham Halsey to Duane, Sept. 24, 1833. Halsey signed the request as cashier, but the draft was in Niles' handwriting; Niles to Duane, Sept. 24, 1833. Letters from Banks, Apr. 1, 1833, through July 1, 1834, NA. Kendall to Niles, Oct. 2, 14, 1833, WP-CHS. Kendall advised that "with equal capital and charters those [banks] which are in hands politically friendly will be preferred." *Hartford Times,* Nov. 11, 1833.

11. As permitted by its charter. See Niles to Duane, Sept. 24, 1833, Letters from Banks, NA; Trumbull (ed.), *Hartford,* Vol. I, p. 341.

12. Roger S. Baldwin to Nathan Smith, Feb. 14, 1834, Baldwin Family papers, Sterling Library, Yale; Welles to William Patton, Mar. 12, 1834, WP-HL.

13. Nathan Smith to David Daggett, Mar. 1834, Daggett papers, Sterling Library, Yale; W. W. Ellsworth to Timothy Pitkin, Mar. 14, 1834, Pitkin papers, HL. The vote: National Republicans, 18,411; Jacksonian Democrats, 15,884; Anti-Masons, 2398.

14. Charles Arnold to Welles, Apr. 20, 1834, WP-LC; *Columbian Register,* May 31, 1834, June 7, 1834; *Hartford Times,* June 9, 1834. For statistics, see Ch. 6, n. 10, above.

15. M. A. DeWolfe Howe, *Life and Letters of George Bancroft* (2 vols.), New York, 1908, Vol. I, pp. 224-25.

16. Both Phelps and Welles congratulated Woodbury on his appointment. On Welles' letter, the new Secretary wrote: "same answer as to Mr. Phelps." Welles would have been shaken if he had known that he stood no higher than Phelps in Woodbury's judgment. Welles to Woodbury, July 2, 1834, LWP-LC.

17. *Columbian Register,* Oct. 18, 1834; Calvin Goddard to David Daggett n.d. (1834), Daggett papers, Sterling Library, Yale.

18. Trumbull (ed.), *Hartford,* Vol. I, p. 620; Schlesinger, *The Age of Jackson,* p. 129; *Hartford Times,* Oct. 27, 1834. John B. Eldridge to Blair, Aug. 29, 1833, BLP, Firestone Library, Princeton.

19. Douglas' disclaimer at the first meeting of National Trades Union, in late March 1834, that the workingmen were "neither disciples of Jacksonism nor Clayism, Van Burenism nor Websterism, nor any other ism but Workeyism," is more rhetorical than real. Earlier in his remarks he had not eschewed politics. "Every good man," he said, "was and ought to be so much of a politician as support measures calculated to increase the sum of human happiness." In his correspondence with Welles, he was quite emphatic that Jacksonian Democracy increased "the sum of human happiness." Commons *et al.* (eds.), *Documentary History,* Vol. VI, pp. 212, 213. Schlesinger, *The Age of Jackson,* pp. 193, 194.

20. Preston King to Welles, Mar. 12, 1832; Niles to Welles, May 22, 1832; Silas Wright to Niles, Sept. 24, 1832, WP-LC.

21. Ari Hoogenboom and Herbert Hershkowitz, "Levi Woodbury's 'Intimate Memoranda of the Jackson Administration," *Pennsylvania Magazine of History and Biography,* Vol. 92, Oct. 1968, pp. 507-15; Cole, *New Hampshire,* pp. 10, 51, 92-93; Kendall to F. P. Blair, Sr., June 24, 1830, BLP.

22. Reynolds Webb to Welles, Jan. 31, 1835, WP-LC.

## CHAPTER 8

1. John Fitch to Woodbury, July 12, 1836, Letters from Banks, NA; Welles to Hill, Feb. 19, 1834; Thomas Mussey to Welles, Jan. 25, 1836, WP-LC. Said Mussey, "You

and the *Times* office are engaged in the same kind of warfare as we have here—in fact since his Satanic Majesty old Nick has lost his empire over the Union, the petty imps are determined if possible to establish *regencies in the several states."*

2. Woodbury to Welles, June 30, 1834; LWP-LC; Niles to Crawford, Jan. 16, 1835; Crawford papers, Connecticut College; Niles to Welles, Dec. 10, 1830; Woodbury to Welles, Oct. 21, 1833; Welles to Van Buren, Mar. 5, 1835; Welles to "Dear Sir," Feb. 17, 1838, WP-LC.

3. Hill to Welles, Nov. 20, 1834, WP-LC.

4. *Hartford Times,* Dec. 20, 22, 1834, Byrdsall, *Loco-Foco,* pp. 44-45.

5. "Address of the State Convention, Middletown, Jan. 28, 1835, to the Democrats of Connecticut," pamphlet, Sterling Library, Yale. *Litchfield Enquirer,* Feb. 5, 1835. The *Times* office printed hundreds of petitions addressed to the county convention, protesting the nomination of "a recent convert" (Luther Loomis) or any man connected in any way with "banks" and "monopolies." These were widely circulated and were signed by hundreds of citizens. Petitions, dated Feb. 1835, WP-CHS; Niles to Cleveland, Feb. 10, 1835, WP-LC; Welles, in the *Times,* sniped constantly at the bank faction. See *Hartford Times,* Feb. 23, 1835, for example.

6. Ellis, by his own admission, was writing Hill at least once a week, and during one day, January 24, he received letters from James K. Polk, Congressmen Aaron Ward (a Van Buren stalwart), and Kendall—all anxious about the Connecticut election; Ellis to Welles, Jan. 24, 1835, WP-LC.

7. For addresses of the various notables in Washington during the 1830's, see E. A. Cohen and Company, *A Full Directory for Washington City, Georgetown and Alexandria,* Washington, D.C., 1834; Hill to Niles, n.d. (Jan.), Feb. 21, 1835; Hill to Welles, Mar. 3, 1835; Welles to Hill, draft, Feb. 1835, WP-LC.

8. *Ibid.;* Hill to Welles, Mar. 3, 1835, WP-LC.

9. Welles to Van Buren, Mar. 5, 1835, VBP-LC. He admitted to the Vice President that certain friends had sent in testimonials for him, among them Niles and ex-Governor Edwards. Henry W. Edwards to Niles, Feb. 12, 1835, WP-LC.

10. Levi Woodbury to Welles, Jan. 17, 1835, WP-LC.

11. *Ibid.,* Jan. 30, 1835; Silas Wright to Welles, Jan. 17, 1835; Ellsworth, who was in Washington, decided to mend a fence or two if he could. He would be happy, he said, to aid Welles in securing a government office if he took himself out of the congressional race. "He has his enemies and so have we all," Ellsworth wrote Niles, "but I do not think Mr. Welles has so many secret enemies as he imagines." Ellsworth to Niles, Feb. 8, 1835, WP-LC.

12. Niles to Welles, Jan. 3, 1837, WP-LC; *Hartford Times,* Mar. 2, 1835; Hartford *Patriot and Democrat,* Mar. 7, 1835; Welles to D. W. Bartlett, Oct. 11, 1837; Welles to Henry Ellsworth, Apr. 22, 1837; Ellsworth to Welles, May 20, 1837, WP-LC; *New Haven Palladium,* Mar. 28, 1835. Significantly, four of the Democratic nominees for state and congressional offices had been "old Federalists."

13. Charles Douglas to Welles, Apr. 12, 1835, WP-LC; Douglas to Welles, May 17, 1835, WP-CHS.

14. William Lyon MacKenzie, *The Life and Times of Martin Van Buren,* Boston, 1846; MacKenzie, *The Times and Opinions of Benjamin Franklin Butler, District Attorney for the Southern District of New York and Jesse Hoyt, Counselor at Law,* Boston, 1845, *passim;* Byrdsall, *Loco-Foco,* p. 20.

15. Welles to Cambreleng, Apr. 6, 13, 1835; Cambreleng to Welles, Apr. 15, 1835, WP-LC.

16. Niles, MS Address, Boston, n.d., WP-CHS.

17. Perry Smith's uncle Nathan was then serving as U. S. Senator from Connecticut, his cousin Truman was a leading Whig politician.

18. Henry W. Edwards to Welles, Apr. 29, 1835; William Ellis to Welles, Feb. 4, 1836, WP-LC.

19. Kendall to Niles, May 11, 1835, WP-LC.

20. Hill to Welles, May 14, 1835, WP-LC.

21. Welles to Van Buren, Apr. 27, 1835, Van Buren papers, LC; F. P. Blair, Sr., to Welles, May 1, 1835; Kendall to Niles, May 11, 1835, WP-LC. Welles wrote that "the great error of Gen'l Jackson was in permitting himself to be importuned into often very improper appointments . . . office-seeking and office-getting was becoming a regular business, where impudence triumphed over worth." Welles to Silas Wright, Apr. 27, 1838, VBP.

22. *Roll of State Officers and Members of the General Assembly of Connecticut from 1776-1881*, pp. 221-85, 462, 464-65.

23. *Hartford Times*, July 29, 1835. See Carl N. Degler, "The Loco-Focos: Urban Agrarians," *Journal of Economic History*, Vol. XVI, Sept. 1956, pp. 322-33.

24. Laws are in *Connecticut Courant, Hartford Times*, Hartford *Patriot and Democrat*, June-July 1835-37; for summaries of the 1835 session, *Columbian Register*, June 13, 1835; *Hartford Times*, July 29, 1835.

25. In 1832, 496 children were employed. *House Exec. Doc.*, 308, No. I, 22nd Cong., 1st sess., pp. 984-87.

26. Hartford *Patriot and Democrat*, July 11, 1835.

27. Welles, MS, miscellaneous writings, 1836, WP-CHS.

28. Anon., "Remarks upon the Address of the Democratic Convention of October, 1838, to the People of Connecticut," pamphlet, Sterling Library, Yale.


CHAPTER 9

1. Toucey to Niles, Dec. 6, 1835, WP-CHS; Arthur G. Staples (ed.), *The Letters of John Fairfield*, Lewiston, Me., 1922, pp. 23, 25.

2. Welles to Edwards, Dec. 10, 1835; William Ellis to Welles, Dec. 1835; Edwards to Niles, Dec. 10, 1835, WP-LC.

3. William Ellis to Welles, Dec. 12, 1835, WP-LC.

4. *New England Weekly Review*, Jan. 16, 1836; William Holland to Van Buren, Nov. 13, 1835, Dec. 30, 1835; VBP-LC; Niles to S. B. Grant, Jan. 26, 1836; Niles to Welles, Feb. 5, 1836, WP-LC.

5. *Ibid.*, Jan. 9, 1836; Elisha Haley to John Russell, Jan. 5, 1836, WP-CHS; Niles to Welles, Jan. 27, 1836, WP-LC; West, *Welles*, pp. 54-55, quoting Silas Wright's version of Jackson's conversation.

6. Hartford *Patriot and Democrat*, Jan. 23, 1836; Albert Day to Niles, Dec. 28, 1835; Kellogg to Niles, Jan. 3, 1836, WP-CHS; Kendall to Jackson, Jan. 7, 1836, WP-LC.

7. *New Haven Palladium*, Jan. 9, 1836; William Ellis to Welles, Dec. 31, 1835; Ralph Ingersoll to Niles, Jan. 14, 15, 1836, WP-LC.

8. Thomas Mussey to Welles, Jan. 25, 1836; Silas Wright to Welles, Jan. 9, 1836; Hill to Welles, Jan. 12, 1836, WP-LC.

9. Hartford *Patriot and Democrat*, Jan. 9, 16, 23, 1836; *Litchfield Enquirer*, Jan. 14, 1836. Welles resigned his Comptrollership as soon as he was confirmed by the U. S. Senate. Welles to "Dear Sir," Jan. 13, 1836, WP-CHS; Niles to Welles, Jan. 27, 1836, WP-LC; Edwards to Welles, Jan. 29, 1836, WP-LC.

10. Hartford *Patriot and Democrat*, Jan. 30, 1836; Schlesinger, *The Age of Jackson*, pp. 149, 213; *Hartford Times*, Jan. 27, Feb. 1, 1836; Niles to Welles, Feb. 3, 1836, WP-LC.

11. Niles to Welles, Jan. 9, Feb. 5, 1836, WP-LC; *New England Weekly Review*, Jan. 9, 1836; *National Intelligencer*, Dec. 2, 1828.

12. Niles to Welles, Jan. 9, 1836, WP-LC.

13. *Ibid.*, Jan. 16, 1836, WP-LC.

14. *Ibid.*, Feb. 15, 1836, WP-LC.

15. Hill to Welles, Feb. 18, 1836, WP-LC; *Register of Debates in Congress*, Vol. 12, 24th Cong., 1st sess., pp. 554-63.

16. Niles to Welles, Feb. 19, 1836; Hill to Welles, Feb. 18, 1836; Henry Ellsworth to Niles, Feb. 22, 1836; Niles to Welles, Feb. 19, 1836, WP-LC.

17. *Ibid.*, Feb. 19, 1836.

18. *Ibid.*, Mar. 7, 16, 1836.

19. For Toucey's position on this and later fusion attempts, see Niles to Welles, Mar. 3, 16, 1836, Dec. 4, 1837; William Ellis to Welles, Apr. 24, 1836, WP-LC.

20. Significant aid did come from an unexpected quarter. In late April the Ingersolls, satisfied that Niles would be elected, decided to discipline the *Register*. Barber was required to accept as his editorial associate his nephew Minott Osborne—at the time a Loco-Foco. William Ellis to Welles, Jan. 30, Apr. 27, 1836, WP-LC; *New Haven Register*, Jan. 30, 1836; *Litchfield Enquirer*, May 12, 1836. The vote: Niles, 121; W. W. Ellsworth, 57; Andrew Judson, 11; scattering, 13; *ibid.*; Niles to Welles, Mar. 7, May 14, 1836, WP-LC; *Litchfield Enquirer*, June 2, 1836.

21. William Ellis to Welles, May 26, 1836; Welles to Niles, June 11, 1836, June 10, 1836, June 23, 1836; Welles to Van Buren, June 9, 1837, WP-LC; *New Haven Palladium*, June 11, 1836.

22. Welles to "Dear Sir," Feb. 17, 1838; Niles to Welles, June 16, 1836, WP-LC.

23. Welles to Van Buren, June 9, 1837, WP-LC.

24. Welles, MS, "Miscellaneous Sketches," WP-CHS.


CHAPTER 10

1. Welles to R. C. Hale, Oct. 16, 1833, WP-LC.

2. Welles wrote an average of five to six letters a night, rarely less than two pages each, in his tiny, cramped hand; see account and receipt for board and room, Oct. 8, 1828, to Jan. 9, 1829, Samuel Welles papers, CSL; E. M. Pease to Welles, Oct. 20, 1832, WP-LC; W. H. Bell to Welles, n. d., WP-CHS.

3. *New England Weekly Review*, Mar. 21, 1831.

4. Welles to Whittier, July 28, 1831, WP-CHS; *Hartford Times*, July 25, 1831; Whittier to Welles, July 1831, WP-CHS; *Columbian Register*, July 23, 1831.

5. Trumbull, *Hartford*, Vol. I, p. 195. Oliver Walcott, Samuel Goodrich, and Thomas H. Seymour were also members. In 1828 Welles had been appointed a lieutenant of the 6th Regiment of Connecticut infantry. Gideon Tomlinson to Welles, May 20, 1828, WP-LC. Four years later he was promoted to Major of the 25th Regiment. By this time his military ardor had spent itself. Governor Peters accepted his resignation on Aug. 10, 1832; Welles to Peters, Aug. 5, 1832; Peters to Welles, Aug. 10, 1832, WP-LC.

6. E. M. Pease to Welles, Oct. 20, 1832; Samuel Kellogg to Niles. For their mutual interest in gardening, see Niles to Welles, Apr. 11, 1847; Welles to Hale, Nov. 17, 1833, WP-LC.

7. Welles to R. C. Hale, Oct. 16, 1832, WP-LC; West, *Welles*, p. 39; Mary Jane Hale to Welles, Apr. 20, 1833; Welles to R. C. Hale, July 3, 1833, WP-LC.

8. Silas Mix to Welles, June 15, 1833; Amos Kendall to Welles, May 11, 1833, WP-LC; Van Buren to Niles, Andrew Judson, William Ellis, and Welles, May 31, 1833, WP-CHS; *Hartford Times*, June 15, 1833.

9. Maunsell B. Field, *Memories of Many Men and Some Women*, New York, 1874, p. 56; See Fletcher Green "On tour with President Andrew Jackson," for a humorous account of the President's trip, *New England Quarterly*, Vol. 36, No. 2, June 1963, pp. 209ff; *Connecticut Courant*, June 24, 1833.

10. Andrew Fitch, partner in a Marseilles mercantile firm which handled a part of the Navy's foreign accounts, happened to be a witness to the Jacksonian celebration in Norwich. He wrote an unsolicited note to Woodbury thanking him for "your kind reception of this gentleman" (Welles) and how pleased all were at the "marked attention paid him by the President, Vice President and Secretary of State." Andrew Fitch, Jr., to Woodbury, July 16, 1833, LWP-LC; *Hartford Times*, July 1, 1833;

Welles to Reuben Hale, July 3, 1833, WP-LC; see also Hoogenboom and Hersh-kowitz, "Levi Woodbury's 'Intimate Memoranda,' " p. 514.

11. Welles to Hale, July 3, 1833, WP-LC.
12. *Ibid.*
13. *Ibid.*
14. *Ibid.*, Nov. 6, 1833.
15. *Ibid.*
16. *Ibid.*
17. *Ibid.*, Nov. 6, 25, 1833.
18. *Ibid.*, Nov. 6, 25, 1833.
19. *Ibid.*, Nov. 6, 25, 1833.
20. R.C. Hale to Welles, Nov. 25, 1833, WP-LC.
21. Welles to Hale, Nov. 17, 25, 1833.
22. *Ibid.*, Dec. 11, 14, 1833.
23. *Ibid.*, Dec. 2, 1833; to "My Dear Aunt and Friends," Dec. 4, 1833.
24. Welles to Hale, Dec. 14, 1833.
25. *Ibid.*, Jan. 6, 9, 14, 1834.
26. Hale to Welles, Jan. 25, 1834; Welles to Hale, Apr. 1, 1834, WP-LC.
27. Welles to Hale, Apr. 1, 1834.
28. *Ibid.*, May 9, July 6, 1834, Jane Hale to Welles, June 28, 1834, WP-LC.
29. Welles to Hale, Aug. 20, 1834, WP-LC.
30. Welles to Niles, Nov. 13, 1834, WP-LC.
31. Henry H. Kinne to Welles, Dec. 4, 1834; see Welles' suggested obituary to Niles in which he says his father acquired "a very handsome property." Welles to Niles, Nov. 13, 1834, WP-LC. Last Will and Testament of Samuel Welles, Probate Records, Hartford County, CSL; see *Connecticut Courant,* July 20, 1835, for announcement of Welles' marriage.

## CHAPTER 11

1. *Connecticut Courant,* July 27, 1835.
2. Mary Welles to Jane Hale, Mar. 1, 1836, Sept. 18, 1837, Sept. 21, 1840, WP-CHS; Welles purchased a home at No. 8 Welles Ave.; Isaac N. Boles, *New Directory and Guidebook for the City of Hartford,* Hartford, 1842, p. 69. For a sketch of Burr and his connection with the *Times,* see Marcus A. Casey, "A Typographical Galaxy," in *Connecticut Quarterly,* Vol. II, No. 1, Jan.-Mar. 1896, pp. 34, 35; see also William F. Henney, *Commonwealth of Connecticut,* Hartford, 1906, pp. 65-68.
3. *Register of Debates,* 24th Cong., 2nd sess., p. 163; Welles to Silas Wright, Jan. 11, 1837, WP-LC.
4. *Hartford Times,* Dec. 10, 1836.
5. Charles Douglas to Welles, Dec. 9, 1836, WP-LC. For complete reporting of the debates over distribution, see *Connecticut Courant,* Dec. 31, 1836.
6. Giles Mansfield to Welles, Dec. 9, 1836; Peleg Cone to Welles, Dec. 17, 1836, WP-LC.
7. J. M. Morse, "Under the Constitution of 1818, the First Decade," Connecticut Tercentenary Publications, No. 17, New Haven, 1933, pp. 10, 11. For debate, see *Connecticut Courant,* May-June 1837.
8. Colin A. Ingersoll to Van Buren, June 21, 1837, VBP-LC. Ingersoll to Woodbury, June 26, 1837; Woodbury to Ingersoll, June 30, 1837, LWP-LC.
9. Niles to Welles, Jan. 25, June 11, 1837, May 1, 1836, Feb. 17, 1837, WP-LC.
10. Charles Douglas to Welles, Nov. 22, 1836, WP-LC.
11. Niles to Welles, May 1, 1836; Loraine T. Pease to Welles, Mar. 8, 1837; Niles to Welles, Mar. 10, 1837, WP-LC.
12. Welles to Wright, Jan. 11, 1837, WP-LC.
13. Niles to Welles, Feb. 17, 1837, WP-LC.

14. J. C. Smith to Welles, May 15, 1837, WP-LC.

15. Welles to Mary Welles, May 30, 1837, WP-LC. A typical Van Buren dinner is described by John Fairfield in Staples (ed.), *Fairfield Letters*, p. 81; Welles to "Dear Sir," June 13, 1837, WP-LC; Welles to Van Buren, June 9, 1837, VBP-LC.

16. *Ibid.*, June 9, 1837; to "Dear Sir," June 13, 1837, WP-LC.

17. *Ibid.*, June 13, 1837; Van Buren to Niles, June 10, 1837, WP-LC; Niles to Van Buren, July 1, 1837, VBP-LC.

18. Hartford *Patriot and Democrat*, June-July 1837; *Washington Globe*, July 22, 1837.

19. Welles to Van Buren, July 24, 1837, VBP-LC; Niles to Welles, Sept. 5, 1837, WP-LC.

20. F. P. Blair, Sr., to Jackson, Oct. 1, 1837, in Bassett (ed.), *Correspondence of Andrew Jackson*, Vol. VI, pp. 513, 514.

21. On Oct. 11, 1837, for instance, Niles attacked paper currency as a swindle. "The creation of currency," he declared, "belongs to the sovereign power of the state and could not" safely be entrusted to individuals. Money was the standard of value, "by which property and contracts are governed." The Constitution clearly reserved this right to the legislative branch of the federal government and specifically defined it in Article I, section eight. "It is as important," he told his fellow Senators, "that we have a uniform standard of value, as it is that we have a uniform standard of weights and measures." *Congressional Globe*, 25th Cong., 1st sess., p. 125, Appendix, p. 193; Van Buren, "Third Annual Message," Dec. 2, 1839, James D. Richardson (comp.), *Compilation of the Messages and Papers of the Presidents, 1789-1897*, 20 vols., Washington, D.C., New York, 1907-16, Vol. IV, p. 1762.

22. Niles to Welles, Sept. 30, Oct. 3, 14, 1837, WP-LC.

23. Welles, "Recollections of Governor William L. Marcy," Learned Coll.; Ivor D. Spencer, *The Victor and the Spoils, a Life of William L. Marcy*, Providence, R.I., 1959, pp. 91-93.

24. Niles to Welles, Sept. 30, 1837, Dec. 4, 6, 1837; William Ellis to Welles, Dec. 26, 1837, WP-LC.

25. Niles to Welles, Apr. 14, 1838; Niles to Welles, n.d. (1838), WP-NYPL; Hartford *Patriot and Democrat*, Apr. 7, 1838; Niles to Welles, Apr. 6, 1838, WP-LC.

26. *Ibid.*, Sept. 11, 1837; Orrin Holt to Welles, Jan. 18, 1840, WP-NYPL; W. V. Pettit to Welles, Apr. 7, 1838, WP-LC.

27. Niles to Welles, Apr. 9, 11, 1838.

28. Woodbury to Andrew Jackson, June 4, 1837, Jackson papers, LC; Silas Wright to Welles, Apr. 24, 1838; Welles to Wright, Apr. 27, 1838, WP-LC. Henry Ellsworth to Welles, Mar. 22, 1838, WP-LC.

29. Niles to Welles, May 1, 1838; Calvin Day to Welles, Jan. 10, 1839, WP-LC; F. P. Blair, Sr., to Jackson, Dec. 23, 1838, Jackson papers, LC; Jackson to Blair, Jan. 5, 1839, Blair Family papers, LC.

30. Capowski, "The Making of a Jacksonian Democrat," p. 192; Niles to Welles, May 27, 29, 1839; Welles to Mary Welles, June 14, 1839, WP-LC.

31. Van Buren may have offered him the Land Office. After the party defeat the previous year, Niles thought the President might offer him "a second grade appointment." He had written Welles at the time that "if he has such an opinion, I do not care how soon he is deceived. . . . I shall accept none unless I think it such, as I am entitled to & as is due to the State." Van Buren wrote Woodbury in September 1839, stating that "the discord in the Land Office is personally troublesome . . . and must be put an end to." He suggested the incumbent be removed and the position offered to Niles. Van Buren to Woodbury, Sept. 1, 1839, LWP-LC.

32. J. C. Smith, Jr., to Welles, Feb. 9, 1839, WP-LC; Welles to Cleveland, Mar. 16, 1840, Simmes Coll., Houghton Library, Harvard; J. C. Smith, Jr., to Welles, Apr. 13, 1840, WP-CHS.

33. William Ellis to Welles, Mar. 23, 1840, WP-LC; Niles to Van Buren, Apr. 8,

1840, VBP-LC; Hartford *Patriot and Democrat,* Apr. 11, 1840; Charles F. Lester to Welles, Apr. 23, 1840, WP-LC.

34. Welles to Niles, May 1840. The independent treasury bill became law on July 4, 1840. Niles to Welles, Mar. 25, 1839; Welles to Van Buren, Mar. 10, 1840; Niles to Welles, May 27, 1839, WP-LC.

35. Van Buren to Welles, May 17, 1843, WP-LC.

36. Niles to Van Buren, May 12, 1840. He acknowledged receipt of Van Buren's letter dated May 9, 1840; Kendall to Van Buren, May 9, 1840; Niles to Van Buren, May 12; Van Buren to Kendall, May 15, 1840, VBP-LC.

37. Niles to Welles, May 30, 1840; Welles to Niles, Aug. 1840, WP-LC.

38. Kendall to Niles, Aug. 9, 1840; Kendall to Welles, Aug. 13, 1840, WP-LC.

39. Niles to Welles, Aug. 12, 1840, WP-LC. Niles was especially irritated at Rives' mark-up on printed speeches and other campaign documents. On one such series in which the Postmaster General was interested, he discovered Blair and Rives were charging 100 per cent more than could be obtained elsewhere.

40. *Ibid.,* Aug. 12, Sept. 24, 1840, WP-LC.

41. Welles to Van Buren, Mar. 10, 1843; Niles to Welles, Sept. 24, 1843; Van Buren to Welles, May 17, 1843, WP-LC.

42. *Hartford Times,* July 18, 1840.


CHAPTER 12

1. Welles to Elias Hale, Dec. 5, 1839, WP-CHS; MS Diary, Oct. 16, 1843, WP-LC, *passim;* West, *Welles,* p. 20; Dr. G. N. Taft to Welles, July 6, 1844, WP-LC.

2 Staples (ed.), *Fairfield Letters,* pp. 355, 360, 361.

3. Niles to Welles, Dec. 7, 1844, WP-LC.

4. *Ibid.,* Dec. 12, 1844.

5. *Ibid.,* Dec. 14, 1844. He did write a long, persuasive letter in Welles' behalf to Polk and secured the signatures of the entire Democratic congressional delegation to back it up, but nothing came of it. Niles to Polk, Dec. 18, 1844, Polk papers, LC.

6. Welles to Niles, Dec. 14, 1844; Welles, MS Diary, Aug. 22, 1841, WP-LC.

7. Welles to Pierce, Mar. 5, 1842, WP-LC.

8. Welles to Cleveland, Apr. 1842, WP-LC; Welles to T. H. Seymour, Feb. 24, 1844, Seymour papers, CHS.

9. Welles to Van Buren, Dec. 7, 1844; R. I. Ingersoll to Niles, Jan. 12, 1842; Welles to Van Buren, Aug. 1, 1843, WP-LC; Welles to Van Buren, Apr. 29, 1843, VBP-LC.

10. Welles entry, Stiles, *Windsor,* Vol. II, p. 534; Welles to Van Buren, June 13, 1843, VBP-LC.

11. Samuel D. Gross (ed.), *Lives of American Physicians and Surgeons,* Philadelphia, 1861, pp. 521-44; Amariah Brigham, *Influence of Religion on Health,* Boston, 1835, pp. 275, 292, 295, 324; Welles to Van Buren, Apr. 29, June 1, Aug. 1, 1843, VBP-LC.

12. Amariah Brigham to Welles, July 31, 1843, WP-LC.

13. *Ibid.,* Mar. 29, Apr. 24, 1844, Niles to Welles, Feb. 14, 26, Mar. 3, 13, 1844, WP-LC.

14. *Ibid.,* Mar. 13, 1844; Amariah Brigham to Welles, Mar. 29, 1844, WP-LC.

15. Welles to Mary Welles, Apr. 14, 1844, WP-LC.

16. *Ibid.*

17. A few days after he and Niles reached Washington, Welles learned that Smith was in town conferring with Jabez Huntington, Connecticut's Whig Senator, and other leading Whigs. W. S. Holabird to Welles, Apr. 10, 1844, WP-LC. On April 11, J. Watson Webb of the *New York Courier and Enquirer* wrote Willie Mangum, President of the Senate, demanding that he refuse to administer the oath to Niles. "Has a magistrate a right to administer an oath to a child of five years of age,"

asked the acerbic editor, "& if not has the presiding officer of a deliberate body a right to administer an oath to a lunatic?" Webb to Mangum, Apr. 11, 1844, in H. T. Shanks (ed.), *The Papers of Willie P. Mangum* (5 vols.), Raleigh, 1950-55; Vol. IV, p. 95. *New York Courier and Enquirer,* Apr. 15, 1844; *Litchfield Enquirer,* Apr. 10, 1844, *New Haven Paladium,* Apr. 16, 1844; Amariah Brigham to Welles, Apr. 29, 1844, WP-LC.

18. Richard Niles to Welles, Apr. 23, 1844, WP-LC.

19. *Ibid.,* Apr. 29, 1844; Simeon E. Baldwin (ed.), *Life and Letters of Simeon Baldwin,* New Haven, 1918, p. 473. Elizur Goodrich, who observed Niles on the Senate floor, thought him "mopish and depressed" but not "an idiot or deranged."

20. Amariah Brigham to Welles, Apr. 29, 1844, WP-LC.

21. Richard Niles to Welles, Apr. 30, 1844, WP-LC; Baldwin, *Baldwin,* p. 473.

22. Richard Niles to Welles, May 16, 1844, WP-LC.

23. See Welles, MS draft, Apr. 1843, opposing extradition of Thomas Dorr; Cleveland rejected it. Learned Coll.

24. H. D. Gilpin to Niles, June 29, 1842; Edmund Burke to Welles, March. 18, 1842, WP-LC; Welles to Van Buren, Apr. 29, 1843, VBP-LC. F. P. Blair, Sr., to Jackson, Dec. 22, 1844, Jackson papers, LC; Welles to Van Buren, Apr. 29, 1843, Dec. 7, 1844, VBP-LC.

25. *Ibid.,* Apr. 29, 1843.

26. *Ibid.;* Edmund Burke to Blair, Dec. 20, 1843. The conservatives of New Hampshire, working with Isaac Hill, wrote Burke: "Have put in nomination Mr. Calhoun for the Presidency and Mr. Woodbury for the Vice Presidency." BLP, Firestone Library, Princeton.

27. Edwin Stearns to Welles, July 13, 1843, WP-LC; Welles to Van Buren, June 13, 1843, VBP-LC.

28. *Ibid.;* Perry Smith to Welles, Aug. 4, 1843, WP-LC; John Danforth to Van Buren, June 14, 1843, VBP-LC.

29. Welles to R. I. Ingersoll, n.d. (1843), WP-LC; Silas Wright to Welles, Aug. 24, 1843, WP-CHS; Ingersoll to Welles, Sept. 30, 1843; Welles to Van Buren, Aug. 1, 1843, WP-LC.

30. *Ibid.,* Oct. 26, 1843; John Danforth to Levi Woodbury, Oct. 17, 1843, LWP-LC; Samuel J. Tilden to Welles, Mar. 21, 1844, WP-LC. The conservatives were beaten in the convention but they would vote against the regular ticket at the polls. Welles to Wright, Mar. 31, 1844, WP-LC. The Democrats gained about 1300 votes over the previous year, while the Whigs gained almost 4500. *Connecticut Courant,* Apr. 27, 1844.

31. Shanks (ed.), *Mangum,* Vol. IV, p. 92; Welles to Wright, May 1, 1844; to "Dear Sir" (Silas Wright), May 1, 1844; Welles to Van Buren, June 15, 1844, WP-LC; Wright to Butler, May 10, 1844, Silas Wright papers, NYPL.

32. For convention proceedings, see New York *Evening Post,* May 30, 1844; *National Intelligencer,* May 29, 30, 1844; Niles to Welles, May 24, 1844, WP-LC; Welles to Van Buren, Dec. 7, 1844, VBP-LC.

33. John T. Adams to Welles, Jan. 8, 1845; Welles to Niles, Jan. 26, 1845, Feb. 13, 1845, WP-LC; *Hartford Weekly Times,* Apr. 2, 1845; Niles to Welles, Feb. 16, 1845, WP-LC.

34. Welles to Van Buren, Feb. 20, 1845, VBP-LC.

35. Welles to Niles, April 21, 1845, WP-LC; Isaac O. Barnes to Woodbury, Feb. 18, 1838, LWP-LC.

36. Welles to Niles, Apr. 28, 1845, WP-LC.

37. Welles to Niles, Apr. 21, 25, 1845, WP-LC; Welles to Van Buren, Apr. 29, 1845, VBP-LC.

38. Niles to Welles, Dec. 8, 15, 1845, WP-LC.

39. *Ibid.,* Jan. 1, 1846. Referring to his conversations with the Secretary, Niles said that Bancroft "is greatly elated with the importance of his station & seems to

think he is the atlas on whose shoulders the destinies of the republic rest." *Ibid.,* Feb. 5, 1846.

40. *Ibid.,* Jan. 25, 28, 1846; Apr. 14, 1846; Welles to Bancroft, Apr. 8, 1846; MS Diary, Aug. 30, 1846, WP-LC.

## CHAPTER 13

1. Welles, MS Diary, Sept. 9, 1848, June 20, 28, 1846, WP-HL.
2. *Ibid.,* July 18, 1846.
3. James Hoppin, *Life of Andrew Hall Foote,* New York, 1874, p. 61.
4. Madeleine Vinton Dahlgren, *Memoir of John A. Dahlgren,* New York, 1891, p. 126.
5. Welles, MS Diary, July 18, 1846, WP-HL.
6. *Ibid.,* May 25, 1846.
7. *Ibid.,* June 19, Sept. 19, 1846.
8. Milo M. Quaife (ed.), *The Diary of James K. Polk* (4 vols.), Chicago, 1910, Vol. II, pp. 429-31. (Hereafter cited as Polk, *Diary.*)
9. See, for instance, Welles to Bancroft, June 8, 1846; John Y. Mason to Welles, Dec. 31, 1846; Welles to Mason, June 19, Aug. 4, Sept. 12, 1847, with endorsement; Bureaux Letters, NA; draft memo to Mason, n.d.; Welles, MS Diary, July 23, 1846, WP-HL.
10. Welles, MS Diary, n.d. (1847), May 23, 1846, WP-HL. It was a matter of principle to Niles; for years he had believed in protection as an incidence to revenue. He had written articles on the subject in 1832 and again in 1841 under the pen name "Colbert" in the *Hartford Times.*
11. "Report from the Secretary of the Treasury," *Senate Exec. Doc.,* Vol. II, 29th Cong., 2nd sess., pp. 9-11.
12. Welles, MS Diary, July 7, 1846, WP-HL.
13. *Ibid.,* July 9, 1846.
14. Niles to Welles, Nov. 12, 1848, WP-LC.
15. *Congressional Globe,* 29th Cong., 1st sess., Appendix, pp. 881, 1157.
16. Ernest P. Muller, "Preston King, A Political Biography," unpublished dissertation, Columbia, 1957, p. 227; *Congressional Globe,* 29th Cong., 1st sess., Appendix, p. 889; Welles to Van Buren, July 28, 1846, VBP-LC.
17. Welles, MS Diary, May 21, 1846, WP-HL.
18. *Hartford Times,* July 8, 1833; Welles to Leggett, Oct. 7, 1835, WP-LC. Welles' strong belief in individual rights, however, led him to defend John Quincy Adams' stand for the right of petition. He also opposed Amos Kendall's circular permitting Southern postmasters to open the mails in search of abolitionist materials; Welles to Burr, June 25, 1848, WP-LC.
19. Welles to Leggett, Oct. 7, 1835; Welles to Burr, June 25, 1848; Welles to Wright, June 21, 1836, WP-LC.
20. Niles to Welles, Feb. 9, 1845; Welles to Van Buren, Feb. 20, 1845, WP-LC.
21. Welles to Van Buren, July 28, 1846, VBP-LC; Welles, MS Diary, May 21, 1846, July 31, 1846, WP-HL.
22. Welles, MS Diary, May 17, 1848, WP-HL; "History of the Polk Administration," Alphabetical Series, WP-LC; Richard R. Stenberg, "The Motivation of the Wilmot Proviso," *Journal of American History,* Vol. XVIII, No. 4, Mar. 1932, pp. 535-40; Niles to Van Buren, Dec. 16, 1847, VBP-LC.
23. Burr was under heavy obligation to both Welles and Niles, who had made him proprietor of the *Times* and lent him the money to purchase it. *Connecticut Quarterly,* Vol. II, No. 1, Jan.-Mar. 1896, pp. 34, 35; Burr to Welles, Oct. 5, 1847; Norris Wilcox to Welles, July 23, 1846; W. J. Hammersley to Welles, Jan. 16, 1847, Burr to Welles, Sept. 11, 1846, Jan. 24, 1847; Welles, MS draft, July 1847; Welles to "My Dear Sir," July 31, 1846; Welles to Niles, Nov. 6, 1846; Welles to Burr, Jan. 27, 1847, WP-LC; *Congressional Globe,* 29th Cong., 2nd sess., pp. 530-32.

24. *Congressional Globe,* 30th Cong., 1st sess., Appendix, pp. 1197-1201. The bill with the Proviso attached passed the Senate by only two votes. Few Northern Democrats could be persuaded to join Niles in maintaining the free-soil position on the floor of the Senate. Dix, one of those who did speak out, found a singular lack of warmth for the Proviso among his colleagues. "Niles made an admirable speech on the Oregon bill," he wrote Azariah Flagg, early in the debate. Dix to Flagg, June 5, 1848, Flagg papers, Butler Library, Columbia. *Congressional Globe,* 30th Cong., 1st sess., Appendix, pp. 1141-43. For Lincoln on Dixon's speech, see Lincoln to Herndon, June 22, 1848, Lincoln papers, LC.

25. W. J. Hammersley to Welles, Feb. 26, 1847; A. E. Burr to Welles, Nov. 5, 1847, WP-LC; Welles to Niles, Sept. 9, 1847, WP-CSL; Burr to Welles, Aug. 31, 1847, WP-LC.

26. Welles, MS Diary, May 17, 1848, WP-HL.

27. *Ibid.,* n.d. (1848).

28. Preston King to Welles, Jan. 31, 1848; Welles to J. J. R. Pease, Feb. 3, 1848, WP-LC; Welles to Flagg, Feb. 4, 1848, Flagg papers, Butler Library, Columbia; Flagg to Welles, Feb. 17, 1848, WP-LC.

29. Welles to Van Buren, July 3, 1848, VBP-LC. Welles, MS Diary, May 22, 1848, WP-HL.

30. Welles to Van Buren, June 5, 1848, June 23, 1848, VBP-LC.

31. Niles to Van Buren, Dec. 16, 1847, VBP-LC.

32. Welles' drafts to Cochrane are all in Welles papers, Huntington Library. Final draft was posted July 13, 1848. On July 22 Welles was importuned again, this time by the Connecticut free-soilers. Niles had immediately identified himself with them, but Welles would not. A. M. Collins, E. H. Owen, Waterman Roberts, Committee, to Welles, July 27, 1848, WP-LC; Welles, MS Diary, Aug. 7, 1848, WP-HL.

33. Welles, MS Diary, Aug. 7, 1848; undated note (Aug. 1848), WP-HL. The Free Soil party, with its motley of Democrats, Whigs, and abolitionists, he thought was "too sudden an amalgamation of parties . . . to be effective."

34. Welles, MS Diary, Sept. 19, 1848, WP-HL; James Dixon to Welles, July 17, 1848; Samuel Kellogg to Welles, July 31, 1848, pp. 9-12, WP-LC.

35. Welles, MS Diary, Mar. 3, 1849, WP-HL; "Recollections of Governor William L. Marcy," pp. 9-12, Learned Coll.

## CHAPTER 14

1. Welles, MS Diary, June 4, 1849, WP-HL. Welles to Niles, Sept. 20, 1849, WP-LC.

2. Welles, MS Diary, Feb. 15, 1850, Oct. 17, 1850, WP-LC; J. H. Trumbull (ed.), *Hartford,* Vol. I, pp. 558, 559, 462; Increase N. Tarbox (ed.), *Diary of Thomas Robbins, D.D., 1746-1854* (2 vols.), Boston, 1886-87, Vol. II, pp. 950, 956.

3. Niles to Welles, June 10, 1849; Welles to Niles, Sept. 20, 1849; Norris Wilcox to Welles, Apr. 9, 1849; Niles to Welles, May 13, WP-LC; Welles, MS Diary, n.d. (Oct. 1849), WP-HL.

4. Welles to D. W. Bartlett, Oct. 11, 1857, Alphabetical Series, WP-LC; Burr to Welles, Nov. 30, 1847, Mar. 24, 1848, WP-LC. By then the President had narrowed the field to Governor Peter Vroom of New Jersey and to Toucey. Again he consulted with his Cabinet. It was now pointed out that Connecticut had received more than its just share of appointments, while New Jersey had been neglected. Convinced by this argument, Polk offered the position to Vroom, who declined. Polk, *Diary,* Vol. III, pp. 431, 468, 455.

5. John Bassett Moore (ed.), *The Works of James Buchanan, Comprising his Speeches, State Papers and Private Correspondence* (12 vols.), Philadelphia and London, 1908-11, Vol. VIII, pp. 362, 363. Welles, draft letter, probably to Preston King, July 19, 1848, WP-HL; Welles to D. W. Bartlett, Oct. 11, 1857, Alphabetical Series, WP-LC.

6. Welles to Burr, June 25, 1848; Welles to Cleveland, Nov. 3, Dec. 19, 1849; Welles to Van Buren, Jan. 2, 1850, WP-HL; Welles to Peleg Child, Dec. 4, 1849, WP-LC.

7. Welles to Cleveland, Feb. 27, 1850, WP-LC; Welles to "Dear Sir," Feb. 1850, WP-CHS; Welles to Cleveland, Feb. 27, 1850, WP-LC.

8. *New-York Tribune,* May 30, June 6, 24, 1850; Norris Wilcox to Welles, June 16, 1850, WP-LC.

9. Welles, MS Diary, Sept. 20, 1850; Welles to Babcock, Mar. 1855, WP-LC.

10. Welles, MS Diary, June 1851, Sept. 20, 21, 1850, Sept., Dec. 1851, Dec. 1852, Feb. 10, 1852, WP-LC.

11. Welles to Niles, Sept. 7, 1851; Welles, MS Diary, Sept. 20, 1851, WP-LC.

12. J. R. Lane, *A Political History of Connecticut During the Civil War,* Washington, D.C., 1941, pp. 34, 35; Cheyney, *Bushnell,* p. 247.

13. Welles to James F. Babcock, Mar. 14, 1855; Welles, "Sound Principles as Against Epithets," Mar. 1855, Alphabetical Series; MS Diary, Aug. 1851, WP-LC; Welles to Van Buren, July 23, 1851; Welles to Mary Welles, June 22, 1851; Welles, MS Diary, June 27, 1851, WP-LC. Eric Foner, *Free Soil, Free Labor, Free Men: The Ideology of the Republican Party Before the Civil War,* New York, 1970, p. 134.

14. A. E. Burr to Welles, Mar. 15, 1847, WP-LC; Welles, MS Diary, Sept. 1848, WP-HL; Welles to Van Buren, Sept. 18, 1848, WP-LC; Burr to Welles, June 23, 1848, July 24, 1848, WP-LC.

15. Welles to "Dear Sir," Oct. 22, 1851; Welles, MS Diary, Sept. 28, 1851, WP-LC.

16. Welles to King, Aug. 5, 1851; Welles to F. P. Blair, Sr., Oct. 5, 1851, WP-CHS; Welles to Samuel J. Tilden, Sept. 29, 1851, Tilden papers, NYPL.

17. John D. Baldwin to Niles, Sept. 19, 1851, WP-LC; Charles Sumner to Bigelow, Aug. 1852, in John Bigelow, *Retrospections of an Active Life* (5 vols.), New York, 1909-13, Vol. I, p. 127. Sumner regretted the fact that John Van Buren had entered the campaign. "Even Welles," wrote Sumner, "with whom he [Van Buren] has been speaking in New Hampshire, says he ought to have gone to Europe."

18. Welles to King, Sept. 9, 1851; see MS Diary, Sept. 28, 1851 (WP-LC) for an attempt by one of Douglas' managers to enlist Welles for his campaign. F. P. Blair, Sr., to Welles, Oct. 4, 1851, WP-LC; Welles to F. P. Blair, Sr., Oct. 1851, WP-CHS; Welles' arguments had so impressed Blair and Dix that both wrote Preston King, backing Houston for the nomination. King remained dubious about taking a candidate from one of the slave states. At this time Benton and Flagg were also supporting Houston. Preston King to Azariah Flagg, Oct. 1, 1851, Flagg papers, Butler Library, Columbia; Niles to Welles, Nov. 4, 1851; E. S. Cleveland to Welles, Nov. 1851, WP-LC. Burke was a former congressman from New Hampshire, Commissioner of Patents during Polk's administration, a close friend of Pierce, and briefly co-editor with "Father" Richie of *The Washington Union;* Burke to Welles, Nov. 5, 1851, WP-LC; James O. Lyford, *Life of Edward H. Rollins, a Political Biography,* Boston, 1906, pp. 47-48; Dix to Welles, Nov. 28, 1851; King to Welles, Dec. 6, 1851, WP-LC.

19. See correspondence of Jonathan D. Williams and Chauncey F. Cleveland to Welles, Dec. 1851-Mar. 1852, WP-LC; William E. Smith, *The Francis Preston Blair Family in Politics* (2 vols.), New York, 1933, Vol. I, p. 273; Welles, MS Diary, Jan. 1852, WP-LC.

20. King to Blair, Feb. 26, 1852, BLP, Firestone Library, Princeton; Sumner to Bigelow, Feb. 2, 1852, in Bigelow, *Retrospections,* Vol. I, p. 124; Colin M. Ingersoll to T. H. Seymour, Feb. 1852, Seymour papers, CHS; Norris Wilcox to Welles, Jan. 25, 1852, WP-LC; Welles to W. M. Pomeroy, Jan. 25, 1852.

21. Welles to "My Dear Sir," Mar. 1, 1852, WP-CHS; Lane, *Connecticut,* pp. 20-21; A. E. Burr to Welles, June 1, 1852, WP-LC.

22. King to Welles, June 12, 1852; Pettit to Niles, June 7, 1852; King to Welles, July 3, 1852, WP-LC; Charles Francis Adams (ed.), *Memoirs of John Quincy Adams* . . . (12 vols.), Philadelphia, 1874-77, Vol. XI, p. 226.

23. Welles to Franklin Pierce, June 5, 1852, Pierce papers, NHHS; to "My Dear Sir," June 15, 1852, WP-CHS.

24. Welles to Pierce, Dec. 20, 1852, WP-LC; Colin Ingersoll was emphatic in asserting that rather than "throw the Northern Democracy into the embrace of abolitionism . . . I am for war."

25. Isaac Toucey to Thomas H. Seymour, Jan. 14, 1853; C. M. Ingersoll to Seymour, Jan. 15, 1853, Seymour papers, CHS. Preston King to Welles, Jan. 21, 1853, WP-LC; Allan Nevins, *The Ordeal of the Union* (2 vols.), New York, 1947. Vol. II, pp. 46, 47; Roy F. Nichols, *Franklin Pierce, Young Hickory of the Granite Hills*, Philadelphia, 1931, pp. 228, 229; Smith, *Blair Family*, Vol. I, p. 289. Blair was one of the few free-soil Democrats who was disgruntled by Marcy's selection. Welles, MS Diary, Feb. 11, 1853, WP-LC.

26. Welles, MS Diary, Apr. 18, 27, 1853, WP-LC. Young Franklin Burr, a brother of the *Times* editor, whom Welles had placed as a clerk in the Pension Office, kept him informed with surprisingly accurate information on Pierce, gleaned from the lower echelons of officeholders. "He allows himself to be influenced too much by bluster and bravado on the part of those who are not his real friends," wrote Burr, "and has hitherto exhibited a vacillating indecision in relation to his appointments, . . ." F. Burr to Welles, Sept. 15, 1853, WP-LC.

27. Welles, "Memorandum," Oct.-Nov. 1853, WP-LC.

28. Welles to "Dear Sir," Feb. 17, 1854, WP-LC.


## CHAPTER 15

1. Nevins, *The Ordeal of the Union*, Vol. II, p. 150; *New-York Tribune*, June 3, 1854.

2. Welles, "Old Parties Are Dead—Principles Are Greater than Parties—but a Party Is Required," and Welles, "Politics, 1854," Alphabetical Series, WP-LC.

3. Welles, MS Diary, Oct. 16, 1853; Dr. F. A. Thomas to Welles, Oct. 31, Nov. 16, 1852, WP-LC; for a sketch of Hall, see Leslie Stephens and Sidney Lee (eds.), *Dictionary of National Biography* (21 vols.), London and New York, 1908-9, Vol. VIII, pp. 964-67; Welles, MS Diary, Oct. 28, Jan. 22, Dec. 31, 1853, WP-LC. The date of Anna Jane's death, as recorded in the family bible, was supplied by Thomas W. Brainard.

4. Theodore D. Bacon, *Leonard Bacon, a Statesman in the Church*, New Haven, 1931, p. 389. Both Toucey and Colin Ingersoll, who represented New Haven in the House, voted for the bill. *New-York Tribune*, May 31, 1854.

5. D. M. Seymour to T. H. Seymour, Mar. 8, Apr. 10, 25, 1854, Seymour papers, CHS.

6. Welles to James T. Pratt, Mar. 1854, WP-LC.

7. B. F. Butler to Welles, July 21, 1854; Henry B. Sanford to Welles, July 28, 1854, WP-LC; Eli Thayer does not list Welles among the directors of the New England Emigrant Aid Company, but Welles' friend Albert Day is so listed. Eli Thayer, *The Kansas Crusade*, New York, 1889, p. 53.

8. W. C. Bryant to Welles, July 17, 1855, WP-LC; John Bigelow, *William Cullen Bryant*, New York, 1899, pp. 104, 105.

9. King freely voiced his personal preferences in talks with Dr. Gamaliel Bailey, editor of Washington's abolitionist newspaper, *The New Era*, but he was most circumspect when it came to launching a campaign. Bailey wrote James Pike, the *Tribune* correspondent, on May 30, 1854, that King "would vote for anybody for President on a distinct anti-slavery issue—whether Seward, Benton, Hale, Houston . . . he suggested a ticket, Benton for President, Seward for Vice President." Bailey to Pike, May 30, 1850, in James S. Pike, *First Blows of the Civil War*, New York, 1879, p. 237; King to Welles, Jan. 10, 1855; Welles to Blair, July 8, 1854; Welles to

King, Sept. 14, 1854; King to Welles, Oct. 21, 1854; John Williams to Welles, Nov. 25, 1854, Jan. 4, 1855; Thomas S. Shankland to Niles, Dec. 3, 1854; Welles to Williams, Dec. 9, 1854; Welles to ' Dear Sir," unfinished draft, Mar. 1855, WP-LC.

10. The *Columbian Register* noted (Aug. 22, 1835) that the New Haven "federal whigs say they intend to have a new name—they mean to be called the *American* party, the main object of which shall be to alter the laws as to naturalized foreigners so that they would be ineligible to hold public office."

11. Cheyney, *Bushnell,* pp. 313, 314.

12. Comparison of election returns in Connecticut from 1835 to 1855 do not reveal the Democrats gaining any particular advantage, though they did attract a major share of the immigrant votes in the cities. Carroll J. Noonan, *A History of Nativism in Connecticut, 1829-1860,* Washington, D.C., 1938, *passim.*

13. Lane, *Connecticut,* p. 45; Edward Blake to S. E. Baldwin, July 1, 1854, Baldwin Family papers, Sterling Library, Yale; Noonan, p. 192.

14. Welles to King, Nov. 25, 1854, WP-LC.

15. Truman Smith to Welles, Dec. 19, 1854, WP-LC.

16. Welles, MS Diary, June 26, 1855, WP-LC.

17. In a letter to Thomas H. Seymour, Pratt displays the animus that was building up against Burr among administration Democrats. If this self-serving ex-congressman had not been so deadly serious, his bantering tone might have been taken for rustic wit. "Old Glastonbury went hindoo," he wrote Seymour, "with damned rascal Thad to lead off & *Gid the spy in the Times office* backing him up . . . those Welles are two as great rascals as state's prison can turn out." (Phrase in italics was underlined in original.) As for Niles, Pratt felt that "the old traitor . . . ought to have been left in a well at Pocquonnock," Pratt to Seymour, July 17, 1855, Seymour papers, CHS.

18. Welles, "An Old Democrat Leaves His Party and Gives His Reasons," Alphabetical Series, WP-LC; see also Welles, MS, "Parties in the U. S., 1857," WP-CHS.

19. Welles to James F. Babcock, Mar. 14, 1855; Welles, "Sound Principles as against Epithets"; "Free Soilers and Abolitionists Are Names Only—the Principles Behind Them Are Vital"; "Constitutionality of the Fugitive Slave Law and the Logical Position an Old Jeffersonian Democrat Should Occupy on that Question." Welles published the latter piece under the pseudonym, "States Rights Democrat." Alphabetical Series, WP-LC.

20. Welles to Babcock, undated draft (Mar. 1855), WP-LC. Welles was referring to John Minor Botts of Virginia. Welles, MS Diary, Sept. 19, 1848, WP-HL.

21. Welles, MS Diary, May 26, 1855, June 12-15, 1855, WP-LC; J. W. Schuckers, *Life and Public Services of Salmon Portland Chase,* New York, 1874, pp. 164-69; *Ohio Statesman,* June-July 1855, *passim.*

22. For example, Welles "sat with a man from Allegheny [sic] county, New York, violent Hunker, but whether Democrat or silver gray did not ascertain." Welles, MS Diary, June 2, 19, 26, 29, 1855, WP-LC.

23. *Ibid.,* July 3, 1855.

24. The legislature, dominated by a Whig Know-Nothing coalition, hearkened to the governor's plea and responded with a resolution calling for the restriction of slavery in the territories. Lane, p. 5; Chase to Welles, Aug. 22, Oct. 26, 1855; Welles to King, Apr. 23, 1855; WP-LC.

25. Welles to "Dear Sir," July 11, 1856, Learned Coll.

26. John Bigelow to Welles, Dec. 27, 1855; Welles to "Dear Sir" (Bigelow), Dec. 28, 1855; WP-LC.

27. Smith, *Blair Family,* Vol. I, pp. 323-24; Preston King to Welles, Jan. 2, 3, 10, 1856, WP-LC.

28. Before he met the Ohio Republican, Welles had expressed his decided preference for Chase; Welles to King, Apr. 23, 1855, WP-LC; Smith, *Blair Family,* Vol. I, p. 324; King to Welles, Jan. 31, 1856, WP-LC.

29. Lane, *Connecticut*, p. 34; *Hartford Republican*, Feb. 7, 1856. "Memo to Editor of the *Times*," Learned Coll., "Chat with B, Who was Expecting to Call but Did Not"; "An Old Democrat Leaves His Party," Alphabetical Series, WP-LC.

30. Chester Birge to Welles, Feb. 20, 1856, WP-LC.

31. For a year John L. Boswell and Faxon jointly published the *Courant*. Indeed, Faxon did more than that, because Boswell became ill and could not function. He ran the *Courant* single-handed—"an active well trained businessman," thought Samuel Bowles, editor of the *Springfield Republican*, "with a talent for details, good address. . . ." Bowles to J. R. Hawley, Feb. 26, 1861, Hawley papers, LC; for prospectus and preliminary organization, see *Evening Press*, Feb. 27, 1856, Learned Coll.; J. H. Trumbull (ed.), *Hartford*, Vol. I, p. 606; *Connecticut Quarterly*, Vol. II, No. 1, Jan.-Mar. 1896, p. 40; Lane, *Connecticut*, pp. 59, 85.

32. Smith, *Blair Family*, Vol. I, pp. 327, 328; Francis Curtis, *The Republican Party*, New York, 1904, pp. 227-29, 252.

33. Welles to James F. Babcock, Feb. 20, 1856, WP-LC. "There were," Welles recalled, "a distinct Whig organization and the Know-Nothing organization as hostile as the Democratic organization to our proceedings," Welles, "An Old Democrat Leaves His Party," Alphabetical Series, WP-LC.

34. Welles, "Declining To Be a Candidate for Governor in 1857," Alphabetical Series, WP-LC; Hartford *Evening Press*, Mar. 18, 1856, Learned Coll.; Lane, *Connecticut*, pp. 60, 61; Noonan, *The Know Nothing Movement*, pp. 349, 242. *New-York Tribune*, Mar. 14, 26, Apr. 4, 1856; New York *Evening Post*, Mar. 13, 31, 1856; Boston *Chronicle*, in the *Press*, Mar. 14, 1856.

35. J. D. Baldwin to Welles, June 26, 1856, WP-LC.

36. Lane, *Connecticut*, p. 68. For the complicated transaction in which the Republicans tried to elect Francis Gillette or Roger Baldwin, see F. G. Wildman to Welles, May 16, 1856; Moses Pierce to Welles, May 17, 24, 1856; Charles L. English to Welles, May 23, 1856, WP-LC.

37. E. D. Morgan to Niles, Mar. 18, 1856, WP-LC.

38. Dr. E. Whitney to Welles, Apr. 5, 1856; Horace Dresser to Welles, Apr. 17, 1856; John R. Pease to Welles, Apr. 23, 1856; Juliet Niles to Welles, May 5, 1856; E. H. Owen to Welles, May 6, 1856, WP-LC; MS Will, John M. Niles, May 2, 1857, Probate Records, CSL. For interesting details on Niles' career and his impact on Welles, see draft obituary, May 31, 1856, WP-HL; see also Welles' sketch of Niles in H. R. Stiles, *Genealogies*, Vol. II, pp. 534-36.

39. E. D. Morgan to Welles, May 1, 1856; Welles, draft letter to E. D. Morgan *et al.*, Apr. 28, 1856; WP-LC. Had Welles known that the Pathfinder's comments were ghost-written by Banks and the pliable Rhode Island Democrat General Charles James, he would not have been so charitable. Fred H. Harrington, *Fighting Politician, General N. P. Banks*, Philadelphia, 1948, p. 35; for another interpretation, see James C. Malin, "Speaker Banks Courts the Free Soilers: The Fremont-Robinson letter of 1856," *New England Quarterly*, Vol. XII, Mar. 1939, pp. 103-12; Preston King to Welles, Apr. 9, 1860, WP-LC; William M. Chace to S. P. Chase, June 21, 1856, Chase papers, LC.

40. E. D. Morgan to James Bunce, May 9, 1856; Welles to Morgan, June 27, 1856, Morgan papers, NYSL.

41. See Charles Johnson (comp.), *Proceedings of the First Three Republican National Conventions, 1856, 1862, 1864*, Minneapolis, 1893, p. 37, for a list of Connecticut delegates. The *Proceedings* are inaccurate on several counts. Niles is listed as a delegate though he had been dead for almost three weeks. Thaddeus Welles is erroneously listed as a member of the platform committee. Gideon Welles is not listed as a delegate. The *New-York Tribune*'s account (June 18, 1856) of the Convention is more accurate. It lists Gideon Welles as a delegate from the Third District and does not carry Niles' name among the delegates at large.

42. For platform, see *Proceedings*, pp. 43-45; for comparisons, see Welles' resolu-

tions on the Fugitive Slave Law, articles signed Jefferson in the *Hartford Times,*
Nov. 1850; Welles to James F. Babcock, Mar. 14, 1855; Welles, "Sound Principles as
against Epithets," and "Constitutionality of the Fugitive Slave Law and the Logical
Position an Old Jeffersonian Democrat Should Occupy on that Question," Alphabetical Series, WP-LC. Except for Joshua Giddings and Alexander Ramsey, the
mayor of St. Paul, Minn., the remaining members were local political wheelhorses,
little known outside of their native states; Charles B. Going, *David Wilmot, Free-
Soiler,* New York, 1924, p. 35.

43. New York *Herald,* May 19, 1860.

44. Welles to E. D. Morgan, Aug. 26, 1856, Morgan papers, NYSL; Welles to "Dear
Sir," Sept. 5, 1856, WP-LC.

45. Welles to E. D. Morgan, Sept. 13, 1856; Morgan papers, NYSL. Major Julius
Rathbun, "The Wide Awakes," *Connecticut Quarterly,* Vol. I, No. 4, Oct.-Dec. 1895,
p. 327; Lane, *Connecticut,* pp. 73, 74; James F. Babcock to Welles, July 23, 1856;
Charles L. English to Welles, July 31, 1856, WP-LC; Welles to E. D. Morgan, July
22, 1856, Morgan papers, NYSL.

46. James Rawley, *Edwin D. Morgan, 1811-1883,* New York, 1955, pp. 62, 64; E. D.
Morgan to Welles, Aug. 8, 1856. When Morgan sent W. M. Chace to the North
American leaders on August 8 for the printed copies of their call so that he could
send a copy to each member of the Republican National Committee, "they backed
square out, saying it was all wrong, ought not to have been sent; no answer wanted."
Morgan to Welles, Sept. 1, 1856, WP-LC.

47. Welles to Moses Pierce, Jan. 24, 1860, WP-LC.


CHAPTER 16

1. Welles to E. D. Morgan, Nov. 7, 1856, Morgan papers, NYSL.

2. Horace Greeley, quoting Stephen A. Douglas, in Greeley, *Recollections of a Busy
Life,* New York, 1869, p. 358.

3. *Hartford Courant,* Mar. 13, 1860.

4. Orris S. Ferry to J. R. Hawley, Oct. 19, 1857, Hawley papers, LC.

5. Moses Pierce to Welles, Mar. 13, 1857; Hartford *Evening Press,* Feb. 19, 1857,
in Learned Coll.

6. *Ibid.,* Feb. 20, 1857.

7. James Dixon to Welles, Mar. 17, 1858, WP-LC.

8. Orris S. Ferry to J. R. Hawley, Oct. 19, Apr. 9, 1857, Hawley papers, LC; Welles
to Edward Pierce, Mar. 13, 1857, WP-LC.

9. Orris S. Ferry to J. R. Hawley, May 14, 1857, Hawley papers, LC.

10. *Ibid.,* Nov. 26, Dec. 23, 1857; James F. Babcock to Welles, Dec. 15, 1857,
WP-LC; Welles' draft of a letter to the editor of the *Hartford Courant,* Dec. 1857,
WP-HL.

11. Orris S. Ferry to J. R. Hawley, May 14, 1857, Hawley papers, LC; *Hartford
Courant,* Jan. 15, 1858.

12. Welles to "Dear Sir," incomplete draft, Jan. 3, 1859, WP-LC. A majority of
those 15,000 or so "ignorant, obstinate and yet mainly honest" Democrats, as Ferry
described them, could, in Welles' opinion, be brought over if the Republicans pursued a more liberal policy. O. S. Ferry to J. R. Hawley, May 14, 1857, Hawley papers,
LC.

13. Welles to S. A. Douglas, Dec. 12, 1857, Douglas papers, Univ. of Chicago.

14. James Dixon to Welles, Dec. 15, 1857; Preston King to Welles, Dec. 18, 1857,
Jan. 2, 1858, WP-LC.

15. J. Dixon to Welles, Mar. 8, 1858, WP-LC.

16. Welles to S. A. Douglas, Mar. 16, 1858, Douglas papers, Univ. of Chicago.

17. J. Dixon to Welles, Apr. 2, 1858; Preston King to Welles, Apr. 12, 1858,
WP-LC.

18. *Ibid.*, Aug. 16, Sept. 30, 1858.

19. Welles to Foster, Mar. 1859, WP-HL.

20. Preston King to Blair, Sept. 1858, BLP, Firestone Library, Princeton; Glyndon G. Van Deusen, *Horace Greeley, Nineteenth Century Crusader*, Philadelphia, 1953, p. 223.

21. Preston King to Welles, July 20, 1858, WP-LC; Welles to King, Aug. 1858, WP-CHS; King to Welles, Aug. 16, Sept. 16, 30, Nov. 16, 1858, WP-LC; to F. P. Blair, Sr., Sept. 1858, BLP, Firestone Library, Princeton; Welles to E. D. Morgan, Dec. 4, 1857, Morgan papers, NYSL; Welles to F. P. Blair, Sr., draft, Jan. 1859, WP-CHS.

22. New York *Evening Post*, Nov. 15, 1858.

23. James Dixon to Welles, Nov. 24, 1858; Welles to Dixon, Dec. 6, 1858; WP-LC; Preston King to Welles, Nov. 16, 1858, WP-LC; Welles to E. D. Morgan, Dec. 4, 1858, Morgan papers, NYSL; Welles to Dixon, Dec. 6, 1858, WP-LC.

24. D. W. Bartlett to Welles, July 9, 12, 1858, WP-LC.

25. "He belongs to a different school of politics from you and I, and . . . a large element of the Republican party"—Welles to F. P. Blair, Sr., draft, June 1858, WP-CHS. "There is a difference between Weed and Morgan," noticed *Tribune* editor Charles A. Dana, "M is not so malleable as was expected"—Dana to James S. Pike, in Pike, *First Blows*, p. 444; James Dixon to Welles, Jan. 24, 29, Feb. 2, 1859, WP-LC.

26. The Burleigh brothers, William Henry and George S., for instance, were active in abolitionist circles and had worked with Welles and Niles in the late 1840's, when both men were trying to convert the Connecticut Democracy to free soil. Welles' name was mentioned favorably by the Burleighs to their radical friends; H. B. Stanton to Chase, Jan. 7, 1861, Chase papers, LC. Stanton, an old Democrat, and a powerful figure in antislavery circles, thought Welles, Bates, and Chase were men "to whom the Republican party is more indebted than any other."

27. John D. Baldwin to Lincoln, Jan. 7, 1861, Lincoln papers, IHS.

28. Samuel E. Staples, *Memorial of John Dennison Baldwin*, Worcester, Mass., 1884, pp. 4-6.

29. *Hartford Courant*, Jan. 14, 1860. A representative group of businessmen met at Middletown on January 18, 1860, where it condemned the raid on Harpers Ferry, repudiated Seward's "Higher Law" doctrine, and, in a sweeping manifest of appeasement, declared against interference of any kind in the internal affairs of the slave states. Representatives of all Republican factions were no less condemnatory, and not one pastor, however radical he might have been on the slavery question, would publicly condone Brown's act. John Niven, *Connecticut for the Union*, New Haven, 1965, p. 16; J. Dixon to Welles, Dec. 17, 1854, WP-LC.

30. The "Wide Awakes" were organized spontaneously in Hartford on Feb. 25, 1860, during a torchlight procession to escort Cassius M. Clay to Touro Hall, where he was to make a campaign speech. Described as "wide awake" by a *Hartford Courant* editorial writer, the Hartford group adopted this slogan. Organization, name, and uniform spread throughout the northern states. For a detailed account, see Major Julius G. Rathbun (an original "Wide Awake"), *Connecticut Quarterly*, Vol. I, pp. 327, 335; see also Niven, *Connecticut for the Union*, pp. 24, 25.

31. West, *Welles*, pp. 70, 71.

32. Rathbun, *Connecticut Quarterly*, Vol. I, pp. 327, 329.

33. J. Doyle DeWitt, *Lincoln in Hartford*, pamphlet, Hartford, 1963, pp. 6, 11; Hartford *Evening Press*, Mar. 8, 1861; O. S. Ferry to J. R. Hawley, Jan. 25, 1860, Hawley papers, LC.

34. See James F. Babcock to Welles, Nov. 10, 1860, WP-LC, in which he all but declares flatly that the two discussed Welles' position in state party circles; Lincoln to A. Chester, Mar. 14, 1860; Lincoln to Babcock, Apr. 14, 1860, in Roy P. Basler (ed.), *The Collected Works of Abraham Lincoln* (8 vols.), New Brunswick, N.J., 1953; Vol. IV, pp. 30, 43, 44. Hereafter cited as Basler, *Works*.

35. Moses Pierce to Welles, Jan. 24, 1860, WP-LC.

36. *Hartford Courant,* Jan. 26, 1860; Preston King to John Bigelow, Mar. 1, 1860, in Bigelow, *Retrospections,* Vol. I, pp. 225, 285.

37. H. S. Bogue to N. P. Banks, Feb. 29, 1860, Banks papers, LC; Welles, *Lincoln and Seward,* New York, 1874, p. 16; Margaret Clapp, *Forgotten First Citizen: John Bigelow,* Boston, 1947, p. 128.

38. As Thurlow Weed soon learned from Samuel Bowles, who reported as early as March 5 that Seward was the favorite of the New England delegates, except those from Connecticut; Harriet Weed and Thurlow Weed Barnes (eds.), *The Life of Thurlow Weed* (2 vols.), Boston, 1883, 84, Vol. II (Memoir), p. 260.

39. O. S. Ferry to Welles, Mar. 1, 1860, WP-LC.

40. Isaac Hazlehurst to Welles, Mar. 8, 1860; S. D. Levering to Welles, Mar. 17, 1860, WP-LC.

41. A. Howard Meneeley, "Three Manuscripts of Gideon Welles," *American Historical Review,* Vol. XXXI, No. 3, Apr. 1926, p. 488. So disgusted was Welles' brother-in-law, George D. Morgan, with the profligate scramble of would-be candidates that he wrote: "Without the slavery question, the Republican party would be swept out of existence almost, so full of schemes and unsound principles are they." George D. Morgan to Welles, Apr. 10, 1860; James T. Sherman to Welles, Mar. 23, 1860, WP-LC; J. R. Hawley to Rev. Francis Hawley, Mar. 4, 1860, Hawley papers, LC.

42. Hawley reflected Welles' views when he wrote his father, "Prefer Chase, then Fremont. Greatly prefer Seward to Bates . . . the old Whig leaders never had either principle or brains. They smashed their own party," *ibid.;* A. A. Burnham to Welles, Mar. 2, 1860, WP-LC; Preston King to Bigelow, May 10, 1860, in Bigelow, *Retrospections,* Vol. I, p. 289.

43. Norman Judd to Welles, Mar. 8, 1860, WP-LC.

44. George H. Noble to Welles, Mar. 5, 1860, WP-LC.

45. A. B. Calef to Welles, Mar. 12, 1860; Edgar S. Tweedy to Welles, Mar. 12, 1860, WP-LC; Chauncey F. Cleveland to Chase, Mar. 19, Apr. 20, 1860, Chase papers, LC.

46. James Dixon to J. R. Hawley, Apr. 6, 1860, Hawley papers, LC; Lane, *Connecticut,* p. 129; William Baringer, *Lincoln's Rise to Power,* Boston, 1937, pp. 175, 176; *New-York Tribune,* Apr. 4, 1860; Dixon rather favored Chase, whom, oddly enough, he thought more conservative than Lincoln. J. Dixon to Welles, May 1, 1860, WP-LC. A second meeting was called at New Haven on May 2, 1860, where with 11 out of 12 present he encountered the same attitude that had prevailed at Hartford. Augustus Chester to Welles, Apr. 17, 1860; Welles to Edgar Welles, Apr. 27, 1860, WP-LC.

47. Welles to E. L. Pierce, Jan. 11, 1861, Pierce papers, Houghton Library, Harvard. Earlier John A. Andrew, chairman of the Massachusetts delegates, had expressed privately that he was for Seward "because he seems the natural head of the party," but then he went on to praise Chase extravagantly, "an admirable executive officer, methodical, direct, clear, judicious." Another close observer of the Massachusetts delegation had long since decided that a majority of the group, though elected as Seward men, "really mean to cut his throat." Henry G. Pearson, *The Life of John A. Andrew* (2 vols.), New York, 1909, Vol. I, p. 112; Preston King to Azariah Flagg, May 7, 1860, Flagg papers, Butler Library, Columbia Univ.; James Dixon to Welles, May 8, 1860, WP-LC; *New York Herald,* May 19, 1860. There is no direct mention of Hawley's participation, but in view of his relationship to Welles and his position in the party, he would certainly not have been excluded. For his attendance at the convention, see Isaac M. Bromley, "The Nomination of Lincoln," *Scribner's Magazine,* Vol. XIV, July-Dec. 1893, p. 648; E. L. Pierce to Welles, Jan. 8, 1861, Lincoln papers, IHS; Dixon to Welles, May 7, 1860, WP-LC; *New York Herald,* May 15, 1860; Henry B. Stanton to Chase, Nov. 30, 1860, Chase papers, LC. Senator James F. Simmons' anti-Seward stance, which was certainly due to Welles' influence, raised him to the status of a Cabinet hopeful, though he was otherwise undistin-

guished and unknown to the public. Pierce was also a close friend of Baldwin and, like Welles, had written articles for Baldwin's *Worcester Spy*. E. L. Pierce to Carl Schurz, Apr. 28, 1859, Huntington Coll., HL.

48. For rivalry between Hamlin and Fessenden, see Charles A. Jellison, *Fessenden of Maine*, Syracuse, 1962, p. 125; C. S. Hamlin, *Life and Times of Hannibal Hamlin*, Cambridge, Mass., 1899, pp. 339, 341; John Goodrich, member of the National Committee from Massachusetts, told Bates that the Massachusetts delegation went to Chicago as friends of Seward, but expected they would have to vote for Bates. Howard K. Beale (ed.), *Annual Report of the American Historical Association* (4 vols.), Vol. IV, *The Diary of Edward Bates, 1859-1866*, Washington, D.C., 1933, p. 132 (hereafter referred to as *Diary of Edward Bates*); Jellison, *Fessenden of Maine*, p. 125.

49. Hamlin, *Hannibal Hamlin*, p. 341; William B. Hesseltine (ed.), *Three Against Lincoln, Murat Halstead Reports of the Caucuses of 1860*, Baton Rouge, 1960, p. 141; William Baringer, *Lincoln's Rise to Power*, p. 216; Edgar Welles to Mary Welles, May 15, 1860; Welles to Mary Welles, May 20, 1860, WP-LC; Hesseltine, *Halstead*, p. 142; *Chicago Tribune*, May 15, 1860; Preston King to Welles, May 4, 1860, WP-LC; Welles was happy to see Edward L. Pierce, whom he had first met in Chase's law office. A close friend of Chase and Sumner, Pierce was an influential member of the Massachusetts delegation. Welles explained his views to Pierce and was highly gratified "to find that we so fully concurred in opinion." Welles to Pierce, Jan. 11, 1861, Pierce papers, Houghton Library, Harvard. There seemed also to have been an undercurrent of opposition to Seward even in the New York delegation; see George Opdyke to Blair, May 10, 1860, BLP, Firestone Library, Princeton.

50. Thomas J. McCormack (ed.), *Memoirs of Gustave Koerner, 1809-1896*, Cedar Rapids, Iowa, 1909, p. 85; Welles, *Lincoln and Seward*, p. 28.

51. Greeley to James S. Pike, May 21, 1861 [misdated], Pike, *First Blows*, pp. 519, 520; Edgar Welles to Mary Welles, May 15, 1860, WP-LC; Van Deusen, *Thurlow Weed: Wizard of the Lobby*, Boston, 1947, p. 251; Van Deusen, *William Henry Seward*, p. 223; Welles to I. N. Arnold, Nov. 27, 1872, ChHS, copy also in Weed papers, Univ. of Rochester; Welles to Mary Welles, May 20, 1860, WP-LC; H. Kreisman to Elihu Washburne, May 15, 1860, Washburne papers, LC. Kreisman was certain that New Hampshire and Connecticut would both go for Lincoln. Lyford, *Rollins*, pp. 102, 104.

52. Samuel Bowles, who reported the convention, noted that all three states concurred that evening and decided not to support Seward. Evidence in Welles' *Lincoln and Seward* and his revealing letter to I. N. Arnold suggest that the Connecticut and Rhode Island caucuses were held earlier than the New Hampshire caucus. Baringer, *Lincoln's Rise to Power*, p. 234; Theodore Calvin Pease (ed.), *The Diary of Orville Hickman Browning* (2 vols.), Coll. of the Ill. State Hist. Lib., XX, Springfield, 1925, Vol. I, pp. 406, 407 (hereafter referred to as Browning, *Diary*). Bowles to H. L. Dawes, Feb. 26, 1861, in George S. Merriam, *The Life and Times of Samuel Bowles* (2 vols.), New York, 1885, Vol. I, p. 318; Hesseltine (ed.), *Halstead*, p. 166; Carl Schurz, *The Reminiscences of Carl Schurz* (3 vols.), New York, 1906, 1908, Vol. II, p. 129.

53. Bessie L. Pierce, *A History of Chicago* (3 vols.), New York, 1940, Vol. II, p. 465.

54. Bromley, "The Nomination of Lincoln," p. 647; New York *Herald*, May 19, 1860; Baringer, *Lincoln's Rise to Power*, pp. 210, 211; R. H. Luthin, *The First Lincoln Campaign*, p. 136; Dr. Humphrey H. Hood, *Reminiscences of Chicago During the Civil War*, Chicago, 1894, pp. 42, 43; Frederick Francis Cook, *By-Gone Days in Chicago*, Chicago, 1910, p. 159; Schurz, *Reminiscences*, Vol. II, p. 180; *New-York Tribune*, May 18, 1860; Welles to Mary Welles, May 20, 1860, WP-LC; Welles to I. N. Arnold, Nov. 27, 1860; Welles to Edgar Welles, Jan. 19, 1871, WP-ChHS.

55. Welles, *Lincoln and Seward*, p. 30; Hesseltine (ed.), *Halstead*, pp. 168, 176; Johnson (comp.), *Proceedings*, p. 153.

56. Weed and Barnes (eds.), *The Life of Thurlow Weed*, Vol. II (*Memoir*), p. 276;

Hamlin, *Hamlin*, p. 345. Some few, like Edward Bates, disagreed; but he was probably disgruntled at having missed the presidential nomination. Said Bates of Hamlin, "He has no general popularity, hardly a general reputation; and his geography is wrong. . . . It was a great blunder to overlook Pennsylvania." *Diary of Edward Bates*, p. 130.

57. Johnson, *Proceedings*, pp. 160, 161; Welles to Mary Welles, May 20, 1860, WP-LC.

## CHAPTER 17

1. Welles to Mary Welles, Mar. 10, 1861, WP-LC; Charles A. Dana, *Lincoln and His Cabinet, A Lecture Delivered before the New Haven Colony Historical Society*, Jamaica, N.Y., 1899, p. 4; Welles' friend Huntington was Chief Clerk of the Court of Claims; *American Almanac*, 1861, p. 143.

2. Welles to Mary Welles, Mar. 10, 1861, WP-LC.

3. *Ibid.*

4. George G. Fogg to Welles, Feb. 27, 1861, Lincoln papers, IHS; *Hartford Courant*, Mar. 2, 1861; Welles to Mary Welles, Mar. 4, 1861; Welles to Edgar Welles, Mar. 4, 1861, WP-LC. Welles, MS Diary, Feb. 18, 1861, WP-HL.

5. Welles to Arnold, Nov. 27, 1872, ChHS; Welles, *Lincoln and Seward*, pp. 27, 28, 30-35; "Nomination of Abraham Lincoln (II)," *The Galaxy*, Vol. XXII, Oct. 1876, pp. 300-388; "Three Manuscripts of Gideon Welles," *American Historical Review*, Vol. XXXI, Oct. 1925-July 1926, pp. 486, 488-89; Weed and Barnes (eds.), *Thurlow Weed*, Vol. I (*Autobiography*), pp. 606, 610, 611.

6. Welles, MS Draft, Lincoln papers, IHS, pp. 14, 15.

7. E. D. Morgan to Welles, Aug. 22, 1860; E. S. Cleveland to Welles, Oct. 2, 1860, WP-LC, indicates that Welles had important financial duties as well; but see James Rawley, *Morgan*, pp. 111, 112.

8. Welles, MS Draft, Lincoln papers, IHS; either from fellow committee member Norman B. Judd or from Dixon through Trumbull.

9. Saratoga corr., New York *Herald*, Aug. 12, 1860. Willard King, in his biography of Davis, *Lincoln's Manager, David Davis*, Cambridge, Mass., 1960, p. 153, describes the meeting with Weed. He says that Davis was at Saratoga but that the others who attended were from Rhode Island, p. 154. But see William E. Baringer, *A House Dividing*, Springfield, Ill., 1945, p. 116; Welles to Arnold, Nov. 27, 1872, and Welles, MS draft, IHS.

10. Welles, MS Draft, Lincoln papers, IHS, p. 16.

11. James Dixon to Welles, May 25, 1860, WP-LC.

12. Van Deusen, *Seward*, pp. 229, 230.

13. E. L. Pierce to Dr. Charles H. Ray, Dec. 7, 1860, Huntington Coll., HL.

14. John Bigelow to Welles, Nov. 14, 1860, WP-LC.

15. See James Madison to J. C. Cabell, Sept. 7, 1829, in Gaillard Hunt (ed.), *Writings* (9 vols.), New York, 1900-1910, Vol. IX, pp. 347-48, also pp. 568, 569.

16. O. S. Ferry to Welles, Dec. 11, 1860, WP-LC.

17. Preston King to Welles, Dec. 15, 1860, WP-LC. Dwight Loomis, congressman from his own district, reported to Hawley, who shared his political letters with Welles, that "Dixon goes much further than his speech and I fear you will be more disappointed still when he comes to vote." Loomis to J. R. Hawley, Dec. 17, 1860, Hawley papers, LC.

18. James Dixon to Welles, Dec. 22, 1860, WP-LC.

19. Dixon had written him on December 8, saying that the South would not budge on the territorial question, that it would demand at the very least the right to expand slavery into "the southern region, which now or hereafter may be under our jurisdiction. . . ." Judging that the Republicans could not accept this, Dixon predicted dire consequences unless the question be delayed long enough for "the hope

of returning reason at the South." Dixon to Welles, Dec. 8, 1860; Welles to Dixon, Dec. 11, 1860, WP-LC.

20. Welles, MS Diary, Jan. 4, 1861, WP-HL.

21. Ferry wrote: "We have got three things to do; first to do right; second to overthrow forever the power of slavery, third to save the Republic. The President is a traitor; traitors are in the Senate; traitors are in the House." Ferry to J. R. Hawley, Dec. 31, 1860, Hawley papers, LC.

22. E. L. Pierce to Dr. Charles H. Ray, Aug. 9, Dec. 7, 1860, Jan. 7, 1861, Huntington Coll., HL. But Welles thought Adams' position was being misunderstood. Welles to E. L. Pierce, Jan. 11, 1861, Pierce papers, Houghton Library, Harvard.

23. See obituary of George Gilman Fogg, *Springfield Republican*, Oct. 10, 1881; James Dixon to Lincoln, Nov. 17, 1860, Lincoln papers, LC; Lincoln endorsed Dixon's letter, "J. Dixon, *Welles*"; Hamlin, *Hannibal Hamlin*, pp. 366-70; Dixon to Welles, Dec. 3, 1860, WP-LC.

24. Welles to Dixon, Dec. 5, 1860; Hannibal Hamlin to Lincoln, Dec. 10, 1860, Lincoln papers, LC. On the envelope, Lincoln wrote "Wells—Adams," for convenience in filing, perhaps, and in view of his reply two weeks later, possibly having more significance than that.

25. Israel Washburn to Lincoln; Richard Yates to Lincoln; Lincoln to Hamlin, Dec. 24, 1860, Lincoln papers, LC; Welles, *Lincoln and Seward*, p. 38; David Davis to Lincoln, Nov. 19, 1860, Lincoln papers, LC; though George Fogg, when he visited Springfield again on December 4, thought Welles the leading contender. Fogg to Lincoln, Dec. 29, 1860, Lincoln papers, IHS. But by early January, he believed Lincoln preferred Banks. Fogg to Lincoln, Jan. 4, 1861; Fogg to Welles, Jan. 5, 1861, WP-HL. Some of those who were pushing for Banks were among Lincoln's closest friends—George M. Gage, a proprietor of the Tremont House, and Isaac N. Arnold. Arnold to Lincoln, Dec. 29, 1860; Gage to Lincoln, Nov. 24, 1860; Lincoln to Hamlin, Dec. 24, 1860; Hamlin to Lincoln, Dec. 14, 1860, Lincoln papers, LC.

26. Earl S. Miers (ed.), *Lincoln Day by Day, A Chronology* (3 vols.), Washington, D.C., 1960, Vol. II, *1849-1860*, p. 302; Weed and Barnes (eds.), *(Autobiography)*, Vol. I, *1809-1865*, pp. 603-11; *Diary of Edward Bates*, pp. 163-68; Baringer, *A House Dividing*, p. 118. See *New-York Tribune*, New York *Herald*, *New York Times*, Dec. 21, 1860, for speculations about Weed's intentions. Hamlin to Lincoln, Dec. 29, 1860; George G. Fogg to Lincoln, Dec. 29, 1860, Lincoln papers, LC; Henry B. Stanton to Welles, Jan. 7, 1860; Fogg to Welles, Dec. 30, 1860, WP-LC.

27. Henry Wilson and others to Lincoln, Jan. 4, 1860; Wilson to Lincoln, Jan. 5, 1860; Leonard Swett to Lincoln, Jan. 5, 1861, Lincoln papers, LC; H. B. Stanton to S. P. Chase, Jan. 7, 1861, Chase papers, LC. Pierce seemed almost beside himself with anger and frustration. In a series of letters to Lincoln's friend, Dr. C. H. Ray, he denounced Banks unsparingly. "Don't you know," he asked, that the sound Republicans here "have groaned under his double-faced conduct . . . he is to us what John Wentworth is to you." E. L. Pierce to Ray, Aug. 9, 1860, Dec. 7, 1860, Jan. 4, 1861, Huntington Coll., HL.

28. George G. Fogg to Welles, Jan. 18, 21, 27, 1861, Lincoln papers, IHS; J. W. Wolcott to Banks, Jan. 9, 1861, Banks papers, LC; Welles, MS Diary, Jan. 19, 1861, WP-HL; William Cullen Bryant, Wilson, Andrew, and Stanton by direct appeal to Lincoln, Sumner through Pierce to Dr. Ray. Bryant to Lincoln, Jan. 4, 1861, Lincoln papers, L.C; E. L. Pierce to Ray, Jan. 1861, Huntington Coll., HL; Pierce to Horace White, Jan. 9, 1861, Lincoln papers, LC; Pierce to Welles, Jan. 8, 1861, Lincoln papers, IHS; Andrew to Lincoln, Jan. 20, 1861, Lincoln papers, LC; the peppery Andrew drew a savage description of Banks—"his know-nothingism, his noncommittalism on every matter of principle in the face of every danger; and his willingness to make everything a subject of doubt by logomachy of sounding and double-meaning phrases. . . ." Even Amos Tuck, who had taken himself out of the competition, attacked Banks. Tuck to Lincoln, Jan. 14, 1861, Lincoln papers, LC.

29. George G. Fogg to Welles, Feb. 1, 1861, Lincoln papers, IHS.

30. Welles to Edgar Welles, Feb. 1861, WP-LC; James Dixon to S. W. Breakman, Jan. 1, 1861, Dixon, miscellaneous papers, NYHS; Welles, MS Diary, Jan. 12, 16, 1861, WP-HL.

31. James Dixon to Welles, Jan. 29, 1861, Lincoln papers, IHS; Welles, MS Diary, Feb. 2, 4, 1861, WP-HL; Allan Nevins, *The Emergence of Lincoln* (2 vols.), New York, 1950, Vol. II, pp. 410-13; Welles to Buckingham, Feb. 2, 1861, WP-LC; George G. Fogg to Welles, Feb. 1, 1861, Lincoln papers, IHS; Fogg to Lincoln, Feb. 2, 1861, Fogg papers, NHHS.

32. George G. Fogg to Lincoln, Feb. 2, 1861, Fogg papers, NHHS.

33. Miers (ed.), *Lincoln Day by Day*, Vol. III, pp. 12-15; Welles, MS Diary, Feb. 18, 1861, WP-HL; E. D. Morgan to Welles, Feb. 19, 20, 1861, Lincoln papers, IHS. But to no avail, according to Governor Morgan, who went over to the Delavan House late in the evening for a private chat with Lincoln. "He intends to offer you an appointment," Morgan wrote the next day, and then maddeningly introduced a note of doubt by adding "I believe he will." Welles heavily underscored this sentence.

34. Mark Howard to Welles, Feb. 24, 25, 27, 1861, Lincoln papers, IHS; J. H. Jordan to S. P. Chase, Feb. 23, 1861, Chase papers, LC.

35. Welles to Edgar Welles, Feb. 26, 27, 1861, WP-LC; G. V. Fox to V.W.F., Oct. 31, 1882, Fox papers, NYHS; Hamlin to Welles, Feb. 28, 1861, Lincoln papers, IHS; Welles to Mary Welles, Apr. 10, 1861, WP-LC; New York *Herald*, Feb. 22, 1861; *New-York Tribune*, Mar. 1, 1861; Welles to Mary Welles, Mar. 10, 1861, WP-LC.

36. Welles to Mary Welles, Mar. 4, 1861; Welles to Edgar Welles, Mar. 4, 1861; Miers (ed.), *Lincoln Day by Day*, Vol. III, p. 23.

37. Welles to Mary Welles, Mar. 4, 1861, WP-LC.

38. Welles to Edgar Welles, Mar. 13, 1861; James F. Babcock to Welles, Mar. 17, 1861, WP-LC; Andrew M. Sallade to Simon Cameron, Apr. 11, 1861, Cameron papers, LC.

39. New York *Herald*, Mar. 11, 1861, and see, for instance, W. P. Fessenden to Welles, Mar. 3, 1861; J. R. Hawley to Welles, Mar. 12, 1861; O. S. Ferry to Welles, Mar. 13, 1861; Mark Howard to Welles, Mar. 16, 1861, WP-LC.

## CHAPTER 18

1. Welles, *Diary*, Vol. I, p. 5. Eventually, over one hundred additional officers of lieutenant's rank or above would resign or be dismissed. "Report of the Secretary of the Navy," 1861; *Senate Exec. Doc.*, 37th Cong., 2nd sess., part 1, pp. 160-69. At least one senior officer, Captain George Magruder, tried to have his resignation accepted on the ground that he would remain neutral. Despite a plea in his behalf by S. P. Chase, Magruder was dismissed. Welles to Magruder, Mar. 19, 1870, WP-LC.

2. Welles, *Diary*, Vol. I, p. 5; but Welles was as forbearing as Toucey had been because of Lincoln's injunction not to offend citizens of the border states. *U.S. Naval Institute Proceedings*, Vol. 49, Oct. 1923, pp. 1676, 1677; S. F. Du Pont to Samuel Mercer, Mar. 13, 1861; Du Pont to H. W. Davis, Mar. 20, 1861, in John D. Hayes (ed.), *Samuel Francis Du Pont, A Selection from His Civil War Letters* (3 vols.), Ithaca, N.Y., 1969, Vol. I, pp. 42-44 (hereafter cited as Du Pont, *Letters*).

3. Welles, *Diary*, Vol. I, p. 4.

4. Fort Taylor at Key West was also in federal hands, but was little known to the Northern public; James Ford Rhodes, *History of the United States from the Compromise of 1850* (9 vols.), New York, 1893-1928, Vol. III, p. 327; S. P. Chase to B. J. Lossing, Aug. 24, 1866, A. Conger Goodyear Coll., Sterling Library, Yale; Lincoln to Welles, Mar. 15, 1861, in *Magazine of History*, Extra, No. 105, 1924, p. 10; Welles to Lincoln, Mar. 15, 1861, Lincoln papers, LC; George P. Bissell to Welles, Mar. 15, 1861, WP-LC; New York *Herald*, Mar. 12, 13, 20, 21, 1861.

5. *Diary of Edward Bates*, p. 180; Montgomery Blair to Welles, May 17, 1873, WP-LC.

6. Mark Howard to Welles, Mar. 19, 1861, WP-LC; Welles to Lincoln, "In Cabinet," Mar. 29, 1861, Lincoln papers, LC.

7. Lincoln to Welles, Mar. 29, 1861, Lincoln papers, LC; Winfield Scott to Fox, Jan. 30, 1861; G. V. Fox to Scott, Feb. 8, 1861; "Mem. for the Relief of Fort Sumpter [*sic*] by G. V. Fox," in R. M. Thompson and R. Wainwright (eds.), *Confidential Correspondence of Gustavus Vasa Fox, Assistant Secretary of the Navy, 1861-1865* (2 vols.), New York, 1920, Vol. I, pp. 3, 7-9 (hereafter cited as Fox, *Confidential Correspondence*). G. V. Fox to Blair, Feb. 23, 1861; "Memorandum of Facts Concerning the Attempt to Send Supplies to Fort Sumter in 1861," Feb. 24, 1866, in *Official Records of the Union and Confederate Navies in the War of the Rebellion*, Series I (27 vols.); Series II (4 vols.), Washington, D.C., 1894-1927 (hereafter cited as *ORN*). *ORN*, Series I, Vol. IV, pp. 223-25, 248.

8. Welles, *Diary*, Vol. I, pp. 17-21.

9. Welles to I. N. Arnold, Nov. 27, 1872, ChHS; Welles, *Diary*, Vol. I, p. 36; *Senate Exec. Doc.*, 37th Cong., 2nd sess., part I, p. 160.

10. Abraham Lincoln, *Message to Congress in Special Session*, July 4, 1861, in Basler, *Works*, Vol. IV, pp. 421-24; David Dixon Porter, *Incidents and Anecdotes of the Civil War*, New York, 1885; David Potter, *Lincoln and His Party in the Secession Crisis* (rev. ed.), New Haven, 1962, pp. 324, 362, 13-14.

11. D. D. Porter to Foote, Apr. 6, 1861, in *ORN*, Series I, Vol. IV, p. 112; Lincoln's responsibility has been a matter of historical controversy for many years. Welles accepted the President's explanation that he had signed the orders brought him by Seward without reading them. Allan Nevins endorsed the Welles thesis, but he feels Lincoln was determined to reinforce Sumter—Allan Nevins, *The War for the Union*, New York, 1959, Vol. I, pp. 57, 58. The most recent interpretation that follows Nevins is Ari Hoogenboom's perceptive treatment, "Gustavus Fox and the Relief of Fort Sumter," *Civil War History*, Vol. IX, No. 4, Dec. 1963. David Potter, in his *Lincoln and His Party in the Secession Crisis*, believes that the President knew what he was doing and that he wanted to avoid confrontation at Sumter, Ch. 12, *passim*. Another analysis of Lincoln's policy is given by Kenneth Stampp, who suggests that the President believed war would come and maneuvered the South into firing the first shot. Stampp gives little credence to Lincoln's own testimony in his July 4, 1861, address to the special session of the 37th Congress, or his later comments to John Hay and C. S. Morehead (Potter, p. 353). Kenneth Stampp, *And the War Came*, Baton Rouge, 1950, pp. 180, 283-86. The crucial orders signed by the President were only six in number, the most important order being but forty-two words. It seems plausible that any trained lawyer would gist each one at a glance and know what he was signing. Circumstantial evidence indicates that Lincoln was fully aware of Seward's plan and approved of it. The orders are in *ORN*, Series I, Vol. IV, pp. 108, 109.

12. A. H. Foote to Welles, Fox, in *Confidential Correspondence*, Vol. I, p. 17; Foote to Welles, Apr. 1, 1861, in *ORN*, Series I, Vol. IV, p. 229.

13. Porter, *Incidents and Anecdotes*, p. 17, *ORN*, Series I, Vol. IV, pp. 109, 229.

14. A. H. Foote to Welles, Apr. 4, 5, 1861; Welles to Foote, Apr. 5, 1861; in *ORN*, Series I, Vol. IV, pp. 234, 236, 237; Welles, *Diary*, Vol. I, pp. 22, 23; D. D. Porter to Foote, Apr. 5, 1861, 8 o'clock, in *ORN*, Series I, Vol. IV, pp. 111, 112.

15. Welles, *Diary*, Vol. I, pp. 23-25; *ORN*, Series I, Vol. IV, pp. 237, 238, 112, 23-25; W. H. Seward to Captain Mercer, Apr. 16, 1861; A. H. Foote to Welles, Apr. 6, 1861, in Fox, *Confidential Correspondence*, Vol. I, p. 27.

16. Porter often stretched the truth if it redounded to his advantage, but he was careful about his official correspondence or anything he wrote that might become part of public record. His letter to Foote and confirming data in Welles' *Diary* make a forceful case that he spoke the truth. D. D. Porter to Seward, Apr. 6, 1861;

Porter to Foote, Apr. 6, 1861, in *ORN*, Series I, Vol. IV, p. 112; Welles, *Diary*, Vol. I, p. 25-36.

17. For professional naval opinion, see S. F. Du Pont to H. W. Davis, Apr. 14, 1861; Samuel Mercer to Du Pont, Apr. 9, 1861, in Du Pont, *Letters*, Vol. I, p. 51.

18. H. A. Adams to Toucey, Feb. 19; Toucey to Adams, Feb. 25; Adams to Welles, Mar. 18, 22, 1861, in *ORN*, Series I, Vol. IV, pp. 85, 88, 97, 98, 100, 101; A. H. Foote to Welles, Mar. 14, 1861. Why Adams did not up-date his report of March 18 is unexplained. That the officer messenger, Washington Gwathmey, carried the report is stated in Adams to Welles, March 18, and again in a note he wrote Welles on March 22, which was apparently sent by mail. Welles confirms that Lt. Gwathmey was the messenger; Welles, *Diary*, Vol. I, p. 29; Welles, "Fort Pickens, Facts in Relation to the Reenforcement of Fort Pickens, in the Spring of 1861," *The Galaxy*, Vol. XI, Jan. 1871, pp. 98, 99, 106, 107.

19. Welles, *Diary*, Vol. I, pp. 30, 31; John L. Worden to Fox, Sept. 20, 1865; H. A. Adams to Welles, Apr. 14, 1861, in *ORN*, Series I, Vol. IV, pp. 111, 115.

20. G. V. Fox to Dr. Lowery, Apr. 3, 1861; "Result of G. V. Fox's Plan for Reinforcing Fort Sumpter [*sic*] In His Own Writing." Fox to Montgomery Blair, Mar. 31, 1861, in Fox, *Confidential Correspondence*, Vol. I, pp. 14, 19, 39.

21. Simon Cameron to Robert S. Chew, Apr. 6, 1861; Lincoln to Curtin, Apr. 8, 1861, in Basler, *Works*, Vol. IV, pp. 323, 324.

22. G. V. Fox to Blair, Apr. 17, 1861, in Fox, *Confidential Correspondence*, pp. 31-35.

23. Welles, *Diary*, Vol. I, pp. 83, 84; Welles, "Mr. Welles in Answer to Mr. Weed. The Facts of the Abandonment of the Gosport Navy Yard," *The Galaxy*, Vol. X, July 1870, pp. 112, 113.

24. Welles, *Diary*, Vol. I, pp. 83, 84, 41, 43; Welles to McCauley, Apr. 10, 1861, in *ORN*, Series I, Vol. IV; "Surrender and Destruction of Navy Yards," *Senate Reports*, No. 37, 37th Cong., 2nd sess., testimony of B. F. Isherwood, p. 77.

25. Welles to C. S. McCauley, Apr. 12, 16, 1861; B. F. Isherwood to Welles, Apr. 18, 1861; Welles to Paulding, Apr. 18, 1861; in Senate *Reports*, 37th Cong., 2nd sess., No. 37, pp. 106-14; William B. Talliaferro to John Letcher, Apr. 23, 1861, in *ORN*, Series I, Vol. IV, p. 308.

26. Welles, *Diary*, Vol. I, pp. 44-49; Welles, "Answer to Mr. Weed," p. 117; James Alden to Welles, Nov. 30, 1861, in *House Reports*, 37th Cong., 3rd sess., pp. 103, 104; Dahlgren, *Dahlgren*, pp. 331, 332; Welles to Samuel L. Breese, Apr. 18, 1861; Welles to W. W. Hunter, Apr. 18, 1861; S. F. Du Pont to Welles, Apr. 19, 1861, in *ORN*, Series I, Vol. IV, pp. 283, 284.

27. Welles to Franklin Buchanan, Apr. 19, 1861; Welles to John A. Dahlgren, Apr. 19, 1861, *ibid.*, p. 284.

28. Rebecca Paulding Davis, *Life of Hiram Paulding, Rear Admiral USN*, New York, 1910, p. 241. A few days later he said, "some times I speak briefly or in monosyllables, and one matter is not disposed of before two more are pressing on me, and this for hours, my mind gets muddy, excited and almost confused" (p. 243). Though Paulding made these comments after his return from Norfolk, it is reasonable to infer that he was not really fit for the command Welles thrust upon him.

29. See his own report, pp. 288, 289, that of Alden, pp. 300-302, and that of Pendergrast in *ORN*, Series I, Vol. IV, pp. 243, 245.

30. C. S. McCauley to Welles, Apr. 23, 1861, *ibid.*, pp. 288, 289.

31. The Virginia militia general William B. Talliaferro, opposing Paulding, could muster only some 600 untrained, unarmed, citizen volunteers, and three or four antique six-pounder field pieces. The militia companies of Norfolk and Portsmouth had not even been called up when Talliaferro arrived on the night of April 18, thirty-six hours before Paulding's appearance. Report of William B. Talliaferro to Governor John Letcher, Apr. 23, 1861, *ibid.*, pp. 306-9.

32. Testimony of James W. Brownley, Testimony of Paymaster Edward C. Doran,

in Senate *Reports,* 37th Cong., 2nd sess., No. 37, pp. 59 and 69-71, Nov. 21, 1861.
33. *ORN,* Series I, Vol. IV, p. 308.
34. Welles to Mary Welles, Apr. 21, 1861, WP-LC; Welles, *Diary,* Vol. I, p. 52.

CHAPTER 19

1. Welles, "Memorandum," Oct. 20, 1861, WP-HL; Welles to Edgar Welles, May 14, 1861, WP-LC.
2. Welles to Mary Welles, Aug. 4, 1861; Welles to Edgar Welles, Nov. 3, 1861, WP-LC.
3. Welles to Fox, Sept. 1861, in Fox, *Confidential Correspondence,* Vol. I, pp. 373, 374; S. F. Du Pont to Davis, Sept. 4, 1861; Du Pont to Mrs. Du Pont, Sept. 17, 18, 1861, in *Du Pont Letters,* pp. 141, 149, 150, 142n; Fox to Stringham, Sept. 14, 1861, in *ORN,* Series I, Vol. IV, p. 210, 211. For a sketch of Goldsborough, see A. Farenholt, " 'And There Were Giants in the Earth in Those Days,' " *U.S. Naval Institute Proceedings,* Vol. 62, Jan.-June 1936, p. 520.
4. Welles to Lot M. Morrill, Dec. 1869, WP-HL.
5. Welles, "Memorandum," Oct. 20, 1861, WP-HL.
6. West, *Welles,* pp. 121, 122; John P. Hale to Welles, Apr. 24, May 29, 1861, WP-LC. Hale had not enjoyed a good reputation in high Republican circles for years. See Horace Greeley's low opinion of Hale in 1858, Greeley to Amos Tuck, Nov. 17, 1858, Greeley papers; Tuck to Fogg, Apr. 26, 1858, Tuck papers, NHHS.
7. C. B. Sedgewick to Welles, May 14, 1861, WP-LC.
8. Welles, "Memorandum," Oct. 20, 1861, WP-HL.
9. W. H. Russell, *My Diary, North and South,* Boston, 1863, pp. 502, 503; *Hartford Courant,* Jan. 6, 1864.
10. Welles, *Diary,* Vol. I, p. 74; *Scientific American,* Apr. 5, 1862, Vol. VI, p. 215; F. A. Roe, *Naval Duties and Discipline with the Policy and Principles of Naval Organization,* New York, 1865, p. 173; Du Pont to Mrs. Du Pont, Nov. 2, 1861, Du Pont, *Letters,* Vol. I, p. 208; Welles to Morrill, Dec. 1869, WP-HL; D. D. Porter to Fox, July 5, 1861, Fox, *Confidential Correspondence,* Vol. II, pp. 76, 77; L. M. Goldsborough to Fox, Dec. 16, 1861, *ibid.,* Vol. I, pp. 221-22.
11. Leonard White, *The Jacksonians: A Study in Administrative History,* New York, 1954, p. 218; *New-York Tribune,* Apr. 4, 1863; Welles, *Diary,* Vol. I, pp. 74, 504, 505; Edward W. Sloan, III, *Benjamin Franklin Isherwood, Navy Engineer,* Annapolis, 1965; Charles O. Paullin, "A Half Century of Naval Administration in America, the Navy Department During the Civil War," *U.S. Naval Institute Proceedings,* Vol. 38, Dec. 1912, p. 1321; C. S. Bushnell to Welles, Mar. 22, 1861, WP-LC.
12. Du Pont to Matthew Maury, Aug. 30, 1862, Du Pont, *Letters,* Vol. I, p. 138; *Register of Officers and Agents, Civil, Military and Naval in the Service of the United States, 1862,* Washington, D.C., 1862, pp. 152-54. By the end of 1863, with three new bureaus, some twenty more personnel were added; *ibid., 1863,* Washington, D.C., 1864, pp. 199-202; Welles to Edgar Welles, Apr. 6, 1872, WP-LC. In August 1861, Welles tried to persuade Dahlgren to take over the Ordnance Bureau. He refused. Dahlgren, *Dahlgren,* p. 342.
13. Faxon to Welles, Mar. 8, 12, 1861; Faxon to Edgar Welles, Apr. 25, 1870, WP-NYPL; Faxon to Mark Howard, Feb. 15, 1865, Howard papers, CHS; *Hartford Courant,* Mar. 20, 1861, July 21, 1862.
14. Berrien had been appointed 4th Auditor in the Treasury Department; Welles to Lincoln, May 8, 1861, Lincoln papers, LC. Fox made thirteen trips from New York to the Isthmus for the United States Mail Steamship Co., New York *Herald,* Oct. 5, 1853-May 5, 1855, *passim.*
15. Fox to Welles, Mar. 25, 1867, WP-LC; Faxon to Edgar Welles, Apr. 25, 1870, WP-NYPL; Lincoln to Welles, May 8, 1861, Basler, *Works,* Vol. IV, p. 363; Fox to Mrs. Fox, May 4, 1861, Fox, *Confidential Correspondence,* Vol. I, pp. 44, 45; Faxon

to Howard, May 10, 1861, Howard papers, CHS; Paullin, "The Navy Department During the Civil War," p. 1316, Sloan, *Isherwood*, pp. 3-4, 20-21, 82-83.

16. Faxon to Howard, May 10, 1861, Howard papers, CHS; Welles to Fox, May 8, 9, 1861; Fox to Mrs. Fox with enclosure, July 25, 1861, in Fox, *Confidential Correspondence*, Vol. I, pp. 45, 46, 363, 364.

17. John Hay, *Letters of John Hay and Extracts from His Diary* (3 vols.), Washington, D.C., 1908, reprinted, New York, 1969, Vol. I, p. 184; Seward to Fox, Feb. 27, 1862, William H. Seward Coll., Univ. of Rochester; Welles, *Diary*, Vol. I, pp. 485, 489; Hiram Paulding to G. D. Morgan, Aug. 21, 1861; Fox to Welles, Jan. 5, 1866, WP-LC; Adm. Joseph Smith to Welles, Oct. 26, 1870, WP-LC; Welles, *Diary*, Vol. I, p. 401; John P. Hale to George G. Fogg, Apr. 27, 1863, Hale papers, NHHS; Henry Villard, *Memoirs of Henry Villard, Journalist and Financier* (2 vols.), Boston and New York, 1904, Vol. I, p. 172.

18. Fox to Mrs. Fox, May 28, 1861, Fox papers, NYHS; C. B. Sedgewick to "My Dear Messmate," Feb. 10, 1867, Henry A. Wise papers, NYHS; Welles to Mary Welles, June 9, 22, 25, 26, July 4, 1861; M. Curtin to Edgar Welles, May 19, 1862; Mary Welles to Edgar Welles, June 1, 1862; Mark Howard to Welles, Jan. 22, 1863; Welles to Edgar Welles, June 14, 1861, WP-LC.

19. Du Pont to Matthew Maury, Aug. 30, 1861, Du Pont, *Letters*, Vol. I, p. 138.

20. Welles, *Lincoln and Seward*, pp. 122-24; Welles to Lincoln, Aug. 5, 1861, Lincoln papers, LC; Lord Newton, *Lord Lyons* (2 vols.), *A Record of British Diplomacy*, London, 1913, Vol. I, pp. 36, 37.

21. *New York Times*, Apr. 20, 1861; Miers (ed.), *Lincoln Day by Day*, Vol. III, p. 35; Van Deusen, *Seward*, pp. 300-301; Stuart L. Bernath, *Squall Across the Atlantic, American Civil War Prize Cases and Diplomacy*, Berkeley and Los Angeles, 1970, pp. 18-23 (hereafter cited as *Civil War Prize Cases*) James C. Welling to Welles, Apr. 7, 1876, WP-LC.

22. For Welles' argument, see his letter to Lincoln, Aug. 5, 1861, Lincoln papers, LC, and his memorandum, "The Interdiction of Commerce with the Insurgent States," Aug. 1861, WP-LC.

23. West, *Welles*, p. 113.

24. Charles Henry Davis, *Life of Charles Henry Davis, Rear Admiral, U.S.N., 1807-1877*, Boston and New York, 1899, p. 124; John C. Frémont to F. P. Blair, May 24, 1861, WP-HL; Du Pont to H. W. Davis, June 1861; Du Pont to William Whetten, June 23, 1861; Du Pont to Mrs. Du Pont, June 27, 1861; G. V. Fox to Du Pont, May 22, 1861; Du Pont to Mrs. Du Pont, June 28, 1861; Du Pont, *Letters*, pp. 71, 75, 78, 85, 86. For texts of reports, see *ORN*, Series I, Vol. XII, pp. 195-206.

25. Davis, *Davis*, pp. 119, 127.

26. Du Pont to Mrs. Du Pont, July 26, 1861, in Du Pont, *Letters*, Vol. I, p. 113; Welles to Du Pont, Aug. 3, 1861, *ORN*, Series I, Vol. XII, p. 207.

27. *Scientific American*, Vol. V, July 13, Aug. 24, 1861; *New-York Tribune*, June 17, 1861; *Hartford Courant*, June 14, 1861; Henry Gildersleeve to Welles, June 15, 1861, WP-LC.

28. F. A. Roe, *Seamanship*, p. 175; C. R. P. Rodgers to C. G. Halpine, Jan. 4, 1864, Huntington Coll., HL; Du Pont to Davis, Jan. 25, 1864, Du Pont, *Letters*, Vol. III, p. 309.

29. F. M. Bennett, *The Steam Navy of the United States*, Pittsburgh, 1896, pp. 214-28; Charles O. Paullin, "The Navy Department During the Civil War (II)," *U.S. Naval Institute Proceedings*, Vol. 39, No. 1, Mar. 1913, pp. 168-70.

## CHAPTER 20

1. Welles, "Notes" regarding Morgan's ship purchasing, Jan. 1862, WP-HL; William Aspinwall to Welles, July 3, 1861; G. D. Morgan to Welles, Nov. 8, Dec. 23, 1861, WP-NYPL.

2. G. D. Morgan to Welles, Apr. 26, 1861, WP-HL; Morgan to Welles, May 2, 1861, WP-LC; Welles to Edgar Welles, Dec. 31, 1864, WP-HL; Welles to Edgar Welles, Nov. 10, 1871, WP-LC; Welles to Morgan, June 4, Oct. 31, 1861, NYHS; Welles to Edgar Welles, Feb. 16, 1862, WP-LC.

3. *New-York Tribune*, May 16, 1862. The American consul in London estimated 5.5 million tons of shipping in 1861. *Congressional Globe*, 41st Cong., 1st sess., Appendix, p. 25.

4. Edgar Welles, "Scrapbook," in possession of the author, pp. 20, 21; G. D. Morgan to Welles, Dec. 24, 1861; Welles to Morgan, Dec. 25, 1861, Jan. 10, 1862; Welles' notes on Morgan's purchase, n.d. (1861); "Memorandum," Oct. 20, 1861, WP-HL; *New-York Tribune*, Jan. 18, Feb. 11, 1862; Albany *Evening Journal*, Aug. 12, 1861; Morgan to Welles, Nov. 7, 1861; Welles to Morgan, Oct. 31, 1861, WP-LC.

5. Joseph F. Durkin, *Stephen R. Mallory, Confederate Navy Chief*, Chapel Hill, 1954, pp. 152-54; *ORN*, Series II, Vol. I, pp. 740-43; Paullin, "The Navy Department During the Civil War (II)," p. 173.

6. Hewitt had written Welles, inquiring if the Navy would need iron plate and beams; Hewitt to Welles, Apr. 18, 1861; Welles to Hewitt, May 9, 1861, Allan Nevins Coll., Butler Library Columbia Univ.; Fox to Welles, Aug. 15, 1863, WP-LC; C. S. Bushnell to Welles, Mar. 9, 23, 1877, WP-HL. Bushnell, writing more than fifteen years after the event, said that it took him a month to lobby the bill through Congress. Although his long and valuable letter to Welles, with its vivid dialogue, bears every evidence of having been composed from notes made at the time, he is obviously exaggerating his role in the lobbying. A good guess as to how much time was required to push the bill through is at most two weeks, probably less. *House Exec. Doc.*, 37th Cong., 1st sess., No. 69; United States *Statutes at Large*, Boston, 1865, Vol. XII, Ch. 38, p. 286.

7. C. S. Bushnell to Welles, Mar. 9, 1877, WP-HL. For a somewhat different version, see William C. Church, *The Life of John Ericsson* (2 vols.), New York, 1906, Vol. I, p. 248.

8. C. S. Bushnell to Welles, Mar. 9, 1877, WP-HL; New York *Herald*, Sept. 12, 1861; Edgar Welles, "Scrapbook," p. 25.

9. C. S. Bushnell to W. A. Stoddard, Sept. 1, 1883, *The Collector*, Vol. LXXXX, Nos. 1-3, 1967, pp. 1, 2; Bushnell to Welles, Mar. 9, 1877, WP-HL.

10. *Ibid.*; Church, *Ericsson*, Vol. I, p. 250.

11. *Ibid.*

12. A. H. Kilty to Welles, Sept. 3, 1868; Mary Louvestre to Welles, Sept. 4, 1868; Welles to Kilty, Aug. 31, 1868, WP-LC; Welles, *Diary*, Vol. I, pp. 213-15.

13. Bennett, *Steam Navy*, pp. 277, 278; Church, *Ericsson*, Vol. I, 246-53, 250-51; J. Leander Bishop, *History of American Manufactures from 1608 to 1860 . . .* (3 vols.), Philadelphia, 1861-68, Vol. III, p. 116; Ericsson to Fox, Jan. 20, 1862, Fox papers, NYHS; Davis, *Davis*, pp. 135-38.

14. Charles W. Maccord, "Ericsson and His Monitor," *North American Review*, Oct. 1889, Vol. 149, No. 395, pp. 462, 463; *ORN*, Series II, Vol. I, pp. 90, 159; Joseph Smith to Ericsson, Oct. 19, 21, Nov. 18, 1861; Ericsson to T. R. Dorlan, Aug. 20, 1874, Misc. papers, HL; see also Ericsson's original contract with his subcontractors, Oct. 28, 1861, Smithsonian; Church, *Ericsson*, Vol. I, pp. 259-71; Edgar Welles, "Scrapbook," p. 25.

15. Welles to Mary Welles, Sept. 1, 1861, WP-LC.

16. John Law to Welles, Aug. 8, 1861, WP-LC; Adam Gurowski, *Diary* (3 vols.), Boston and Washington, D.C., 1862-66, Vol. I, p. 91.

17. Davis, *Davis*, p. 146; Du Pont to Mrs. Du Pont, Sept. 15, 1861, Du Pont, *Letters*, Vol. I, p. 147; Davis, *Davis*, pp. 132, 133.

18. By early September the dispatches to Morgan assumed such an urgent tone that even he became discouraged. "I cannot buy as cheap as if I had a week to do it in," he complained, adding, "I have done all in my power to buy cheap, always

have bought trustfully & carefully." Morgan to Welles, Sept. 10, 1861, WP-LC.

19. Du Pont to Henry Winter Davis, Oct. 8, 1861, Du Pont papers, EML. A comparison of the original letter, with the published version of the Du Pont letters shows that punctuation and abbreviations differ from the printed text in Du Pont, *Letters*, Vol. I, pp. 162-64. For McClellan's continued opposition to the joint expedition, see his note to Thomas A. Scott, Oct. 17, 1861, *ORN*, Series I, Vol. IV, p. 179; see also McClellan's plan for attack on the Southern coast in his memorandum to Lincoln, Aug. 2, 1861, George B. McClellan, *McClellan's Own Story*, New York, 1887, p. 103. Until the meeting on October 7, Lincoln had been pushing the Du Pont–Sherman operation. Du Pont to Mrs. Du Pont, Sept. 17, 1861, Du Pont, *Letters*, Vol. I, p. 149; Lincoln to Simon Cameron, Sept. 18, 1861; Lincoln to Welles, Sept. 18, 1861, Lincoln papers, LC.

20. Welles, "Admiral Farragut and New Orleans. With an Account of the Origin and Command of the First Three Naval Expeditions of the War. First Paper," *The Galaxy*, Vol. XII, Nov. 1871, pp. 672, 673; Du Pont to Henry Du Pont, Oct. 15, 1861, Du Pont, *Letters*, Vol. I, pp. 164-65; Du Pont to Fox, Oct. 24, 1861, Fox, *Confidential Correspondence*, Vol. I, p. 58. In all, 78 vessels, ranging from converted Brooklyn-Manhattan ferryboats to four of the new Lenthall gunboats just out of the yards. There were 23 colliers, 29 transports, and 26 warships. "I am astounded myself at the magnitude of the affair," wrote Du Pont. Du Pont to Mrs. Du Pont, Oct. 24, 26, 1861, Du Pont, *Letters*, Vol. I, pp. 184, 188. Percival Drayton to L. M. Hoyt, Oct. 25, 1861, "Naval Letters of Captain Percival Drayton," *Bulletin of the New York Public Library*, Vol. X, No. 11, Nov. 1906, p. 593.

21. H. W. Davis reported that "by the 10th we got enough from the leaky rumors of the Secesh to know you were successful." Davis to Du Pont, Nov. 15, 1861, Du Pont papers, EML. Du Pont to Welles, Nov. 8, 21, 1861, *ORN*, Series I, Vol. XII, pp. 265, 266. Du Pont's fleet captain, Charles H. Davis, said: "We came here with plans matured at the Department which we executed almost *au pied de la lettre. . . .*" Davis to Welles, n.d. (1861), WP-LC.

22. C. F. Adams, Jr., to Henry Adams, Nov. 5, 1861, W. C. Ford (ed.), *C. F. and Henry Adams, A Cycle of Adams Letters* (2 Vols.), Boston, 1920, Vol. I, p. 63; Welles to Edgar Welles, Dec. 8, 1861, WP-LC; Washington *Evening Star*, Aug. 2, 1861. Bushnell owned a quarter-interest in Ericsson's ironclad *Monitor*, which was then under construction. He held the contract for the *Galena*, an ironclad gunboat, and had made a tidy sum for himself as the middleman in the charter and sale of several steamers to the government. Everything Bushnell had done was perfectly legal, but he was excoriated, and deservedly so, for making exorbitant profits at the Navy's expense. *House Reports*, 37th Cong., 2nd sess., Vol. I, No. 2, pt. I, pp. 23, 24, 673, 286; pt. II, pp. 1510-13. G. D. Morgan to Welles, Sept. 7, 1861, WP-NYHS.

23. *Congressional Globe*, 37th Cong., 1st sess., p. 1.

24. Dexter A. Hawkins to Elihu B. Washburne, Jan. 6, 1862, Washburne papers, LC.

25. Welles, n.d., "Memorandum," WP-HL; New York *Evening Post*, Jan. 19, 1862; *Hartford Courant*, Feb. 12, 1862. See, for instance, Morgan's explanation of his course in four separate purchases. G. D. Morgan to Welles, Dec. 23, 1861, WP-NYPL; *Senate Exec. Doc.*, No. 15, Jan. 14, 1862, 37th Cong., 2nd sess.; *Senate Reports*, 37th Cong., 2nd sess., Nos. 9, 15. *Congressional Globe*, 37th Cong., 2nd sess., Appendix, pp. 124ff; Edgar Welles, "Scrapbook," pp. 31-33.

26. G. D. Morgan to Welles, Dec. 24, 1861; Welles to Morgan, Dec. 30, 1861, WP-LC; *Hartford Courant*, Jan. 13, 1862; Fox to Welles, Jan. 15, 1867; James Holbrook to Welles, Mar. 14, 1861; Mark Howard to Welles, May 3, July 25, 1861, Jan. 31, 1862, WP-LC; *Hartford Courant*, May 30, July 3, 1861, Apr. 28, 1862; *New-York Tribune*, Aug. 29, 1861, Mar. 19, 1862; *Hartford Courant*, Feb. 12, 1862; W. L. Barnes to Erastus Corning, June 28, 1862; George Barnard to Howard, Aug. 17, 1861; Howard to Welles, Aug. 19, 1861; Welles to Howard, Sept. 22, 1861; Charles Eames to

Welles, Oct. 5, 1861, WP-LC; James Grimes to Fox, Aug. 1862, Fox papers, NYHS; Welles to Fox, July 25, 1871, WP-NYPL; William Salter, *The Life of James W. Grimes*, New York, 1876, pp. 290-291; J. M. Forbes to Ripley, Feb. 17, 1862, in Sarah F. Hughes (ed.), *Letters and Recollections of John Murray Forbes* (2 vols.), Boston and New York, 1899, 1900, Vol. I, pp. 289, 290; Forbes to C. B. Sedgewick, Jan. 18, 1862, WP-LC; Forbes had written an earlier private letter to Sedgewick, making a much more spirited defense. Sedgewick, a New York congressman and a member of the House naval affairs committee, defended Welles on the floor of the House. *Congressional Globe*, 37th Cong., 2nd sess., Appendix, pp. 124ff. See also John Ericcson to James Gordon Bennett, *New York Herald*, Apr. 26, 1862.

27. James M. Merrill, *Battle Flags South*, Rutherford, N.J., 1970, pp. 31-35; Gurowski, *Diary*, Vol. I, p. 91.

28. Welles to Edgar Welles, Feb. 5, 9, 1862; to G. D. Morgan (draft), Dec. 25, 1861; Mrs. D. G. Farragut to "Dr. Sir," Feb. 1, 1881, WP-LC; *Diary of Edward Bates*, p. 227; *Congressional Globe*, 37th Cong., 2nd sess., p. 821; A. H. Foote to Welles, Feb. 15, 1862, *ORN*, Series I, Vol. XXII, pp. 585-87; L. M. Goldsborough to Fox, Feb. 20, 1862, Fox, *Confidential Correspondence*, Vol. I, pp. 240-42. Du Pont had been probing the Georgia coastline since early December 1861. C. H. Davis to Welles, Dec. 6, 1861, WP-LC; Farragut to Fox, Feb. 17, 1862; Charles Lee Lewis, *David Glasgow Farragut, Our First Admiral*, Annapolis, 1943, pp. 20-21.

29. Thomas Scott to E. M. Stanton, Feb. 11, 1862, Apr. 16, 19, 1862, Stanton papers, LC; A. H. Foote to Welles, June 20, 1862; James B. Eads to Welles, May 8, 1861, WP-LC; Davis, *Davis*, pp. 216, 217; Fletcher Pratt, *Civil War on Western Waters*, New York, 1956, p. 14; Merrill, *Battle Flags South*, pp. 21-22; Foote to Welles, July 2, 1862, WP-LC; James M. Hoppin, *Life of Andrew Hull Foote, Rear Admiral United States Navy*, pp. 178-88.

30. *Diary of Edward Bates*, pp. 182, 183; Welles to Simon Cameron, May 14, 1861; Welles to James B. Eads, Apr. 29, 1861; Cameron to George B. McClellan, May 14, 1861; Welles to John Rodgers, May 16, 1861; Welles to S. M. Pook, May 30, 1861; J. K. Moorhead to Cameron, May 27, 1861; Rodgers to Welles, June 8, 1861; Welles to Rodgers, June 12, 1861; S. L. Phelps to Rodgers, July 21, 1861; Fox to J. P. Sanford, Sept. 24, 1861, all *ORN*, Series I, Vol. XII, pp. 277-350; McClellan, *McClellan's Own Story*, pp. 44, 45; John C. Frémont to Montgomery Blair, n.d., NYHS; see also Frémont to Blair, Aug. 9, 1861, *ORN*, Series I, Vol. XII, p. 297; A. H. Foote to Fox, Sept. 27, Nov. 2, 4, Dec. 30, 1861, Jan. 4, 11, 27, 31, 1862; Fox to Foote, Jan. 27, Mar. 7, 1862; Fox to D. D. Porter, Nov. 8, 1862, Fox, *Confidential Correspondence*, Vol. II, pp. 20-42, 147.

31. McClellan, *McClellan's Own Story*, pp. 101-5; Pratt, *Western Waters*, pp. 46-51; Edward Devens to Fox, Oct. 28, 1861, Fox, *Confidential Correspondence*, Vol. I, pp. 391-96; *New York Times*, Oct. 28, 1861; *New York Herald*, Oct. 27, 1861; Welles, "Admiral Farragut and New Orleans . . . First Paper," p. 675.

32. Fox to Welles, June 19, 1871, WP-HL; Welles, "Admiral Farragut and New Orleans . . . First Paper," pp. 677, 678; D. D. Porter to Fox, July 5, 14, 1861, Fox, *Confidential Correspondence*, Vol. II, pp. 73-80; Fox to Welles, Dec. 1, 1870, Jan. 24, June 19, 1871, WP-LC; Fox to Welles, June 19, July 8, 1871, WP-HL; Bigelow, *Retrospections*, Vol. I, p. 490; Welles to Morrill, Dec. 1869, WP-HL; Hay, *Letters and Diary*, Vol. I, p. 246. Welles, writing in the *Galaxy* ten years later, states that the personnel at the meeting were himself, Fox, Porter, Lincoln, and McClellan. But Dahlgren wrote in his journal on Nov. 14, 1861, that he went to the meeting with Welles, Fox, and Porter. Porter has a different version in his *Incidents and Anecdotes of the Civil War*, 1885, in which he has Hale and Grimes also present, but not Fox. Testimony of Welles, Fox, and Dahlgren all controvert this. Welles would never have asked Hale to any such conference, Porter, *Incidents*, pp. 64-66. Lincoln brought Seward with him, Dahlgren, *Dahlgren*, p. 348.

33. Samuel Breeze was senior and had commanded a squadron, but had not been

to sea for over three years; see Lewis R. Hamersly, *The Records of Living Officers of the U.S. Navy and the Marine Corps*, Philadelphia, 1870.

34. Welles to Fox, July 8, 1871, WP-HL; D. D. Porter to Fox, Mar. 28, 1862, Fox papers, NYHS; Welles, *Diary*, Vol. II, pp. 116, 117; Welles, "Admiral Farragut and New Orleans (I)," pp. 679ff, 681. Charles Lee Lewis, *David Glasgow Farragut, Our First Admiral*, p. 7; *David Glasgow Farragut, Admiral in the Making*, Annapolis, 1941, pp. 264-66; *Register of the Commissioned and Warrant Officers of the Navy of the United States, Including Officers of the Marine Corps and Others for the Year 1861*, Washington, D.C., 1861, pp. 16, 17; *House Exec. Doc.*, No. 24, 1861-62, 37th Cong., 2nd sess., pp. 2-4; Welles, *Diary*, Vol. II, Aug. 23, 1864, pp. 116, 117, 134, 135; Lewis, *Farragut* (1943), pp. 8, 9.

35. Dahlgren, *Dahlgren*, pp. 349, 350; Fox to Welles, Jan. 24, 1871, WP-LC; Lewis, *Farragut, Our First Admiral*, pp. 8, 9, 12-14; Welles, *Diary*, Vol. I, p. 440.

36. Welles to Mary Welles, Sept. 10, 1862, WP-LC.

37. Loyall Farragut, *The Life of David Glasgow Farragut, First Admiral of the United States Navy*, New York, 1879, p. 217; Farragut to Fox, Jan. 30, Feb. 12, Mar. 5, 21, 1862; Fox, *Confidential Correspondence*, Vol. I, pp. 209-301, 304, 305, 307; Fox to Porter, Feb. 24, 1862, Porter papers, HL; Porter to Fox, Mar. 28, Apr. 8, 1862, Fox papers, NYHS.

38. Farragut to Fox, Mar. 21, Apr. 7, 8, 1862, Fox papers, NYHS; William Hunter, Jr., to Welles, Oct. 24, 1862, WP-HL.

39. Farragut, *Life of Farragut*, p. 216; Lewis, *Farragut, Our First Admiral*, pp. 30, 31; Fox to Welles, Dec. 1, 1870, Jan. 24, 1871, WP-LC.

40. C. H. Davis to Du Pont, Apr. 1, 1862 quoted in Davis, *Davis*, pp. 209, 210.

41. Dahlgren, *Dahlgren*, p. 366.

42. Fox to Farragut, May 17, 1862, Farragut papers, HL. Welles to Farragut, Jan. 20, 1862, *ORN*, Series I, Vol. XVIII, pp. 7, 8.

43. Welles, *Diary*, Vol. I, p. 440; Welles, "Admiral Farragut at New Orleans . . . Second Paper," *The Galaxy*, Vol. XII, Dec. 1871, pp. 824, 828; Welles to Edgar Welles, May 25, 1862, WP-LC.


CHAPTER 21

1. New York *Herald*, Jan. 3, 1863. Welles, *Diary*, Vol. I, p. 212, Jan. 1, 1863.

2. See Montgomery Blair's opinion on the creation of West Virginia, WP-LC, Dec. 26, 1862; Welles, *Diary*, Vol. I, pp. 191, 208-9, 212-13; Lincoln to Members of the Cabinet, Dec. 23, 1862; Welles to Lincoln, Dec. 29, 1862, Lincoln papers, LC; *Diary of Edward Bates*, p. 271; Washington *Evening Star*, Jan. 1, 1863. The Lincoln papers have two copies of Welles' opinion; one is in microfilm, series I, reel 46, the other, which Lincoln actually read, is in microfilm, series III, reel 97.

3. When fortifications expert General Mansfield said to Welles that "we must . . . establish our military lines; [make them] frontiers between the belligerents as between the countries of Continental Europe," Welles strenuously opposed his viewpoint. Attributing Mansfield's statement to the teachings of West Point, Welles remarked at the time, "we become by the process rapidly two [hostile] nations. All beyond the frontiers are considered . . . as enemies, although large sections and in some instances whole states have a Union majority." Welles, *Diary*, Vol. I, pp. 84, 85.

4. *Ibid.*, p. 209.

5. W. C. Bryant to J. M. Forbes, Aug. 21, 1861, in Hughes (ed.), *Forbes*, Vol. I, p. 237.

6. A. Howard Meneeley, *The War Department, 1861, a Study in Mobilization and Administration*, New York, 1928, Ch. IX; Field, *Memories of Many Men*, pp. 220, 266, 267.

7. J. M. Forbes to Bryant, Aug. 24, 1861, in Hughes (ed.), *Forbes*, Vol. I, p. 241.

8. Welles to Stringham, Sept. 25, 1861; Welles to Du Pont, Sept. 25, 1861, *ORN*, Series I, Vol. VI, p. 25; Vol. XII, p. 210.

9. Welles to Howard, Sept. 23, 1861, WP-LC.

10. Lincoln urged Senator Orville H. Browning to have Forney elected Secretary of the Senate. Browning, *Diary*, Vol. I, pp. 478, 481, 482.

11. Smith wrote to the New York Democrat S. L. M. Barlow that he had "replied with some warmth, advocating the position that the government had nothing to do with slavery & that the rebellion could & ought to be crushed by the arms of free white men alone." Caleb Smith to Barlow, Nov. 22, 23, 1861, Barlow papers, HL.

12. "Report of the Secretary of the Navy," *Senate Exec. Doc.*, No. 1, 37th Cong., 2nd sess., 1861, p. 21.

13. George W. Julian, *Political Recollections, 1840 to 1872*, Chicago, 1884, p. 198.

14. Percival Drayton to L. M. Hoyt, Jan. 18, 1862, *Bulletin of the New York Public Library*, Vol. X, No. 11, Nov. 1906, p. 597.

15. Welles to Edgar Welles, Dec. 8, 1861, WP-LC; Welles, "The History of Emancipation," *The Galaxy*, Vol. XIV, No. 6, Dec. 1872, pp. 838, 839.

16. Welles to Blair, n. d., WP-NYPL; Welles to Blair, Sept. 24, 1870; Alexander McClure to Welles, Nov. 14, 1870, WP-LC; Meneeley, "Three Manuscripts of Gideon Welles," pp. 486-88; *Diary of Edward Bates*, pp. 203, 206; Nevins, *The War for the Union*, Vol. I, pp. 397-402.

17. David Donald, *Charles Sumner and the Rights of Man*, New York, 1970, p. 50; Welles, *Lincoln and Seward*, pp. 42, 201; Welles, *Diary*, Vol. I, p. 58; Benjamin Thomas and Harold Hyman, *Stanton: The Life and Times of Lincoln's Secretary of War*, New York, 1962, pp. 100, 110, 111; Van Deusen, *Seward*, p. 244.

18. Nevins, *The War for the Union*, Vol. I, p. 409; Field, *Memories of Many Men*, pp. 264, 268; Welles, *Diary*, Vol. I, pp. 56-59; Fanny Seward, MS Diary, Apr. 4, 1862, Seward papers, Univ. of Rochester.

19. Meneeley, "Three Manuscripts of Gideon Welles," p. 588; Welles to Blair, Jan. 9, 1861, Blair Family papers, LC.

20. Welles, *Diary*, Vol. I, p. 54.

21. *Diary of Edward Bates*, p. 227.

22. For pertinent contemporary comments on Stanton, see Fanny Seward, MS Diary, Apr. 6, 1862, Seward papers, Univ. of Rochester; Welles, *Diary*, Vol. I, pp. 54-60; *Diary of Edward Bates*, p. 227; Dennis Hart Mahan to W. C. Church, n. d. (1863), Church papers, NYPL.

23. Meneeley, "Three Manuscripts of Gideon Welles," p. 493.

24. Thomas and Hyman, *Stanton*, p. 134.

25. *Ibid.*, pp. 148, 149; H. L. Trefousse, *Benjamin Franklin Wade, Radical Republican from Ohio*, New York, 1963, pp. 161, 162.

26. Nevins, *The War for the Union*, Vol. I, pp. 406-7; Trefousse, *Wade*, pp. 159-67.

27. Thomas and Hyman, *Stanton*, p. 134.

28. Julian, *Recollections*, p. 205.

29. Mahan, a professor at West Point, had conferred with Chase in November 1861, and at that time he presented the Secretary with a plan for the organization of the armies into corps. Mahan breakfasted with Stanton on his first day in office and again urged this plan; Dennis H. Mahan to W. C. Church, n.d. (1863), Church papers, NYPL.

30. Welles, *Diary*, Vol. I, p. 61.

31. *Ibid.*, Vol. I, p. 69.

32. Percival Drayton to Mrs. Hoyt, Oct. 12, 1861; *Bulletin of the New York Public Library*, Vol. X, No. 11, Nov. 1906, p. 592; Dahlgren, *Dahlgren*, p. 349; G. W. Blunt in the *New-York Tribune*, Jan. 27, 1866.

33. Welles, *Diary*, Vol. I, p. 61; Fox to Welles, July 10, 1869, WP-LC; June 19, 1871, WP-HL.

34. Welles, *Diary*, Vol. I, p. 64.

## CHAPTER 22

1. Welles, *Diary*, Vol. I, pp. 61, 62; West, *Welles*, p. 156.
2. Browning, *Diary*, Vol. I, pp. 532, 533; Dahlgren, *Dahlgren*, pp. 358-59; J. K. F. Mansfield to John E. Wool, March 8, 1862; Wool to Stanton, March 8, 1862; John L. Worden to Welles, March 8, 1862, *ORN*, Series I, Vol. 7, pp. 4, 5.
3. Welles, *Diary*, Vol. I, pp. 62-76; Dahlgren, *Dahlgren*, pp. 359, 360; Fox to Welles, Mar. 9, 1862; Fox to G. B. McClellan, Mar. 9, 1862; Fox to Montgomery Blair, Mar. 10, 1862, Fox, *Confidential Correspondence*, Vol. I, pp. 434-36; John A. Dahlgren to Ulrich Dahlgren, Mar. 11, 1862, Dahlgren papers, LC; Hay, *Letters and Diary*, Vol. I, p. 54. Quite likely the *Monitor* would have sunk the *Merrimack* had Dahlgren permitted wrought iron to replace cast iron shot. He feared that the wrought iron shot was too heavy, and he would not risk the bursting of the *Monitor*'s guns. Later it was proved not only that wrought iron shot was safe but that the guns could have been loaded with twice the amount of powder. Dahlgren to Fox, Mar. 11, 1862, Huntington Coll., HL.
4. J. G. Bernard to Fox, Feb. 12, 1862; McClellan to Fox, Mar. 14, 1862, *Confidential Correspondence*, Vol. I, pp. 419-22, 438-39; Welles, *Diary*, Vol. I, p. 120; Vol. III, p. 674; Stephen E. Ambrose, *Halleck, Lincoln's Chief of Staff*, Baton Rouge, 1962, pp. 5-9.
5. Welles, *Diary*, Vol. I, pp. 83, 107, 119-21.
6. *Ibid.*, p. 102.
7. Hyman and Thomas, *Stanton*, pp. 143, 170, 171; J. W. Schuckers, *Life and Public Services of Salmon Portland Chase*, pp. 434-37; Welles, *Diary*, Vol. I, pp. 101-4.
8. Nevins, *The War for the Union*, Vol. IV, p. 125; Welles, *Diary*, Vol. I, p. 108.
9. *Ibid.*, p. 93.
10. *Ibid.*, pp. 94-96; E. G. Bourne (ed.), *Diary and Correspondence of Salmon P. Chase, Annual Report of the American Historical Association* (2 vols.), Washington, D.C., 1903, Vol. II, p. 62.
11. Welles, *Diary*, Vol. I, pp. 98, 99; Edgar Welles to Mary Welles, Aug. 31, 1862; Welles to Mary Welles, Aug. 31, 1862, WP-LC; Welles, quoting Lincoln on the figures, *Diary*, Vol. I, p. 117.
12. *Ibid.*, pp. 100-102; undated circular, Stanton papers, LC; Chase, *Diary and Correspondence*, pp. 62, 63.
13. Welles, *Diary*, Vol. I, p. 104.
14. Edward Bates to Lieber, Sept. 2, 3, 1862, Lieber papers, HL.
15. Welles, *Diary*, Vol. I, pp. 104-5.
16. Welles, *Lincoln and Seward*, p. 196.
17. Welles, *Diary*, Vol. I, pp. 107-12; Welles, *Lincoln and Seward*, pp. 193-98; Welles to Mary Welles, Sept. 2, 1862, WP-LC.
18. Welles, *Diary*, Vol. I, p. 118.
19. *Ibid.*, pp. 114, 115. Commenting on the alarm in Pennsylvania, Welles wrote his wife, who was visiting her old home: "Governor Curtin is a very excitable man, and not capable of looking at things deliberately. It is one of the misfortunes of times like these, to have men in responsible positions who are easily panic stricken. Weakness of judgment and necessary prompt decisions are qualities that do not always couple." Welles to Mary Welles, Sept. 14, 1862, WP-LC.
20. *Ibid.*, July 13, 1862, WP-LC.
21. Welles, *Diary*, Vol. I, pp. 70, 71.
22. Welles to Mary Welles, July 13, 1862, WP-LC.
23. Thomas and Hyman, *Stanton*, pp. 234, 235.
24. It is unclear whether Lincoln consulted with other members of the Cabinet before he presented his "order" before the Cabinet on July 22, 1862; Allan Nevins, *The War for the Union*, Vol. II, pp. 163-65. There is evidence that he had spoken

about it to Stanton, possibly as early as May. Stanton seems to have had an inkling that Lincoln would propose emancipation before the Cabinet meeting on July 22, 1862. He took F. B. Cutting, formerly a pro-slavery Democrat from New York but now a fervid emancipationist, to visit Lincoln on July 22, hoping apparently that Cutting would convince the President to act. Since Lincoln had already drafted a proclamation, there would have seemed to be no need for the Cutting interview if Stanton had known this. He himself expressed surprise at the scope of Lincoln's draft. Stanton, "Memo," Cabinet meeting, Tuesday, July 22, 1862, Stanton papers, LC; see Thomas and Hyman, *Stanton*, pp. 238, 239, for a different interpretation of the Cutting letter. Cutting to Stanton, Feb. 20, 1867, Stanton papers, LC.

25. Welles, "Administration of Abraham Lincoln," *The Galaxy*, Vol. XXIII, Feb. 1877, pp. 155, 156; *New-York Tribune*, May 3, 1862.

26. E. M. Stanton, "Memorandum," Stanton papers, LC; Welles, "Administration of Abraham Lincoln (III)," *The Galaxy*, Oct. 1877, Vol. XXIII, p. 441; Chase, *Diary*, pp. 48, 49; Thomas and Hyman, pp. 239, 240.

27. Welles, *Diary*, Vol. I, p. 142.

28. Chase, *Diary*, pp. 87-89; E. M. Stanton, "Memorandum"; Cutting to Stanton, Feb. 20, 1867, Stanton papers, LC; Welles, *Diary*, Vol. I, pp. 142-45.

## CHAPTER 23

1. *Report of the Joint Committee on the Conduct of the War*, Vol. IV, part 3, p. 415; 37th Cong., 3rd sess.

2. Fox to Du Pont, May 12, 1862, Fox, *Confidential Correspondence*, Vol. I, p. 119.

3. Welles to Du Pont, May 13, 1862, in *Report of the Secretary of the Navy in Relation to Armored Vessels*, Washington, D.C., 1864, p. 51 (hereafter cited as *Armored Vessels*), also published as *House Exec. Doc.* No. 69, 38th Cong., 1st sess.

4. Dahlgren, *Dahlgren*, p. 381.

5. Du Pont to Mrs. Du Pont, in *Letters*, June 22, 1862, Vol. II, p. 129.

6. Fox to Du Pont, May 12, June 3, 1862, Fox, *Confidential Correspondence*, Vol. I, pp. 119, 120, 126-28.

7. Welles, *Diary*, Vol. I, p. 160.

8. Du Pont to Mrs. Du Pont, Oct. 16, 17, 22, 1862, Du Pont, *Letters*, Vol. II, pp. 245-58.

9. *Ibid.*, p. 258.

10. Du Pont to H. W. Davis, Oct. 25, 1862, Du Pont, *Letters*, Vol. II, p. 259.

11. Fox to Du Pont, Dec. 13, 1862; Jan. 6, 1863, Fox, *Confidential Correspondence*, Vol. I, pp. 168-70, 172, 173.

12. Welles to Du Pont, Jan. 6, 1863, in *Armored Vessels*, p. 52.

13. Du Pont to Welles, Du Pont, *Letters*, Vol. II, p. 377.

14. Du Pont to Mrs. Du Pont, Feb. 15, 1863, Du Pont, *Letters*, Vol. II, p. 436; Welles to Du Pont, Jan. 31, 1863, *Armored Vessels*, pp. 53, 54.

15. G. W. Childs (comp.), *The National Almanac Record for the Year 1863-1864*, Philadelphia, 1863-64, p. 116; J. Thomas Scharf, *History of the Confederate Navy from Its Organization to the Surrender of Its Last Vessel*, Albany, 1894, pp. 505-13. Welles, *Diary*, Vol. I, pp. 220-30; Fox to Farragut, Fox, *Confidential Correspondence*, Vol. I, pp. 324-26; George S. Denison to Chase, Jan. 8, 1863, Chase papers, LC.

16. Scharf, *Confederate Navy*, p. 981.

17. New York *Herald*, Feb. 4-6; *New-York Tribune*, Feb. 5, 6; *New York Times*, Feb. 5, 1863.

18. Welles, *Diary*, Vol. I, p. 232.

19. See, for instance, Du Pont to Fox, Dec. 22, 1862, Feb. 25, Mar. 3, 1863, Fox, *Confidential Correspondence*, Vol. I, 170-72, 182-84, 187-89.

20. Fox to Du Pont, Feb. 16, 1863, Fox, *Confidential Correspondence,* Vol. I, pp. 179, 180; Welles, *Diary,* Vol. I, p. 236.

21. *Ibid.;* Thomas Turner to Du Pont, Jan. 19, 1863, *Armored Vessels,* pp. 171, 172.

22. Du Pont to Fox, Feb. 24, 1862, Fox, *Confidential Correspondence,* Vol. I, pp. 182, 183.

23. Percival Drayton to Du Pont, Mar. 4, 1863, *Armored Vessels,* p. 187; Du Pont to Mrs. Du Pont, Mar. 4, 1863, Du Pont, *Letters,* Vol. II, pp. 465-67.

24. Welles, *Diary,* Vol. I, p. 249.

25. Stimers was also concerned about their slow rate of fire; Stimers to Fox, Feb. 28, 1863, Fox papers, NYHS.

26. Welles, *Diary,* Vol. I, p. 247.

27. Du Pont to Mrs. Du Pont, Mar. 27, 1863, Du Pont, *Letters,* Vol. II, pp. 518, 519; Welles, *Diary,* Vol. I, p. 247. Some members of the "lobby" are identified in Faxon to Welles, June 2, 1872, WP-LC. See also Welles' testimony, *House Misc. Doc.,* 42nd Cong., 2nd sess., p. 262.

28. Du Pont to Fox, Mar. 2, 1863, Fox, *Confidential Correspondence,* Vol. I, pp. 185-86.

29. Fox to Du Pont, Mar. 18, 1863, Fox, *Confidential Correspondence,* Vol. I, pp. 193, 194.

30. Welles, *Diary,* Vol. I, p. 259; Dahlgren, *Dahlgren,* p. 389; Halleck joined the chorus of critics when he told Lincoln that Du Pont "had serious doubts as to the capture of Charleston," Fox to Du Pont, Mar. 26, 1863, Fox, *Confidential Correspondence,* Vol. I, p. 196; Fox to Ericsson, Apr. 9, 1863, Pierpont Morgan Library, New York.

31. Du Pont to Mrs. Du Pont, Mar. 27, 1863, Du Pont, *Letters,* Vol. II, pp. 519-20.

32. After the fact, Du Pont recognized that he should have "told the department what I thought: that the attack would be futile and might be disastrous." Du Pont to Mrs. Du Pont, Apr. 10, 1863, Du Pont, *Letters,* Vol. III, p. 14.

33. Du Pont to Mrs. Du Pont, Apr. 8, 1863, Du Pont, *Letters,* Vol. III, pp. 3-6; Du Pont to Welles, with reports, Apr. 8, 1863, *Armored Vessels,* pp. 55-81.

34. Fox to Du Pont, Apr. 2, 1863, Du Pont, *Letters,* Vol. II, p. 538.

35. John Hay to Lincoln, Apr. 10, 1863, Hay, *Letters and Diary,* Vol. I, pp. 75-78.

36. For a dramatic account of the battle and subsequent events, see Villard, *Memoirs,* Vol. II, pp. 27-51.

37. Du Pont to Mrs. Du Pont, Apr. 25, 1863, Du Pont, *Letters,* Vol. III, pp. 59, 60; Welles, *Diary,* Vol. I, pp. 267, 268; *Armored Vessels,* p. 77; Du Pont to Welles, Apr. 16, 1863, Du Pont, *Letters,* Vol. III, p. 39; John Hay to Nicolay, Apr. 23, 1863, in Hay *Letters and Diary,* Vol. I, p. 83; Lincoln to Hunter and Du Pont, Apr. 14, 1863, *Armored Vessels,* p. 78.

38. Charles O. Boutelle to Du Pont, Apr. 22, 1863, *ORN,* Series I, Vol. IV, p. 56; John Hay to Nicolay, Apr. 23, 1863, *Hay Letters and Diary,* Vol. I, pp. 83-84; Stimers differed with the captains; see his report, *Armored Vessels,* pp. 80, 81; John Rodgers to Welles, May 1863, WP-HL; Welles, *Diary,* Vol. I, p. 296.

39. Fulton had filed copies of his stories with Fox, though he was not required to do so. He had also corresponded with Fox and with Montgomery Blair. But the story that was so critical of Du Pont had not been read by Fox or by Welles. Admiral Charles H. Davis, who also did not read it until after publication, thought that, if it had, they would have censored it. Fulton to Fox, Mar. 24, 1863, Apr. 13, 1863, Fox papers, NYHS; Fox to Welles, May 13, 1863, Welles misc. papers, NYHS; Horatio Bridge to Du Pont, May 15, 1863; Benjamin Gerhard to Du Pont, June 18, 1863, Du Pont papers, EML; Welles, *Diary,* Vol. I, p. 288.

40. *Armored Vessels,* pp. 99-101.

41. Gerald S. Henig, "Henry Winter Davis: A Biography," unpubl. doctoral dissertation, CUNY, 1971, p. 358; Carman and Luthin, *Lincoln and the Patronage,* p. 209; H. W. Davis to Du Pont, May 3, 1863, Du Pont papers, EML; Davis to Lincoln, May 4, 1863, Lincoln papers, LC; Welles, *Diary,* Vol. I, pp. 312, 341, 342.

## CHAPTER 24

1. Welles, *Diary*, Vol. I, p. 107; *Diary of Edward Bates*, pp. 258, 259; Welles to Reuben Hale, May 24, 1862, Welles papers, Univ. of Chicago Library; Welles to Edgar Welles, Feb. 25, 1862, WP-LC.

2. Mary Welles to Edgar Welles, June 1, 1862; Joseph D. Hull to Welles, June 19, 1862, WP-LC.

3. Welles to Mary Welles, Sept. 8, 12, 1862; Welles to George S. Blake, Sept. 15, 1862, WP-LC.

4. Welles to Edgar Welles, Oct. 12, 1862, WP-LC; Hubert Welles died Nov. 18, 1862; Welles to Edgar Welles, Nov. 18, 1862, WP-HL; *New-York Tribune*, Nov. 18, 1862; *Hartford Courant*, Nov. 20, 1862; Welles, *Diary*, Vol. I, p. 182.

5. Anna I. Boyden, *Echoes from Hospital and White House*, Boston, 1884, p. 52.

6. Lincoln to Welles, Feb. 21, 1862, WP-CHS.

7. Dr. Robert Kingston to Mary Welles, Feb. 21, 1862, WP-LC.

8. *Diary of Edward Bates*, p. 236; Welles to Edgar Welles, Feb. 23, 1862, WP-LC.

9. Mary Lincoln to Mary Welles, Feb. 21, 1862, July 11, 1865, WP-LC; Boyden, *Echoes*, pp. 70, 71, 74-76; Ruth Painter Randall, *Mary Lincoln: The Biography of a Marriage*, Boston, 1953, pp. 67, 245.

10. Welles, *Lincoln and Seward*, pp. 186, 187.

11. John Hooker to Welles, Nov. 25, 1861, WP-LC; C. F. Adams, "The Trent Affair," *American Historical Review*, Vol. XVII, Apr. 1912, pp. 544-48; Welles, "The Capture and Release of Mason and Slidell," *The Galaxy*, Vol. XV, May 1873, pp. 648, 649; *ORN*, Series I, Vol. I, p. 148.

12. James P. Baxter, III, "Papers Relating to Belligerent and Neutral Rights," *American Historical Review*, Vol. XXXIV, Oct. 1928, pp. 84-87; Van Deusen, *Seward*, pp. 310-15; Welles, *Diary*, Vol. I, p. 299; Welles, *Lincoln and Seward*, p. 185. For an opposing view, see Percival Drayton to L. M. Hoyt, Jan. 18, 1862, *Bulletin of the New York Public Library*, Vol. X, No. 11, Nov. 1906, p. 599.

13. See Charles J. Hoadley to "Dear Sir," Oct. 4, 1861, CHS, for the boredom, loneliness, and general unpleasantness of blockade duty; Paullin, "The Navy Department During the Civil War (II)," pp. 186-88.

14. Welles, *Diary*, Vol. I, pp. 207, 230.

15. *Scientific American*, Vol. IX, Oct. 24, 1863, p. 260; Welles to Edgar Welles, Mar. 19, 1863; Welles to Aspinwall and Forbes, Mar. 16, 1863; Forbes to Welles, Mar. 28, Apr. 1, 10, 1863, WP-LC. Their mission was unsuccessful. L. M. Case and W. F. Spencer, *The United States and France: Civil War Diplomacy*, Philadelphia, 1970, pp. 433-36.

16. Welles, *Diary*, Vol. I, pp. 246-47; Sumner to Welles, Mar. 11, 1863, WP-LC; Welles, *Diary*, Vol. I, p. 254; Welles to Seward, Mar. 31, 1863, WP-LC (also reprinted in Welles, *Diary*, Vol. I, pp. 252-56, and in Welles, *Lincoln and Seward*, pp. 155-60).

17. W. W. McKean to Welles, Nov. 1, 1861; Welles to McKean, Nov. 25, 1861, WP-NYPL; Bernath, *Civil War Prize Cases*, p. 53.

18. Welles, *Diary*, Vol. I, pp. 79, 80.

19. *Ibid.*; Welles, "Instructions to Squadron Commanders," Aug. 18, 1862, *ORN*, Series I, Vol. VII, pp. 656, 657.

20. Welles, *Diary*, Vol. I, p. 82; *New-York Tribune*, Oct. 24, 1862.

21. *New-York Tribune*, Feb. 12, 1863; Welles, *Lincoln and Seward*, pp. 132-37.

22. Scharf, *Confederate Navy*, p. 797; Seward to Welles, Oct. 31, 1862, WP-LC; Welles, *Lincoln and Seward*, p. 86; Welles to Blair, Apr. 21, 1872, Oct. 29, 1873, WP-LC.

23. Welles to Seward, May 12, 1862, WP-LC; Welles, *Diary*, Vol. I, pp. 266, 267; Welles, *Lincoln and Seward*, pp. 86-88; Welles to Blair, Apr. 21, 1872, Blair Family papers, LC; Welles to Blair, Oct. 29, 1873, BLP, Firestone Library, Princeton; Welles, *Lincoln and Seward*, pp. 85-96; Welles, *Diary*, Vol. I, pp. 266-86; Welles, *Lincoln and*

*Seward,* pp. 92-115; Bernath, *Civil War Prize Cases,* pp. 63-84; Donald, *Sumner,* pp. 108, 111; *New-York Tribune,* Apr. 16, 1863.

24. Percival Drayton to Alexander Hamilton, Jr., Jan. 13, 1864, *Bulletin of the New York Public Library,* Vol. X, No. 12, Dec. 1906, pp. 639, 643; Basler, *Works,* Vol. V, pp. 210, 211; Ludwell H. Johnson, "Northern Profit and Profiteers: The Cotton Rings of 1864-1865," *Civil War History,* Vol. XII, No. 2, June 1966, p. 101.

25. Welles to Edgar Welles, Oct. 18, 1863, WP-LC; Welles, *Diary,* Vol. I, pp. 165, 166, 173-75.

26. *Ibid.,* pp. 177, 183, 318.

27. J. L. McPhail to Foxhall Parker, Feb. 5, 1864; Parker to Welles, Feb. 12, 1864, *ORN,* Series V, Vol. I, pp. 391, 392; Welles, *Diary,* Vol. I, p. 527.

28. Welles to Chase, Feb. 18, 1864, WP-LC; Welles, *Diary,* Vol. I, pp. 527, 528; Field, *Memories of Many Men,* pp. 272, 273; see also Chase to Welles, Mar. 5, 1864; Welles to Chase, Mar. 17, 1864, WP-LC; Welles, *Diary,* Vol. I, pp. 537, 543-48.

29. Welles, *Diary,* Vol. I, pp. 544, 545.

30. Thomas H. O'Connor, "Lincoln and the Cotton Trade," *Civil War History,* Vol. VII, No. 1, Mar. 1961, pp. 23-26; Welles, *Diary,* Vol. I, pp. 14, 98, 510, 511; Basler, *Works,* 1863-64, Vol. VII, pp. 148, 151.

31. Welles, *Diary,* Vol. II, p. 66.

32. Percival Drayton to H. A. Wise, Oct. 23, 1863, n. d. (1864); John H. Missroon to Wise, Oct. 13, 1863, Apr. 16, 1864, Mar. 22, 1865, Wise papers, NYHS; Welles to W. C. Bryant, June 27, 1864; John M. S. Williams to Welles, June 27, 1864; Welles to Mrs. Smith, June 23, 1864, WP-LC; *New-York Tribune,* Nov. 29, 1864, July 29, 1865; H. S. Olcott to Welles, Jan. 29, 1865, WP-LC; Olcott to W. E. Chandler, Feb. 10, 1865, Chandler papers, LC; Chandler to Charles Eames, Feb. 20, 1864; Chandler to Welles, Feb. 25, 1865, WP-LC; Chandler to Olcott, Mar. 28, 1965, Chandler papers, NHHS.

33. Welles to Edgar Welles, Feb. 14, 1864, WP-LC.

34. Welles, *Diary,* Vol. II, p. 179.

## CHAPTER 25

1. Welles, *Diary,* Vol. I, p. 381.

2. *The American Annual Cyclopaedia and Register of Important Events of the Year 1863* (Vols. 1-14), New York, 1862-75; Vol. III, pp. 836-43.

3. Welles, *Diary,* Vol. I, p. 377.

4. Edward McPherson, *The Political History of the United States of America During the Great Rebellion,* Washington, D.C., and New York, 1864, p. 323; Welles, *Diary,* Vol. I, pp. 407-8.

5. Chase to W. C. Noyes, Apr. 7, 1863, Chase to Major B. C. Ludlow, Apr. 7, 1863, Chase to Lincoln, Apr. 12, 1865, Schuckers, *Chase,* pp. 465-67, 516-18; Welles, *Diary,* Vol. II, pp. 410-15; Herman Belz, *Reconstructing the Union, Theory and Policy During the Civil War,* Ithaca, 1969, pp. 97, 98; David Donald (ed.), *Inside Lincoln's Cabinet: The Civil War Diaries of Salmon P. Chase,* New York, 1954, pp. 50, 51.

6. Welles, *Diary,* Vol. I, p. 469; Welles, "Administration of Abraham Lincoln," *The Galaxy,* Vol. XXIII, Feb. 1877, p. 154; Chase to Joshua Levitt, Oct. 7, 1863, Chase to Greeley, Oct. 9, 1863, Schuckers, *Chase,* pp. 303, 304, 394, 395.

7. Dana to Stanton, Dec. 19, 1862, Stanton papers, LC. Dana had written Stanton that Weed had gone over to the "secession democracy. They conspired with them to defeat Wadsworth, and Seward was a party to the conspiracy. These men to defeat the emancipation policy and for the sake of slavery are willing to destroy the government." Welles agreed. See Welles, *Diary,* Vol. I, pp. 154, 219.

8. For example, see Montgomery Blair to S. L. M. Barlow, May 4, 20, 27, 1864, Barlow papers, HL; Welles, *Diary,* Vol. I, p. 205; Vol. II, pp. 20, 370; H. W. Davis

to Du Pont, Sept. 28 or 29, 1864, Du Pont, *Letters*, Vol. III, pp. 393-97; Hay, *Letters and Diary*, Vol. I, pp. 228, 229.

9. *Diary of Edward Bates*, pp. 311-13; H. W. Davis to Du Pont, Nov. 4, 1863, Du Pont papers, EML.

10. *National Intelligencer*, Oct. 5, 1863; Washington *Evening Star*, Oct. 5, 1863; *New-York Tribune*, Oct. 5, 1863.

11. Hay, *Letters and Diary*, Vol. I, pp. 235-45.

12. H. W. Davis to Du Pont, Nov. 20, 1863, Du Pont, *Letters*, Vol. III, p. 286; R. H. Luthin, "A Discordant Chapter in Lincoln's Administration: The Davis and Blair Controversy," *Maryland Historical Magazine*, Vol. XXXIX, No. 1, Mar. 1944, pp. 35, 36.

13. Welles, *Diary*, Vol. I, p. 467; Governor Andrew Curtin was quoted as saying that if Blair had made his speech a month earlier, the Republicans would have lost 20,000 votes in Pennsylvania. But Blair received a surprisingly temperate letter from Sumner and was even congratulated by W. E. Chandler, a rising radical politician in New Hampshire. P. J. Straudenraus (ed.), *Mr. Lincoln's Washington: Selections from the Writings of Noah Brooks, Civil War Correspondent*, New York, 1967, p. 248; Sumner to Blair, Oct. 28, 1863, Chandler to Blair, Oct. 28, 1863, Nov. 20, 1863, Blair Family papers, LC.

14. J. R. Hawley to Welles, Aug. 31, Oct. 2, 1863, Hawley papers, LC; Dahlgren to Welles, Nov. 30, 1863, Jan. 22, Feb. 1, 1864, WP-LC.

15. Du Pont to Welles, Oct. 22, 1863, Welles to Du Pont, Nov. 4, 1863, *Armored Vessels*, pp. 260-70; Welles, *Diary*, Vol. I, pp. 476-78.

16. H. W. Davis to Du Pont, Nov. 4, 1863, Du Pont papers, EML; Charles B. Clark, "Politics in Maryland During the Civil War," *Maryland Historical Magazine*, Vol. XXXVIII, No. 3, Sept. 1943, pp. 251-58; Davis to Du Pont, Jan. 28, 1864, Du Pont papers, EML.

17. Welles, *Diary*, Vol. II, p. 41; Donald, *Sumner*, p. 178; Belz, *Reconstructing the Union*, pp. 155, 156; Hans L. Trefousse, *The Radical Republicans: Lincoln's Vanguard for Social Justice*, New York, 1969, pp. 155, 156; H. W. Davis to Du Pont, Dec. 11, 1863, Du Pont papers, EML.

18. *New-York Tribune*, Dec. 28, 1864.

19. Welles, *Diary*, Vol. I, pp. 481, 482; H. W. Davis to Du Pont, Dec. 11, 1863, Du Pont papers, EML.

20. Richard H. Sewell, *John P. Hale and the Politics of Abolition*, Cambridge, Mass., 1965, pp. 204-7; Hale to G. G. Fogg, Apr. 27, 1863, Hale papers, NHHS; Welles, *Diary*, Vol. I, pp. 484-89; H. W. Davis to Du Pont, Dec. 31, 1863, Du Pont papers, EML; Hale to Elizabeth Hale, Dec. 17, 1863, Hale papers, NHHS. Davis claimed that Stanton was "as much disgusted with Fox & the Secretary as you are & laughs at Grimes' ferocious flutter like a hen with one chicken at the crooking of a finger against the Navy Department." Davis to Du Pont, Mar. 4, 1864; Dec. 31, 1863, Jan. 9, 1864, Du Pont papers, EML. E. L. Pierce, *Memoirs and Letters of Charles Sumner* (4 vols.), Cambridge, Mass., 1877-93, Vol. IV, p. 216.

21. H. W. Davis to Du Pont, Dec. 18 or 19, 1863, Du Pont papers, EML; *Congressional Globe*, 38th Cong., 1st sess., pp. 38, 42; "Report of the Secretary of the Navy, 1863," *House Exec. Doc.*, No. 1, 38th Cong., 1st sess., Vol. IV, *passim*.

22. Welles, *Diary*, Vol. I, pp. 504-5. After Du Pont and other ranking naval officers warned him of the pitfalls, Davis lost interest in the controversy. Davis to Du Pont, Jan. 9, 1864; Du Pont to Davis, Jan. 25, 1864, Du Pont papers, EML. For a full and objective discussion of the controversy, see Sloan, *Isherwood*, Ch. V; see also the not-so-objective account in Bennett, *Steam Navy*, pp. 161, 517-26. John P. Hale was "hot for a blow at Fox and Welles," but Davis, who lacked confidence in his prudence, gave him only the general outlines of his scheme, no details; Davis to Du Pont, Jan. 9, 1864, Du Pont papers, EML.

23. Welles, *Diary*, Vol. I, pp. 507, 508, 522, 523.

24. Welles' decision also required yet another resolution, one that would again reflect on Du Pont's apparent failure to obey orders. Welles probably drafted the resolution himself. Davis to Du Pont, Mar. 1, 1864, Du Pont papers, EML. As a final thrust at his enemies in Congress, Welles chose Frank Blair, Jr., to offer the resolution. William E. Smith, *Blair Family*, Vol. II, pp. 251-52; *Armored Vessels*, Preface, i-iii. The resolution passed handily after Thaddeus Stevens, at Davis' request, withdrew his opposition.

25. The department anticipated the resolution of the House and Senate to print 5000 copies. It was approved April 21, 1864. *Armored Vessels*, Preface, i; H. W. Davis to Du Pont, Apr. 4, 8, 11, 13, 1864, Du Pont papers, EML; *Armored Vessels*, Preface, iii, v; Davis to Du Pont, Jan. 9, Apr. 13, 1864, Du Pont papers, EML.

26. Twice more during his tenure, Davis tried to force a reorganization of the Navy Department by interposing a Board of Admiralty between the Secretary and the bureaus. He failed in both attempts, even though reform along the lines he suggested was long overdue.

On December 9, 1863, a central committee, with Schenck as a prominent member, was formed in Washington to promote Chase's candidacy. Wade, Davis, Stevens, Sumner, and other prominent radicals did not at first associate themselves with this movement, but by early January the Chase boom had gained enough strength among opinion-makers that Senators John Sherman of Ohio and Samuel C. Pomeroy of Kansas, leading Chase men, felt secure enough to engineer a conference. It was well attended. E. L. Pierce, *Sumner*, p. 195. Pomeroy then signed a circular puffing Chase that was widely distributed. The organization also published a pamphlet, *The Next Presidential Election*, a vitriolic attack on Lincoln. Charles R. Wilson, "The Original Chase Organization Meeting and *The Next Presidential Election*," *Journal of American History*, Vol. 23, 1936, pp. 64-76.

27. Welles, *Diary*, Vol. I, p. 501; Welles to Hale, Aug. 13, 1862, Hale papers, NHHS. For the importance of navy yard influence in congressional elections, see, for instance, Samuel Hooper to Welles, Nov. 10, 1864, WP-NYPL.

28. A. H. Foote to Welles, June 12, 1861, WP-LC; John J. Almy to Fox, Sept. 2, 1861, Fox papers, NYHS; Paulding to Welles, Oct. 27, 1862, Aug. 20, 1864; Fox to Welles, Jan. 15, 1867; Francis Bacon to Fessenden, Aug. 26, 1863; WP-LC; Welles to E. D. Morgan, Oct. 26, Dec. 29, 1863, Morgan papers, NYSL.

29. John P. Hale to Blair, Sept. 20, 1863, Blair Family papers, LC; *New-York Tribune*, Sept. 3, 1863; Welles to Edgar Welles, June 12, 1864, WP-LC; *New-York Tribune*, July 18, 1863; W. E. Chandler to Blair, Nov. 20, 1863, Blair Family papers, LC; Carman and Luthin, *Lincoln and the Patronage*, pp. 231-34; Welles, *Diary*, Vol. I, pp. 366, 384, 386, 486-89; Welles to Edgar Welles, Dec. 13, 1863, WP-LC; Fox to Blair, Apr. 12, 1871, Blair Family papers, LC; Leon B. Richardson, *William E. Chandler, Republican*, New York, 1940, pp. 42-44; Chandler to Welles, Feb. 25, 1865, WP-LC.

30. Nehemiah Ordway, Chairman of the Republican state committee, told Blair that at a recent Republican caucus Hale had moved to strike out a resolution endorsing the administration. Only four members out of seventy joined him. Ordway, C. H. Rollins, and Chandler formed the "drug store" clique in Concord which was in the process of taking over the Republican party in the state. Montgomery Blair to Hale, Sept. 22, 1863, Blair Family papers, LC; Lyford, *Rollins*, pp. 166, 170-72; Welles, *Diary*, Vol. II, p. 51.

31. For one side of the feud, see a splenetic pamphlet by Mark Howard, "Despotic Doctrines Declared by the United States Senate Exposed and Senator Dixon Unmasked," Hartford, 1863, WP-HL; Howard to Welles, Feb. 29, Jan. 19, 1864, WP-LC; *Hartford Courant*, Jan. 18, 1864; Welles to Howard, Jan. 15; Welles to Charles Dudley Warner, Jan. 19, 1864; Welles to Edgar Welles, Jan. 17, 1864; Howard to Welles, Jan. 19, 1864; James G. Bolles to Welles, Feb. 18, 1864, WP-LC. Not knowing how irritated Lincoln was by the whole affair, Faxon was critical of Welles' effort

to mediate. "I suppose that he would not want to make as much of a fight as you would—it is not his nature," Faxon wrote Howard. Faxon to Howard, Feb. 3, 1864, Howard papers, CHS; Carman and Luthin, *Lincoln and the Patronage*, pp. 236-39; Calvin Day to J. R. Hawley, Apr. 1, 1864, Hawley papers, LC; Lane, *Connecticut*, pp. 256, 257.

32. Faxon to J. R. Hawley, Mar. 8, 1864, Hawley papers, LC; Chase to James A. Hamilton, Jr., Feb. 29, 1864, Chase papers, NYPL; Mary Welles to Edgar Welles, Feb. 29, 1864, WP-LC; Donald (ed.), *Civil War Diaries of Salmon P. Chase*, p. 211.

33. Welles, *Diary*, Vol. I, pp. 529, 530; Faxon to Howard, Mar. 1, 1864, Howard papers, CHS; Carman and Luthin, *Lincoln and the Patronage*, p. 229; Welles to Hawley, Mar. 27, 1864; Hawley to Welles, Mar. 16, 1864, Hawley papers, LC; Welles to Edgar Welles, Feb. 28, 1864, WP-LC. Adam Gurowski, *Diary, 1863, 64, 65*, Washington, D.C., 1866, p. 199. Welles had the same low opinion of Frémont that H. W. Davis did. "There is a striving to make Frémont a candidate," wrote Davis, "under the delusion that he can be elected." Davis to Du Pont, Apr. 4, 1864, Du Pont papers, EML.

34. Welles, *Diary*, Vol. II, p. 4.

35. "The losses of Grant are appalling," wrote Hawley, who exclaimed, with some irony, that "perhaps the first of July may see Grant with as few men as McClellan had in '62 on that day and near the same place." J. R. Hawley to Welles, June 19, 1864, WP-LC. For confirmation of Hawley's radical views, see Francis Hawley to Hawley, May 29, 1864, Hawley papers, LC. Welles was somewhat surprised at Johnson's nomination. Although he had little use for Hamlin, he expected his renomination. He understood that Seward had been for Hamlin and had induced Lincoln to express no preference; Welles to Edgar Welles, June 12, 1864, WP-LC; Johnson (comp.), *Republican Conventions*, pp. 222-26; Alexander K. McClure, *Our Presidents and How We Make Them*, New York, 1905, pp. 188, 189; Burton J. Hendrick, *Lincoln's War Cabinet*, Boston, 1946, p. 441; Welles to Hawley, July 12, 1864, Hawley papers, LC; Allan Nevins, *The War for the Union*, Vol. IV, New York, 1971, pp. 78-80; Welles, *Diary*, Vol. II, pp. 62, 63; Basler, *Works*, Vol. VI, pp. 433-34; Welles, *Diary*, Vol. II, pp. 46-52. See also E. D. Morgan to Welles, May 11, 1864, WP-LC; Welles to Morgan, May 11, 1864, Morgan papers, NYSL; Welles, *Diary*, Vol. II, p. 30. Radicals were not enthusiastic about Lincoln but, as Faxon wrote Howard, they had little choice. "I don't know who else could be run to advantage—Chase seems to be the only one prominently named, and I confess I would like him for his brains—but yet his Department has been *no better managed* than some others." Faxon to Howard, Jan. 5, 1864, Howard papers, CHS. For two versions of the complex intrigue that resulted in Johnson's nomination, see Hamlin, *Hamlin*, pp. 464-71; Chauncey M. Depew to Edgar Welles, Feb. 25, 1910, WP-LC.

36. Montgomery Blair to Barlow, May 1, 11, 1864, Barlow papers, HL; Smith, *Blair Family*, Vol. II, pp. 279, 281.

37. Welles outlined his policy to Hiram Paulding, Commandant of the Brooklyn Navy Yard: "I do not feel it a duty to make war," he wrote, "on quiet, skilful artizans who honestly discharge their duty, because their opinions of men do not square with mine." Welles to Paulding, Aug. 17, 1864, WP-LC; see also Henry J. Raymond to Seward, Aug. 5, 1864, Seward papers, NYPL.

38. Welles, *Diary*, Vol. II, pp. 95, 98.

39. Allan Nevins, *The War for the Union*, Vol. IV, pp. 106, 107.

40. Mark Howard to Welles, Aug. 24, 1864; James R. Doolittle to Welles, Sept. 24, 1864, WP-LC; Basler, *Works*, Vol. VII, p. 514; Nevins, *The War for the Union*, Vol. IV, pp. 92, 93; Welles, *Diary*, Vol. II, pp. 41-43; Howard to Welles, Aug. 24, 1864, WP-LC. Fear of defeat brought the Weed faction together briefly with the radicals under the leadership of H. W. Davis. At a series of meetings in New York, Davis managed to secure an uneasy consensus of radicals and conservatives on a harebrained scheme. Lincoln and Frémont would be forced to withdraw and a new

candidate would be nominated at Cincinnati on September 28. Davis to Du Pont, Aug. 10, 18, 25, 31, 1864, Du Pont papers, EML; Henry H. Elliot to Welles, Aug. 31, 1864, WP-LC; Nevins, *The War for the Union*, Vol. IV, pp. 107-8.

41. Welles, *Diary*, Vol. II, p. 132.

42. Moses Pierce to Welles, Oct. 4, 1864; Faxon to Welles, Nov. 7, 1864; Welles to Edgar Welles, Sept. 4, 1864, WP-LC. As late as September 24, after Sheridan's victory over Early in the Shenandoah valley, Browning and Trumbull still had not declared for Lincoln. "It is a matter of deep sorrow to me," wrote Senator James R. Doolittle of Wisconsin to Welles, "that any question as to their position should have arisen." Doolittle to Welles, Sept. 24, 1864, WP-LC.

43. H. W. Davis to Du Pont, Sept. 28, 29, 1864, Du Pont papers, EML; Faxon to Howard, Sept. 25, 1864, Howard papers, CHS; Welles, *Diary*, and note to entry, Vol. II, p. 158.

44. Davis to Du Pont, Sept. 28, 29, 1864, Du Pont papers, EML.

45. Welles, *Diary*, Vol. II, pp. 179, 181, 193; Basler, *Works*, Vol. VIII, pp. 136-52; Montgomery Blair to S. L. M. Barlow, Jan. 12, 1865, Barlow papers, HL; Davis to Du Pont, Feb. 15, 1865, Du Pont papers, EML; *New-York Tribune*, Feb. 6, 1865.

46. Fox to W. E. Chandler, Feb. 23, 1864, Chandler papers, LC; Fox told Lincoln that if Welles left the Cabinet, he would leave too. Welles, *Diary*, Vol. II, pp. 239, 242, 248, 251; Charles L. Jellison, *Fessenden*, pp. 194, 195.

47. Lately Thomas, *The First President Johnson*, New York, 1968, pp. 294-99; Welles, *Diary*, Vol. II, pp. 251-52; Thomas and Hyman, *Stanton*, p. 349; John B. Henderson, "Emancipation and Impeachment," *The Century Magazine*, Vol. LXXXV, No. 2, Dec. 1914, p. 198; John W. Forney, *Anecdotes of Public Men*, New York, 1874, p. 39; Straudenraus, *Noah Brooks*, pp. 418-24; New York *Herald*, Mar. 5, 1865; *Chicago Tribune*, Mar. 5, 1865; New York *Evening Post*, Mar. 5, 1865.

48. Welles, *Diary*, Vol. II, p. 278; Basler, *Works*, Vol. VIII, pp. 399-405, 399-400n, 589, 406-8n; Welles, *Diary*, Vol. II, pp. 270-81.

49. Mary Welles, MS, "Memorandum," Apr. 14, 1865, WP-LC; Welles, draft narrative, n. d., WP-HL; Welles, *Diary*, Apr. 17, 1865, Vol. II, pp. 283-88. Thomas Hutchinson (comp.), *Boyd's Washington and Georgetown Directory*, Washington, D.C., 1865, p. 142.

50. Field, *Memories of Many Men*, pp. 322-27.


CHAPTER 26

1. Welles, *Diary*, Vol. II, pp. 289, 290; Benjamin C. Truman, "Anecdotes of Andrew Johnson," *The Century Magazine*, Vol. LXXXV, No. 3, Jan. 1913, p. 435; Welles, *Diary*, Vol. II, pp. 289-90; Welles, MS Diary fragment, Apr. 15, 1865, WP, Univ. of Chicago Library; H. W. Davis to Du Pont, Apr. 15, 1865, Du Pont papers, EML.

2. Welles, "Lincoln and Johnson, Their Plan of Reconstruction and the Resumption of National Authority . . . First Paper," *The Galaxy*, Vol. XIII, Apr. 1872, pp. 526, 527; Thomas and Hyman, *Stanton*, pp. 357, 358; Welles, *Diary*, Vol. II, p. 282.

3. H. Greeley to Blair, Apr. 17, 1865, Blair Family papers, LC; Welles to Blair, draft, Dec. 1876, WP-LC.

4. J. R. Hawley to Harriet Hawley, Jan. 9, 1863; Warner to Hawley, Sept. 8, 1865, Hawley papers, LC.

5. Welles, *Diary*, Vol. II, pp. 291, 394.

6. Thomas and Hyman, *Stanton*, p. 403; Gideon Welles, "Lincoln and Johnson (I)," pp. 528-30; untitled MS draft in Welles papers, John Hay Library, Brown Univ.; Welles, *Diary*, Apr. 14, probably written Apr. 18, 1865, Vol. II, pp. 291, 292; Welles to Lt. Com. Eastman, Apr. 22, 1865; Edgar Welles to George Harrington, Apr. 20, 1865, WP-LC; Thomas and Hyman, *Stanton*, p. 404.

7. Welles, *Diary*, Vol. II, pp. 294-98; *New York Times, New-York Tribune, National Intelligencer*, Apr. 23, 1865.

8. H. W. Davis to Du Pont, Apr. 15, 19, 22, May 22, 1865, Du Pont papers, EML.

9. Donald, *Sumner*, pp. 214, 220; Calvin Day to Welles, Apr. 27, 1865, WP-LC; C. D. Warner to Welles, Apr. 26, 1865, WP-CHS.

10. Welles, *Diary*, Vol. II, pp. 302, 303.

11. Basler, *Works*, Vol. VII, p. 55; Welles, "Lincoln and Johnson," pp. 521-28, 530-32; Welles, *Diary*, Vol. II, pp. 301-3.

12. Welles, *Diary*, Vol. II, p. 310; see Welles' comment on a letter Sumner wrote to Mrs. Charles Eames, *ibid.*, p. 363.

13. *Ibid.*, Vol. II, pp. 303-5, 308-11.

14. James D. Richardson (comp.), *A Compilation of the Messages and Papers of the Presidents*, New York, 1916, Vol. VIII, p. 3511; Calvin Day to Welles, June 20, 1865, WP-LC.

15. Welles to Lot M. Morrill, Dec. 1869, WP-HL; Welles, *Diary*, Vol. II, pp. 340, 341; Fox to Henry T. Blow, Feb. 3, 1865, Fox papers, NYHS; Welles, draft MS, June 1862, WP-HL; *New-York Tribune*, June 13, 1862.

16. Welles to Edgar Welles, Feb. 5, 1863, WP-LC, Fox to Ericsson, Jan. 8, 1865, Harbeck Coll., HL; Fox to Seward, Apr. 8, 1867, Seward papers, Univ. of Rochester; James King to Fox, Aug. 26, 1864, WP-LC; Lord Newton, *Lord Lyons*, Vol. I, pp. 120, 121, 128-30; "Report of the Secretary of the Navy, 1864," *House Exec. Doc.*, No. 1, 38th Cong., 2nd sess., XXVI, XXVII; Bennett, *Steam Navy*, p. 572; Welles, *Diary*, Vol. II, pp. 340, 341. For brief specifications of these vessels, see *ORN*, Series II, Vol. I; James B. Eads to Welles, May 10, 1864, WP-LC.

17. "Report of the Secretary of the Navy, 1865," *House Exec. Doc.*, No. 1, 39th Cong., 1st sess., Washington, D.C., IV, XI, XXIII, XXXII.

18. Sumner to Welles, June 15, July 4, 1865, WP-LC; Richardson, *Messages and Papers*, Vol. VIII, pp. 3516-26; Welles to Sumner, June 30, 1865; Sumner to Welles, July 4, 5, 1865, WP-LC.

19. Welles, *Diary*, Vol. II, p. 330.

20. *Chicago Tribune*, July 5, 1865; Welles, *Diary*, Vol. II, p. 324.

21. Mark Howard to Welles, July 27, 1865, WP-LC.

22. Welles, *Diary*, Vol. II, pp. 347, 348.

23. Sumner to Francis Lieber, Aug. 11, 1865, Lieber papers, HL. Despite their opposing views, Sumner's relations with Welles remained excellent. Welles, *Diary*, Vol. II, p. 369; Edward L. Pierce, *Memoir and Letters of Charles Sumner*, Boston, 1893, Vol. IV, p. 269.

24. Thomas T. Eckert to Stanton, Sept. 5, 1865, Stanton papers, LC.

25. Welles, *Diary*, Vol. II, pp. 579, 580; *Hartford Times, New Haven Register*, Sept. 20, 1865. That same day, he received a similar query from the moderate Republican *New Haven Palladium*. Charles Dudley Warner to Welles, Sept. 30, 1865; C. A. Croffut to Welles, Sept. 20, 1865, WP-LC.

26. Welles to Croffut, Welles to Warner, Sept. 22, 1865, WP-LC; Warner to Welles, Sept. 26, 1865, WP-CHS; *Hartford Courant*, Sept. 26, 1865; Welles to Warner, Oct. 10, 1865, WP-HL; Welles, *Diary*, Vol. II, pp. 373-75.

27. W. E. Chandler to Boutwell, Oct. 7, 1865, Chandler papers, LC.

28. Edward McPherson, *The Political History of the United States of America During the Period of Reconstruction*, Washington, D.C., 1880, pp. 48, 49; *New-York Tribune*, Oct. 7, 23, 1865, Sept. 16, 1865.

29. Welles to Warner, Oct. 10, 1865, WP-HL.

30. Mark Howard to Welles, Nov. 13, Dec. 2, 1865, WP-LC.

## CHAPTER 27

1. Benjamin B. Kendrick, *The Journal of the Joint Committee of Fifteen on Reconstruction, 39th Congress 1865-1867*, New York, 1914, pp. 141, 37.

2. Welles, *Diary*, Vol. II, pp. 387, 388, Charles R. Williams (ed.), *Diary and Letters of Rutherford Birchard Hayes* (5 vols.), Columbus, Ohio, 1922-26, Vol. III, p. 7; Richardson (comp.), *Messages and Papers,* Vol. VIII, pp. 3551-69.

3. William A. Dunning, "A Little More Light on Andrew Johnson," Massachusetts Historical Society *Proceedings,* Second Series, Vol. XIX, Boston, 1905; *New-York Tribune,* Dec. 6, 1865.

4. Welles, *Diary,* Vol. II, pp. 393-95.

5. *Ibid.,* p. 298; Welles, "Lincoln and Johnson, Second Paper," *The Galaxy,* Vol. XIII, May 1872, pp. 667-68.

6. *Ibid.,* pp. 669, 670, 672; Schurz, *Reminiscences of Carl Schurz,* Vol. III, p. 214; *New-York Tribune,* June 20, 1866.

7. Welles, "Administration of Abraham Lincoln," *The Galaxy,* Vol. XXIII, Feb. 1877, pp. 158, 159.

8. Welles, *Diary,* Vol. II, June 30, 1864, p. 325; Trefousse, *Wade,* pp. 234, 235, 268; Mary Land, "Bluff Ben Wade's New England Background," *New England Quarterly,* Vol. 27 (Dec. 1954), pp. 484ff.; Jellison, *Fessenden,* p. 199; Welles, *Diary,* Vol. II, p. 381.

9. See, for instance, J. R. Hawley to Welles, Feb. 26, 1866, Hawley papers, LC; Calvin Day to Welles, Feb. 26, 1866, WP-LC; Greeley to Blair, Feb. 16, 1867, Blair Family papers, LC; Andrew Johnson to Benjamin Truman, Aug. 3, 1868, *The Century Magazine,* Jan. 1913, p. 438.

10. Welles, *Diary,* Vol. II, pp. 447-49; James W. Grimes to Welles, Oct. 14, 1866, WP-LC; Faxon to Mark Howard, Feb. 22, 1866, Howard papers, CHS; Jellison, *Fessenden,* p. 198.

11. McPherson, *Political History: Reconstruction,* pp. 51, 52; Welles, *Diary,* Vol. II, p. 415.

12. *New-York Tribune,* Jan. 29, 31, 1866; *New York Times,* Jan. 29, 1866; Welles, *Diary,* Vol. II, p. 422.

13. *New-York Tribune,* Jan. 31, 1866.

14. "Impeachment of the President," *House Reports,* 40th Cong., 1st sess., pp. 269, 270.

15. Welles, *Diary,* Vol. II, p. 425.

16. *Ibid.,* p. 432; Andrew Johnson, "Veto Message and Papers," Mar. 19, 1866, Johnson papers, LC; John H. and LaWanda Cox, "Andrew Johnson and His Ghost Writers: An Analysis of the Freedmen's Bureau and Civil Rights, Veto Messages," *Journal of American History,* Vol. XLVIII, Dec. 1961, pp. 462, 463.

17. Welles, *Diary,* Vol. II, pp. 434, 435, 437; Welles to Browning, Dec. 24, 1870, WP-CHS; Welles to Montgomery Blair, May 15, 1871, WP-LC.

18. Welles, *Diary,* Vol. II, p. 437; Montgomery Blair to Barlow, Feb. 17, 1866, Barlow papers, HL.

19. Kendrick, *The Journal of the Joint Committee,* Ch. V, *passim;* see Calvin Day's reply to Welles' letter of Feb. 5, 1866; Day to Welles, Feb. 15, 1866, WP-LC.

20. Welles, *Diary,* Vol. II, pp. 449-50.

21. *Washington Chronicle,* Feb. 23, 1866; *New-York Tribune,* Mar. 1, 1866; Welles, *Diary,* Vol. II, pp. 460, 461.

22. "Civil Rights Bill," drafts of Welles and Seward, Mar. 27, 1866, Johnson papers, LC; for the act itself, see *United States Statutes at Large,* Vol. XIV, Ch. 31, pp. 27-30, Boston, 1868. Veto message, Richardson (comp.), *Messages and Papers,* Vol. VIII, pp. 3603-11.

23. John H. and LaWanda Cox, "Andrew Johnson and His Ghost Writers," pp. 474-79.

24. J. R. Hawley to Welles, Feb. 26, Mar. 12, 22, 1866, Hawley papers, LC.

25. A. E. Burr to Welles, Mar. 12, 1866; Welles to Hawley, Mar. 24, 30, 1866, WP-LC; *National Intelligencer,* Mar. 20, 24, 1866; Welles, *Diary,* Vol. II, pp. 452-62; *New-York Tribune,* Mar. 26, 30, 1866. For an opposing view on the consequences of

new party alignments, see George D. Morgan to Welles, Mar. 20, 1866, WP-LC. Welles ignored Morgan's advice.

26. Welles, *Diary*, Vol. II, pp. 480-83.

27. *Ibid.*, pp. 496, 497.

28. *National Intelligencer*, May 2, 1866; Thomas and Hyman, *Stanton*, pp. 479-83.

29. Welles, *Diary*, Vol. II, pp. 502-10; A. E. Burr to Welles, Apr. 27, May 8, 10, 16, 1866; James F. Babcock to Welles, May 14, 15, 17, 19, 24, 1866; Norris Wilcox to Welles, May 15, 1866, WP-LC.

30. *Trial of Andrew Johnson, President of the United States, Before the Senate of the United States on Impeachment by the House of Representatives for High Crimes and Misdemeanors* (3 vols.), Washington, D.C., 1868, Vol. I, pp. 152-54; Thomas and Hyman, *Stanton*, pp. 494-97; David Miller De Witt, *The Impeachment and Trial of Andrew Johnson, Seventeenth President of the United States*, New York, 1903, pp. 110, 111; Welles, *Diary*, Vol. II, pp. 563-69.

31. *Ibid.*, p. 568; Thomas and Hyman, *Stanton*, pp. 485, 486; LaWanda and John H. Cox, *Politics, Principle and Prejudice, 1865-1866*, New York, 1963, pp. 220-23; Kendrick, *Journal of the Joint Committee*, pp. 203, 204; Fawn M. Brodie, *Thaddeus Stevens, Scourge of the South*, New York, 1959, pp. 269, 270; Mark M. Krug, *Lyman Trumbull, Conservative Radical*, New York, 1965, p. 246.

32. Welles, *Diary*, Vol. II, pp. 501, 521; *New York Times*, June 14, 1866; J. R. Doolittle to Welles, July 11, 1866; Welles to Doolittle, July 11, 1866, WP-LC; Welles, *Diary*, Vol. II, pp. 528-41, 573. For Welles' work on the draft for the call, see miscellaneous memoranda, June 1866, WP-NYPL.

33. Welles, *Diary*, Vol. II, pp. 588-92, 595, 603; Dixon to Welles, Sept. 26, 1866, WP-LC; Welles, *Diary*, Vol. II, pp. 608-9; W. Patton to Welles, Oct. 10, 1866; James W. Grimes to Welles, Oct. 14, 1866, WP-LC; Welles, *Diary*, Vol. II, p. 598; Philip Dorsheimer to Welles, Sept. 25, Oct. 20, 1866; Albert Smith to Welles, Sept. 25; Welles to T. C. Selfridge, Sept. 24, 1866, WP-LC; Faxon to Mark Howard, Oct. 12, 1866, Howard papers, CHS; Welles, *Diary*, Vol. II, p. 590.

34. James W. Grimes to Welles, Oct. 14, 1866, WP-LC.

### CHAPTER 28

1. Welles, *Diary*, Vol. II, p. 651; *Hartford Courant*, July 20, 1863.

2. Welles, *Diary*, Vol. II, pp. 550, 551, 651, 652.

3. Welles to Bates, Jan. 21, 1867, WP-LC.

4. Welles to Grimes, Oct. 19, 1866, WP-LC.

5. See, for instance, his telegram to Gov. Parsons of Alabama, Jan. 17, 1867, McPherson, *Political History: Reconstruction*, p. 352.

6. *Congressional Globe*, 39th Cong., 2nd sess., pp. 250, 1075, 1076.

7. Thomas and Hyman, *Stanton*, pp. 514, 515.

8. George S. Boutwell, "Johnson's Plot and Motives," *North American Review*, Dec. 1885, Vol. 141, No. 349, pp. 572, 573.

9. Francis Fessenden, *Life and Public Service of William Pitt Fessenden* (2 vols.), New York, 1907, Vol. II, p. 251. For instance, see conflicting opinions of John Sherman, W. P. Fessenden, Orris S. Ferry, and James R. Doolittle in *Trial of Andrew Johnson*, Vol. III, pp. 3-31, 121-23, 244-46.

10. Welles, *Diary*, Vol. III, pp. 8-11.

11. The radicals had tried to admit Colorado but had run into unexpected opposition from Sumner and were unable to pass the bill over Johnson's veto. Donald, *Sumner*, pp. 259, 284; DeWitt, *Impeachment*, pp. 65, 66, 89, 90.

12. Welles, *Diary*, Vol. III, pp. 25, 26; Fox to Welles, Feb. 5, 1867, WP-LC; *New York Times*, Jan. 17, 1867; Richard N. Current, *Old Thad Stevens*, Madison, Wisc., 1942, p. 269. Seward was lobbying for the Alaskan purchase.

13. Montgomery Blair to Barlow, Feb. 14, 1867, Barlow papers, HL. For Johnson's admiration of Seward and Stanton, see Col. W. G. Moore, MS Notebook, July 14, 1866, May 7, 1867, Johnson papers, LC.

14. Williams (ed.), *Hayes*, Vol. III, p. 25. Compare Johnson's abortive attempt to head off the 14th Amendment in Jan. 1867, by having the ex-Confederate states pass amendments guaranteeing limited Negro suffrage, with what Congress would have accepted in March 1866; Fox to Welles, Feb. 5, 1867, WP-LC; *New York Times*, Jan. 17, 1867; Current, *Old Thad Stevens*, p. 269; "Notes of Colonel W. G. Moore, Private Secretary to President Johnson, 1865-1868," *American Historical Review*, Vol. XIX, No. 1, Oct. 1913, p. 102.

15. "Notes of Colonel W. G. Moore," p. 105. For Andrew Johnson's pro-Seward position, see Montgomery Blair to Barlow, June 3, 1866, Feb. 14, 1867, Barlow papers, HL; Smith, *Blair Family*, Vol. II, pp. 332, 333; Andrew Johnson to Benjamin Truman, Aug. 3, 1868, Benjamin Truman "Anecdotes of President Johnson," *The Century Magazine*, Jan. 1913, pp. 438, 439.

16. John A. Carpenter, *Sword and Olive Branch*, Pittsburgh, 1964, p. 129; Welles, *Diary*, Vol. III, pp. 42-46; "Notes of Colonel W. G. Moore," p. 109.

17. Browning, *Diary*, Vol. II, p. 130.

18. "Notes of Colonel W. G. Moore," p. 105; Welles, *Diary*, Vol. III, pp. 42-49.

19. Welles, *Diary*, Vol. III, p. 49; Eric McKitrick, *Andrew Johnson and Reconstruction*, Chicago, 1960, pp. 476-85; Fessenden, *Fessenden*, Vol. II, p. 138; Browning, *Diary*, Vol. II, p. 131; "Notes of Colonel W. G. Moore," p. 110; Thomas and Hyman, *Stanton*, p. 524.

20. Hugh McCulloch, *Men and Measures of Half a Century*, New York, 1900, p. 401; Thomas and Hyman, *Stanton*, p. 526.

21. Welles, *Diary*, Vol. III, pp. 50, 51; Welles to Johnson, draft, Aug. 4, 1867, WP-HL. Stanbery worked with Black on the message. Johnson heavily edited their copy. Moore, MS Notebook, Mar. 2, 1867, Johnson papers, LC; Welles, *Diary*, Vol. III, p. 205; *Impeachment Investigation*, Testimony taken before the Judiciary Committee of the House of Representatives in the Investigation of the Charges against Andrew Johnson, *House Reports*, 40th Cong., 1st sess., pp. 271, 272.

22. McCulloch, *Men and Measures*, p. 391.

23. Browning, *Diary*, Vol. II, p. 134; Welles, *Diary*, Vol. III, p. 58; "Notes of Colonel W. G. Moore," p. 106. For a complete text of the Act and the accompanying protest, see McPherson, *Political History: Reconstruction*, p. 178.

24. Browning, *Diary*, Vol. II, p. 135; Welles, *Diary*, Vol. III, p. 62.

25. Thomas and Hyman, *Stanton*, p. 530; Welles, *Diary*, Vol. III, pp. 64, 66; Welles to Johnson, draft, Aug. 4, 1867, July 27, Aug. 16, 1869; Johnson to Welles, Dec. 8, 1869; Welles to Johnson, Jan. 14, 1870, Johnson papers, LC.

26. Thomas and Hyman, *Stanton*, p. 531. For the text of the Act, see McPherson, *Political History: Reconstruction*, pp. 192-94. The Senate remained in special session, but only to consider appointments. It adjourned April 20, 1867. Browning, *Diary*, Vol. II, p. 144.

27. Welles, *Diary*, Vol. III, p. 91; Welles to Joseph S. Fowler, Nov. 9, 1875, WP-HL; Moore, MS Notebook, May 7, 1867, Johnson papers, LC.

28. Welles, *Diary*, Vol. III, pp. 93, 94, 96, 98.

29. Stanton, MS "Minutes," June 20, 1867, Stanton papers, LC.

30. Welles, *Diary*, Vol. III, pp. 109-14; Grant to Sheridan, June 24, 1867, Johnson papers, LC.

31. *National Intelligencer*, June 21, 1867; *New-York Tribune*, June 21, 1867; Welles, *Diary*, Vol. III, pp. 110-14; G. C. Gorham, *Life and Public Services of Edwin M. Stanton* (2 vols.), Boston, 1899, Vol. II, pp. 360-71; Thomas and Hyman, *Stanton*, pp. 537, 539, 542-45; Stanton, MS "Minutes," June 19-20, 1867, Stanton papers, LC.

## CHAPTER 29

1. For the text of the Act, see McPherson, *Political History: Reconstruction*, pp. 335-36; For Johnson's veto, see Richardson, *Compilation of Messages and Papers*, Vol. IX, pp. 3734-43; Welles, *Diary*, Vol. III, pp. 137, 138.

2. Williams (ed.), *Hayes*, Vol. III, pp. 6, 7.

3. Browning, *Diary*, Vol. II, pp. 152-53; Welles, *Diary*, Vol. III, pp. 143-45; M. T. E. Chandler to Welles, Aug. 1867, Johnson papers, LC; De Witt, *Impeachment*, p. 281.

4. McCulloch, *Men and Measures*, pp. 404, 405.

5. Welles, *Diary*, Vol. III, p. 145; Browning, *Diary*, Vol. II, pp. 152, 153.

6. W. B. Hesseltine, *Ulysses S. Grant, Politician*, New York, 1935, pp. 87, 88; McPherson, *Political History: Reconstruction*, pp. 306-8; Welles, *Diary*, Vol. III, pp. 154, 155; "Notes of Colonel W. G. Moore," pp. 103, 104.

7. Thomas and Hyman, *Stanton*, p. 599; Welles, *Diary*, Vol. III, pp. 149-57; "Notes of Colonel W. G. Moore," p. 108; Thomas and Hyman absolve Stanton of any guilt in withholding the Surratt clemency petition; they contend that Holt was solely responsible.

8. Browning, *Diary*, Vol. II, p. 154.

9. "Notes of Colonel W. G. Moore," p. 108.

10. Welles, *Diary*, Vol. III, pp. 158-68; Thomas and Hyman, *Stanton*, p. 549.

11. Montgomery Blair to Mrs. Blair, Aug. 10, 1867, Blair Family papers, LC. But Blair told Welles after the meeting that Johnson was "intensely ambitious and all his thoughts are bent on renomination and election." Since this conflicts with what Blair wrote his wife, and since Johnson was not the type of man to be frank with Blair about his intentions, this remark seems to be one of Blair's offhand inferences. His record in this respect is long and well documented. Welles, *Diary*, Vol. III, p. 166.

12. *Ibid.*, p. 167; "Notes of Colonel W. G. Moore," p. 109; Gorham, *Stanton*, Vol. II, pp. 405-9.

13. Stanton declared that "much as the general commanding the armies of the United States has been appointed *ad interim*, and has notified me that he has accepted the appointment, I have no alternative but to submit, under protest to superior force." Grant was disturbed by the language. "Notes of Colonel W. G. Moore," p. 114; Johnson to Stanton, Aug. 12, 1867, Stanton to Johnson, Aug. 12, 1867, Johnson papers, LC; "Notes of Colonel W. G. Moore," p. 109; Thomas and Hyman, *Stanton*, pp. 550-53; Welles, *Diary*, Vol. III, p. 169.

14. Smith, *Blair Family*, Vol. II, pp. 319, 330 ff; Adam Badeau, *Grant in Peace from Appomattox to Mount McGregor, a Personal Memoir*, Hartford, 1887, pp. 77-82; Welles, *Diary*, Vol. II, p. 529.

15. McKitrick, *Johnson*, p. 502; Hesseltine, *Grant*, pp. 87, 88; Thomas and Hyman, *Stanton*, pp. 534, 535.

16. Welles, *Diary*, Vol. I, p. 539.

17. *Ibid.*, Vol. II, pp. 397, 593; Grant to Johnson, Dec. 18, 1865, McPherson, *Political History: Reconstruction*, pp. 67, 68; Donald M. Fairfax to Edgar Welles, Oct. 26, 1885, WP-LC.

18. Welles, *Diary*, Vol. III, p. 5. Welles' opinion that Grant had thrown in with the moderate radicals is confirmed by Rutherford B. Hayes, then an Ohio congressman, Williams (ed.), *Hayes*, Vol. III, p. 4, and also by Col. Cyrus B. Comstock, a member of Grant's staff, Comstock, MS Diary, Mar. 1, 1867, LC.

19. Welles, *Diary*, Vol. III, pp. 141, 167.

20. Browning, *Diary*, Vol. II, p. 156; Welles, *Diary*, Vol. III, p. 176.

21. Grant to Johnson (copy), Aug. 26, 1867, Johnson papers, LC; "Notes of Colonel

W. G. Moore," pp. 111-13; Hesseltine, *Grant,* pp. 95, 96; *Washington Chronicle,* Aug. 25, 1867.

22. His assessment proved to be completely correct. Browning, *Diary,* Vol. II, pp. 161, 162; Thomas and Hyman, *Stanton,* p. 559; James Merrill, *William Tecumseh Sherman,* New York, 1971, pp. 320, 321.

23. Welles, *Diary,* Vol. III, pp. 232-35.

24. S. J. Randall to Edgar Welles, Nov. 14, 1867, Phineas J. Horwitz to Edgar Welles, Nov. 25, 1867, WP-HL; Welles, *Diary,* Vol. III, p. 237; Mary Welles to Edgar Welles, Nov. 12, 1867, James F. Babcock to Welles, Nov. 28, 1867, WP-LC; Browning, *Diary,* Vol. II, pp. 164, 167.

25. *Ibid.;* Boutwell, "Johnson's Plot and Motives," pp. 578, 579.

26. Greeley to J. R. Hawley, Nov. 27, 1867, Hawley papers, LC.

27. Welles, *Diary,* Vol. III, p. 238; MS, dated Nov. 30, 1867, Johnson papers, LC.

28. Welles, *Diary,* Vol. III, p. 258; Col. Moore, MS Notebook, Jan. 11, 1868, Johnson papers, LC.

29. Thomas Ewing to "My Dear General" (Sherman), Jan. 25, 1868, Johnson papers, LC; Montgomery Blair to Edgar Welles, June 14, 1878, WP-LC; Browning, *Diary,* Vol. II, p. 162.

30. Thomas and Hyman, *Stanton,* pp. 568, 569; W. T. Sherman, *Memoirs of Gen. W. T. Sherman, Written by Himself* (2 vols.), New York, 1892, Vol. II, pp. 421, 422; Hesseltine, *Grant,* pp. 103, 104.

31. Johnson confirmed that both Reverdy Johnson and Sherman had urged him to nominate Cox. Both said that they had come after consulting Grant. As Welles recorded it, "they thought that the Senate might be induced to consent that he might have Cox and in that way dispose of Stanton." Browning, *Diary,* Vol. II, pp. 173-75; Welles, *Diary,* Vol. III, pp. 259-61; "Notes of Colonel W. G. Moore," p. 115; Merrill, *Sherman,* p. 322.

32. *National Intelligencer,* Jan. 15, 1868.

33. Sherman, *Memoirs,* Vol. II, p. 423.

34. Hesseltine, *Grant,* pp. 94, 95; Welles, *Diary,* Vol. III, pp. 167, 169.

35. Badeau, *Grant in Peace,* pp. 113, 114. For correspondence between Grant and Johnson, see Johnson papers, Jan. 27-Feb. 3, 1868; see also McPherson, *Political History: Reconstruction,* pp. 282-93. Scrapbook containing a large file of newspaper clippings is in Johnson papers, LC. Even Thaddeus Stevens thought the evidence favored Johnson. Brodie, *Stevens,* p. 333. Sherman, *Memoirs,* Vol. II, contains further correspondence bearing on the break and subsequent developments, pp. 423-33. Merrill, *Sherman,* pp. 323, 324; Thomas Ewing to "My Dear General," Jan. 25, 1868, Johnson papers, LC. That Ewing's letter advising Sherman to keep clear of the controversy should be in the Johnson papers is firm evidence that Johnson wanted Sherman for the War Department.

36. Welles to Cox, Feb. 26, 1870, Welles to John Bigelow, Oct. 31, 1869, Bigelow papers, NYPL; Welles to Blair, Jan. 25, 1870, Jan. 4, 1871, WP-LC.

37. Browning, *Diary,* Vol. II, p. 182. Both Stanbery and McCulloch strongly urged Johnson not to remove Stanton.

38. Welles, *Diary,* Vol. III, p. 280.

39. *Trial of Andrew Johnson,* Vol. I, pp. 235, 663, 664, 704-6; Welles, *Diary,* Vol. III, p. 289.

40. Welles, *Diary,* Vol. III, pp. 290, 291.

41. Welles to Johnson, Feb. 5, 1868, Johnson papers, LC; Welles to John Welles, Mar. 8, May 10, 1868, Stanbery to Welles, Apr. 2, 1868, WP-LC; *Trial of Andrew Johnson,* pp. 663-704.

42. Welles, *Diary,* Vol. III, pp. 357, 362, 367-69; Browning, *Diary,* Vol. II, p. 199.

43. Even such an outspoken radical as Samuel Pomeroy of Kansas had his own doubts about deposing the President. He had tried without success to head off impeachment. If Johnson had given in and asked his Cabinet to resign, as Pomeroy

proposed, the trial would never have taken place. Pomeroy was quoted as saying, "we are not satisfied with Stanton; we are not satisfied with our position in respect to him. We would be glad to have an excuse to get rid of him in some way and there must be a general change in the Cabinet before that can be done." "Notes of Colonel W. G. Moore," p. 126. Pomeroy's vote was also up for sale. Moore, MS Notebook, May 2, 1868, Johnson papers, LC; Fox, MS Diary, Apr. 5, 1868, Fox papers, NYHS; Welles, *Diary*, Vol. III, pp. 338, 339. S. P. Chase to J. E. Snodgrass; Chase to Col. William B. Thomas, Mar. 10, 1868; Chase to J. E. Snodgrass, Mar. 16, 1868; Chase to Gerritt Smith, Apr. 19, 1868, in Schuckers, *Chase*, pp. 574-78; James C. Kennedy to Johnson, Feb. 22, 1868, Johnson papers, LC; De Witt, *Impeachment*, pp. 389, 524. For the articles of impeachment, see *Trial of Andrew Johnson*, Vol. I, pp. 6-10; for the roll call votes in the Senate on Articles XI, II, and III, pp. 486, 487, 496, 497.

44. Johnson to Truman, Aug. 3, 1868, *Century Magazine*, Jan. 1913, p. 438; John Bigelow, MS Diary, Sept. 23, 1868, Bigelow papers, NYPL.

45. Welles, *Diary*, Vol. III, pp. 398, 399; Welles to Samuel J. Tilden, Oct. 14, 1868, WP-CHS; Welles to Edgar Welles, June 9, 1868; Welles to John A. Welles, June 28, 1868; A. E. Burr to Welles, July 4, 1868; Fox to Welles, Nov. 2, 1868, WP-LC.

46. Welles, *Diary*, Vol. III, Mar. 3, 1869, pp. 539-40.


### CHAPTER 30

1. *General Orders and Circulars Issued by the Navy Department from 1868 to 1887*, Washington, D.C., 1887, p. 307.

2. Speech of Aaron F. Stevens, *Congressional Globe*, 41st Cong., 3rd sess., Appendix, pp. 46-47.

3. Sloan, *Isherwood*, p. 232; Welles, *Diary*, Vol. III, pp. 551, 552; Fox to Welles, Jan. 14, 1870, WP-LC; Welles to L. M. Morrill, Dec. 1869, WP-LC.

4. Welles, *Diary*, Vol. III, p. 570; *Congressional Globe*, 41st Cong., 3rd sess., Appendix, pp. 45-54.

5. Welles, *Diary*, Vol. III, p. 547; Welles to Edgar Welles, Mar. 25, 1869, WP-LC.

6. Welles, *Diary*, Vol. III, pp. 546, 551.

7. Faxon to Welles, Mar. 22, 1869, WP-LC.

8. Welles to "My Dear Sons," Mar. 29, 1869, WP-LC.

9. Welles, *Diary*, Vol. III, pp. 582-87; Welles to Edgar Welles, June 4, 1869, Welles to Joseph Smith, July 27, 1870, WP-LC.

10. Welles to Edgar Welles, Aug. 22, Nov. 29, 1869, WP-LC; James B. Eads to Welles, June 10, 1869, WP-LC.

11. Howard K. Beale's introduction to Welles, *Diary*, Vol. I, xxiii-xxx; Welles to Edgar Welles, Apr. 20, 1873, WP-LC.

12. Welles, *Diary*, Vol. II, p. 87; Welles to Bigelow, Oct. 21, 1869; Bigelow, MS Diary, June 22, 1869, Bigelow papers, NYPL; *New York Times*, Sept. 23, 1869; Bigelow to Welles, Oct. 4, 1869, WP-LC.

13. Welles to Edgar Welles, June 6, 1870; Fox to Welles, June 15, 1870; Welles to Smith, July 23, 1870, WP-LC.

14. Welles to Edgar Welles, Oct. 21, 1870, WP-LC.

15. Allan Nevins, *Hamilton Fish: The Inner History of the Grant Administration*, New York, 1936, p. 281.

16. Joseph Smith to Welles, Jan. 20, 1870, WP-LC.

17. Welles to Edgar Welles, Feb. 19, 1870, WP-LC.

18. Fox to Welles, Dec. 3, 1870, WP-LC.

19. Fox to Welles, Jan. 28, 1870, WP-LC; *Hartford Courant*, Jan. 12, 1870; *New-York Tribune*, Jan. 13, 1870; C. C. Chaffee to Welles, Jan. 29, 1870, WP-LC; Joseph Smith to Welles, Jan. 20, 1870, Chaffee to Welles, Jan. 21, 1870; *Congressional Globe*, 41st Cong., 2nd sess., Appendix, pp. 49-52.

20. George F. Hoar, *Autobiography of Seventy Years* (2 vols.), New York, 1903, Vol. I, p. 209.

21. Welles, *Diary*, Vol. II, pp. 178, 653; Vol. III, pp. 139, 325; Welles to Smith, July 27, 1870; Smith to Welles, Dec. 13, 1870, WP-LC.

22. John Lenthall to Welles, Jan. 25, 1872, WP-NYPL; Bennett, *Steam Navy*, pp. 399, 544-45; Leonard W. Swann, Jr., *John Roach, Maritime Entrepreneur*, Annapolis, 1965, pp. 125-34.

23. John Lenthall to Welles, Jan. 25, 1872, WP-NYPL.

24. Welles to Edgar Welles, Apr. 5, 8, May 18, 22, 1872, WP-LC; Norman Wiard to W. C. Church, May 20, 1872, Church papers, LC; Welles to O. S. Ferry, May 6, 1872; Charles A. Dana to Welles, Aug. 17, 1872, WP-LC.

25. *House Misc. Doc.* 201, Vol. IV, 42nd Cong., 2nd sess., p. 257.

26. James G. Blaine, *Twenty Years of Congress*, Norwich, Conn., 1884-86, Vol. II, p. 638.

27. *House Misc. Doc.* 201, p. 212.

28. *Ibid.*, p. 264.

29. *Ibid.*, p. 255.

30. Faxon to Welles, June 2, 1872, WP-LC.

31. Welles to Edgar Welles, Apr. 5, 8, May 18, 1872; Charles A. Dana to Welles, Aug. 17, 1872, WP-LC; *House Misc. Doc.*, No. 201, Vol. IV, 42nd Cong., 2nd sess., pp. 245-65; *House Misc. Doc.* 170, Vol. II, pt. 5, 44th Cong., 1st sess., pp. 212-18; Welles to Mary Welles, Mar. 10, 12, 1876, WP-LC.

32. Welles to Edgar Welles, Feb. 12, 1875, WP-LC.

33. See miscellaneous drafts, Jan.-Mar. 1870 and other dates in Alphabetical Series, WP-LC.

34. Welles, "Memorandum," June 6, 1872; invitation to Welles, signed by Carl Schurz, Jacob D. Cox, and others, June 6, 1872, WP-CHS; Hiram Barney to Welles, June 17, 1872; Welles to James B. Eads, Sept. 3, 1871, WP-LC.

35. Welles to Edgar Welles, Apr. 20, 1870; Charles Francis Adams, "Memorial Address on the Life, Character and Public Services of William H. Seward," Albany, 1873; Welles to W. C. Bryant, Mar. 14, 1874, WP-LC.

36. Welles, *Lincoln and Seward*, Preface, iii, iv.

37. *Ibid.*, p. v; Welles to "My Dear Sir," Mar. 19, 1874, Thomas G. Welles Coll., Coventry, Conn.

38. O. H. Browning to Welles, May 20, 1874, WP-LC; R. T. Lincoln to Welles, Mar. 21, 1874, WP-CHS.

39. Welles, "Administration of Abraham Lincoln," *The Galaxy*, Feb. 1877, p. 158; Welles to D. L. Phillips, Secretary, Aug. 31, 1874, WP-LC; Welles to I. N. Arnold, Nov. 27, 1872, ChHS; Welles to W. C. Bryant, Mar. 14, 1874, WP-LC.

40. Beale, introduction, Welles, *Diary*, Vol. I, xxv, xxvi, xxx; Welles to Edgar Welles, Apr. 20, 1873, WP-LC.

41. *Ibid.*, Feb. 12, 1875, WP-LC.

42. *Ibid.*, Feb. 6, 1875, WP-LC.

43. Welles was asked to act as a pallbearer at the Chase funeral. William Sprague to Welles, May 7, 1873, WP-LC.

44. Welles to "Dr. Sir," May 26, 1838; G. D. Morgan to Welles, Sept. 29, 1876, WP-NYPL; M. J. W. Peabody to H. B. Learned, Aug. 14, 1906, Learned Coll.; W. B. Franklin to Edgar Welles, Dec. 26, 1877, WP-LC; G. D. Morgan to Welles, Feb. 5, 1878, WP-NYPL.

45. *Hartford Times*, Feb. 12, 1878; *New-York Tribune*, Feb. 12, 1878; Fox, MS Diary, Feb. 14, Fox papers, NYHS.

# BIBLIOGRAPHY

## I. PRIMARY SOURCES

### A. *Welles Papers*

1. The Library of Congress collection is by far the most valuable and extensive body of papers, numbering as it does some 45,000 items, including manuscript diaries from 1827 to 1869, the papers of Edgar Welles and the H. Barrett Learned collection of papers relating to Gideon Welles. The collection consists of the chronological series (33 reels of microfilm), the Alphabetical Series (4 reels of microfilm), and the H. Barrett Learned papers (3 reels of microfilm). In all, 70 volumes and 21 boxes of letters and documents. Manuscript diaries 1827-54 are included, but not the memoirs and the diaries from 1861 to 1869, which number several thousand manuscript pages.

2. The Connecticut Historical Society has about 5000 items, among which are the papers of John M. Niles and some correspondence of Mrs. Gideon Welles.

3. The New York Public Library with 1400 items covers Welles' career, but is primarily concerned with his tenure as Secretary of the Navy.

4. The Huntington Library, San Marino, California, is a small but choice (600 items) collection that includes Diaries for 1846-48, and 1861, significant political and personal correspondence, miscellaneous drafts of editorials, memos, and letters. In the collection is an invaluable, heavily edited, account of the events surrounding the Lincoln assassination that is much fuller than the diary entry.

5. The Thomas G. Welles Collection of about 500 items, owned by Thomas G. Welles of Coventry, Connecticut, is largely concerned with family and business affairs. It contains an interesting, almost daily, account of affairs in Washington during 1864 and early 1865 in letters Welles wrote to his son, Thomas G. Welles, who was serving in the Army of the Potomac.

6. Other important Welles papers are 150 letters, accounts, and a diary for the year 1836 in the Connecticut State Library, about 100 items at the Research Library, UCLA; letters and manuscript memoirs concerning the nomination of Abraham Lincoln in the Lincoln papers, Illinois Historical Society; family and political letters in the University of Chicago Library; letters Welles wrote as a youth at the Lincoln Shrine, Redlands, California; and a scattering of items primarily political at the Chicago Historical Society, New York Historical Society, Sterling Library, Yale, John Hay Library, Brown, Houghton Library, Harvard.

7. Welles corresponded with politicians, newspaper editors, and state and national officials, naval and army officers. These letters and documents are included under the heading of other manuscript collections. But the major sources of Welles' correspondence outside of the special collections enumerated are: the G. V. Fox papers, New York Historical Society, J. R. Hawley papers and the Blair Family papers, Library of Congress, the John M. Niles papers, New York Public Library, and the Mark Howard papers, Connecticut Historical Society.

### B. *Published Papers and Works of Gideon Welles*

Howard K. Beale (ed.), *The Diary of Gideon Welles* (3 vols.), New York, 1960.

John T. Morse (ed.), *The Diary of Gideon Welles* (3 vols.), Boston, 1909-11.

"Mr. Welles in Answer to Mr. Weed. The Facts of the Abandonment of Gosport Navy-Yard," *The Galaxy*, Vol. X (July 1870), pp. 109-19.

"Fort Sumter. Facts in Relation to the Expedition Ordered by the Administration of President Lincoln for the Relief of the Garrison in Fort Sumter," *The Galaxy*, Vol. X (Nov. 1870), pp. 613-37.

"Fort Pickens. Facts in Relation to the Reinforcement of Fort Pickens, in the Spring of 1861," *The Galaxy*, Vol. XI (Jan. 1871), pp. 92-107.

"Admiral Farragut and New Orleans. With an Account of the Origin and Command of the First Three Naval Expeditions of the War. First Paper," *The Galaxy*, Vol. XII (Nov. 1871), pp. 669-83.

"Admiral Farragut and New Orleans. With an Account of the Origin and Command of the First Three Naval Expeditions of the War. Second Paper," *The Galaxy*, Vol. XII (Dec. 1871), pp. 817-32.

"Lincoln and Johnson. Their Plan of Reconstruction and the Resumption of National Authority. First Paper," *The Galaxy*, Vol. XIII (Apr. 1872), pp. 520-32.

"Lincoln and Johnson. Their Plan of Reconstruction and the Resumption of National Authority. Second Paper," *The Galaxy*, Vol. XIII (May 1872), pp. 663-73.

"History of Emancipation," *The Galaxy*, Vol. XIV (Dec. 1872), pp. 838-51.

"The Capture of Mason and Slidell," *The Galaxy*, Vol. XIV (May 1873), pp. 642-51.

"Mr. Lincoln and Mr. Seward. Remarks on the Memorial Address of Charles Francis Adams on the Late William H. Seward. First Paper," *The Galaxy*, Vol. XVI (Oct. 1873), pp. 518-30.

"Mr. Lincoln and Mr. Seward. Remarks on the Memorial Address of Charles Francis Adams on the Late William H. Seward. Second Paper," *The Galaxy*, Vol. XVI (Nov. 1873), pp. 687-700.

"Mr. Lincoln and Mr. Seward. Remarks on the Memorial Address of Charles Francis Adams on the Late William H. Seward. Third Paper," *The Galaxy*, Vol. XVI (Dec. 1873), pp. 792-804.

*The Galaxy* articles October, November, and December 1873 were edited and reprinted in *Lincoln and Seward*, New York, 1874.

"Nomination and Election of Abraham Lincoln. Account of His Administration. No. 1," *The Galaxy*, Vol. XXII (Sept. 1876), pp. 300-308.

"Nomination and Election of Abraham Lincoln. Account of His Administration. No. 2," *The Galaxy*, Vol. XXII (Oct. 1876), pp. 437-46.

"Administration of Abraham Lincoln," *The Galaxy*, Vol. XXIII (Jan. 1877), pp. 5-23.

"Administration of Abraham Lincoln," *The Galaxy*, Vol. XXIII (Feb. 1877), pp. 149-59.

"Administration of Abraham Lincoln," *The Galaxy*, Vol. XXIII (Oct. 1877), pp. 437-50.

"Administration of Abraham Lincoln. Radical Plottings against Mr. Lincoln," *The Galaxy*, Vol. XXIV (Nov. 1877), pp. 608-24.

"The Opposition to Lincoln in 1864," the *Atlantic Monthly*, Vol. LXI (Mar. 1878), pp. 366-76.

"Lincoln's Triumph in 1864," the *Atlantic Monthly*, Vol. XLI (Apr. 1878), pp. 454-68.

### C. *Other Manuscripts Collections Used*

| | |
|---|---|
| N. P. Banks papers | New York Historical Society |
| Baldwin Family papers | Sterling Library, Yale |
| S. L. M. Barlow papers | Huntington Library |
| John Bigelow papers | New York Public Library |
| Blair Family papers | Library of Congress |
| Blair-Lee papers | Firestone Library, Princeton |
| William A. Buckingham papers | Connecticut State Library |
| Simon Cameron papers | Library of Congress |
| William E. Chandler papers | Library of Congress |
| Salmon P. Chase papers | A. Conger Goodyear Coll., Sterling |
| Salmon P. Chase papers | Library of Congress |
| Salmon P. Chase papers | New York Public Library |
| Salmon P. Chase papers | New York Historical Society |
| W. C. Church papers | New York Public Library |
| W. C. Church papers | Library of Congress |
| Chauncey F. Cleveland papers | Connecticut Historical Society |
| Connnecticut Miscellaneous papers | New York Public Library |
| C. G. Comstock papers | Library of Congress |
| Ingoldsby W. Crawford papers | Connecticut College Library |
| David Daggett papers | Sterling Library, Yale |
| John A. Dahlgren papers | Library of Congress |
| John A. Dix papers | Butler Library, Columbia |
| James Dixon Miscellaneous papers | New York Historical Society |
| Stephen A. Douglas papers | Chicago Historical Society |
| Percival Drayton papers | New York Public Library |
| S. F. Du Pont papers (microfilm) | Eleutheran Mills Historical Library |
| John Ericsson papers | New York Historical Society |
| D. G. Farragut papers | Huntington Library |
| Azariah Flagg papers | Butler Library, Columbia |
| George G. Fogg papers | New Hampshire Historical Society |

| | |
|---|---|
| Gustavus Vasa Fox papers | New York Historical Society |
| A. Conger Goodyear collection | Sterling Library, Yale |
| Horace Greeley papers | New Hampshire Historical Society |
| Duff Green papers | Library of Congress |
| William Hammersley papers | Connecticut Historical Society |
| John P. Hale papers | New Hampshire Historical Society |
| Isaac Hill papers | New Hampshire Historical Society |
| Mark Howard papers | Connecticut Historical Society |
| Joseph R. Hawley papers | Library of Congress |
| Andrew Jackson papers | Library of Congress |
| Andrew Johnson papers (microfilm) | Library of Congress |
| Preston King papers | New York Public Library |
| Francis Lieber papers | Huntington Library |
| Abraham Lincoln papers | Library of Congress |
| Abraham Lincoln papers (Xerox) | Illinois Historical Society |
| E. D. Morgan papers (microfilm) | New York State Library |
| John M. Niles papers | New York Public Library |
| Edward L. Pierce papers | Houghton Library, Howard |
| Edward L. Pierce papers | Huntington Library |
| Franklin Pierce papers (microfilm) | Library of Congress |
| Franklin Pierce papers | New Hampshire Historical Society |
| James K. Polk papers (microfilm) | Library of Congress |
| David Dixon Porter papers | Library of Congress |
| David Dixon Porter papers | Huntington Library |
| Charles H. Ray papers | Huntington Library |
| Frances Seward (diary—microfilm) | Univ. of Rochester Library |
| W. H. Seward papers (Xerox) | Univ. of Rochester Library |
| T. H. Seymour papers | Connecticut Historical Society |
| Edwin M. Stanton papers | Library of Congress |
| Samuel J. Tilden papers | New York Public Library |
| Amos Tuck papers | New Hampshire Historical Society |
| Martin Van Buren papers (microfilm) | Library of Congress |
| Elihu Washburne papers | Library of Congress |
| Levi Woodbury papers | Library of Congress |
| Silas Wright papers | New York Public Library |
| | |
| Letters from Banks, 1833-36 | National Archives |
| Bureaux Letters, 1846-49 | National Archives |
| Record Group 45 | National Archives |
| Probate Records, 1835, 1878 | Connecticut State Library |
| Autograph Coll. | Pierpont Morgan Library |

## D. *Printed Manuscripts, Public Documents, Diaries, Recollections, Memoirs, etc.*

Charles Francis Adams (ed.), *Memoirs of John Quincy Adams . . .* (12 vols.), Philadelphia, 1874-77.

Charles Francis Adams, "Memorial Address on the Life, Character and Public Services of William H. Seward," Albany, 1873.

———, "Address of the State Convention, Middletown, Jan. 28, 1835, to the Democrats of Connecticut," pamphlet, Sterling Library, Yale.

*The American Annual Cyclopaedia and Register of Important Events of the Year 1863* (Vols. 1-14), New York, 1862-75; Vol. III.

William W. Andrews (ed.), *The Correspondence and Miscellanies of the Hon. John Cotton Smith,* New York, 1847.

P. T. Barnum, *The Life of P. T. Barnum Written by Himself,* New York, 1855.

Roy P. Basler (ed.), *The Collected Works of Abraham Lincoln* (8 vols.; Index), New Brunswick, 1953.

John Spencer Bassett (ed.), *Correspondence of Andrew Jackson* (7 vols.), Washington, D.C., 1926-35.

Howard K. Beale (ed.), *The Diary of Edward Bates, 1859-1866,* American Historical Association, *Annual Report,* 1940 (4 vols.), Washington, D.C., 1933, Vol. IV.

————— (ed.), *Diary of Gideon Welles* (3 vols.), New York, 1960.

John Bigelow, *Retrospections of an Active Life* (5 vols.), New York, 1909-13.

James G. Blaine, *Twenty Years of Congress,* Norwich, Conn.; 1884-86.

Anna J. Borden, *Echoes From Hospital and White House,* Boston, 1884.

E. G. Bourne (ed.), *Diary and Correspondence of Salmon P. Chase,* American Historical Association, *Annual Report,* 1903 (2 vols.), Vol. II.

George S. Boutwell, "Johnson's Plot and Motives," *North American Review* (December 1885), Vol. CXL, No. CCCXLIX.

Elihu Burritt, *Thoughts and Things at Home and Abroad . . . with a Memoir by Mary Howitt,* Boston and New York, 1854.

*Catalogue,* American Literary, Scientific and Military Academy, 1821, Norwich, Vermont.

—————, "Catalogue of the Officers and Cadets, Together With the Prospectus and Internal Regulations of the American Literary, Scientific and Military Academy at Middletown, Connecticut," Middletown, 1825.

Mary B. Cheney, *Life and Letters of Horace Bushnell* (1st ed., 1880), New York, 1905.

Michel Chevalier, *Society, Manners and Politics in the United States: Being a Series of Letters on North America,* Boston, 1839.

Lucius E. Chittenden, *Recollections of President Lincoln and His Administration,* New York, 1891.

John R. Commons, *et al.* (ed.), *Documentary History of American Industrial Society* (10 vols.), Cleveland, Ohio, 1910-11.

*Congressional Globe,* 25th Cong., 1st sess., *Appendix.*

*Congressional Globe,* 29th Cong., 1st sess.

*Congressional Globe,* 29th Cong., 2nd sess.

*Congressional Globe,* 30th Cong., 1st sess., *Appendix.*

*Congressional Globe,* 37th Cong., 1st sess.

*Congressional Globe,* 37th Cong., 2nd sess., *Appendix.*

*Congressional Globe,* 38th Cong., 1st sess.

*Congressional Globe,* 41st Cong., 1st sess., *Appendix.*

Francis H. Curtis, "Glastonbury," pamphlet, Glastonbury, 1928, Sterling Library, Yale.

Madeleine Vinton Dahlgren, *Memoir of John A. Dahlgren,* New York, 1891.

Charles Henry Davis, *Life of Charles Henry Davis, Rear Admiral, U.S.N., 1807-1877,* Boston and New York, 1899.

David Donald (ed.), *Inside Lincoln's Cabinet: The Civil War Diaries of Salmon P. Chase,* New York, 1954.

Lorenzo Dow, *Biography and Miscellany,* Norwich, Conn., 1834.

————, *Analectic History; Touching Nullification, Northern and Southern: The Last Warning of Lorenzo Dow,* Washington, D.C., 1834.

————, *The Dealings of God, Man and the Devil* . . . (4th ed.), Norwich, 1833.

Maunsell B. Field, "Memories of Many Men and Some Women," New York, 1874.

J. C. Fitzpatrick (ed.), *Autobiography of Martin Van Buren,* American Historical Association, *Annual Report* (2 vols.), 1918, Vol. II, Washington, D.C., 1920.

John W. Forney, *Anecdotes of Public Men,* New York, 1874.

"General Chauncey Whittlesey's Renunciation of Free Masonry and Appeal to the Public," pamphlet No. 3, Connecticut Anti-Masonic Tract Association, Hartford, 1834.

————, *General Orders and Circulars Issued by the Navy Department from 1868 to 1887,* Washington, D.C., 1887.

Ransome H. Gillet, *The Life and Times of Silas Wright* (2 vols.), Albany, 1874.

S. G. Goodrich, *Recollections of a Lifetime* (2 vols.), New York and Auburn, 1857.

U. S. Grant, Personal Memoirs of U. S. Grant (2 vols.), New York, 1885, 1886.

Horace Greeley, *Recollections of a Busy Life,* New York, 1869.

Adam Gurowski, *Diary* (3 vols.), Boston and Washington, D.C., 1862-66.

Nathaniel Hawthorne, *Works* (22 vols.), Boston and New York, 1900.

John Hay, *Letters of John Hay and Extracts from His Diary* (3 vols.), pr. Washington, D.C., 1908, repr., New York, 1969.

John D. Hayes (ed.), *Samuel Francis Du Pont, A Selection from His Civil War Letters* (3 vols.), Ithaca, New York, 1969.

John B. Henderson, "Emancipation and Impeachment," *Century Magazine* (Dec. 1914), Vol. LXXXV.

W. B. Hesseltine (ed.), *Three Against Lincoln, Murat Halstead Reports of the Caucuses of 1860,* Baton Rouge, 1960.

George F. Hoar, *Autobiography of Seventy Years* (2 vols.), New York, 1903.

Dr. Humphrey H. Hood, *Reminiscences of Chicago During the Civil War,* Chicago, 1894.

Ari Hoogenboom and Herbert Hershkowitz, "Levi Woodbury's Intimate Memoranda of the Jackson Administration," *Pennsylvania Magazine of History and Biography* (Oct. 1968), Vol. 92.

John Hooker, *Reminiscences,* Hartford, 1899.

*House Exec. Doc.,* No. 69, 37th Cong., 1st sess.

*House Exec. Doc.,* No. 24, 37th Cong., 2nd sess.

*House Misc. Doc.,* No. 201, Vol. IV, 42nd Cong., 2nd sess.

*House Misc. Doc.,* No. 170, part 5, Vol. II, 44th Cong., 1st sess.

*House Reports,* Vol. I, No. 2, pts. I, II, 37th Cong., 2nd sess.

Sarah F. Hughes (ed.), *Letters and Recollections of John Murray Forbes* (2 vols.), Boston and New York, 1899, 1900.

Gaillard Hunt (ed.), *James Madison Writings* (9 vols.), New York, 1900-1910.

————, "Impeachment of the President," *House Reports,* 40th Cong., 1st sess.

———— (ed.), *James Madison Writings* (9 vols.), New York, 1900-1910.

Charles Johnson (comp.), *The Proceedings of the First Three Republican National Conventions, 1856, 1860, 1864,* Minneapolis, 1893.

George W. Julian, *Political Recollections, 1840 to 1872,* Chicago, 1884.

Benjamin B. Kendrick, *The Journal of the Joint Committee of Fifteen on Reconstruction, 39th Congress, 1865-1867,* New York, 1914.

Leonard W. Labaree (comp.), *The Public Records of the State of Connecticut for the Years 1783 and 1784,* Hartford, 1943.

William Lyon MacKenzie, *The Life and Times of Martin Van Buren,* Boston, 1846.

————, *The Times and Opinions of Benjamin Franklin Butler, District Attorney for the Southern District of New York and Jesse Hoyt, Counselor at Law,* Boston, 1845.

George B. McClellan, *McClellan's Own Story,* New York, 1887.

Charles W. Maccord, "Ericsson and His Monitor," *North American Review* (October 1889), Vol. CXLIX, No. CCCXCV.

Thomas J. McCormack (ed.), *Memoirs of Gustave Koerner, 1809-1896,* Cedar Rapids, Iowa, 1909.

Hugh McCulloch, *Men and Measures of Half a Century,* New York, 1900.

Edward McPherson, *The Political History of the United States of America During the Great Rebellion,* Washington, D.C., and New York, 1864.

Edward McPherson, *The Political History of the United States During the Period of Reconstruction,* Washington, D.C., 1880.

Harriet Martineau, *Retrospect of Western Travel* (3 vols.), London, 1838.

J. P. Mayer (ed.), *Alexis De Tocqueville, Journey to America,* New Haven, 1960.

A. Howard Meneeley, "Three Manuscripts of Gideon Welles," *American Historical Review* (Apr. 1926), Vol. XXXI, No. 3.

George S. Merriam, *The Life and Times of Samuel Bowles* (2 vols.), New York, 1885.

John Bassett Moore (ed.), *The Works of James Buchanan, Comprising his Speeches, State Papers and Private Correspondence* (12 vols.), Phila. and London, 1908-11.

"Naval Letters of Captain Percival Drayton, 1861-1865," *Bulletin of the*

*New York Public Library* (Nov. 1906), Vol. X, No. 11, Nov. 1906; Vol. X, No. 12, Dec. 1906.

————, *Official Records of the Union and Confederate Navies in the War of the Rebellion*, Series I (27 vols.), Series II (4 vols.), Washington, D.C., 1894-1927.

Saul K. Padover (ed.), *Thomas Jefferson on Democracy*, New York, 1946.

T. J. Page, "Autobiographical Sketch of Thomas Jefferson Page," *U.S. Naval Institute Proceedings* (Oct. 1923), Vol. 49.

T. N. Parmelee, "Recollections of an Old Stager," *Harper's Magazine*, Aug. 1872-June 1874.

Theodore Calvin Pease (ed.), *The Diary of Orville Hickman Browning* (2 vols.), Coll. of the Ill. State Hist. Lib., XX, Springfield, 1925.

James S. Pike, *First Blows of the Civil War*, New York, 1879.

"Perley" Poore, *Perley's Reminiscences of Sixty Years in the National Metropolis* (2 vols.), Philadelphia, 1886.

David Dixon Porter, *Incidents and Anecdotes of the Civil War*, New York, 1885.

————, "Proceedings of the State Convention of the National Republican Young Men, Hartford, 1832," pamphlet, Sterling Library, Yale.

Milo M. Quaife (ed.), *The Diary of James K. Polk* (4 vols.), Chicago, 1910.

————, *Record of Service of Connecticut Men in the War of the Revolution, War of 1812, Mexican War*, Hartford, 1889.

————, *Register of Officers and Agents, Civil, Military and Naval in the Service of the United States, 1862*, Washington, D.C., 1862.

————, "Remarks upon the Address of the Democratic Convention of October, 1838, to the People of Connecticut," pamphlet, Sterling Library, Yale.

*Register of Debates in Congress*, 24th Cong., 1st sess.; 2nd sess.

"Report of the Joint Committee on the Conduct of the War," Vol. IV, part 3, *Senate Doc.*, No. 108, 37th Cong., 3rd sess.

"Report of the Secretary of the Navy, July 5, 1861," *Senate Doc.*, No. 1, 37th Cong., 1st sess.

"Report of the Secretary of the Navy, Dec. 3, 1861," *Senate Doc.*, No. 1, Vol. 3, 37th Cong., 2nd sess.

"Report of the Secretary of the Navy, Dec. 1, 1862," *House Exec. Doc.*, No. 1, Vol. 3, 37th Cong., 3rd sess.

"Report of the Secretary of the Navy, Dec. 5, 1863," *House Exec. Doc.*, No. 1, Vol. 5, 39th Cong., 1st sess.

"Report of the Secretary of the Navy, Dec. 5, 1864," *House Exec. Doc.*, No. 1, Pt. 6, Vol. 6, 38th Cong., 2nd sess.

"Report of the Secretary of the Navy, Dec. 4, 1865," *House Exec. Doc.*, No. 1, Vol. 5, 39th Cong., 1st sess.

"Report of the Secretary of the Navy, Dec. 3, 1866," *House Exec. Doc.*, No. 1, Vol. 4, 39th Cong., 2nd sess.

"Report of the Secretary of the Navy, Dec. 7, 1868," *House Exec. Doc.*, No. 1, Vol. 4, 40th Cong., 3rd sess.

*Report of the Secretary of the Navy in Relation to Armored Vessels*, Washington, D.C., 1864.

"Report from the Secretary of the Treasury," *Senate Exec. Doc.*, Vol. II, 29th Cong., 2nd sess.

James D. Richardson (comp.), *A Compilation of the Messages and Papers of the Presidents* (20 vols.), New York, 1911-16.

Albert G. Riddle, *Recollections of War Times; Reminiscences of Men and Events in Washington, 1860-1865*, New York, 1895.

————, *Roll of the State Officers and General Assembly of Connecticut, 1776-1881*, Hartford, 1881.

Gurdon W. Russell, "Up Neck in 1825," Hartford, 1890.

Nathan Sargent, *Public Men and Events from the Commencement of Mr. Monroe's Administration, in 1817 to the Close of Mr. Fillmore's Administration in 1853*, Philadelphia, 1875.

J. W. Schuckers, *Life and Public Service of Salmon Portland Chase*, New York, 1874.

Carl Schurz, *The Reminiscences of Carl Schurz* (3 vols.), New York, 1906, 1908.

*Senate Reports*, 37th Cong., 2nd sess., Nos. 9, 15.

*Senate Exec. Doc.*, insert No. 15, 37th Cong., 2nd sess.

H. T. Shanks (ed.), *The Papers of Willie P. Mangum* (5 vols.), Raleigh, N.C., 1950-55.

W. T. Sherman, *Memoirs of W. T. Sherman, Written by Himself* (2 vols.), New York, 1892.

Henry B. Stanton, *Random Recollections*, New York, 1887.

Arthur G. Staples (ed.), *The Letters of John Fairfield*, Lewiston, Me., 1922.

William Stickney (ed.), *Autobiography of Amos Kendall*, New York, 1872.

P. J. Straudenraus (ed.), *Mr. Lincoln's Washington: Selections from the Writings of Noah Brooks, Civil War Correspondent*, New York, 1967.

Increase N. Tarbox (ed.), *Diary of Thomas Robbins, D.D., 1746-1854* (2 vols.), Boston, 1886-87.

R. M. Thompson and R. Wainwright (eds.), *Confidential Correspondence of Gustavus Vasa Fox, Assistant Secretary of the Navy, 1861-1865* (2 vols.), New York, 1920.

Minton Thrift (ed.), *Memoir of the Rev. Jesse Lee, With Extracts from his Journals*, New York, 1823.

————, *Trial of Andrew Johnson, President of the United States, Before the Senate of the United States on Impeachment by the House of Representatives for High Crimes and Misdemeanors* (3 vols.), Washington, D.C., 1868.

Benjamin C. Truman, "Anecdotes of Andrew Johnson," *The Century Magazine* (Jan. 1913), Vol. LXXXV, No. 3.

William Tudor, *Letters on the Eastern States*, Boston, 1821.

Henry Villard, *Memoirs of Henry Villard, Journalist and Financier* (2 vols.), Boston and New York, 1904.

Harriet Weed and Thurlow Weed Barnes (eds.), *The Life of Thurlow Weed* (2 vols.), Boston, 1883-84, Vol. I (Memoir), Vol. II (Autobiography).

Charles R. Williams (ed.), *Diary and Letters of Rutherford Birchard Hayes* (5 vols.), Columbus, 1922-26.

*United States Statutes at Large,* Vol. XII, Boston, 1865.

*United States Statutes at Large,* Vol. XIII, Boston, 1868.

*Army and Navy Journal,* 1863-65
Boston *Commonwealth,* 1854-55
Bridgeport *Republican Farmer,* 1826-45
*Charter Oak,* 1843-45
*Chicago Tribune,* 1861-65
Columbus *Ohio Statesman,* June-July 1855
*Connecticut Herald,* 1826-36
Hartford *American Mercury,* 1826-36
Hartford *Connecticut Courant* (weekly), 1826-48; (daily), 1848-67
Hartford *Evening Press,* 1856-65
Hartford *Jeffersonian,* 1832-33
Hartford *Mirror,* 1826-32
Hartford *Patriot and Democrat,* 1836-40
Hartford *Republican,* 1849-51; Jan.-Feb. 1856
*Hartford Times,* 1828-68
Hartford *Times and Weekly Advertizer,* 1820-28
Litchfield *Enquirer,* 1824-45
*Middlesex Gazette,* 1828-34
Middletown *American Sentinel and Witness,* 1828-32
*New England Weekly Review,* 1827-31

*New Hampshire Patriot,* 1828-31
New Haven *Columbian Register* (weekly), 1826-36
New Haven *Connecticut Herald*
New Haven *Connecticut Journal*
*New Haven Palladium,* 1829-67
*New Haven Register (Columbian Register—*weekly), 1836-67
New London *Gazette,* 1829-36
New York *Courier and Enquirer,* 1828-31
New York *Evening Post,* 1850-68
New York *Herald,* 1845-67
New York *Sun,* 1870-72
*New York Times,* 1854-70
*New-York Tribune,* 1845-78
*Richmond Whig,* 1831
*Scientific American,* 1861-65
*United States Telegraph,* 1827-32
Washington *Evening Star,* 1860-69
*Washington Globe,* 1830-45
Washington, D.C. *Chronicle,* 1867-68
Washington, D.C. *National Era,* 1850-60
Washington, D.C., *National Intelligencer,* 1829-68
Worcester *Massachusetts Spy,* 1854-61

## II. SECONDARY WORKS

C. F. Adams, "The Trent Affair," *American Historical Review* (Apr. 1912), Vol. XVII.

Robert G. Albion, *The Rise of New York Port,* New York, 1939.

Theodore D. Bacon, *Leonard Bacon, a Statesman in the Church,* New Haven, 1931.

Adam Badeau, *Grant in Peace from Appomattox to Mount McGregor, a Personal Memoir,* Hartford, 1887.

Bernard Bailyn, *Education in the Forming of American Society,* Chapel Hill, 1950.

William E. Baringer, *A House Dividing,* Springfield, Ill., 1945.

————, *Lincoln's Rise to Power,* Boston, 1937.

James P. Baxter, III, "Papers Relating to Belligerent and Neutral Rights," *American Historical Review* (Oct. 1928), Vol. XXXIV.

William Beardsley (comp.), *Officers, Teachers, and Alumni of the Episcopal Academy of Connecticut, 1796-1916,* New Haven, 1916.

Herman Belz, *Reconstructing the Union, Theory and Policy During the Civil War,* Ithaca, 1969.

F. M. Bennett, *The Steam Navy of the United States,* Pittsburgh, 1896.

Stuart L. Bernath, *Squall Across the Atlantic, American Civil War Prize Cases and Diplomacy,* Berkeley and Los Angeles, 1970.

J. Leander Bishop, *History of American Manufactures, 1608-1860* (3 vols.), Philadelphia, 1861-68.

Cyrus P. Bradley, *Biography of Isaac Hill of New Hampshire,* Concord, N.H., 1835.

Newton C. Brainard, *The Hartford State House of 1796,* Hartford, 1964.

Amariah Brigham, *Influence of Religion on Health,* Boston, 1835.

Fawn M. Brodie, *Thaddeus Stevens, Scourge of the South,* New York, 1959.

Isaac M. Bromley, "The Nomination of Lincoln," *Scribner's Magazine* (July-Dec. 1893), Vol. XIV.

Charles W. Burpee, *A Century in Hartford,* Hartford, 1931.

Fitzwilliam Byrdsall, *History of the Loco-Foco or Equal Rights Party,* New York, 1842.

V. J. Capowski, "The Era of Good Feelings in New Hampshire: Gubernatorial Campaigns of Levi Woodbury, 1823-1824," *Historical New Hampshire* (Winter 1966), Vol. XXI, No. 4.

John A. Carpenter, *Sword and Olive Branch,* Pittsburgh, 1964.

L. M. Case and W. F. Spencer, *The United States and France: Civil War Diplomacy,* Philadelphia, 1970.

Marcus A. Casey, "A Typographical Galaxy," *The Connecticut Quarterly* (Jan.-Mar. 1896), Vol. II, No. 1.

Frances M. Caulkins, *History of New London, Connecticut from the First Survey of the Coast in 1612 to 1852,* Hartford, 1852.

G. W. Childs (comp.), *The National Almanac and Annual Record for the Year 1863-64,* Philadelphia, 1863-64.

William C. Church, *The Life of John Ericsson* (2 vols.), New York, 1906.

Margaret Clapp, *Forgotten First Citizen: John Bigelow,* Boston, 1947.

Charles B. Clark, "Politics in Maryland During the Civil War," *The Maryland Historical Magazine* (Sept. 1943), Vol. XXXVIII, No. 3.

Donald B. Cole, *Jacksonian Democracy in New Hampshire, 1800-1851,* Cambridge, Mass., 1970.

John H. and LaWanda Cox, "Andrew Johnson and His Ghost Writers: An Analysis of the Freedman's Bureau and Civil Rights, Veto Messages," *Journal of American History* (Dec. 1961), Vol. XLVIII.

LaWanda and John H. Cox, *Politics, Principle and Prejudice, 1865-1866,* New York, 1963.

Richard N. Current, *Old Thad Stevens,* Madison, Wisc., 1942.

Francis Curtis, *The Republican Party,* New York, 1904.

Charles A. Dana, *Lincoln and His Cabinet, A Lecture Delivered before the New Haven Colony Historical Society,* Jamaica, N.Y., 1899.

Carl N. Degler, "The Loco-Focos: Urban Agrarians," *Journal of Economic History* (Sept. 1936), Vol. XVI.

David Miller De Witt, *The Impeachment and Trial of Andrew Johnson, Seventeenth President of the United States,* New York, 1903.

J. Doyle De Witt, *Lincoln in Hartford,* pamphlet, Hartford, 1963.

David Donald, *Charles Sumner and the Rights of Man,* New York, 1970.

William A. Dunning, "A Little More Light on Andrew Johnson," *Massachusetts Historical Society Proceedings,* Second Series, Vol. XIX, Boston, 1905.

Joseph F. Durkin, *Stephen R. Mallory, Confederate Navy Chief,* Chapel Hill, 1954.

Franklin Ellis (ed.), *History of That Part of the Susquehanna and Juniata Valleys Embraced in the Counties of Mifflin, Juniata, Perry, and Snyder in the Commonwealth of Pennsylvania* (2 vols.), Philadelphia, 1886.

William A. Ellis (ed.), *Norwich University 1819-1911, Her History, Her Graduates, Her Roll of Honor* (2 vols.), Montpelier, Vt., 1911.

A. Farenholt, " 'And There Were Giants in the Earth in Those Days,' " *U.S. Naval Institute Proceedings* (Jan.-June 1936), Vol. 62.

———, *The Farmer's Almanac,* Boston, 1847.

Loyall Farragut, *The Life of David Glasgow Farragut, First Admiral of the United States Navy,* New York, 1879.

Eric Foner, *Free Soil, Free Labor, Free Men: The Ideology of the Republican Party Before the Civil War,* New York, 1970.

Sidney Forman, *West Point: A History of the United States Military Academy,* New York, 1950.

M. E. Goddard and H. V. Partridge, *A History of Norwich,* Hanover, N.H., 1905.

G. C. Gorham, *Life and Public Services of Edwin M. Stanton* (2 vols.), Boston, 1899.

Constance Green, *Washington Village and Capital, 1800-1878,* Princeton, 1962.

Samuel D. Gross (ed.), *Lives of American Physicians and Surgeons,* Philadelphia, 1861.

Gordon S. Haight, *Mrs. Lydia Huntley Sigourney, the Sweet Singer of Hartford,* New Haven, 1930.

Charles E. Hamlin, *Life and Times of Hannibal Hamlin,* Cambridge, Mass., 1899.

Fred H. Harrington, *Fighting Politician, General N. P. Banks,* Philadelphia, 1948.

Albert Bushnell Hart, *Salmon Portland Chase,* New York, 1899.

William F. Henney, *Commonwealth of Connecticut,* Hartford, 1906.

C. F. Heverly, *History of the Towandas, 1776-1886* (Towanda, Pa., 1886).

James M. Hoppin, *Life of Andrew Hull Foote, Rear Admiral United States Navy,* New York, 1874.

M. A. De Wolfe Howe, *Life and Letters of George Bancroft* (2 vols.), New York, 1908.

Frederic Hudson, *Journalism in the United States from 1690-1782,* New York, 1873.

# BIBLIOGRAPHY

Thomas Hutchinson (comp.), *Boyd's Washington and Georgetown Directory*, Washington, D.C., 1865.

Charles A. Jellison, *Fessenden of Maine*, Syracuse, 1962.

Ludwell H. Johnson, "Northern Profit and Profiteers: The Cotton Rings of 1864-1865," *Civil War History* (June 1966), Vol. XII.

Willard King, *Lincoln's Manager, David Davis*, Cambridge, Mass., 1960.

Edward C. Kirkland, *Men, Cities and Transportation, A Study in New England History, 1820-1900* (2 vols.), New York, 1968.

Mark M. Krug, *Lyman Trumbull, Conservative Radical*, New York, 1965.

Mary Land, "Bluff Ben Wade's New England Background," *New England Quarterly* (Dec. 1954), Vol. 27.

J. R. Lane, *A Political History of Connecticut During the Civil War*, Washington, D.C., 1941.

Richard Leopold, *Robert Dale Owen*, Boston, 1940.

Charles Lee Lewis, *David Glasgow Farragut, Admiral in the Making*, Annapolis, 1941.

————, *David Glasgow Farragut, Our First Admiral*, Annapolis, 1943.

R. H. Luthin, "A Discordant Chapter in Lincoln's Administration: The Davis and Blair Controversy," *Maryland Historical Magazine* (Mar. 1944), Vol. XXXIX, No. 1.

————, *The First Lincoln Campaign*, Cambridge, Mass., 1944.

James O. Lyford, *Life of Edward H. Rollins, a Political Biography*, Boston, 1906.

Alexander K. McClure, *Our Presidents and How We Make Them*, New York, 1905.

Eric McKitrick, *Andrew Johnson and Reconstruction*, Chicago, 1960.

James C. Malin, "Speaker Banks Courts the Free Soilers: The Frémont-Robinson Letter of 1856," *New England Quarterly* (Mar. 1939), Vol. XII.

Carlos Martyr, *William E. Dodge: The Christian Merchant*, New York, 1890.

A. Howard Meneeley, *The War Department, 1861, a Study in Mobilization and Administration*, New York, 1928.

James M. Merrill, *Battle Flags South*, Rutherford, N.J., 1970.

————, *William Tecumseh Sherman*, New York, 1971.

Earl S. Miers (ed.), *Lincoln Day by Day, A Chronology, 1809-1865* (3 vols.), Washington, D.C.

John W. Moore (comp.), *Printers, Printing, Publishing and Editing*, Concord, N.H., 1886.

J. M. Morse, "Under the Constitution of 1818, the First Decade," *Connecticut Tercentary Publications, No. 17*, New Haven, 1933.

F. L. Mott, *A History of American Magazines, 1741-1850*, New York, 1930.

Allan Nevins, *The Emergence of Lincoln* (2 vols.), New York, 1950.

————, *Hamilton Fish: The Inner History of the Grant Administration*, New York, 1936.

————, *The Ordeal of the Union* (2 vols.), New York, 1947.

————, *The War for the Union* (4 vols.), New York, 1959-71.

Lord Newton, *Lord Lyons, a Record of British Diplomacy* (2 vols.), London, 1913.

Roy F. Nichols, *Franklin Pierce, Young Hickory of the Granite Hills,* Philadelphia, 1931.

John Niven, *Connecticut for the Union,* New Haven, 1965.

Carroll J. Noonan, *A History of Nativism in Connecticut, 1829-1860,* Washington, D.C., 1938.

James Parton, *The Life of Andrew Jackson* (3 vols.), New York, 1861.

Charles O. Paullin, "A Half Century of Naval Administration in America. The Navy Department During the Civil War," *U.S. Naval Institute Proceedings* (Dec. 1912), Vol. 38.

————, "The Navy Department During the Civil War (II)," *U.S. Naval Institute Proceedings* (Mar. 1913), Vol. 39, No. 1.

Henry G. Pearson, *The Life of John A. Andrew* (2 vols.), New York, 1909.

John C. Pease and John M. Niles, *A Gazetteer of the States of Connecticut and Rhode Island,* Hartford, 1819.

Francois Peyre-Ferry and Alden Partridge, *The Art of Epistolary Composition and a Discourse on Education,* Middletown, Conn., 1826.

Bessie L. Pierce, *A History of Chicago* (3 vols.), New York, 1937-57.

David Potter, *Lincoln and His Party in the Secession Crisis* (rev. ed.), New Haven, 1962.

Fletcher Pratt, *Civil War on Western Waters,* New York, 1956.

Ruth Painter Randall, *Mary Lincoln: The Biography of a Marriage,* Boston, 1953.

Julius G. Rathbun, "The Wide Awakes," *Connecticut Quarterly* (Oct.-Dec. 1895), Vol. I, No. 4.

Robert V. Remini, *The Election of Andrew Jackson,* New York, 1963.

James Ford Rhodes, *History of the United States from the Compromise of 1850* (9 vols.), New York, 1893-1928.

Leon B. Richardson, *William E. Chandler, Republican,* New York, 1940.

Caroline Robbins, *The Eighteenth-Century Commonwealthman,* Cambridge, Mass., 1959.

F. A. Roe, *Naval Duties and Disciplines with the Policy and Principles of Naval Organization,* New York, 1865.

Clinton Rossiter, *The Seed Time of the Republic,* New York, 1953.

J. Thomas Scharf, *History of the Confederate Navy from Its Organization to the Surrender of Its Last Vessel,* Albany, 1894.

A. M. Schlesinger, Jr., *The Age of Jackson,* Boston, 1945.

Charles C. Sellers, *Lorenzo Dow, the Bearer of the Word,* New York, 1928.

Frederick W. Seward, *Seward at Washington as Senator and Secretary of State . . . ,* New York, 1891.

Richard H. Sewell, *John P. Hale and the Politics of Abolition,* Cambridge, Mass., 1965.

Edward W. Sloan, III, *Benjamin Franklin Isherwood, Navy Engineer,* Annapolis, 1965.

William A. Smith, *Secondary Education in the United States,* New York, 1932.

William E. Smith, *The Francis Preston Blair Family in Politics* (2 vols.), New York, 1933.

Ivor D. Spencer, *The Victor and the Spoils, A Life of William L. Marcy,* Providence, R.I., 1959.

Everett S. Stackpole, *History of New Hampshire* (4 vols.), New York, 1917.

Kenneth Stampp, *And the War Came,* Baton Rouge, 1950.

Samuel E. Staples, *Memorial of John Dennison Baldwin,* Worcester, Mass., 1884.

Bernard C. Steiner, *The History of Education in Connecticut,* Washington, D.C., 1893.

Leonard W. Swann, Jr., *John Roach, Maritime Entrepreneur,* Annapolis, 1965.

Bayard Taylor, *Critical Essays,* New York, 1880.

Benjamin Thomas and Harold Hyman, *Stanton: The Life and Times of Lincoln's Secretary of War,* New York, 1962.

Lately Thomas, *The First President Johnson,* New York, 1968.

H. L. Trefousse, *Benjamin Franklin Wade, Radical Republican from Ohio,* New York, 1963.

———, *The Radical Republicans: Lincoln's Vanguard for Social Justice,* New York, 1969.

John Trenchard and Richard Gordon, *The Independent Whig,* Hartford, 1816.

J. Hammond Trumbull (ed.), *Memorial History of Hartford County, 1633-1884* (2 vols.), Boston, 1886.

Glyndon G. Van Deusen, *Horace Greeley, Nineteenth Century Crusader,* Philadelphia, 1953.

———, *Thurlow Weed: Wizard of the Lobby,* Boston, 1947.

———, *William Henry Seward,* New York, 1967.

Glenn Weaver, "America's First 'Junior College': The Episcopal Academy of Connecticut," *Connecticut Historical Society Bulletin,* Vol. 27, No. 1, Jan. 1962.

Thomas Weaver, *Historical Sketch of the Police Service of Hartford,* Hartford, 1901.

Richard S. West, Jr., *Gideon Welles, Lincoln's Navy Department,* Indianapolis and New York, 1943.

Homer White, *The Norwich Cadets: A Tale of the Rebellion,* St. Albans, Vt., 1873.

Leonard White, *The Jacksonians: A Study in Administrative History,* New York, 1954.

Charles R. Wilson, "The Original Chase Organization Meeting and the Next Presidential Election," *Journal of American History* (June 1936), Vol. 23, No. 1.

### III. UNPUBLISHED DOCTORAL DISSERTATIONS

Alan W. Brownsword, "Connecticut Political Patterns, 1817-1826," University of Wisconsin, 1961.

Vincent J. Capowski, "The Making of a Jacksonian Democrat: Levi Woodbury, 1789-1831," Fordham University, 1966.

Gerald S. Henig, "Henry Winter Davis: A Biography," City University of New York, 1971.

Ernest P. Muller, "Preston King, a Political Biography," Columbia University, 1957.

# APPENDIX I

*Gideon Welles, Not Gustavus Vasa Fox, Ran the Navy Department During the Civil War: A Random Sampling of Documents in the National Archives, Navy Department, 1861-65*

EVER SINCE ABRAHAM LINCOLN in casual conversation praised Gustavus Vasa Fox extravagantly, a legend has grown up that he, not Welles, ran the Navy Department during the Civil War. Although Welles has had his advocates, David Dixon Porter, Mrs. David G. Farragut, and more recently, Charles O. Paullin, able historian of naval administration, Fox has generally been considered the more influential figure in directing the Navy's role. Formerly a professional naval officer, Fox was also a dynamic individual, much more in the public eye than the more retiring Welles. His personal qualities and his obvious professional talents have had their impact on naval historians, many of whom are professional naval officers themselves. The consensus has been that Fox, not Welles, was the driving force behind the Navy's effort. But a random sampling of Navy Department documents in the National Archives (Record Group 45) demonstrates that Welles was no figurehead secretary. The two men acted as a team, but Welles was the senior decision-maker, and the final authority on all matters great and small.

Of the thousands of letters, memoranda and dispatches that flowed in and out of the Department, Welles personally read about one-third, Fox at best one-sixth, the Bureau Chiefs and the clerical force handled the remainder. Fox conducted a heavy unofficial correspondence with squadron commanders, far more than Welles, and no doubt many of his verbal suggestions, orders, decisions shaped in part the correspondence of the Bureau Chiefs. But Departmental records reveal that Welles was the chief in fact as well as in name.

Welles gave particular attention to correspondence with other departments and with the President. During August 1861, for instance, of the 93 executive letters received, Welles read 31, many of which had eight- to ten-page enclosures. He almost always wrote minutes, some of them extensive, all directing what action should be taken. Fox read only six of these letters. His record for

September was better—14 letters out of 88 received, but during the same period Welles read 24. As the war intensified and the responsibilities of the various departments increased, so did their communications with each other. In December 1863 out of 82 executive letters received, 49 passed through Welles' office. Two were initialed by Fox and one by Faxon.

An example of Welles' handling of executive business was the following draft he wrote on the back of a request from Chase for the Navy to supply coal to the revenue cutters, *Reliance* and *Hercules*—"can not the Treasury Department buy coal and charter vessels as the Army and Navy do?" asked Welles. "Our coal contract is nearly expended and our hands are full to supply our squadrons." Fox disagreed. In a second endorsement he replied, "It is a small quantity (20 tons for each vessel per month) & must be allowed to the treasury." Welles approved in a third endorsement. In another example, Secretary of State Seward enclosed a note from Louis de Geoffroy, French *Chargé* in Washington, claiming that a deserter from a French naval vessel, one François Minoret, was serving under an assumed name on the U.S.S. *North Carolina*. Seward asked that Minoret be turned over to the French. Welles denied the request. He wrote Seward on October 15, 1864, that "a late refusal on the part of English authorities to deliver up desertions from the *Iroquois* raises the question whether it is right on our part to surrender and send back for punishment those who came to us." For the month of September 1864 the Department received 350 executive letters and documents. Welles read 105 of these, Fox only 9. On a majority of the letters he read, Welles wrote minutes, some only a line or two, some filling up an entire page with his small, cramped hand.

Examination of other categories of official correspondence to the Department—Officers' Letters, Commanders' Letters, Captains', Commodores', and Admirals' Letters, Bureau Letters, and Miscellaneous Letters—indicates that Welles read and acted upon from three to six times as many dispatches as Fox. These documents dealt with all kinds of naval matters. There were, for instance, 342 letters in the Miscellaneous correspondence file of the Department for October-December 1864. Welles read and acted upon 115, Fox 26, Faxon 62.

The three men performed much routine work that should have been delegated to others. For example, under miscellaneous letters December 1864, we find that Neape and Levy of the Penn Works, Philadelphia, wrote Welles on December 22, 1864, complaining that they delivered eight propellors to the Mississippi Squadron at a cost of $1,067.32; all received and duly acknowledged; shipment had been made during February and March 1864; but they had received no payment after ten months! Welles in pencil ordered Francis Stickney, warrant clerk, to draft a reply for his signature, using the following language: "Paymaster Boggs has been disabled most of the summer and unable to attend to business. He is now at St. Louis engaged in settling all claims arising during his connection with the Mississippi Flotilla and it is presumed that prompt attention will now be given to this."

Bureau letters which involved the internal administration of the Department, like Executive letters, were of special interest to the Secretary. In fact, Welles wrote more and longer minutes on these documents than on any others. And more frequently appear those terse questions and comments that run throughout his endorsements—"What are the facts? Be more specific! Make clear recommendations!" An example of Welles' insistence on clarity was his rather abrupt reply to an endorsement of Isherwood, regarding the payment of a bill for steam gauges. "The inference is that the Chief of the Bureau is in favor of the payment of the bill," wrote Welles below Isherwood's ambiguous endorsement on February 6, 1864, "if so let it be distinctly recommended—if no as distinctly disapproved." Isherwood approved the payment three days later.

Welles kept a careful check on employment and work in progress in the various Navy Yards as reported weekly by the various commandants and by Admiral Gregory's ironclad office. He and Fox read all of Ericsson's correspondence with the Department except what may have been purposefully sidetracked. There were 227 individual items in Commanders' Letters, November-December 1863. Welles read 60 of these and wrote minutes on 34. Fox read 19 and wrote minutes on 12. Two hundred and eight items are filed in Admirals', Commodores', and Captains' Letters, January-February 1863. Of these Welles read 35, Fox read 5. An example of Welles' instructions in this category is his endorsement on a letter from Admiral Gregory who informed the Department that the contractors were falling behind schedule: "Write sharp letter to these contractors," Welles directed Faxon who drafted such a letter for his signature. Gregory's report was dated January 23, 1863, Welles' letter went out on January 28, 1863.

Welles, Fox, Faxon, and the Bureau Chiefs initialed every document that passed over their desks. Thus, it was simple to make a tabulation. Sometimes Fox initialed F; at other times, G.F. in pencil or occasionally in pen. Faxon's initialing is easily distinguished from Fox's. Welles used pencil exclusively and always initialed "W."

All of the above conclusions were derived from a random sampling of the Naval letter groups between the years 1861 and 1865. The author scanned 2367 letters and about 1000 enclosures. He tabulated the initialing of the documents and the endorsements by Welles, Fox, Faxon, and the Bureau Chiefs. If the endorsement seemed significant, then he studied both letter and endorsement. In this way a fairly comprehensive picture of Department administration emerges. The roles of Welles, Fox, Faxon, the Bureau Chiefs and the clerks can be evaluated with some degree of accuracy. *Record group 45, National Archives.* Officers' letters, Dec. 1861 (305 letters), Commanders' letters, Nov.-Dec. 1863 (227 letters), Admirals', Commodores', and Captains' letters, Jan.-Feb. 1863 (208 letters). Executive letters, Aug.-Oct., Dec. 1861; Sept.-Oct. 1864 (553 letters), Bureau letters, Jan.-Apr. 1862; Aug.-Oct. 1862; Jan.-Apr. 1864 (578 letters), Miscellaneous letters, Dec. 1864 (496 letters), all exclusive of enclosures.

# INDEX